W9-BGD-791

# Object-Oriented & Classical Software Engineering

Seventh Edition

**Stephen R. Schach**
*Vanderbilt University*

Boston   Burr Ridge, IL   Dubuque, IA   New York   San Francisco   St. Louis
Bangkok   Bogotá   Caracas   Kuala Lumpur   Lisbon   London   Madrid   Mexico City
Milan   Montreal   New Delhi   Santiago   Seoul   Singapore   Sydney   Taipei   Toronto

# Higher Education

OBJECT-ORIENTED & CLASSICAL SOFTWARE ENGINEERING, SEVENTH EDITION

Published by McGraw-Hill, a business unit of The McGraw-Hill Companies, Inc., 1221 Avenue of the Americas, New York, NY 10020. Copyright © 2007 by The McGraw-Hill Companies, Inc. All rights reserved. Previous editions © 1990, 1993, 1996, 1999, 2002, and 2005. No part of this publication may be reproduced or distributed in any form or by any means, or stored in a database or retrieval system, without the prior written consent of The McGraw-Hill Companies, Inc., including, but not limited to, in any network or other electronic storage or transmission, or broadcast for distance learning.

Some ancillaries, including electronic and print components, may not be available to customers outside the United States.

This book is printed on acid-free paper.

3 4 5 6 7 8 9 0 DOC/DOC 0 9 8 7

ISBN-13   978–0–07–319126–3
ISBN-10   0–07–319126–4


Publisher: *Alan R. Apt*
Developmental Editor: *Rebecca Olson*
Executive Marketing Manager: *Michael Weitz*
Project Manager: *Lora Kalb*
Senior Production Supervisor: *Kara Kudronowicz*
Senior Coordinator of Freelance Design: *Michelle D. Whitaker*
Cover Designer: *Christopher Reese*
(USE) Cover Image: *Royalty-Free/CORBIS*
Compositor: *ICC Macmillan Inc.*
Typeface: *10/12 Times Roman*
Printer: *R. R. Donnelley Crawfordsville, IN*


**Library of Congress Cataloging-in-Publication Data**

Schach, Stephen R.
   Object-oriented and classical software engineering / Stephen R. Schach. — 7th ed.
      p.    cm.
   Includes index.
   ISBN 978–0–07–319126–3 —  ISBN 0–07–319126–4 (hard copy : alk. paper)
    1. Software engineering. 2. Object oriented programming (Computer science). 3. UML (Computer science).
    4. C++ and Java (Computer program language). I. Title.

QA76.758.S318      2007
005.1—dc22                                                      2006012083
                                                                CIP

www.mhhe.com

To Jackson

# Preface

The sixth edition of this book, published in 2004, was vastly different to the fifth edition. More than half of the sixth edition consisted of new material, much of it on the Unified Process, and the topics that were retained from the fifth edition were rewritten from a more modern viewpoint.

Many instructors were kind enough to provide feedback on the sixth edition. They approved of the drastic changes I had made in the sixth edition, but suggested that the aim of the seventh edition should be to update the sixth edition, rather than once again make widespread changes. In addition, a number of instructors have asked for a new running case study in Part 2 of the book.

Accordingly, there are two types of changes in the seventh edition:

- The book has been updated throughout. In particular, I have considerably expanded the material on agile processes and open-source software development in Chapters 2 and 4. The references have been updated, and there are new problems in every chapter.

- I have replaced the Osbert Oglesby case study, used to illustrate the techniques of software development in Chapters 10 through 15, with the MSG Foundation case study.

## Features Retained from the Sixth Edition

- The Unified Process is still largely the methodology of choice for object-oriented software development. Throughout this book, the student is therefore exposed to both the theory and the practice of the Unified Process.

- In Chapter 1, the strengths of the object-oriented paradigm are analyzed in depth.

- The iterative-and-incremental life-cycle model has been introduced as early as possible, namely, in Chapter 2. Furthermore, as with all previous editions, numerous other life-cycle models are presented, compared, and contrasted.

- In Chapter 3 ("The Software Process"), the workflows (activities) and processes of the Unified Process are introduced, and the need for two-dimensional life-cycle models is explained.

- A wide variety of ways of organizing software teams are presented in Chapter 4 ("Teams"), including teams for agile processes and for open-source software development.

- Chapter 5 ("The Tools of the Trade") includes information on important classes of CASE tools.

- The importance of continual testing is stressed in Chapter 6 ("Testing").

- Objects continue to be the focus of attention in Chapter 7 ("From Modules to Objects").

- The material on interoperability, which was removed from Chapter 8 ("Reusability and Portability") in the sixth edition, has not been replaced. In both the fourth and the fifth editions, these sections became hopelessly out of date during the 6 months it took to publish the books. In my opinion, the field is moving too fast to be included in a textbook; an instructor wishing to include interoperability in a software engineering course should obtain up-to-the-minute material from the Internet.

- The new IEEE standard for software project management plans is again presented in Chapter 9 ("Planning and Estimating").
- Chapter 10 ("Requirements"), Chapter 12 ("Object-Oriented Analysis"), and Chapter 13 ("Design") are largely devoted to the workflows (activities) of the Unified Process. For obvious reasons, Chapter 11 ("Classical Analysis") has not been changed, other than the case study.
- The material in Chapter 14 ("Implementation") clearly distinguishes between implementation and integration.
- The importance of postdelivery maintenance is stressed in Chapter 15.
- Chapter 16 provides additional material on UML to prepare the student thoroughly for employment in the software industry. This chapter is of particular use to instructors who utilize this book for the two-semester software engineering course sequence. In the second semester, in addition to developing the team-based term project or a capstone project, the student can acquire additional knowledge of UML, beyond what is needed for this book.
- As before, there are two running case studies. The MSG Foundation case study and the elevator problem case study have been developed using the Unified Process. As usual, Java and C++ implementations are available online at www.mhhe.com/schach.
- In addition to the two running case studies that are used to illustrate the complete life cycle, seven mini case studies highlight specific topics, such as the moving-target problem, stepwise refinement, and postdelivery maintenance.
- In all the previous editions, I have stressed the importance of documentation, maintenance, reuse, portability, testing, and CASE tools. In this edition, all these concepts are stressed equally firmly. It is no use teaching students the latest ideas unless they appreciate the importance of the basics of software engineering.
- As in the sixth edition, particular attention is paid to object-oriented life-cycle models, object-oriented analysis, object-oriented design, management implications of the object-oriented paradigm, and the testing and maintenance of object-oriented software. Metrics for the object-oriented paradigm also are included. In addition, many briefer references are made to objects, a paragraph or even only a sentence in length. The reason is that the object-oriented paradigm is not concerned just with how the various phases are performed but rather permeates the way we think about software engineering. Object technology again pervades this book.
- The software process still is the concept that underlies the book as a whole. To control the process, we have to be able to measure what is happening to the project. Accordingly, the emphasis on metrics is retained. With regard to process improvement, the material on the capability maturity model (CMM), ISO/IEC 15504 (SPICE), and ISO/IEC 12207 has been retained; the people capability maturity model (P–CMM) has been added to the chapter on teams.
- The book is still language independent; the few code examples are presented in C++ and Java, and I have made every effort to smooth over language-dependent details and ensure that the code examples are equally clear to C++ and Java users. For example, instead of using cout for C++ output and System.out.println for Java output, I have utilized the pseudocode instruction *print*. (The one exception is the new case study, where complete implementation details are given in both C++ and Java, as before.)

- As in the sixth edition, this book contains over 600 references. I have selected current research papers as well as classic articles and books whose message remains fresh and relevant. There is no question that software engineering is a rapidly moving field, and students therefore need to know the latest results and where in the literature to find them. At the same time, today's cutting-edge research is based on yesterday's truths, and I see no reason to exclude an older reference if its ideas are as applicable today as they originally were.

- With regard to prerequisites, it is assumed that the reader is familiar with one high-level programming language such as C, C++, Ada, or Java. In addition, the reader is expected to have taken a course in data structures.

## Why the Classical Paradigm Still Is Included

There is now almost unanimous agreement that the object-oriented paradigm is superior to the classical paradigm. Nevertheless, I feel that attempting to eliminate all mention of the classical paradigm is unwise.

First, it is impossible to appreciate why object-oriented technology is superior to classical technology without fully understanding the classical approach and how it differs from the object-oriented approach. For example, the object-oriented paradigm uses an iterative and incremental life-cycle model. To show why such a life-cycle model is needed, it is essential to explain in detail the differences between classical life-cycle models like the waterfall model and the iterative and incremental life-cycle model of the object-oriented paradigm. Therefore, all through the book, I have included material on the classical paradigm so that the student can clearly appreciate the differences between the classical paradigm and the object-oriented paradigm.

The second reason why I have included both paradigms is that technology transfer is a slow process. Notwithstanding the impact of Y2K on accelerating the switch to the object-oriented paradigm, the majority of software organizations still have not yet adopted the object-oriented paradigm. It therefore is likely that many of the students who use this book will be employed by organizations that use classical software engineering techniques. Furthermore, even when an organization uses the object-oriented approach for developing new software, existing software still has to be maintained, and this legacy software is not object oriented. Therefore, excluding classical material would be unfair to many of the students who use this text.

A third reason for including both paradigms is that a student who is employed at an organization considering making the transition to object-oriented technology will be able to advise that organization regarding both the strengths and the weaknesses of the new paradigm. So, as in the previous edition, the classical and object-oriented approaches are compared, contrasted, and analyzed.

## How the Seventh Edition Is Organized

Like the sixth edition of this book, the seventh edition is written for both the traditional one-semester and the newer two-semester software engineering curriculum, now growing in popularity. In the traditional one-semester (or one-quarter) course, the instructor has to rush through the theoretical material to provide the students the knowledge and skills needed for the term project as soon as possible. The need for haste is so that the students can commence the term project early enough to complete it by the end of the semester. To cater to a one-semester, project-based software engineering course, Part 2 of this book covers the software life cycle, workflow by workflow, and Part 1 contains the theoretical material needed to understand Part 2. For example, Part 1 introduces the reader to CASE, metrics, and testing; each chapter of Part 2 contains a section on CASE tools for that workflow, a section on metrics for that workflow, and a section on testing during that workflow. Part 1 is kept short to enable the instructor to start Part 2 relatively early in the semester. Furthermore, the last two chapters of Part 1 (Chapters 8 and 9) may be postponed, and then taught in parallel with Part 2. As a result, the class can begin developing the term project as soon as possible.

We turn now to the two-semester software engineering curriculum. More and more computer science and computer engineering departments are realizing that the overwhelming preponderance of their graduates find employment as software engineers. As a result, many colleges and universities have introduced a two-semester (or two-quarter) software engineering sequence. The first course is largely theoretical (but often includes a small project of some sort). The second course comprises a major team-based term project. This is usually a capstone project. When the term project is in the second course, there is no need for the instructor to rush to start Part 2.

Therefore, an instructor teaching a one-semester (or one-quarter) sequence using the seventh edition covers most of Chapters 1 through 7 and then starts Part 2 (Chapters 10 through 16). Chapters 8 and 9 can be taught in parallel with Part 2 or at the end of the course while the students are implementing the term project. When teaching the two-semester sequence, the chapters of the book are taught in order; the class now is fully prepared for the team-based term project that they will develop in the following semester.

To ensure that the key software engineering techniques of Part 2 truly are understood, each is presented twice. First, whenever a technique is introduced, it is illustrated by means of the elevator problem. The elevator problem is the correct size for the reader to be able to see the technique applied to a complete problem, and it has enough subtleties to highlight both the strengths and weaknesses of the technique being taught. Then, the relevant portion of the MSG Foundation case study is presented. This detailed solution provides the second illustration of each technique.

# The Problem Sets

As in the previous edition, this book has five types of problems. First, there are running object-oriented analysis and design projects at the end of Chapters 10, 12, and 13. These have been included because the only way to learn how to perform the requirements, analysis, and design workflows is from extensive hands-on experience.

Second, the end of each chapter contains a number of exercises intended to highlight key points. These exercises are self-contained; the technical information for all the exercises can be found in this book.

Third, there is a software term project. It is designed to be solved by students working in teams of three, the smallest number of team members that cannot confer over a standard telephone. The term project comprises 15 separate components, each tied to the relevant chapter. For example, design is the topic of Chapter 13, so in that chapter the component of the term project is concerned with software design. By breaking a large project into smaller, well-defined pieces, the instructor can monitor the progress of the class more closely. The structure of the term project is such that an instructor may freely apply the 15 components to any other project that he or she chooses.

Because this book has been written for use by graduate students as well as upper-class undergraduates, the fourth type of problem is based on research papers in the software engineering literature. In each chapter, an important paper has been chosen; wherever possible, a paper related to object-oriented software engineering has been selected. The student is asked to read the paper and answer a question relating to its contents. Of course, the instructor is free to assign any other research paper; the For Further Reading section at the end of each chapter includes a wide variety of relevant papers.

The fifth type of problem relates to the case study. This type of problem was first introduced in the third edition in response to a number of instructors who feel that their students learn more by modifying an existing product than by developing a new product from scratch. Many senior software engineers in the industry agree with that viewpoint. Accordingly, each chapter in which the case study is presented has problems that require the student to modify the case study in some way. For example, in one chapter the student is asked to redesign the case study using a different design technique from the one used for the case study. In another chapter, the student is asked what the effect would have been of performing the steps of the object-oriented analysis in a different order. To make it easy to modify the source code of the case study, it is available on the World Wide Web at www.mhhe.com/schach.

The website also has material for instructors, including a complete set of PowerPoint lecture notes and detailed solutions to all the exercises as well as to the term project.

## Material on UML

This book makes substantial use of the Unified Modeling Language (UML). If the students do not have previous knowledge of UML, this material may be taught in two ways. I prefer to teach UML on a just-in-time basis; that is, each UML concept is introduced just before it is needed. The following table describes where the UML constructs used in this book are introduced.

| Construct | Section in Which the Corresponding UML Diagram Is Introduced |
|---|---|
| Class diagram, note, inheritance (generalization), aggregation, association, navigation triangle | Section 7.7 |
| Use case | Section 10.4.3 |
| Use-case diagram, use-case description | Section 10.7 |
| Stereotype | Section 12.1 |
| Statechart | Section 12.6 |
| Interaction diagram (sequence diagram, collaboration diagram) | Section 12.15 |

Alternatively, Chapter 16 contains an introduction to UML, including material above and beyond what is needed for this book. Chapter 16 may be taught at any time; it does not depend on material in the first 15 chapters. The topics covered in Chapter 16 are as given in the following table.

| Construct | Section in Which the Corresponding UML Diagram Is Introduced |
|---|---|
| Class diagram, aggregation, multiplicity, composition, generalization, association | Section 16.2 |
| Note | Section 16.3 |
| Use-case diagram | Section 16.4 |
| Stereotype | Section 16.5 |
| Interaction diagram | Section 16.6 |
| Statechart | Section 16.7 |
| Activity diagram | Section 16.8 |
| Package | Section 16.9 |
| Component diagram | Section 16.10 |
| Deployment diagram | Section 16.11 |

# Acknowledgments

I greatly appreciate the constructive criticisms and many helpful suggestions of the reviewers of the six previous editions, including

**Arvin Agah**
*University of Kansas*

**Kiumi Akingbehin**
*University of Michigan, Dearborn*

**Phil Bernhard**
*Clemson University*

**Dan Berry**
*The Technion*

**Don Bickerstaff**
*Eastern Washington University*

**Richard J. Botting**
*California State University, San Bernardino*

**Michael Buckley**
*State University New York, Buffalo*

**Catherine Lowry Campbell**
*New Jersey Institute of Technology*

**James Cardow**
*Air Force Institute of Technology*

**Betty Cheng**
*Michigan State University*

**David Cheriton**
*Stanford University*

**Thaddeus R. Crews, Jr.**
*Western Kentucky University*

**Buster Dunsmore**
*Purdue University*

**Eduardo B. Fernandez**
*Florida Atlantic University*

**Michael Godfrey**
*Cornell University*

**Bob Goldberg**
*IBM*

**Donald Gotterbarn**
*East Tennessee State University*

**Frances Grodzinsky**
*Sacred Heart University*

**Jim Han**
*Florida Atlantic University*

**Scott Hawker**
*University of Alabama*

**Thomas B. Horton**
*Florida Atlantic University*

**Greg Jones**
*Utah State University*

**Peter E. Jones**
*University of Western Australia*

**Gail Kaiser**
*Columbia University*

**Laxmikant V. Kale**
*University of Illinois*

**Helene Kershner**
*University of Buffalo*

**Werner Krandick**
*Drexel University*

**Owen Lavin**
*DePaul University*

**Chung Lee**
*California State Polytechnic, Pomona*

**Richar A. Lejk**
*University of North Carolina, Chapel Hill*

**Michael McCracken**
*Georgia Institute of Technology*

**Susan Mengel**
*Texas Tech University*

**Everald E. Mills**
*Seattle University*

**Fred Mowle**
*Purdue University*

**Donald Needham**
*United States Naval Academy*

**Ron New**
*Johns Hopkins University*

**David Notkin**
*University of Washington*

**Andy Podgurski**
*Case Western Reserve University*

**Hal Render**
*University of Colorado, Colorado Springs*

**David C. Rine**
*George Mason University*

**David S. Rosenblum**
*University of California, Irvine*

**Shmuel Rotenstreich**
*George Washington University*

**Mansur Samadzadeh**
*Oklahoma State University*

**John H. Sayler**
*University of Michigan*

**Wendel Scarborough**
*Azusa Pacific University*

**Bob Schuerman**
*State College, Pennsylvania*

**Gerald B. Sheble**
*Iowa State*

**Fred Strauss**
*Polytechnic University*

**K. C. Tai**
*North Carolina State University*

**Toby Teorey**
*University of Michigan*

**Jie We**
*City University of New York*

**Laurie Werth**
*University of Texas, Austin*

**Lee White**
*Case Western Reserve University*

**David Workman**
*University of Central Florida*

**George W. Zobrist**
*University of Missouri, Rolla*

In addition, special thanks go to the reviewers of this edition, including

**Robert M. Cubert**
*University of Florida*

**Michael Hoffman**
*California State University, Long Beach*

**Saeed S. Monemi**
*California State Polytechnic University, Pomona*

**Linda Ott**
*Michigan Technological University*

**James Purtilo**
*University of Maryland*

**Steven Shaffer**
*Pennsylvania State University*

**Fred Strauss**
*Polytechnic University*

I would like to thank the numerous instructors from all over the world who sent me e-mail regarding the sixth edition. As always, I am exceedingly appreciative of their suggestions, comments, and criticisms. In particular, I thank Professor Michael Haugrud (Minnesota State University Moorhead) for suggesting improvements to the Winburg mini case study. I look forward with anticipation to receiving instructors' feedback on this edition also. My e-mail address is srs@vuse.vanderbilt.edu.

Students, too, continue to be most helpful. Once more I thank my students at Vanderbilt University for their provocative questions and constructive suggestions, both inside and outside the classroom. I also am most appreciative of the questions and comments on the sixth edition e-mailed to me by students from all over the world. Special thanks go to Benjamin Polak, a student at the University of Erlangen, Germany, for suggesting improvements to the elevator problem case study. As with the previous editions, I look forward keenly to student feedback on this edition, too.

I warmly thank three individuals who have also made significant contributions to previous editions of this book. First, Kris Irwin once again provided a complete solution to the term project, including implementing it in both Java and C++. Second, Jeff Gray implemented the MSG Foundation case study. Third, Lauren Ryder was again a co-author of the *Instructor's Solution Manual* and contributor to the PowerPoint slides.

I turn now to McGraw-Hill. My publisher Alan Apt and my developmental editor Rebecca Olson provided assistance and guidance throughout the project. I thank copyeditor Lucy Mullins for her many helpful suggestions. It was a pleasure to work with marketing manager Michael Weitz, media manager Christina Nelson, production supervisor Kara Kudronowicz, and proofreader Carrie Barker. The striking cover of this book was designed by Michelle Whitaker and Christopher Reese, both of whom I warmly thank. Finally, I particularly wish to thank production manager Lora Kalb for her endless help and for keeping the project on schedule. She invariably went the extra mile—and more.

As always, I enjoyed working with the highly competent compositors at Interactive Composition Corporation. I also thank ICC project manager Deepti Hingle.

Finally, as always, I thank my wife, Sharon, for her continual support. As with all my previous books, I did my utmost to try to ensure that family commitments took precedence over writing. However, when deadlines loomed, this was sometimes not possible. At such times, she was always understanding, and for this I am most grateful.

It is my privilege to dedicate my thirteenth book to my grandson, Jackson, with love.

*Stephen R. Schach*

# Contents

The following are registered trademarks:

ADF
Analyst/Designer
Ant
Apache
Apple
AS/400
AT&T
Bachman Product Set
Bell Laboratories
Borland
Bugzilla
Capability Maturity Model
ClearCase
ClearQuest
CMM
Coca-Cola
CORBA
CppUnit
CVS
DB2
Eclipse
e-Components
Emeraude
Enterprise JavaBeans
eServer
Excel
Firefox
Focus
Ford
Foundation Class Library
FoxBASE
GCC
Hewlett-Packard
IBM
IMS/360
Jackpot Source Code Metrics

Java
JBuilder
JUnit
Linux
Lotus 1-2-3
Lucent Technologies
MacApp
Macintosh
Macintosh Toolbox
MacProject
Microsoft
Motif
MS-DOS
MVS/360
Natural
Netscape
*New York Times*
Object C
Objective-C
ObjectWindows Library
1-800-flowers.com
Oracle
Oracle Developer Suite
OS/360
OS/370
OS/VS2
Palm Pilot
Parasoft
Post-it Note
PowerBuilder
PREfix
PREfast
Project
PureCoverage
PVCS
QARun

Rational
Requisite Pro
Rhapsody
Rose
SBC Communications
SilkTest
SLAM
Software through Pictures
Solaris
SourceSafe
SPARCstation
Sun
Sun Enterprise
Sun Microsystems
Sun ONE Studio
System Architect
Together
UNIX
VAX
Visual Component Library
Visual C++
Visual J++
VM/370
VMS
*Wall Street Journal*
WebSphere
Win32
Windows 95
Windows 2000
Windows NT
X11
Xrunner
XUnit
Zip disk
ZIP Code
zSeries

# Part 1

## Introduction to Software Engineering

The first nine chapters of this book play a dual role: They introduce the reader to the software process, and they provide the foundation for the material in the second half of the book, where the workflows (activities) of software development are described.

The software process is the way we produce software. It starts with concept exploration and ends when the product is finally decommissioned. During this period, the product goes through a series of steps such as requirements, analysis (specification), design, implementation, integration, postdelivery maintenance, and ultimately, retirement. The software process includes the tools and techniques we use to develop and maintain software as well as the software professionals involved.

Chapter 1, "The Scope of Software Engineering," points out that techniques for software production must be cost effective and promote constructive interaction between the members of the software production team. The importance of objects is stressed throughout the book, starting with this chapter.

A variety of different software life-cycle models are discussed in detail in Chapter 2, "Software Life-Cycle Models." These include the evolution-tree model, the waterfall model, the rapid-prototyping model, the synchronize-and-stabilize model, the open-source model, the agile process model, the spiral model, and most important of all, the iterative-and-incremental model. To enable the reader to decide on an appropriate life-cycle model for a specific project, the various life-cycle models are compared and contrasted.

"The Software Process" is the title of Chapter 3. The emphasis in this chapter is on the Unified Process, currently the most promising way of developing software. Agile processes, an alternative approach to software development gaining in popularity, are also treated in detail. The chapter concludes with material on software process improvement.

Chapter 4 is entitled "Teams." Today's projects are too large to be completed by a single individual within the given time constraints. Instead, a team of software professionals collaborate on the project. The major topic of this chapter is how teams should be organized so that team members work together productively. Various ways of organizing teams are discussed, including democratic teams, chief programmer teams, synchronize-and-stabilize teams, open-source teams, and agile process teams.

A software engineer needs to be able to use a number of different tools, both analytical and practical. In Chapter 5, "The Tools of the Trade," the reader is introduced to a variety of software engineering tools. One such tool is stepwise refinement, a technique for decomposing a large problem into smaller, more tractable problems. Another tool is cost–benefit analysis, a technique for determining whether a software project is financially feasible. Then, computer-aided software engineering (CASE) tools are described. A CASE tool is a software product that assists software engineers to develop and maintain software. Finally, to manage the software process, it is necessary to measure various quantities to determine whether the project is on track. These measures (metrics) are critical to the success of a project.

The last two topics of Chapter 5, CASE tools and metrics, are treated in detail in Chapters 10 through 15, which describe the specific workflows of the software life cycle. There is a discussion of the CASE tools that support each workflow, as well as a description of the metrics needed to manage that workflow adequately.

Chapter 6, "Testing," discusses the concepts underlying testing. The consideration of testing techniques specific to each workflow of the software life cycle is deferred until Chapters 10 through 15.

Chapter 7, "From Modules to Objects," gives a detailed explanation of classes and objects and why the object-oriented paradigm is proving more successful than the classical paradigm. The concepts of this chapter are utilized in the rest of the book, particularly Chapter 10, "Requirements"; Chapter 12, "Object-Oriented Analysis"; and Chapter 13, "Design," in which object-oriented design is presented.

The ideas of Chapter 7 are extended in Chapter 8, "Reusability and Portability." It is important to be able to write reusable software that can be ported to a variety of different hardware. The first part of the chapter is devoted to reuse; the topics include a variety of reuse case studies as well as reuse strategies such as object-oriented patterns and frameworks. Portability is the second major topic; portability strategies are presented in some depth. A recurring theme of this chapter is the role of objects in achieving reusability and portability.

The last chapter in Part 1 is Chapter 9, "Planning and Estimating." Before starting a software project, it is essential to plan the entire operation in detail. Once the project begins, management must closely monitor progress, noting deviations from the plan and taking corrective action where necessary. Also, it is vital that the client be provided accurate estimates of how long the project will take and how much it will cost. Different estimation techniques are presented, including function points and COCOMO II. A detailed description of a software project management plan is given. The material of this chapter is utilized in Chapters 11 and 12. When the classical paradigm is used, major planning and estimating activities take place at the end of the classical analysis phase, as explained in Chapter 11. When software is developed using the object-oriented paradigm, this planning takes place at the end of the object-oriented analysis workflow (Chapter 12).

# Chapter 1

# The Scope of Software Engineering

## Learning Objectives

After studying this chapter, you should be able to

- Define what is meant by software engineering.
- Describe the classical software engineering life-cycle model.
- Explain why the object-oriented paradigm is now so widely accepted.
- Discuss the implications of the various aspects of software engineering.
- Distinguish between the classical and modern views of maintenance.
- Discuss the importance of continual planning, testing, and documentation.
- Appreciate the importance of adhering to a code of ethics.

A well-known story tells of an executive who received a computer-generated bill for $0.00. After having a good laugh with friends about "idiot computers," the executive tossed the bill away. A month later, a similar bill arrived, this time marked 30 days. Then came the third bill. The fourth bill arrived a month later, accompanied by a message hinting at possible legal action if the bill for $0.00 was not paid at once.

The fifth bill, marked 120 days, did not hint at anything—the message was rude and forthright, threatening all manner of legal actions if the bill was not immediately paid. Fearful of his organization's credit rating in the hands of this maniacal machine, the executive called an acquaintance who was a software engineer and related the whole sorry story. Trying not to laugh, the software engineer told the executive to mail a check for $0.00. This had the desired effect, and a receipt for $0.00 was received a few days later. The executive meticulously filed it away in case at some future date the computer might allege that $0.00 was still owed.

This well-known story has a less well-known sequel. A few days later, the executive was summoned by his bank manager. The banker held up a check and asked, "Is this your check?"

The executive agreed that it was.

"Would you mind telling me why you wrote a check for $0.00?" asked the banker.

So the whole story was retold. When the executive had finished, the banker turned to him and she quietly asked, "Have you any idea what your check for $0.00 did to *our* computer system?"

A computer professional can laugh at this story, albeit somewhat nervously. After all, every one of us has designed or implemented a product that, in its original form, would have resulted in the equivalent of sending dunning letters for $0.00. Up to now, we have always caught this sort of fault during testing. But our laughter has a hollow ring to it, because at the back of our minds is the fear that someday we will not detect the fault before the product is delivered to the customer.

A decidedly less humorous software fault was detected on November 9, 1979. The Strategic Air Command had an alert scramble when the worldwide military command and control system (WWMCCS) computer network reported that the Soviet Union had launched missiles aimed toward the United States [Neumann, 1980]. What actually happened was that a simulated attack was interpreted as the real thing, just as in the movie *WarGames* some 5 years later. Although the U.S. Department of Defense understandably has not given details about the precise mechanism by which test data were taken for actual data, it seems reasonable to ascribe the problem to a software fault. Either the system as a whole was not designed to differentiate between simulations and reality or the user interface did not include the necessary checks for ensuring that end users of the system would be able to distinguish fact from fiction. In other words, a software fault, if indeed the problem was caused by software, could have brought civilization as we know it to an unpleasant and abrupt end. (See Just in Case You Wanted to Know Box 1.1 for information on disasters caused by other software faults.)

Whether we are dealing with billing or air defense, much of our software is delivered late, over budget, and with residual faults, and does not meet the client's needs. Software engineering is an attempt to solve these problems. In other words, **software engineering** is a discipline whose aim is the production of fault-free software, delivered on time and within budget, that satisfies the client's needs. Furthermore, the software must be easy to modify when the user's needs change.

The scope of software engineering is extremely broad. Some aspects of software engineering can be categorized as mathematics or computer science; other aspects fall into the areas of economics, management, or psychology. To display the wide-reaching realm of software engineering, we now examine five different aspects.

## 1.1 Historical Aspects

It is a fact that electric power generators fail, but far less frequently than payroll products. Bridges sometimes collapse but considerably less often than operating systems. In the belief that software design, implementation, and maintenance could be put on the same footing as traditional engineering disciplines, a NATO study group in 1967 coined the term

In the case of the WWMCCS network, disaster was averted at the last minute. However, the consequences of other software faults have been fatal. For example, between 1985 and 1987, at least two patients died as a consequence of severe overdoses of radiation delivered by the Therac-25 medical linear accelerator [Leveson and Turner, 1993]. The cause was a fault in the control software.

Also, during the 1991 Gulf War, a Scud missile penetrated the Patriot antimissile shield and struck a barracks near Dhahran, Saudi Arabia. In all, 28 Americans were killed and 98 wounded. The software for the Patriot missile contained a cumulative timing fault. The Patriot was designed to operate for only a few hours at a time, after which the clock was reset. As a result, the fault never had a significant effect and therefore was not detected. In the Gulf War, however, the Patriot missile battery at Dhahran ran continuously for over 100 hours. This caused the accumulated time discrepancy to become large enough to render the system inaccurate.

During the Gulf War, the United States shipped Patriot missiles to Israel for protection against the Scuds. Israeli forces detected the timing problem after only 8 hours and immediately reported it to the manufacturer in the United States. The manufacturer corrected the fault as quickly as it could, but tragically, the new software arrived the day after the direct hit by the Scud [Mellor, 1994].

Fortunately, it is extremely rare for death or serious injury to be caused by a software fault. However, one fault can cause major problems for thousands and thousands of people. For example, in February 2003, a software fault resulted in the U.S. Treasury Department mailing 50,000 Social Security checks that had been printed without the name of the beneficiary, so the checks could not be deposited or cashed [St. Petersburg Times Online, 2003]. In April 2003, borrowers were informed by SLM Corp. (commonly known as Sallie Mae) that the interest on their student loans had been miscalculated as a consequence of a software fault from 1992 but detected only at the end of 2002. Nearly 1 million borrowers were told that they would have to pay more, either in the form of higher monthly payments or extra interest payments on loans extending beyond their original 10-year terms [GJSentinel.com, 2003]. Both faults were quickly corrected, but together they resulted in nontrivial financial consequences for about a million people.

---

*software engineering*. The claim that building software is similar to other engineering tasks was endorsed by the 1968 NATO Software Engineering Conference held in Garmisch, Germany [Naur, Randell, and Buxton, 1976]. This endorsement is not too surprising; the very name of the conference reflected the belief that software production should be an engineering-like activity (but see Just in Case You Wanted to Know Box 1.2). A conclusion of the conferees was that software engineering should use the philosophies and paradigms of established engineering disciplines to solve what they termed the **software crisis**, namely, that the quality of software generally was unacceptably low and that deadlines and budgets were not being met.

Despite many software success stories, an unacceptably large proportion of software products still are being delivered late, over budget, and with residual faults. For example, the Standish Group is a research firm that analyzes software development projects. Their study of 9236 development projects completed in 2004 is summarized in Figure 1.1 [Hayes, 2004]. Only 29 percent of the projects were successfully completed, whereas 18 percent were canceled before completion or were never implemented. The remaining 53 percent of the projects were completed and installed on the client's computer. However, those projects

As stated in Section 1.1, the aim of the Garmisch conference was to make software development as successful as traditional engineering. But by no means are all traditional engineering projects successful. For example, consider bridge building.

In July 1940, construction of a suspension bridge over the Tacoma Narrows in Washington State was completed. Soon after, it was discovered that the bridge swayed and buckled dangerously in windy conditions. Approaching cars would alternately disappear into valleys and then reappear as that part of the bridge rose again. From this behavior, the bridge was given the nickname "Galloping Gertie." Finally, on November 7, 1940, the bridge collapsed in a 42 mile per hour wind; fortunately, the bridge had been closed to all traffic some hours earlier. The last 15 minutes of its life were captured on film, now stored in the U.S. National Film Registry.

A somewhat more humorous bridge construction failure was observed in January 2004. A new bridge was being built over the Upper Rhine River near the German town of Laufenberg, to connect Germany and Switzerland. The German half of the bridge was designed and constructed by a team of German engineers; the Swiss half by a Swiss team. When the two parts were connected, it immediately became apparent that the German half was some 21 inches (54 centimeters) higher than the Swiss half. Major reconstruction was needed to correct the problem, which was caused by wrongly correcting for the fact that "sea level" is taken by Swiss engineers to be the average level of the Mediterranean Sea, whereas German engineers use the North Sea. To compensate for the difference in sea levels, the Swiss side should have been raised 10.5 inches. Instead, it was lowered 10.5 inches, resulting in the gap of 21 inches [Spiegel Online, 2004].

were over budget, late, or had fewer features and functionality than initially specified. In other words, during 2004, less than one in three software development projects was successful; more than half the projects displayed one or more symptoms of the software crisis.

The financial implications of the software crisis are horrendous. In a survey conducted by the Cutter Consortium [2002], the following was reported:

- An astounding 78 percent of information technology organizations have been involved in disputes that ended in litigation.

- In 67 percent of those cases, the functionality or performance of the software products as delivered did not meet up to the claims of the software developers.

**FIGURE 1.1**

The outcomes of over 9000 development projects completed in 2004.

Source: [Hayes, 2004].

Canceled 18%

Successful 29%

Completed late, over budget, and/or with features missing 53%

- In 56 percent of those cases, the promised delivery date slipped several times.
- In 45 percent of those cases, the faults were so severe that the software product was unusable.

It is clear that far too little software is delivered on time, within budget, fault free, and meeting its client's needs. To achieve these goals, a software engineer has to acquire a broad range of skills, both technical and managerial. These skills have to be applied not just to programming but to every step of software production, from requirements to postdelivery maintenance.

That the software crisis still is with us, some 40 years later, tells us two things. First, the software production process, while resembling traditional engineering in many respects, has its own unique properties and problems. Second, the software crisis perhaps should be renamed the **software depression**, in view of its long duration and poor prognosis.

We now consider economic aspects of software engineering.

## 1.2 Economic Aspects

A software organization currently using coding technique $CT_{old}$ discovers that new coding technique $CT_{new}$ would result in code being produced in only nine-tenths of the time needed by $CT_{old}$ and, hence, at nine-tenths the cost. Common sense seems to dictate that $CT_{new}$ is the appropriate technique to use. In fact, although common sense certainly dictates that the faster technique is the technique of choice, the economics of software engineering may imply the opposite.

- One reason is the cost of introducing new technology into an organization. The fact that coding is 10 percent faster when technique $CT_{new}$ is used may be less important than the costs incurred in introducing $CT_{new}$ into the organization. It may be necessary to complete two or three projects before recouping the cost of training. Also, while attending courses on $CT_{new}$, software personnel are unable to do productive work. Even when they return, a steep learning curve may be involved; it may take many months of practice with $CT_{new}$ before software professionals become as proficient with $CT_{new}$ as they currently are with $CT_{old}$. Therefore, initial projects using $CT_{new}$ may take far longer to complete than if the organization had continued to use $CT_{old}$. All these costs need to be taken into account when deciding whether to change to $CT_{new}$.

- A second reason why the economics of software engineering may dictate that $CT_{old}$ be retained is the maintenance consequence. Coding technique $CT_{new}$ indeed may be 10 percent faster than $CT_{old}$ and the resulting code may be of comparable quality from the viewpoint of satisfying the client's current needs. But the use of technique $CT_{new}$ may result in code that is difficult to maintain, making the cost of $CT_{new}$ higher over the life of the product. Of course, if the software developer is not responsible for any postdelivery maintenance, then, from the viewpoint of just that developer, $CT_{new}$ is a more attractive proposition. After all, the use of $CT_{new}$ would cost 10 percent less. The client should insist that technique $CT_{old}$ be used and pay the higher initial costs with the expectation that the total lifetime cost of the software will be lower. Unfortunately, often the sole aim of both the client and the software provider is to produce code as quickly as possible. The long-term effects of using a particular technique generally are ignored in the interests of short-term gain. Applying economic principles to software engineering requires the client to choose techniques that reduce long-term costs.

This example deals with coding, which constitutes less than 10 percent of the software development effort. The economic principles, however, apply to all other aspects of software production as well.

We now consider the importance of maintenance.

## 1.3    Maintenance Aspects

In this section, we describe maintenance within the context of the software life cycle. A **life-cycle model** is a description of the steps that should be performed when building a software product. Many different life-cycle models have been proposed; several of them are described in Chapter 2. Because it is almost always easier to perform a sequence of smaller tasks than one large task, the overall life-cycle model is broken into a series of smaller steps, called **phases**. The number of phases varies from model to model—from as few as four to as many as eight. In contrast to a life-cycle model, which is a theoretical description of what should be done, the actual series of steps performed on a specific software product, from concept exploration through final retirement, is termed the **life cycle** of that product. In practice, the phases of the life cycle of a software product may not be carried out exactly as specified in the life-cycle model, especially when time and cost overruns are encountered. It has been claimed that more software projects have gone wrong from lack of time than for all other reasons combined [Brooks, 1975].

Until the end of the 1970s, most organizations were producing software using as their life-cycle model what now is termed the **waterfall model**. There are many variations of this model, but by and large, a product developed using this classical life-cycle model goes through the six phases shown in Figure 1.2. These phases probably do not correspond exactly to the phases of any one particular organization, but they are sufficiently close to most practices for the purposes of this book. Similarly, the precise name of each phase varies from organization to organization. The names used here for the various phases have been chosen to be as general as possible in the hope that the reader will feel comfortable with them.

1. *Requirements phase.* During the **requirements phase**, the concept is explored and refined, and the client's requirements are elicited.

2. *Analysis (specification) phase.* The client's requirements are analyzed and presented in the form of the **specification document**, "what the product is supposed to do." The

**FIGURE 1.2**
The six phases of the classical life-cycle model.

1. Requirements phase
2. Analysis (specification) phase
3. Design phase
4. Implementation phase
5. Postdelivery maintenance
6. Retirement

**analysis phase** sometimes is called the **specification phase**. At the end of this phase, a plan is drawn up, the **software project management plan**, describing the proposed software development in full detail.

3. *Design phase*. The specifications undergo two consecutive design processes during the **design phase**. First comes **architectural design**, in which the product as a whole is broken down into components, called **modules**. Then, each module is designed; this process is termed **detailed design**. The two resulting **design documents** describe "how the product does it."

4. *Implementation phase*. The various components undergo **coding** and testing (**unit testing**) separately. Then, the components of the product are combined and tested as a whole; this is termed **integration**. When the developers are satisfied that the product functions correctly, it is tested by the client (**acceptance testing**). The **implementation phase** ends when the product is accepted by the client and installed on the client's computer. (We see in Chapter 14 that coding and integration should be performed in parallel.)

5. *Postdelivery maintenance*. The product is used to perform the tasks for which it was developed. During this time, it is maintained. **Postdelivery maintenance** includes all changes to the product once the product has been delivered and installed on the client's computer and passes its acceptance test. Postdelivery maintenance includes **corrective maintenance** (or **software repair**), which consists of the removal of residual faults while leaving the specifications unchanged, as well as **enhancement** (or software update), which consists of changes to the specifications and the implementation of those changes. There are, in turn, two types of enhancement. The first is **perfective maintenance**, changes that the client thinks will improve the effectiveness of the product, such as additional functionality or decreased response time. The second is **adaptive maintenance**, changes made in response to changes in the environment in which the product operates, such as a new hardware/operating system or new government regulations. (For an insight into the three types of postdelivery maintenance, see Just in Case You Wanted to Know Box 1.3.)

6. *Retirement*. **Retirement** occurs when the product is removed from service. This occurs when the functionality provided by the product no longer is of any use to the client organization.

Now we examine the definition of *maintenance* in greater detail.

## 1.3.1  Classical and Modern Views of Maintenance

In the 1970s, software production was viewed as consisting of two distinct activities performed sequentially: *development* followed by *maintenance*. Starting from scratch, the software product was developed, and then installed on the client's computer. Any change to the software after installation on the client's computer and acceptance by the client, whether to fix a residual fault or extend the functionality, constituted classical maintenance [IEEE 610.12, 1990]. Hence, the way that software was developed classically can be described as the **development-then-maintenance model**.

This is a **temporal definition**; that is, an activity is classified as development or maintenance depending on when it is performed. Suppose that a fault in the software is detected and corrected a day after the software has been installed. By definition, this constitutes

One of the most widely quoted results in software engineering is that 17.4 percent of the postdelivery maintenance effort is corrective in nature; 18.2 percent is adaptive; 60.3 percent is perfective; and 4.1 percent can be categorized as "other." This result is taken from a paper published in 1978 [Lientz, Swanson, and Tompkins, 1978].

However, the result in that paper was not derived from *measurements* on maintenance data. Instead, the authors conducted a survey of maintenance managers who were asked to *estimate* how much time was devoted to each category within their organization as a whole and state how confident they felt about their estimate. More specifically, the participating software maintenance managers were asked whether their response was based on reasonably accurate data, minimal data, or no data; 49.3 percent stated that their answer was based on reasonably accurate data, 37.7 percent on minimal data, and 8.7 percent on no data.

In fact, one should seriously question whether any respondents had "reasonably accurate data" regarding the percentage of time devoted to the categories of maintenance included in the survey; most of them probably did not have even "minimal data." In that survey, participants were asked to state what percentage of maintenance consisted of items like "emergency fixes" or "routine debugging"; from this raw information, the percentage of adaptive, corrective, and perfective maintenance was deduced. Software engineering was just starting to emerge as a discipline in 1978, and it was the exception for software maintenance managers to collect the detailed information needed to respond to such a survey. Indeed, in modern terminology, in 1978 virtually every organization was still at CMM level 1 (see Section 3.13).

Hence, we have strong grounds for questioning whether the actual distribution of postdelivery maintenance activities back in 1978 was anything like the estimates of the managers who took part in the survey. The distribution of maintenance activities is certainly nothing like that today. For example, results on actual maintenance data for the Linux kernel [Schach et al., 2002] and the gcc compiler [Schach et al., 2003b] show that at least 50 percent of postdelivery maintenance is corrective, as opposed to the 17.4 percent figure of the survey.

---

classical maintenance. But if the identical fault is detected and corrected the day before the software is installed, in terms of the definition, this constitutes classical development. Now suppose that a software product has just been installed but the client wants to increase the functionality of the software product. Classically, that would be described as "perfective maintenance." However, if the client wants the same change to be made just before the software product is installed, this would be classical development. Again, there is no difference whatsoever between the nature of the two activities, but classically one is considered development, the other perfective maintenance.

In addition to such inconsistencies, two other reasons explain why the development-then-maintenance model is unrealistic today:

1. Nowadays, it is certainly not unusual for construction of a product to take a year or more. During this time, the client's requirements may well change. For example, the client might insist that the product now be implemented on a faster microprocessor, which has just become available. Alternatively, the client organization may have expanded into Belgium while development was under way, and the product now has to be modified so it also can handle sales in Belgium. To see how a change in requirements can affect the

software life cycle, suppose that the client's requirements change while the design is being developed. The software engineering team has to suspend development and modify the specification document to reflect the changed requirements. Furthermore, it then may be necessary to modify the design as well, if the changes to the specifications necessitate corresponding changes to those portions of the design already completed. Only when these changes have been made can development proceed. In other words, developers have to perform "maintenance" long before the product is installed.

2. A second problem with the classical development-then-maintenance model arose as a result of the way in which we now construct software. In classical software engineering, a characteristic of development was that the development team built the target product starting from scratch. In contrast, as a consequence of the high cost of software production today, wherever possible developers try to reuse parts of existing software products in the software product to be constructed (reuse is discussed in detail in Chapter 8). Therefore, the development-then-maintenance model is inappropriate today because reuse is so widespread.

A more realistic way of looking at maintenance is that given in the standard for life-cycle processes published by the International Organization for Standardization (ISO) and the International Electrotechnical Commission (IEC). That is, maintenance is the process that occurs when "software undergoes modifications to code and associated documentation due to a problem or the need for improvement or adaptation" [ISO/IEC 12207, 1995]. In terms of this **operational definition**, maintenance occurs whenever a fault is fixed or the requirements change, irrespective of whether this takes place before or after installation of the product. The Institute for Electrical and Electronics Engineers (IEEE) and the Electronic Industries Alliance (EIA) subsequently adopted this definition [IEEE/EIA 12207.0-1996, 1998] when IEEE standards were modified to comply with ISO/IEC 12207. (See Just in Case You Wanted to Know Box 1.4 for more on ISO.)

In this book, the term *postdelivery maintenance* refers to the 1990 IEEE definition of maintenance as any change to the software after it has been delivered and installed on the client's computer, and *modern maintenance*, or just **maintenance**, refers to the 1995 ISO/IEC definition of corrective, perfective, or adaptive activities performed at any time. Postdelivery maintenance is therefore a subset of (modern) maintenance.

## 1.3.2 The Importance of Postdelivery Maintenance

It is sometimes said that only bad software products undergo postdelivery maintenance. In fact, the opposite is true: Bad products are thrown away, whereas good products are repaired and enhanced, for 10, 15, or even 20 years. Furthermore, a software product is a model of the real world, and the real world is perpetually changing. As a consequence, software has to be maintained constantly for it to remain an accurate reflection of the real world.

For instance, if the sales tax rate changes from 6 to 7 percent, almost every software product that deals with buying or selling has to be changed. Suppose the product contains the C++ statement

**const float** salesTax = 6.0;

or the equivalent Java statement

**public static final float** salesTax = **(float)** 6.0;

The International Organization for Standardization (ISO) is a network of the national standards institutes of 147 countries, with a central secretariat based in Geneva, Switzerland. ISO has published over 13,500 internationally accepted standards, ranging from standards for photographic film speed ("ISO number") to many of the standards presented in this book. For example, ISO 9000 is discussed in Chapter 3.

ISO is not an acronym. It is derived from the Greek word ἴσος, meaning "equal," the root of the English prefix iso- found in words such as *isotope*, *isobar*, and *isosceles*. The International Organization for Standardization chose ISO as the short form of its name to avoid having multiple acronyms arising from the translation of the name "International Organization for Standardization" into the languages of the different member countries. Instead, to achieve international standardization, a universal short form of its name was chosen.

---

declaring that salesTax is a floating-point constant initialized to the value 6.0. In this case, maintenance is relatively simple. With the aid of a text editor the value 6.0 is replaced by 7.0 and the code is recompiled and relinked. However, if instead of using the name salesTax, the actual value 6.0 has been used in the product wherever the value of the sales tax is invoked, then such a product is extremely difficult to modify. For example, there may be occurrences of the value 6.0 in the source code that should be changed to 7.0 but are overlooked or instances of 6.0 that do not refer to sales tax but incorrectly are changed to 7.0. Finding these faults almost always is difficult and time consuming. In fact, with some software, it might be less expensive in the long run to throw away the product and recode it rather than try to determine which of the many constants need to be changed and how to make the modifications.

The real-time real world also is constantly changing. The missiles with which a jet fighter is armed may be replaced by a new model, requiring a change to the weapons control component of the associated avionics system. A six-cylinder engine is to be offered as an option in a popular four-cylinder automobile; this implies changing the onboard computers that control the fuel injection system, timing, and so on.

But just how much time (= money) is devoted to postdelivery maintenance? The pie chart in Figure 1.3(a) shows that, some 30 years ago, approximately two-thirds of total software costs went to postdelivery maintenance; the data were obtained by averaging information from various sources, including [Elshoff, 1976; Daly, 1977; Zelkowitz, Shaw, and Gannon, 1979; and Boehm, 1981]. Newer data show that an even larger proportion is devoted to postdelivery maintenance. Many organizations devote 70–80 percent or more of their software budget to postdelivery maintenance [Yourdon, 1992; Hatton, 1998], as shown in Figure 1.3(b).

Surprisingly, the average cost percentages of the classical development phases have hardly changed. This is shown in Figure 1.4, which compares the data used to derive Figure 1.3(a) with more recent data on 132 Hewlett-Packard projects [Grady, 1994].

Now consider again the software organization currently using coding technique $CT_{old}$ that learns that $CT_{new}$ will reduce coding time by 10 percent. Even if $CT_{new}$ has no adverse effect on maintenance, an astute software manager will think twice before changing coding practices. The entire staff has to be retrained, new software development tools purchased, and perhaps additional staff members hired who are experienced in the new technique. All this

**FIGURE 1.3**
Approximate average cost percentages of development and postdelivery maintenance (a) between 1976 and 1981 and (b) between 1992 and 1998.

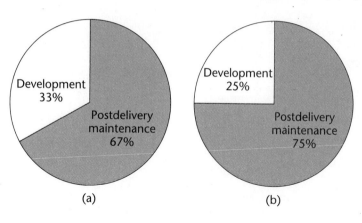

(a)                    (b)

**FIGURE 1.4**  A comparison of the approximate average cost percentages of the classical development phases for various projects between 1976 and 1981 and for 132 more recent Hewlett-Packard projects.

|  | Various Projects between 1976 and 1981 | 132 More Recent Hewlett-Packard Projects |
|---|---|---|
| Requirements and analysis (specification) phases | 21% | 18% |
| Design phase | 18 | 19 |
| Implementation phase | | |
|   Coding (including unit testing) | 36 | 34 |
|   Integration | 24 | 29 |

expense and disruption has to be endured for a decrease of at most 0.85 percent in software costs because, as shown in Figures 1.3(b) and 1.4, coding together with unit testing constitutes on average only 34 percent of 25 percent or 8.5 percent of total software costs.

Now suppose a new technique that reduces postdelivery maintenance costs by 10 percent is developed. This probably should be introduced at once, because on average, it will reduce overall costs by 7.5 percent. The overhead involved in changing to this technique is a small price to pay for such large overall savings.

Because postdelivery maintenance is so important, a major aspect of software engineering consists of those techniques, tools, and practices that lead to a reduction in postdelivery maintenance costs.

## 1.4  Requirements, Analysis, and Design Aspects

Software professionals are human and therefore sometimes make a mistake while developing a product. As a result, there will be a fault in the software. If the mistake is made while eliciting the requirements, the resulting fault will probably also appear in the specifications, the design, and the code. Clearly, the earlier we correct a fault, the better.

The relative costs of fixing a fault at various phases in the classical software life cycle are shown in Figure 1.5 [Boehm, 1981]. The figure reflects data from IBM [Fagan, 1974],

**FIGURE 1.5**   The relative cost of fixing a fault at each phase of the classical software life cycle. The solid line is the best fit for the data relating to the larger software projects, and the dashed line is the best fit for the smaller software projects.

Source: Barry Boehm, *Software Engineering Economics,* © 1981, p. 40. Adapted by permission of Prentice Hall, *Englewood Cliffs,* NJ.

GTE [Daly, 1977], the Safeguard project [Stephenson, 1976], and some smaller TRW projects [Boehm, 1980]. The solid line in Figure 1.5 is the best fit for the data relating to the larger projects, and the dashed line is the best fit for the smaller projects. For each of the phases of the classical software life cycle, the corresponding relative cost to detect and correct a fault is depicted in Figure 1.6. Each step on the solid line in Figure 1.6 is constructed by taking the corresponding point on the solid straight line of Figure 1.5 and plotting the data on a linear scale.

Suppose it costs $40 to detect and correct a specific fault during the design phase. From the solid line in Figure 1.6 (projects between 1974 and 1980), that same fault would cost only about $30 to fix during the analysis phase. But, during postdelivery maintenance, that fault would cost around $2000 to detect and correct. Newer data show that now it is even more important to detect faults early. The dashed line in Figure 1.6 shows the cost of detecting and correcting a fault during the development of system software for the IBM AS/400 [Kan et al., 1994]. On average, the same fault would have cost $3680 to fix during postdelivery maintenance of the AS/400 software.

The reason that the cost of correcting a fault increases so steeply is related to what has to be done to correct a fault. Early in the development life cycle, the product essentially exists only on paper, and correcting a fault may simply mean making a change to a document. The other extreme is a product already delivered to a client. At the very least, correcting a fault at that time means editing the code, recompiling and relinking it, and then carefully testing that the problem is solved. Next, it is critical to check that making the change has

**FIGURE 1.6**
The solid line depicts the points on the solid line of Figure 1.5 plotted on a linear scale. The dashed line depicts newer data.

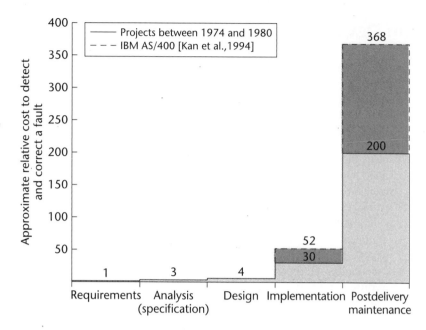

not created a new problem elsewhere in the product. All the relevant documentation, including manuals, needs to be updated. Finally, the corrected product must be delivered and reinstalled. The moral of the story is this: We must find faults early or else it will cost us money. We therefore should employ techniques for detecting faults during the requirements and analysis (specification) phases.

There is a further need for such techniques. Studies have shown [Boehm, 1979] that between 60 and 70 percent of all faults detected in large projects are requirements, analysis, or design faults. Newer results from inspections bear out this preponderance of requirements, analysis, or design faults (an inspection is a meticulous examination of a document by a team, as described in Section 6.2.3). During 203 inspections of Jet Propulsion Laboratory software for the NASA unmanned interplanetary space program, on average, about 1.9 faults were detected per page of a specification document, 0.9 faults per page of a design, but only 0.3 faults per page of code [Kelly, Sherif, and Hops, 1992].

Therefore it is important that we improve our requirements, analysis, and design techniques, not only so that faults can be found as early as possible but also because requirements, analysis, and design faults constitute such a large proportion of all faults. Just as the example in Section 1.3 showed that reducing postdelivery maintenance costs by 10 percent reduces overall costs by about 7.5 percent, reducing requirements, analysis, and design faults by 10 percent reduces the overall number of faults by 6–7 percent.

That so many faults are introduced early in the software life cycle highlights another important aspect of software engineering: techniques that yield better requirements, specifications, and designs.

Most software is produced by a team of software engineers rather than by a single individual responsible for every aspect of the development and maintenance life cycle. We now consider the implications of this.

## 1.5   Team Development Aspects

The cost of hardware continues to decrease rapidly. A mainframe computer of the 1950s that cost in excess of a million preinflation dollars was considerably less powerful in every way than a laptop computer of today costing less than $1000. As a result, organizations easily can afford hardware that can run large products, that is, products too large to be written by one person within the allowed time constraints. For example, if a product has to be delivered within 18 months but would take a single software professional 15 years to complete, then the product must be developed by a team. However, team development leads to interfacing problems among code components and communication problems among team members.

For example, Jeff and Juliet code modules p and q, respectively, where module p calls module q. When Jeff codes p, he writes a call to q with five arguments in the argument list. Juliet codes q with five arguments, but in a different order from those of Jeff. Some software tools, such as the Java interpreter and loader, or *lint* for C (Section 8.7.4), detect such a type violation but only if the interchanged arguments are of different types; if they are of the same type, then the problem may not be detected for a long period of time. It may be debated that this is a design problem, and if the modules had been more carefully designed, this problem would not have happened. That may be true, but in practice a design often is changed after coding commences, but notification of a change may not be distributed to all members of the development team. Therefore, when a design that affects two or more programmers has been changed, poor communication can lead to the interface problems Jeff and Juliet experienced. This sort of problem is less likely to occur when only one individual is responsible for every aspect of the product, as was the case before powerful computers that can run huge products became affordable.

But interfacing problems are merely the tip of the iceberg when it comes to problems that can arise when software is developed by teams. Unless the team is properly organized, an inordinate amount of time can be wasted in conferences between team members. Suppose that a product takes a single programmer 1 year to complete. If the same task is assigned to a team of six programmers, the time for completing the task frequently is closer to 1 year than the expected 2 months, and the quality of the resulting code may well be lower than if the entire task had been assigned to one individual (see Section 4.1). Because a considerable proportion of today's software is developed and maintained by teams, the scope of software engineering must include techniques for ensuring that teams are properly organized and managed.

As has been shown in the preceding sections, the scope of software engineering is extremely broad. It includes every step of the software life cycle, from requirements to postdelivery retirement. It also includes human aspects, such as team organization; economic aspects; and legal aspects, such as copyright law. All these aspects implicitly are incorporated in the definition of software engineering given at the beginning of this chapter, that software engineering is a discipline whose aim is the production of fault-free software delivered on time, within budget, and satisfying the user's needs.

We return to the classical phases of Figure 1.2 to ask why there is no planning, testing, or documentation phase.

## 1.6   Why There Is No Planning Phase

Clearly it is impossible to develop a software product without a plan. Accordingly, it appears to be essential to have a **planning phase** at the very beginning of the project.

The key point is that, until it is known exactly what is to be developed, there is no way an accurate detailed plan can be drawn up. Therefore, three types of planning activities take place when a software product is developed using the classical paradigm:

1. At the beginning of the project, preliminary planning takes place for managing the requirements and analysis phases.
2. Once what is going to be developed is known precisely, the *software project management plan* (SPMP) is drawn up. This includes the budget, staffing requirements, and detailed schedule. The earliest we can draw up the project management plan is when the specification document has been approved by the client, that is, at the end of the analysis phase. Until that time, planning has to be preliminary and partial.
3. All through the project, management needs to monitor the SPMP and be on the watch for any deviation from the plan.

For example, suppose that the SPMP for a specific project states the project as a whole will take 16 months and that the design phase will take 4 of those months. After a year, management notices that the project as a whole seems to be progressing considerably slower than anticipated. A detailed investigation shows that, so far, 8 months have been devoted to the design phase, which is still far from complete. The project almost certainly will have to be abandoned, and the funds spent to date are wasted. Instead, management should have tracked progress by phase, and noticed, after at most 2 months, a serious problem in the design phase. At that time, a decision could have been made how best to proceed. The usual initial step in such a situation is to call in a consultant to determine if the project is feasible and whether the design team is competent to carry out the task or the risk of proceeding is too great. Based on the report of the consultant, various alternatives are now considered, including reducing the scope of the target product and then designing and implementing a less ambitious one. Only if all other alternatives are considered unworkable does the project have to be canceled. In the case of the specific project, this cancellation would have taken place some 6 months earlier if management had monitored the plan closely, saving a considerable sum of money.

In conclusion, there is no separate planning phase. Instead, planning activities are carried out all through the life cycle. However, there are times when planning activities predominate. These include the beginning of the project (preliminary planning) and directly after the specification document has been signed off on by the client (software project management plan).

## 1.7   Why There Is No Testing Phase

It is essential to check a software product meticulously after it has been developed. Accordingly, it is reasonable to ask why there is no testing phase after the product has been implemented.

Unfortunately, checking a software product once it is ready to be delivered to the client is far too late. For instance, if there is a fault in the specification document, this fault will have been carried forward into the design and implementation. There are times in the process when testing is carried out almost to the total exclusion of other activities. This occurs toward the end of each phase (**verification**) and is especially true before the product is handed over to the client (**validation**). Although there are times when testing predominates, there should never be times when no testing is being performed. If testing is treated as a separate **testing phase**, then there is a very real danger that testing will not be carried out constantly throughout every phase of the product development and maintenance process.

But, even this is not enough. What is needed is continual checking of a software product. Meticulous checking should be an automatic accompaniment of every software development and maintenance activity. Conversely, a separate testing phase is incompatible with the goal of ensuring that a software product is as fault free as possible at all times.

Every software development organization should contain an independent group whose primary responsibility is to ensure that the delivered product is what the client needs and that the product has been built correctly in every way. This group is called the *software quality assurance* (SQA) group. The **quality** of software is the extent to which it meets its specifications. Quality and software quality assurance are described in more detail in Chapter 6, as is the role of SQA in setting and enforcing standards.

## 1.8    Why There Is No Documentation Phase

Just as there should never be a separate planning phase or testing phase, there also should never be a separate **documentation phase**. On the contrary, at all times, the documentation of a software product must be complete, correct, and up to date. For instance, during the analysis phase, the specification document must reflect the current version of the specifications and similarly for the other phases.

1. One reason why it is essential to ensure that the documentation is always up to date is the large turnover in personnel in the software industry. For example, suppose that the design documentation has not been kept current and the chief designer leaves to take another job. It is now extremely hard to update the design document to reflect all the changes made while the system was being designed.

2. It is almost impossible to perform the steps of a specific phase unless the documentation of the previous phase is complete, correct, and up to date. For instance, an incomplete specification document must inevitably result in an incomplete design and then in an incomplete implementation.

3. It is virtually impossible to test whether a software product is working correctly unless documents are available that state how that software product is supposed to behave.

4. Maintenance is almost impossible unless there is a complete and correct set of documentation that describes precisely what the current version of the product does.

Therefore, just as there is no separate planning phase or testing phase, there is no separate documentation phase. Instead, planning, testing, and documentation should be activities that accompany all other activities while a software product is being constructed.

Now we examine the object-oriented paradigm.

# 1.9   The Object-Oriented Paradigm

Before 1975, most software organizations used no specific techniques; each individual worked his or her own way. Major breakthroughs were made between approximately 1975 and 1985, with the development of the so-called **structured** or **classical paradigm**. The techniques constituting the classical paradigm include structured systems analysis (Section 11.3), data flow analysis (Section 13.3), structured programming, and structured testing (Section 14.13.2). These techniques seemed extremely promising when first used. However, as time passed, they proved to be somewhat less successful in two respects:

1. The techniques sometimes were unable to cope with the increasing size of software products. That is, the classical techniques were adequate when dealing with small-scale products (typically 5000 lines of code) or even medium-scale products of 50,000 lines of code. Today, however, large-scale products of 500,000 lines of code are relatively common; even products of 5 million or more lines of code are not considered unusual. However, the classical techniques frequently could not scale up sufficiently to handle the development of today's larger products.

2. The classical paradigm did not live up to earlier expectations during postdelivery maintenance. A major driving force behind the development of the classical paradigm 30 years ago was that, on average, two-thirds of the software budget was being devoted to postdelivery maintenance (see Figure 1.3). Unfortunately, the classical paradigm has not solved this problem; as pointed out in Section 1.3.2, many organizations still spend 70–80 percent or more of their time and effort on postdelivery maintenance [Yourdon, 1992; Hatton, 1998].

A major reason for the limited success of the classical paradigm is that classical techniques are either operation oriented or attribute (data) oriented but not both. The basic components of a software product are the operations of the product and the attributes on which those operations operate. For example, determine_average_height[1] is an operation that operates on a collection of heights (attributes) and returns the average of those heights (attribute). Some classical techniques, such as data flow analysis (Section 13.3), are operation oriented. That is, such techniques concentrate on the operations of the product; the attributes are of secondary importance. Conversely, techniques such as Jackson system development (Section 13.5) are attribute oriented. The emphasis here is on the attributes; the operations that operate on the attributes are less significant.

In contrast, the object-oriented paradigm considers both attributes and operations to be equally important. A simplistic way of looking at an object is as a unified software artifact that incorporates both the attributes and the operations performed on the attributes (an **artifact** is a component of a software product, such as a specification document, a code module, or a manual). This definition of an object is incomplete and is fleshed out later in

---

[1] In this book, the name of a variable in a classical software product is written using the classical convention of separating the parts of a variable name with underscores, for example, this_is_a_classical_variable. A variable in an object-oriented software product is written using the object-oriented convention of using an uppercase letter to mark the start of a new part of the name of a variable, for example, thisIsAnObjectOrientedVariable.

**FIGURE 1.7**  A comparison of implementations of a bank account using (a) the classical paradigm and (b) the object-oriented paradigm. The solid black line surrounding the object denotes that details as to how accountBalance is implemented are not known outside the object.

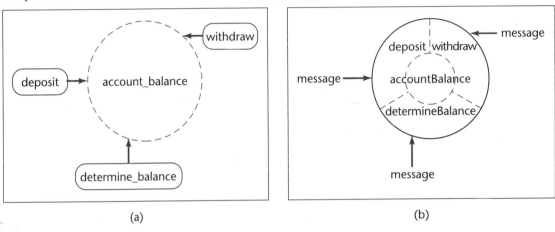

(a)                                                                        (b)

the book, once *inheritance* has been defined (Section 7.8). Nevertheless, the definition captures much of the essence of an object.

A bank account is one example of an object (see Figure 1.7). The attribute component of the object is the accountBalance. The operations that can be performed on that account balance include deposit money in the account, withdraw money from the account, and determineBalance. The bank account object combines an attribute together with the three operations performed on that attribute in a single artifact. From the viewpoint of the classical paradigm, a product that deals with banking would have to incorporate an attribute, the account_balance, and three operations, deposit, withdraw, and determine_balance.

Up to now, there seems to be little difference between the two approaches. However, a key point is the way in which an object is implemented. Specifically, details as to how the attributes of an object are stored are not known from outside the object. This is an instance of "information hiding," discussed in more detail in Section 7.6. In the case of the bank account object shown in Figure 1.7(b), the rest of the software product is aware that there is such a thing as a balance within a bank account object, but it has no idea as to the format of accountBalance. That is, there is no knowledge outside the object as to whether the account balance is implemented as an integer or a floating-point number or a field (component) of some larger structure. This information barrier surrounding the object is denoted by the solid black line in Figure 1.7(b), which depicts an implementation using the object-oriented paradigm. In contrast, a dashed line surrounds account_balance in Figure 1.7(a), because all the details of account_balance are known to the modules in the implementation using the classical paradigm, and the value of account_balance therefore can be changed by any of them.

Returning to Figure 1.7(b), the object-oriented implementation, if a customer deposits $10 in an account, then a **message** is sent to the deposit method of the relevant object telling it to increment the accountBalance attribute by $10 (a **method** is an implementation of an operation). The deposit method is within the bank account object and knows how the accountBalance is implemented; this is denoted by the dashed circular line inside the object. But no entity external to the object needs this knowledge. That the three methods in Figure 1.7(b) shield accountBalance from the rest of the product symbolizes this localization of knowledge. The fact that implementation details are local to an object leads the first of the many strengths of the object-oriented paradigm:

1. Consider postdelivery maintenance. Suppose that the banking product has been constructed using the classical paradigm. If the way an account_balance is represented is changed from (say) an integer to a field of a structure, then every part of that product with anything to do with an account_balance has to be changed and these changes have to be made consistently. In contrast, if the object-oriented paradigm is used, then changes need be made only within the bank account object itself. No other part of the product has knowledge of how an accountBalance is implemented, so no other part can have access to an accountBalance. Consequently, no other part of the banking product needs to be changed. Accordingly, the object-oriented paradigm makes maintenance quicker and easier, and the chance of introducing a **regression fault** (that is, a fault inadvertently introduced into one part of a product as a consequence of making an apparently unrelated change to another part of the product) is greatly reduced.

2. In addition to maintenance, the object-oriented paradigm also makes development easier. In many instances, an object has a physical counterpart. For example, a bank account object in the bank product corresponds to an actual bank account in the bank for which this product is being written. As will be shown in Part 2, modeling plays a major role in the object-oriented paradigm. The close correspondence between the objects in a product and their counterparts in the real world should lead to better-quality software.

3. Well-designed objects are independent units. As has been explained, an object consists of both attributes and the operations performed on the attributes. If all the operations performed on the attributes of an object are included in that object, then the object can be considered a conceptually independent entity. Everything in the product that relates to the portion of the real world modeled by that object can be found in the object itself. This conceptual independence sometimes is termed **encapsulation** (Section 7.4). But there is an additional form of independence, physical independence. In a well-designed object, information hiding ensures that implementation details are hidden from everything outside that object. The only allowable form of communication is sending a message to the object to carry out a specific operation. The way that the operation is carried out is entirely the responsibility of the object itself. For this reason, object-oriented design sometimes is referred to as **responsibility-driven design** [Wirfs-Brock, Wilkerson, and Wiener, 1990] or **design by contract** [Meyer, 1992]. (For another view of responsibility-driven design, see Just in Case You Wanted to Know Box 1.5, derived from an example in [Budd, 2002].)

4. A product built using the classical paradigm is implemented as a set of modules, but conceptually it is essentially a single unit. This is one reason why the classical paradigm has been less successful when applied to larger products. In contrast, when the object-oriented paradigm is used correctly, the resulting product consists of a number of smaller, largely independent units. The object-oriented paradigm reduces the level of complexity of a software product and hence simplifies both development and maintenance.

Suppose that you live in New Orleans, and you want to send a Mother's Day bouquet to your mother in Chicago. One strategy would be to consult the Chicago yellow pages (on the World Wide Web), determine which florist is located closest to your mother's apartment, and place your order with that florist. A more convenient way is to order the flowers at **1-800-flowers.com**, leaving the total responsibility for delivering the flowers to that company. It is irrelevant where **1-800-flowers.com** is physically located or which florist is given your order to deliver. In any event, the company does not divulge that information, an instance of information hiding.

In exactly the same way, when a message is sent to an object, not only is it entirely irrelevant how the request is carried out, but the unit that sends the message is not even allowed to know the internal structure of the object. The object itself is entirely responsible for every detail of carrying out the message.

5. The object-oriented paradigm promotes reuse; because objects are independent entities, they can be utilized in future products. This reuse of objects reduces the time and cost of both development and maintenance, as explained in Chapter 8.

When the object-oriented paradigm is utilized, the classical software life cycle of Figure 1.2 has to be modified. Figure 1.8 compares the life-cycle model of the classical paradigm with that of the object-oriented paradigm.

The first difference appears to be purely terminological; the word *phase* is used for the classical paradigm, whereas *workflow* is used for the object-oriented paradigm. In fact, as will be explained in detail in Chapter 2, there is no correspondence between a phase and a workflow. On the contrary, the two terms are totally distinct, and this distinction epitomizes the differences between the life-cycle models that underlie the two paradigms.

In this chapter, we consider another difference between the two paradigms, the role played by modules (in the classical paradigm) versus that played by objects (in the object-oriented paradigm). First consider the design phase of the classical paradigm. As stated in Section 1.3, this phase is divided into two subphases: architectural design followed by detailed design. In the architectural design subphase, the product is decomposed into components, called *modules*. Then, during the detailed design subphase, the data structures and algorithms of each module are designed in turn. Finally, during the implementation phase, these modules are implemented.

If the object-oriented paradigm is used instead, one of the steps of the object-oriented analysis workflow is to determine the classes. Because a class is a kind of module, architectural

**FIGURE 1.8**

Comparison of the life-cycle models of the classical paradigm and the object-oriented paradigm.

| Classical Paradigm | Object-Oriented Paradigm |
|---|---|
| 1. Requirements phase | 1. Requirements workflow |
| 2. Analysis (specification) phase | 2′. Object-oriented analysis workflow |
| 3. Design phase | 3′. Object-oriented design workflow |
| 4. Implementation phase | 4′. Object-oriented implementation workflow |
| 5. Postdelivery maintenance | 5. Postdelivery maintenance |
| 6. Retirement | 6. Retirement |

**FIGURE 1.9**
Differences
between the
classical
paradigm and
the object-
oriented
paradigm.

| Classical Paradigm | Object-Oriented Paradigm |
|---|---|
| 2. Analysis (specification) phase<br>• Determine what the product is to do | 2′. Object-oriented analysis workflow<br>• Determine what the product is to do<br>• Extract the classes |
| 3. Design phase<br>• Architectural design (extract the modules)<br>• Detailed design | 3′. Object-oriented design workflow<br>• Detailed design |
| 4. Implementation phase<br>• Code the modules in an appropriate programming language<br>• Integrate | 4′. Object-oriented implementation workflow<br>• Code the classes in an appropriate object-oriented programming language<br>• Integrate |

design is performed during the object-oriented analysis workflow. Consequently, object-oriented analysis goes further than the corresponding analysis (specification) phase of the classical paradigm. This is shown in Figure 1.9.

This difference between the two paradigms has major consequences. When the classical paradigm is used, there almost always is a sharp transition between the analysis phase and the design phase. After all, the aim of the analysis phase is to determine *what* the product is to do, whereas the purpose of the design phase is to decide *how* to do it. In contrast, when object-oriented analysis is used, objects enter the life cycle from the very beginning. The objects are extracted in the analysis workflow, designed in the design workflow, and coded in the implementation workflow. The object-oriented paradigm is therefore an integrated approach; the transition from workflow to workflow is far smoother than with the classical paradigm, reducing the number of faults introduced during development.

As already mentioned, it is inadequate to define an object merely as a software artifact that encapsulates both attributes and operations and implements the principle of information hiding. A more complete definition is given in Chapter 7, where objects are examined in depth.

## 1.10   The Object-Oriented Paradigm in Perspective

Figure 1.1 is evidence of the many shortcomings of the classical (structured) paradigm. However, the object-oriented paradigm is by no means a panacea of all ills:

- Like all approaches to software production, the object-oriented paradigm has to be used correctly; it is just as easy to misuse the object-oriented paradigm as any other paradigm.
- When correctly applied, the object-oriented paradigm can solve some (but not all) of the problems of the classical paradigm.
- The object-oriented paradigm has some problems of its own, as described in Section 7.9.
- The object-oriented paradigm is the best approach available today. However, like all technologies, it is certain to be superseded by a superior technology in the future.

In this book, strengths and weaknesses of both the classical and the object-oriented paradigm are pointed out within the context of the specific topic under discussion.

Consequently, the comparison of the two paradigms does not appear in one single place but is spread over the entire book.

We now define a number of software engineering terms.

# 1.11   Terminology

The **client** is the individual who wants a product to be built (developed). The **developers** are the members of a team responsible for building that product. The developers may be responsible for every aspect of the process, from the requirements onward, or they may be responsible for only the implementation of an already designed product.

Both the client and developers may be part of the same organization. For example, the client may be the head actuary of an insurance company and the developers a team headed by the vice-president for software development of that insurance company. This is termed **internal software development**. On the other hand, with **contract software** the client and developers are members of totally independent organizations. For instance, the client may be a senior official in the Department of Defense and the developers employees of a major defense contractor specializing in software for weapons systems. On a much smaller scale, the client may be an accountant in a one-person practice and the developer a student who earns income by writing software on a part-time basis.

The third party involved in software production is the **user**. The user is the person or persons on whose behalf the client has commissioned the product and who will utilize the software. In the insurance company example, the users may be insurance agents, who will use the software to select the most appropriate policy. In some instances, the client and the user are the same person (for example, the accountant discussed previously).

As opposed to expensive custom software written for one client, multiple copies of software, such as word processors or spreadsheets, are sold at much lower prices to a large numbers of buyers. That is, the manufacturers of such software (such as Microsoft or Borland) recover the cost of developing a product by volume selling. This type of software usually is called **commercial off-the-shelf (COTS) software**. The earlier term for this type of software was **shrink-wrapped software**, because the box containing the CD or diskettes, the manuals, and the license agreement almost always was shrink-wrapped. Nowadays, COTS software often is downloaded over the World Wide Web—there is no box to shrink-wrap. For this reason, COTS software nowadays sometimes is referred to as **clickware**. COTS software is developed for "the market"; that is, there are no specific clients or users until the software has been developed and is available for purchase.

**Open-source software** is becoming extremely popular. An open-source software product is developed and maintained by a team of volunteers and may be downloaded and used free of charge by anyone. Widely used open-source products include the Linux operating system, the Firefox Web browser, and the Apache Web server. The term *open source* refers to the availability of the source code to all, unlike most commercial products where only the executable version is sold. Because any user of an open-source product can scrutinize the source code and report faults to the developers, many open-source software products are of high quality. The expected consequence of the public nature of faults in open-source software was formalized by Raymond in *The Cathedral and the Bazaar* as *Linus's Law*, named after Linus Torvalds, the creator of Linux [Raymond, 2000].

**Linus's Law** states that "given enough eyeballs, all bugs are shallow." In other words, if enough individuals scrutinize the source code of an open-source software product, someone should be able to locate that fault and suggest how to fix it. A related principle is "Release early. Release often" [Raymond, 2000]. That is, open-source developers tend to spend less time on testing than closed-source developers, preferring to release a new version of a product virtually as soon as it is finished, leaving much of the responsibility for testing to users.

A word used on almost every page of this book is **software**. Software consists of not just code in machine-readable form but also all the documentation that is an intrinsic component of every project. Software includes the specification document, the design document, legal and accounting documents of all kinds, the software project management plan, and other management documents as well as all types of manuals.

Since the 1970s, the difference between a **program** and a **system** has become blurred. In the "good old days," the distinction was clear. A program was an autonomous piece of code, generally in the form of a deck of punched cards that could be executed. A system was a related collection of programs. A system might consist of programs P, Q, R, and S. Magnetic tape $T_1$ was mounted, and then program P was run. It caused a deck of data cards to be read in and produced as output tapes $T_2$ and $T_3$. Tape $T_2$ then was rewound, and program Q was run, producing tape $T_4$ as output. Program R now merged tapes $T_3$ and $T_4$ into tape $T_5$; $T_5$ served as input for program S, which printed a series of reports.

Compare that situation with a product, running on a machine with a front-end communications processor and a back-end database manager, that performs real-time control of a steel mill. The single piece of software controlling the steel mill does far more than the old-fashioned system, but in terms of the classic definitions of program and system, this software undoubtedly is a program. To add to the confusion, the term *system* now is also used to denote the hardware–software combination. For example, the flight control system in an aircraft consists of both the in-flight computers and the software running on them. Depending on who is using the term, the flight control system also may include the controls, such as the joystick, that send commands to the computer and the parts of the aircraft, such as the wing flaps, controlled by the computer. Furthermore, within the context of traditional software development, the term **systems analysis** refers to the first two phases (requirements and analysis phases) and **systems design** refers to the third phase (design phase).

To minimize confusion, this book uses the term **product** to denote a nontrivial piece of software. There are two reasons for this convention. The first is simply to obviate the program versus system confusion by using a third term. The second reason is more important. This book deals with the **process** of software production, and the end result of a process is termed a *product*. Finally, the term *system* is used in its modern sense, that is, the combined hardware and software, or as part of universally accepted phrases, such as operating system and management information system.

Two words widely used within the context of software engineering are *methodology* and *paradigm*. In the 1970s, the word **methodology** began to be used in the sense of "a way of developing a software product"; the word actually means the "science of methods." Then, in the 1980s, the word **paradigm** became a major buzzword of the business world, as in the phrase, "It's a whole new paradigm." The software industry soon started using the word *paradigm* in the phrases **object-oriented paradigm** and classical (or **traditional**) **paradigm** to mean "a style of software development." This was another unfortunate

The first use of the word *bug* to denote a fault is attributed to the late Rear Admiral Grace Murray Hopper, one of the designers of COBOL. On September 9, 1945, a moth flew into the Mark II computer that Hopper and her colleagues used at Harvard and lodged between the contact plates of a relay. Thus, there was actually a bug in the system. Hopper taped the bug to the log book and wrote, "First actual case of bug being found." The log book, with moth still attached, is in the Naval Museum at the Naval Surface Weapons Center, in Dahlgren, Virginia.

Although this may have been the first use of *bug* in a computer context, the word was used in engineering slang in the 19th century [Shapiro, 1994]. For example, Thomas Alva Edison wrote on November 18, 1878, "This thing gives out and then that—'Bugs'—as such little faults and difficulties are called ..." [Josephson, 1992]. One of the definitions of *bug* in the 1934 Edition of *Webster's New English Dictionary* is, "A defect in apparatus or its operation." It is clear from Hopper's remark that she, too, was familiar with the use of the word in that context; otherwise, she would have explained what she meant.

choice of terminology, because a paradigm is a model or a pattern. Erudite readers offended by this corruption of the English language are warmly invited to take up the cudgels of linguistic accuracy on the author's behalf; he is tired of tilting at windmills.

A methodology or a paradigm applies to the process as a whole. In contrast, a **technique** is applicable to a portion of the software process. Examples include coding techniques, documentation techniques, and planning techniques.

When a programmer makes a **mistake**, the consequence of that mistake is a **fault** in the code. Executing the software product then results in a **failure**, that is, the observed incorrect behavior of the product as a consequence of the fault. An **error** is the amount by which a result is incorrect. The terms *mistake, fault, failure,* and *error* are defined in IEEE Standard 610.12, "A Glossary of Software Engineering Terminology" [IEEE 610.12, 1990], reaffirmed in 2002 [IEEE Standards, 2003]. The word **defect** is a generic term that refers to a fault, failure, or error. In the interests of precision, in this book we therefore minimize use of the umbrella term *defect*.

One term that is avoided as far as possible is **bug** (the history of this word is in Just in Case You Wanted to Know Box 1.6). The term *bug* nowadays is simply a euphemism for a *fault*. Although there generally is no real harm in using euphemisms, the word bug has overtones that are not conducive to good software production. Specifically, instead of saying, "I made a mistake," a programmer will say, "A bug crept into the code" (not *my* code but *the* code), thereby transferring responsibility for the mistake from the programmer to the bug. No one blames a programmer for coming down with a case of influenza, because the flu is caused by the flu bug. Referring to a mistake as a bug is a way of casting off responsibility. In contrast, the programmer who says, "I made a mistake," is a computer professional who takes responsibility for his or her actions.

Considerable confusion surrounds object-oriented terminology. For example, in addition to the term **attribute** for a data component of an object, the term **state variable** sometimes is used in the object-oriented literature. In Java, the term is **instance variable**. In C++ the term **field** is used, and in Visual Basic .NET, the term is **property**. With regard to the implementation of the operations of an object, the term *method* usually is used; in C++, however, the term is **member function**. In C++, a member of an object refers to either an attribute ("field") or a method. In Java, the term *field* is used to denote either an attribute ("instance variable") or a method. To avoid confusion, wherever possible, the generic terms *attribute* and *method* are used in this book.

Fortunately, some terminology is widely accepted. For example, when a method within an object is invoked, this almost universally is termed **sending a message** to the object.

## 1.12   Ethical Issues

We conclude this chapter on a cautionary note. Software products are developed and maintained by humans. If those individuals are hard working, intelligent, sensible, up to date, and above all, *ethical*, then the chances are good that the way that the software products they develop and maintain will be satisfactory. Unfortunately, the converse is equally true.

Most societies for professionals have a code of **ethics** to which all its members must adhere. The two major societies for computer professionals, the Association for Computing Machinery (ACM) and the Computer Society of the Institute of Electrical and Electronics Engineers (IEEE-CS) jointly approved a Software Engineering Code of Ethics and Professional Practice as the standard for teaching and practicing software engineering [IEEE/ACM, 1999]. It is lengthy, so a short version, consisting of a preamble and eight principles, was also produced. Here is the short version:

**Software Engineering Code of Ethics and Professional Practice[2] (Version 5.2)**

**as recommended by the IEEE-CS/ACM Joint Task Force on
Software Engineering Ethics and Professional Practices
Short Version
Preamble**

The short version of the code summarizes aspirations at a high level of abstraction; the clauses that are included in the full version give examples and details of how these aspirations change the way we act as software engineering professionals. Without the aspirations, the details can become legalistic and tedious; without the details, the aspirations can become high sounding but empty; together, the aspirations and the details form a cohesive code.

Software engineers shall commit themselves to making the analysis, specification, design, development, testing and maintenance of software a beneficial and respected profession. In accordance with their commitment to the health, safety and welfare of the public, software engineers shall adhere to the following Eight Principles:

1. *Public*—Software engineers shall act consistently with the public interest.
2. *Client and Employer*—Software engineers shall act in a manner that is in the best interests of their client and employer consistent with the public interest.
3. *Product*—Software engineers shall ensure that their products and related modifications meet the highest professional standards possible.
4. *Judgment*—Software engineers shall maintain integrity and independence in their professional judgment.
5. *Management*—Software engineering managers and leaders shall subscribe to and promote an ethical approach to the management of software development and maintenance.

---

[2] © 1999 by the Institute of Electrical and Electronics Engineers, Inc., and the Association for Computing Machinery, Inc.

6. *Profession*—Software engineers shall advance the integrity and reputation of the profession consistent with the public interest.
7. *Colleagues*—Software engineers shall be fair to and supportive of their colleagues.
8. *Self*—Software engineers shall participate in lifelong learning regarding the practice of their profession and shall promote an ethical approach to the practice of the profession.

The codes of ethics of other societies for computer professionals express similar sentiments. It is vital for the future of our profession that we adhere rigorously to such codes of ethics.

In Chapter 2, we examine various life-cycle models in order to shed further light on the differences between the classical and the object-oriented paradigm.

---

**Chapter Review**

Software engineering is defined (Section 1.1) as a discipline whose aim is the production of fault-free software that satisfies the user's needs and is delivered on time and within budget. To achieve this goal, appropriate techniques have to be used throughout software production, including when performing analysis (specification) and design (Section 1.4) and postdelivery maintenance (Section 1.3). Software engineering addresses all the steps of the software life cycle and incorporates aspects of many different areas of human knowledge, including economics (Section 1.2) and the social sciences (Section 1.5). There is no separate planning phase (Section 1.6), no testing phase (Section 1.7), and no documentation phase (Section 1.8). In Section 1.9, objects are introduced, and a comparison between the classical and object-oriented paradigms is made. Then the object-oriented paradigm is evaluated (Section 1.10). Next, in Section 1.11, the terminology used in this book is explained. Finally, ethical issues are discussed in Section 1.12.

---

**For Further Reading**

The earliest source of information on the scope of software engineering is [Boehm, 1976]. For an analysis of the extent to which software engineering can be considered to be a true engineering discipline, see [Wasserman, 1996] and [Ebert, Matsubara, Pezzé, and Bertelsen, 1997]. The future of software engineering is discussed in [Brereton et al., 1999; Kroeker et al., 1999; and Finkelstein, 2000]. The current state of the practice of software engineering is described in a variety of articles in the November/December 2003 issue of *IEEE Software*.

For a view on the importance of postdelivery maintenance in software engineering and how to plan for it, see [Parnas, 1994]. The unreliability of software and the resulting risks (especially in safety-critical systems) are discussed in [Mellor, 1994] and [Neumann, 1995]. Software development for COTS-based products is the subject of [Brownsword, Oberndorf, and Sledge, 2000]. Acquiring COTS components is described in [Ulkuniemi and Seppanen, 2004] and in [Keil and Tiwana, 2005].

Risks in enterprise systems are described in [Scott and Vessey, 2002] and in information systems in general in [Longstaff, Chittister, Pethia, and Haimes, 2000]. A modern view of the software crisis appears in [Glass, 1998]. Zvegintzov [1998] explains just how little accurate data on software engineering practice actually are available.

The fact that mathematics underpins software engineering is stressed in [Devlin, 2001]. The importance of economics in software engineering is discussed in [Boehm, 1981; Baetjer, 1996; and Boehm and Huang, 2003]. The November/December 2002 issue of *IEEE Software* contains a number of articles on software engineering economics.

Two classic books on the social sciences and software engineering are [Weinberg, 1971], and [Shneiderman, 1980]. Neither book requires prior knowledge of psychology or the behavioral sciences in general. A newer book on the topic is [DeMarco and Lister, 1987].

Brooks's [1975] timeless work, *The Mythical Man-Month*, is a highly recommended introduction to the realities of software engineering. The book includes sections on all the topics mentioned in this chapter.

An excellent introduction to open-source software is [Raymond, 2000]. Paulsen, Succi, and Eberlein [2004] present an empirical study comparing open- and closed-source software products. Reuse of open-source components is described in [Madanmohan and De', 2004]. A variety of articles on open-source software appears in the January/February 2004 issue of *IEEE Software* and in issue No. 2, 2005, of *IBM Systems Journal*.

Excellent introductions to the object-oriented paradigm include [Meyer, 1997] and [Budd, 2002]. A balanced perspective of the paradigm is given in [Radin, 1996]. Khan, Al-A'ali, and Girgis [1995] explain the differences between the classical and object-oriented paradigms. Three successful projects carried out using the object-oriented paradigm are described in [Capper, Colgate, Hunter, and James, 1994], with a detailed analysis. A survey of the attitudes of 150 experienced software developers toward the object-oriented paradigm is reported in [Johnson, 2000]. Lessons learned from developing large-scale object-oriented products are presented in [Maring, 1996] and [Fichman and Kemerer, 1997]. Potential pitfalls of the object-oriented paradigm are described in [Webster, 1995].

## Key Terms

| | | |
|---|---|---|
| acceptance testing *9* | error *26* | phase *8* |
| adaptive maintenance *9* | ethics *27* | planning phase *17* |
| analysis phase *9* | failure *26* | postdelivery maintenance *9* |
| architectural design *9* | fault *26* | process *25* |
| artifact *19* | field *26* | product *25* |
| attribute *26* | implementation phase *9* | program *25* |
| bug *26* | instance variable *26* | property *26* |
| classical paradigm *19* | integration *9* | quality *18* |
| clickware *24* | internal software | regression fault *21* |
| client *24* |   development *24* | requirements phase *8* |
| coding *9* | life cycle *8* | responsibility-driven |
| commercial-off-the-shelf | life-cycle model *8* |   design *21* |
|   (COTS) software *24* | Linus's Law *25* | retirement *9* |
| contract software *24* | maintenance *11* | send a message *27* |
| corrective maintenance *9* | member function *26* | shrink-wrapped software *24* |
| defect *26* | message *20* | software *25* |
| design by contract *21* | method *20* | software crisis *5* |
| design document *9* | methodology *25* | software depression *7* |
| design phase *9* | mistake *26* | software engineering *4* |
| detailed design *9* | module *9* | software project management |
| developer *24* | object-oriented paradigm *25* |   plan *9* |
| development-then- | open-source software *24* | software repair *9* |
|   maintenance model *9* | operational definition (of | specification document *8* |
| documentation phase *18* |   maintenance) *11* | specification phase *9* |
| encapsulation *21* | paradigm *25* | state variable *26* |
| enhancement *9* | perfective maintenance *9* | structured paradigm *19* |

system *25*
systems analysis *25*
systems design *25*
technique *26*
temporal definition
   (of maintenance) *9*

testing phase *18*
traditional paradigm *25*
unit testing *9*
user *24*

validation *18*
verification *18*
waterfall model *8*

**Problems**

1.1   You are in charge of automating a large bakery. The cost of developing the software has been estimated to be $425,000. Approximately how much additional money will be needed for post-delivery maintenance of the software?

1.2   Is there a way of reconciling the classical temporal definition of maintenance with the operational definition we now use? Explain your answer.

1.3   You are a software-engineering consultant. The chief information officer of a regional gasoline distribution corporation wants you to develop a software product that will carry out all the accounting functions of the company and provide online information to the head office staff regarding orders and inventory in the various company storage tanks. Computers are required for 21 accounting clerks, 15 order clerks, and 37 storage tank clerks. In addition, 14 managers need access to the data. The company is willing to pay $30,000 for the hardware and the software together and wants the complete software product in 4 weeks. What do you tell him? Bear in mind that your company wants his corporation's business, no matter how unreasonable his request.

1.4   You are a vice-admiral in the Velorian Navy. It has been decided to call in a software development organization to develop the control software for a new generation of ship-to-ship missiles. You are in charge of supervising the project. In order to protect the government of Veloria, what clauses do you include in the contract with the software developers?

1.5   You are a software engineer whose job is to supervise the development of the software in Problem 1.4. List ways your company can fail to satisfy the contract with the navy. What are the probable causes of such failures?

1.6   Seven months after delivery, a fault is detected in the software of a product that analyses DNA using the Stein–Röntgen reagent. The cost of fixing the fault is $16,700. The cause of the fault is an ambiguous sentence in the specification document. Approximately how much would it have cost to have corrected the fault during the analysis phase?

1.7   Suppose that the fault in Problem 1.6 had been detected during the implementation phase. Approximately how much would it have cost to have fixed it then?

1.8   You are the president of an organization that builds large-scale software. You show Figure 1.6 to your employees, urging them to find faults early in the software life cycle. Someone responds that it is unreasonable to expect anyone to remove faults before they have entered the product. For example, how can anyone remove a fault while the design is being produced if the fault in question is a coding fault? What do you reply?

1.9   Describe a situation in which the client, developer, and user are the same person.

1.10   What problems can arise if the client, developer, and user are the same person? How can these problems be solved?

1.11   What potential advantages accrue if the client, developer, and user are the same person?

1.12   Look up the word *system* in a dictionary. How many different definitions are there? Write down those definitions that are applicable within the context of software engineering.

1.13   It is your first day at your first job. Your manager hands you a program listing and says, "See if you can find the bug." What do you reply?

1.14  You are in charge of developing the product in Problem 1.1. Will you use the object-oriented paradigm or the classical paradigm? Give reasons for your answer.

1.15  Instead of implementing component c9 of a software product, the developers decide to buy a COTS component with the same specifications as component c9. What are the advantages and disadvantages of this approach?

1.16  Instead of implementing component c37 of a software product, the developers decide to utilize an open-source component with the same specifications as component c37. What are the advantages and disadvantages of this approach?

1.17  (Term Project) Suppose that the product for Osric's Office Appliances and Decor of Appendix A has been implemented exactly as described. Now Osric wants the product to be modified so that the priority of a customer in the queue can be manually changed. In what ways will the existing product have to be changed? Would it be better to discard everything and start again from scratch?

1.18  (Readings in Software Engineering) Your instructor will distribute copies of Schach et al. [2003b]. What is your opinion of the relative merits of results based on managers' estimates compared to results computed from actual data?

## References

[Baetjer, 1996] H. BAETJER, *Software as Capital: An Economic Perspective on Software Engineering,* IEEE Computer Society Press, Los Alamitos, CA, 1996.

[Boehm, 1976] B. W. BOEHM, "Software Engineering," *IEEE Transactions on Computers* **C-25** (December 1976), pp. 1226–41.

[Boehm, 1979] B. W. BOEHM, "Software Engineering, R & D Trends and Defense Needs," in: *Research Directions in Software Technology,* P. Wegner (Editor), The MIT Press, Cambridge, MA, 1979.

[Boehm, 1980] B. W. BOEHM, "Developing Small-Scale Application Software Products: Some Experimental Results," *Proceedings of the Eighth IFIP World Computer Congress,* October 1980, pp. 321–26.

[Boehm, 1981] B. W. BOEHM, *Software Engineering Economics,* Prentice Hall, Englewood Cliffs, NJ, 1981.

[Boehm and Huang, 2003] B. BOEHM AND L. G. HUANG, "Value-Based Software Engineering: A Case Study," *IEEE Computer* **36** (March 2003), pp. 33–41.

[Brereton et al., 1999] P. BRERETON, D. BUDGEN, K. BENNETT, M. MUNRO, P. LAYZELL, L. MACAULAY, D. GRIFFITHS, AND C. STANNETT, "The Future of Software," *Communications of the ACM* **42** (December 1999), pp. 78–84.

[Brooks, 1975] F. P. BROOKS, JR., *The Mythical Man-Month: Essays on Software Engineering,* Addison-Wesley, Reading, MA, 1975; Twentieth Anniversary Edition, Addison-Wesley, Reading, MA, 1995.

[Brownsword, Oberndorf, and Sledge, 2000] L. BROWNSWORD, T. OBERNDORF, AND C. A. SLEDGE, "Developing New Process for COTS-Based Systems," *IEEE Software* **17** (July/August 2000), pp. 40–47.

[Budd, 2002] T. A. BUDD, *An Introduction to Object-Oriented Programming,* 3rd ed., Addison-Wesley, Reading, MA, 2002.

[Capper, Colgate, Hunter, and James, 1994] N. P. CAPPER, R. J. COLGATE, J. C. HUNTER, AND M. F. JAMES, "The Impact of Object-Oriented Technology on Software Quality: Three Case Histories," *IBM Systems Journal* **33** (No. 1, 1994), pp. 131–57.

[Cutter Consortium, 2002] Cutter Consortium, "78% of IT Organizations Have Litigated," *The Cutter Edge,* www.cutter.com/research/2002/edge020409.html,[3] April 09, 2002.

[Daly, 1977] E. B. DALY, "Management of Software Development," *IEEE Transactions on Software Engineering* **SE-3** (May 1977), pp. 229–42.

[DeMarco and Lister, 1987] T. DEMARCO AND T. LISTER, *Peopleware: Productive Projects and Teams,* Dorset House, New York, 1987.

[Devlin, 2001] K. DEVLIN, "The Real Reason Why Software Engineers Need Math," *Communications of the ACM* **44** (October 2001), pp. 21–22.

[Ebert, Matsubara, Pezzé, and Bertelsen, 1997] C. EBERT, T. MATSUBARA, M. PEZZÉ, AND O. W. BERTELSEN, "The Road to Maturity: Navigating between Craft and Science," *IEEE Software* **14** (November/December 1997), pp. 77–88.

[Elshoff, 1976] J. L. ELSHOFF, "An Analysis of Some Commercial PL/I Programs," *IEEE Transactions on Software Engineering* **SE-2** (June 1976), pp. 113–20.

[Fagan, 1974] M. E. FAGAN, "Design and Code Inspections and Process Control in the Development of Programs," Technical Report IBM-SSD TR 21.572, IBM Corporation, December 1974.

[Fichman and Kemerer, 1997] R. G. FICHMAN and C. F. KEMERER, "Object Technology and Reuse: Lessons from Early Adopters," *IEEE Computer* **30** (July 1997), pp. 47–57.

[Finkelstein, 2000] A. FINKELSTEIN (Editor), *The Future of Software Engineering,* IEEE Computer Society Press, Los Alamitos, CA, 2000.

[GJSentinel.com, 2003] "Sallie Mae's Errors Double Some Bills," www.gjsentinel.com/news/content/coxnet/headlines/0522_salliemae.html, May 22, 2003.

[Glass, 1998] R. L. GLASS, "Is There Really a Software Crisis?" *IEEE Software* **15** (January/February 1998), pp. 104–5.

[Grady, 1994] R. B. GRADY, "Successfully Applying Software Metrics," *IEEE Computer* **27** (September 1994), pp. 18–25.

[Hatton, 1998] L. HATTON, "Does OO Sync with How We Think?" *IEEE Software* **15** (May/June 1998), pp. 46–54.

[Hayes, 2004] F. HAYES, "Chaos Is Back," *Computerworld,* www.computerworld.com/managementtopics/management/project/story/0,10801,97283,00.html, November 8, 2004.

[IEEE 610.12, 1990] "A Glossary of Software Engineering Terminology," IEEE 610.12-1990, Institute of Electrical and Electronic Engineers, Inc., 1990.

[IEEE Standards, 2003] "Products and Projects Status Report," standards.ieee.org/db/status/status.txt, June 3, 2003.

[IEEE/ACM, 1999] "Software Engineering Code of Ethics and Professional Practice, Version 5.2, as Recommended by the IEEE-CS/ACM Joint Task Force on Software Engineering Ethics and Professional Practice," www.computer.org/tab/seprof/code.htm, 1999.

[IEEE/EIA 12207.0-1996, 1998] "IEEE/EIA 12207.0-1996 Industry Implementation of International Standard ISO/IEC 12207:1995," Institute of Electrical and Electronic Engineers, Electronic Industries Alliance, New York, 1998.

[ISO/IEC 12207, 1995] "ISO/IEC 12207:1995, Information Technology—Software Life-Cycle Processes," International Organization for Standardization, International Electrotechnical Commission, Geneva, 1995.

---

[3] This and the other URLs cited in this book were correct at the time of going to press. However, Web addresses tend to change all too frequently and without prior or subsequent notification. If this happens, the reader should use a search engine to locate the new URL.

[Johnson, 2000] R. A. JOHNSON, "The Ups and Downs of Object-Oriented System Development," *Communications of the ACM* **43** (October 2000), pp. 69–73.

[Josephson, 1992] M. JOSEPHSON, *Edison, A Biography,* John Wiley and Sons, New York, 1992.

[Kan et al., 1994] S. H. KAN, S. D. DULL, D. N. AMUNDSON, R. J. LINDNER, and R. J. HEDGER, "AS/400 Software Quality Management," *IBM Systems Journal* **33** (No. 1, 1994), pp. 62–88.

[Keil and Tiwana, 2005] M. KEIL AND A. TIWANA, "Beyond Cost: The Drivers of COTS Application Value," *IEEE Software* **22** (May/June 2005), pp. 64–69.

[Kelly, Sherif, and Hops, 1992] J. C. KELLY, J. S. SHERIF, AND J. HOPS, "An Analysis of Defect Densities Found during Software Inspections," *Journal of Systems and Software* **17** (January 1992), pp. 111–17.

[Khan, Al-A'ali, and Girgis, 1995] E. H. KHAN, M. AL-A'ALI, AND M. R. GIRGIS, "Object-Oriented Programming for Structured Procedural Programming," *IEEE Computer* **28** (October 1995), pp. 48–57.

[Kroeker et al., 1999] K. K. KROEKER, L. WALL, D. A. TAYLOR, C. HORN, P. BASSETT, J. K. OUSTERHOUT, M. L. GRISS, R. M. SOLEY, J. WALDO, AND C. SIMONYI, "Software [R]evolution: A Roundtable," *IEEE Computer* **32** (May 1999), pp. 48–57.

[Leveson and Turner, 1993] N. G. LEVESON AND C. S. TURNER, "An Investigation of the Therac-25 Accidents," *IEEE Computer* **26** (July 1993), pp. 18–41.

[Lientz, Swanson, and Tompkins, 1978] B. P. LIENTZ, E. B. SWANSON, AND G. E. TOMPKINS, "Characteristics of Application Software Maintenance," *Communications of the ACM* **21** (June 1978), pp. 466–71.

[Longstaff, Chittister, Pethia, and Haimes, 2000] T. A. LONGSTAFF, C. CHITTISTER, R. PETHIA, AND Y. Y. HAIMES, "Are We Forgetting the Risks of Information Technology?" *IEEE Computer* **33** (December 2000), pp. 43–51.

[Madanmohan and De', 2004] T. R. MADANMOHAN AND R. DE', "Open Source Reuse in Commercial Firms," *IEEE Software* **21** (November/December 2004), pp. 62–69.

[Maring, 1996] B. MARING, "Object-Oriented Development of Large Applications," *IEEE Software* **13** (May 1996), pp. 33–40.

[Mellor, 1994] P. MELLOR, "CAD: Computer-Aided Disaster," Technical Report, Centre for Software Reliability, City University, London, July 1994.

[Meyer, 1992] B. MEYER, "Applying 'Design by Contract'," *IEEE Computer* **25** (October 1992), pp. 40–51.

[Meyer, 1997] B. MEYER, *Object-Oriented Software Construction*, 2nd ed., Prentice Hall, Upper Saddle River, NJ, 1997.

[Naur, Randell, and Buxton, 1976] P. NAUR, B. RANDELL, AND J. N. BUXTON (Editors), *Software Engineering: Concepts and Techniques: Proceedings of the NATO Conferences*, Petrocelli-Charter, New York, 1976.

[Neumann, 1980] P. G. NEUMANN, Letter from the Editor, *ACM SIGSOFT Software Engineering Notes* **5** (July 1980), p. 2.

[Neumann, 1995] P. G. NEUMANN, *Computer-Related Risks*, Addison-Wesley, Reading, MA, 1995.

[Parnas, 1994] D. L. PARNAS, "Software Aging," *Proceedings of the 16th International Conference on Software Engineering*, Sorrento, Italy, May 1994, pp. 279–87.

[Paulson, Succi, and Eberlein, 2004] J. W. PAULSON, G. SUCCI, AND A. EBERLEIN, "An Empirical Study of Open-Source and Closed-Source Software Products," *IEEE Transactions on Software Engineering* **30** (April 2004), pp. 246–56.

[Radin, 1996] G. RADIN, "Object Technology in Perspective," *IBM Systems Journal* **35** (No. 2, 1996), pp. 124–26.

[Raymond, 2000] E. S. RAYMOND, *The Cathedral and the Bazaar: Musings on Linux and Open Source by an Accidental Revolutionary*, O'Reilly & Associates, Sebastopol, CA, 2000; also available at www.catb.org/~esr/writings/cathedral-bazaar/cathedral-bazaar/.

[Schach et al., 2002] S. R. SCHACH, B. JIN, D. R. WRIGHT, G. Z. HELLER, AND A. J. OFFUTT, "Maintainability of the Linux Kernel," *IEE Proceedings—Software* **149** (February 2002), pp. 18–23.

[Schach et al., 2003b] S. R. SCHACH, B. JIN, G. Z. HELLER, L. YU, AND J. OFFUTT, "Determining the Distribution of Maintenance Categories: Survey versus Measurement," *Empirical Software Engineering* **8** (December 2003), pp. 351–66.

[Scott and Vessey, 2002] J. E. SCOTT AND I. VESSEY, "Managing Risks in Enterprise Systems Implementations," *Communications of the ACM* **45** (April 2002), pp. 74–81.

[Shapiro, 1994] F. R. SHAPIRO, "The First Bug," *Byte* **19** (April 1994), p. 308.

[Shneiderman, 1980] B. SHNEIDERMAN, *Software Psychology: Human Factors in Computer and Information Systems*, Winthrop Publishers, Cambridge, MA, 1980.

[Spiegel Online, 2004] "Rheinbrücke mit Treppe—54 Zentimeter Höhenunterschied," www.spiegel.de/panorama/0,1518,281837,00.html.

[St. Petersburg Times Online, 2003] "Thousands of Federal Checks Uncashable," www.sptimes.com/2003/02/07/Worldandnation/Thousands_of_federal_.shtml, February 07, 2003.

[Stephenson, 1976] W. E. STEPHENSON, "An Analysis of the Resources Used in Safeguard System Software Development," Bell Laboratories, Draft Paper, August 1976.

[Ulkuniemi and Seppanen, 2004] P. ULKUNIEMI, AND V. SEPPANEN, "COTS Component Acquisition in an Emerging Market," *IEEE Software* **21** (November/December 2004), pp. 76–82.

[Wasserman, 1996] A. I. WASSERMAN, "Toward a Discipline of Software Engineering," *IEEE Software* **13** (November/December 1996), pp. 23–31.

[Webster, 1995] B. F. WEBSTER, *Pitfalls of Object-Oriented Development*, M&T Books, New York, 1995.

[Weinberg, 1971] G. M. WEINBERG, *The Psychology of Computer Programming*, Van Nostrand Reinhold, New York, 1971.

[Wirfs-Brock, Wilkerson, and Wiener, 1990] R. WIRFS-BROCK, B. WILKERSON, AND L. WIENER, *Designing Object-Oriented Software*, Prentice Hall, Englewood Cliffs, NJ, 1990.

[Yourdon, 1992] E. YOURDON, *The Decline and Fall of the American Programmer*, Yourdon Press, Upper Saddle River, NJ, 1992.

[Zelkowitz, Shaw, and Gannon, 1979] M. V. ZELKOWITZ, A. C. SHAW, AND J. D. GANNON, *Principles of Software Engineering and Design,* Prentice Hall, Englewood Cliffs, NJ, 1979.

[Zvegintzov, 1998] N. ZVEGINTZOV, "Frequently Begged Questions and How to Answer Them," *IEEE Software* **15** (January/February 1998), pp. 93–96.

# Chapter

# 2

---

# Software Life-Cycle Models

## Learning Objectives

After studying this chapter, you should be able to

- Describe how software products are developed in practice.
- Understand the evolution-tree life-cycle model.
- Appreciate the negative impact of change on software products.
- Utilize the iterative-and-incremental life-cycle model.
- Comprehend the impact of Miller's Law on software production.
- Describe the strengths of the iterative-and-incremental life-cycle model.
- Realize the importance of mitigating risks early.
- Describe agile processes, including extreme programming.
- Compare and contrast a variety of other life-cycle models.

---

Chapter 1 describes how software products would be developed in an ideal world. The theme of this chapter is what happens in practice. As will be explained, there are vast differences between theory and practice.

## 2.1 Software Development in Theory

In an ideal world, a software product is developed as described in Chapter 1. As depicted schematically in Figure 2.1, the system is developed from scratch; $\varnothing$ denotes the empty set. (See Just in Case You Wanted to Know Box 2.1 if you want to know the origin of the term *from scratch*.) First the client's Requirements are determined, and then the Analysis is performed. When the analysis artifacts are complete, the Design is produced. This is followed

The term *from scratch,* meaning "starting with nothing," comes from 19th century sports terminology. Before roads (and running tracks) were paved, races had to be held on open ground. In many cases, the starting line was a scratch in the sand. A runner who had no advantage or handicap had to start from that line, that is, "from [the] scratch."

The term *scratch* has a different sporting connotation nowadays. A "scratch golfer" is one whose golfing handicap is zero.

**FIGURE 2.1**
Idealized
software
development.

by the Implementation of the complete software product, which is then installed on the client's computer.

However, software development is considerably different in practice for two reasons. First, software professionals are human and therefore make mistakes. Second, the client's requirements can change while the software is being developed. In this chapter, both these issues are discussed in some depth, but first we present a mini case study, based on the case study in [Tomer and Schach, 2000], that illustrates the issues involved.

*Mini*  *ase Study*

| 2.2 | *Winburg Mini Case Study* |

To reduce traffic congestion in downtown Winburg, Indiana, the mayor convinces the city to set up a public transportation system. Bus-only lanes are to be established, and commuters will be encouraged to "park and ride"; that is, to park their cars in suburban parking lots and then take buses from there to work and back at a cost of one dollar per ride. Each bus is to have a fare machine that accepts only dollar bills. Passengers insert a bill into the slot as they enter the bus. Sensors inside the fare machine scan the bill, and the software in the machine uses an image recognition algorithm to decide whether the passenger has indeed inserted a valid dollar bill into the slot. It is important that the fare machine be accurate because, once the news gets out that any piece of paper will do the trick, fare income will plummet to effectively zero. Conversely, if the machine regularly rejects valid dollar bills, passengers will be reluctant to use the buses. In addition, the fare machine must be rapid. Passengers will be equally reluctant to use the buses if the machine spends 15 seconds coming to a decision regarding the validity of a dollar bill—it would take even a relatively small number of passengers many minutes to board a bus. Therefore, the requirements for the fare machine software include an average response time of less than 1 second, and an average accuracy of at least 98 percent.

*Episode 1* The first version of the software is implemented.

*Episode 2* Tests show that the required constraint of an average response time of 1 second for deciding on the validity of a dollar bill is not achieved. In fact, on average, it takes 10 seconds to get a response. Senior management discovers the cause. It seems that, to get the required 98 percent accuracy, a programmer has been instructed by her manager to use double-precision numbers for all mathematical calculations. As a result, every operation takes at least twice as long as it would with the usual single-precision numbers. The result is that the program is much slower than it should be, resulting in the long response time. Calculations then show that, despite what the manager told the programmer, the stipulated 98 percent accuracy can be attained even if single-precision numbers are used. The programmer starts to make the necessary changes to the implementation.

*Episode 3* Before the programmer can complete her work, further tests of the system show that, even if the indicated changes to the implementation were made, the system would still have an average response time of over 4.5 seconds, nowhere near the stipulated 1 second. The problem is the complex image recognition algorithm. Fortunately, a faster algorithm has just been discovered, so the fare machine software is redesigned and rewritten using the new algorithm. This results in the average response time being successfully achieved.

*Episode 4* By now, the project is considerably behind schedule and way over budget. The mayor, a successful entrepreneur, has the bright idea of asking the software development team to try to increase the accuracy of the dollar bill recognition component of the system as much as possible, to sell the resulting package to vending machine companies. To meet this new requirement, a new design is adopted that improves the average accuracy to over 99.5 percent. Management decides to install that version of the software in the fare machines. At this point, development of the software is complete. The city is later able to sell its system to two small vending machine companies, defraying about one-third of the cost overrun.

*Epilogue* A few years later, the sensors inside the fare machine become obsolete and need to be replaced by a newer model. Management suggests taking advantage of the change to upgrade the hardware at the same time. The software professionals point out that changing the hardware means that new software also is needed. They suggest rewriting the software in a different programming language. At the time of writing, the project is 6 months behind schedule and 25 percent over budget.

**FIGURE 2.2** The evolution-tree life-cycle model for the Winburg mini case study. (The rectangle drawn with a dotted line denotes the implementation not completed.)

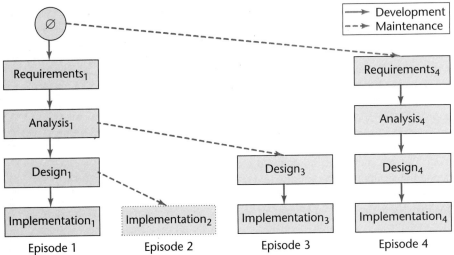

| | | | |
|---|---|---|---|
| Episode 1 | Episode 2 | Episode 3 | Episode 4 |

However, everyone involved is confident that the new system will be more reliable and of higher quality, despite "minor discrepancies" in meeting its response time and accuracy requirements.

Figure 2.2 depicts the **evolution-tree life-cycle model** of the mini case study. The leftmost boxes represent Episode 1. As shown in the figure, the system was developed from scratch ($\varnothing$). The requirements (Requirements$_1$), analysis (Analysis$_1$), design (Design$_1$), and implementation (Implementation$_1$) followed in turn. Next, as previously described, trials of the first version of the software showed that the average response time of 1 second could not be achieved and the implementation had to be modified. The modified implementation appears in Figure 2.2 as Implementation$_2$. However, Implementation$_2$ was never completed. That is why the rectangle representing Implementation$_2$ is drawn with a dotted line.

In Episode 3, the design had to be changed. Specifically, a faster image recognition algorithm was used. The modified design (Design$_3$) resulted in a modified implementation (Implementation$_3$).

Finally, in Episode 4, the requirements were changed (Requirements$_4$) to increase the accuracy. This resulted in modified specifications (Analysis$_4$), modified design (Design$_4$), and modified implementation (Implementation$_4$).

In Figure 2.2, the solid arrows denote development and the dashed arrows denote maintenance. For example, when the design is changed in Episode 3, Design$_3$ replaced Design$_1$ as the design of Analysis$_1$.

The evolution-tree model is an example of a **life-cycle model** (or **model**, for short), that is, the series of steps to be performed while the software product is developed and maintained. Another life-cycle model that can be used for the mini case study is the **waterfall life-cycle model** [Royce, 1970]; a simplified version of the waterfall model is depicted in Figure 2.3. This classical life-cycle model can

**FIGURE 2.3**
A simplified version of the waterfall life-cycle model.

be viewed as the linear model of Figure 2.1 with feedback loops. Then, if a fault is found during the design that was caused by a fault in the requirements, following the dashed upward arrows, the software developers can backtrack from the design up to the analysis and hence to the requirements and make the necessary corrections there. Then, they move down to the analysis, correct the specification document to reflect the corrections to the requirements, and in turn, correct the design document. Design activities can now resume where they were suspended when the fault was discovered. Again, the solid arrows denote development; the dashed arrows, maintenance.

The waterfall model can certainly be used to represent the Winburg mini case study, but, unlike the evolution-tree model of Figure 2.2, it cannot show the order of events. The evolution-tree model has a further advantage over the waterfall model. At the end of each episode we have a **baseline**, that is, a complete set of artifacts (recall that an **artifact** is a constituent component of a software product). There are four baselines in Figure 2.2. They are

At the end of Episode 1: $\text{Requirements}_1$, $\text{Analysis}_1$, $\text{Design}_1$, $\text{Implementation}_1$
At the end of Episode 2: $\text{Requirements}_1$, $\text{Analysis}_1$, $\text{Design}_1$, $\text{Implementation}_2$
At the end of Episode 3: $\text{Requirements}_1$, $\text{Analysis}_1$, $\text{Design}_3$, $\text{Implementation}_3$
At the end of Episode 4: $\text{Requirements}_4$, $\text{Analysis}_4$, $\text{Design}_4$, $\text{Implementation}_4$

The first baseline is the initial set of artifacts; the second baseline reflects the modified (but never completed) $\text{Implementation}_2$ of Episode 2, together with the unchanged requirements, analysis, and design of Episode 1. The third baseline is the same as the first baseline but with the design and implementation changed. The fourth baseline is the complete set of new artifacts shown in Figure 2.2. We revisit the concept of a baseline in Chapters 5 and 15.

## 2.3   Lessons of the Winburg Mini Case Study

The Winburg mini case study depicts the development of a software product that goes awry for a number of unrelated causes, such as a poor implementation strategy (the unnecessary use of double-precision numbers) and the decision to use an algorithm that was too slow. In the end, the project was a success. However, the obvious question is, Is software development really as chaotic in practice? In fact, the mini case study is far less traumatic than many, if not the majority of, software projects. In the Winburg mini case study, there were only two new versions of the software because of faults (the inappropriate use of double-precision numbers; the utilization of an algorithm that could not meet the response time requirement), and only one new version because of a change made by the client (the need for increased accuracy).

Why are so many changes to a software product needed? First, as previously stated, software professionals are human and therefore make mistakes. Second, a software product is a model of the real world, and the real world is continually changing. This issue is discussed at greater length in Section 2.4.

Mini Case Study

2.4   *Teal Tractors Mini Case Study*

Teal Tractors, Inc., sells tractors in most areas of the United States. The company has asked its software division to develop a new product that can handle all aspects of its business. For example, the product must be able to handle sales, inventory, and commissions paid to the sales staff, as well as providing all necessary accounting functions. While this software product is being implemented, Teal Tractors buys a Canadian tractor company. The management of Teal Tractors decides that, to save money, the Canadian operations are to be integrated into the U.S. operations. That means that the software has to be changed before it is completed:

1. It must be modified to handle additional sales regions.
2. It must be extended to handle those aspects of the business that are handled differently in Canada, such as taxes.
3. It must be extended to handle two different currencies, U.S. dollars and Canadian dollars.

Teal Tractors is a rapidly growing company with excellent future prospects. The takeover of the Canadian tractor company is a positive development, one that may well lead to even greater profits in future years. But, from the viewpoint of the software division, the purchase of the Canadian company could be disastrous. Unless the requirements, analysis, and design have been performed with a view to incorporating possible future extensions, the work involved in adding the Canadian sales regions may be so great that it might be more effective to discard everything done to date and start from scratch. The reason is that changing the product at this stage is similar to trying to fix a software product late in its life cycle (see Figure 1.6). Extending the software to handle aspects specific to the Canadian market, as well as Canadian currency, may be equally hard.

Even if the software has been well thought out and the original design is indeed extensible, the design of the resulting patched-together product cannot be as cohesive as it would have been if it had been developed from the very beginning to cater to both the United States and Canada. This can have severe implications for future maintenance.

The software division of Teal Tractors is a victim of the **moving-target problem**. That is, while the software is being developed, the requirements change. It does not matter that the reason for the change is otherwise extremely worthwhile. The fact is that the takeover of the Canadian company could well be detrimental to the quality of the software being developed.

In some cases, the reason for the moving target is less benign. Sometimes a powerful senior manager within an organization keeps changing his or her mind regarding the functionality of a software product being developed. In other cases, there is **feature creep**, a succession of small, almost trivial, additions to the requirements. But, whatever the reason may be, frequent changes, no matter how minor they may seem, are harmful to the health of a software product. It is important that a software product be designed as a set of components that are as independent as possible, so that a change to one part of the software does not induce a fault in an apparently unrelated part of the code, a so-called **regression fault**. When numerous changes are made, the effect is to induce dependencies within the code. Finally, there are so many dependencies that virtually any change induces one or more regression faults. At that time, the only thing that can be done is to redesign the entire software product and reimplement it.

Unfortunately, there is no known solution to the moving-target problem. With regard to positive changes to requirements, growing companies are always going to change, and these changes have to be reflected in the mission-critical software products of the company. As for negative changes, if the individual calling for those changes has sufficient clout, nothing can be done to prevent the changes being implemented, to the detriment of the further maintainability of the software product.

## 2.5   Iteration and Incrementation

As a consequence of both the moving-target problem and the need to correct the inevitable mistakes made while a software product is being developed, the life cycle of actual software products resembles the evolution-tree model of Figure 2.2 or the waterfall model of Figure 2.3, rather than the idealized chain of Figure 2.1. One consequence of this reality is that it does not make much sense to talk about (say) "*the* analysis phase." Instead, the operations of the analysis phase are spread out over the life cycle. Similarly, Figure 2.2 shows four different versions of the implementation, one of which (Implementation$_2$) was never completed because of the moving-target problem.

Consider successive versions of an artifact, for example, the specification document or a code module. From this viewpoint, the basic process is iterative. That is, we produce the first version of the artifact, then we revise it and produce the second version, and so on. Our intent is that each version is closer to our target than its predecessor and finally we construct a version that is satisfactory. **Iteration** is an intrinsic aspect of software engineering, and iterative life-cycle models have been used for over 30 years [Larman and Basili, 2003]. For example, the waterfall model, which was first put forward in 1970, is iterative (but not incremental).

A second aspect of developing real-world software is the restriction imposed on us by **Miller's Law**. In 1956, George Miller, a professor of psychology, showed that, at any one time, we humans are capable of concentrating on only approximately seven chunks (units of information) [Miller, 1956]. However, a typical software artifact has far more than seven chunks. For example, a code artifact is likely to have considerably more than seven variables, and a requirements document is likely to have many more than seven requirements. One way we humans handle this restriction on the amount of information we can handle at any one time is to use **stepwise refinement**. That is, we concentrate on those aspects that are currently the most important and postpone until later those aspects that are currently less critical. In other words, every aspect is eventually handled but in order of current importance. This means that we start off by constructing an artifact that solves only a small part of what we are trying to achieve. Then, we consider further aspects of the problem and add the resulting new pieces to the existing artifact. For example, we might construct a requirements document by considering the seven requirements we consider the most important. Then, we would consider the seven next most important requirements, and so on. This is an incremental process. **Incrementation** is also an intrinsic aspect of software engineering; incremental software development is over 45 years old [Larman and Basili, 2003].

In practice, iteration and integration are used in conjunction with one another. That is, an artifact is constructed piece by piece (incrementation), and each increment goes through multiple versions (iteration). These ideas are illustrated in Figure 2.2, which represents the life cycle for the Winburg mini case study (Sections 2.2 and 2.3). As shown in that figure, there is no single "requirements phase" as such. Instead, the client's requirements are extracted and analyzed twice, yielding the original requirements (Requirements$_1$) and the modified requirements (Requirements$_4$). Similarly, there is no single "implementation phase," but rather four separate episodes in which the code is produced and then modified.

These ideas are generalized in Figure 2.4, which reflects the basic concepts underlying the **iterative-and-incremental life-cycle model** [Jacobson, Booch, and Rumbaugh, 1999]. The figure shows the development of a software product in four increments, labeled Increment A, Increment B, Increment C, and Increment D. The horizontal axis is time and the vertical axis is person-hours (one person-hour is the amount of work that one person can do in 1 hour), so the shaded area under each curve is the total effort for that increment.

It is important to appreciate that Figure 2.4 depicts just one possible way a software product can be decomposed into increments. Another software product may be constructed in just 2 increments, whereas a third may require 13. Furthermore, the figure is not intended to be an accurate representation of precisely how a software product is developed. Instead, it shows how the emphasis changes from iteration to iteration.

The sequential phases of Figure 2.1 are artificial constructs. Instead, as explicitly reflected in Figure 2.4, we must acknowledge that different **workflows** (activities) are performed over the entire life cycle. There are five **core workflows**, the **requirements workflow**, **analysis workflow**, **design workflow**, **implementation workflow**, and **test workflow**, and, as stated in the previous sentence, all five are performed over the life

**FIGURE 2.4** The construction of a software product in four increments.

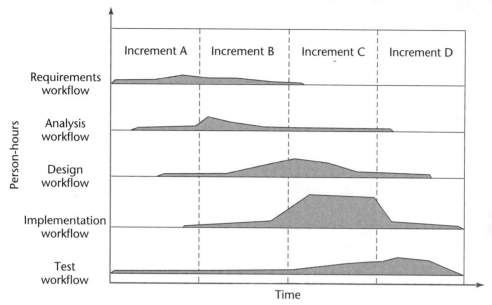

cycle of a software product. However, there are times when one workflow predominates over the other four.

For example, at the beginning of the life cycle, the software developers extract an initial set of requirements. In other words, at the beginning of the iterative-and-incremental life cycle, the requirements workflow predominates. These requirements artifacts are extended and modified during the remainder of the life cycle. During that time, the other four workflows (analysis, design, implementation, and test) predominate. In other words, the requirements workflow is the major workflow at the beginning of the life cycle, but its relative importance decreases thereafter. Conversely, the implementation and test workflows occupy far more of the time of the members of the software development team toward the end of the life cycle than they do at the beginning.

Planning and documentation activities are performed throughout the iterative-and-incremental life cycle. Furthermore, testing is a major activity during each iteration, and particularly at the end of each iteration. In addition, the software as a whole is thoroughly tested once it has been completed; at that time, testing and then modifying the implementation in the light of the outcome of the various tests is virtually the sole activity of the software team. This is reflected in the test workflow of Figure 2.4.

Figure 2.4 shows four increments. Consider Increment A, depicted by the column on the left. At the beginning of this increment, the requirements team members determine the client's requirements. Once most of the requirements have been determined, the first version of part of the analysis can be started. When sufficient progress has been made with the analysis, the first version of the design can be started. Even some coding is often done during this first increment, perhaps in the form of a proof-of-concept prototype to test the feasibility of part of the proposed software product. Finally, as previously mentioned,

**FIGURE 2.5**

The three
iterations of
Increment B of
the iterative-
and-incremental
life-cycle model
of Figure 2.4.

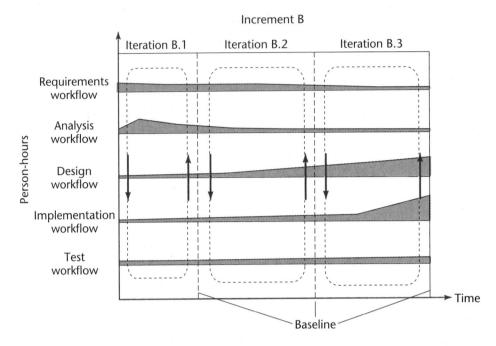

planning, testing, and documentation activities start on Day One and continue from then on, until the software product is finally delivered to the client.

Similarly, the primary concentration during Increment B is on the requirements and analysis workflows, and then on the design workflow. The emphasis during Increment C is first on the design workflow, and then on the implementation workflow and test workflow. Finally, during Increment D, the implementation workflow and test workflow dominate.

As reflected in Figure 1.4, about one-fifth of the total effort is devoted to the requirements and analysis workflows (together), another one-fifth to the design workflow, and about three-fifths to the implementation workflow. The relative total sizes of the shaded areas in Figure 2.4 reflect these values.

There is iteration during each increment of Figure 2.4. This is shown in Figure 2.5, which depicts three iterations during Increment B. (Figure 2.5 is an enlarged view of the second column of Figure 2.4.) As shown in Figure 2.5, each iteration involves all five workflows but again in varying proportions.

Again, it must be stressed that Figure 2.5 is not intended to show that every increment involves exactly three iterations. The number of iterations varies from increment to increment. The purpose of Figure 2.5 is to show the iteration within each increment and repeat that all five workflows (requirements, analysis, design, implementation, and testing, together with planning and documentation) are carried out during almost every iteration, although in varying proportions each time.

As previously explained, Figure 2.4 reflects the incrementation intrinsic to the development of every software product. Figure 2.5 explicitly displays the iteration that underlies incrementation. Specifically, Figure 2.5 depicts three consecutive iterative steps, as opposed to one large incrementation. In more detail, Iteration B.1 consists of requirements, analysis, design, implementation, and test workflows, represented by the leftmost dashed rectangle with rounded corners. The iteration continues until the artifacts of each of the five workflows are satisfactory.

Next, all five sets of artifacts are iterated in Iteration B.2. This second iteration is similar in nature to the first. That is, the requirements artifacts are improved, which in turn triggers improvements to the analysis artifacts, and so on, as reflected in the second iteration of Figure 2.5, and similarly for the third iteration.

The process of iteration and incrementation starts at the beginning of Increment A and continues until the end of Increment D. The completed software product is then installed on the client's computer.

 *Mini Case Study*

## 2.6   Winburg Mini Case Study Revisited

Figure 2.6 shows the evolution-tree model of the Winburg mini case study (Figure 2.2) superimposed on the iterative-and-incremental model (the test workflow is not shown because the evolution-tree model assumes continual testing, explained in Section 1.7). Figure 2.6 sheds additional light on the nature of incrementation:

- Increment A corresponds to Episode 1, Increment B corresponds to Episode 2, and so on.

**FIGURE 2.6**   The evolution-tree life-cycle model for the Winburg mini case study (Figure 2.2) superimposed on the iterative-and-incremental life-cycle model.

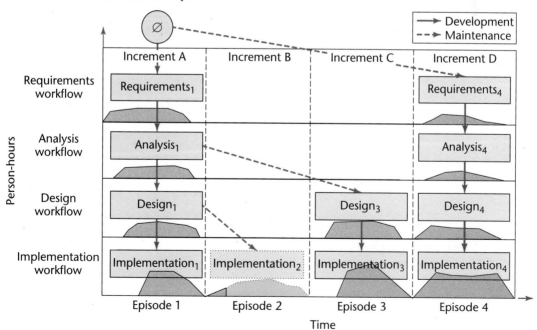

- From the viewpoint of the iterative-and-incremental model, two of the increments do not include all four workflows. In more detail, Increment B (Episode 2) includes only the implementation workflow, and Increment C (Episode 3) includes only the design workflow and the implementation workflow. The iterative-and-incremental model does not require that every workflow be performed during every increment.

- Furthermore, in Figure 2.4 most of the requirements workflow is performed in Increment A and Increment B, whereas in Figure 2.6 it is performed in Increment A and Increment D. Also, in Figure 2.4 most of the analysis is performed in Increment B, whereas in Figure 2.6 the analysis workflow is performed in Increment A and Increment D. This accentuates that neither Figure 2.4 nor Figure 2.6 represents the way every software product is built. Instead, each figure shows the way that one particular software product is built, highlighting the underlying iteration and incrementation.

- The small size and abrupt termination of the implementation workflow during Increment B (Episode 2) of Figure 2.6 shows that Implementation$_2$ was not completed. The gray piece reflects the part of the implementation workflow that was not performed.

- The three dashed arrows of the evolution-tree model show that each increment constitutes maintenance of the previous increment. In this example, the second and third increments are instances of corrective maintenance. That is, each increment corrects faults in the previous increment. As previously explained, Increment B (Episode 2) corrects the implementation workflow by replacing double-precision variables with the usual single-precision variables. Increment C (Episode 3) corrects the design workflow by using a faster image recognition algorithm, thereby enabling the response time requirement to be met. Corresponding changes then have to be made to the implementation workflow. Finally, in Increment D (Episode 4) the requirements are changed to stipulate improved overall accuracy, an instance of perfective maintenance. Corresponding changes are then made to the analysis workflow, design workflow, and implementation workflow.

# 2.7 Risks and Other Aspects of Iteration and Incrementation

Another way of looking at iteration and incrementation is that the project as a whole is divided into smaller mini projects (or increments). Each mini project extends the requirements, analysis, design, implementation, and testing artifacts. Finally, the resulting set of artifacts constitutes the complete software product.

In fact, each mini project consists of more than just extending the artifacts. It is essential to check that each artifact is correct (the test workflow) and make any necessary changes to the relevant artifacts. This process of checking and modifying, then rechecking and remodifying, and so on, is clearly iterative in nature. It continues until the members of the development team are satisfied with all the artifacts of the current mini project (or increment). When that happens, they proceed to the next increment.

Comparing Figure 2.3 (the waterfall model) with Figure 2.5 (view of the iterations within Increment B) shows that each iteration can be viewed as a small but complete waterfall model. That is, during each iteration the members of the development team go through the classical requirements, analysis, design, and implementation phases on a specific portion of the software product. From this viewpoint, the iterative-and-incremental model of Figures 2.4 and 2.5 can be viewed as a consecutive series of waterfall models.

The iterative-and-incremental model has many strengths:

1. Multiple opportunities are offered for checking that the software product is correct. Every iteration incorporates the test workflow, so every iteration is another chance to check all the artifacts developed up to this point. The later faults are detected and corrected, the higher is the cost, as shown in Figure 1.6. Unlike the classical waterfall model, each of the many iterations of the iterative-and-incremental model offers a further opportunity to find faults and correct them, thereby saving money.

2. The robustness of the underlying architecture can be determined relatively early in the life cycle. The **architecture** of a software product includes the various component artifacts and how they fit together. An analogy is the architecture of a cathedral, which might be described as Romanesque, Gothic, or Baroque, among other possibilities. Similarly, the architecture of a software product might be described as object-oriented (Chapter 7), pipes and filters (UNIX or Linux components), or client–server (with a central server providing file storage for a network of client computers). The architecture of a software product developed using the iterative-and-incremental model must have the property that it can be extended continually (and, if necessary, easily changed) to incorporate the next increment. Being able to handle such extensions and changes without falling apart is called **robustness**. Robustness is an important quality during development of a software product; it is vital during postdelivery maintenance. So, if a software product is to last through the usual 12, 15, or more years of postdelivery maintenance, the underlying architecture has to be robust. When an iterative-and-incremental model is used, it soon becomes apparent whether or not the architecture is robust. If, in the course of incorporating (say) the third increment, it is clear that the software developed to date has to be drastically reorganized and large parts rewritten, then it is clear that the architecture is not sufficiently robust. The client must decide whether to abandon the project or start again from scratch. Another possibility is to redesign the architecture to be more robust, and then reuse as much of the current artifacts as possible before proceeding to the next increment. Another reason why a robust architecture is so important is the moving-target problem (Section 2.4). It is all but certain that the client's requirements will change, either because of growth within the client's organization or because the client keeps changing his or her mind as to what the target software has to do. The more robust the architecture, the more resilient to change the software will be. It is not possible to design an architecture that can cope with too many drastic changes. But, if the required changes are reasonable in scope, a robust architecture should be capable of incorporating those changes without having to be drastically restructured.

3. The iterative-and-incremental model enables us to **mitigate risks** early. **Risks** are invariably involved in software development and maintenance. In the Winburg mini case study, for example, the original image recognition algorithm was not fast enough; there is an ever-present risk that a completed software product will not meet its time constraints. Developing a software product incrementally enables us to mitigate such risks early in the life cycle. For example, suppose a new local area network (LAN) is being developed and there is concern that the current network hardware is inadequate for the new software product. Then, the first one or two iterations are directed toward constructing those parts of the software that interface with the network hardware. If it turns out that, contrary to the developers' fears, the network has the necessary capability, the developers can proceed with the project, confident that this risk has been mitigated. On the other hand, if the network indeed cannot cope with the additional traffic that the new LAN generates, this is reported to the client early in the life cycle, when only a small proportion of the budget has been spent. The client can now decide whether to cancel the project, extend the capabilities of the existing network, buy a new and more powerful network, or take some other action.

4. We always have a working version of the software. Suppose a software product is developed using the classical life-cycle model of Figure 2.1. Only at the very end of the project is there a working version of the software product. In contrast, when the iterative-and-incremental life-cycle model is used, at the end of each iteration, there is a working version of part of the overall target software product. The client and the intended users can experiment with that version and determine what changes are needed to ensure that the future complete implementation meets their needs. These changes can be made to a subsequent increment, and the client and users can then determine if further changes are needed. A variation on this is to deliver partial versions of the software product, not only for experimentation but to smooth the introduction of the new software product in the client organization. Change is almost always perceived as a threat. All too frequently, users fear that the introduction of a new software product within the workplace will result in them losing their jobs to a computer. However, introducing a software product gradually can have two benefits. First, the understandable fear of being replaced by a computer is diminished. Second, it is generally easier to learn the functionality of a complex software product if that functionality is introduced stepwise over a period of months, rather than as a whole.

5. There is empirical evidence that the iterative-and-incremental life-cycle model works. The pie chart of Figure 1.1 shows the results of the report from the Standish Group on projects completed in 2004 [Hayes, 2004]. In fact, this report (the so-called CHAOS Report—see Just in Case You Wanted to Know Box 2.2) is produced every 2 years. Figure 2.7 shows the results for 1994 through 2004. The percentage of successful products increased steadily from 16 percent in 1994 to 34 percent in 2002, but then decreased to 29 percent in 2004. In both the 2002 [Softwaremag.com, 2004] and 2004 [Hayes, 2004] reports, one of the factors associated with the successful projects was the use of an iterative process. (The reasons given for the decrease in the percentage of successful projects in 2004 included more large projects than in 2002, use of the waterfall model, lack of user involvement, and lack of support from senior executives [Hayes, 2004].)

The term *CHAOS* is an acronym. For some unknown reason, the Standish Group keeps the acronym top secret. They state [Standish, 2003]:

> Only a few people at The Standish Group, and any one of the 360 people who received and saved the T-shirts we gave out after they completed the first survey in 1994, know what the CHAOS letters represent.

**FIGURE 2.7**
Results of the Standish Group CHAOS Report from 1994 to 2004.

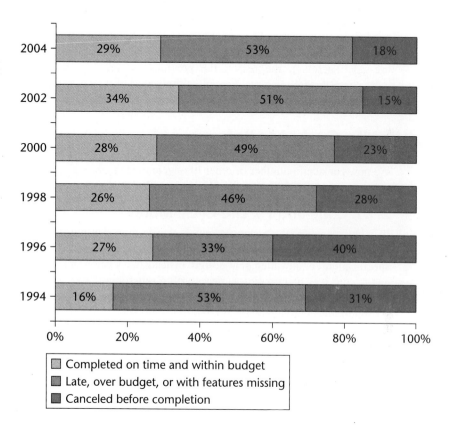

## 2.8 Managing Iteration and Incrementation

At first glance, the iterative-and-incremental model of Figures 2.4 and 2.5 looks totally chaotic. Instead of the orderly progression from requirements to implementation of the waterfall model (Figure 2.3), it appears that developers do whatever they like, perhaps some coding in the morning, an hour or two of design after lunch, and then half an hour of specifying before going home. That is *not* the case. On the contrary, the iterative-and-incremental model is as regimented as the waterfall model, because as previously pointed out, developing a software product using the iterative-and-incremental model is nothing more or less than developing a series of smaller software products, all using the waterfall model.

In more detail, as shown in Figure 2.3, developing a software product using the waterfall model means successively performing the requirements, analysis, design, and implementation phases (in that order) on the software product as a whole. If a problem is encountered, the feedback loops of Figure 2.3 (dashed arrows) are followed; that is, iteration (maintenance) is performed. However, if the same software product is developed using the iterative-and-incremental model, the software product is treated as a set of increments. For each increment in turn, the requirements, analysis, design, and implementation phases (in that order) are repeatedly performed *on that increment* until it is clear that no further iteration is needed. In other words, the project as a whole is broken up into a series of waterfall mini projects. During each mini project, iteration is performed as needed, as shown in Figure 2.5. Therefore, the reason the previous paragraph stated that the iterative-and-incremental model is as regimented as the waterfall model is because the iterative-and-incremental model *is* the waterfall model, applied successively.

# 2.9   Other Life-Cycle Models

We now consider a number of other life-cycle models, including the spiral model and the synchronize-and-stabilize model. We begin with the infamous code-and-fix model.

## 2.9.1 Code-and-Fix Life-Cycle Model

It is unfortunate that so many products are developed using what might be termed the **code-and-fix life-cycle model**. The product is implemented without requirements or specifications, or any attempt at design. Instead, the developers simply throw code together and rework it as many times as necessary to satisfy the client. This approach is shown in Figure 2.8, which clearly displays the absence of requirements, specifications, and design. Although this approach may work well on short programming exercises 100 or 200 lines long, the code-and-fix model is totally unsatisfactory for products of any reasonable size. Figure 1.6 shows that the cost of changing a software product is relatively small if the change is made during the requirements, analysis, or design phases but grows unacceptably large if changes are made after the product has been coded or, worse, if it has already been

**FIGURE 2.8**
The code-and-fix life-cycle model.

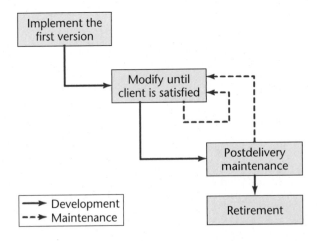

delivered and installed on the client's computer. Hence, the cost of the code-and-fix approach is actually far greater than the cost of a properly specified and meticulously designed product. In addition, maintenance of a product can be extremely difficult without specification or design documents, and the chances of a regression fault occurring are considerably greater. Instead of the code-and-fix approach, it is essential that, before development of a product begins, an appropriate life-cycle model be chosen.

Regrettably, all too many projects use the code-and-fix model. The problem is particularly acute in organizations that measure progress solely in terms of lines of code, so members of the software development team are pressured into churning out as many lines of code as possible, starting on Day One of the project. The code-and-fix model is the easiest way to develop software—and by far the worst way.

A simplified version of the waterfall model was presented in Section 2.2. We now consider that model in more detail.

## 2.9.2  Waterfall Life-Cycle Model

The waterfall life-cycle model was first put forward by Royce [1970]. Figure 2.9 shows the feedback loops for maintenance while the product is being developed, as reflected in Figure 2.3, the simplified waterfall model. Figure 2.9 also shows the feedback loops for postdelivery maintenance.

A critical point regarding the waterfall model is that no phase is complete until the documentation for that phase has been completed and the products of that phase have been approved by the software quality assurance (SQA) group. This carries over into modifications; if the products of an earlier phase have to be changed as a consequence of following a feedback loop, that earlier phase is deemed to be complete only when the documentation for the phase has been modified and the modifications have been checked by the SQA group.

**FIGURE 2.9**
The full waterfall life-cycle model.

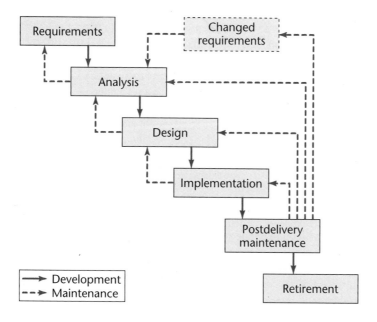

Inherent in every phase of the waterfall model is testing. Testing is not a separate phase to be performed only after the product has been constructed, nor is it to be performed only at the end of each phase. Instead, as stated in Section 1.7, testing should proceed continually throughout the software process. In particular, during maintenance, it is necessary to ensure not only that the modified version of the product still does what the previous version did—and still does it correctly (regression testing)—but that it also satisfies any new requirements imposed by the client.

The waterfall model has many strengths, including the enforced disciplined approach— the stipulation that documentation be provided at each phase and the requirement that all the products of each phase (including the documentation) be meticulously checked by SQA. However, the fact that the waterfall model is documentation driven can also be a weakness. To see this, consider the following two somewhat bizarre scenarios.

First, Joe and Jane Johnson decide to build a house. They consult with an architect. Instead of showing them sketches, plans, and perhaps a scale model, the architect gives them a 20-page single-spaced typed document describing the house in highly technical terms. Even though both Joe and Jane have no previous architectural experience and hardly understand the document, they enthusiastically sign it and say, "Go right ahead, build the house!"

Another scenario is as follows. Mark Marberry buys his suits by mail order. Instead of mailing him pictures of their suits and samples of available cloths, the company sends Mark a written description of the cut and the cloth of their products. Mark then orders a suit solely on the basis of a written description.

The preceding two scenarios are highly unlikely. Nevertheless, they typify precisely the way software is often constructed using the waterfall model. The process begins with the specifications. In general, specification documents are long, detailed, and quite frankly, boring to read. The client is usually inexperienced in the reading of software specifications, and this difficulty is compounded by the fact that specification documents are usually written in a style with which the client is unfamiliar. The difficulty is even worse when the specifications are written in a formal specification language like Z [Spivey, 1992] (Section 11.9). Nevertheless, the client proceeds to sign off on the specification document, whether properly understood or not. In many ways there is little difference between Joe and Jane Johnson contracting to have a house built from a written description that they only partially comprehend and clients approving a software product described in terms of a specification document that they only partially understand.

Mark Marberry and his mail-order suits may seem bizarre in the extreme, but that is precisely what happens when the waterfall model is used in software development. The first time that the client sees a working product is only after the entire product has been coded. Small wonder that software developers live in fear of the sentence, "I know this is what I asked for, but it isn't really what I wanted."

What has gone wrong? There is a considerable difference between the way a client understands a product as described by the specification document and the actual product. The specifications exist only on paper; the client therefore cannot really understand what the product itself will be like. The waterfall model, depending as it does so crucially on written specifications, can lead to the construction of products that simply do not meet the client's real needs.

In fairness it should be pointed out that, just as an architect can help a client understand what is to be built by providing scale models, sketches, and plans, so the software engineer can use graphical techniques, such as data flow diagrams (Section 11.3) or UML diagrams (Chapter 16), to communicate with the client. The problem is that these graphical aids do not describe how the finished product will work. For example, there is a considerable difference between a flowchart (a diagrammatic description of a product) and the working product itself. In this book, two solutions are put forward for solving the problem that the specification document generally does not describe a product in a way that enables the client to determine whether the proposed product meets his or her needs. The object-oriented solution is described in Chapters 10 and 12. The classical solution is the rapid-prototyping model, described in Section 2.9.3.

### 2.9.3 Rapid-Prototyping Life-Cycle Model

A **rapid prototype** is a working model that is functionally equivalent to a subset of the product. For example, if the target product is to handle accounts payable, accounts receivable, and warehousing, then the rapid prototype might consist of a product that performs the screen handling for data capture and prints the reports, but does no file updating or error handling. A rapid prototype for a target product that is to determine the concentration of an enzyme in a solution might perform the calculation and display the answer, but without doing any validation or reasonableness checking of the input data.

The first step in the **rapid-prototyping life-cycle model** depicted in Figure 2.10 is to build a rapid prototype and let the client and future users interact and experiment with the rapid prototype. Once the client is satisfied that the rapid prototype indeed does most of what is required, the developers can draw up the specification document with some assurance that the product meets the client's real needs.

Having constructed the rapid prototype, the software process continues as shown in Figure 2.10. A major strength of the rapid-prototyping model is that the development of

**FIGURE 2.10**
The rapid-prototyping life-cycle model.

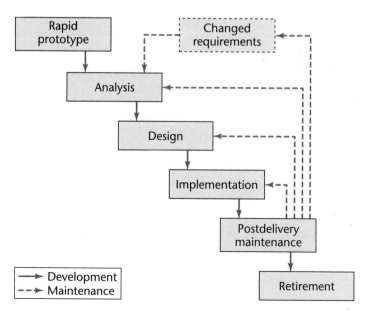

the product is essentially linear, proceeding from the rapid prototype to the delivered product; the feedback loops of the waterfall model (Figure 2.9) are less likely to be needed in the rapid-prototyping model. There are a number of reasons for this. First, the members of the development team use the rapid prototype to construct the specification document. Because the working rapid prototype has been validated through interaction with the client, it is reasonable to expect that the resulting specification document will be correct. Second, consider the design. Even though the rapid prototype has (quite rightly) been hurriedly assembled, the design team can gain insight from it—at worst it will be of the "how not to do it" variety. Again, the feedback loops of the waterfall model are less likely to be needed here.

Implementation comes next. In the waterfall model, implementation of the design sometimes leads to design faults coming to light. In the rapid-prototyping model, the fact that a preliminary working version of the software product has already been built tends to lessen the need to repair the design during or after implementation. The prototype has given some insights to the design team, even though it may reflect only partial functionality of the complete target product.

Once the product has been accepted by the client and installed, postdelivery maintenance begins. Depending on the specific maintenance task that has to be performed, the cycle is reentered either at the requirements, analysis, design, or implementation phase.

An essential aspect of a rapid prototype is embodied in the word *rapid*. The developers should endeavor to construct the rapid prototype as rapidly as possible to speed up the software development process. After all, the sole use of the rapid prototype is to determine what the client's real needs are; once this has been determined, the rapid prototype implementation is discarded but the lessons learned are retained and used in subsequent development phases. For this reason, the internal structure of the rapid prototype is not relevant. What is important is that the prototype be built rapidly and modified rapidly to reflect the client's needs. Therefore, speed is of the essence.

Rapid prototyping is discussed in greater detail in Chapter 10.

### 2.9.4 Open-Source Life-Cycle Model

Almost all successful **open-source software** projects go through two informal phases. First, a single individual has an idea for a program, such as an operating system (Linux), a Net browser (Firefox), or a Web server (Apache). He or she builds an initial version, which is then made available for distribution free of charge to anyone who would like a copy; nowadays, this is done via the Internet, at sites like SourceForge.net and FreshMeat.net. If someone downloads a copy of the initial version and thinks that the program fulfills a need, he or she will start to use that program.

If there is sufficient interest in the program, the project moves gradually into informal phase two. Users become co-developers, in that some users report defects and others suggest ways of fixing those defects. Some users put forward ideas for extending the program, and others implement those ideas. As the program expands in functionality, yet other users port the program so that it can run on additional operating system–hardware combinations. A key aspect is that individuals work on an open-source project in their spare time on a voluntary basis; they are not paid to participate.

**FIGURE 2.11**
The open-source life-cycle model.

Now look more closely at the three activities of the second informal phase:

1. Reporting and correcting defects is corrective maintenance.
2. Adding additional functionality is perfective maintenance.
3. Porting the program to a new environment is adaptive maintenance.

In other words, the second informal phase of the open-source life-cycle model consists solely of postdelivery maintenance, as shown in Figure 2.11. In fact, the term co-developers in the second paragraph of this section should rather be *co-maintainers*.

There a number of key differences between closed-source and open-source software life-cycle models:

- Closed-source software is maintained and tested by teams of employees of the organization that owns the software. Users sometimes submit defect reports. However, these are restricted to **failure reports** (reports of observed incorrect behavior); users have no access to the source code, so they cannot possibly submit **fault reports** (reports that describe where the source code is incorrect and how to correct it).

  In contrast, open-source software is generally maintained by unpaid volunteers. Users are strongly encouraged to submit defect reports. Although all users have access to the source code, only the minority have the inclination and the time, as well as the necessary skills, to peruse the source code and submit fault reports ("fixes"); most defect reports are therefore failure reports. There is generally a **core group** of dedicated maintainers who take responsibility for managing the open-source project. Some members of the **peripheral group**, that is, the users who are not members of the core group, choose to submit defect reports from time to time. The members of the core group are responsible for ensuring that these defects are corrected. In more detail, when a fault report is submitted, a core group member checks that the fix indeed solves the problem and modifies the source code appropriately. When a failure report is submitted, a member of the core group will either personally determine the fix or assign that task to another volunteer, often a member of the peripheral group who is eager to become more involved in the open-source project. Again, the power to install the fix in the software is restricted to members of the core group.

- New versions of closed-source software are typically released roughly once a year. Each new version is carefully checked by the software quality assurance group before release; a wide variety of test cases are run.

  In contrast, a dictum of the open-source movement is "Release early. Release often" [Raymond, 2000]. That is, the core group releases a new version of an open-source product as soon as it is ready, which may be a month or even only a day after the previous version was released. This new version is released after minimal testing; it is assumed that more extensive testing will be performed by the members of the peripheral group. A new version may be installed by literally hundreds of thousands of users within a day or two of its release. These users do not run test cases as such. However, in the course of utilizing the new version on their computer, they encounter failures, which they report via e-mail. In this way, faults in the new version (as well as deeper faults in previous versions) come to light and are corrected.

Comparing Figures 2.8, 2.10, and 2.11, we see that the open-source life-cycle model has features in common with both the code-and-fix model and the rapid-prototyping model. In all three life-cycle models, an initial working version is produced. In the case of the rapid-prototyping model, this initial version is discarded, and the target product is then specified and designed before being coded. In both the code-and-fix and open-source life-cycle models, the initial version is reworked until it becomes the target product. Accordingly, in an open-source project, there are generally no specifications or design.

Bearing in mind the great importance of having specifications and designs, how have some open-source projects been so successful? In the closed-source world, some software professionals are more skilled and some are less skilled (see Section 9.2). The challenge of producing open-source software has attracted some of the finest software experts. In other words, an open-source project can be successful, despite the lack of specifications or design, if the skills of the individuals who work on that project are so superb that they can function effectively without specifications or design. However, notwithstanding the abilities of the members of the core group, eventually a point will be reached when the open-source product is no longer maintainable [Yu et al., 2004].

The open-source life-cycle model is restricted in its applicability. On the one hand, the open-source model has been extremely successfully used for certain infrastructure software projects, such as operating systems (Linux, OpenBSD, Mach, Darwin), Web browsers (Firefox, Netscape), compilers (gcc), Web servers (Apache), or database management systems (MySQL). On the other hand, it is hard to conceive of open-source development of a software product to be used in one commercial organization. A key to open-source software development is that the members of both the core group and the periphery are users of the software being developed. Consequently, the open-source life-cycle model is inapplicable unless the target product is viewed by a wide range of users as useful to them.

At the time of writing, there are more than 100,000 open-source projects at Sourge-Forge.net and FreshMeat.net. About half them have never even attracted a team to work on the project. Of those where work has started, the overwhelming preponderance have never been completed and are unlikely to ever progress much further. But when the open-source model has worked, it has sometimes been incredibly successful. The open-source products listed in parentheses in the previous paragraph are extremely widely used; most of them are utilized on a regular basis by literally millions of users.

Explanations for the success of the open-source life-cycle model are presented in Chapter 4 within the context of team organizational aspects of open-source software projects.

## 2.9.5 Agile Processes

**Extreme programming** [Beck, 2000] is a somewhat controversial new approach to software development based on the iterative-and-incremental model. The first step is that the software development team determines the various features (**stories**) the client would like the product to support. For each such feature, the team informs the client how long it will take to implement that feature and how much it will cost. This first step corresponds to the requirements and analysis workflows of the iterative-and-incremental model (Figure 2.4).

The client selects the features to be included in the each successive build using cost–benefit analysis (Section 5.2), that is, on the basis of the time and the cost estimates provided by the development team as well as the potential benefits of the feature to his or her business. The proposed build is broken down into smaller pieces termed **tasks**. A programmer first draws up test cases for a task; this is termed **test-driven development** (TDD). Two programmers work together on one computer (**pair programming**) [Williams, Kessler, Cunningham, and Jeffries, 2000], implementing the task and ensuring that all the test cases work correctly. The two programmers alternate typing every 15 or 20 minutes; the programmer who is not typing carefully checks the code while it is being entered by his or her partner. The task is then integrated into the current version of the product. Ideally, implementing and integrating a task should take no more than a few hours. In general, a number of pairs will implement tasks in parallel, so integration takes place essentially continuously. Team members change coding partners daily, if possible; learning from the other team members increases everyone's skill level. The TDD test cases used for the task are retained and utilized in all further integration testing.

Some drawbacks to pair programming have been observed in practice [Drobka, Noftz, and Raghu, 2004]. For example, pair programming requires large blocks of uninterrupted time, and software professionals can have difficulty in finding 3- to 4-hour blocks of time. In addition, pair programming does not always work well with shy or overbearing individuals, or with two inexperienced programmers.

A number of features of extreme programming (XP) are somewhat different to the way that software is usually developed:

- The computers of the XP team are set up in the center of a large room lined with small cubicles.
- A client representative works with the XP team at all times.
- No individual can work overtime for two successive weeks.
- There is no specialization. Instead, all members of the XP team work on requirements, analysis, design, code, and testing.
- There is no overall design step before the various builds are constructed. Instead, the design is modified while the product is being built. This procedure is termed **refactoring**. Whenever a test case will not run, the code is reorganized until the team is satisfied that the design is simple, straightforward, and runs all the test cases satisfactorily.

Two acronyms now associated with extreme programming are YAGNI (you aren't gonna need it) and DTSTTCPW (do the simplest thing that could possibly work). In other words, a principle of extreme programming is to minimize the number of features; there is no need to build a product that does any more than what the client actually needs.

Extreme programming is one of a number of new paradigms that are collectively referred to as **agile processes**. Seventeen software developers (later dubbed the Agile Alliance) met at a Utah ski resort for two days in February 2001 and produced the *Manifesto for Agile Software Development* [Beck et al., 2001]. Many of the participants had previously authored their own software development methodologies, including Extreme Programming [Beck, 2000], Crystal [Cockburn, 2001], and Scrum [Schwaber, 2001]. Consequently, the Agile Alliance did not prescribe a specific life-cycle model, but rather laid out a group of underlying principles that were common to their individual approaches to software development.

Agile processes are characterized by considerably less emphasis on analysis and design than in almost all other modern life-cycle models. Implementation starts much earlier in the life cycle, because working software is considered more important than detailed documentation. Responsiveness to changes in requirements is another major goal of agile processes, and so is the importance of collaborating with the client.

One of the principles in the *Manifesto* is to deliver working software frequently, ideally every 2 or 3 weeks. One way of achieving this is to use **timeboxing** [Jalote, Palit, Kurien, and Peethamber, 2004], which has been used for many years as a time management technique. A specific amount of time is set aside for a task, and the team members then do the best job they can during that time. Within the context of agile processes, typically 3 weeks are set aside for each iteration. On the one hand, it gives the client confidence to know that a new version with additional functionality will arrive every 3 weeks. On the other hand, the developers know that they will have 3 weeks (but no more) to deliver a new iteration without client interference of any kind; once the client has chosen the work for an iteration, it cannot be changed or increased. However, if it is impossible to complete the entire task in the timebox, the work may be reduced ("descoped"). In other words, agile processes demand fixed time, not fixed features.

Another common feature of agile processes is to have a short meeting at a regular time each day. All team members have to attend the meeting. Making all the participants stand in a circle, rather than sit around a table, helps to ensure that the meeting lasts no more than the stipulated 15 minutes. Each team member in turn answers five questions:

- What have I done since yesterday's meeting?
- What am I working on today?
- What problems are preventing me from achieving this?
- What have we forgotten?
- What did I learn that I would like to share with the team?

The aim of the **stand-up meeting** is to raise problems, not solve them; solutions are found at follow-up meetings, preferably held directly after the stand-up meeting. Like timeboxing, stand-up meetings are a successful management technique now utilized within the context of agile processes. Both timeboxed iterations and stand-up meetings are instances of two basic principles that underlie all agile methods: communication and satisfying the client's needs as quickly as possible.

Agile processes have been successfully used on a number of small-scale projects. However, agile processes have not yet been used widely enough to determine whether this approach will fulfill its early promise. Furthermore, even if agile processes turn out to be good for small-scale software products, that does not necessarily mean that they can be used for medium- or large-scale software products, as will now be explained.

To appreciate why many software professionals have expressed doubts about agile processes within the context of medium- and especially large-scale software products [Reifer, Maurer, and Erdogmus, 2003], consider the following analogy by Grady Booch [2000]. Anyone can successfully hammer together a few planks to build a doghouse, but it would be foolhardy to build a three-bedroom home without detailed plans. In addition, skills in plumbing, wiring, and roofing are needed to build a three-bedroom home, and inspections are essential. (That is, being able to build small-scale software products does not necessarily mean that one has the skills for building medium-scale software products.) Furthermore, the fact that a skyscraper is the height of 1000 doghouses does not mean that one can build a skyscraper by piling 1000 doghouses on top of one another. In other words, building large-scale software products requires even more specialized and sophisticated skills than those needed to cobble together small-scale software products.

A key determinant in deciding whether agile processes are indeed a major breakthrough in software engineering will be the cost of future postdelivery maintenance (Section 1.3.2). That is, if the use of agile processes results in a reduction in the cost of postdelivery maintenance, XP and other agile processes will become widely adopted. On the other hand, refactoring is an intrinsic component of agile processes. As previously explained, the product is not designed as a whole; instead, the design is developed incrementally, and the code is reorganized whenever the current design is unsatisfactory for any reason. This refactoring then continues during postdelivery maintenance. If the design of a product when it passes its acceptance test is open-ended and flexible, then perfective maintenance should be easy to achieve at a low cost. However, if the design has to be refactored whenever additional functionality is added, then the cost of postdelivery maintenance of that product will be unacceptably high. As a consequence of the newness of the approach, as yet only a small amount of experimental data exist on development using agile processes, and almost none on maintenance. However, preliminary data indicate that refactoring can consume a large percentage of the overall cost [Li and Alshayeb, 2002].

Nevertheless, experiments have shown that certain features of agile processes work well. For example, Williams, Kessler, Cunningham, and Jeffries [2000] have shown that pair programming leads to the development of higher-quality code in a shorter time, with greater job satisfaction. Accordingly, even if agile processes as a whole prove to be disappointing, some features of agile processes may be adopted as mainstream software engineering practices in the future.

The *Manifesto for Agile Software Development* essentially claims that agile processes are superior to more disciplined processes like the Unified Process (Chapter 3). Skeptics respond that proponents of agile processes are little more than hackers. However, there is a middle ground. The two approaches are not incompatible; it is possible to incorporate proven features of agile processes within the framework of disciplined processes. This integration of the two approaches is described in books such as the one by Boehm and Turner [2003].

In conclusion, agile processes appear to be a useful approach to building small-scale software products when the client's requirements are vague. In addition, some of the features of agile processes can be effectively utilized within the context of other life-cycle models.

## 2.9.6 Synchronize-and-Stabilize Life-Cycle Model

Microsoft, Inc., is the world's largest manufacturer of COTS software. The majority of its packages are built using a version of the iterative-and-incremental model that has been termed the **synchronize-and-stabilize life-cycle model** [Cusumano and Selby, 1997].

The requirements analysis phase is conducted by interviewing numerous potential clients for the package and extracting a list of features of highest priority to the clients. A specification document is now drawn up. Next, the work is divided into three or four builds. The first build consists of the most critical features, the second build consists of the next most critical features, and so on. Each build is carried out by a number of small teams working in parallel. At the end of each day, all the teams **synchronize**; that is, they put the partially completed components together and test and debug the resulting product. **Stabilization** is performed at the end of each of the builds. Any remaining faults that have been detected so far are fixed, and they now **freeze** the build; that is, no further changes will be made to the specifications.

The repeated synchronization step ensures that the various components always work together. Another advantage of this regular execution of the partially constructed product is that the developers obtain early insight into the operation of the product and can modify the requirements if necessary during the course of a build. The life-cycle model can even be used if the initial specification is incomplete. The synchronize-and-stabilize model is considered further in Section 4.5, where team organizational details are discussed.

The spiral model has been left to last because it incorporates aspects of all the other models described in Section 2.9.

## 2.9.7 Spiral Life-Cycle Model

As stated in Section 2.5, an element of risk is always involved in the development of software. For example, key personnel can resign before the product has been adequately documented. The manufacturer of hardware on which the product is critically dependent can go bankrupt. Too much, or too little, can be invested in testing and quality assurance. After spending hundreds of thousands of dollars on developing a major software product, technological breakthroughs can render the entire product worthless. An organization may research and develop a database management system, but before the product can be marketed, a lower-priced, functionally equivalent package is announced by a competitor. The components of a product may not fit together when integration is performed. For obvious reasons, software developers try to minimize such risks wherever possible.

One way of minimizing certain types of risk is to construct a prototype. As described in Section 2.9.3, one approach to reducing the risk that the delivered product will not satisfy the client's real needs is to construct a rapid prototype during the requirements phase. During subsequent phases, other sorts of prototypes may be appropriate. For example, a telephone company may devise a new, apparently highly effective algorithm for routing calls through a long-distance network. If the product is implemented but does not work as expected, the telephone company will have wasted the cost of developing the product. In addition, angry or inconvenienced customers may take their business elsewhere. This outcome can be avoided by constructing a **proof-of-concept prototype** to handle only the routing of calls and testing it on a simulator. In this way, the actual system is not disturbed; and for the cost of implementing just the routing algorithm, the telephone company can determine whether it is worthwhile to develop an entire network controller incorporating the new algorithm.

A proof-of-concept prototype is not a rapid prototype constructed to be certain that the requirements have been accurately determined, as described in Section 2.9.3. Instead, it is more like an engineering prototype, that is, a scale model constructed to test the feasibility of construction. If the development team is concerned whether a particular part of the proposed software product can be constructed, a proof-of-concept prototype is constructed. For example, the developers may be concerned whether a particular computation can be performed quickly enough. In that case, they build a prototype to test the timing of just that computation. Or they may be worried that the font they intend to use for all screens will be too small for the average user to read without eyestrain. In this instance, they construct a prototype to display a number of different screens and determine by experiment whether the users find the font uncomfortably small.

The idea of minimizing risk via the use of prototypes and other means is the idea underlying the **spiral life-cycle model** [Boehm, 1988]. A simplified way of looking at this life-cycle model is as a waterfall model with each phase preceded by risk analysis, as shown in Figure 2.12. Before commencing each phase, an attempt is made to mitigate (control) the risks. If it is impossible to mitigate all the significant risks at that stage, then the project is immediately terminated.

**FIGURE 2.12**
A simplified version of the spiral life-cycle model.

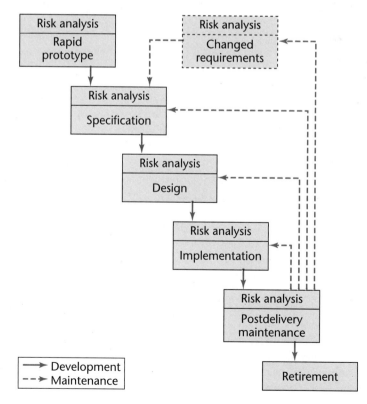

Prototypes can be used effectively to provide information about certain classes of risk. For example, timing constraints can generally be tested by constructing a prototype and measuring whether the prototype can achieve the necessary performance. If the prototype is an accurate functional representation of the relevant features of the product, then measurements made on the prototype should give the developers a good idea as to whether the timing constraints can be achieved.

Other areas of risk are less amenable to prototyping, for example, the risk that the software personnel necessary to build the product cannot be hired or that key personnel may resign before the project is complete. Another potential risk is that a particular team may not be competent enough to develop a specific large-scale product. A successful contractor who builds single-family homes would probably not be able to build a high-rise office complex. In the same way, there are essential differences between small-scale and large-scale software, and prototyping is of little use. This risk cannot be mitigated by testing team performance on a much smaller prototype, in which team organizational issues specific to large-scale software cannot arise. Another area of risk for which prototyping cannot be employed is evaluating the delivery promises of a hardware supplier. A strategy the developer can adopt is to determine how well previous clients of the supplier have been treated, but past performance is by no means a certain predictor of future performance. A penalty clause in the delivery contract is one way of trying to ensure that essential hardware is delivered on time, but what if the supplier refuses to sign an agreement that includes such a clause? Even with a penalty clause, late delivery may occur and eventually lead to legal action that can drag on for years. In the meantime, the software developer may have gone bankrupt because nondelivery of the promised hardware caused nondelivery of the promised software. In short, whereas prototyping helps reduce risk in some areas, in other areas it is at best a partial answer, and in still others it is no answer at all.

The full spiral model is shown in Figure 2.13. The radial dimension represents cumulative cost to date, and the angular dimension represents progress through the spiral. Each cycle of the spiral corresponds to a phase. A phase begins (in the top left quadrant) by determining objectives of that phase, alternatives for achieving those objectives, and constraints imposed on those alternatives. This process results in a strategy for achieving those objectives. Next, that strategy is analyzed from the viewpoint of risk. Attempts are made to mitigate every potential risk, in some cases by building a prototype. If certain risks cannot be mitigated, the project may be terminated immediately; under some circumstances, however, a decision could be made to continue the project but on a significantly smaller scale. If all risks are successfully mitigated, the next development step is started (bottom right quadrant). This quadrant of the spiral model corresponds to the classical waterfall model. Finally, the results of that phase are evaluated and the next phase is planned.

The spiral model has been used successfully to develop a wide variety of products. In one set of 25 projects in which the spiral model was used in conjunction with other means of increasing productivity, the productivity of every project increased by at least 50 percent over previous productivity levels and by 100 percent in most of the projects [Boehm, 1988]. To be able to decide whether the spiral model should be used for a given project, the strengths and weaknesses of the spiral model are now assessed.

The spiral model has a number of strengths. The emphasis on alternatives and constraints supports the reuse of existing software (Section 8.1) and the incorporation of software

**FIGURE 2.13**  Full spiral life-cycle model.

Source: [Boehm, 1988] (© 1988 IEEE).

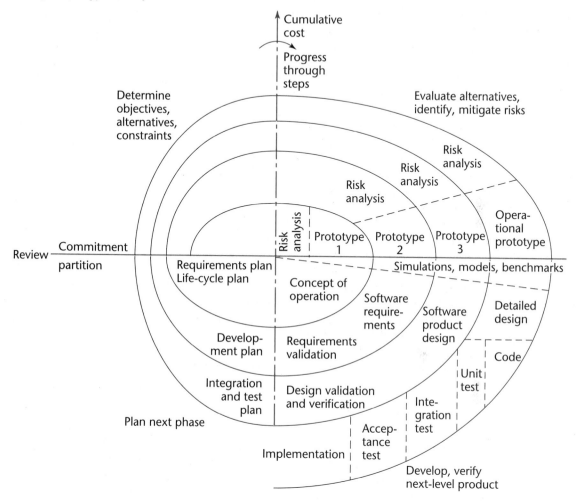

quality as a specific objective. In addition, a common problem in software development is determining when the products of a specific phase have been adequately tested. Spending too much time on testing is a waste of money, and delivery of the product may be unduly delayed. Conversely, if too little testing is performed, then the delivered software may contain residual faults, resulting in unpleasant consequences for the developers. The spiral model answers this question in terms of the risks that would be incurred by not doing enough testing or by doing too much testing. Perhaps most important, within the structure of the spiral model, postdelivery maintenance is simply another cycle of the spiral; there is essentially no distinction between postdelivery maintenance and development. Therefore, the problem that postdelivery maintenance is sometimes maligned by ignorant software professionals does not arise, because postdelivery maintenance is treated the same way as development.

There are restrictions on the applicability of the spiral model. Specifically, in its present form, the model is intended exclusively for internal development of large-scale software [Boehm, 1988]. Consider an internal project, that is, one where the developers and client are members of the same organization. If risk analysis leads to the conclusion that the project should be terminated, then in-house software personnel can simply be reassigned to a different project. However, once a contract has been signed between a development organization and an external client, an attempt by either side to terminate that contract can lead to a breach-of-contract lawsuit. Therefore, in the case of contract software, all risk analysis must be performed by both client and developers before the contract is signed, not as in the spiral model.

A second restriction on the spiral model relates to the size of the project. Specifically, the spiral model is applicable to only large-scale software. It makes no sense to perform risk analysis if the cost of performing the risk analysis is comparable to the cost of the project as a whole, or if performing the risk analysis would significantly affect the profit potential. Instead, the developers should first decide how much is at risk and then how much risk analysis, if any, to perform.

A major strength of the spiral model is that it is risk driven, but this can also be a weakness. Unless the software developers are skilled at pinpointing the possible risks and analyzing the risks accurately, there is a real danger that the team may believe that all is well at a time when the project, in fact, is headed for disaster. Only if the members of the development team are competent risk analysts should management decide to use the spiral model.

Overall, however, the major weakness of the spiral model, as well as the waterfall model and the rapid-prototyping model, is that it assumes that software is developed in discrete phases. In reality, however, software development is iterative and incremental, as reflected in the evolution-tree model (Section 2.2) or the iterative-and-incremental model (Section 2.5).

## 2.10   Comparison of Life-Cycle Models

Nine different software life-cycle models have been examined with special attention paid to some of their strengths and weaknesses. The code-and-fix model (Section 2.9.1) should be avoided. The waterfall model (Section 2.9.2) is a known quantity. Its strengths are understood, and so are its weaknesses. The rapid-prototyping model (Section 2.9.3) was developed as a reaction to a specific perceived weakness in the waterfall model, namely, that the delivered product may not be what the client really needs. However, there is still insufficient evidence that this approach is superior to the waterfall model in other respects. The open-source life-cycle model has been incredibly successful in a small number of cases when used to construct infrastructure software (Section 2.9.4). Agile processes (Section 2.9.5) are a set of controversial new approaches that, so far, appear to work, but for only small-scale software. The synchronize-and-stabilize model (Section 2.9.6) has been used with great success by Microsoft, but as yet there is no evidence of comparable success in other corporate cultures. Yet another alternative is to use the spiral model (Section 2.9.7), but only if the developers are adequately trained in risk analysis and risk resolution. The evolution-tree model (Section 2.2) and the iterative-and-incremental model (Section 2.5) are closest to the way that software is produced in the real world. An overall comparison appears in Figure 2.14.

**FIGURE 2.14**
Comparison of life-cycle models described in this chapter, including the section in which each is defined.

| Life-Cycle Model | Strengths | Weaknesses |
|---|---|---|
| Evolution-tree model (Section 2.2) | Closely models real-world software production Equivalent to the iterative-and-incremental model | |
| Iterative-and-incremental life-cycle model (Section 2.5) | Closely models real-world software production Underlies the Unified Process | |
| Code-and-fix life-cycle model (Section 2.9.1) | Fine for short programs that require no maintenance | Totally unsatisfactory for nontrivial programs |
| Waterfall life-cycle model (Section 2.9.2) | Disciplined approach Document driven | Delivered product may not meet client's needs |
| Rapid-prototyping life-cycle model (Section 2.9.3) | Ensures that the delivered product meets the client's needs | Not yet proven beyond all doubt |
| Open-source life-cycle model (Section 2.9.4) | Has worked extremely well in a small number of instances | Limited applicability Usually does not work |
| Agile processes (Section 2.9.5) | Works well when the client's requirements are vague | Appears to work on only small-scale projects |
| Synchronize-and-stabilize life-cycle model (Section 2.9.6) | Future users' needs are met Ensures that components can be successfully integrated | Has not been widely used other than at Microsoft |
| Spiral life-cycle model (Section 2.9.7) | Risk driven | Can be used for only large-scale, in-house products Developers have to be competent in risk analysis and risk resolution |

Each software development organization should decide on a life-cycle model that is appropriate for that organization, its management, its employees, and its software process and should vary the life-cycle model depending on the features of the specific product currently under development. Such a model incorporates appropriate aspects of the various life-cycle models, utilizing their strengths and minimizing their weaknesses.

**Chapter Review**

There are significant differences between the way that software is developed in theory (Section 2.1) and the way it is developed in practice. The Winburg mini case study is used to introduce the evolution-tree model (Section 2.2). Lessons of this mini case study, especially that requirements change, are presented in Section 2.3. Change is discussed in greater detail in Section 2.4, where the moving-target problem is presented using the Teal Tractors mini case study. In Section 2.5, the importance of iteration and incrementation in real-world software engineering is stressed, and the iterative-and-incremental model is presented. The Winburg mini case study is then re-examined in Section 2.6 to illustrate the equivalence of the evolution-tree model and the iterative-and-incremental model. In Section 2.7, the strengths of the iterative-and-incremental model are presented, particularly that it enables us to resolve risks early. Management of the iterative-and-incremental model is discussed in Section 2.8. A number of different life-cycle models are now described, including the code-and-fix life-cycle model (Section 2.9.1), waterfall life-cycle model (Section 2.9.2), rapid-prototyping life-cycle model (Section 2.9.3), open-source life-cycle model (Section 2.9.4), agile processes (Section 2.9.5), synchronize-and-stabilize life-cycle model (Section 2.9.6), and spiral life-cycle model (Section 2.9.7). In Section 2.10, these life-cycle models are compared and suggestions are made regarding the choice of a life-cycle model for a specific project.

**For Further Reading**

The waterfall model was first put forward in [Royce, 1970]. An analysis of the waterfall model is given in the first chapter of [Royce, 1998].

For an introduction to rapid prototyping, a suggested book is [Connell and Shafer, 1989].

The synchronize-and-stabilize model is outlined in [Cusumano and Selby, 1997] and described in detail in [Cusumano and Selby, 1995]. Insight into the synchronize-and-stabilize model can be obtained from [McConnell, 1996]. The spiral model is explained in [Boehm, 1988], and its application to the TRW Software Productivity System appears in [Boehm et al., 1984].

Extreme programming is described in [Beck, 2000]; refactoring is the subject of [Fowler et al., 1999]. The *Manifesto for Agile Software Development* may be found at [Beck et al., 2001]. Books have been published on a variety of agile methods, including [Cockburn, 2001] and [Schwaber, 2001]. Agile methods are advocated in [Highsmith and Cockburn, 2001; Boehm, 2002; DeMarco and Boehm, 2002; and Boehm and Turner, 2003], whereas the case against agile methods is presented in [Stephens and Rosenberg, 2003]. Refactoring is surveyed in [Mens and Tourwe, 2004]. The use of XP in four mission-critical projects is described in [Drobka, Noftz, and Raghu, 2004]. Issues that can arise when introducing agile processes within an organization that currently is using traditional methodologies are discussed in [Nerur, Mahapatra, and Mangalaraj, 2005]. A number of papers on extreme programming appear in the May/June 2003 issue of *IEEE Software,* including [Murru, Deias, and Mugheddu, 2003] and [Rasmusson, 2003], both of which describe successful projects developed using extreme programming. The effectiveness of test-driven development is discussed in [Erdogmus, Morisio, and Torchiano, 2005]. The June 2003 issue of *IEEE Computer* contains several articles on agile processes. The May/June 2005 issue of *IEEE Software* has four articles on agile processes, especially [Ceschi, Sillitti, Succi, and De Panfilis, 2005] and [Karlström and Runeson, 2005].

Risk analysis is described in [Ropponen and Lyttinen, 2000; Longstaff, Chittister, Pethia, and Haimes, 2000; and Scott and Vessey, 2002]. The May/June 1997 issue of *IEEE Software* contains 10 articles on risk management.

A major iterative and incremental model is described in detail in [Jacobson, Booch, and Rumbaugh, 1999]. However, many other iterative and incremental models have been put forward over the past 30 years, as recounted in [Larman and Basili, 2003]. The use of an incremental model to build an air-traffic control system is discussed in [Goth, 2000]. An iterative approach to re-engineering legacy systems is given in [Bianchi, Caivano, Marengo, and Visaggio, 2003].

Many other life-cycle models have been put forward. For example, Rajlich and Bennett [2000] describe a maintenance-oriented life-cycle model. The July/August 2000 issue of *IEEE Software* has a variety of papers on software life-cycle models, including [Williams, Kessler, Cunningham, and Jeffries, 2000] which describes an experiment on pair programming, one component of agile methods.

The proceedings of the International Software Process Workshops are a useful source of information on life-cycle models. [ISO/IEC 12207, 1995] is a widely accepted standard for software life-cycle processes.

**Key Terms**

agile process *58*
analysis workflow *42*
architecture *47*
artifact *39*
baseline *39*
code-and-fix life-cycle
    model *50*
core group *55*
core workflow *42*
design workflow *42*
evolution-tree life-cycle
    model *38*
extreme programming *57*
failure report *55*
fault report *55*
feature creep *41*
freeze *60*
implementation workflow *42*

incrementation *42*
iteration *42*
iterative-and-incremental
    life-cycle model *42*
life-cycle model *38*
Miller's Law *42*
mitigate risk *48*
model *38*
moving-target problem *41*
open-source software *54*
pair programming *57*
peripheral group *55*
proof-of-concept
    prototype *60*
rapid prototype *53*
rapid-prototyping life-cycle
    model *53*
refactoring *57*

regression fault *41*
requirements workflow *42*
risk *48*
robustness *47*
spiral life-cycle model *61*
stabilize *60*
stand-up meeting *58*
stepwise refinement *42*
story *57*
synchronize *60*
synchronize-and-stabilize
    life-cycle model *60*
task *57*
test-driven development *57*
test workflow *42*
timeboxing *58*
waterfall life-cycle model *38*
workflow *42*

**Problems**

2.1  Represent the Winburg mini case study of Section 2.3 using the waterfall model. Is this more or less effective than the evolution-tree model? Explain your answer.

2.2  Assume that the programmer in the Winburg mini case study had used single-precision numbers from the beginning. Draw the resulting evolution tree.

2.3  What is the connection between Miller's Law and stepwise refinement?

2.4  Does stepwise refinement correspond to iteration or incrementation?

2.5  How are a workflow, an artifact, and a baseline related?

2.6  What is the connection between the waterfall model and the iterative-and-incremental model?

2.7  Suppose you have to build a product to determine the inverse of 653.8231 to five decimal places. Once the product has been implemented and tested, it will be thrown away. Which life-cycle model would you use? Give reasons for your answer.

2.8  You are a software engineering consultant and have been called in by the vice-president for finance of a corporation that manufactures and sells boots. She wants your organization to build a product that will monitor the company's stock, starting with the purchasing of the leather and keeping track of the boots as they are manufactured, distributed to the individual stores, and sold to customers. What criteria would you use in selecting a life-cycle model for the project?

2.9  List the risks involved in developing the software of Problem 2.8. How would you attempt to mitigate each risk?

2.10 Your development of the stock control product for the bootwear chain is so successful that your organization decides that it must be rewritten as a package to be sold to a variety of different organizations that manufacture and sell products via their own retailers. The new product must therefore be portable and easily adapted to new hardware and/or operating systems. How would the criteria you use in selecting a life-cycle model for this project differ from those in your answer to Problem 2.7?

2.11 Describe the sort of product that would be an ideal application for open-source software development.

2.12 Now describe the type of situation where open-source software development is inappropriate.

2.13 Describe the sort of product that would be an ideal application for an agile process.

2.14 Now describe the type of situation where an agile process is inappropriate.

2.15 Describe the sort of product that would be an ideal application for the spiral model.

2.16 Now describe the type of situation where the spiral model is inappropriate.

2.17 (Term Project) Which software life-cycle model would you use for the Osric's Office Appliances and Decor product described in Appendix A? Give reasons for your answer.

2.18 (Readings in Software Engineering) Your instructor will distribute copies of [Mens and Tourwe, 2004]. What are the implications of this paper for agile processes?

**References**

[Beck, 2000] K. BECK, *Extreme Programming Explained: Embrace Change,* Addison-Wesley Longman, Reading, MA, 2000.

[Beck et al., 2001] K. BECK, M. BEEDLE, A. COCKBURN, W. CUNNINGHAM, M. FOWLER, J. GRENNING, J. HIGHSMITH, A. HUNT, R. JEFFRIES, J. KERN, B. MARICK, R. C. MARTIN, S. MELLOR, K. SCHWABER, J. SUTHERLAND, D. THOMAS, AND A. VAN BENNEKUM, *Manifesto for Agile Software Development,* agilemanifesto.org, 2001.

[Bianchi, Caivano, Marengo, and Visaggio, 2003] A. BIANCHI, D. CAIVANO, V. MARENGO, AND G. VISAGGIO, "Iterative Reengineering of Legacy Systems," *IEEE Transactions on Software Engineering* **29** (March 2003), pp. 225–41.

[Boehm, 1988] B. W. BOEHM, "A Spiral Model of Software Development and Enhancement," *IEEE Computer* **21** (May 1988), pp. 61–72.

[Boehm, 2002] B. W. BOEHM, "Get Ready for Agile Methods, with Care," *IEEE Computer* **35** (January 2002), pp. 64–69.

[Boehm and Turner, 2003] B. BOEHM AND R. TURNER, *Balancing Agility and Discipline: A Guide for the Perplexed,* Addison-Wesley Professional, Boston, MA, 2003.

[Boehm et al., 1984] B. W. BOEHM, M. H. PENEDO, E. D. STUCKLE, R. D. WILLIAMS, AND A. B. PYSTER, "A Software Development Environment for Improving Productivity," *IEEE Computer* **17** (June 1984), pp. 30–44.

[Booch, 2000] G. BOOCH, "The Future of Software Engineering," keynote address, International Conference on Software Engineering, Limerick, Ireland, May 2000.

[Ceschi, Sillitti, Succi, and De Panfilis, 2005] M. CESCHI, A. SILLITTI, G. SUCCI, AND S. DE PANFILIS, "Project Management in Plan-Based and Agile Companies," *IEEE Software* **22** (May/June 2005), pp. 21–27.

[Cockburn, 2001] A. COCKBURN, *Agile Software Development,* Addison-Wesley Professional, Reading, MA, 2001.

[Connell and Shafer, 1989] J. L. CONNELL AND L. SHAFER, *Structured Rapid Prototyping: An Evolutionary Approach to Software Development*, Yourdon Press, Englewood Cliffs, NJ, 1989.

[Cusumano and Selby, 1995] M. A. CUSUMANO AND R. W. SELBY, *Microsoft Secrets: How the World's Most Powerful Software Company Creates Technology, Shapes Markets, and Manages People,* The Free Press/Simon and Schuster, New York, 1995.

[Cusumano and Selby, 1997] M. A. CUSUMANO AND R. W. SELBY, "How Microsoft Builds Software," *Communications of the ACM* **40** (June 1997), pp. 53–61.

[DeMarco and Boehm, 2002] T. DEMARCO AND B. BOEHM, "The Agile Methods Fray," *IEEE Computer* **35** (June 2002), pp. 90–92.

[Drobka, Noftz, and Raghu, 2004] J. DROBKA, D. NOFTZ, AND R. RAGHU, "Piloting XP on Four Mission-Critical Projects," *IEEE Software* **21** (November/December 2004), pp. 70–75.

[Erdogmus, Morisio, and Torchiano, 2005] H. ERDOGMUS, M. MORISIO, AND M. TORCHIANO, "On the Effectiveness of the Test-First Approach to Programming," *IEEE Transactions on Software Engineering* **31** (March 2005), pp. 226–237.

[Fowler et al., 1999] M. FOWLER WITH K. BECK, J. BRANT, W. OPDYKE, AND D. ROBERTS, *Refactoring: Improving the Design of Existing Code*, Addison-Wesley, Reading, MA, 1999.

[Goth, 2000] G. GOTH, "New Air Traffic Control Software Takes an Incremental Approach," *IEEE Software* **17** (July/August 2000), pp. 108–111.

[Hayes, 2004] F. HAYES, "Chaos Is Back," *Computerworld,* www.computerworld.com/managementtopics/management/project/story/0,10801,97283,00.html, November 8, 2004.

[Highsmith and Coburn, 2001] J. HIGHSMITH AND A. COCKBURN, "Agile Software Development: The Business of Innovation," *IEEE Computer* **34** (September 2001), pp. 120–22.

[ISO/IEC 12207, 1995] "ISO/IEC 12207:1995, Information Technology—Software Life-Cycle Processes," International Organization for Standardization, International Electrotechnical Commission, Geneva, 1995.

[Jacobson, Booch, and Rumbaugh, 1999] I. JACOBSON, G. BOOCH, AND J. RUMBAUGH, *The Unified Software Development Process,* Addison-Wesley, Reading, MA, 1999.

[Jalote, Palit, Kurien, and Peethamber, 2004] P. JALOTE, A. PALIT, P. KURIEN, AND V. T. PEETHAMBER, "Timeboxing: A Process Model for Iterative Software Development," *Journal of Systems and Software* **70** (February 2004), pp. 117–27.

[Karlström and Runeson, 2005] D. KARLSTRÖM AND P. RUNESON, "Combining Agile Methods with Stage-Gate Project Management," *IEEE Software* **22** (May/June 2005), pp. 43–49.

[Larman and Basili, 2003] C. LARMAN AND V. R. BASILI, "Iterative and Incremental Development: A Brief History," *IEEE Computer* **36** (June 2003), pp. 47–56.

[Longstaff, Chittister, Pethia, and Haimes, 2000] T. A. LONGSTAFF, C. CHITTISTER, R. PETHIA, AND Y. Y. HAIMES, "Are We Forgetting the Risks of Information Technology?" *IEEE Computer* **33** (December 2000), pp. 43–51.

[McConnell, 1996] S. MCCONNELL, "Daily Build and Smoke Test," *IEEE Software* **13** (July/August 1996), pp. 144, 143.

[Mens and Tourwe, 2004] T. MENS AND T. TOURWE, "A Survey of Software Refactoring," *IEEE Transactions on Software Engineering* **30** (February 2004), pp. 126–39.

[Miller, 1956] G. A. MILLER, "The Magical Number Seven, Plus or Minus Two: Some Limits on Our Capacity for Processing Information," *The Psychological Review* **63** (March 1956), pp. 81–97; reprinted in: www.well.com/user/smalin/miller.html.

[Murru, Deias, and Mugheddu, 2003] O. MURRU, R. DEIAS, AND G. MUGHEDDU, "Assessing XP at a European Internet Company," *IEEE Software* **20** (May/June, 2003), pp. 37–43.

[Nerur, Mahapatra, and Mangalaraj, 2005] S. NERUR, R. MAHAPATRA, G. MANGALARAJ, "Challenges of Migrating to Agile Methodologies," *Communications of the ACM* **48** (May 2005), pp. 72–78.

[Rajlich and Bennett, 2000] V. RAJLICH AND K. H. BENNETT, "A Staged Model for the Software Life Cycle," *IEEE Computer* **33** (July 2000), pp. 66–71.

[Rasmusson, 2003] J. RASMUSSON, "Introducing XP into Greenfield Projects: Lessons Learned," *IEEE Software* **20** (May/June, 2003), pp. 21–29.

[Raymond, 2000] E. S. RAYMOND, *The Cathedral and the Bazaar: Musings on Linux and Open Source by an Accidental Revolutionary,* O'Reilly & Associates, Sebastopol, CA, 2000; also available at www.catb.org/~esr/writings/cathedral-bazaar/cathedral-bazaar/.

[Reifer, Maurer, and Erdogmus, 2003] D. REIFER, F. MAURER, AND H. ERDOGMUS, "Scaling Agile Methods," *IEEE Software* **20** (July/August 2004), pp. 12–14.

[Ropponen and Lyttinen, 2000] J. ROPPONEN AND K. LYTTINEN, "Components of Software Development Risk: How to Address Them? A Project Manager Survey," *IEEE Transactions on Software Engineering* **26** (February 2000), pp. 96–111.

[Royce, 1970] W. W. ROYCE, "Managing the Development of Large Software Systems: Concepts and Techniques," *1970 WESCON Technical Papers, Western Electronic Show and Convention,* Los Angeles, August 1970, pp. A/1-1–A/1-9; reprinted in: *Proceedings of the 11th International Conference on Software Engineering,* Pittsburgh, May 1989, IEEE, pp. 328–38.

[Royce, 1998] W. ROYCE, *Software Project Management: A Unified Framework*, Addison-Wesley, Reading, MA, 1998.

[Schwaber, 2001] K. SCHWABER, *Agile Software Development with Scrum,* Prentice Hall, Upper Saddle River, NJ, 2001.

[Scott and Vessey, 2002] J. E. SCOTT AND I. VESSEY, "Managing Risks in Enterprise Systems Implementations," *Communications of the ACM* **45** (April 2002), pp. 74–81.

[Softwaremag.com, 2004] "Standish: Project Success Rates Improved Over 10 Years," www.softwaremag.com/L.cfm?Doc=newsletter/2004-01-15/Standish, January 15, 2004.

[Spivey, 1992] J. M. SPIVEY, *The Z Notation: A Reference Manual,* Prentice Hall, New York, 1992.

[Standish, 2003] STANDISH GROUP INTERNATIONAL, "Introduction," www.standishgroup.com/chaos/introduction.pdf, 2003.

[Stephens and Rosenberg, 2003] M. STEPHENS AND D. ROSENBERG, *Extreme Programming Refactored: The Case against XP,* Apress, Berkeley, CA, 2003.

[Tomer and Schach, 2000] A. TOMER AND S. R. SCHACH, "The Evolution Tree: A Maintenance-Oriented Software Development Model," in: *Proceedings of the Fourth European Conference on Software Maintenance and Reengineering (CSMR 2000),* Zürich, Switzerland, February/March 2000, pp. 209–14.

[Williams, Kessler, Cunningham, and Jeffries, 2000] L. WILLIAMS, R. R. KESSLER, W. CUNNINGHAM, AND R. JEFFRIES, "Strengthening the Case for Pair Programming," *IEEE Software* **17** (July/August 2000), pp. 19–25.

[Yu, Schach, Chen, and Offutt, 2004] L. YU, S. R. SCHACH, K. CHEN, AND J. OFFUTT, "Categorization of Common Coupling and Its Application to the Maintainability of the Linux Kernel," *IEEE Transactions on Software Engineering* **30** (October 2004), pp. 694–706.

# Chapter 3

# The Software Process

## Learning Objectives

After studying this chapter, you should be able to

- Explain why two-dimensional life-cycle models are important.
- Describe the five core workflows of the Unified Process.
- List the artifacts tested in the test workflow.
- Describe the four phases of the Unified Process.
- Explain the difference between the workflows and the phases of the Unified Process.
- Appreciate the importance of software process improvement
- Describe the capability maturity model (CMM).

The software process is the way we produce software. It incorporates the methodology (Section 1.11) with its underlying software life-cycle model (Chapter 2) and techniques, the tools we use (Sections 5.4 through 5.10), and most important of all, the individuals building the software.

Different organizations have different software processes. For example, consider the issue of documentation. Some organizations consider the software they produce to be self-documenting, that is, the product can be understood simply by reading the source code. Other organizations, however, are documentation intensive. They punctiliously draw up specifications and check them methodically. Then they perform design activities painstakingly, check and recheck their designs before coding commences, and give extensive descriptions of each code artifact to the programmers. Test cases are preplanned, the result of each test run is logged, and the test data are meticulously filed away. Once the product has been delivered and installed on the client's computer, any suggested change must be proposed in writing, with detailed reasons for making the change. The proposed change can be made only with written authorization, and the modification is not integrated into the product until the documentation has been updated and the changes to the documentation approved.

Intensity of testing is another measure by which organizations can be compared. Some organizations devote up to half their software budgets to testing software, whereas others feel that only the user can thoroughly test a product. Consequently, some companies devote minimal time and effort to testing the product but spend a considerable amount of time fixing problems reported by users.

Postdelivery maintenance is a major preoccupation of many software organizations. Software that is 10, 15, or even 20 years old is continually enhanced to meet changing needs; in addition, residual faults continue to appear, even after the software has been successfully maintained for many years. Almost all organizations move their software to newer hardware every 3 to 5 years; this, too, constitutes postdelivery maintenance.

In contrast, yet other organizations essentially are concerned with research, leaving development—let alone maintenance—to others. This applies particularly to university computer science departments, where graduate students build software to prove that a particular design or technique is feasible. The commercial exploitation of the validated concept is left to other organizations. (See Just in Case You Wanted to Know Box 3.1 regarding the wide variation in the ways different organizations develop software.)

However, regardless of the exact procedure, the software development process is structured around the five workflows of Figure 2.4: requirements, analysis (specification), design, implementation, and testing. In this chapter, these workflows are described, together with potential challenges that may arise during each workflow. Solutions to the challenges associated with the production of software usually are nontrivial, and the rest of this book is devoted to describing suitable techniques. In the first part of this chapter, only the challenges are highlighted, but the reader is guided to the relevant sections or chapters for solutions. Thus, this part of the chapter not only is an overview of the software process, but a guide to much of the rest of the book. The chapter concludes with national and international initiatives to improve the software process.

We now examine the Unified Process.

# 3.1 The Unified Process

As stated at the beginning of this chapter, methodology is one component of a software process. The primary object-oriented methodology today is the **Unified Process**. As explained in Just in Case You Wanted to Know Box 3.2, the Unified "Process" is actually a methodology, but the name Unified Methodology already had been used as the name of the first version of the **Unified Modeling Language** (UML). The three precursors of the Unified Process (OMT, Booch's method, and Objectory) are no longer supported, and the other object-oriented methodologies have had little or no following. As a result, the Unified Process is usually the primary choice today for object-oriented software production. Fortunately, as will be demonstrated in Part 2 of this book, the Unified Process is an excellent object-oriented methodology in almost every way.

The Unified Process is not a specific series of steps that, if followed, result in the construction of a software product. In fact, no such single "one size fits all" methodology could exist because of the wide variety of types of software products. For example, there are many different application domains, such as insurance, aerospace, and manufacturing. Also, a methodology for rushing a COTS package to market ahead of its competitors is different from one used to construct a high-security electronic funds transfer network. In addition, the skills of software professionals can vary widely.

Instead, the Unified Process should be viewed as an adaptable methodology. That is, it is modified for the specific software product to be developed. As will be seen in Part 2, some features of the Unified Process are inapplicable to small- and even medium-scale software. However, much of the Unified Process is used for software products of all sizes. The emphasis in this book is on this common subset of the Unified Process, but aspects of the Unified Process applicable to only large-scale software also are discussed, to ensure that the issues that need to be addressed when larger software products are constructed are thoroughly appreciated.

# 3.2 Iteration and Incrementation within the Object-Oriented Paradigm

The object-oriented paradigm uses modeling throughout. A **model** is a set of UML diagrams that represent one or more aspects of the software product to be developed. (UML diagrams are introduced in Chapter 7.) Recall that UML stands for Unified *Modeling* Language. That is, UML is the tool that we use to represent (model) the target software product. A major reason for using a graphical representation like UML is best expressed by the old proverb, a picture is worth a thousand words. UML diagrams enable software professionals to communicate with one another more quickly and more accurately than if only verbal descriptions were used.

The object-oriented paradigm is an iterative and incremental methodology. Each workflow consists of a number of steps, and to carry out that workflow, the steps of the workflow are repeatedly performed until the members of the development team are satisfied that they have an accurate UML model of the software product they want to develop. That is, even the most experienced software professionals iterate and reiterate until they are finally satisfied that the UML diagrams are correct. The implication is that software engineers, no

Until recently, the most popular object-oriented software development methodologies were object modeling technique (OMT) [Rumbaugh et al., 1991] and Grady Booch's method [Booch, 1994]. OMT was developed by Jim Rumbaugh and his team at the General Electric Research and Development Center in Schenectady, New York, whereas Grady Booch developed his method at Rational, Inc., in Santa Clara, California. All object-oriented software development methodologies essentially are equivalent, so the differences between OMT and Booch's method are small. Nevertheless, there always was a friendly rivalry between the supporters of the two camps.

This changed in October 1994, when Rumbaugh joined Booch at Rational. The two methodologists immediately began to work together to develop a methodology that would combine OMT and Booch's method. When a preliminary version of their work was published, it was pointed out that they had not developed a methodology but merely a notation for representing an object-oriented software product. The name *Unified Methodology* was quickly changed to *Unified Modeling Language* (UML). In 1995, they were joined at Rational by Ivar Jacobson, author of the Objectory methodology. Booch, Jacobson, and Rumbaugh, affectionately called the "Three Amigos" (after the 1986 John Landis movie *Three Amigos!* with Chevy Chase and Steve Martin), then worked together. Version 1.0 of UML, published in 1997, took the software engineering world by storm. Until then, there had been no universally accepted notation for the development of a software product. Almost overnight UML was used all over the world. The Object Management Group (OMG), an association of the world's leading companies in object technology, took the responsibility for organizing an international standard for UML, so that every software professional would use the same version of UML, thereby promoting communication among individuals

matter how outstanding they may be, almost never get the various work products right the first time. How can this be?

The nature of software products is such that virtually everything has to be developed iteratively and incrementally. After all, software engineers are human, and therefore subject to Miller's Law (Section 2.5). That is, it is impossible to consider everything at the same time, so just seven or so chunks (units of information) are handled initially. Then, when the next set of chunks is considered, more knowledge about the target software product is gained, and the UML diagrams are modified in the light of this additional information. The process continues in this way until eventually the software engineers are satisfied that all the models for a given workflow are correct. In other words, initially the best possible UML diagrams are drawn in the light of the knowledge available at the beginning of the workflow. Then, as more knowledge about the real-world system being modeled is gained, the diagrams are made more accurate (iteration) and extended (incrementation). Accordingly, no matter how experienced and skillful a software engineer may be, he or she repeatedly iterates and increments until satisfied that the UML diagrams are an accurate representation of the software product to be developed.

Ideally, by the end of this book, the reader would have the software engineering skills necessary for constructing the large, complex software products for which the Unified Process was developed. Unfortunately, there are three reasons why this is not feasible.

1. Just as it is not possible to become an expert on calculus or a foreign language in one single course, gaining proficiency in the Unified Process requires extensive study and, more important, unending practice in object-oriented software engineering.

within an organization as well as companies worldwide. UML [Booch, Rumbaugh, and Jacobson, 1999] is today the unquestioned international standard notation for representing object-oriented software products.

An orchestral score shows which musical instruments are needed to play the piece, the notes each instrument is to play and when it is to play them, as well as a whole host of technical information such as the key signature, tempo, and loudness. Could this information be given in English, rather than a diagram? Probably, but it would be impossible to play music from such a description. For example, there is no way a pianist and a violinist could perform a piece described as follows: "The music is in march time, in the key of B minor. The first bar begins with the A above middle C on the violin (a quarter note). While this note is being played, the pianist plays a chord consisting of seven notes. The right hand plays the following four notes: E sharp above middle C . . ."

It is clear that, in some fields, a textual description simply cannot replace a diagram. Music is one such field; software development is another. And for software development, the best modeling language available today is UML.

Taking the software engineering world by storm with UML was not enough for the Three Amigos. Their next endeavor was to publish a complete software development methodology that unified their three separate methodologies. This unified methodology was first called the *Rational Unified Process* (RUP); *Rational* is in the name of the methodology not because the Three Amigos considered all other approaches to be irrational, but because at that time all three were senior managers at Rational, Inc. (Rational was bought by IBM in 2003). In their book on RUP [Jacobson, Booch, and Rumbaugh, 1999], the name *Unified Software Development Process* (USDP) was used. The term *Unified Process* is generally used today, for brevity.

2. The Unified Process was developed primarily for use in developing large, complex software products. To be able to handle the many intricacies of such software products, the Unified Process is itself large. It would be hard to cover every aspect of the Unified Process in a textbook of this size.

3. To teach the Unified Process, it is necessary to present a case study that illustrates the features of the Unified Process. To illustrate the features that apply to large software products, such a case study would have to be large. For example, just the specifications typically would take over 1000 pages.

For these three reasons, this book presents most, but not all, of the Unified Process.

The five **core workflows** of the Unified Process (requirements workflow, analysis workflow, design workflow, implementation workflow, and test workflow) and their challenges are now discussed.

## 3.3    The Requirements Workflow

Software development is expensive. The development process usually begins when the client approaches a development organization with regard to a software product that, in the opinion of the client, is either essential to the profitability of his or her enterprise or somehow can be justified economically. The aim of the **requirements workflow** is for the development organization to determine the client's needs.

The first task of the development team is to acquire a basic understanding of the **application domain** (**domain** for short), that is, the specific environment in which the target software product is to operate. The domain could be banking, automobile manufacturing, or nuclear physics.

At any stage of the process, if the client stops believing that the software will be cost effective, development will terminate immediately. Throughout this chapter the assumption is made that the client feels that the cost is justified. Therefore, a vital aspect of software development is the **business model**, a document that demonstrates the cost-effectiveness of the target product. (In fact, the "cost" is not always purely financial. For example, military software often is built for strategic or tactical reasons. Here, the cost of the software is the potential damage that could be suffered in the absence of the weapon being developed.)

At an initial meeting between client and developers, the client outlines the product as he or she conceptualizes it. From the viewpoint of the developers, the client's description of the desired product may be vague, unreasonable, contradictory, or simply impossible to achieve. The task of the developers at this stage is to determine exactly what the client needs and to find out from the client what constraints exist.

- A major constraint is almost always the **deadline**. For example, the client may stipulate that the finished product must be completed within 14 months. In almost every application domain, it is now commonplace for a target software product to be mission critical. That is, the client needs the software product for core activities of his or her organization, and any delay in delivering the target product is detrimental to the organization.

- A variety of other constraints often are present such as **reliability** (for example, the product must be operational 99 percent of the time or the mean time between failures must be at least 4 months). Another common constraint is the size of the executable load image (for example, it has to run on the client's personal computer or on the hardware inside the satellite).

- The **cost** is almost invariably an important constraint. However, the client rarely tells the developers how much money is available to build the product. Instead, a common practice is that, once the specifications have been finalized, the client asks the developers to name their price for completing the project. Clients follow this bidding procedure in the hope that the amount of the developers' bid is lower than the amount the client has budgeted for the project.

The preliminary investigation of the client's needs sometimes is called **concept exploration**. In subsequent meetings between members of the development team and the client team, the functionality of the proposed product is successively refined and analyzed for technical feasibility and financial justification.

Up to now, everything seems to be straightforward. Unfortunately, the requirements workflow frequently is performed inadequately. When the product finally is delivered to the user, perhaps a year or two after the specifications have been signed off on by the client, the client may say to the developers, "I know that this is what I asked for, but it isn't really what I wanted." What the client asked for and, therefore, what the developers thought the client wanted, was not what the client actually *needed*. There can be a number of reasons for this predicament. First, the client may not truly understand what is going on in his or her own organization. For example, it is no use asking the software developers for a faster operating system if the cause of the current slow turnaround is a badly designed database. Or, if the client operates an unprofitable chain of retail stores, the client may ask for a financial management information system that reflects such items as sales, salaries, accounts payable, and accounts receivable. Such a product will be of little use if the real reason for the losses is shrinkage (theft by employees and shoplifting). If that is the case, then a stock control system rather than a financial management information system is required.

But the major reason why the client frequently asks for the wrong product is that software is complex. If it is difficult for a software professional to visualize a piece of software and its functionality, the problem is far worse for a client who is barely computer literate. As will be shown in Chapter 10, the Unified Process can help in this regard; the many UML diagrams of the Unified Process assist the client in gaining the necessary detailed understanding of what needs to be developed.

## 3.4   The Analysis Workflow

The aim of the **analysis workflow** is to analyze and refine the requirements to achieve the detailed understanding of the requirements essential for developing a software product correctly and maintaining it easily. At first sight, however, there is no need for an analysis workflow. Instead, an apparently simpler way to proceed would be to develop a software product by continuing with further iterations of the requirements workflow until the necessary understanding of the target software product has been obtained.

The key point is that the output of the requirements workflow must be totally comprehended by the client. In other words, the artifacts of the requirements workflow must be expressed in the language of the client, that is, in a natural (human) language such as English, Armenian, or Zulu. But all natural languages, without exception, are somewhat imprecise and lend themselves to misunderstanding. For example, consider the following paragraph:

> A part record and a plant record are read from the database. If it contains the letter A directly followed by the letter Q, then calculate the cost of transporting that part to that plant.

At first sight, this requirement seems perfectly clear. But to what does *it* (the second word in the second sentence) refer: the part record, the plant record, or the database?

Ambiguities of this kind cannot arise if the requirements are expressed (say) in a mathematical notation. However, if a mathematical notation is used for the requirements, then the client is unlikely to understand much of the requirements. As a result, there may well be miscommunication between client and developers regarding the requirements, and consequently, the software product developed to satisfy those requirements may not be what the client needs.

The solution is to have two separate workflows. The requirements workflow is couched in the language of the client; the analysis workflow, in a more precise language that ensures that the design and implementation workflows are correctly carried out. In addition, more details are added during the analysis workflow, details not relevant to the client's understanding of the target software product but essential for the software professionals who will develop the software product. For example, the initial state of a statechart (Section 12.6) would surely not concern the client in any way but has to be included in the specifications if the developers are to build the target product correctly.

The specifications of the product constitute a contract. The software developers are deemed to have completed the contract when they deliver a product that satisfies the acceptance criteria of the specifications. For this reason, the specifications should not include imprecise terms like *suitable, convenient, ample*, or *enough*, or similar terms that sound exact but in practice are equally imprecise, such as *optimal* or *98 percent complete*. Whereas contract software development can lead to a lawsuit, there is no chance of the specifications forming the basis for legal action when the client and developers are from the same organization. Nevertheless, even in the case of internal software development, the specifications always should be written as if they will be used as evidence in a trial.

More important, the specifications are essential for both testing and maintenance. Unless the specifications are precise, there is no way to determine whether they are correct, let alone whether the implementation satisfies the specifications. And it is hard to change the specifications unless some document states exactly what the specifications currently are.

When the Unified Process is used, there is no specification document in the usual sense of the term. Instead, a set of UML artifacts are shown to the client, as described in Chapter 12. These UML diagrams and their descriptions can obviate many (but by no means all) of the problems of the classical specification document.

One mistake that can be made by a classical analysis team is that the specifications are ambiguous; as previously explained, **ambiguity** is intrinsic to natural languages. **Incompleteness** is another problem in the specifications; that is, some relevant fact or requirement may be omitted. For instance, the specification document may not state what actions are to be taken if the input data contain errors. Moreover, the specification document may contain **contradictions**. For example, one place in the specification document for a product that controls a fermentation process states that if the pressure exceeds 35 psi, then valve M17 immediately must be shut. However, another place states that, if the pressure exceeds 35 psi, then the operator immediately must be alerted; only if the operator takes no remedial action within 30 seconds should valve M17 be shut automatically. Software development cannot proceed until such problems in the specifications have been corrected. As pointed out in the previous paragraph, many of these problems can be reduced by using the Unified Process. This is because UML diagrams together with descriptions of those diagrams are less likely to contain ambiguity, incompleteness, and contradictions.

Once the client has approved the specifications, detailed planning and estimating commences. No client authorizes a software project without knowing in advance how long the project will take and how much it will cost. From the viewpoint of the developers, these two items are just as important. If the developers underestimate the cost of a project, then the client pays the agreed-upon fee, which may be significantly less than the developers' actual cost. Conversely, if the developers overestimate what the project costs, then the client may turn down the project or have the job done by other developers whose estimate is more reasonable. Similar issues arise with regard to duration estimates. If the developers underestimate how long completing a project will take, then the resulting late delivery of the product, at best, results in a loss of confidence by the client. At worst, lateness penalty clauses in the contract are invoked, causing the developers to suffer financially. Again, if the developers overestimate how long it will take for the product to be delivered, the client may well award the job to developers who promise faster delivery.

For the developers, merely estimating the duration and total cost is not enough. The developers need to assign the appropriate personnel to the various workflows of the development process. For example, the implementation team cannot start until the relevant design artifacts have been approved by the SQA group, and the design team is not needed until the analysis team has completed its task. In other words, the developers have to plan ahead. A software project management plan (SPMP) must be drawn up that reflects the separate workflows of the development process and shows which members of the development organization are involved in each task, as well as the deadlines for completing each task.

The earliest that such a detailed plan can be drawn up is when the specifications have been finalized. Before that time, the project is too amorphous for complete planning. Some aspects of the project certainly must be planned right from the start, but until the developers know exactly what is to be built, they cannot specify all aspects of the plan for building it.

Therefore, once the specifications have been approved by the client, preparation of the software project management plan commences. Major components of the plan are the **deliverables** (what the client is going to get), the **milestones** (when the client gets them), and the **budget** (how much it is going to cost).

The plan describes the software process in fullest detail. It includes aspects such as the life-cycle model to be used, the organizational structure of the development organization, project responsibilities, managerial objectives and priorities, the techniques and CASE tools to be used, and detailed schedules, budgets, and resource allocations. Underlying the entire plan are the duration and cost estimates; techniques for obtaining such estimates are described in Section 9.2.

The analysis workflow is described in Chapters 11 and 12: classical analysis techniques are described in Chapter 11, and object-oriented analysis is the subject of Chapter 12. A major artifact of the analysis workflow is the software project management plan. An explanation of how to draw up the SPMP is given in Sections 9.3 though 9.5.

Now the design workflow is examined.

## 3.5 The Design Workflow

The specifications of a product spell out *what* the product is to do; the design shows *how* the product is to do it. More precisely, the aim of the **design workflow** is to refine the artifacts of the analysis workflow until the material is in a form that can be implemented by the programmers.

As explained in Section 1.3, during the classical design phase, the design team determines the internal structure of the product. The designers decompose the product into **modules**, independent pieces of code with well-defined interfaces to the rest of the product. The interface of each module (that is, the arguments passed to the module and the arguments returned by the module) must be specified in detail. For example, a module might measure the water level in a nuclear reactor and cause an alarm to sound if the level is too low. A module in an avionics product might take as input two or more sets of coordinates of an incoming enemy missile, compute its trajectory, and invoke another module to advise the pilot as to possible evasive action. Once the team has completed the decomposition into modules (the **architectural design**), the **detailed design** is performed. For each module, algorithms are selected and data structures chosen.

Turning now to the object-oriented paradigm, the basis of that paradigm is the **class**, a specific type of module. Classes are extracted during the analysis workflow and designed during the design workflow. Consequently, the object-oriented counterpart of architectural design is performed as a part of the object-oriented analysis workflow, and the object-oriented counterpart of detailed design is part of the object-oriented design workflow.

The design team must keep a meticulous record of the design decisions that are made. This information is essential for two reasons.

1. While the product is being designed, a dead end will be reached at times and the design team must backtrack and redesign certain pieces. Having a written record of why specific decisions were made assists the team when this occurs and helps it get back on track.

2. Ideally, the design of the product should be open-ended, meaning future enhancements (postdelivery maintenance) can be done by adding new classes or replacing existing classes without affecting the design as a whole. Of course, in practice, this ideal is difficult to achieve. Deadline constraints in the real world are such that designers struggle against the clock to complete a design that satisfies the original specifications, without worrying about any later enhancements. If future enhancements (to be added after the product is delivered to the client) are included in the specifications, then these must be allowed for in the design, but this situation is extremely rare. In general, the specifications, and hence the design, deal with only present requirements. In addition, while the product is still being designed, there is no way to determine all possible future enhancements. Finally, if the design has to take *all* future possibilities into account, at best it will be unwieldy; at worst, it will be so complicated that implementation is impossible. So the designers have to compromise, putting together a design that can be extended in many reasonable ways without the need for total redesign. But, in a product that undergoes major enhancement, the time will come when the design simply cannot handle further changes. When this stage is reached, the product must be redesigned as a whole. The task of the redesign team is considerably easier if the team members are provided a record of the reasons for all the original design decisions.

## 3.6 The Implementation Workflow

The aim of the **implementation workflow** is to implement the target software product in the chosen implementation language(s). A small software product is sometimes implemented by the designer. In contrast, a large software product is partitioned into smaller subsystems, which are then implemented in parallel by coding teams. The subsystems, in turn, consist of **components** or **code artifacts** implemented by an individual programmer.

Usually, the only documentation given a programmer is the relevant design artifact. For example, in the case of the classical paradigm, the programmer is given the detailed design of the module he or she is to implement. The detailed design usually provides enough information for the programmer to implement the code artifact without too much difficulty. If there are any problems, they can quickly be cleared up by consulting the responsible designer. However, there is no way for the individual programmer to know if the architectural design is correct. Only when integration of individual code artifacts commences do the shortcomings of the design as a whole start coming to light.

Suppose that a number of code artifacts have been implemented and integrated and the parts of the product integrated so far appear to be working correctly. Suppose further that a programmer has correctly implemented artifact a45, but when this artifact is integrated with the other existing artifacts, the product fails. The cause of the failure lies not in artifact a45 itself, but rather in the way that artifact a45 interacts with the rest of the product, as specified in the architectural design. Nevertheless, in this type of situation the programmer who just coded artifact a45 tends to be blamed for the failure. This is unfortunate, because the programmer has simply followed the instructions provided by the designer and implemented the artifact exactly as described in the detailed design for that artifact. The members of the programming team are rarely shown the "big picture," that is, the architectural design, let alone asked to comment on it. Although it is grossly unfair to expect an individual programmer to be aware of the implications for the product as a whole of a specific artifact, this unfortunately happens in practice all too often. This is yet another reason why it is so important for the design to be correct in every respect.

The correctness of the design (as well as the other artifacts) is checked as part of the test workflow.

# 3.7    The Test Workflow

As shown in Figure 2.4, in the Unified Process testing is carried out in parallel with the other workflows, starting from the beginning. There are two major aspects to testing.

1. Every developer and maintainer is personally responsible for ensuring that his or her work is correct. Therefore, a software professional has to test and retest each artifact he or she develops or maintains.
2. Once the software professional is convinced that an artifact is correct, it is handed over to the software quality assurance group for independent testing, as described in Chapter 6.

The nature of the **test workflow** changes depending on the artifacts being tested. However, a feature important to all artifacts is traceability.

## 3.7.1 Requirements Artifacts

If the requirements artifacts are to be testable over the life cycle of the software product, then one property they must have is **traceability**. For example, it must be possible to trace every item in the analysis artifacts back to a requirements artifact and similarly for the design artifacts and the implementation artifacts. If the requirements have been presented methodically, properly numbered, cross-referenced, and indexed, then the developers should have little difficulty tracing through the subsequent artifacts and ensuring that they are indeed a true reflection of the client's requirements. When the work of the members of the requirements team is subsequently checked by the SQA group, traceability simplifies their task, too.

## 3.7.2 Analysis Artifacts

As pointed out in Chapter 1, a major source of faults in delivered software is faults in the specifications that are not detected until the software has been installed on the client's computer and used by the client's organization for its intended purpose. Both the analysis team and the SQA group must therefore check the analysis artifacts assiduously. In addition, they must ensure that the specifications are feasible, for example, that a specific hardware component is fast enough or that the client's current online disk storage capacity is adequate to handle the new product. An excellent way of checking the analysis artifacts is by means of a review. Representatives of the analysis team and of the client are present. The meeting usually is chaired by a member of the SQA group. The aim of the review is to determine whether the analysis artifacts are correct. The reviewers go through the analysis artifacts, checking to see if there are any faults. Walkthroughs and inspections are two types of reviews, and they are described in Section 6.2.

We turn now to the checking of the detailed planning and estimating that takes place once the client has signed off on the specifications. Whereas it is essential that every aspect of the SPMP be meticulously checked by the development team and then by the SQA group, particular attention must be paid to the plan's duration and cost estimates. One way to do this is for management to obtain two (or more) independent estimates of both duration and cost when detailed planning starts, and then reconcile any significant differences. With regard to the SPMP document, an excellent way to check it is by a review similar to the review of the analysis artifacts. If the duration and cost estimates are satisfactory, the client will give permission for the project to proceed.

### 3.7.3 Design Artifacts

As mentioned in Section 3.7.1, a critical aspect of testability is traceability. In the case of the design, this means that every part of the design can be linked to an analysis artifact. A suitably cross-referenced design gives the developers and the SQA group a powerful tool for checking whether the design agrees with the specifications and whether every part of the specifications is reflected in some part of the design.

Design reviews are similar to the reviews that the specifications undergo. However, in view of the technical nature of most designs, the client usually is not present. Members of the design team and the SQA group work through the design as a whole as well as through each separate design artifact, ensuring that the design is correct. The types of faults to look for include logic faults, interface faults, lack of exception handling (processing of error conditions), and most important, nonconformance to the specifications. In addition, the review team always should be aware of the possibility that some analysis faults were not detected during the previous workflow. A detailed description of the review process is given in Section 6.2.

### 3.7.4 Implementation Artifacts

Each component should be tested while it is being implemented (desk checking); and after it has been implemented, it is run against test cases. This informal testing is done by the programmer. Thereafter, the quality assurance group tests the component methodically; this is termed **unit testing**. A variety of unit-testing techniques are described in Chapter 14.

In addition to running test cases, a code review is a powerful, successful technique for detecting programming faults. Here, the programmer guides the members of the review team through the listing of the component. The review team must include an SQA representative. The procedure is similar to reviews of specifications and designs described previously. As in all the other workflows, a record of the activities of the SQA group are kept as part of the test workflow.

Once a component has been coded, it must be combined with the other coded components so that the SQA group can determine whether the (partial) product as a whole functions correctly. The way in which the components are integrated (all at once or one at a time) and the specific order (from top to bottom or from bottom to top in the component interconnection diagram or class hierarchy) can have a critical influence on the quality of the resulting product. For example, suppose the product is integrated bottom up. A major design fault, if present, will show up late, necessitating an expensive rewrite. Conversely, if the components are integrated top down, then the lower-level components usually do not receive as thorough a testing as would be the case if the product were integrated bottom up. These and other problems are discussed in detail in Chapter 14. A detailed explanation is given there as to why coding and integration must be performed in parallel.

The purpose of this **integration testing** is to check that the components combine correctly to achieve a product that satisfies its specifications. During integration testing, particular care must be paid to testing the component interfaces. It is important that the number, order, and types of formal arguments match the number, order, and types of actual arguments. This strong type checking [van Wijngaarden et al., 1975] is best performed by the compiler and linker. However, many languages are not strongly typed. When such a language is used, checking the interfaces must be done by members of the SQA group.

When the integration testing has been completed (that is, when all the components have been coded and integrated), the SQA group performs **product testing**. The functionality of the product as a whole is checked against the specifications. In particular, the constraints listed in the specifications must be tested. A typical example is whether the response time has been met. Because the aim of product testing is to determine whether the specifications have been correctly implemented, many of the test cases can be drawn up once the specifications are complete.

Not only must the correctness of the product be tested but also its robustness. That is, intentionally erroneous input data are submitted to determine whether the product will crash or whether its error-handling capabilities are adequate for dealing with bad data. If the product is to be run together with the client's currently installed software, then tests also must be performed to check that the new product will have no adverse effect on the client's existing computer operations. Finally, a check must be made as to whether the source code and all other types of documentation are complete and internally consistent. Product testing is discussed in Section 14.21. On the basis of the results of the product test, a senior manager in the development organization decides whether the product is ready to be released to the client.

The final aspect of integration testing is **acceptance testing**. The software is delivered to the client, who tests it on the actual hardware, using actual data as opposed to test data. No matter how methodical the development team or the SQA group might be, there is a significant difference between test cases, which by their very nature are artificial, and actual data. A software product cannot be considered to satisfy its specifications until the product has passed its acceptance test. More details about acceptance testing are given in Section 14.22.

In the case of COTS software (Section 1.11), as soon as product testing is complete, versions of the complete product are supplied to selected possible future clients for testing on site. The first such version is termed the **alpha release**. The corrected alpha release is called the **beta release**; in general, the beta release is intended to be close to the final version. (The terms *alpha release* and *beta release* are generally applied to all types of software products, not just COTS.)

Faults in COTS software usually result in poor sales of the product and huge losses for the development company. So that as many faults as possible come to light as early as possible, developers of COTS software frequently give alpha or beta releases to selected companies, in the expectation that on-site tests will uncover any latent faults. In return, the alpha and beta sites frequently are promised free copies of the delivered version of the software. Risks are involved for a company participating in alpha or beta testing. In particular, alpha releases can be fault laden, resulting in frustration, wasted time, and possible damage to databases. However, the company gets a head start in using the new COTS software, which can give it an advantage over its competitors. A problem occurs sometimes when software organizations use alpha testing by potential clients in place of thorough product testing by the SQA group. Although alpha testing at a number of different sites usually brings to light a large variety of faults, there is no substitute for the methodical testing that the SQA group can provide.

## 3.8   Postdelivery Maintenance

Postdelivery maintenance is not an activity grudgingly carried out after the product has been delivered and installed on the client's computer. On the contrary, it is an integral part of the software process that must be planned for from the beginning. As explained in Section 3.5, the design, as far as is feasible, should take future enhancements into account. Coding must be performed with future maintenance kept in mind. After all, as pointed out in Section 1.3, more money is spent on postdelivery maintenance than on all other software activities combined. It therefore is a vital aspect of software production. Postdelivery maintenance must never be treated as an afterthought. Instead, the entire software development effort must be carried out in such a way as to minimize the impact of the inevitable future postdelivery maintenance.

A common problem with postdelivery maintenance is documentation or, rather, lack of it. In the course of developing software against a time deadline, the original analysis and design artifacts frequently are not updated and, consequently, are almost useless to the maintenance team. Other documentation such as the database manual or the operating manual may never be written, because management decided that delivering the product to the client on time was more important than developing the documentation in parallel with the software. In many instances, the source code is the only documentation available to the maintainer. The high rate of personnel turnover in the software industry exacerbates the maintenance situation, in that none of the original developers may be working for the organization at the time when maintenance is performed. Postdelivery maintenance frequently is the most challenging aspect of software production for these reasons and the additional reasons given in Chapter 15.

Turning now to testing, there are two aspects to testing changes made to a product when postdelivery maintenance is performed. The first is checking that the required changes have been implemented correctly. The second aspect is ensuring that, in the course of making the required changes to the product, no other inadvertent changes were made. Therefore, once the programmer has determined that the desired changes have been implemented, the product must be tested against previous test cases to make certain that the functionality of the rest of the product has not been compromised. This procedure is called **regression testing**. To assist in regression testing, it is necessary that all previous test cases be retained, together with the results of running those test cases. Testing during post-delivery maintenance is discussed in greater detail in Chapter 15.

A major aspect of postdelivery maintenance is a record of all the changes made, together with the reason for each change. When software is changed, it has to be regression tested. Therefore, the regression test cases are a central form of documentation.

## 3.9   Retirement

The final stage in the software life cycle is **retirement**. After many years of service, a stage is reached when further postdelivery maintenance no longer is cost effective.

- Sometimes, the proposed changes are so drastic that the design as a whole would have to be changed. In such a case, it is less expensive to redesign and recode the entire product.
- So many changes may have been made to the original design that interdependencies inadvertently have been built into the product, and even a small change to one minor component might have a drastic effect on the functionality of the product as a whole.
- The documentation may not have been adequately maintained, thereby increasing the risk of a regression fault to the extent that it would be safer to recode than maintain.
- The hardware (and operating system) on which the product runs is to be replaced; it may be more economical to rewrite from scratch than to modify.

In each of these instances the current version is replaced by a new version, and the software process continues.

True retirement, on the other hand, is a somewhat rare event that occurs when a product has outgrown its usefulness. The client organization no longer requires the functionality provided by the product, and it finally is removed from the computer.

## 3.10   The Phases of the Unified Process

Figure 3.1 differs from Figure 2.4 in that the labels of the increments have been changed. Instead of Increment A, Increment B, and so on, the four increments are now labeled Inception phase, Elaboration phase, Construction phase, and Transition phase. In other words, the phases of the Unified Process correspond to increments.

Although in theory the development of a software product could be performed in any number of increments, development in practice often seems to consist of four increments. The increments or phases are described in Sections 3.10.1 through 3.10.4, together with the deliverables of each phase, that is, the artifacts that should be completed by the end of that phase.

Every step performed in the Unified Process falls into one of five core workflows and *also* into one of four phases, the inception phase, elaboration phase, construction phase, and transition phase. The various steps of these four phases are already described in Sections 3.3 through 3.7. For example, building a business model is part of the requirements

**FIGURE 3.1**

The core
workflows and
the phases of
the Unified
Process.

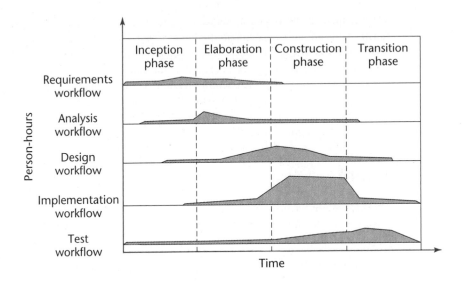

workflow (Section 3.3). It is also part of the inception phase. Nevertheless, each step has to be considered twice, as will be explained.

Consider the requirements workflow. To determine the client's needs, one of the steps is, as just stated, to build a business model. In other words, within the framework of the requirements workflow, building a business model is presented within a *technical* context. In Section 3.10.1, a description is presented of building a business model within the framework of the inception phase, the phase in which management decides whether or not to develop the proposed software product. That is, building a business model shortly is presented within an *economic* context (Section 1.2).

At the same time, there is no point in presenting each step twice, both times at the same level of detail. Accordingly, the inception phase is described in depth to highlight the difference between the technical context of the workflows and the economic context of the phases, but the other three phases are simply outlined.

## 3.10.1 The Inception Phase

The aim of the **inception phase** is to determine whether it is worthwhile to develop the target software product. In other words, the primary aim of this phase is to determine whether the proposed software product is economically viable.

Two steps of the requirements workflow are to understand the domain and build a business model. Clearly, there is no way the developers can give any kind of opinion regarding a possible future software product unless they first understand the domain in which they are considering developing the target software product. It does not matter if the domain is a television network, a machine tool company, or a hospital specializing in liver disease—if the developers do not fully understand the domain, little reliance can be placed on what they subsequently build. Hence, the first step is to obtain domain knowledge. Once the developers have a full comprehension of the domain, the second step is to build a business model. In other words, the first need is to understand the domain itself, and the second need is to understand precisely how the client organization operates in that domain.

Now the scope of the target project has to be delimited. For example, consider a proposed software product for a new highly secure ATM network for a nationwide chain of banks. The size of the business model of the banking chain as a whole is likely to be huge. To determine what the target software product should incorporate, the developers have to focus on only a subset of the business model, namely, the subset covered by the proposed software product. Therefore, delimiting the scope of the proposed project is the third step.

Now the developers can begin to make the initial business case. The questions that need to be answered before proceeding with the project include [Jacobson, Booch, and Rumbaugh, 1999]:

- Is the proposed software product cost effective? That is, will the benefits to be gained as a consequence of developing the software product outweigh the costs involved? How long will it take to obtain a return on the investment needed to develop the proposed software product? Alternatively, what will be the cost to the client if he or she decides not to develop the proposed software product? If the software product is to be sold in the marketplace, have the necessary marketing studies been performed?

- Can the proposed software product be delivered in time? That is, if the software product is delivered late to the market, will the organization still make a profit or will a competitive software product obtain the lion's share of the market? Alternatively, if the software product is to be developed to support the client organization's own activities (presumably including mission-critical activities), what is the impact if the proposed software product is delivered late?

- What risks are involved in developing the software product, and how can these risks be mitigated? Do the team members who will develop the proposed software product have the necessary experience? Is new hardware needed for this software product and, if so, is there a risk that it will not be delivered in time? If so, is there a way to mitigate that risk, perhaps by ordering backup hardware from another supplier? Are software tools (Chapter 5) needed? Are they currently available? Do they have all the necessary functionality? Is it likely that a COTS package (Section 1.11) with all (or almost all) the functionality of the proposed custom software product will be put on the market while the project is under way, and how can this be determined?

By the end of the inception phase the developers need answers to these questions so that the initial business case can be made.

The next step is to identify the risks. There are three major risk categories:

1. *Technical risks*. Examples of technical risks were just listed.
2. *Not getting the requirements right*. This risk can be mitigated by performing the requirements workflow correctly.
3. *Not getting the architecture right*. The architecture may not be sufficiently robust. (Recall from Section 2.7 that the architecture of a software product consists of the various components and how they fit together, and that the property of being able to handle extensions and changes without falling apart is its robustness.) In other words, while the software product is being developed, there is a risk that trying to add the next piece to what has been developed so far might require the entire architecture to be redesigned from scratch. An analogy would be to build a house of cards, only to find the entire edifice tumbling down when an additional card is added.

The risks need to be ranked so that the critical risks are mitigated first.

As shown in Figure 3.1, a small amount of the analysis workflow is performed during the inception phase. All that is usually done is to extract the information needed for the design of the architecture. This design work is also reflected in Figure 3.1.

Turning now to the implementation workflow, during the inception phase frequently no coding is performed. However, on occasion, it is necessary to build a proof-of-concept prototype to test the feasibility of part of the proposed software product, as described in Section 2.9.7.

The test workflow commences at the start of the inception phase. The major aim here is to ensure that the requirements are accurately determined.

Planning is an essential part of every phase. In the case of the inception phase, the developers have insufficient information at the beginning of the phase to plan the entire development, so the only planning done at the start of the project is the planning for the inception phase itself. For the same reason, a lack of information, the only planning that can meaningfully be done at the end of the inception phase is to plan for just the next phase, the elaboration phase.

Documentation, too, is an essential part of every phase. The deliverables of the inception phase include [Jacobson, Booch, and Rumbaugh, 1999]

- The initial version of the domain model.
- The initial version of the business model.
- The initial version of the requirements artifacts.
- A preliminary version of the analysis artifacts.
- A preliminary version of the architecture.
- The initial list of risks.
- The initial use cases (see Chapter 10).
- The plan for the elaboration phase.
- The initial version of the business case.

Obtaining the last item, the initial version of the business case, is the overall aim of the inception phase. This initial version incorporates a description of the scope of the software product as well as financial details. If the proposed software product is to be marketed, the business case includes revenue projections, market estimates, and initial cost estimates. If the software product is to be used in-house, the business case includes the initial cost–benefit analysis (Section 5.2).

### 3.10.2 The Elaboration Phase

The aim of the **elaboration phase** is to refine the initial requirements, refine the architecture, monitor the risks and refine their priorities, refine the business case, and produce the software project management plan. The reason for the name *elaboration phase* is clear; the major activities of this phase are refinements or elaborations of the previous phase.

Figure 3.1 shows that these tasks correspond to all but completing the requirements workflow (Chapter 10), performing virtually the entire analysis workflow (Chapter 12), and then starting the design of the architecture (Section 8.5.4).

The deliverables of the elaboration phase include [Jacobson, Booch, and Rumbaugh, 1999]

- The completed domain model.
- The completed business model.
- The completed requirements artifacts.
- The completed analysis artifacts.
- An updated version of the architecture.
- An updated list of risks.
- The software project management plan (for the remainder of the project).
- The completed business case.

### 3.10.3 The Construction Phase

The aim of the **construction phase** is to produce the first operational-quality version of the software product, the so-called beta release (Section 3.7.4). Consider Figure 3.1 again. Even though the figure is only a symbolic representation of the phases, it is clear that the emphasis in this phase is on implementation and testing the software product. That is, the various components are coded and unit tested. The code artifacts are then compiled and linked (integrated) to form subsystems, which are integration tested. Finally, the subsystems are combined into the overall system, which is product tested. This was described in Section 3.7.4.

The deliverables of the construction phase include [Jacobson, Booch, and Rumbaugh, 1999]

- The initial user manual and other manuals, as appropriate.
- All the artifacts (beta release versions).
- The completed architecture.
- The updated risk list.
- The software project management plan (for the remainder of the project).
- If necessary, the updated business case.

### 3.10.4 The Transition Phase

The aim of the **transition phase** is to ensure that the client's requirements have indeed been met. This phase is driven by feedback from the sites at which the beta version has been installed. (In the case of a custom software product developed for a specific client, there is just one such site.) Faults in the software product are corrected. Also, all the manuals are completed. During this phase, it is important to try to discover any previously unidentified risks. (The importance of uncovering risks even during the transition phase is highlighted in Just in Case You Wanted to Know Box 3.3.)

The deliverables of the transition phase include [Jacobson, Booch, and Rumbaugh, 1999]

- All the artifacts (final versions).
- The completed manuals.

A real-time system frequently is more complex than most people, even its developers, realize. As a result, sometimes subtle interactions take place among components that even the most skilled testers usually would not detect. An apparently minor change therefore can have major consequences.

A famous example of this is the fault that delayed the first space shuttle orbital flight in April 1981 [Garman, 1981]. The space shuttle avionics are controlled by four identical synchronized computers. Also, an independent fifth computer is ready for backup in case the set of four computers fails. Two years earlier, a change had been made to the module that performs initialization before the avionics computers are synchronized. An unfortunate side effect of this change was that a record containing a time just slightly later than the current time was erroneously sent to the data area used for synchronization of the avionics computers. The time sent was sufficiently close to the actual time for this fault not to be detected. About 1 year later, the time difference was slightly increased, just enough to cause a 1 in 67 chance of a failure. Then, on the day of the first space shuttle launch, with hundreds of millions of people watching on television all over the world, the synchronization failure occurred and three of the four identical avionics computers were synchronized one cycle late relative to the first computer.

A fail-safe device that prevents the independent fifth computer from receiving information from the other four computers unless they are in agreement had the unanticipated consequence of preventing initialization of the fifth computer, and the launch had to be postponed. An all too familiar aspect of this incident was that the fault was in the initialization module, a module that apparently had no connection whatsoever with the synchronization routines.

Unfortunately, this was by no means the last real-time software fault affecting a space launch. For example, in April 1999, a Milstar military communications satellite was hurled into a uselessly low orbit at a cost of $1.2 billion; the cause was a software fault in the upper stage of the Titan 4 rocket [*Florida Today*, 1999].

Not just space launches are affected by real-time faults but landings, too. In May 2003, a Soyuz TMA-1 spaceship launched from the international space station landed 300 miles off course in Kazakhstan after a ballistic descent. The cause of the landing problems was, yet again, a real-time software fault [CNN.com, 2003].

## 3.11   One- versus Two-Dimensional Life-Cycle Models

A classical life-cycle model (like the waterfall model of Section 2.9.2) is a one-dimensional model, as represented by the single axis in Figure 3.2(a). Underlying the Unified Process is a two-dimensional life-cycle model, as represented by the two axes in Figure 3.2(b).

The one-dimensional nature of the waterfall model is clearly reflected in Figure 2.3. In contrast, Figure 2.2 shows the evolution-tree model of the Winburg mini case study. This model is two-dimensional and should therefore be compared to Figure 3.2(b).

Are the additional complications of a two-dimensional model necessary? The answer was given in Chapter 2, but this is such an important issue that it is repeated here. When developing a software product, in an ideal world, the requirements workflow would be completed before proceeding to the analysis workflow. Similarly, the analysis workflow would be completed before starting the design workflow, and so on. In reality, however, all but the

**FIGURE 3.2**
Comparison of
(a) a classical
one-dimensional
life-cycle model
and (b) the two-
dimensional
Unified Process
life-cycle
model.

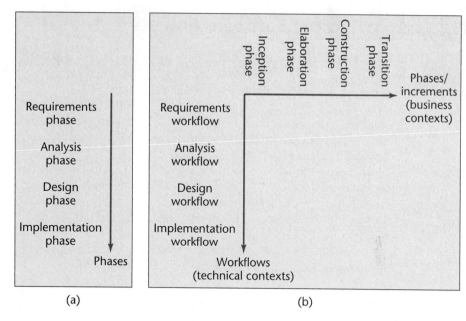

most trivial software products are too large to handle as a single unit. Instead, the task has to be divided into increments (phases), and within each increment the developers have to iterate until they have completed the task under construction. As humans, we are limited by Miller's Law [Miller, 1956], which states that we can actively process only seven concepts at a time. We therefore cannot deal with software products as a whole, but instead we have to break those systems into subsystems. Even subsystems can be too large at times—components may be all that we can handle until we have a fuller understanding of the software product as a whole.

The Unified Process is the best solution to date for treating a large problem as a set of smaller, largely independent subproblems. It provides a framework for incrementation and iteration, the mechanism used to cope with the complexity of large software products.

Another challenge that the Unified Process handles well is the inevitable changes. One aspect of this challenge is changes in the client's requirements while a software product is being developed, the so-called moving-target problem (Section 2.4).

For all these reasons, the Unified Process is currently the best methodology available. However, in the future, the Unified Process will doubtless be superseded by some new methodology. Today's software professionals are looking beyond the Unified Process to the next major breakthrough. After all, in virtually every field of human endeavor, the discoveries of today are often superior to anything that was put forward in the past. The Unified Process is sure to be superseded, in turn, by the methodologies of the future. The important lesson is that, based on *today's* knowledge, the Unified Process appears to be better than the other alternatives currently available.

The remainder of this chapter is devoted to national and international initiatives aimed at process improvement.

## 3.12   Improving the Software Process

Our global economy depends critically on computers and hence on software. For this reason, the governments of many countries are concerned about the software process. For example, in 1987, a task force of the U.S. Department of Defense (DoD) reported, "After two decades of largely unfulfilled promises about productivity and quality gains from applying new software methodologies and technologies, industry and government organizations are realizing that their fundamental problem is the inability to manage the software process" [Brooks et al., 1987].

In response to this and related concerns, the DoD founded the Software Engineering Institute (SEI) and set it up at Carnegie Mellon University in Pittsburgh on the basis of a competitive procurement process. A major success of the SEI has been the capability maturity model (CMM) initiative. Related software process improvement efforts include the ISO 9000-series standards of the International Organization for Standardization, and ISO/IEC 15504, an international software improvement initiative involving more than 40 countries. We begin by describing the CMM.

## 3.13   Capability Maturity Models

The **capability maturity models** of the SEI are a related group of strategies for improving the software process, irrespective of the actual life-cycle model used. (The term **maturity** is a measure of the goodness of the process itself.) The SEI has developed CMMs for software (SW–CMM), for management of human resources (P–CMM; the *P* stands for "people"), for systems engineering (SE–CMM), for integrated product development (IPD–CMM), and for software acquisition (SA–CMM). There are some inconsistencies between the models, and an inevitable level of redundancy. Accordingly, in 1997, it was decided to develop a single integrated framework for maturity models, capability maturity model integration (CMMI), which incorporates all five existing capability maturity models. Additional disciplines may be added to CMMI in the future [SEI, 2002].

For reasons of space, only one capability maturity model, SW–CMM, is examined here, and an overview of the P–CMM is given in Section 4.8. The SW–CMM was first put forward in 1986 by Watts Humphrey [Humphrey, 1989]. Recall that a software process encompasses the activities, techniques, and tools used to produce software. It therefore incorporates both technical and managerial aspects of software production. Underlying the SW–CMM is the belief that the use of new software techniques in itself will not result in increased productivity and profitability, because our problems are caused by how we manage the software process. The strategy of the SW–CMM is to improve the management of the software process in the belief that improvements in technique are a natural consequence. The resulting improvement in the process as a whole should result in better-quality software and fewer software projects that suffer from time and cost overruns.

Bearing in mind that improvements in the software process cannot occur overnight, the SW–CMM induces change incrementally. More specifically, five levels of maturity are defined, and an organization advances slowly in a series of small evolutionary steps toward the higher levels of process maturity [Paulk, Weber, Curtis, and Chrissis, 1995]. To understand this approach, the five levels now are described.

## *Maturity Level 1. Initial Level*

At the **initial level**, the lowest level, essentially no sound software engineering management practices are in place in the organization. Instead, everything is done on an ad hoc basis. A specific project that happens to be staffed by a competent manager and a good software development team may be successful. However, the usual pattern is time and cost overruns caused by a lack of sound management in general and planning in particular. As a result, most activities are responses to crises rather than preplanned tasks. In level-1 organizations, the software process is unpredictable, because it depends totally on the current staff; as the staff changes, so does the process. As a consequence, it is impossible to predict with any accuracy such important items as the time it will take to develop a product or the cost of that product.

It is unfortunate that the vast majority of software organizations all over the world are still level-1 organizations.

## *Maturity Level 2. Repeatable Level*

At the **repeatable level**, basic software project management practices are in place. Planning and management techniques are based on experience with similar products, hence, the name *repeatable*. At level 2, measurements are taken, an essential first step in achieving an adequate process. Typical measurements include the meticulous tracking of costs and schedules. Instead of functioning in a crisis mode, as in level 1, managers identify problems as they arise and take immediate corrective action to prevent them from becoming crises. The key point is that, without measurements, it is impossible to detect problems before they get out of hand. Also, measurements taken during one project can be used to draw up realistic duration and cost schedules for future projects.

## *Maturity Level 3. Defined Level*

At the **defined level**, the process for software production is fully documented. Both the managerial and technical aspects of the process are clearly defined, and continual efforts are made to improve the process wherever possible. Reviews (Section 6.2) are used to achieve software quality goals. At this level, it makes sense to introduce new technology, such as CASE environments (Section 5.6), to increase quality and productivity further. In contrast, "high tech" only makes the crisis-driven level-1 process even more chaotic.

Although a number of organizations have attained maturity levels 2 and 3, few have reached levels 4 or 5. The two highest levels therefore are targets for the future.

## *Maturity Level 4. Managed Level*

A **managed-level** organization sets quality and productivity goals for each project. These two quantities are measured continually and corrective action is taken when there are unacceptable deviations from the goal. Statistical quality controls [Deming, 1986; Juran, 1988] are in place to enable management to distinguish a random deviation from a meaningful violation of quality or productivity standards. (A simple example of a statistical quality control measure is the number of faults detected per 1000 lines of code. A corresponding objective is to reduce this quantity over time.)

## *Maturity Level 5. Optimizing Level*

The goal of an **optimizing-level** organization is continuous process improvement. Statistical quality and process control techniques are used to guide the organization. The

FIGURE 3.3
The five levels
of the capability
maturity model
and their key
process areas
(KPAs).

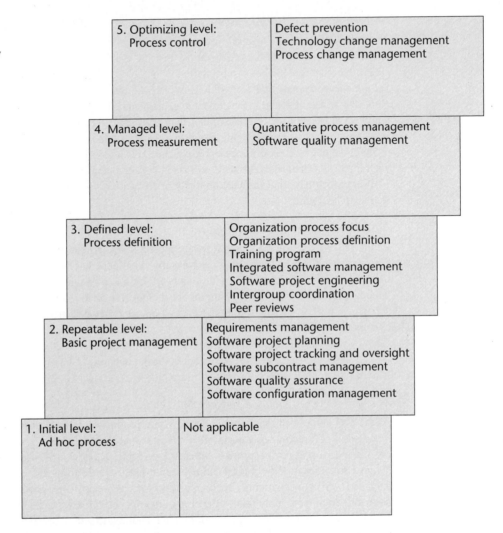

5. Optimizing level:
   Process control

Defect prevention
Technology change management
Process change management

4. Managed level:
   Process measurement

Quantitative process management
Software quality management

3. Defined level:
   Process definition

Organization process focus
Organization process definition
Training program
Integrated software management
Software project engineering
Intergroup coordination
Peer reviews

2. Repeatable level:
   Basic project management

Requirements management
Software project planning
Software project tracking and oversight
Software subcontract management
Software quality assurance
Software configuration management

1. Initial level:
   Ad hoc process

Not applicable

knowledge gained from each project is utilized in future projects. The process therefore incorporates a positive feedback loop, resulting in a steady improvement in productivity and quality.

These five maturity levels are summarized in Figure 3.3, which also shows the key process areas (KPAs) associated with each maturity level. To improve its software process, an organization first attempts to gain an understanding of its current process, and then formulates the intended process. Next, actions to achieve this process improvement are determined and ranked in priority. Finally, a plan to accomplish this improvement is drawn up and executed. This series of steps is repeated, with the organization successively improving its software process; this progression from level to level is reflected in Figure 3.3. Experience with the capability maturity model has shown that advancing a complete maturity level usually takes from 18 months to 3 years, but moving from level 1 to level 2 can sometimes take 3 or even 5 years. This is a reflection of how difficult it is to instill a methodical approach in an organization that up to now has functioned on a purely ad hoc and reactive basis.

For each maturity level, the SEI has highlighted a series of **key process areas** (KPAs) that an organization should target in its endeavor to reach the next maturity level. For example, as shown in Figure 3.3, the KPAs for level 2 (repeatable level) include configuration management (Section 5.8), software quality assurance (Section 6.1.1), project planning (Chapter 9), project tracking (Section 9.2.5), and requirements management (Chapter 10). These areas cover the basic elements of software management: Determine the client's needs (requirements management), draw up a plan (project planning), monitor deviations from that plan (project tracking), control the various pieces that make up the software product (configuration management), and ensure that the product is fault free (quality assurance). Within each KPA is a group of between two and four related goals that, if achieved, result in that maturity level being attained. For example, one project planning goal is the development of a plan that appropriately and realistically covers the activities of software development.

At the highest level, maturity level 5, the KPAs include fault prevention, technology change management, and process change management. Comparing the KPAs of the two levels, it is clear that a level-5 organization is far in advance of one at level 2. For example, a level-2 organization is concerned with software quality assurance, that is, with detecting and correcting faults (software quality is discussed in more detail in Chapter 6). In contrast, the process of a level-5 organization incorporates fault prevention, that is, trying to ensure that no faults are in the software in the first place. To aid an organization to reach the higher maturity levels, the SEI has developed a series of questionnaires that form the basis for an assessment by an SEI team. The purpose of the assessment is to highlight current shortcomings in the organization's software process and to indicate ways in which the organization can improve its process.

The CMM program of the Software Engineering Institute was sponsored by the U.S. Department of Defense. One of the original goals of the CMM program was to raise the quality of defense software by evaluating the processes of contractors who produce software for the DoD and awarding contracts to those contractors who demonstrate a mature process. The U.S. Air Force stipulated that any software development organization that wished to be an Air Force contractor had to conform to SW–CMM level 3 by 1998, and the DoD as a whole subsequently issued a similar directive. Thus, pressure is put on organizations to improve the maturity of their software processes. However, the SW–CMM program has moved far beyond the limited goal of improving DoD software and is being implemented by a wide variety of software organizations that wish to improve software quality and productivity.

# 3.14   Other Software Process Improvement Initiatives

A different attempt to improve software quality is based on the **International Organization for Standardization** (ISO) 9000-series standards, a series of five related standards applicable to a wide variety of industrial activities, including design, development, production, installation, and servicing; ISO 9000 certainly is not just a software standard.

Within the ISO 9000 series, standard **ISO 9001** [1987] for quality systems is the standard most applicable to software development. Because of the broadness of ISO 9001, ISO has published specific guidelines to assist in applying ISO 9001 to software: **ISO 9000-3** [1991]. (For more information on ISO, see Just in Case You Wanted to Know Box 1.4.)

ISO 9000 has a number of features that distinguish it from the CMM [Dawood, 1994]. ISO 9000 stresses documenting the process in both words and pictures to ensure consistency and comprehensibility. Also, the ISO 9000 philosophy is that adherence to the standard does not guarantee a high-quality product but rather reduces the risk of a poor-quality product. ISO 9000 is only part of a quality system. Also required are management commitment to quality, intensive training of workers, and setting and achieving goals for continual quality improvement. ISO 9000-series standards have been adopted by over 60 countries, including the United States, Japan, Canada, and the countries of the European Union (EU). This means, for example, that if a U.S. software organization wishes to do business with a European client, the U.S. organization must first be certified as ISO 9000 compliant. A certified registrar (auditor) has to examine the company's process and certify that it complies with the ISO standard.

Following their European counterparts, more and more U.S. organizations are requiring ISO 9000 certification. For example, General Electric Plastic Division insisted that 340 vendors achieve the standard by June 1993 [Dawood, 1994]. It is unlikely that the U.S. government will follow the EU lead and require ISO 9000 compliance for non-U.S. companies that wish to do business with organizations in the United States. Nevertheless, pressures both within the United States and from its major trading partners ultimately may result in significant worldwide ISO 9000 compliance.

**ISO/IEC 15504** is an international process improvement initiative, like ISO 9000. The initiative was formerly known as **SPICE**, an acronym formed from Software Process Improvement Capability dEtermination. Over 40 countries actively contributed to the SPICE endeavor. SPICE was initiated by the British Ministry of Defence (MOD) with the long-term aim of establishing SPICE as an international standard (MOD is the UK counterpart of the U.S. DoD, which initiated the CMM). The first version of SPICE was completed in 1995. In July 1997, the SPICE initiative was taken over by a joint committee of the International Organization for Standardization and the International Electrotechnical Commission. For this reason, the name of the initiative was changed from SPICE to ISO/IEC 15504, or 15504 for short.

# 3.15   Costs and Benefits of Software Process Improvement

Does implementing software process improvement lead to increased profitability? Results indicate that this indeed is the case. For example, the Software Engineering Division of Hughes Aircraft in Fullerton, California, spent nearly $500,000 between 1987 and 1990 for assessments and improvement programs [Humphrey, Snider, and Willis, 1991]. During this 3-year period, Hughes Aircraft moved up from maturity level 2 to level 3, with every expectation of future improvement to level 4 and even level 5. As a consequence of improving its process, Hughes Aircraft estimated its annual savings to be of the order of $2 million. These savings accrued in a number of ways, including decreased overtime hours, fewer crises, improved employee morale, and lower turnover of software professionals.

**FIGURE 3.4**   Results of 34 Motorola GED projects (MEASL stands for "million equivalent assembler source lines").
Source: [Diaz and Sligo, 1997] (© 1997, IEEE).

| CMM Level | Number of Projects | Relative Decrease in Duration | Faults per MEASL Detected during Development | Relative Productivity |
|---|---|---|---|---|
| Level 1 | 3 | 1.0 | — | — |
| Level 2 | 9 | 3.2 | 890 | 1.0 |
| Level 3 | 5 | 2.7 | 411 | 0.8 |
| Level 4 | 8 | 5.0 | 205 | 2.3 |
| Level 5 | 9 | 7.8 | 126 | 2.8 |

Comparable results have been reported at other organizations. For example, the Equipment Division at Raytheon moved from level 1 in 1988 to level 3 in 1993. A twofold increase in productivity resulted, as well as a return of $7.70 for every dollar invested in the process improvement effort [Dion, 1993]. As a consequence of results like these, the capability maturity models are being applied relatively widely within the U.S. software industry and abroad.

For example, Tata Consultancy Services in India used both the ISO 9000 framework and CMM to improve its process [Keeni, 2000]. Between 1996 and 2000, the errors in effort estimation decreased from about 50 percent to only 15 percent. The effectiveness of reviews (that is, the percentage of faults found during reviews) increased from 40 to 80 percent. The percentage of effort devoted to reworking projects dropped from nearly 12 percent to less than 6 percent.

Motorola Government Electronics Division (GED) has been actively involved in SEI's software process improvement program since 1992 [Diaz and Sligo, 1997]. Figure 3.4 depicts 34 GED projects, categorized according to the maturity level of the group that developed each project. As can be seen from the figure, the relative duration (that is, the duration of a project relative to a baseline project completed before 1992) decreased with increasing maturity level. Quality was measured in terms of faults per million equivalent assembler source lines (MEASL); to be able to compare projects implemented in different languages, the number of lines of source code was converted into the number of equivalent lines of assembler code [Jones, 1996]. As shown in Figure 3.4, quality increased with increasing maturity level. Finally, productivity was measured as MEASL per person-hour. For reasons of confidentiality, Motorola does not publish actual productivity figures, so Figure 3.4 reflects productivity relative to the productivity of a level-2 project. (No quality or productivity figures are available for the level-1 projects because these quantities cannot be measured when the team is at level 1.)

As a consequence of published studies such as those described in this section and those listed in the For Further Reading section of this chapter, more and more organizations worldwide are realizing that process improvement is cost effective.

An interesting side effect of the process improvement movement has been the interaction between software process improvement initiatives and software engineering standards. For example, in 1995 the International Organization for Standardization published ISO/IEC 12207, a full life-cycle software standard [ISO/IEC 12207, 1995]. Three years later, a

There are constraints on the speed of hardware because electrons cannot travel faster than the speed of light. In a famous article entitled "No Silver Bullet," Brooks [1986] suggested that inherent problems exist in software production, and that these problems can never be solved because of analogous constraints on software. Brooks argued that intrinsic properties of software, such as its complexity, the fact that software is invisible and unvisualizable, and the numerous changes to which software is typically subjected over its lifetime, make it unlikely that there will ever be an order-of-magnitude increment (or "silver bullet") in software process improvement.

U.S. version of the standard [IEEE/EIA 12207, 1998] was published by the Institute of Electrical and Electronic Engineers (IEEE) and the Electronic Industries Alliance (EIA). This version incorporates U.S. software "best practices," many of which can be traced back to CMM. To achieve compliance with IEEE/EIA 12207, an organization must be at or near CMM capability level 3 [Ferguson and Sheard, 1998]. Also, ISO 9000-3 now incorporates parts of ISO/IEC 12207. This interplay between software engineering standards organizations and software process improvement initiatives surely will lead to even better software processes.

Another dimension of software process improvement appears in Just in Case You Wanted to Know Box 3.4.

**Chapter Review**

After some preliminary definitions, the Unified Process is introduced in Section 3.1. The importance of iteration and incrementation within the object-oriented paradigm is described in Section 3.2. Now the core workflows of the Unified Process are explained in detail; the requirements workflow (Section 3.3), analysis workflow (Section 3.4), design workflow (Section 3.5), implementation workflow (Section 3.6), and test workflow (Section 3.7). The various artifacts tested during the test workflow are described in Sections 3.7.1 through 3.7.4. Postdelivery maintenance is discussed in Section 3.8, and retirement in Section 3.9. The relationship between the workflows and the phases of the Unified Process is analyzed in Section 3.10, and a detailed description is given of the four phases of the Unified Process: the inception phase (Section 3.10.1), the elaboration phase (Section 3.10.2), the construction phase (Section 3.10.3), and the transition phase (Section 3.10.4). The importance of two-dimensional life-cycle models is discussed in Section 3.11.

The last part of the chapter is devoted to software process improvement (Section 3.12). Details are given of various national and international software improvement initiatives, including the capability maturity models (Section 3.13), and ISO 9000 and ISO/IEC 15504 (Section 3.14). The cost-effectiveness of software process improvement is discussed in Section 3.15.

**For Further Reading**

The review articles in the For Further Reading section of Chapter 1 [Brooks, 1975; Boehm, 1976; Wasserman, 1996; and Ebert, Matsubara, Pezzé, and Bertelsen, 1997] also highlight the problems associated with the software process. The March/April 2003 issue of *IEEE Software* contains a number of articles on the software process, including [Eickelmann and Anant, 2003], a discussion of statistical process control. Practical applications of statistical process control are described in [Weller, 2000] and [Florac, Carleton, and Barnard, 2000].

With regard to testing during each workflow, a good general source is [Beizer, 1990]. More specific references are given in Chapter 6 of this book and in the For Further Reading section at the end of that chapter.

A detailed description of the original SEI capability maturity model is given in [Humphrey, 1989]. Capability maturity model integration is described in [SEI, 2002]. Humphrey [1996] describes a personal software process (PSP); results of applying the PSP appear in [Ferguson et al., 1997]. Some potential problems with the PSP are discussed in [Johnson and Disney, 1998]. The PSP and the team software process (TSP) are described in [Humphrey, 1999]. The results of an experiment to measure the effectiveness of PSP training are presented in [Prechelt and Unger, 2000]. Extensions needed to the Unified Process for it to comply with CMM levels 2 and 3 are presented in [Manzoni and Price, 2003]. Implementing SW–CMM in a small organization is described in [Guerrero and Eterovic, 2004]. The July/August 2000 issue of *IEEE Software* has three papers on software process maturity, and there are four papers on the PSP in the November/December 2000 issue of *IEEE Software*.

An overview of SEI software process assessments appears in [Herbsleb et al., 1997]. A number of articles have been written on industry experiences from the viewpoint of a specific company that introduced the SEI process improvement program; typical examples include Shlumberger [Wohlwend and Rosenbaum, 1993] and Raytheon [Haley, 1996]. The impact of SEI on the software industry is discussed in [Saiedian and Kuzara, 1995] and [Johnson and Brodman, 2000]. An interesting view of the CMM is given in [Bamberger, 1997]. [Bamford and Deibler, 1993b] is a detailed comparison of ISO 9000 and the CMM; an overview appears in [Bamford and Deibler, 1993a]. Paulk [1995] details another comparison. Pitterman [2000] describes how a group at Telecordia Technologies reached level 5; a study of how a Computer Sciences Corporation group attained level 5 appears in [McGarry and Decker, 2002]. Insights into the nature of level-5 organizations appear in [Eickelmann, 2003]. Cost–benefit analysis of software process improvement is described in [van Solingen, 2004]. An empirical investigation of the key factors for success in software process improvement is presented in [Dybå, 2005].

Problems of software product improvement appear in [Conradi and Fuggetta, 2002]. The results of 18 different software process improvement initiatives conducted at Ericsson are described in [Borjesson and Mathiassen, 2004]. A wealth of information on the CMM is available at the SEI CMM website www.sei.cmu.edu. The ISO/IEC 15504 (SPICE) home page is at www.sei.cmu.edu/technology/process/spice/.

A comparison between CMM and IEEE/EIA 12207 is given in [Ferguson and Sheard, 1998], and a comparison between CMM and Six Sigma (another approach to process improvement) appears in [Murugappan and Keeni, 2003]. A repository containing the results of some 400 software improvement experiments is described in [Blanco, Gutiérrez, and Satriani, 2001].

**Key Terms**

| | | |
|---|---|---|
| acceptance testing *83* | class *80* | design workflow *79* |
| alpha release *83* | code artifact *80* | detailed design *79* |
| ambiguity *78* | component *80* | domain *76* |
| analysis workflow *77* | concept exploration *76* | elaboration phase *88* |
| application domain *76* | construction phase *89* | implementation workflow *80* |
| architectural design *79* | contradiction *78* | inception phase *86* |
| beta release *83* | core workflow *75* | incompleteness *78* |
| budget *79* | cost *76* | initial level *93* |
| business model *76* | deadline *76* | integration testing *83* |
| capability maturity model (CMM) *92* | defined level *93* | International Organization for Standardization (ISO) *95* |
| | deliverable *79* | |

ISO 9000-3 *96*
ISO 9001 *96*
ISO/IEC 15504 *96*
key process area (KPA) *95*
managed level *93*
maturity *92*
milestone *79*
model *73*

module *79*
optimizing level *93*
product testing *83*
regression testing *85*
reliability *76*
repeatable level *93*
requirements workflow *75*
retirement *85*

SPICE *96*
test workflow *81*
traceability *81*
transition phase *89*
Unified Modeling Language
 (UML) *73*
Unified Process *73*
unit testing *82*

## Problems

3.1   Consider the requirements workflow and the analysis workflow. Would it make more sense to combine these two activities into one workflow than to treat them separately?

3.2   More testing is performed during the implementation workflow than in any other workflow. Would it be better to divide this workflow into two separate workflows, one incorporating the nontesting aspects, the other all the testing?

3.3   Maintenance is the most important activity of software production and the most difficult to perform. Nevertheless, it is looked down on by many software professionals, and maintenance programmers often are paid less than developers. Do you think that this is reasonable? If not, how would you try to change it?

3.4   Why do you think that, as stated in Section 3.9, true retirement is a rare event?

3.5   Because of a fire at Elmer's Software, all documentation for a product is destroyed just before it is delivered. What is the impact of the resulting lack of documentation?

3.6   You have just purchased Antedeluvian Software Developers, an organization on the verge of bankruptcy because the company is at maturity level 1. What is the first step you will take to restore the organization to profitability?

3.7   Section 3.13 states that it makes little sense to introduce CASE environments within organizations at maturity level 1 or 2. Explain why this is so.

3.8   What is the effect of introducing CASE tools (as opposed to environments) within organizations with a low maturity level?

3.9   Maturity level 1, the initial level, refers to an absence of good software engineering management practices. Would it not have been better for the SEI to have labeled the initial level as maturity level 0?

3.10  (Term Project) What differences would you expect to find if the Osric's Office Appliances and Decor product of Appendix A were developed by an organization at CMM level 1, as opposed to an organization at level 5?

3.11  (Readings in Software Engineering) Your instructor will distribute copies of [Eickelmann, 2003]. Would you choose to work in a level-5 organization? Explain your answer.

## References

[Bamberger, 1997] J. BAMBERGER, "Essence of the Capability Maturity Model," *IEEE Computer* **30** (June 1997), pp. 112–14.

[Bamford and Deibler, 1993a] R. C. BAMFORD AND W. J. DEIBLER, II, "Comparing, Contrasting ISO 9001 and the SEI Capability Maturity Model," *IEEE Computer* **26** (October 1993), pp. 68–70.

[Bamford and Deibler, 1993b] R. C. BAMFORD AND W. J. DEIBLER, II, "A Detailed Comparison of the SEI Software Maturity Levels and Technology Stages to the Requirements for ISO 9001 Registration," Software Systems Quality Consulting, San Jose, CA, 1993.

[Beizer, 1990] B. Beizer, *Software Testing Techniques,* 2nd ed., Van Nostrand Reinhold, New York, 1990.

[Blanco, Gutiérrez, and Satriani, 2001] M. Blanco, P. Gutiérrez, and G. Satriani, "SPI Patterns: Learning from Experience," *IEEE Software* **18** (May/June 2001), pp. 28–35.

[Boehm, 1976] B. W. Boehm, "Software Engineering," *IEEE Transactions on Computers* **C-25** (December 1976), pp. 1226–41.

[Booch, 1994] G. Booch, *Object-Oriented Analysis and Design with Applications,* 2nd ed., Benjamin/ Cummings, Redwood City, CA, 1994.

[Booch, Rumbaugh, and Jacobson, 1999] G. Booch, J. Rumbaugh, and I. Jacobson, *The UML Users Guide,* Addison-Wesley, Reading, MA, 1999.

[Borjesson and Mathiassen, 2004] A. Borjesson and L. Mathiassen, "Successful Process Implementation," *IEEE Software* **21** (July/August 2004), pp. 36–44.

[Brooks, 1975] F. P. Brooks, Jr., *The Mythical Man-Month: Essays on Software Engineering,* Addison-Wesley, Reading, MA, 1975; twentieth Anniversary Edition, Addison-Wesley, Reading, MA, 1995.

[Brooks, 1986] F. P. Brooks, Jr., "No Silver Bullet," in: *Information Processing '86,* H.-J. Kugler (Editor), Elsevier North-Holland, New York, 1986; reprinted in *IEEE Computer* **20** (April 1987), pp. 10–19.

[Brooks et al., 1987] F. P. Brooks, V. Basili, B. Boehm, E. Bond, N. Eastman, D. L. Evans, A. K. Jones, M. Shaw, and C. A. Zraket, "Report of the Defense Science Board Task Force on Military Software," Department of Defense, Office of the Under Secretary of Defense for Acquisition, Washington, DC, September 1987.

[CNN.com, 2003] "Russia: Software Bug Made Soyuz Stray," edition.cnn.com/2003/TECH/ space/05/06/soyuz.landing.ap/.

[Conradi and Fuggetta, 2002] R. Conradi and A. Fuggetta, "Improving Software Process Improvement," *IEEE Software* **19** (July/August 2002), pp. 92–99.

[Dawood, 1994] M. Dawood, "It's Time for ISO 9000," *CrossTalk* (March 1994), pp. 26–28.

[Deming, 1986] W. E. Deming, *Out of the Crisis,* MIT Center for Advanced Engineering Study, Cambridge, MA, 1986.

[Diaz and Sligo, 1997] M. Diaz and J. Sligo, "How Software Process Improvement Helped Motorola," *IEEE Software* **14** (September/October 1997), pp. 75–81.

[Dion, 1993] R. Dion, "Process Improvement and the Corporate Balance Sheet," *IEEE Software* **10** (July 1993), pp. 28–35.

[Dybå, 2005] T. Dybå, "An Empirical Investigation of the Key Factors for Success in Software Process Improvement," *IEEE Transactions in Software Engineering* **31** (May 2005), pp. 410–24.

[Ebert, Matsubara, Pezzé, and Bertelsen, 1997] C. Ebert, T. Matsubara, M. Pezzé, and O. W. Bertelsen, "The Road to Maturity: Navigating between Craft and Science," *IEEE Software* **14** (November/December 1997), pp. 77–88.

[Eickelmann, 2003] N. Eickelmann, "An Insider's View of CMM Level 5," *IEEE Software* **20** (July/August 2003), pp. 79–81.

[Eickelmann and Anant, 2003] N. Eickelmann and A. Anant, "Statistical Process Control: What You Don't Know Can Hurt You!" *IEEE Software* **20** (March/April 2003), pp. 49–51.

[Ferguson and Sheard, 1998] J. Ferguson and S. Sheard, "Leveraging Your CMM Efforts for IEEE/EIA 12207," *IEEE Software* **15** (September/October 1998), pp. 23–28.

[Ferguson et al., 1997] P. Ferguson, W. S. Humphrey, S. Khajenoori, S. Macke, and A. Matvya, "Results of Applying the Personal Software Process," *IEEE Computer* **30** (May 1997), pp. 24–31.

[Florac, Carleton, and Barnard, 2000] W. A. FLORAC, A. D. CARLETON, AND J. BARNARD, "Statistical Process Control: Analyzing a Space Shuttle Onboard Software Process," *IEEE Software* **17** (July/August 2000), pp. 97–106.

[*Florida Today*, 1999] "Milstar Satellite Lost during Air Force Titan 4b Launch from Cape," *Florida Today*, www.floridatoday.com/space/explore/uselv/titan/b32/, June 5, 1999.

[Garman, 1981] J. R. GARMAN, "The 'Bug' Heard 'Round the World," *ACM SIGSOFT Software Engineering Notes* **6** (October 1981), pp. 3–10.

[Guerrero and Eterovic, 2004] F. GUERRERO AND Y. ETEROVIC, "Adopting the SW-CMM in a Small IT Organization," *IEEE Software* **21** (July/August 2004), pp. 29–35.

[Haley, 1996] T. J. HALEY, "Raytheon's Experience in Software Process Improvement," *IEEE Software* **13** (November 1996), pp. 33–41.

[Herbsleb et al., 1997] J. HERBSLEB, D. ZUBROW, D. GOLDENSON, W. HAYES, AND M. PAULK, "Software Quality and the Capability Maturity Model," *Communications of the ACM* **40** (June 1997), pp. 30–40.

[Humphrey, 1989] W. S. HUMPHREY, *Managing the Software Process*, Addison-Wesley, Reading, MA, 1989.

[Humphrey, 1996] W. S. HUMPHREY, "Using a Defined and Measured Personal Software Process," *IEEE Software* **13** (May 1996), pp. 77–88.

[Humphrey, 1999] W. S. HUMPHREY, "Pathways to Process Maturity: The Personal Software Process and Team Software Process," *SEI Interactive* **2** (No. 4, December 1999), interactive.sei.cmu.edu/Features/1999/June/Background/Background.jun99.htm.

[Humphrey, Snider, and Willis, 1991] W. S. HUMPHREY, T. R. SNIDER, AND R. R. WILLIS, "Software Process Improvement at Hughes Aircraft," *IEEE Software* **8** (July 1991), pp. 11–23.

[IEEE/EIA 12207, 1998] "IEEE/EIA 12207.0-1996 Industry Implementation of International Standard ISO/IEC 12207:1995," Institute of Electrical and Electronics Engineers, Electronic Industries Alliance, New York, 1998.

[ISO 9000-3, 1991] "ISO 9000-3, Guidelines for the Application of ISO 9001 to the Development, Supply, and Maintenance of Software," International Organization for Standardization, Geneva, 1991.

[ISO 9001, 1987] "ISO 9001, Quality Systems—Model for Quality Assurance in Design/Development, Production, Installation, and Servicing," International Organization for Standardization, Geneva, 1987.

[ISO/IEC 12207, 1995] "ISO/IEC 12207:1995, Information Technology—Software Life-Cycle Processes," International Organization for Standardization, International Electrotechnical Commission, Geneva, 1995.

[Jacobson, Booch, and Rumbaugh, 1999] I. JACOBSON, G. BOOCH, AND J. RUMBAUGH, *The Unified Software Development Process,* Addison-Wesley, Reading, MA, 1999.

[Johnson and Brodman, 2000] D. JOHNSON AND J. G. BRODMAN, "Applying CMM Project Planning Practices to Diverse Environments," *IEEE Software* **17** (July/August 2000), pp. 40–47.

[Johnson and Disney, 1998] P. M. JOHNSON AND A. M. DISNEY, "The Personal Software Process: A Cautionary Tale," *IEEE Software* **15** (November/December 1998), pp. 85–88.

[Jones, 1996] C. JONES, *Applied Software Measurement,* McGraw-Hill, New York, 1996.

[Juran, 1988] J. M. JURAN, *Juran on Planning for Quality,* Macmillan, New York, 1988.

[Keeni, 2000] G. KEENI, "The Evolution of Quality Processes at Tata Consultancy Services," *IEEE Software* **17** (July/August 2000), pp. 79–88.

[Manzoni and Price, 2003] L. V. MANZONI AND R. T. PRICE, "Identifying Extensions Required by RUP (Rational Unified Process) to Comply with CMM (Capability Maturity Model) Levels 2 and 3," *IEEE Transactions on Software Engineering* **29** (February 2003), pp. 181–92.

[McGarry and Decker, 2002] F. MCGARRY AND B. DECKER, "Attaining Level 5 in CMM Process Maturity," *IEEE Software* **19** (2002), pp. 87–96.

[Miller, 1956] G. A. MILLER, "The Magical Number Seven, Plus or Minus Two: Some Limits on Our Capacity for Processing Information," *The Psychological Review* **63** (March 1956), pp. 81–97. Reprinted in: www.well.com/user/smalin/miller.html.

[Murugappan and Keeni, 2003] M. MURUGAPPAN AND G. KEENI, "Blending CMM and Six Sigma to Meet Business Goals," *IEEE Software* **20** (March/April 2003), pp. 42–48.

[Paulk, 1995] M. C. PAULK, "How ISO 9001 Compares with the CMM," *IEEE Software* **12** (January 1995), pp. 74–83.

[Paulk, Weber, Curtis, and Chrissis, 1995] M. C. PAULK, C. V. WEBER, B. CURTIS, AND M. B. CHRISSIS, *The Capability Maturity Model: Guidelines for Improving the Software Process,* Addison-Wesley, Reading, MA, 1995.

[Pitterman, 2000] B. PITTERMAN, "Telecordia Technologies: The Journey to High Maturity," *IEEE Software* **17** (July/August 2000), pp. 89–96.

[Prechelt and Unger, 2000] L. PRECHELT AND B. UNGER, "An Experiment Measuring the Effects of Personal Software Process (PSP) Training," *IEEE Transactions on Software Engineering* **27** (May 2000), pp. 465–72.

[Rumbaugh et al., 1991] J. RUMBAUGH, M. BLAHA, W. PREMERLANI, F. EDDY, AND W. LORENSEN, *Object-Oriented Modeling and Design,* Prentice Hall, Englewood Cliffs, NJ, 1991.

[Saiedian and Kuzara, 1995] H. SAIEDIAN AND R. KUZARA, "SEI Capability Maturity Model's Impact on Contractors," *IEEE Computer* **28** (January 1995), pp. 16–26.

[SEI, 2002] "CMMI Frequently Asked Questions (FAQ)," Software Engineering Institute, Carnegie Mellon University, Pittsburgh, June 2002.

[van Solingen, 2004] R. VAN SOLINGEN, "Measuring the ROI of Software Process Improvement," *IEEE Software* **21** (May/June 2004), pp. 32–38.

[van Wijngaarden et al., 1975] A. VAN WIJNGAARDEN, B. J. MAILLOUX, J. E. L. PECK, C. H. A. KOSTER, M. SINTZOFF, C. H. LINDSEY, L. G. L. T. MEERTENS, AND R. G. FISKER, "Revised Report on the Algorithmic Language ALGOL 68," *Acta Informatica* **5** (1975), pp. 1–236.

[Wasserman, 1996] A. I. WASSERMAN, "Toward a Discipline of Software Engineering," *IEEE Software* **13** (November/December 1996), pp. 23–31.

[Weller, 2000] E. F. WELLER, "Practical Applications of Statistical Process Control," *IEEE Software* **18** (May/June 2000), pp. 48–55.

[Wohlwend and Rosenbaum, 1993] H. WOHLWEND AND S. ROSENBAUM, "Software Improvements in an International Company," *Proceedings of the 15th International Conference on Software Engineering,* Baltimore, MD, May 1993, pp. 212–20.

# Chapter 4

# Teams

**Learning Objectives**

After studying this chapter, you should be able to

- Explain the importance of a well-organized team.
- Describe how modern hierarchical teams are organized.
- Analyze the strengths and weaknesses of a variety of different team organizations.
- Appreciate the issues that arise when choosing an appropriate team organization.

Without competent, well-trained software engineers, a software project is doomed to failure. However, having the right people is not enough; teams must be organized in such a way that the team members can work productively in cooperation with one another. Team organization is the subject of this chapter.

## 4.1 Team Organization

Most products are too large to be completed by a single software professional within the given time constraints. As a result, the product must be assigned to a group of professionals organized as a **team**. For example, consider the analysis workflow. To specify the target product within 2 months, it may be necessary to assign the task to three analysis specialists organized as a team under the direction of the analysis manager. Similarly, the design task may be shared between members of the design team.

Suppose now that a product has to be coded within 3 months, even though 1 person-year of coding is involved (a person-year is the amount of work that can be done by one person in 1 year). The solution is apparently simple: If one programmer can code the product in 1 year, four programmers can do it in 3 months.

This, of course, does not work. In practice, the four programmers may take nearly a year, and the quality of the resulting product well may be lower than if one programmer had coded the entire product. The reason is that some tasks can be shared, but others must be done individually. For instance, if one farmhand can pick a strawberry field in 10 days, the same strawberry field can be picked by 10 farmhands in 1 day. On the other hand, one elephant can produce a calf in 22 months, but this feat cannot possibly be accomplished in 1 month by 22 elephants.

In other words, tasks like strawberry picking can be fully shared; others, like elephant production, cannot be shared at all. Unlike elephant production, it is possible to share implementation tasks between members of a team by distributing the coding among the team members. However, team programming also is unlike strawberry picking in that team members have to interact with one another in a meaningful and effective way. For example, suppose Sheila and Harry have to code two modules, m1 and m2. A number of things can go wrong. For instance, both Sheila and Harry may code m1 and ignore m2. Or Sheila may code m1, and Harry may code m2. But when m1 calls m2, it passes four arguments; Harry has coded m2 in such a way that it requires five arguments. Or the order of the arguments in m1 and m2 may be different. Or the order may be the same, but the data types may be slightly different. Such problems usually are caused by a decision made while the design workflow is performed that is not propagated throughout the development organization. The issue has nothing whatsoever to do with the technical competency of the programmers. Team organization is a managerial issue; management must organize the programming teams so that each team is highly productive.

A different type of difficulty that arises from team development of software is shown in Figure 4.1. Three channels of communication exist between the three computer professionals working on the project. Now, suppose that the work is slipping, a deadline is rapidly approaching, and the task is not nearly complete. The obvious thing to do is to add a fourth professional to the team. But the first thing that must happen when the fourth professional joins the team is for the other three to explain in detail what has been accomplished to date and what is still incomplete. In other words, adding personnel to a late software project makes it even later. This principle is known as **Brooks's Law** after Fred Brooks who observed it while managing the development of OS/360 [Brooks, 1975], an operating system for IBM 360 mainframe computers.

In a large organization, teams are used in every workflow of software production, but especially when the implementation workflow is performed; during that workflow, programmers work independently on separate code artifacts. Accordingly, the implementation

**FIGURE 4.1**
Communication paths between three computer professionals (solid lines) and when a fourth professional joins them (dashed lines).

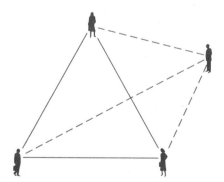

Some 40 years ago, when software was still input on punched cards, all too many programmers regarded "bugs" in software in the same light as insects that would invade their card deck unless prevented from doing so. This attitude was amusingly lampooned by the marketing of an aerosol spray named *Shoo-Bug*. The instructions on the label solemnly explained that spraying one's card deck with Shoo-Bug would ensure that no bugs could possibly infest the code. Of course, the spray can contained nothing but air.

workflow is a prime candidate for sharing the task among several computer professionals. In some smaller organizations, one individual may be responsible for the requirements, analysis, and design, after which the implementation is done by a team of two or three programmers. Because teams are used most heavily when performing the implementation workflow, the problems of team organization are felt most acutely during implementation. In the remainder of this chapter, team organization therefore is presented within the context of implementation, even though the problems and their solutions are equally applicable to all the other workflows.

There are two extreme approaches to programming-team organization, democratic teams and chief programmer teams. The approach taken here is to describe each of the two approaches, highlight its strengths and weaknesses, and then suggest other ways of organizing a programming team that incorporate the best features of the two extremes.

## 4.2  Democratic Team Approach

The democratic team organization was first described by Weinberg in 1971 [Weinberg, 1971]. The basic concept underlying the democratic team is **egoless programming**. Weinberg points out that programmers can be highly attached to their code. Sometimes, they even name their modules after themselves: They therefore see their modules as an extension of themselves. The difficulty with this is that a programmer who sees a module as an extension of his or her ego is certainly not going to try to find all the faults in "his" code or "her" code. And, if there is a fault, it is termed a *bug*, like some insect that crept unasked into the code and could have been prevented if only the code had been guarded more zealously against invasion (see Just in Case You Wanted to Know Box 4.1).

Weinberg's solution to the problem of programmers being too closely attached to their own code is egoless programming. The social environment must be restructured and so must programmer values. Every programmer must encourage the other members of the team to find faults in his or her code. The presence of a fault must not be considered something bad but a normal and accepted event; the attitude of the reviewer should be appreciation at being asked for advice, rather than ridicule of the programmer for making coding mistakes. The team as a whole thus develops an ethos, a group identity; and modules belong to the team as a whole rather than to any one individual.

A group of up to 10 egoless programmers constitutes a **democratic team**. Weinberg warns that management may have difficulty working with such a team. After all, consider the managerial career path. When a programmer is promoted to a management position, his or her fellow programmers are not promoted and must strive to attain the higher level at the next round of promotions. In contrast, a democratic team is a group working for a common cause with no single leader, with no programmers trying to get promoted to the next level. What is important is team identity and mutual respect.

Weinberg tells of a democratic team that developed an outstanding product. Management decided to give a cash award to the team's nominal manager (by definition, a democratic team has no leader). He refused to accept it personally, saying that it had to be shared equally among all members of the team. Management thought that he was angling for more money and that the team (and especially its nominal manager) had some rather unorthodox ideas. Management forced the nominal manager to accept the money, which he then divided equally among the team. Next, the entire team resigned and joined another company as a team.

The strengths and weaknesses of democratic teams are now presented.

### 4.2.1 Analysis of the Democratic Team Approach

A major strength of the democratic team approach is the positive attitude toward the finding of faults. The more found, the happier are the members of a democratic team. This positive attitude leads to more rapid detection of faults and hence to high-quality code. But there are some major problems. As pointed out previously, managers may have difficulty accepting egoless programming. In addition, a programmer with, say, 15 years of experience is likely to resent having his or her code appraised by fellow programmers, especially beginners.

Weinberg feels that egoless teams spring up spontaneously and cannot be imposed from outside. Little experimental research has been done on democratic programming teams, but the experience of Weinberg is that democratic teams are enormously productive. Mantei [1981] has analyzed the democratic team organization using arguments based on theories of and experiments on group organization in general rather than specifically on programming teams. She points out that decentralized groups work best when the problem is difficult and suggests that democratic teams should function well in a research environment. It has been my experience that a democratic team also works well in an industrial setting when a hard problem must be solved. On a number of occasions I have been a member of democratic teams that have sprung up spontaneously among computer professionals with research experience. But, once the task has been reduced to the implementation of a hard-won solution, the team must then be reorganized in a more hierarchical fashion, such as the chief programmer team approach described in Section 4.3.

## 4.3   Classical Chief Programmer Team Approach

Consider the six-person team shown in Figure 4.2, with 15 two-person communication channels. In fact, the total number of two-, three-, four-, five-, and six-person groups is 57. This multiplicity of communication channels is the major reason why a six-person team structured as in Figure 4.2 is unlikely to be able to perform 36 person-months of work in 6 months; many hours are wasted in meetings involving two or more team members at a time.

Now consider the six-person team shown in Figure 4.3. Again, there are six programmers, but now only five lines of communication. This is the basic concept behind what now is termed the **chief programmer team**. A related idea was put forward by Brooks [1975], who drew the analogy of a chief surgeon directing an operation. The surgeon is assisted by other surgeons, the anesthesiologist, and a variety of nurses. In addition, when

**FIGURE 4.2**
Communication
paths between
six computer
professionals.

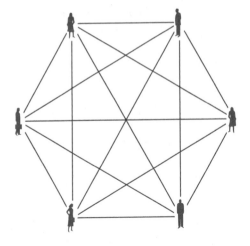

**FIGURE 4.3**
The structure of
a classical chief
programmer
team.

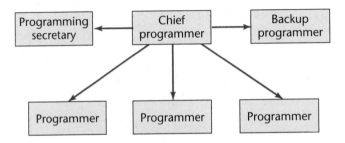

necessary, the team uses experts in other areas, such as cardiologists or nephrologists. This analogy highlights two key aspects of a chief programmer team. The first is **specialization**: Each member of the team carries out only those tasks for which he or she has been trained. The second aspect is **hierarchy**: The chief surgeon directs the actions of all the other members of the team and is responsible for every aspect of the operation.

The chief programmer team concept was formalized by Mills [Baker, 1972]. A classical chief programmer team, as described by Baker some 30 years ago, is shown in Figure 4.3. It consisted of the chief programmer, who was assisted by the backup programmer, the programming secretary, and from one to three programmers. When necessary, the team was assisted by specialists in other areas, such as legal or financial matters, or the job control language (JCL) statements used to give operating system commands to the mainframe computers of that era. The **chief programmer** was both a successful manager and a highly skilled programmer who did the architectural design and any critical or complex sections of the code. The other team members worked on the detailed design and the coding, under the direction of the chief programmer. As shown in Figure 4.3, no lines of communication existed between the programmers; all interfacing issues were handled by the chief programmer. Finally, the chief programmer reviewed the work of the other team members, because the chief programmer was personally responsible for every line of code.

The position of **backup programmer** was necessary only because the chief programmer was human and could therefore become ill, fall under a bus, or change jobs. Therefore, the backup programmer had to be as competent as the chief programmer in every respect and had to know as much about the project as the chief programmer. In addition, to free the chief programmer to concentrate on the architectural design, the backup programmer did black-box test case planning (Section 14.11) and other tasks independent of the design process.

The word *secretary* has a number of meanings. On the one hand, a secretary assists a busy executive by answering the telephone, typing correspondence, and so on. But when we talk about the American Secretary of State or the British Foreign Secretary, we refer to one of the most senior members of the Cabinet. The **programming secretary** was not a part-time clerical assistant but a highly skilled, well-paid, central member of a chief programmer team. The programming secretary was responsible for maintaining the project production library, the documentation of the project. This included source code listings, JCL, and test data. The programmers handed their source code to the secretary, who was responsible for its conversion to machine-readable form, compilation, linking, loading, execution, and running test cases. **Programmers** therefore did nothing but program. All other aspects of their work were handled by the programming secretary. (Because the programming secretary maintained the project production library, some organizations used the title **librarian**.)

Recall that what is described here are Mills's and Baker's original ideas, dating back to 1971, when keypunches still were widely used. Coding no longer is done that way. Programmers now have their own terminals or workstations in which they enter their code, edit it, test it, and so on. A modern version of the classical chief programmer team is described in Section 4.4.

## 4.3.1 The *New York Times* Project

The chief programmer team concept was first used in 1971 by IBM to automate the clipping file ("morgue") of the *New York Times*. The clipping file contains abstracts and full articles from the *New York Times* and other publications. Reporters and other members of the editorial staff use this information bank as a reference source.

The facts of the project are astounding. For example, 83,000 lines of code (LOC) were written in 22 calendar months, an effort of 11 person-years. After the first year, only the file maintenance system consisting of 12,000 LOC had been written. Most of the code was written in the last 6 months. Only 21 faults were detected in the first 5 weeks of acceptance testing; only 25 further faults were detected in the first year of operation. Principal programmers averaged one detected fault and 10,000 LOC per person-year. The file maintenance system, delivered 1 week after coding was completed, operated 20 months before a single fault was detected. Almost half the subprograms, usually 200 to 400 lines of PL/I, a language developed by IBM, were correct on the first compilation [Baker, 1972].

Nevertheless, after this fantastic success, no comparable claims for the chief programmer team concept have been made. Yes, many successful projects have been carried out using chief programmer teams, but the figures reported, although satisfactory, are not as impressive as those obtained for the *New York Times* project. Why was the *New York Times* project such a success, and why have similar results not been obtained on other projects?

One possible explanation is that this was a prestige project for IBM. It was the first real trial for PL/I. An organization known for its superb software experts, IBM set up a team comprising what can only be described as its crème de la crème from one division. Second, technical backup was extremely strong. PL/I compiler writers were on hand to assist the programmers in every way they could, and JCL experts assisted with the job control language. A third possible explanation was the expertise of the chief programmer, F. Terry Baker. He is what is now called a **superprogrammer**, a programmer whose output is four or five times that of an average good programmer. In addition, Baker is a superb manager and leader, and his skills, enthusiasm, and personality could be the reasons underlying the success of the project.

If the chief programmer is competent, then the chief programmer team organization works well. Although the remarkable success of the *New York Times* project has not been repeated, many successful projects have employed variants of the chief programmer approach. The reason for the phrase *variants of the approach* is that the classical chief programmer team as described in [Baker, 1972] is impractical in many ways.

### 4.3.2 Impracticality of the Classical Chief Programmer Team Approach

Consider the chief programmer, a combination of a highly skilled programmer and successful manager. Such individuals are difficult to find due to a shortage of highly skilled programmers as well as a shortage of successful managers; and the job description of a chief programmer requires both abilities. Also, the qualities needed to be a highly skilled programmer appear to be different from those needed to be a successful manager; therefore, the chances of finding a chief programmer are small.

If chief programmers are hard to find, backup programmers are as rare as hen's teeth. After all, the backup programmer is expected to be as good as the chief programmer but has to take a back seat and a lower salary while waiting for something to happen to the chief programmer. Few top programmers or top managers would accept such a role.

A programming secretary also is difficult to find. Software professionals are notorious for their aversion to paperwork, and the programming secretary is expected to do nothing but paperwork all day.

Therefore, chief programmer teams, at least as proposed by Baker, are impractical to implement. Democratic teams also were shown to be impractical but for different reasons. Furthermore, neither technique seems to be able to handle products that require 20, let alone 120, programmers for the implementation workflow. What is needed is a way of organizing programming teams that uses the strengths of democratic teams and chief programmer teams and can be extended to the implementation of larger products.

## 4.4 Beyond Chief Programmer and Democratic Teams

Democratic teams have a major strength: a positive attitude toward finding faults. A number of organizations use chief programmer teams in conjunction with code reviews (Section 6.2), creating a potential pitfall. The chief programmer is personally responsible for every line of code and, therefore, must be present during all code reviews. However, a chief programmer also is a manager and, as explained in Chapter 6, reviews should not be used for any sort of performance appraisal. So, because the chief programmer is also the manager responsible for the primary evaluation of the team members, it is strongly inadvisable for that individual to be present at a code review.

**FIGURE 4.4**
The structure of
a modern
programming
team.

The way out of this contradiction is to remove much of the managerial role from the chief programmer. After all, the difficulty of finding one individual who is both a highly skilled programmer and successful manager has been pointed out. Instead, the chief programmer should be replaced by two individuals: a **team leader** in charge of the technical aspects of the team's activities and a **team manager** responsible for all nontechnical managerial decisions. The structure of the resulting team is shown in Figure 4.4. It is important to realize that this organizational structure does not violate the fundamental managerial principle that no employee should report to more than one manager. The areas of responsibility are clearly delineated. The team leader is responsible for only technical management. Consequently, budgetary and legal issues are not handled by the team leader nor are performance appraisals. On the other hand, the team leader has sole responsibility on technical issues. The team manager therefore has no right to promise, say, that the product will be delivered within 4 weeks; promises of that sort have to be made by the team leader. The team leader naturally participates in all code reviews; after all, he or she is personally responsible for every aspect of the code. At the same time, the team manager is not permitted at a review, because programmer performance appraisal is a function of the team manager. Instead, the team manager acquires knowledge of the technical skills of each programmer in the team during regularly scheduled team meetings.

Before implementation begins, it is important to demarcate clearly those areas that appear to be the responsibility of both the team manager and the team leader. For example, consider the issue of annual leave. The situation can arise that the team manager approves a leave application because leave is a nontechnical issue, only to find the application vetoed by the team leader because a deadline is approaching. The solution to this and related issues is for higher management to draw up a policy regarding areas that both the team manager and the team leader consider to be their responsibility.

What about larger projects? This approach can be scaled up as shown in Figure 4.5, which shows the technical managerial organizational structure; the nontechnical side is similarly organized. Implementation of the product as a whole is under the direction of the project leader. The programmers report to their team leaders, and the team leaders report to the project leader. For even larger products, additional levels can be added to the hierarchy.

Another way of drawing on the best features of both democratic and chief programmer teams is to decentralize the decision-making process where appropriate. The resulting channels of communication are shown in Figure 4.6. This scheme is useful for the sorts of

**FIGURE 4.5** The technical managerial organizational structure for larger projects.

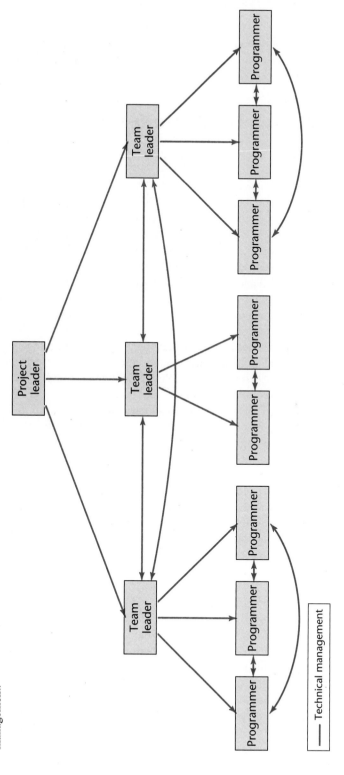

**FIGURE 4.6**  The decentralized decision-making version of the team organization of Figure 4.5 showing the communication channels for technical management.

problems for which the democratic approach is good, that is, in a research environment or whenever a hard problem requires the synergistic effect of group interaction for its solution. Notwithstanding the decentralization, the arrows from level to level still point downward; allowing programmers to dictate to the project leader can lead only to chaos.

## 4.5  Synchronize-and-Stabilize Teams

An alternative approach to team organization is the synchronize-and-stabilize team utilized by Microsoft [Cusumano and Selby, 1997]. Microsoft builds large products; for example, Windows 2000 consists of more than 30 million lines of code, built by over 3000 programmers and testers, reusing much of Windows NT 4.0 [Business Week Online, 1999]. Team organization is a vital aspect of the successful construction of a product of this size.

The synchronize-and-stabilize life-cycle model was described in Section 2.9.6. The success of this model is largely a consequence of the way the teams are organized. Each of the three or four sequential builds of the synchronize-and-stabilize model is constructed by a number of small parallel teams led by a manager and consisting of between three and eight developers together with three to eight testers who work one-to-one with the developers. The team is provided the specifications of its overall task; individual team members then are given the freedom to design and implement their portions of that task as they wish. The reason that this does not rapidly devolve into hacker-induced chaos is the synchronization step performed each day: The partially completed components are tested and debugged on a daily basis. Accordingly, even though individual creativity and autonomy are nurtured, the individual components always work together.

The strength of this approach is that, on the one hand, individual programmers are encouraged to be creative and innovative, a characteristic of a democratic team. On the other hand, the daily synchronization step ensures that the hundreds of developers work together toward a common goal without requiring the communication and coordination characteristic of a chief programmer team (Figure 4.3).

Microsoft developers must follow very few rules, but one of them is that they must adhere strictly to the time laid down to enter their code into the product database for that day's synchronization. Cusumano and Selby [1997] liken this to telling children that they can do what they like all day but have to be in bed by 9 P.M. Another rule is that, if a developer's code prevents the product from being compiled for that day's synchronization, the problem must be fixed immediately so that the rest of the team can test and debug that day's work.

Will use of the synchronize-and-stabilize model and associated team organization guarantee that every other software organization will be as successful as Microsoft? This is extremely unlikely. Microsoft, Inc., is more than just the synchronize-and-stabilize model. It is an organization consisting of a highly talented set of managers and software developers with an evolved group ethos. Merely using the synchronize-and-stabilize model does not magically turn an organization into another Microsoft. At the same time, the use of many of the features of the model in other organizations could lead to process improvement. On the other hand, it has been suggested that the synchronize-and-stabilize model is simply a way of allowing a group of hackers to develop large products and that Microsoft's success is due to superb marketing, rather than quality software.

## 4.6 Teams for Agile Processes

Section 2.9.5 gives an overview of agile processes [Beck et al., 2001]. In this section, we describe how teams are organized when agile processes are used.

A somewhat unusual feature of agile processes is that all code is written by a team of two programmers sharing a single computer; this is referred to as **pair programming** [Williams, Kessler, Cunningham, and Jeffries, 2000]. The reasons for this approach include:

- As explained in Section 2.9.5, pair programmers first draw up test cases, and then implement that piece of code (**task**). As explained in Section 6.6, it is highly inadvisable for a programmer to test his or her own code. Agile processes get around this problem by having one pair programmer in a team draw up the test cases for a task and the other pair programmer jointly implement the code using those test cases.

- In a more conventional life-cycle model, when a developer leaves a project, all the knowledge accumulated by that developer leaves as well. In particular, the software on which that developer was working may not yet have been documented and may have to be redeveloped from scratch. In contrast, if one member of a pair programming team leaves, the other is sufficiently knowledgeable to continue working on the same part of the software with a new pair programmer. Furthermore, the presence of the test cases assist in highlighting a fault, should the new team accidentally damage the software by making an ill-advised modification.

- Working closely in pairs enables a less experienced software professional to acquire the skills of the more experienced team member.

- As mentioned in Section 2.9.5, all the computers used by the various pair teams are placed together in the middle of a large room. This promotes group ownership of code, a positive feature of egoless teams (Section 4.2).

So, even though the idea of two programmers working together on the same computer may seem somewhat unusual, the practice has distinct advantages.

## 4.7 Open-Source Programming Teams

It is surprising that *any* open-source projects have succeeded, let alone that some of the most successful software products ever were developed using the open-source life-cycle model. After all, open-source projects are generally staffed by teams of unpaid volunteers. They communicate asynchronously (i.e., via e-mail), with no team meetings and no managers—informality reigns in every respect. Furthermore, no specifications or designs exist; in fact, documentation of any kind is extremely rare, even in mature projects. But despite these virtually insurmountable obstacles, a small number of open-source projects such as Linux and Apache have attained the highest levels of success.

Individuals volunteer to take part in an open-source project for two main reasons: for the sheer enjoyment of accomplishing a worthwhile task, or for the learning experience.

- In order to attract volunteers to an open-source project and keep them interested, it is essential that at all times they view the project as "worthwhile." Individuals are unlikely to devote a considerable portion of their spare time to a project unless they truly believe that the project will succeed and that the product will be widely utilized. Participants will start to drift away if they start viewing the project as futile.

- With regard to the second reason, many software professionals join an open-source project in order to gain skills in a technology that is new to them, such as a modern programming language or an operating system with which they are unfamiliar. They can then leverage the knowledge they gain to obtain a promotion within their own organization or acquire a better position in another organization. After all, employers frequently view experience gained working on a large, successful open-source project as more desirable than acquiring additional academic qualifications. Conversely, there is no point in devoting months of hard work to a project that ultimately fails.

In other words, unless a project is viewed at all times as a winner, it will not attract and retain volunteers to work on that project. Furthermore, the members of the open-source team must at all times feel that they are making a contribution. For all these reasons, it is essential that the key individual behind an open-source project be a superb motivator. Unless this is the case, the project is doomed to inevitable failure.

Another prerequisite for successful open-source development is the skills of the team members. As explained in detail in Section 9.2, large differences in skill levels have been observed between programmers. Bearing in mind the obstacles to successful open-source software production listed in the first paragraph of this section, there is virtually no way that an open-source project can succeed unless the members of the core group (Section 2.9.4) are top-caliber individuals with finely honed skills of the highest order. Such top-class individuals will thrive in almost any environment, including one as unstructured as an open-source team.

In other words, an open-source project succeeds because of the nature of the target product, the personality of the instigator, and the talents of the members of the core group. The way that a successful open-source team is organized is essentially irrelevant.

# 4.8 People Capability Maturity Model

The people capability maturity model (P–CMM) describes best practices for managing and developing the workforce of an organization [Curtis, Helfey, and Miller, 2002]. As with the software capability maturity model, SW–CMM (Section 3.13), an organization progresses through five maturity levels with the aim of continuously improving individual skills and engendering effective teams.

Every maturity level has its own **key process areas** (KPAs), each of which needs to be addressed satisfactorily before an organization can be deemed to have attained that maturity level. For example, for level 2, the managed level, the KPAs are staffing, communication and coordination, work environment, performance management, training and development, and compensation. In contrast, the KPAs for level 5, the optimizing level, are continuous capability improvement, organizational performance alignment, and continuous workforce innovation.

The SW–CMM is a framework for improving an organization's software process—no specific process or methodology is recommended. In the same way, the P–CMM is a framework for improving an organization's processes for managing and developing its workforce, and no specific approach to team organization is put forward.

# 4.9  Choosing an Appropriate Team Organization

A comparison of the various types of team organization appears in Figure 4.7, which also shows the section in which each team organization is described. Unfortunately, no one solution solves the problem of programming team organization or, by extension, the problem of organizing teams for all the other workflows. The optimal way of organizing a team depends on the product to be built, previous experience with various team structures, and most important, the culture of the organization. For example, if senior management is uncomfortable with decentralized decision making, then it will not be implemented.

In practice, most teams are currently organized as described in Section 4.4. That is, some variant of the chief programmer team is the usual practice.

Not much research has been done on software development team organization, and many of the generally accepted principles are based on research on group dynamics in

**FIGURE 4.7**
Comparison of approaches to team organization and the section in this chapter in which each is described.

| Team Organization | Strengths | Weaknesses |
|---|---|---|
| Democratic teams (Section 4.2) | High-quality code as consequence of positive attitude to finding faults<br>Particularly good with hard problems | Experienced staff resent their code being appraised by beginners<br>Cannot be externally imposed |
| Classical chief programmer teams (Section 4.3) | Major success of *New York Times* project | Impractical |
| Modified chief programmer teams (Section 4.3.1) | Many successes | No successes comparable to the *New York Times* project |
| Modern hierarchical programming teams (Section 4.4) | Team manager/team leader structure obviates need for chief programmer<br>Scales up<br>Supports decentralization when needed | Problems can arise unless areas of responsibility of the team manager and the team leader are clearly delineated |
| Synchronize-and-stabilize teams (Section 4.5) | Encourages creativity<br>Ensures that a huge number of developers can work toward a common goal | No evidence so far that this method can be utilized outside Microsoft |
| Agile process teams (Section 4.6) | Programmers do not test their own code<br>Knowledge is not lost if one programmer leaves<br>Less-experienced programmers can learn from others<br>Group ownership of code | Still too little evidence regarding efficacy |
| Open-source teams (Section 4.7) | A few projects are extremely successful | Narrowly applicable<br>Must be led by a superb motivator<br>Requires top caliber participants |

general and not on software development teams. Even when studies on software teams have been conducted, the sample sizes have generally been small, so the results have not been convincing.

Until experimental results on team organization have been obtained within the software industry, it will not be easy to determine the optimal team organization for a specific product.

**Chapter Review**

The issue of team organization (Section 4.1) is approached by first considering democratic teams (Section 4.2) and chief programmer teams (Section 4.3). The success of the *New York Times* project (Section 4.3.1) is contrasted with the impracticality of classic chief programmer teams (Section 4.3.2). A team organization that uses the strengths of both approaches is suggested in Section 4.4. Synchronize-and-stabilize teams (used by Microsoft) are described in Section 4.5. Teams for agile processes are discussed in Section 4.6 and for open-source software in Section 4.7. The people capability maturity model (P–CMM) is described in Section 4.8. Finally, Section 4.9 describes the factors involved in choosing the optimal team organization for a given project.

**For Further Reading**

The classic works on team organization are [Weinberg, 1971; Baker, 1972; and Brooks, 1975]. Newer books on the subject include [DeMarco and Lister, 1987] and [Cusumano and Selby, 1995]. An interesting description of how team interactions evolve is found in [Mackey, 1999]. Articles on team organization and management can be found in the October 1993 issue of the *Communications of the ACM*. Chapter 11 of [Royce, 1998] contains useful information on the roles played by team members. A promising approach is the use of personality type analysis in selecting team members; see, for example, [Gorla and Lam, 2004].

Synchronize-and-stabilize teams are outlined in [Cusumano and Selby, 1997] and described in detail in [Cusumano and Selby, 1995]. Insight into synchronize-and-stabilize teams can be obtained from [McConnell, 1996]. Extreme programming teams are described in [Beck, 2000]. The May/June 2003 issue of *IEEE Software* includes a number of papers on extreme programming, especially [Reifer, 2003] and [Murru, Deias, and Mugheddue, 2003]. Views on agile processes are expressed in [Boehm, 2002] and [DeMarco and Boehm, 2002], and in the May/June 2005 issue of *IEEE Software*. Williams, Kessler, Cunningham, and Jeffries [2000] describe an experiment on pair programming, one component of extreme programming. Strengths and weaknesses of pair programming are described in [Drobka, Noftz, and Raghu, 2004]. P–CMM is described in [Curtis, Hefley, and Miller, 2002].

**Key Terms**

| | | |
|---|---|---|
| backup programmer *108* | hierarchy *108* | specialization *108* |
| Brooks's Law *105* | key process area (KPA) *116* | superprogrammer *110* |
| chief programmer *108* | librarian *109* | task *115* |
| chief programmer team *107* | pair programming *115* | team *104* |
| democratic team *106* | programmer *109* | team leader *111* |
| egoless programming *106* | programming secretary *109* | team manager *111* |

**Problems**

4.1   How would you organize a team to develop a payroll project? Explain your answer.

4.2   How would you organize a team for developing state-of-the-art military communications software? Explain your answer.

4.3   You have just started a new software company. All your employees are recent college graduates; this is their first programming job. Is it possible to implement democratic teams in your organization, and if so, how?

4.4   A student programming team is organized as a democratic team. What can be deduced about the students in the team?

4.5   A student programming team is organized as a chief programming team. What can be deduced about the students in the team?

4.6   To compare two different team organizations, $TO_1$ and $TO_2$, within a large software company, the following experiment is proposed. The same software product will be built by two different teams, one organized according to $TO_1$ and the other according to $TO_2$. The company estimates that each team will take about 18 months to build the product. Give three reasons why this experiment is impractical and unlikely to yield meaningful results.

4.7   Why do teams for agile processes have to share a computer?

4.8   What are the differences between a democratic team and an open-source team?

4.9   Would you like to work in an organization that uses synchronize-and-stabilize teams? Explain your answer.

4.10  (Term Project) What type of team organization would be appropriate for developing Osric's Office Appliances and Decor product described in Appendix A?

4.11  (Readings in Software Engineering) Your instructor will distribute copies of [Drobka, Noftz, and Raghu, 2004]. Would you like to be a member of an extreme programming team? Explain your answer.

**References**

[Baker, 1972] F. T. BAKER, "Chief Programmer Team Management of Production Programming," *IBM Systems Journal* **11** (No. 1, 1972), pp. 56–73.

[Beck, 2000] K. BECK, *Extreme Programming Explained: Embrace Change,* Addison-Wesley Longman, Reading, MA, 2000.

[Beck et al., 2001] K. BECK, M. BEEDLE, A. COCKBURN, W. CUNNINGHAM, M. FOWLER, J. GRENNING, J. HIGHSMITH, A. HUNT, R. JEFFRIES, J. KERN, B. MARICK, R. C. MARTIN, S. MELLOR, K. SCHWABER, J. SUTHERLAND, D. THOMAS, AND A. VAN BENNEKUM, *Manifesto for Agile Software Development,* agilemanifesto.org, 2001.

[Boehm, 2002] B. W. BOEHM, "Get Ready for Agile Methods, with Care," *IEEE Computer* **35** (January 2002), pp. 64–69.

[Brooks, 1975] F. P. BROOKS, JR., *The Mythical Man-Month: Essays in Software Engineering,* Addison-Wesley, Reading, MA, 1975; Twentieth Anniversary Edition, Addison-Wesley, Reading, MA, 1995.

[Business Week Online, 1999] *Business Week Online*, www.businessweek.com/1999/99_08/b3617025.htm, February 2, 1999.

[Curtis, Hefley, and Miller, 2002] B. CURTIS, W. E. HEFLEY, AND S. A. MILLER, *The People Capability Maturity Model: Guidelines for Improving the Workforce*, Addison-Wesley, Reading, MA, 2002.

[Cusumano and Selby, 1995] M. A. CUSUMANO AND R. W. SELBY, *Microsoft Secrets: How the World's Most Powerful Software Company Creates Technology, Shapes Markets, and Manages People*, The Free Press/Simon and Schuster, New York, 1995.

[Cusumano and Selby, 1997] M. A. CUSUMANO AND R. W. SELBY, "How Microsoft Builds Software," *Communications of the ACM* **40** (June 1997), pp. 53–61.

[DeMarco and Boehm, 2002] T. DEMARCO AND B. BOEHM, "The Agile Methods Fray," *IEEE Computer* **35** (June 2002), pp. 90–92.

[DeMarco and Lister, 1987] T. DEMARCO AND T. LISTER, *Peopleware: Productive Projects and Teams,* Dorset House, New York, 1987.

[Drobka, Noftz, and Raghu, 2004] J. DROBKA, D. NOFTZ, AND R. RAGHU, "Piloting XP on Four Mission-Critical Projects," *IEEE Software* **21** (November/December 2004), pp. 70–75.

[Gorla and Lam, 2004] N. GORLA AND Y. W. LAM, "Who Should Work with Whom?" *Communications of the ACM* **47** (June 2004), pp. 79–82.

[Mackey, 1999] K. MACKEY, "Stages of Team Development," *IEEE Software* **16** (July/August 1999), pp. 90–91.

[Mantei, 1981] M. MANTEI, "The Effect of Programming Team Structures on Programming Tasks," *Communications of the ACM* **24** (March 1981), pp. 106–13.

[McConnell, 1996] S. MCCONNELL, "Daily Build and Smoke Test," *IEEE Software* **13** (July/August 1996), pp. 144, 143.

[Murru, Deias, and Mugheddue, 2003] O. MURRU, R. DEIAS, AND G. MUGHEDDUE, "Assessing XP at a European Internet Company," *IEEE Software* **20** (May/June 2003), pp. 37–43.

[Reifer, 2003] D. REIFER, "XP and the CMM," *IEEE Software* **20** (May/June 2003), pp. 14–15.

[Royce, 1998] W. ROYCE, *Software Project Management: A Unified Framework*, Addison-Wesley, Reading, MA, 1998.

[Weinberg, 1971] G. M. WEINBERG, *The Psychology of Computer Programming*, Van Nostrand Reinhold, New York, 1971.

[Williams, Kessler, Cunningham, and Jeffries, 2000] L. WILLIAMS, R. R. KESSLER, W. CUNNINGHAM, AND R. JEFFRIES, "Strengthening the Case for Pair Programming," *IEEE Software* **17** (July/August 2000), pp. 19–25.

# Chapter 5

# The Tools of the Trade

## Learning Objectives

After studying this chapter, you should be able to

- Appreciate the importance of stepwise refinement and utilize it in practice.
- Apply cost–benefit analysis.
- Select appropriate software metrics.
- Discuss the scope and taxonomy of CASE.
- Describe version-control tools, configuration-control tools, and build tools.
- Understand the importance of CASE.

Software engineers need two types of tools. First are the analytical tools used in software development, such as stepwise refinement and cost–benefit analysis. Then come the software tools, that is, products that assist the teams of software engineers in developing and maintaining software. These usually are termed **CASE** tools (CASE is an acronym that stands for computer-aided software engineering). This chapter is devoted to these two types of tools of the trade, first theoretical (analytical) tools and then software (CASE) tools. We begin with stepwise refinement.

## 5.1 Stepwise Refinement

Stepwise refinement, introduced in Section 2.5, is a problem-solving technique that underlies many software engineering techniques. **Stepwise refinement** can be defined as a means to postpone decisions on details until as late as possible to concentrate on the important issues. As a consequence of Miller's Law (Section 2.5), we can concentrate on only approximately seven chunks (units of information) at a time. Accordingly, we use stepwise refinement to defer nonessential decisions until later while focusing on the key issues.

As will be seen during the course of this book, stepwise refinement underlies many analysis techniques, design and implementation techniques, and even testing and integration techniques. Stepwise refinement is of critical importance within the context of the object-oriented paradigm, because the underlying life-cycle model is iterative and incremental.

The following mini case study illustrates how stepwise refinement can be used in the design of a product.

## Mini Case Study

### 5.1.1    *Stepwise Refinement Mini Case Study*

The mini case study presented in this section may seem almost trivial in that it involves updating a sequential master file, a common operation in many application areas. This choice of a simple, familiar problem is to enable you to concentrate on stepwise refinement rather than on the application domain.

Design a product to update the sequential master file containing name and address data for the monthly magazine *True Life Software Disasters*. There are three types of transactions: insertions, modifications, and deletions, with transaction codes 1, 2, and 3, respectively. The transaction types are

Type 1: INSERT (a new subscriber into the master file)

Type 2: MODIFY (an existing subscriber record)

Type 3: DELETE (an existing subscriber record)

Transactions are sorted into alphabetical order by name of subscriber. If more than one transaction is performed for a given subscriber, the transactions for that subscriber are sorted so that insertions occur before modifications and modifications before deletions.

The first step in designing a solution is to set up a typical file of input transactions, such as that shown in Figure 5.1. The file contains five records: DELETE Brown, INSERT Harris, MODIFY Jones, DELETE Jones, and INSERT Smith. (It is not unusual to perform both a modification and a deletion of the same subscriber in one run.)

**FIGURE 5.1**
Input transaction records for the sequential master file update.

| Transaction Type | Name | Address |
|---|---|---|
| 3 | Brown | |
| 1 | Harris | 2 Oak Lane, Townsville |
| 2 | Jones | Box 345, Tarrytown |
| 3 | Jones | |
| 1 | Smith | 1304 Elm Avenue, Oak City |

**FIGURE 5.2**

A representation of the sequential master file update.

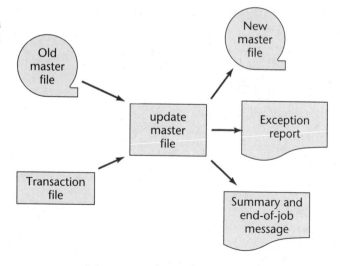

**FIGURE 5.3**

First refinement of the design.

The problem may be represented as shown in Figure 5.2. There are two input files:

1. Old master file name and address records
2. Transaction file

and three output files:

3. New master file name and address records
4. Exception report
5. Summary and end-of-job message

To begin the design process, the starting point is the single box update master file shown in Figure 5.3. This box can be decomposed into three boxes, input, process, and output. The assumption is that, when process requires a record, our level of competence is such that the correct record can be produced at the right time. Similarly, we are capable of writing the correct record to the correct file at the right time. Therefore, the technique is to separate out the input and output aspects and concentrate on the process. What is this process? To determine what it does, consider the example shown in Figure 5.4. The key of the first transaction record (Brown) is compared with the key of the first old master file record (Abel). Because Brown comes after Abel, the Abel record is written to the new master file, and the next old master file record

**FIGURE 5.4**

The transaction file, old master file, new master file, and exception report.

| Transaction file | Old master file | New master file |
|---|---|---|
| 3  Brown | Abel | Abel |
| 1  Harris | Brown | Harris |
| 2  Jones | James | James |
| 3  Jones | Jones | Smith |
| 1  Smith | Smith | Townsend |
|  | Townsend |  |

Exception report

| |
|---|
| Smith |

**FIGURE 5.5**

A diagrammatic representation of the process.

| | |
|---|---|
| Transaction record key = old master file record key | 1. INSERT: Print error message<br>2. MODIFY: Change master file record<br>3. DELETE: *Delete master file record |
| Transaction record key > old master file record key | Copy old master file record to new master file |
| Transaction record key < old master file record key | 1. INSERT: Write transaction record to new master file<br>2. MODIFY: Print error message<br>3. DELETE: Print error message |

*Deletion of a master file record is implemented by not copying the record onto the new master file.

(Brown) is read. In this case, the key of the transaction record matches the key of the old master file record, and because the transaction type is 3 (DELETE), the Brown record must be deleted. This is implemented by not copying the Brown record onto the new master file. The next transaction record (Harris) and old master file record (James) are read, overwriting the Brown records in their respective buffers. Harris comes before James and, therefore, is inserted into the new master file; the next transaction record (Jones) is read. Because Jones comes after James, the James record is written to the new master file, and the next old master file record is read; this is Jones. As can be seen from the transaction file, the Jones record is to be modified and then deleted, so the next transaction record (Smith) and the next old master file record (also Smith) are read. Unfortunately, the transaction type is 1 (INSERT), but Smith already is in the master file. So there is an error of some sort in the data, and the Smith record is written to the exception report. To be more precise, the Smith transaction record is written to the exception report, and the Smith old master file record is written to the new master file.

Now that the process is understood, it may be represented as in Figure 5.5. Next, the process box of Figure 5.3 may be refined, resulting in the second refinement shown in Figure 5.6. The dashed lines to the input and output boxes denote that decisions as to how to handle input and output have been deferred until a later refinement. The remainder of the figure is the flowchart of the process, or rather, an

**FIGURE 5.6**   The second refinement of the design.

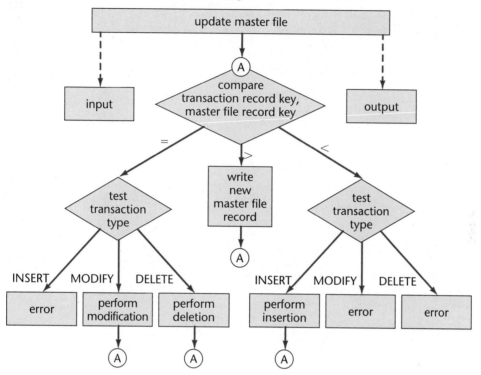

early refinement of the flowchart. As already pointed out, input and output have been deferred. Also, there is no provision for an end-of-file condition, nor has it yet been specified what to do when an error condition is encountered. The strength of stepwise refinement is that these and similar problems can be solved in later refinements.

The next step is to refine the input and output boxes of Figure 5.6, resulting in Figure 5.7. End-of-file conditions still have not been handled nor has the writing of the end-of-job message. Again, these can be done at a later iteration. What is critical, however, is that the design of Figure 5.7 has a major fault. To see this, consider the situation with regard to the data of Figure 5.4 when the current transaction is 2 Jones, that is, modify Jones, and the current old master file record is Jones. In the design of Figure 5.7, because the key of the transaction record is the same as the key of the old master file record, the leftmost path is followed to the test transaction type decision box. Because the current transaction type is MODIFY, the old master file record is modified and written to the new master file, and the next transaction record is read. This record is 3 Jones, that is, delete Jones. But the modified Jones record has already been written to the new master file.

The reader may wonder why an incorrect refinement deliberately is presented. The point is that, when using stepwise refinement, it is necessary to check each successive refinement before proceeding to the next. If a particular refinement turns out to

**FIGURE 5.7** The third refinement of the design (the design has a major fault).

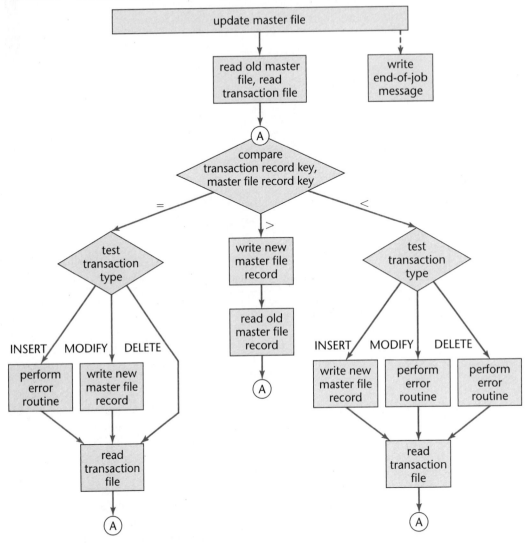

be faulty, it is not necessary to restart the process from the beginning but merely to go back to the previous refinement and proceed from there. In this instance, the second refinement (Figure 5.6) is correct, so it may be used as the basis for another attempt at a third refinement. This time, the design uses level-1 **lookahead**; that is, a transaction record is processed only after the next transaction record has been analyzed. The details are left as an exercise; see Problem 5.1.

In the fourth refinement, details that have been ignored up to now, such as opening and closing files, have to be introduced. With stepwise refinement, such details are handled last, after the logic of the design has been fully developed. Obviously, it is impossible to execute the product without opening and closing files. However, what is important here is the stage in the design process at which such details as file openings and closings are handled. While the design is being developed, the seven or so chunks on which the designer can concentrate at once should *not* include details like opening and closing files. File openings and closings have nothing to do with the design itself; they are merely implementation details that are part of any design. However, in later refinements, opening and closing files becomes vital. In other words, stepwise refinement can be considered a technique for setting the priorities of the various problems that have to be solved within a workflow. Stepwise refinement ensures that every problem is solved and each is solved at the appropriate time, without having to handle more than $7 \pm 2$ chunks at any one time.

The term *stepwise refinement* was first introduced by Wirth [1971]. In the preceding mini case study, stepwise refinement was applied to a flowchart, whereas Wirth applied the technique to pseudocode. The specific representation to which stepwise refinement is applied is not important; stepwise refinement is a general technique that can be used for every workflow and with almost every representation.

Miller's Law is a fundamental restriction on the mental powers of humans. Because we cannot fight our nature, we must live with it, accepting our limitations and doing the best we can under the circumstances.

The power of stepwise refinement is that it helps the software engineer concentrate on the relevant aspects of the current development task and ignore details that, although essential in the overall scheme, need not be considered, and in fact should be ignored, until later. Unlike a divide-and-conquer technique, in which the problem as a whole is decomposed into subproblems of essentially equal importance, in stepwise refinement, the importance of a particular aspect of the problem changes from refinement to refinement. Initially, a particular issue may be irrelevant, but later that same issue is of critical importance. The challenge with stepwise refinement is deciding which issues must be handled in the current refinement and which can be postponed until a later refinement.

Like stepwise refinement, cost–benefit analysis is a fundamental theoretical software engineering technique used throughout the software life cycle. This technique is described in Section 5.2.

## 5.2 Cost–Benefit Analysis

One way of determining whether a possible course of action would be profitable is to compare estimated future benefits against projected future costs. This is termed **cost–benefit analysis**. As an example of cost–benefit analysis within the computer context, consider how Krag Central Electric Company (KCEC) decided in 1965 whether or not to computerize its billing system. Billing was being done manually by 80 clerks who mailed bills every 2 months to KCEC customers. Computerization would require KCEC to buy or lease the necessary software and hardware, including data-capture equipment for recording the input data on punch cards or magnetic tape.

One advantage of computerization would be that bills could be mailed monthly instead of every 2 months, improving the company's cash flow considerably. Furthermore, the

**FIGURE 5.8**
Cost–benefit analysis data for KCEC.

| Benefits | | Costs | |
|---|---|---|---|
| Salary savings (7 years) | 1,575,000 | Hardware and software (7 years) | 1,250,000 |
| Improved cash flow (7 years) | 875,000 | Conversion cost (first year only) | 350,000 |
| | | Explanations to customers (first year only) | 125,000 |
| Total benefits | $2,450,000 | Total costs | $1,725,000 |

80 billing clerks would be replaced by 11 data-capture clerks. As shown in Figure 5.8, salary savings over the next 7 years were estimated to be $1.575 million, and improved cash flow was projected to be worth $875,000. The total benefits therefore were estimated at $2.45 million. On the other hand, a complete data processing department would have to be set up, staffed by well-paid computer professionals. Over a 7-year period, costs were estimated as follows. The cost of hardware and software, including postdelivery maintenance, was estimated to be $1.25 million. In the first year, there would be a conversion cost of $350,000, and the cost of explaining the new system to customers was estimated at an additional $125,000. Total costs were estimated at $1.725 million, about $750,000 less than the estimated benefits for that 7-year period. KCEC immediately decided to computerize.

Cost–benefit analysis is not always straightforward. On the one hand, a management consultant can estimate salary savings, an accountant can project cash flow improvements, net present value (NPV) can be used to handle the change in the cost of money, and a software engineering consultant can estimate the costs of hardware, software, and conversion. But how are we to determine the cost of dealing with customers trying to adjust to computerization? How can we measure the benefits of inoculating an entire population against measles? And how can we make estimates regarding a market window, that is, the benefit of being first on the market with a new product or the cost of not being the first (and hence losing customers)?

The point is that tangible benefits are easy to measure, but intangible benefits can be hard to quantify directly. A practical way of assigning a dollar value to intangible benefits is to make **assumptions**. These assumptions always must be stated in conjunction with the resulting estimates of the benefits. After all, managers have to make decisions. If no data are available, then making assumptions from which such data can be determined usually is the best that can be done under the circumstances. This approach has the further advantage that, if someone else reviewing the data and the underlying assumptions can come up with better assumptions, then better data can be produced and the associated intangible benefits can be computed more accurately. The same technique can be used for intangible costs.

Cost–benefit analysis is a fundamental technique in deciding whether a client should computerize his or her business, and if so, in what way. The costs and benefits of various alternative strategies are compared. For example, a product for storing the results of drug trials can be implemented in a number of different ways, including flat files and various database management systems. For each possible strategy, the costs and benefits are computed, and the one for which the difference between benefits and costs is the largest is selected as the optimal strategy.

The final theoretical tool described in this chapter is software metrics.

## 5.3  Software Metrics

As explained in Section 3.13, without measurements (or **metrics**) it is impossible to detect problems early in the software process, before they get out of hand. Metrics thus can serve as an early warning system for potential problems. A wide variety of metrics can be used. For example, lines of code (LOC) is one way of measuring the size of a product (see Section 9.2.1). If LOC measurements are taken at regular intervals, they provide a measure of how fast the project is progressing. In addition, the number of faults per 1000 lines of code is a measure of software quality. After all, it is of little use if a programmer consistently turns out 2000 lines of code a month but half of them have to be thrown away because they are unacceptable. Accordingly, LOC in isolation is not a very meaningful metric.

Once the product has been installed on the client's computer, a metric such as mean time between failures provides management an indication of its reliability. If a certain product fails every other day, its quality is clearly lower than that of a similar product that on average runs for 9 months without a failure.

Certain metrics can be applied throughout the software process. For example, for each workflow, we can measure the effort in person-months (1 person-month is the amount of work done by one person in 1 month). Staff turnover is another important metric. High turnover adversely affects current projects because it takes time for a new employee to learn the relevant facts about the project (see Section 4.1). In addition, new employees may have to be trained in aspects of the software process; if new employees are less educated in software engineering than the individuals they replace, then the process as a whole may suffer. Of course, cost is an essential metric that must also be monitored continually throughout the entire process.

A number of different metrics are described in this book. Some are **product metrics**; they measure some aspect of the product itself, such as its size or its reliability. Others are **process metrics** used by the developers to deduce information about the software process. A typical metric of this kind is the efficiency of fault detection during development, that is, the ratio of the number of faults detected during development to the total number of faults detected in the product over its lifetime.

Many metrics are specific to a given workflow. For example, lines of code cannot be used before the implementation workflow, and the number of faults detected per hour in reviewing specifications is relevant to only the analysis workflow. In subsequent chapters describing each of the various workflows of the software process, the metrics relevant to that workflow are discussed.

A cost is involved in gathering the data needed to compute the values of metrics. Even if the data gathering is fully automated, the CASE tool (Section 5.4) that accumulates the required information is not free and interpreting the output from the tool consumes human resources. Bearing in mind that hundreds (if not thousands) of metrics have been put forward, an obvious question is, What should a software organization measure? There are five essential, fundamental metrics:

1. Size (in lines of code or, better, in a more meaningful metric, such as those of Section 9.2.1).
2. Cost (in dollars).

As explained in Section 1.11, for software engineers the term *system* is frequently used to mean a software–hardware combination. The field of **systems engineering** spans a wide range of activities, starting with defining the client's needs and requirements until they have been fully implemented in the constructed system. Subsequently, after the system has been delivered to the client, following successful acceptance tests, it undergoes extensive modifications throughout its entire life cycle, to remove defects or add needed improvements or adaptations [Tomer and Schach, 2002].

Accordingly, there are strong similarities between systems engineering and software engineering. It is therefore not surprising that, for systems engineers, the acronym CASE stands for "computer-aided systems engineering." Because of the major role often played by software in systems engineering, within the context of systems engineering it is sometimes hard to know which version of the CASE acronym is meant.

3. Duration (in months).
4. Effort (in person-months).
5. Quality (number of faults detected).

Each of these metrics must be measured by workflow. On the basis of the data from these fundamental metrics, management can identify problems within the software organization, such as high fault rates during the design workflow or code output that is well below the industry average. Once problem areas have been highlighted, a strategy to correct these problems can be considered. To monitor the success of this strategy, more-detailed metrics can be introduced. For example, it may be deemed appropriate to collect data on the fault rates of each programmer or to conduct a survey of user satisfaction. Consequently, in addition to the five fundamental metrics, more detailed data gathering and analysis should be performed only toward a specific objective.

Finally, one aspect of metrics is still fairly controversial. Questions have been raised as to the validity of some popular metrics; these issues are discussed in Section 14.13.2. Although it is agreed that we cannot control the software process unless we can measure it, there is still some disagreement as to precisely what should be measured [Fenton and Pfleeger, 1997].

We now turn from theoretical tools to software (CASE) tools.

## 5.4   CASE

During the development of a software product, a number of very different operations have to be carried out. Typical activities include estimating resource requirements, drawing up the specification document, performing integration testing, and writing the user manual. Unfortunately, none of these activities, nor the others in the software process, can be fully automated and performed by a computer without human intervention.

However, computers can *assist* every step of the way. The title of this section, "CASE," stands for computer-aided (or computer-assisted) software engineering (but see Just in Case You Wanted to Know Box 5.1). Computers can help by carrying out much of the drudge work associated with software development, including the creation and organization of artifacts of all kinds, such as plans, contracts, specifications, designs, source code, and management information. Documentation is essential for software development and maintenance, but the majority of individuals involved in software development are not fond of creating or updating documentation. Maintaining diagrams on the computer is especially useful as it allows changes to be made with ease.

But CASE is not restricted to assisting with documentation. In particular, computers can assist software engineers to cope with the complexity of software development, especially in managing all the details. CASE involves all aspects of computer support for software engineering. At the same time, it is important to remember that CASE stands for computer-*aided* software engineering, and not computer-*automated* software engineering— no computer yet can replace a human with respect to development or maintenance of software. For the foreseeable future at least, the computer must remain a tool of the software professional.

## 5.5    Taxonomy of CASE

The simplest form of CASE is the software **tool**, a product that assists in just one aspect of the production of software. CASE tools currently are being used with every workflow of the life cycle. For example, a variety of tools are on the market, many of them for use with personal computers, that assist in the construction of graphical representations of software products, such as flowcharts and UML diagrams. CASE tools that help the developer during the earlier workflows of the process (the requirements, analysis, and design workflows) sometimes are termed **upperCASE** or **front-end tools**, whereas those that assist with the implementation workflow and postdelivery maintenance are termed **lowerCASE** or **back-end tools**. Figure 5.9(a) represents a CASE tool that assists with part of the requirements workflow.

An important class of CASE tools is the **data dictionary**, a computerized list of all data defined within the product. A large product contains tens (if not hundreds) of thousands of data items, and the computer is ideal for storing information such as variable names and types, and the location where each is defined, as well as procedure names and parameters and their types. An important part of every data dictionary entry is a description of the item; for example, This procedure takes as input the body weight of

**FIGURE 5.9**
A representation of (a) a tool, (b) a workbench, and (c) an environment.

the newborn infant and computes the appropriate dosage of the drug or List of aircraft arrival times sorted with earliest times first.

The power of a data dictionary can be enhanced by combining it with a **consistency checker**, a tool to check that every data item in the specification document is reflected in the design and, conversely, every item in the design has been defined in the specification document.

Another use of a data dictionary is to provide the data for report generators and screen generators. A **report generator** is used to generate the code needed for producing a report. A **screen generator** is used to assist the software developer in producing the code for a data capture screen. Suppose that a screen is being designed to enter the weekly sales at each branch of a chain of book stores. The branch number is a four-digit integer in the range 1000–4500 or 8000–8999, entered on the screen three lines from the top. This information is given to the screen generator. The screen generator then automatically generates code to display the string BRANCH NUMBER _ _ _ _ three lines from the top and position the cursor at the first underline character. As the user enters each digit, it is displayed; and the cursor moves on to the next underline. The screen generator also generates code for checking that the user enters only digits and that the resulting four-digit integer is in the specified range. If the data entered are invalid or the user presses the ? key, help information is displayed.

Use of such generators can result in the implementation being quickly constructed. Furthermore, a graphical representation tool combined with a data dictionary, consistency checker, report generator, and screen generator constitute a requirements, analysis, and design **workbench** that supports the first three core workflows. An example of a commercial workbench that incorporates all these features is Software through Pictures.[1]

Another class of workbench is a requirements management workbench. Such a workbench allows systems analysts to organize and track the requirements of a software development project. RequisitePro is a commercial example of such a workbench.

A CASE workbench therefore is a collection of tools that together support one or two activities, where an **activity** is a related collection of tasks. For example, the coding activity includes editing, compiling, linking, testing, and debugging. An activity is not the same as a workflow of a life-cycle model. In fact, the tasks of an activity can even cross workflow boundaries. For example, a project management workbench is used for every workflow of the project, and a coding workbench can be used for building a proof-of-concept prototype, as well as for the implementation workflow and postdelivery maintenance. Figure 5.9(b) represents a workbench of upperCASE tools. The workbench includes the requirements workflow tool of Figure 5.9(a), as well as tools for parts of the analysis and design workflows.

Continuing the progression of CASE technology from tools to workbenches, the next item is the CASE environment. Unlike the workbench, which supports one or two activities, an **environment** supports the complete software process or, at the very least, a large portion of the software process [Fuggetta, 1993]. Figure 5.9(c) depicts an environment that

---

[1] The fact that a specific CASE tool is cited in this book in no way implies any form of endorsement of that CASE tool by the author or publisher. Each CASE tool mentioned in this book has been included because it is a typical example of the class of CASE tools of which it is an instance.

supports all aspects of all workflows of the life cycle. Environments are discussed in greater detail in Chapter 14.

Having set up a CASE taxonomy (tools, workbenches, and environments), the scope of CASE now is considered.

## 5.6   Scope of CASE

As mentioned previously, the need to have accurate and up-to-date documentation available at all times is a primary reason for implementing CASE technology. For example, suppose that specifications are produced manually. A member of the development team has no way of telling whether a particular specification document is the current version or an older version. There is no way of knowing if the handwritten changes on that document are part of the current specification or merely a suggestion later rejected. On the other hand, if the specifications of the product are produced using a CASE tool, then at any time, there is only one copy of the specifications, the online version accessed via the CASE tool. Then, if the specifications are changed, members of the development team easily can access the document and be sure that they are seeing the current version. In addition, the consistency checker will flag any design changes without corresponding changes to the specification document.

Programmers also need **online documentation**. For example, online help information must be provided for the operating system, editor, programming language, and so on. In addition, programmers have to consult manuals of many kinds, such as editor manuals and programming manuals. It is highly desirable that, wherever possible, these manuals be available online. Apart from the convenience of having everything at one's fingertips, it generally is quicker to query by computer than to try to find the appropriate manual and plow through it to find the needed item. In addition, it usually is much easier to update an online manual than to try to find all hard-copy versions of a manual within an organization and make the necessary page changes. As a result, online documentation is likely to be more accurate than hard-copy versions of the same material—another reason for providing online documentation to programmers. An example of such online documentation is the UNIX *manual* pages [Sobell, 1995]. CASE also can assist with communication among team members. **E-mail** is as much a part of an office today as a computer or a fax machine. There are many advantages to e-mail. From the viewpoint of software production, storing copies of all e-mail relevant to a specific project in a particular mailbox provides a written record of the decisions made during the project. This can be used to resolve conflicts that may arise later. Many CASE environments and some CASE workbenches now incorporate e-mail systems. In other organizations, the e-mail system is implemented via a World Wide Web browser such as Netscape or Firefox. Other tools that are equally essential are **spreadsheets** and **word processors**.

The term **coding tools** refers to CASE tools such as text editors, debuggers, and pretty printers designed to simplify the programmer's task, reduce the frustration many programmers experience in their work, and increase programmer productivity. Before discussing such tools, three definitions are required. **Programming-in-the-small** refers to software development at the level of the code of a single module, whereas **programming-in-the-large** is software development at the module level [DeRemer and Kron, 1976]. The latter includes aspects such as architectural design and integration. **Programming-in-the-many** refers to software production by a team. At times, the team works at the module level; at times, at the code level. Accordingly, programming-in-the-many incorporates aspects of both programming-in-the-large and programming-in-the-small.

A **structure editor** is a text editor that "understands" the implementation language. That is, a structure editor can detect a syntax fault as soon as it has been keyed in by the programmer, speeding the implementation because time is not wasted on futile compilations. Structure editors exist for a wide variety of languages, operating systems, and hardware. Because a structure editor has knowledge of the programming language, it is easy to incorporate a **pretty printer** (or **formatter**) into the editor to ensure that the code always has a good visual appearance. For example, a pretty printer for C++ ensures that each } is indented the same amount as its corresponding {. Reserved words are automatically put in boldface so that they stand out, and indentation has been designed to aid readability. Nowadays, structure editors of this kind form part of numerous programming workbenches, such as Visual C++ and JBuilder.

Now consider the problem of invoking a method within the code, only to discover at linkage time that either the method does not exist or it has been wrongly specified in some way. What is needed is for the structure editor to support **online interface checking**. That is, just as the structure editor has information regarding the name of every variable declared by the programmer, so it must also know the name of every method defined within the product. For example, if the programmer enters a call such as

average = dataArray.computeAverage (numberOfValues);

but method computeAverage has not yet been defined, then the editor immediately responds with a message such as

Method computeAverage not known

At this point, the programmer is given two choices, either to correct the name of the method or to declare a new method named computeAverage. If the second option is chosen, the programmer also must specify the arguments of the new method. Argument types must be supplied when declaring a new method because the major reason for having online interface checking is precisely to be able to check full interface information, not just the names of methods. A common fault is for method p to call method q passing, say, four arguments, whereas method q has been specified with five arguments. It is more difficult to detect the fault when the call correctly uses four arguments, but two of the arguments are transposed. For example, the declaration of method q might be

**void** q (**float** floatVar, **int** intVar, string s1, string s2)

whereas the call is

q (intVar, floatVar, s1, s2);

The first two arguments have been transposed in the call statement. Java compilers and linkers detect this fault but only when they are invoked later. In contrast, an online interface checker immediately detects this and similar faults. In addition, if the editor has a help facility, the programmer can request online information as to the precise arguments of method q before attempting to code the call to q. Better yet, the editor should generate a template for the call, showing the type of each argument. The programmer merely has to replace each formal argument by an actual argument of the correct type.

A major advantage of online interface checking is that hard-to-detect faults caused by calling methods with the wrong number of arguments or arguments of the wrong type are immediately flagged. Online interface information is important for the efficient production of high-quality software, particularly when the software is produced by a team (programming-in-the-many). It is essential that online interface information regarding all code artifacts be available to all programming team members at all times. Furthermore, if one programmer changes the interface of method vaporCheck, perhaps by changing the type of one argument from **int** to **float** or by adding an additional argument, then every component that calls vaporCheck must automatically be disabled until the relevant call statements have been altered to reflect the new state of affairs.

Even with a **syntax-directed editor** incorporating an online interface checker, the programmer still has to exit from the editor and invoke the compiler and linker. Clearly, there can be no compilation faults, but the compiler still has to be invoked to perform code generation. Then the linker has to be called. Again, the programmer can be sure that all external references will be satisfied as a consequence of the presence of the online interface checker, but the linker still is needed to link the product. The solution to this is to incorporate an **operating system front end** within the editor. That is, a programmer should be able to give operating system commands from within the editor. To cause the editor to invoke the compiler, linker, loader, and any other system software needed to cause the code artifact to be executed, the programmer should be able to type a single command, named go or run, or use the mouse to choose the appropriate icon or menu selection. In UNIX, this can be achieved by using the *make* command (Section 5.9) or by invoking a shell script [Sobell, 1995]. Such front ends can be implemented in other operating systems, as well.

One of the most frustrating computing experiences is for a product to execute for a second or so and then terminate abruptly, printing a message such as

Overflow at 506

The programmer is working in a high-level language such as Java or C++ not a low-level language like assembler or machine code. But when debugging support is of the Overflow at 506 variety, the programmer is forced to examine machine code core dumps, assembler listings, linker listings, and a variety of similar low-level documentation, thereby destroying the whole advantage of programming in a high-level language. A similar situation arises when the only information provided is the infamous UNIX message

Core dumped

or the equally uninformative

Segmentation fault

Here again, the user is forced to examine low-level information.

In the event of a failure, the message shown in Figure 5.10 is a great improvement over the earlier terse error messages. The programmer immediately can see that the method failed because of an attempt to divide by 0. Even more useful is for the operating system to enter edit mode and automatically display the line at which the failure was detected, line 6, together with the preceding and following four or five lines. The programmer probably can then see what caused the failure and make the necessary changes.

Another type of source-level debugging is tracing. Before the advent of CASE tools, programmers had to insert appropriate print statements into their code by hand that, at

**FIGURE 5.10**
Output from a
source-level
debugger.

```
OVERFLOW ERROR

  Class:   cyclotronEnergy
 Method:   performComputation
 Line 6:   newValue = (oldValue + tempValue) / tempValue;
           oldValue = 3.9583       tempValue = 0.0000
```

execution time, would indicate the line number and the values of relevant variables. This now can be done by giving commands to a **source-level debugger** that automatically causes trace output to be produced. Even better is an **interactive source-level debugger**. Suppose that the value of variable escapeVelocity seems to be incorrect and that method computeTrajectory seems to be faulty. Using the interactive source-level debugger, the programmer can set breakpoints in the code. When a breakpoint is reached, execution stops and debugging mode is entered. The programmer now asks the debugger to trace the variable escapeVelocity and the method computeTrajectory. That is, every time the value of escapeVelocity subsequently is either used or changed, execution again halts. The programmer then has the option of entering further debugging commands, for example, to request that the value of a specific variable be displayed. Alternatively, the programmer may choose to continue execution in debugging mode or return to normal execution mode. The programmer similarly can interact with the debugger whenever the method compute-Trajectory is entered or exited. Such an interactive source-level debugger offers almost every conceivable type of assistance to the programmer when a product fails. The UNIX debugger *dbx* is an example of such a CASE tool.

As pointed out many times, it is essential that documentation of all kinds be available online. In the case of programmers, all documentation they might need should be accessible from within the editor.

What has now been described—a structure editor with online interface checking capabilities, operating system front end, source-level debugger, and online documentation—constitutes an adequate and effective programming workbench.

This sort of workbench is by no means new. All these features were supported by the FLOW software development workbench as far back as 1980 [Dooley and Schach, 1985]. Therefore, what has been put forward as a minimal but essential programming workbench does not require many years of research before a prototype can be tentatively produced. Quite the contrary, the necessary technology has been in place for over 20 years, and it is somewhat surprising that there are programmers who still implement code the "old-fashioned way," instead of using a workbench like Sun ONE Studio.

An essential tool, especially when software is developed by a team, is a version-control tool.

## 5.7 Software Versions

Whenever a product is maintained, there will be at least two **versions** of the product: the old version and the new version. Because a product is composed of code artifacts, there will also be two or more versions of each of the component artifacts that have been changed.

Version control is described first within the context of postdelivery maintenance, and then broadened to include earlier parts of the process.

## 5.7.1 Revisions

Suppose a product has been installed at a number of different sites. If a fault is found in an artifact, then that artifact has to be fixed. After appropriate changes have been made, there will be two versions of the artifact, the old version and the new version intended to replace it. The new version is termed a **revision**. The presence of multiple versions apparently is easy to solve—any old versions should be thrown away, leaving just the correct one. But that would be most unwise. Suppose that the previous version of the artifact was revision $n$, and that the new version is revision $n + 1$. First, there is no guarantee that revision $n + 1$ is any more correct than revision $n$. Even though revision $n + 1$ may have been thoroughly tested by the software quality assurance group, both in isolation and linked to the rest of the product, there may be disastrous consequences when the new version of the product is run by the user on actual data. Revision $n$ must be kept for a second reason. The product may have been distributed to a variety of sites, and not all of them may have installed revision $n + 1$. If a fault report is received from a site still using revision $n$, then to analyze this new fault, it is necessary to configure the product in exactly the same way it is configured at the user's site, that is, incorporating revision $n$ of the artifact. It therefore is necessary to retain a copy of every revision of each artifact.

As described in Section 1.3, perfective maintenance is performed to extend the functionality of a product. In some instances, new artifacts are written; in other cases, existing artifacts are changed to incorporate this additional functionality. These new versions also are revisions of existing artifacts. So are artifacts changed when performing adaptive maintenance; that is, changes that are made to the product in response to changes in the environment in which the product operates. As with corrective maintenance, all previous versions must be retained because issues arise not just during postdelivery maintenance but from implementation onward. After all, once an artifact has been coded, it continually undergoes changes as a consequence of faults being detected and corrected. As a result, there are numerous versions of every artifact, and it is vital to have some sort of control to ensure that every member of the development team knows which is the current version of a given artifact. Before we can present a solution to this problem, a further complication must be taken into account.

## 5.7.2 Variations

Consider the following example. Most computers support more than one type of printer. For example, a personal computer may support an ink-jet printer and a laser printer. The operating system therefore must contain two **variations** of the printer driver, one for each type of printer. Unlike revisions, each of which is written specifically to replace its predecessor, variations are designed to coexist. Another situation where variations are needed is when a product is to be ported to a variety of different operating systems and hardware. A different variation of many of the artifacts may have to be produced for each operating system–hardware combination.

Versions are schematically depicted in Figure 5.11, which shows both revisions and variations. To complicate matters further, in general, there are multiple revisions of each variation. For a software organization to avoid drowning in a morass of multiple versions, a CASE tool is needed.

**FIGURE 5.11**
A schematic
representation
of multiple
versions of
artifacts,
showing
(a) revisions and
(b) variations.

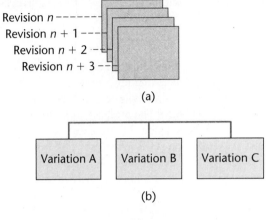

**FIGURE 5.12**
Components of
an executable
load image.

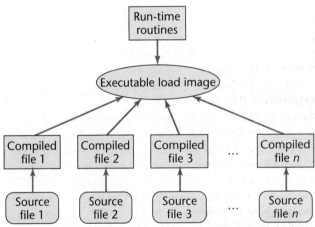

## 5.8   Configuration Control

The code for every artifact exists in three forms. First is the source code, nowadays generally written in a high-level language like C++ or Java. Next comes the object code, produced by compiling the source code. In this book, because of possible confusion of the word *object,* we refer to object code as *compiled code*. Finally, the compiled code for each artifact is combined with run-time routines to produce an executable load image. This is shown in Figure 5.12. The programmer can use various different versions of each artifact. The specific version of each artifact from which a given version of the complete product is built is called the **configuration** of that version of the product.

Suppose that a programmer is given a test report from the SQA group stating that an artifact failed on a specific set of test data. One of the first things to do is attempt to re-create the failure. But how can the programmer determine which revisions of which variations went into the version of the product that crashed? Unless a configuration-control tool (described in the following discussion) is used, the only way to pinpoint the cause of the failure is to look at the executable load image, in octal or hexadecimal format, and compare it to the compiled code, also in octal or hexadecimal. Specifically, the various versions of

**FIGURE 5.13**    Multiple revisions and variations. (a) Four revisions of artifact acknowledgeMessage. (b) Two variations of artifact printerDriver, with three revisions of variation printerDriver (laser).

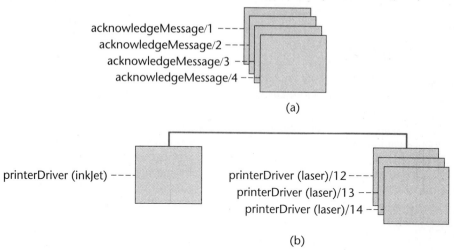

acknowledgeMessage/1  – – – –
acknowledgeMessage/2  – –
acknowledgeMessage/3  –
acknowledgeMessage/4  – –

(a)

printerDriver (inkJet)  – – –

printerDriver (laser)/12 – – –
printerDriver (laser)/13 – –
printerDriver (laser)/14 – –

(b)

the source code have to be compiled and compared to the compiled code that went into the executable load image. Although this can be done, it can take a long time, particularly if the product has dozens (if not hundreds) of code artifacts, each with multiple versions. Therefore, two problems must be solved when dealing with multiple versions. First, we must distinguish between versions so that the correct version of each code artifact is compiled and linked to the product. Second, there is the inverse problem: Given an executable load image, determine which version of each of its components went into it.

The first item needed to solve this problem is a version-control tool. Many operating systems, particularly for mainframe computers, support version control. But many do not, in which case a separate version-control tool is needed. A common technique used in version control is for the name of each file to consist of two pieces, the file name itself and the revision number. For example, an artifact that acknowledges receipt of a message has revisions acknowledgeMessage/1, acknowledgeMessage/2, and so on, as depicted in Figure 5.13(a). A programmer then can specify exactly which revision is needed for a given task.

With regard to multiple variations (slightly changed versions that fulfill the same role in different situations), one useful notation is to have a basic file name, followed by a variation name in parentheses [Babich, 1986]. Thus two printer drivers are given the names printerDriver (inkJet) and printerDriver (laser).

Of course, there will be multiple revisions of each variation, such as printerDriver (laser)/12, printerDriver (laser)/13, and printerDriver (laser)/14. This is depicted in Figure 5.13(b).

A version-control tool is the first step toward being able to manage multiple versions. Once it is in place, a detailed record (or **derivation**) of every version of the product must be kept. The derivation contains the name of each source code element, including the variation and revision, the versions of the various compilers and linkers used, the name of the person who constructed the product, and of course, the date and the time at which it was constructed.

Version control is a great help in managing multiple versions of artifacts and the product as a whole. But more than just version control is needed, because of additional problems associated with maintaining multiple variations.

Consider the two variations printerDriver (inkJet) and printerDriver (laser). Suppose that a fault is found in printerDriver (inkJet), and suppose that the fault occurs in a part of the artifact common to both variations. Then it is necessary to fix not only printerDriver (inkJet) but also printerDriver (laser). In general, if there are $v$ variations of an artifact, all $v$ of them have to be fixed. Not only that, they have to be fixed in exactly the same way.

One solution to this problem is to store just one variation, say, printerDriver (inkJet). Then any other variation is stored in terms of the list of changes that have to be made to go from the original to that variation. The list of differences is termed a *delta*. What is stored is one variation and $v - 1$ deltas. Variation printerDriver (laser) is retrieved by accessing printerDriver (inkJet) and applying the delta. A change made just to printerDriver (laser) is implemented by changing the appropriate delta. However, any change made to printerDriver (inkJet), the original variation, automatically applies to all the other variations.

A **configuration-control tool** can automatically manage multiple variations. But **configuration control** goes beyond multiple variations. A configuration-control tool also can handle problems caused by development and maintenance by teams, as described in Section 5.8.1.

### 5.8.1 Configuration Control during Postdelivery Maintenance

All sorts of difficulties can arise when more than one programmer simultaneously maintains a product. For example, suppose each of two programmers is assigned a different fault report on a Monday morning. By coincidence, both localize the fault they are to fix to different parts of the same artifact mDual. Each programmer makes a copy of the current version of the artifact, mDual/16, and they start to work on the faults. The first programmer fixes the first fault, has the changes approved, and replaces the artifact, now called mDual/17. A day later the second programmer fixes the second fault, has the changes approved, and installs artifact mDual/18. Unfortunately, revision 17 contains the changes of only the first programmer, whereas revision 18 contains those of only the second programmer. None of the changes of the first programmer are in mDual/18, because the second programmer made changes to mDual/16, instead of to mDual/17.

Although the idea of each programmer making individual copies of an artifact is far better than both working together on the same piece of software, clearly it is inadequate for maintenance by a team. What is needed is some mechanism that allows only one user at a time to change an artifact.

### 5.8.2 Baselines

The maintenance manager must set up a **baseline**, a configuration (set of versions) of all the artifacts in the product. When trying to find a fault, a maintenance programmer puts copies of any needed artifacts into his or her **private workspace**. In this private workspace, the programmer can change anything at all without having an impact on any other programmer in any way, because all changes are made to the programmer's private copy; the baseline version is left untouched.

Once it has been decided which artifact has to be changed to fix the fault, the programmer **freezes** the current version of the artifact he or she is going to alter. No other programmer may make changes to any frozen version. After the maintenance programmer has made changes and they have been tested, the new version of the artifact is installed, thereby modifying the baseline. The previous version, now frozen, is retained because it may be needed in the future, as explained previously, but it cannot be altered. Once a new version has been installed, any other maintenance programmer can freeze the new version and make changes to it. The resulting artifact, in turn, becomes the next baseline version. A similar procedure is followed if two or more artifacts have to be changed simultaneously.

This scheme solves the problem with artifact mDual. Both programmers make private copies of mDual/16 and use those copies to analyze the respective faults that they have been assigned to fix. The first programmer decides what changes to make, freezes mDual/16 and makes those changes to repair the first fault. After the changes have been tested, the resulting revision, mDual/17, becomes the baseline version. In the meantime, the second programmer has found the second fault by experimenting with a private copy of mDual/16. However, changes cannot now be made to mDual/16 because it was frozen by the first programmer. Once mDual/17 becomes the baseline, it is frozen by the second programmer whose changes are made to mDual/17. The resulting artifact now is installed as mDual/18, a version that incorporates the changes of both programmers. Revisions mDual/16 and mDual/17 are retained for possible future reference, but they can never be altered.

### 5.8.3 Configuration Control during Development

While an artifact is in the process of being coded, versions are changing too rapidly for configuration control to be helpful. Once coding of the artifact has been completed, it should immediately be tested informally by its programmer, as described in Section 6.6. During this informal testing, the artifact again passes through numerous versions. When the programmer is satisfied, the artifact is handed over to the SQA group for methodical testing. As soon as the artifact has been passed by the SQA group, it is ready to be integrated into the product. From then on, it should be subject to the same configuration-control procedures as those of postdelivery maintenance. Any change to an integrated artifact can have an impact on the product as a whole in the same way as a change made during postdelivery maintenance. Therefore, configuration control is needed not only during postdelivery maintenance but also during implementation. Furthermore, management cannot monitor the development process adequately unless every artifact is subject to configuration control as soon as is reasonable, that is, after it has been passed by the SQA group. When configuration control is properly applied, management is aware of the status of every artifact and can take early corrective action if project deadlines seem to be slipping.

The three major UNIX version-control tools are *sccs* (source code control system) [Rochkind, 1975], *rcs* (revision control system) [Tichy, 1985], and *cvs* (concurrent versions system) [Loukides and Oram, 1997]. PVCS is a popular, commercially available configuration-control tool. Microsoft SourceSafe is a configuration-control tool for personal computers. *cvs* is an open-source configuration management tool. (Open-source software is described in Section 1.11.)

## 5.9   Build Tools

If a software organization does not wish to purchase a complete configuration-control tool, then at the very least, a version-control tool must be used in conjunction with a **build tool**, that is, a tool that assists in selecting the correct version of each compiled-code artifact to be linked to form a specific version of the product. At any time, multiple variations and revisions of each artifact are in the product library. All version-control tools assist users in distinguishing among different versions of artifacts of source code. But keeping track of compiled code is more difficult, because some version-control tools do not attach revision numbers to compiled versions.

To cope with this, some organizations automatically compile the latest version of each artifact every night, thereby ensuring that all the compiled code is up to date. Although this technique works, it can be extremely wasteful of computer time because frequently a large number of unnecessary compilations are performed. The UNIX tool *make* can solve this problem [Feldman, 1979]. For each executable load image, the programmer sets up a Makefile specifying the hierarchy of source and compiled files that go into that particular configuration; such a hierarchy is shown in Figure 5.12. More complex dependencies, such as included files in C or C++, also can be handled by *make*. When invoked by a programmer, the tool works as follows: UNIX, like virtually every other operating system, attaches a date and time stamp to each file. Suppose that the stamp on a source file is Friday, June 6, at 11:24 A.M., whereas the stamp on the corresponding compiled file is Friday, June 6, at 11:40 A.M. Then it is clear that the source file has not been changed since the compiled file was created by the compiler. On the other hand, if the date and time stamp on the source file is later than that on the compiled file, then *make* calls the appropriate compiler or assembler to create a version of the compiled file that corresponds to the current version of the source file.

Next, the date and time stamp on the executable load image is compared to those on every compiled file in that configuration. If the executable load image was created later than all the compiled files, then there is no need to relink. But if a compiled file has a later stamp than that of the load image, then the load image does not incorporate the latest version of that compiled file. In this case, *make* calls the linker and constructs an updated load image.

In other words, *make* checks whether the load image incorporates the current version of every artifact. If so, then nothing further is done and no CPU time is wasted on needless compilations and linkage. If not, then *make* calls the relevant system software to create an up-to-date version of the product.

In addition, *make* simplifies the task of building a compiled file. The user need not specify each time what artifacts are to be used and how they are to be connected, because this information already is in the Makefile. Therefore, a single *make* command is all that is needed to build a product with hundreds of artifacts and ensure that the complete product is put together correctly.

Tools like *make* have been incorporated into an endless variety of programming environments, including Visual Java and Visual C++. An open-source version of *make* is Ant (a product of the Apache project).

## 5.10 Productivity Gains with CASE Technology

Reifer (as reported in [Myers, 1992]) conducted an investigation into productivity gains as a consequence of introducing CASE technology. He collected data from 45 companies in 10 industries. Half the companies were in the field of information systems, 25 percent in scientific areas, and 25 percent in real-time aerospace. Average annual productivity gains varied from 9 percent (real-time aerospace) to 12 percent (information systems). If only productivity gains are considered, then these figures do not justify the cost of $125,000 per user of introducing CASE technology. However, the companies surveyed felt that the justification for CASE is not merely increased productivity but also shorter development time and improvement in software quality. In other words, the introduction of CASE environments boosted productivity, although less than some proponents of CASE technology have claimed. Nevertheless, other, equally important reasons were given for introducing CASE technology into a software organization, such as faster development, fewer faults, better usability, easier maintenance, and improved morale.

Newer results on the effectiveness of CASE technology from over 100 development projects at 15 Fortune 500 companies reflect the importance of training and the software process [Guinan, Cooprider, and Sawyer, 1997]. When teams using CASE were given training in application development in general as well as tool-specific training, user satisfaction increased and development schedules were met. However, when training was not provided, software was delivered late and users were less satisfied. Also, performance increased by 50 percent when teams used CASE tools in conjunction with a structured methodology. These results support the assertion in Section 3.13 that CASE environments should not be used by groups at maturity levels 1 or 2. To put it bluntly, a fool with a tool is still a fool [Guinan, Cooprider, and Sawyer, 1997]. The final figure in this chapter, Figure 5.14, is an alphabetical list of the theoretical tools and CASE tools described in this chapter, together with the section in which each is described.

**FIGURE 5.14**
Summary of the theoretical (analytical) tools and software (CASE) tools presented in this chapter and the section in which each is described.

**Analytical Tools**

Cost–benefit analysis (Section 5.2)
Metrics (Section 5.3)
Stepwise refinement (Section 5.1)

**CASE Taxonomy**

Environment (Section 5.5)
LowerCASE tool (Section 5.5)
UpperCASE tool (Section 5.5)
Workbench (Section 5.5)

**CASE Tools**

Build tool (Section 5.9)
Coding tool (Section 5.6)
Configuration-control tool (Section 5.8)
Consistency checker (Section 5.5)
Data dictionary (Section 5.5)
E-mail (Section 5.6)
Interface checker (Section 5.6)
Online documentation (Section 5.6)
Operating system front end (Section 5.6)
Pretty printer (Section 5.6)
Report generator (Section 5.5)
Screen generator (Section 5.5)
Source-level debugger (Section 5.6)
Spreadsheet (Section 5.6)
Structure editor (Section 5.6)
Version-control tool (Section 5.7)
Word processor (Section 5.6)
World Wide Web browser (Section 5.6)

**Chapter Review**

First, a number of analytical tools are presented. Stepwise refinement, based on Miller's Law, is described in Section 5.1 and illustrated by means of an example in Section 5.1.1. Another analytical tool, cost–benefit analysis, is presented in Section 5.2. Software metrics are introduced in Section 5.3.

Computer-aided software engineering (CASE) is defined in Section 5.4, and the taxonomy and scope of CASE are described in Sections 5.5 and 5.6, respectively. A variety of CASE tools are next described. When large products are constructed, version-control tools, configuration-control tools, and build tools are essential; these are presented in Sections 5.7 through 5.9. Productivity gains, as a consequence of the use of CASE technology, are described in Section 5.10.

**For Further Reading**

For further information regarding Miller's Law and his theory of how the brain operates on chunks, consult [Tracz, 1979] and [Moran, 1981] as well as Miller's original paper [Miller, 1956].

Wirth's [1971] paper on stepwise refinement is a classic of its kind and deserves detailed study. Equally significant from the viewpoint of stepwise refinement are the books by Dijkstra [1976] and Wirth [1975]. Stepwise design of real-time systems is described in [Kurki-Suonio, 1993].

Studies of tool evaluation are presented in [Kitchenham, Pickard, and Pfleeger, 1995]. The extent to which CASE is used in the software industry is described in [Sharma and Rai, 2000].

In this book, CASE tools for the separate workflows of the software process are described in the chapters on each workflow. For information on workbenches or CASE environments, consult the For Further Reading section of Chapter 14.

[Whitgift, 1991] is a good introduction to configuration management. Newer articles include [van der Hoek, Carzaniga, Heimbigner, and Wolf, 2002; Mens, 2002; and Walrad and Strom, 2002]. The proceedings of the International Workshops on Software Configuration Management are a useful source of information.

There are many excellent books on cost–benefit analysis, including [Gramlich, 1997]. Cost–benefit analysis of software product lines (Section 8.5.4) is discussed in [Bockle et al., 2004]. Van Solingen [2004] presents cost–benefit analysis of software process improvement.

Important books on metrics include [Shepperd, 1996] and [Fenton and Pfleeger, 1997]. Jones [1994] highlights unworkable and invalid metrics that nevertheless continue to be mentioned in the literature. The validity of object-oriented metrics is discussed in [El Emam, Benlarbi, Goel, and Rai, 2001] and [Alshayeb and Li, 2003]. The March/April 1997 issue of *IEEE Software* contains a number of papers on metrics, including [Pfleeger, Jeffrey, Curtis, and Kitchenham, 1997], an assessment of software measurement. Kilpi [2001] describes how a metrics program was implemented at Nokia. Metrics for COTS-based systems are presented in [Sedigh-Ali and Paul, 2001].

A number of articles from the Seventh International Software Metrics Symposium appear in the November 2001 issue of *IEEE Transactions on Software Engineering;* of particular interest is [Briand and Wüst, 2001].

**Key Terms**

| | | |
|---|---|---|
| activity *132* | configuration *138* | e-mail *133* |
| assumptions *128* | configuration control *140* | environment *132* |
| back-end tool *131* | configuration-control tool *140* | formatter *134* |
| baseline *140* | consistency checker *132* | freeze *140* |
| build tool *141* | cost–benefit analysis *127* | front-end tool *131* |
| CASE *121* | data dictionary *131* | interactive source-level |
| coding tool *133* | derivation *139* | debugger *136* |

**Problems**

5.1 Consider the effect of introducing lookahead to the design of the corrected third refinement of the sequential master file update problem. That is, before processing a transaction the next transaction must be read. If both transactions apply to the same master file record, then the decision regarding the processing of the current transaction depends on the type of the next transaction. Draw up a 3 × 3 table with the rows labeled by the type of the current transaction and the columns labeled by the type of the next transaction and fill in the action to be taken in each instance. For example, two successive insertions of the same record clearly are an error. But two modifications may be perfectly valid; for example, a subscriber can change address more than once in a given month. Now develop a flowchart for the third refinement that incorporates lookahead.

5.2 Check whether your answer to Problem 5.1 can correctly handle a modification transaction followed by a deletion transaction, both transactions being applied to the same master file record. If not, modify your answer.

5.3 Check whether your answer to Problem 5.1 also can handle correctly an insertion followed by a modification followed by a deletion, all applied to the same master file record. If not, modify your answer.

5.4 Check whether your answer to Problem 5.1 can also correctly handle *n* insertions, modifications, or deletions, *n* > 2, all applied to the same master file record. If not, modify your answer.

5.5 The last transaction record has no successor. Check whether your flowchart for Problem 5.1 takes this into account and processes the last transaction record correctly. If not, modify your answer.

5.6 In some applications, an alternative to lookahead can be achieved by cleverly ordering the transactions. For example, the original problem caused by a modification followed by a deletion of the same master file record could have been solved by processing a deletion before a modification. This would have resulted in the master file being written correctly and an error message appearing in the exception report. Investigate whether there is an ordering of the transactions that can solve all the difficulties listed in Problems 5.2 through 5.4.

5.7 A new form of gastrointestinal disease is sweeping the country of Concordia. Like histoplasmosis, it is transmitted as an airborne fungus. Although the disease is almost never fatal, an attack is extremely painful and the sufferer is unable to work for about 2 weeks. The government of Concordia wishes to determine how much money, if any, to spend on attempting to eradicate the disease. The committee charged with advising the Department of Public Health is considering four aspects of the problem: health care costs (Concordia provides free health care to all its citizens), loss of earnings (and hence loss of taxes), pain and discomfort, and gratitude toward the government. Explain how cost–benefit analysis can assist the committee. For each benefit or cost, suggest how a dollar estimate for that benefit or cost could be obtained.

5.8 Does a one-person software production organization need a version-control tool, and if so, why?

5.9 Does a one-person software production organization need a configuration-control tool, and if so, why?

5.10 You are the manager in charge of the software that controls the navigation system for a midget submarine. Three different user-reported faults have to be fixed, and you assign one each to Paul, Quentin, and Rachel. A day later you learn that, to implement each of the three fixes, the same four artifacts must be changed. However, your configuration-control tool is inoperative, so you will have to manage the changes yourself. How will you do it?

5.11 Which of the case tools listed in Figure 5.14 promote stepwise refinement during software development? Justify your answer.

5.12 (Term Project) What types of CASE tools would be appropriate for developing the Osric's Office Appliances and Decor product described in Appendix A?

5.13 (Readings in Software Engineering) Your instructor will distribute copies of [Wirth, 1971]. List the differences between Wirth's approach and the approach to stepwise refinement presented in this chapter.

## References

[Alshayeb and Li, 2003] M. ALSHAYEB, AND W. LI "An Empirical Validation of Object-Oriented Metrics in Two Different Iterative Software Processes," *IEEE Transactions on Software Engineering* **29** (November 2003), pp. 1043–49.

[Babich, 1986] W. A. BABICH, *Software Configuration Management: Coordination for Team Productivity,* Addison-Wesley, Reading, MA, 1986.

[Bockle et al., 2004] G. BOCKLE, P. CLEMENTS, J. D. MCGREGOR, D. MUTHIG, AND K. SCHMID, "Calculating ROI for Software Product Lines," *IEEE Software* **21** (May/June 2004), pp. 23–31.

[Briand and Wüst, 2001] L. C. BRIAND AND J. WÜST, "Modeling Development Effort in Object-Oriented Systems Using Design Properties," *IEEE Transactions on Software Engineering* **27** (November 2001), pp. 963–86.

[DeRemer and Kron, 1976] F. DEREMER AND H. H. KRON, "Programming-in-the-Large versus Programming-in-the-Small," *IEEE Transactions on Software Engineering* **SE-2** (June 1976), pp. 80–86.

[Dijkstra, 1976] E. W. DIJKSTRA, *A Discipline of Programming,* Prentice Hall, Englewood Cliffs, NJ, 1976.

[Dooley and Schach, 1985] J. W. M. DOOLEY AND S. R. SCHACH, "FLOW: A Software Development Environment Using Diagrams," *Journal of Systems and Software* **5** (August 1985), pp. 203–19.

[El Emam, Benlarbi, Goel, and Rai, 2001] K. EL EMAM, S. BENLARBI, N. GOEL, AND S. N. RAI, "The Confounding Effect of Class Size on the Validity of Object-Oriented Metrics," *IEEE Transactions on Software Engineering* **27** (July 2001), pp. 630–50.

[Feldman, 1979] S. I. FELDMAN, "Make—A Program for Maintaining Computer Programs," *Software—Practice and Experience* **9** (April 1979), pp. 225–65.

[Fenton and Pfleeger, 1997] N. E. FENTON AND S. L. PFLEEGER, *Software Metrics: A Rigorous and Practical Approach*, 2nd ed., IEEE Computer Society, Los Alamitos, CA, 1997.

[Fuggetta, 1993] A. FUGGETTA, "A Classification of CASE Technology," *IEEE Computer* **26** (December 1993), pp. 25–38.

[Gramlich, 1997] E. M. GRAMLICH, *A Guide to Benefit–Cost Analysis,* 2nd ed., Waveland Books, Prospect Heights, IL, 1997.

[Guinan, Cooprider, and Sawyer, 1997] P. J. GUINAN, J. G. COOPRIDER, AND S. SAWYER, "The Effective Use of Automated Application Development Tools," *IBM Systems Journal* **36** (No. 1, 1997), pp. 124–39.

[Jones, 1994] C. JONES, "Software Metrics: Good, Bad, and Missing," *IEEE Computer* **27** (September 1994), pp. 98–100.

[Kilpi, 2001] T. KILPI, "Implementing a Software Metrics Program at Nokia," *IEEE Software* **18** (November/December 2001), pp. 72–76.

[Kitchenham, Pickard, and Pfleeger, 1995] B. KITCHENHAM, L. PICKARD, AND S. L. PFLEEGER. "Case Studies for Method and Tool Evaluation," *IEEE Software* **12** (July 1995), pp. 52–62.

[Kurki-Suonio, 1993] R. KURKI-SUONIO, "Stepwise Design of Real-Time Systems," *IEEE Transactions on Software Engineering* **19** (January 1993), pp. 56–69.

[Loukides and Oram, 1997] M. K. LOUKIDES AND A. ORAM, *Programming with GNU Software,* O'Reilly and Associates, Sebastopol, CA, 1997.

[Mens, 2002] T. MENS, "A State-of-the-Art Survey on Software Merging," *IEEE Transactions on Software Engineering* **28** (May 2002), pp. 449–62.

[Miller, 1956] G. A. MILLER, "The Magical Number Seven, Plus or Minus Two: Some Limits on Our Capacity for Processing Information," *The Psychological Review* **63** (March 1956), pp. 81–97. Reprinted in: www.well.com/user/smalin/miller.html.

[Moran, 1981] T. P. MORAN (Editor), Special Issue: The Psychology of Human-Computer Interaction, *ACM Computing Surveys* **13** (March 1981).

[Myers, 1992] W. MYERS, "Good Software Practices Pay off—or Do They?" *IEEE Software* **9** (March 1992), pp. 96–97.

[Pfleeger, Jeffrey, Curtis, and Kitchenham, 1997] S. L. PFLEEGER, R. JEFFREY, B. CURTIS, AND B. KITCHENHAM, "Status Report on Software Measurement," *IEEE Software* **14** (March/April 1997), pp. 33–44.

[Rochkind, 1975] M. J. ROCHKIND, "The Source Code Control System," *IEEE Transactions on Software Engineering* **SE-1** (October 1975), pp. 255–65.

[Sedigh-Ali and Paul, 2001] S. SEDIGH-ALI AND R. A. PAUL, "Software Engineering Metrics for COTS-Based Systems," *IEEE Computer* **34** (May 2001), pp. 44–50.

[Sharma and Rai, 2000] S. SHARMA AND A. RAI, "CASE Deployment in IS Organizations," *Communications of the ACM* **43** (January 2000), pp. 80–88.

[Shepperd, 1996] M. SHEPPERD, *Foundations of Software Measurement,* Prentice Hall, Upper Saddle River, NJ, 1996.

[Sobell, 1995] M. G. SOBELL, *A Practical Guide to the UNIX System,* 3rd ed., Benjamin/Cummings, Menlo Park, CA, 1995.

[Tichy, 1985] W. F. TICHY, "RCS—A System for Version Control," *Software—Practice and Experience* **15** (July 1985), pp. 637–54.

[Tomer and Schach, 2002] A. TOMER AND S. R. SCHACH, "A Three-Dimensional Model for System Design Evolution," *Systems Engineering* **5** (No. 4, 2002), pp. 264–273.

[Tracz, 1979] W. J. TRACZ, "Computer Programming and the Human Thought Process," *Software—Practice and Experience* **9** (February 1979), pp. 127–37.

[van der Hoek, Carzaniga, Heimbigner, and Wolf, 2002] A. VAN DER HOEK, A. CARZANIGA, D. HEIMBIGNER, AND A. L. WOLF, "A Testbed for Configuration Management Policy Programming," *IEEE Transactions on Software Engineering* **28** (January 2002), pp. 79–99.

[van Solingen, 2004] R. VAN SOLINGEN, "Measuring the ROI of Software Process Improvement," *IEEE Software* **21** (May/June 2004), pp. 32–38.

[Walrad and Strom, 2002] C. WALRAD AND D. STROM, "The Importance of Branching Models in SCM," *IEEE Computer* **35** (September 2002), pp. 31–38.

[Whitgift, 1991] D. WHITGIFT, *Methods and Tools for Software Configuration Management,* John Wiley and Sons, New York, 1991.

[Wirth, 1971] N. WIRTH, "Program Development by Stepwise Refinement," *Communications of the ACM* **14** (April 1971), pp. 221–27.

[Wirth, 1975] N. WIRTH, *Algorithms + Data Structures = Programs,* Prentice Hall, Englewood Cliffs, NJ, 1975.

# Chapter  6

# Testing

### Learning Objectives

After studying this chapter, you should be able to

- Describe quality assurance issues.
- Describe how to perform non-execution-based testing (inspections) of artifacts.
- Describe the principles of execution-based testing.
- Explain what needs to be tested.

Classical software life-cycle models all too frequently include a separate testing phase, after integration and before postdelivery maintenance. Nothing could be more dangerous from the viewpoint of trying to achieve high-quality software. Testing is an integral component of the software process and an activity that must be carried out throughout the life cycle: During the requirements workflow, the requirements must be checked; during the analysis workflow, the specifications must be checked; and the software production management plan must undergo similar scrutiny. The design workflow requires meticulous checking at every stage. During the implementation workflow, each code artifact certainly must be tested; and the product as a whole needs testing when it has been fully integrated. After passing the acceptance test, the product is installed and postdelivery maintenance begins. And hand in hand with maintenance goes repeated checking of modified versions of the product.

In other words, it is not sufficient to test the product of a workflow merely at the end of that workflow. For example, consider the design workflow. The members of the design team must consciously and conscientiously check the design while they develop it. It is not much use for the team to develop the complete design artifacts only to find, weeks or months later, that a mistake made early in the process necessitates redesigning almost the entire product. Therefore, continual testing must be carried out by the development team while it performs each workflow, in addition to more methodical testing at the end of each workflow.

The terms *verification* and *validation* were introduced in Section 1.7. **Verification** refers to the process of determining whether a workflow has been correctly carried out; this takes place at the end of each workflow. On the other hand, **validation** is the intensive evaluation process that takes place just before the product is delivered to the client. Its purpose is to determine whether the product as a whole satisfies its specifications. Even though both terms are defined in the IEEE software engineering glossary [IEEE 610.12, 1990] in this way, and notwithstanding the common usage of the term **V & V** to denote testing, the words *verification* and *validation* are used as little as possible in this book. One reason is that, as explained in Section 6.5, the word *verification* has another meaning within the context of testing. A second reason is that the phrase *verification and validation* (or *V & V*) implies that the process of checking a workflow can wait until the end of that workflow. On the contrary, it is essential that this checking be carried out in parallel with all software development and maintenance activities. Therefore, to avoid the undesirable implications of the phrase *V & V,* the term **testing** is used. A second reason why we use the word *testing* is that this is the terminology of the Unified Process. For example, the fifth core workflow is the **test workflow**.

Essentially there are two types of testing: execution-based testing and non-execution-based testing. For example, it is impossible to execute a written specification document; the only alternatives are to review it as carefully as possible or subject it to some form of analysis. However, once there is executable code, it becomes possible to run test cases, that is, to perform execution-based testing. Nevertheless, the existence of code does not preclude non-execution-based testing, because as will be explained, methodically reviewing code uncovers at least as many faults as running test cases. In this chapter, the principles of both execution-based and non-execution-based testing are described. These principles are applied in Chapters 10 through 15, where a description is given of each workflow of the process model and the specific testing practices applicable to it. The first two faults described in Just in Case You Wanted to Know Box 1.1 led to fatal consequences. Fortunately, in most cases, the result of delivering software with residual faults is considerably less catastrophic. Nevertheless, the importance of testing cannot be stressed too strongly.

## 6.1   Quality Issues

We begin this section by expanding on the definitions of Section 1.11 that relate to testing. A **fault** is injected into the software when a human makes a **mistake** [IEEE 610.12, 1990]. One mistake on the part of a software professional may cause several faults; conversely, various mistakes may cause the identical fault. A **failure** is the observed incorrect behavior of the software product as a consequence of a fault, and the **error** is the amount by which a result is incorrect [IEEE 610.12, 1990]. A specific failure may be caused by several faults, and some faults may never cause a failure. The word **defect** is a generic term for a fault, failure, or error.

Now we turn to quality issues. The term *quality* frequently is misunderstood when used within the software context. After all, quality implies excellence of some sort, but this unfortunately is infrequently the meaning intended by software engineers. To put it bluntly, all that many software development organizations can achieve is merely to get the software to function correctly—excellence is an order of magnitude more than what is generally possible for organizations at CMM level 1 (Section 3.13).

The **quality** of software is the extent to which the product satisfies its specifications (see Just in Case You Wanted to Know Box 6.1). However, this is not enough. For example, to ensure that a product can be easily maintained, the product must be well designed and meticulously coded. Therefore, it is necessary that software have high quality, but this is by no means sufficient.

The task of every software professional is to ensure high-quality software at all times. That is, each developer and maintainer is personally responsible for checking that his or her work is correct. Quality is not something added afterward by the **software quality assurance (SQA)** group but rather must be built in by the developers from the very beginning. One role of the SQA group is to ensure that the developers are indeed doing high-quality work. The SQA group has additional responsibilities, too, as described in Section 6.1.1.

## 6.1.1 Software Quality Assurance

As previously stated, one aspect of the role of the SQA group is to test that the developers' product is correct. More precisely, once the developers have completed a workflow and carefully checked their work, members of the SQA group have to ensure that the workflow has indeed been carried out correctly. Also, when the product is complete and the developers are confident that the product as a whole is correct, the SQA group has to make sure that this is so. However, software quality assurance goes further than just testing (or V & V) at the end of a workflow or the end of the development process. SQA applies to the software process itself. For example, the responsibilities of the SQA group include the development of the various standards to which the software must conform as well as the establishment of the monitoring procedures for ensuring compliance with those standards. In brief, the role of the SQA group is to ensure the quality of the software process and thereby ensure the quality of the product.

## 6.1.2 Managerial Independence

It is important to have **managerial independence** between the development team and the SQA group. That is, development should be under one manager, SQA under a different manager, and neither manager should be able to overrule the other. The reason is that, all too frequently, serious defects are found in a product as the delivery deadline approaches. The software organization must now choose between two unsatisfactory options. Either the product can be released on time but full of faults, leaving the client to struggle with faulty software, or the developers can fix the software but deliver it late. No matter what, the client probably will lose confidence in the software organization. The decision to deliver faulty software on time should not be made by the manager responsible for development, nor should the SQA manager be able to make the decision to perform further testing and deliver the product late. Instead, both managers should report to a more senior manager who can decide which choice would be in the best interests of both the software development organization and the client.

At first sight, having a separate SQA group would appear to add considerably to the cost of software development, but this is not so. The additional cost is relatively small compared to the resulting benefit—higher-quality software. Without an SQA group, every member of the software development organization would have to be involved to some extent with quality assurance activities. Suppose an organization has 100 software professionals and each devotes about 30 percent of his or her time to quality assurance activities. Instead, the 100 individuals should be divided into two groups, with 70 individuals performing software development and the other 30 people responsible for SQA. The same amount of time is devoted to SQA, the only additional expense being a manager to lead the SQA group. Quality assurance now can be performed by an independent group of specialists, leading to products of higher quality than when SQA activities are performed throughout the organization.

In the case of a very small software company (four employees or fewer), it may simply not be economically viable to have a separate SQA group. The best that can be done under such circumstances is to ensure that the analysis artifacts are checked by someone other than the person responsible for producing those artifacts and similarly for the design artifacts, code artifacts, and so on. The reason for this is explained in Section 6.2.

## 6.2   Non-Execution-Based Testing

Testing software without running test cases is termed **non-execution-based testing**. Examples of non-execution-based testing methods include reviewing software (carefully reading through it) and analyzing software mathematically (Section 6.5).

It is not a good idea for the person responsible for drawing up a document to be the only one responsible for reviewing it. Almost everyone has blind spots that allow faults to creep into the document, and those same blind spots prevent the faults from being detected on review. Therefore, the review task must be assigned to someone other than the original author of the document. In addition, having only one reviewer may not be adequate; we all have had the experience of reading through a document many times while failing to detect a blatant spelling mistake that a second reader picks up almost immediately. This is one principle underlying review techniques like walkthroughs or inspections. In both types of review, a document (such as a specification document or design document) is painstakingly checked by a team of software professionals with a broad range of skills. The strength of a review by a team of experts is that the different skills of the participants increase the chances of finding a fault. In addition, a team of skilled individuals working together often generates a synergistic effect.

Walkthroughs and inspections are two types of reviews. The fundamental difference between them is that walkthroughs have fewer steps and are less formal than inspections.

## 6.2.1 Walkthroughs

A walkthrough team should consist of four to six individuals. An analysis walkthrough team should include at least one representative from the team responsible for drawing up the specifications, the manager responsible for the analysis workflow, a client representative, a representative of the team that will perform the next workflow of the development (in this instance the design team), and a representative of the software quality assurance group. For reasons that will be explained in Section 6.2.2, the SQA group member should chair the walkthrough.

The members of the walkthrough team should, as far as possible, be experienced senior technical staff members because they tend to find the important faults. That is, they detect the faults that would have a major negative impact on the project [R. New, personal communication, 1992].

The material for the walkthrough must be distributed to the participants well in advance to allow for thorough preparation. Each reviewer should study the material and develop two lists: a list of items the reviewer does not understand and a list of items the reviewer believes are incorrect.

## 6.2.2 Managing Walkthroughs

The walkthrough should be chaired by the SQA representative because the SQA representative has the most to lose if the walkthrough is performed poorly and faults slip through. In contrast, the representative responsible for the analysis workflow may be eager to have the specification document approved as quickly as possible to start some other task. The client representative may decide that any faults not detected at the review probably will show up during acceptance testing and be fixed at that time at no cost to the client organization. But the SQA representative has the most at stake: The quality of the product is a direct reflection of the professional competence of the SQA group.

The person leading the walkthrough guides the other members of the walkthrough team through the document to uncover any faults. It is not the task of the team to correct faults, but merely to record them for later correction. There are four reasons for this:

1. A correction produced by a committee (that is, the walkthrough team) within the time constraints of the walkthrough is likely to be lower in quality than a correction produced by an individual trained in the necessary techniques.
2. A correction produced by a walkthrough team of five individuals takes at least as much time as a correction produced by one person and, therefore, costs five times as much when the salaries of the five participants are considered.
3. Not all items flagged as faults actually are incorrect. In accordance with the dictum, "If it ain't broke, don't fix it," it is better for faults to be analyzed methodically and corrected only if there really is a problem, rather than have a team attempt to "fix" something that is completely correct.
4. There simply is not enough time in a walkthrough to both detect and correct faults. No walkthrough should last longer than 2 hours. The time should be spent detecting and recording faults, not correcting them.

There are two ways of conducting a walkthrough. The first is participant driven. Participants present their lists of unclear items and items they think are incorrect. The representative of the analysis team must respond to each query, clarifying what is unclear to the reviewer and either agreeing that indeed there is a fault or explaining why the reviewer is mistaken.

The second way of conducting a review is document driven. A person responsible for the document, either individually or as part of a team, walks the participants through that document, with the reviewers interrupting either with their prepared comments or comments triggered by the presentation. This second approach is likely to be more thorough. In addition, it generally leads to the detection of more faults because the majority of faults at a document-driven walkthrough are spontaneously detected by the presenter. Time after time, the presenter will pause in the middle of a sentence, his or her face will light up, and a fault, one that has lain dormant through many readings of the document, suddenly becomes obvious. A fruitful field for research by a psychologist would be to determine why verbalization so often leads to fault detection during walkthroughs of all kinds, including requirements walkthroughs, analysis walkthroughs, design walkthroughs, plan walkthroughs, and code walkthroughs. Not surprisingly, the more thorough document-driven review is the technique prescribed in the IEEE Standard for Software Reviews [IEEE 1028, 1997].

The primary role of the walkthrough leader is to elicit questions and facilitate discussion. A walkthrough is an interactive process; it is not supposed to be one-sided instruction by the presenter. It also is essential that the walkthrough not be used as a means of evaluating the participants. If that happens, the walkthrough degenerates into a point-scoring session and does not detect faults, no matter how well the session leader tries to run it. It has been suggested that the manager who is responsible for the document being reviewed should be a member of the walkthrough team. If this manager also is responsible for the annual evaluations of the members of the walkthrough team (and particularly of the presenter), the fault detection capabilities of the team will be compromised, because the primary motive of the presenter will be to minimize the number of faults that show up. To prevent this conflict of interests, the person responsible for a given workflow should not also be directly responsible for evaluating any member of the walkthrough team for that workflow.

## 6.2.3 Inspections

Inspections were first proposed by Fagan [1976] for testing designs and code. An **inspection** goes far beyond a walkthrough and has five formal steps.

1. An **overview** of the document to be inspected (requirements, specification, design, code, or plan) is given by one of the individuals responsible for producing that document. At the end of the overview session, the document is distributed to the participants.

2. In the **preparation**, the participants try to understand the document in detail. Lists of fault types found in recent inspections, with the fault types ranked by frequency, are excellent aids. These lists help team members concentrate on the areas where the most faults have occurred.

3. To begin the inspection, one participant walks through the document with the inspection team, ensuring that every item is covered and that every branch is taken at least once. Then fault finding commences. As with walkthroughs, the purpose is to find and document the

faults, not to correct them. Within one day the leader of the inspection team (the **moderator**) must produce a written report of the inspection to ensure meticulous follow-through.

4. In the **rework**, the individual responsible for the document resolves all faults and problems noted in the written report.

5. In the **follow-up**, the moderator must ensure that every issue raised has been resolved satisfactorily, by either fixing the document or clarifying items incorrectly flagged as faults. All fixes must be checked to ensure that no new faults have been introduced [Fagan, 1986]. If more than 5 percent of the material inspected has been reworked, then the team must reconvene for a 100 percent reinspection.

The inspection should be conducted by a team of four. For example, in the case of a design inspection, the team consists of a moderator, designer, implementer, and tester. The moderator is both manager and leader of the inspection team. There must be a representative of the team responsible for the current workflow as well as a representative of the team responsible for the next workflow. The designer is a member of the team that produced the design, whereas the implementer is responsible, either individually or as part of a team, for translating the design into code. Fagan suggests that the tester be any programmer responsible for setting up test cases; it is, of course, preferable that the tester be a member of the SQA group. The IEEE standard recommends a team of between three and six participants [IEEE 1028, 1997]. Special roles are played by the moderator, the **reader** who leads the team through the design, and the **recorder** responsible for producing a written report of the detected faults.

An essential component of an inspection is the checklist of potential faults. For example, the checklist for a design inspection should include items such as these: Is each item of the specification document adequately and correctly addressed? For each interface, do the actual and formal arguments correspond? Have error-handling mechanisms been adequately identified? Is the design compatible with the hardware resources or does it require more hardware than actually is available? Is the design compatible with the software resources; for example, does the operating system stipulated in the analysis artifacts have the functionality required by the design?

An important component of the inspection procedure is the record of fault statistics. Faults must be recorded by severity (major or minor; an example of a major fault is one that causes premature termination or damages a database) and fault type. In the case of a design inspection, typical fault types include interface faults and logic faults. This information can be used in a number of useful ways:

- The number of faults in a given product can be compared with averages of faults detected at the same stage of development in comparable products, giving management an early warning that something is amiss and allowing timely corrective action to be taken.

- If inspecting two or three code artifacts results in the discovery of a disproportionate number of faults of a particular type, management can begin checking other code artifacts and take corrective action.

- If the inspection of a particular code artifact reveals far more faults than were found in any other code artifact in the product, there is usually a strong case for redesigning that artifact from scratch and implementing the new design.

• Information regarding the number and types of faults detected at an inspection of a design artifact aids the team performing the code inspection of the implementation of that artifact at a later stage.

The first experiment of Fagan [1976] was performed on a systems product. One hundred person-hours were devoted to inspections, at a rate of two 2-hour inspections per day by a four-person team. Of all the faults found during the development of the product, 67 percent were located by inspections before unit testing was started. Furthermore, during the first 7 months after the product was installed, 38 percent fewer faults were detected in the inspected product than in a comparable product reviewed using informal walkthroughs.

Fagan [1976] conducted another experiment on an applications product and found that 82 percent of all detected faults were discovered during design and code inspections. A useful side effect of the inspections was that programmer productivity rose because less time had to be spent on unit testing. Using an automated estimating model, Fagan determined that, as a result of the inspection process, the savings on programmer resources were 25 percent despite the time that had to be devoted to the inspections. In a different experiment Jones [1978] found that over 70 percent of detected faults could be detected by conducting design and code inspections.

Subsequent studies have produced equally impressive results. In a 6000-line business data processing application, 93 percent of all detected faults were found during inspections [Fagan, 1986]. As reported in [ Ackerman, Buchwald, and Lewski, 1989], the use of inspections rather than testing during the development of an operating system decreased the cost of detecting a fault by 85 percent; in a switching system product, the decrease was 90 percent [Fowler, 1986]. At the Jet Propulsion Laboratory (JPL), on average, each 2-hour inspection exposed 4 major faults and 14 minor faults [Bush, 1990]. Translated into dollar terms, this meant a savings of approximately $25,000 *per inspection*. Another JPL study [Kelly, Sherif, and Hops, 1992] showed that the number of faults detected decreased exponentially by classical phase. In other words, with the aid of inspections, faults can be detected early in the software process. The importance of this early detection is reflected in Figure 1.6.

One advantage that code inspections have over running test cases (execution-based testing) is that the testers need not deal with failures. It frequently happens that, when a product under test is executed, it fails. The fault that caused the failure must now be located and fixed before execution-based testing can continue. In contrast, a fault found in the code during non-execution-based testing is logged and the review continues.

A risk of the inspection process is that, like the walkthrough, it might be used for performance appraisal. The danger is particularly acute in the case of inspections because of the detailed fault information available. Fagan dismisses this fear by stating that, over a period of 3 years, he knew of no IBM manager who used such information against a programmer, or as he put it, no manager tried to "kill the goose that lays the golden eggs" [Fagan, 1976]. However, if inspections are not conducted properly, they may not be as wildly successful as they have been at IBM. Unless top management is aware of the potential problem, misuse of inspection information is a distinct possibility.

## 6.2.4 Comparison of Inspections and Walkthroughs

Superficially, the difference between an inspection and a walkthrough is that the inspection team uses a checklist of queries to aid it in finding the faults. But the difference goes deeper than that. A walkthrough is a two-step process: preparation followed by team analysis of the document. An inspection is a five-step process: overview, preparation, inspection, rework, and follow-up; and the procedure to be followed in each step is formalized. Examples of such formalization are the methodical categorization of faults and the use of that information in inspection of the documents of the succeeding workflows as well as in inspections of future products.

The inspection process takes much longer than a walkthrough. Is inspection worth the additional time and effort? The data of Section 6.2.3 clearly indicate that inspections are a powerful, cost-effective tool to detect faults.

### 6.2.5 Strengths and Weaknesses of Reviews

There are two major strengths of a **review** (walkthrough or inspection). First, a review is an effective way to detect a fault; second, faults are detected early in the software process, that is, before they become expensive to fix. For example, design faults are detected before implementation commences and coding faults are found before the artifact is integrated into the product.

However, the effectiveness of a review can be reduced if the software process is inadequate. First, large-scale software is extremely hard to review unless it consists of smaller, largely independent components. A strength of the object-oriented paradigm is that, if correctly carried out, the resulting product consists of largely independent pieces. Second, a design review team sometimes has to refer to the analysis artifacts; a code review team often needs access to the design documents. Unless the documentation of the previous workflows is complete, updated to reflect the current version of the project, and available online, the effectiveness of review teams is severely hampered.

### 6.2.6 Metrics for Inspections

To determine the effectiveness of inspections, a number of different metrics can be used. The first is the **inspection rate**. When specifications and designs are inspected, the number of pages inspected per hour can be measured; for code inspections, an appropriate metric is lines of code inspected per hour. A second metric is the **fault density**, measured in faults per page inspected or faults per 1000 lines of code (KLOC) inspected. This metric can be subdivided into major faults per unit of material and minor faults per unit of material. Another useful metric is the **fault detection rate**, that is, the number of major and minor faults detected per hour. A fourth metric is the **fault detection efficiency**, that is, the number of major and minor faults detected per person-hour.

Although the purpose of these metrics is to measure the effectiveness of the inspection process, the results instead may reflect deficiencies of the development team. For example, if the fault detection rate suddenly rises from 20 faults per thousand lines of code to 30, this does not necessarily mean that the inspection team has suddenly become 50 percent more efficient. Another explanation could be that the quality of code has decreased and there simply are more faults to be detected.

Having discussed non-execution-based testing, the next topic is execution-based testing.

## 6.3    Execution-Based Testing

It has been claimed that testing is a demonstration that faults ("bugs") are not present. Even though some organizations spend up to 50 percent of their software budget on testing, delivered "tested" software is notoriously unreliable.

The reason for this contradiction is simple. As Dijkstra put it, "Program testing can be a very effective way to show the presence of bugs, but it is hopelessly inadequate for showing their absence" [Dijkstra, 1972]. What Dijkstra is saying is that, if a product is executed with test data and the output is wrong, then the product definitely contains a fault. But, if the output is correct, then there still may be a fault in the product; the only information that can be deduced from that particular test is that the product runs correctly on that particular set of test data.

## 6.4   What Should Be Tested?

To be able to describe what properties should be tested, it is first necessary to give a precise description of execution-based testing. According to Goodenough [1979], **execution-based testing** is a process of inferring certain behavioral properties of a product based, in part, on the results of executing the product in a known environment with selected inputs. This definition has three troubling implications.

1. First, the definition states that testing is an inferential process. The tester takes the product, runs it with known input data, and examines the output. The tester has to infer what, if anything, is wrong with the product. From this viewpoint, testing is comparable to trying to find the proverbial black cat in a dark room, but without knowing whether or not a cat is in the room in the first place. The tester has few clues to help find any faults: perhaps 10 or 20 sets of inputs and corresponding outputs, possibly a user fault report, and thousands of lines of code. From this, the tester has to deduce if there is a fault and, if so, what it is.

2. A problem with the definition arises from the phrase *in a known environment*. We never really can know our environment, either the hardware or the software. We never can be certain that the operating system is functioning correctly or that the run-time routines are correct. An intermittent hardware fault may lie in the main memory of the computer. So what is observed as the behavior of the product in fact may be a correct product interacting with a faulty compiler or faulty hardware or some other faulty component of the environment.

3. Another worrisome part of the definition of execution-based testing is the phrase *with selected inputs*. In the case of a real-time system, frequently no control is possible over the inputs to the system. Consider avionics software. The flight control system has two types of inputs. The first type of input is what the pilot wants the aircraft to do. If the pilot pulls back on the joystick to climb or opens the throttle to increase the speed of the aircraft, these mechanical motions are transformed into digital signals sent to the flight control computer. The second type of input is the current physical state of the aircraft, such as its altitude, speed, and the elevation of the wing flaps. The flight control software uses the values of such quantities to compute what signals should be sent to the components of the aircraft, such as the wing flaps and the engines, to implement the pilot's directives. Whereas the pilot's inputs easily can be set to any desired values simply by setting the aircraft's controls appropriately, the inputs corresponding to the current physical state of the aircraft cannot be manipulated so easily. In fact, there is no way one can force the aircraft to provide "selected inputs."

How then can such a real-time system be tested? The answer is to use a simulator. A **simulator** is a working model of the environment in which the product, in this case the flight control software, executes. The flight control software can be tested by causing the simulator to send selected inputs to the flight control software. The simulator has controls that allow the operator to set an input variable to any selected value. If the purpose of the test is to determine how the flight control software performs if one engine catches fire, then the controls of the simulator are set so that the inputs sent to the flight control software are indistinguishable from the inputs that would be sent if an engine of the actual aircraft were on fire. The output is analyzed by examining the output signals sent from the flight control software to the simulator. But, at best, a simulator can be a good approximation of a faithful model of some aspect of the system; it never can be the system itself. Using a simulator means that, whereas there indeed is a "known environment," there is little likelihood that this known environment is in every way identical to the actual environment in which the product will be installed.

The preceding definition of *testing* speaks of "behavioral properties." What behavioral properties must be tested? An obvious answer is, Test whether the product functions correctly. But, as will be shown, correctness is neither necessary nor sufficient. Before discussing correctness, four other behavioral properties are considered: utility, reliability, robustness, and performance [Goodenough, 1979].

## 6.4.1  Utility

**Utility** is the extent to which a user's needs are met when a correct product is used under conditions permitted by its specifications. In other words, a product that is functioning correctly is now subjected to inputs that are valid in terms of the specifications. The user may test, for example, how easy the product is to use, whether the product performs useful functions, and whether the product is cost effective compared to competing products. Irrespective of whether the product is correct or not, these vital issues have to be tested. If the product is not cost effective, then there is no point in buying it. And unless the product is easy to use, it will not be used at all or it will be used incorrectly. Therefore, when considering buying an existing product (including shrink-wrapped software), the utility of the product should be tested first, and if the product fails on that score, testing should stop.

## 6.4.2  Reliability

Another aspect of a product that must be tested is its reliability. **Reliability** is a measure of the frequency and criticality of product failure; recall that a failure is an unacceptable effect or behavior, under permissible operating conditions, that occurs as a consequence of a fault. In other words, it is necessary to know how often the product fails (**mean time between failures**) and how bad the effects of that failure can be. When a product fails, an important issue is how long it takes, on average, to repair it (**mean time to repair**). But, often more important is how long it takes to repair the *results* of the failure. This last point frequently is overlooked. Suppose that the software running on a communications front end fails, on average, only once every 6 months; but when it fails, it completely wipes out a database. At best, the database can be reinitialized to its status when the last checkpoint dump was taken, and the audit trail can then be used to put the database into a state that is virtually up to date. But, if this recovery process takes the better part of 2 days, during which time the database and communications front end are inoperative, then the reliability of the product is low, notwithstanding that the mean time between failures is 6 months.

An embedded computer is an integral part of a larger system whose primary purpose is not computation. The function of embedded software is to control the device in which the computer is embedded. Military examples include a network of avionics computers on board a warplane or a computer built into an intercontinental ballistic missile. The embedded computer in the nose cone of a missile controls only that missile; it cannot be used, say, for printing the payroll checks for the soldiers on the missile base.

More familiar examples are the computer chip in a digital watch or a washing machine. Again, the chip in a washing machine is used exclusively to control the washing machine. There is no way that the owner of that washing machine could use the chip to balance a checkbook.

### 6.4.3 Robustness

Another aspect of every product that requires testing is its robustness. Although it is difficult to come up with a precise definition, **robustness** essentially is a function of a number of factors, such as the range of operating conditions, the possibility of unacceptable results with valid input, and the acceptability of effects when the product is given invalid input. A product with a wide range of permissible operating conditions is more robust than a more-restrictive product. A robust product should not yield unacceptable results when the input satisfies its specifications; for example, giving a valid command should not have disastrous consequences. A robust product should not crash when the product is *not* used under permissible operating conditions. To test for this aspect of robustness, test data that do not satisfy the input specifications are deliberately entered, and the tester determines how badly the product reacts. For example, when the product solicits a name, the tester may reply with a stream of unacceptable characters, such as control-A escape-% ?$#@. If the computer responds with a message such as Incorrect data—Try again or, better, informs the user as to why the data do not conform to what was expected, it is more robust than a product that crashes whenever the data deviate even slightly from what is required.

### 6.4.4 Performance

**Performance** is another aspect of the product that must be tested. For example, it is essential to know the extent to which the product meets its constraints with regard to response time or space requirements. For an embedded computer system such as an onboard computer in a handheld antiaircraft missile, the space constraints of the system may be such that only 128 megabytes (MB) of main memory are available for the software. No matter how excellent the software may be, if it needs 256 MB of main memory, then it cannot be used at all. (For more information on embedded software, see Just in Case You Wanted to Know Box 6.2.)

Real-time software is characterized by hard time constraints, that is, time constraints of such a nature that, if a constraint is not met, information is lost. For example, a nuclear reactor control system may have to sample the temperature of the core and process the data every 10th of a second. If the system is not fast enough to handle interrupts from the temperature sensor every 10th of a second, then data are lost, and there is no way of ever recovering the data; the next time the system receives temperature data, it will be the current temperature, not the reading that was missed. If the reactor is on the point of a meltdown, then it is critical that all relevant information be both received and processed as laid down in the specifications. With all real-time systems, the performance must meet every time constraint listed in the specifications.

## 6.4.5 Correctness

Finally, a definition of **correctness** can be given. A product is correct if it satisfies its output specifications, independent of its use of computing resources, when operated under permitted conditions [ [Goodenough, 1979]. In other words, if input that satisfies the input specifications is provided and the product is given all the resources it needs, then the product is correct if the output satisfies the output specifications.

This definition of *correctness*, like the definition of *testing* itself, has worrisome implications. Suppose a product has been tested successfully against a broad variety of test data. Does this mean that the product is acceptable? Unfortunately, it does not. If a product is correct, all that means is that it satisfies its specifications. But what if the specifications themselves are incorrect? To illustrate this difficulty, consider the specification shown in Figure 6.1. The specifications state that the input to the sort is an array p of n integers, whereas the output is another array q sorted in nondecreasing order. Superficially, the specifications seem perfectly correct. But consider method trickSort shown in Figure 6.2. In that method, all n elements of array q are set to 0. The method satisfies the specifications of Figure 6.1 and is therefore correct.

What happened? Unfortunately, the specifications of Figure 6.1 are wrong. What has been omitted is a statement that the elements of q, the output array, are a permutation (rearrangement) of the elements of the input array p. An intrinsic aspect of sorting is that it is a rearrangement process. And the method of Figure 6.2 capitalizes on this specification fault. In other words, the method trickSort is correct, but the specifications of Figure 6.1 are wrong. Corrected specifications appear in Figure 6.3. From this example, it is clear that the consequences of specification faults are nontrivial. After all, the correctness of a product is meaningless if its specifications are incorrect.

The fact that a product is correct is not *sufficient*, because the specifications in terms of which it was shown to be correct may be wrong. But is it *necessary*? Consider the following example. A software organization has acquired a superb new C++ compiler. The new

**FIGURE 6.1**
Incorrect specifications for a sort.

| Input specification: | p : array of n integers, n > 0. |
|---|---|
| Output specification: | q : array of n integers such that $q[0] \leq q[1] \leq \cdots \leq q[n - 1]$ |

**FIGURE 6.2**
Method trickSort, which satisfies the specifications of Figure 6.1.

```
void trickSort (int p[ ], int q[ ])
{
    int i;
    for (i = 0; i < n; i++)
        q[i] = 0;
}
```

**FIGURE 6.3**
Corrected
specifications
for the sort.

| | |
|---|---|
| *Input specification:* | p : array of n integers, n > 0. |
| *Output specification:* | q : array of n integers such that<br>$q[0] \leq q[1] \leq \cdots \leq q[n-1]$ |
| | The elements of array q are a permutation of the elements of array p, which are unchanged. |

compiler can translate twice as many lines of source code per second as the old compiler, the object code runs nearly 45 percent faster, and the size of the object code is about 20 percent smaller. In addition, the error messages are much clearer and the cost of postdelivery maintenance and updates is less than half of that of the old compiler. There is one problem, however; the first time that a **for** statement appears in any class, the compiler prints a spurious error message. The compiler therefore is not correct, because the specifications for a compiler implicitly or explicitly require that error messages be printed if, and only if, there is a fault in the source code. It is certainly possible to use the compiler—in fact, in every way but one the compiler is absolutely ideal. Furthermore, it is reasonable to expect that this minor fault will be corrected in the next release. In the meantime, the programmers learn to ignore the spurious error message. Not only can the organization live with the incorrect compiler, but if anyone were to suggest replacing it by the old correct compiler, there would be an outcry. Therefore, the correctness of a product is neither necessary nor sufficient.

Both preceding examples admittedly are somewhat artificial. But they do make the point that correctness simply means that the product is a correct implementation of its specifications. In other words, there is more to testing than just showing that the product is correct.

With all the difficulties associated with execution-based testing, computer scientists have tried to come up with other ways of ensuring that a product does what it is supposed to do. One such non-execution-based alternative that has received considerable attention for more than 40 years is correctness proving.

## 6.5 Testing versus Correctness Proofs

A **correctness proof** is a mathematical technique for showing that a product is correct, in other words, that it satisfies its specifications. The technique is sometimes termed *verification*. However, as previously pointed out, the term has another meaning within the testing context. In addition, *verification* is also often used to denote all non-execution-based techniques, not only correctness proving. For clarity, this mathematical procedure will be termed *correctness proving*, to remind the reader that it is a mathematical proof process.

### 6.5.1 Example of a Correctness Proof

To see how correctness is proven, consider the code fragment shown in Figure 6.4. The flowchart equivalent to the code is given in Figure 6.5. We now show that the code fragment is correct—after the code has been executed, the variable s will contain the sum of the n

**FIGURE 6.4**
A code
fragment to be
proven correct.

```
int k, s;
int y[n];
k = 0;
s = 0;
while (k < n)
{
    s = s + y[k];
    k = k + 1;
}
```

**FIGURE 6.5**
The flowchart of
Figure 6.4.

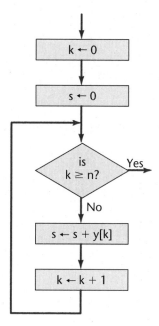

elements of the array y. In Figure 6.6, an *assertion* is placed before and after each state-ment, at the places labeled with the letters *A* through *H*; that is, a claim has been made at each place that a certain mathematical property holds there. The correctness of each asser-tion is now proven.

The input specification, the condition that holds at *A* before the code is executed, is that the variable n is a positive integer; that is,

$$A: \quad n \in \{1, 2, 3, \ldots\} \tag{6.1}$$

An obvious output specification is that, if control reaches point *H*, the value of s contains the sum of the n values stored in array y, that is,

$$H: \quad s = y[0] + y[1] + \cdots + y[n-1] \tag{6.2}$$

In fact, the code fragment can be proven correct with respect to a stronger output specification:

$$H: \quad k = n \text{ and } s = y[0] + y[1] + \cdots + y[n-1] \tag{6.3}$$

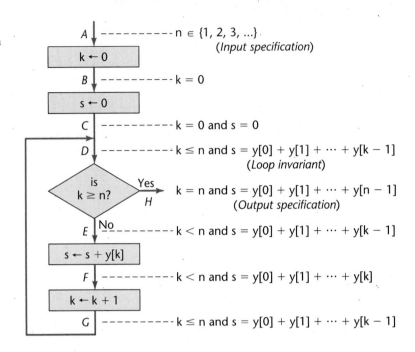

A     $n \in \{1, 2, 3, \ldots\}$
            *(Input specification)*

$k \leftarrow 0$

B     $k = 0$

$s \leftarrow 0$

C     $k = 0$ and $s = 0$

D     $k \leq n$ and $s = y[0] + y[1] + \cdots + y[k-1]$
             *(Loop invariant)*

is $k \geq n?$    Yes   $k = n$ and $s = y[0] + y[1] + \cdots + y[n-1]$
H             *(Output specification)*

E   No    $k < n$ and $s = y[0] + y[1] + \cdots + y[k-1]$

$s \leftarrow s + y[k]$

F     $k < n$ and $s = y[0] + y[1] + \cdots + y[k]$

$k \leftarrow k + 1$

G     $k \leq n$ and $s = y[0] + y[1] + \cdots + y[k-1]$

A natural reaction to the last sentence is to ask, From where did output specification (6.3) come? By the end of the proof, we hope you have the answer to that question; also see Problems 6.10 and 6.11.

In addition to the input and output specifications, a third aspect of the proof process is to provide an invariant for the loop. That is, a mathematical expression must be provided that holds at point *D* irrespective of whether the loop has been executed 0, 1, or many times. The **loop invariant** that will be proven to hold is

$$D: \quad k \leq n \text{ and } s = y[0] + y[1] + \cdots + y[k-1] \qquad \textbf{(6.4)}$$

Now it will be shown that if input specification (6.1) holds at point *A*, then output specification (6.3) will hold at point *H*; that is, the code fragment will be proven to be correct.

First, the assignment statement $k \leftarrow 0$ is executed. Control now is at point *B*, where the following assertion holds:

$$B: \quad k = 0 \qquad \textbf{(6.5)}$$

To be more precise, at point *B*, the assertion should read $k = 0$ and $n \in \{1, 2, 3, \ldots\}$. However, the input specification (6.1) holds at all points in the flowchart. For brevity, the and $n \in \{1, 2, 3, \ldots\}$ therefore is omitted from now on.

At point *C*, as a consequence of the second assignment statement, $s \leftarrow 0$, the following assertion is true:

$$C: \quad k = 0 \text{ and } s = 0 \qquad \textbf{(6.6)}$$

Now the loop is entered. It will be proven by induction that the loop invariant (6.4) indeed is correct. Just before the loop is executed for the first time, assertion (6.6) holds;

that is, $k = 0$ and $s = 0$. Now consider loop invariant (6.4). Because $k = 0$ by assertion (6.6) and $n \geq 1$ from input specification (6.1), it follows that $k \leq n$ as required. Furthermore, because $k = 0$, it follows that $k - 1 = -1$, so the sum in (6.4) is empty and $s = 0$ as required. Loop invariant (6.4) therefore is true just before the first time the loop is entered.

Next, the inductive hypothesis step is performed. Assume that, at some stage during the execution of the code fragment, the loop invariant holds. That is, for $k$ equal to some value $k_0$, $0 \leq k_0 \leq n$, execution is at point $D$, and the assertion that holds is

$$D: \quad k_0 \leq n \text{ and } s = y[0] + y[1] + \cdots + y[k_0 - 1] \quad \textbf{(6.7)}$$

Control now passes to the test box. If $k_0 \geq n$, then because $k_0 \leq n$ by hypothesis, it follows that $k_0 = n$. By inductive hypothesis (6.7), this implies that

$$H: \quad k_0 = n \text{ and } s = y[0] + y[1] + \cdots + y[n - 1] \quad \textbf{(6.8)}$$

which is precisely the output specification (6.3).

On the other hand, if the test is $k_0 \geq n$? fails, then control passes from point $D$ to point $E$. Because $k_0$ is not greater than or equal to $n$, $k_0 < n$ and (6.7) becomes

$$E: \quad k_0 < n \text{ and } s = y[0] + y[1] + \cdots + y[k_0 - 1] \quad \textbf{(6.9)}$$

The statement $s \leftarrow s + y[k_0]$ now is executed, so from assertion (6.9), at point $F$, the following assertion must hold:

$$F: \quad k_0 < n \text{ and } s = y[0] + y[1] + \cdots + y[k_0 - 1] + y[k_0]$$

$$= y[0] + y[1] + \cdots + y[k_0] \quad \textbf{(6.10)}$$

The next statement to be executed is $k_0 \leftarrow k_0 + 1$. To see the effect of this statement, suppose that the value of $k_0$ before executing this statement is 17. Then the last term in the sum in (6.10) is $y[17]$. Now the value of $k_0$ is increased by 1 to 18. The sum $s$ is unchanged, so the last term in the sum still is $y[17]$, which is now $y[k_0 - 1]$. Also, at point $F$, $k_0 < n$. Increasing the value of $k_0$ by 1 means that if the inequality is to hold at point $G$, then $k_0 \leq n$. Therefore, the effect of increasing $k_0$ by 1 is that the following assertion holds at point $G$:

$$G: \quad k_0 \leq n \text{ and } s = y[0] + y[1] + \cdots + y[k_0 - 1] \quad \textbf{(6.11)}$$

Assertion (6.11) that holds at point $G$ is identical to assertion (6.7) that, by assumption, holds at point $D$. But point $D$ is topologically identical to point $G$. In other words, if (6.7) holds at $D$ for $k = k_0$, then it again will hold at $D$ with $k = k_0 + 1$. It has been shown that the loop invariant holds for $k = 0$. By induction, it follows that loop invariant (6.4) holds for all values of $k$, $0 \leq k \leq n$.

All that remains is to prove that the loop terminates. Initially, by assertion (6.6), the value of $k$ is equal to 0. Each iteration of the loop increases the value of $k$ by 1 when the statement $k \leftarrow k + 1$ is executed. Eventually, $k$ must reach the value $n$, at which time the loop is exited and the value of $s$ is given by assertion (6.8), thereby satisfying output specification (6.3).

To review, given the input specification (6.1), it was proven that loop invariant (6.4) holds whether the loop has been executed 0, 1, or more times. Furthermore, it was proven that after $n$ iterations the loop terminates; and when it does, the values of $k$ and $s$ satisfy the output specification (6.3). In other words, the code fragment of Figure 6.4 has been mathematically proven to be correct.

*Mini Case Study*

### 6.5.2 Correctness Proof Mini Case Study

An important aspect of correctness proofs is that they should be done in conjunction with design and coding. As Dijkstra put it, "The programmer should let the program proof and program grow hand in hand" [Dijkstra, 1972]. For example, when a loop is incorporated into the design, a loop invariant is put forward; and as the design is refined stepwise, so is the invariant. Developing a product in this way gives the programmer confidence that the product is correct and tends to reduce the number of faults. Quoting Dijkstra again, "The only effective way to raise the confidence level of a program significantly is to give a convincing proof of its correctness" [Dijkstra, 1972]. But even if a product is proven to be correct, it must be thoroughly tested as well. To illustrate the necessity for testing in conjunction with correctness proving, consider the following.

In 1969, Naur reported on a technique for constructing and proving a product correct [Naur, 1969]. The technique was illustrated by what Naur termed a *line-editing problem;* today this would be considered a text-processing problem. It may be stated as follows:

> Given a text consisting of words separated by blank characters or by newline (new line) characters, convert it to line-by-line form in accordance with the following rules:
>
> 1. Line breaks must be made only where the given text contains a blank or newline;
> 2. Each line is filled as far as possible, as long as
> 3. No line will contain more than maxpos characters

Naur constructed a procedure using his technique and informally proved its correctness. The procedure consisted of approximately 25 lines of code. The paper then was reviewed by Leavenworth in *Computing Reviews* [Leavenworth, 1970]. The reviewer pointed out that, in the output of Naur's procedure, the first word of the first line is preceded by a blank unless the first word is exactly maxpos characters long. Although this may seem a trivial fault, it is a fault that surely would have been detected had the procedure been tested, that is, executed with test data rather than only proven correct. But worse was to come. London [1971] detected three additional faults in Naur's procedure. One is that the procedure does not terminate unless a word longer than maxpos characters is encountered. Again, this fault is likely to have been detected if the procedure had been tested. London then presented a corrected version of the procedure and proved formally that the resulting procedure was correct; recall that Naur had used only informal proof techniques.

The next episode in this saga is that Goodenough and Gerhart [1975] found three faults that London had not detected, despite his formal "proof." These included the fact that the last word is not output unless it is followed by a blank or newline. Yet again, a reasonable choice of test data would have detected this fault without much difficulty. In fact, of the total of seven faults collectively detected by Leavenworth, London, and Goodenough and Gerhart, four could have been detected simply by running the procedure on test data, such as the illustrations given in Naur's original paper. The lesson from this saga is clear. Even if a product has been proven correct, it still must be tested thoroughly.

The example in Section 6.5.1 showed that proving the correctness of even a small code fragment can be a lengthy process. Furthermore, the mini case study of this section showed that it is a difficult, error-prone process, even for a 25-line procedure. The following issue therefore must be put forward: Is correctness proving just an interesting research idea or is it a powerful software engineering technique whose time has come? This is answered in Section 6.5.3.

## 6.5.3  Correctness Proofs and Software Engineering

A number of software engineering practitioners have put forward reasons why correctness proving should not be viewed as a standard software engineering technique. First, it is claimed that software engineers lack adequate mathematical training. Second, it is suggested that proving is too expensive to be practical; and third, proving is too hard. Each of these reasons will be shown to be an oversimplification:

1. Although the proof given in Section 6.5.1 can be understood with hardly more than high school algebra, nontrivial proofs require that input specifications, output specifications, and loop invariants be expressed in first- or second-order predicate calculus or its equivalent. Not only does this make the proof process simpler for a mathematician, it allows correctness proving to be done by a computer. To complicate matters further, predicate calculus now is somewhat outdated. To prove the correctness of concurrent products, techniques using temporal or other modal logics are required [Manna and Pnueli, 1992]. There is no doubt that correctness proving requires training in mathematical logic. Fortunately, most computer science majors today either take courses in the requisite material or have the background to learn correctness-proving techniques on the job. Therefore, colleges now are turning out computer science graduates with sufficient mathematical skills for correctness proving. The claim that practicing software engineers lack the necessary mathematical training may have been true in the past, but it no longer applies in the light of the thousands of computer science majors joining the industry each year.

2. The claim that proving is too expensive for use in software development also is false. On the contrary, the economic viability of correctness proving can be determined on a project-by-project basis using cost–benefit analysis (Section 5.2). For example, consider the software for the international space station. Human lives are at stake, and if something goes wrong, a space shuttle rescue mission may not arrive in time. The cost of proving life-critical space station software correct is large. But the potential cost of a software fault that might be overlooked if correctness proving is not performed is even larger.

3. Despite the claim that correctness proving is too hard, many nontrivial products successfully have been proven correct, including operating system kernels, compilers, and communications systems [Landwehr, 1983; Berry and Wing, 1985]. Furthermore, many tools such as theorem provers assist in correctness proving. A theorem prover takes as input a product, its input and output specifications, and loop invariants. The theorem prover then attempts to prove mathematically that the product, when given input data satisfying the input specifications, produces output data satisfying the output specifications.

**FIGURE 6.7**
"Theorem
prover."

```
void theoremProver ( )
{
    print "This product is correct";
}
```

At the same time, there are some difficulties with correctness proving:

- For example, how can we be sure that a theorem prover is correct? If the theorem prover prints out This product is correct, can we believe it? To take an extreme case, consider the so-called theorem prover shown in Figure 6.7. No matter what code is submitted to this theorem prover, it will print out This product is correct. In other words, what reliability can be placed on the output of a theorem prover? One suggestion is to submit a theorem prover to itself and see whether it is correct. Apart from the philosophical implications, a simple way of seeing that this will not work is to consider what would happen if the theorem prover of Figure 6.7 were submitted to itself for proving. As always, it would print out This product is correct, thereby "proving" its own correctness.

- A further difficulty is finding the input and output specifications, and especially the loop invariants or their equivalents in other logics such as modal logic. Suppose a product is correct. Unless a suitable invariant for each loop can be found, there is no way of proving the product correct. Yes, tools do exist to assist in this task. But even with state-of-the-art tools, a software engineer simply may not be able to come up with a correctness proof. One solution to this problem is to develop the product and proof in parallel, as advocated in Section 6.5.2. When a loop is designed, an invariant for that loop is specified at the same time. With this approach, it is somewhat easier to prove that a code artifact is correct.

- Worse than not being able to find loop invariants, what if the specifications themselves are incorrect? An example of this is method trickSort (Figure 6.2). A good theorem prover, when given the incorrect specifications of Figure 6.1, undoubtedly will declare that the method shown in Figure 6.2 is correct.

Manna and Waldinger [1978] stated that, "We can never be sure that the specifications are correct" and "We can never be certain that a verification system is correct." These statements from two leading experts in the field encapsulate the various points made previously.

Does all this mean that there is no place for correctness proofs in software engineering? Quite the contrary. Proving products correct is an important, and sometimes vital, software engineering tool. Proofs are appropriate where human lives are at stake or where otherwise indicated by cost–benefit analysis. If the cost of proving software correct is less than the probable cost if the product fails, then the product should be proven. However, as the text-processing mini case study shows, proving alone is not enough. Instead, correctness proving should be viewed as an important component of the set of techniques that must be utilized together to check that a product is correct. Because the aim of software engineering is the production of quality software, correctness proving is indeed an important software engineering technique.

Even when a full formal proof is not justified, the quality of software can be markedly improved through the use of informal proofs. For example, a proof similar to that of

One feature of languages such as Java (but not C or C++) is bounds checking. An example of bounds checking is examining every array index during execution to ensure that it is within its declared range.

Hoare suggested that using bounds checking while developing a product but turning it off once the product is working correctly can be likened to learning to sail on dry land wearing a life jacket and then taking the life jacket off when actually at sea. In his Turing Award lecture, Hoare [1981] described a compiler he developed in 1961. When users later were offered the opportunity to turn off bounds checking after the final version of the compiler had been installed, they unanimously refused, because they had experienced so many incidents of values out of range during test runs of earlier versions of the compiler.

Bounds checking can be viewed as a special case of a more general concept, assertion checking. Hoare's life jacket analogy is equally applicable to turning off assertion checking once the final version has been installed.

Hoare's remarks were sadly prophetic. Today, a major technique used by hackers to penetrate computers is to send a long stream of data to an operating system to deliberately cause a buffer to overflow and overwrite a portion of the operating system with malicious executable code. This technique can work only if the programmers omitted to include bounds checking in the code for reading data into the buffer of an operating system written in C or C++, or turned off bounds checking.

Section 6.5.1 assists in checking that a loop is executed the correct number of times. A second way of improving software quality is to insert assertions such as those of Figure 6.6 into the code. Then, if at execution time an assertion does not hold, the product is halted and the software team can investigate whether the assertion that terminated execution is incorrect or whether indeed a fault in the code was detected by triggering the assertion. Languages such as Java (from version 1.4 onward) support assertions directly by means of an **assert** statement. Suppose that an informal proof requires that the value of variable xxx be positive at a particular point in the code. Even though the members of the design team may be convinced that there is no way for xxx to be negative, for additional reliability they may specify that the statement

$$\textbf{assert } (\text{xxx} > 0)$$

must appear at that point in the code. If xxx is less than or equal to 0, execution terminates, and the situation can be investigated by the software team. Unfortunately, *Assert* in C++ is a debugging statement, similar to *assert* in C; it is not part of the language itself. Ada 95 supports assertions via a **pragma**.

Once the users are confident that the product works correctly, they have the option of switching off assertion checking. This speeds up execution, but any fault that would have been detected by an assertion may not be found if assertion checking is switched off. Therefore, there is a trade-off between run-time efficiency and continuing assertion checking even after the product has been installed on the client's computer. (Just in Case You Wanted to Know Box 6.3 gives an interesting insight on this issue.)

A fundamental issue in execution-based testing is which members of the software development team should be responsible for carrying it out.

## 6.6 Who Should Perform Execution-Based Testing?

Suppose a programmer is asked to test a code artifact he or she has written. Testing has been described by Myers [1979] as the process of executing a product with the intention of finding faults. Testing therefore is a destructive process. On the other hand, the programmer doing the testing ordinarily does not wish to destroy his or her work. If the fundamental attitude of the programmer toward the code is the usual protective one, then the chances of that programmer using test data that will highlight faults is considerably lower than if the major motivation were truly destructive. A successful test finds faults. This, too, poses a difficulty. It means that, if the code artifact passes the test, then the test has failed. Conversely, if the code artifact does not perform according to specifications, then the test succeeds. A programmer who is asked to test a code artifact he or she has written is being asked to execute the code artifact in such a way that a failure (incorrect behavior) ensues. This goes against the creative instincts of programmers.

An inescapable conclusion is that programmers should not test their own code artifacts. After a programmer has been *con*structive and built a code artifact, testing that code artifact requires the creator to perform a *de*structive act and attempt to destroy that creation. A second reason why execution-based testing should be done by someone else is that the programmer may have misunderstood some aspect of the design or specifications. If testing is done by someone else, such faults may be discovered. Nevertheless, debugging (finding the cause of the failure and correcting the fault) is best done by the original programmer, the person most familiar with the code.

The statement that a programmer should not test his or her own code must not be taken too far. Consider the programming process. The programmer begins by reading the detailed design of the code artifact; this may be in the form of a flowchart or, more likely, pseudocode. But, whatever technique is used, the programmer must certainly **desk check** the code artifact before entering it into the computer. That is, the programmer must try out the flowchart or pseudocode with various test cases, tracing through the detailed design to check that each test case is executed correctly. Only when the programmer is satisfied that the detailed design is correct should the text editor be invoked to code the artifact.

Once the code artifact is in machine-readable form, it undergoes a series of tests. Test data are used to determine that the code artifact works successfully, probably the same test data used to desk check the detailed design. Next, if the code artifact executes correctly when correct test data are used, then the programmer tries out incorrect data to test the robustness of the code artifact. When the programmer is satisfied that the code artifact operates correctly, systematic testing commences. This **systematic testing** should not be performed by the programmer.

If the programmer is not to perform this systematic testing, who is to do it? As stated in Section 6.1.2, independent testing must be performed by the SQA group. The key word here is *independent*. Only if the SQA group truly is independent of the development team can its members fulfill their mission of ensuring that the product indeed satisfies its specifications, without software development managers applying pressures such as product deadlines that might hamper their work. SQA personnel must report to their own manager and thus protect their independence.

How is systematic testing performed? An essential part of a test case is a statement of the expected output before the test is executed. It is a complete waste of time for the tester to sit at a terminal, execute the code artifact, enter haphazard test data, and then peer at the screen and say, "I guess that looks right." Equally futile is for the tester to plan test cases with great care and execute each test case in turn, look at the output, and say, "Yes, that certainly looks right." It is far too easy to be fooled by plausible results. If programmers are allowed to test their own code, then there always is the danger that the programmer will see what he or she wants to see. The same danger can occur even when the testing is done by someone else. The solution is for management to insist that, before a test is performed, both the test data and the expected results of that test be recorded. After the test has been performed, the actual results should be recorded and compared with the expected results.

Even in small organizations and with small products, it is important that this recording be done in machine-readable form, because test cases should never be thrown away. The reason for this is postdelivery maintenance. While the product is being maintained, **regression testing** must be performed. Stored test cases that the product has previously executed correctly must be rerun to ensure that the modifications made to add new functionality to the product have not destroyed the product's existing functionality. This is discussed further in Chapter 15.

## 6.7   When Testing Stops

After a product has been successfully maintained for many years, it eventually may lose its usefulness and be superseded by a totally different product, in much the same way that electronic valves were replaced by transistors. Alternatively, a product still may be useful, but the cost of porting it to new hardware or running it under a new operating system may be more than the cost of constructing a new product, using the old one as a prototype. So, finally, the software product is decommissioned and removed from service. Only at that point, when the software has been irrevocably discarded, is it time to stop testing.

Now that all the necessary background material has been covered, objects can be examined in greater detail. This is the subject of Chapter 7.

**Chapter Review**

A key theme of this chapter is that testing must be carried out in parallel with all activities of the software process. The chapter begins with a description of quality issues (Section 6.1). Next, non-execution-based testing is described (Section 6.2), with a careful discussion of walkthroughs and inspections. This is followed by a definition of execution-based testing (Sections 6.3 and 6.4) and a discussion of behavioral properties of a product that must be tested, including utility, reliability, robustness, performance, and correctness (Sections 6.4.1 through 6.4.5). In Section 6.5, correctness proving is introduced and an example of such a proof is given in Section 6.5.1. The role of correctness proofs in software engineering then is analyzed (Sections 6.5.2 and 6.5.3). Another important issue is that systematic execution-based testing must be performed by the independent SQA group and not by the programmer (Section 6.6). Finally, the issue of when testing can finally stop is discussed in Section 6.7.

**For Further Reading**

The attitude of software producers to the testing process has changed over the years, from viewing testing as a means of showing that a product runs correctly to the modern attitude that testing should be used to prevent requirements, analysis, design, and implementation faults. This progression is described in [Gelperin and Hetzel, 1988]. The nature of software testing and the reasons why it is so hard are discussed in [Whittaker, 2000]. The pervasiveness of faults is described in [Lieberman and Fry, 2001]. Ways to reduce the number of faults appear in [Boehm and Basili, 2001].

Myths regarding software quality are discussed in [Voas, 1999]. Whittaker and Voas [2000] present an interesting theory of reliability.

[Baber, 1987] is a good introduction to proving programs correct. A standard technique of correctness proving uses the so-called Hoare logic, as described in [Hoare, 1969]. An alternative approach to ensuring that products satisfy their specifications is to construct the product stepwise, checking that each step preserves correctness. This is described in [Dijkstra, 1968] and [Wirth, 1971]. An important article regarding acceptance of correctness proofs by the software engineering community is [DeMillo, Lipton, and Perlis, 1979].

The IEEE *Standard for Software Reviews* [IEEE 1028, 1997] is an excellent source of information on non-execution-based testing. Experiments evaluating inspections of a large-scale software product are described in [Perry et al., 2002]. Vitharana and Ramamurthy [2003] suggest that inspections should be anonymous and computer mediated. The impact of group process support on inspections is presented in [Tyran and George, 2002]. The selection of inspection team members is discussed in [Miller and Yin, 2004]. A review of inspections is given in [Parnas and Lawford, 2003], and the state of the practice is described in [Ciolkowski, Laitenberger, and Biffl, 2003]. Object-oriented code inspections are discussed in [Dunsmore, Roper, and Wood, 2003].

The classic work on execution-based testing is [Myers, 1979], a work that has had a significant impact on the field of testing. [DeMillo, Lipton, and Sayward, 1978] remains an excellent source of information on selection of test data. [Beizer, 1990] is a compendium on testing, a true handbook on the subject. A similar work is [Hetzel, 1988].

Turning specifically to the object-oriented paradigm, [Kung, Hsia, and Gao, 1998] is a book on object-oriented testing, and so is [Sykes and McGregor, 2000].

The proceedings of the International Symposium on Software Testing and Analysis cover a similar broad spectrum of testing issues. The February 2002 issue of *IEEE Transactions on Software Engineering* contains a variety of papers from the 2000 Symposium; [Elbaum, Malishevsky, and Rothermel, 2002] is of particular interest.

**Key Terms**

correctness *161*
correctness proof *162*
defect *150*
desk check *170*
error *150*
execution-based testing *158*
failure *150*
fault *150*
fault density *157*
fault detection efficiency *157*
fault detection rate *157*
follow-up *155*
inspection *154*
inspection rate *157*
loop invariant *164*

managerial independence *151*
mean time between failures *159*
mean time to repair *159*
mistake *150*
moderator *155*
non-execution-based
   testing *152*
overview *154*
performance *160*
preparation *154*
quality *151*
reader *155*
recorder *155*
regression testing *171*
reliability *159*

review *157*
rework *155*
robustness *160*
simulator *159*
software quality
   assurance (SQA) *151*
systematic testing *170*
test workflow *150*
testing *150*
utility *159*
V & V *150*
validation *150*
verification *150*

**Problems**

6.1 How are the terms *correctness proving, verification,* and *validation* used in this book?

6.2 A software development organization currently employs 96 software professionals, including 19 managers, all of whom develop as well as test software. The latest figures show that 27 percent of their time is spent on testing activities. The average annual cost to the company of a manager is $144,000, whereas nonmanagerial professionals cost $107,000 a year on average; both figures include overhead. Use cost–benefit analysis to determine whether a separate SQA group should be set up within the organization.

6.3 Repeat the cost–benefit analysis of Problem 6.2 for a firm with only seven software professionals, including two managers. Assume that the other figures remain unchanged.

6.4 You have been testing a code artifact for 11 days and found two faults. What does this tell you about the existence of other faults?

6.5 What are the similarities between a walkthrough and an inspection? What are the differences?

6.6 You are a member of the SQA group at Ye Olde Fashioned Software. You suggest to your manager that inspections be introduced. He responds that he sees no reason why four people should waste their time looking for faults when one person can run test cases on the same piece of code. How do you respond?

6.7 You are the SQA manager at Hardy Hardware, a regional chain of 754 hardware stores. Your organization is considering buying a stock-control package for use throughout the organization. Before authorizing the purchase of the package, you decide to test it thoroughly. What properties of the package do you investigate?

6.8 All 754 stores in the Hardy Hardware organization are now to be connected by a communications network. A sales representative is offering you a 4-week free trial to experiment with the communications package he is trying to sell you. What sort of software tests would you perform and why?

6.9 You are a rear admiral in the Valerian Navy in charge of developing the software for controlling the ship-to-ship missile of Problem 1.4. The software has been delivered to you for acceptance testing. What properties of the software do you test?

6.10 What happens to the correctness proof of Section 6.5.1 if loop invariant

$$s = y[0] + y[1] + \cdots + y[k - 1]$$

is used instead of (6.4)?

6.11 Assume that you have some experience with loop invariants and know that invariant (6.4) is the correct invariant for the loop of Figure 6.6. Show that output specification (6.3) is a natural consequence of the loop invariant.

6.12 Consider the following code fragment:

```
k = 0;
g = 1;
while (k < n)
{
    k = k + 1;
    g = g * k;
}
```

Prove that this code fragment correctly computes $g = n!$ if n is a positive integer.

6.13 Can correctness proving solve the problem that the product as delivered to the client may not be what the client really needs? Give reasons for your answer.

6.14 How should Dijkstra's statement (Section 6.3) be changed to apply to correctness proofs rather than testing? Bear in mind the mini case study of Section 6.5.2.

6.15 Design and implement a solution to the Naur text-processing problem (Section 6.5.2) using the language specified by your instructor. Execute it against test data and record the number of faults you find and the cause of each fault (e.g., logic fault, loop counter fault). Do not correct any of the faults you detect. Now exchange products with a fellow student and see how many faults each of you finds in the other's product and whether or not they are new faults. Again record the cause of each fault and compare the fault types found by each of you. Tabulate the results for the class as a whole.

6.16 Why is there a need to distinguish between a fault, a failure, and an error? Surely the use of the umbrella term *defect* simplifies matters?

6.17 (Term Project) Explain how you would test the utility, reliability, robustness, performance, and correctness of the Osric's Office Appliances and Decor product in Appendix A.

6.18 (Readings in Software Engineering) Your instructor will distribute copies of [Miller and Yin, 2004]. Would you use a cognitively based inspection team selection mechanism? Justify your answer.

## References

[Ackerman, Buchwald, and Lewski, 1989] A. F. ACKERMAN, L. S. BUCHWALD, AND F. H. LEWSKI, "Software Inspections: An Effective Verification Process," *IEEE Software* **6** (May 1989), pp. 31–36.

[Baber, 1987] R. L. BABER, *The Spine of Software: Designing Provably Correct Software: Theory and Practice,* John Wiley and Sons, New York, 1987.

[Beizer, 1990] B. BEIZER, *Software Testing Techniques,* 2nd ed., Van Nostrand Reinhold, New York, 1990.

[Berry and Wing, 1985] D. M. BERRY AND J. M. WING, "Specifying and Prototyping: Some Thoughts on Why They Are Successful," in: *Formal Methods and Software Development, Proceedings of the International Joint Conference on Theory and Practice of Software Development,* Vol. 2, Springer-Verlag, Berlin, 1985, pp. 117–28.

[Boehm and Basili, 2001] B. BOEHM AND V. R. BASILI, "Software Defect Reduction Top Ten List," *IEEE Computer* **34** (January 2001), pp. 135–37.

[Bush, 1990] M. BUSH, "Improving Software Quality: The Use of Formal Inspections at the Jet Propulsion Laboratory," *Proceedings of the 12th International Conference on Software Engineering,* Nice, France, March 1990, pp. 196–99.

[Ciolkowski, Laitenberger, and Biffl, 2003] M. CIOLKOWSKI, O. LAITENBERGER, S. BIFFL, "Software Reviews, the State of the Practice," *IEEE Software* **20** (November/December 2003), pp. 46–51.

[DeMillo, Lipton, and Perlis, 1979] R. A. DEMILLO, R. J. LIPTON, AND A. J. PERLIS, "Social Processes and Proofs of Theorems and Programs," *Communications of the ACM* **22** (May 1979), pp. 271–80.

[DeMillo, Lipton, and Sayward, 1978] R. A. DEMILLO, R. J. LIPTON, AND F. G. SAYWARD, "Hints on Test Data Selection: Help for the Practicing Programmer," *IEEE Computer* **11** (April 1978), pp. 34–43.

[Dijkstra, 1968] E. W. DIJKSTRA, "A Constructive Approach to the Problem of Program Correctness," *BIT* **8** (No. 3, 1968), pp. 174–86.

[Dijkstra, 1972] E. W. DIJKSTRA, "The Humble Programmer," *Communications of the ACM* **15** (October 1972), pp. 859–66.

[Dunsmore, Roper, and Wood, 2003] A. DUNSMORE, M. ROPER, AND M. WOOD, "The Development and Evaluation of Three Diverse Techniques for Object-Oriented Code Inspection," *IEEE Transactions on Software Engineering* **29** (August 2003), pp. 677–86.

[Elbaum, Malishevsky, and Rothermel, 2002] A. ELBAUM, A. G. MALISHEVSKY, AND G. ROTHERMEL, "Test Case Prioritization: A Family of Empirical Studies," *IEEE Transactions on Software Engineering* **28** (2002), pp. 159–82.

[Fagan, 1976] M. E. FAGAN, "Design and Code Inspections to Reduce Errors in Program Development," *IBM Systems Journal* **15** (No. 3, 1976), pp. 182–211.

[Fagan, 1986] M. E. FAGAN, "Advances in Software Inspections," *IEEE Transactions on Software Engineering* **SE-12** (July 1986), pp. 744–51.

[Fowler, 1986] P. J. FOWLER, "In-Process Inspections of Workproducts at AT&T," *AT&T Technical Journal* **65** (March/April 1986), pp. 102–12.

[Gelperin and Hetzel, 1988] D. GELPERIN AND B. HETZEL, "The Growth of Software Testing," *Communications of the ACM* **31** (June 1988), pp. 687–95.

[Goodenough, 1979] J. B. GOODENOUGH, "A Survey of Program Testing Issues," in: *Research Directions in Software Technology,* P. Wegner (Editor), The MIT Press, Cambridge, MA, 1979, pp. 316–40.

[Goodenough and Gerhart, 1975] J. B. GOODENOUGH AND S. L. GERHART, "Toward a Theory of Test Data Selection," *Proceedings of the Third International Conference on Reliable Software,* Los Angeles, 1975, pp. 493–510; also published in *IEEE Transactions on Software Engineering* **SE-1** (June 1975), pp. 156–73. Revised version: J. B. Goodenough and S. L. Gerhart, "Toward a Theory of Test Data Selection: Data Selection Criteria," in: *Current Trends in Programming Methodology,* Vol. 2, R. T. Yeh (Editor), Prentice Hall, Englewood Cliffs, NJ, 1977, pp. 44–79.

[Hetzel, 1988] W. HETZEL, *The Complete Guide to Software Testing,* 2nd ed., QED Information Systems, Wellesley, MA, 1988.

[Hoare, 1969] C. A. R. HOARE, "An Axiomatic Basis for Computer Programming," *Communications of the ACM* **12** (October 1969), pp. 576–83.

[Hoare, 1981] C. A. R. HOARE, "The Emperor's Old Clothes," *Communications of the ACM* **24** (February 1981), pp. 75–83.

[IEEE 610.12, 1990] "A Glossary of Software Engineering Terminology," IEEE 610.12-1990, Institute of Electrical and Electronic Engineers, New York, 1990.

[IEEE 1028, 1997] *Standard for Software Reviews,* IEEE 1028, Institute of Electrical and Electronic Engineers, New York, 1997.

[Jones, 1978] T. C. JONES, "Measuring Programming Quality and Productivity," *IBM Systems Journal* **17** (No. 1, 1978), pp. 39–63.

[Kelly, Sherif, and Hops, 1992] J. C. KELLY, J. S. SHERIF, AND J. HOPS, "An Analysis of Defect Densities Found during Software Inspections," *Journal of Systems and Software* **17** (January 1992), pp. 111–17.

[Kung, Hsia, and Gao, 1998] D. C. KUNG, P. HSIA, AND J. GAO, *Testing Object-Oriented Software,* IEEE Computer Society Press, Los Alamitos, CA, 1998.

[Landwehr, 1983] C. E. LANDWEHR, "The Best Available Technologies for Computer Security," *IEEE Computer* **16** (July 1983), pp. 86–100.

[Leavenworth, 1970] B. LEAVENWORTH, Review #19420, *Computing Reviews* **11** (July 1970), pp. 396–97.

[Lieberman and Fry, 2001] H. LIEBERMAN AND C. FRY, "Will Software Ever Work?" *Communications of the ACM* **44** (March 2001), pp. 122–24.

[London, 1971] R. L. LONDON, "Software Reliability through Proving Programs Correct," *Proceedings of the IEEE International Symposium on Fault-Tolerant Computing,* March 1971.

[Manna and Pnueli, 1992] Z. MANNA AND A. PNUELI, *The Temporal Logic of Reactive and Concurrent Systems,* Springer-Verlag, New York, 1992.

[Manna and Waldinger, 1978] Z. MANNA AND R. WALDINGER, "The Logic of Computer Programming," *IEEE Transactions on Software Engineering* **SE-4** (1978), pp. 199–229.

[Miller and Yin, 2004] J. MILLER AND Z. YIN, "A Cognitive-Based Mechanism for Constructing Software Inspection Teams," *IEEE Transactions on Software Engineering* **30** (November 30), pp. 811–25.

[Myers, 1979] G. J. MYERS, *The Art of Software Testing,* John Wiley and Sons, New York, 1979.

[Naur, 1969] P. NAUR, "Programming by Action Clusters," *BIT* **9** (No. 3, 1969), pp. 250–58.

[Parnas and Lawford, 2003] D. L. PARNAS AND M. LAWFORD, "The Role of Inspection in Software Quality Assurance," *IEEE Transactions on Software Engineering* **29** (August 2003), pp. 674–76.

[Perry et al., 2002] D. E. PERRY, A. PORTER, M. W. WADE, L. G. VOTTA, AND J. PERPICH, "Reducing Inspection Interval in Large-Scale Software Development," *IEEE Transactions on Software Engineering* **28** (July 2002), pp. 695–705.

[Sykes and McGregor, 2000] D. A. SYKES AND J. D. MCGREGOR, *Practical Guide to Testing Object-Oriented Software,* Addison-Wesley, Reading, MA, 2000.

[Tyran and George, 2002] C. K. TYRAN AND J. F. GEORGE, "Improving Software Inspections with Group Process Support," *Communications of the ACM* **45** (September 2002), pp. 87–92.

[Vitharana and Ramamurthy, 2003] P. VITHARANA AND K. RAMAMURTHY, "Computer-Mediated Group Support, Anonymity and the Software Inspection Process: An Empirical Investigation," *IEEE Transactions on Software Engineering* **29** (March 2003), pp. 167–80.

[Voas, 1999] J. VOAS, "Software Quality's Eight Greatest Myths," *IEEE Software* **16** (September/October 1999), pp. 118–20.

[Whittaker, 2000] J. A. WHITTAKER, "What Is Software Testing? And Why Is It So Hard?" *IEEE Software* **17** (January/February 2000), pp. 70–79.

[Whittaker and Voas, 2000] J. A. WHITTAKER AND J. VOAS, "Toward a More Reliable Theory of Software Reliability," *IEEE Computer* **33** (December 2000), pp. 36–42.

[Wirth, 1971] N. WIRTH, "Program Development by Stepwise Refinement," *Communications of the ACM* **14** (April 1971), pp. 221–27.

# Chapter 7

# From Modules to Objects

## Learning Objectives

After studying this chapter, you should be able to

- Design modules and classes with high cohesion and low coupling.
- Understand the need for information hiding.
- Describe the software engineering implications of inheritance, polymorphism, and dynamic binding.
- Distinguish between generalization, aggregation, and association.
- Discuss the object-oriented paradigm in greater depth than before.

Some of the more lurid computer magazines seem to suggest that the object-oriented paradigm was a sudden, dramatic new discovery of the mid-1980s, a revolutionary alternative to the then-popular classical paradigm. That is not the case. Instead, the theory of modularity underwent steady progress during the 1970s and the 1980s, and objects were simply an evolutionary development within the theory of modularity (but see Just in Case You Wanted to Know Box 7.1). This chapter describes objects within the context of modularity.

This approach is taken because it is extremely difficult to use objects correctly without understanding why the object-oriented paradigm is superior to the classical paradigm. And, to do that, it is necessary to appreciate that an object is merely the next logical step in the body of knowledge that begins with the concept of a module.

## 7.1 What Is a Module?

When a large product consists of a single monolithic block of code, maintenance is a nightmare. Even for the author of such a monstrosity, attempting to debug the code is extremely difficult; for another programmer to understand it is virtually impossible. The solution is to

Object-oriented concepts were introduced as early as 1966 in the simulation language Simula 67 [Dahl and Nygaard, 1966]. However, at that time, the technology was too radical for practical use, so it lay dormant until the early 1980s, when it essentially was reinvented within the context of the theory of modularity.

This chapter includes other examples of the way leading-edge technology lies dormant until the world is ready for it. For example, information hiding (Section 7.6) was first proposed in 1971 within the software context by Parnas [1971], but the technology was not widely adopted until about 10 years later, when encapsulation and abstract data types had become part of software engineering.

We humans seem to adopt new ideas only when we are ready to use them, not necessarily when they are first presented.

---

break the product into smaller pieces, called *modules*. What is a module? Is the way a product is broken into modules important in itself or is it important only to break a large product into smaller pieces of code?

Stevens, Myers, and Constantine [1974] made an early attempt to describe modules. They defined a **module** as "a set of one or more contiguous program statements having a name by which other parts of the system can invoke it, and preferably having its own distinct set of variable names." In other words, a module consists of a single block of code that can be invoked in the way that a procedure, function, or method is invoked. This definition seems to be extremely broad. It includes procedures and functions of all kinds, whether internal or separately compiled. It includes COBOL paragraphs and sections, even though they cannot have their own variables, because the definition states that the property of possessing a distinct set of variable names is merely "preferable." It also includes modules nested inside other modules. But, broad as it is, the definition does not go far enough. For example, an assembler macro is not invoked and therefore, by the preceding definition, is not a module. In C and C++, a header file of declarations that is **#include**d in a product similarly is not invoked. In short, this definition is too restrictive.

Yourdon and Constantine [1979] give a broader definition: "A module is a lexically contiguous sequence of program statements, bounded by boundary elements, having an aggregate identifier." Examples of boundary elements are begin . . . end pairs in a block-structured language like Pascal or {. . .} pairs in C++ or Java. This definition not only includes all the cases excluded by the previous definition but is broad enough to be used throughout this book. In particular, procedures and functions of the classical paradigm are modules. In the object-oriented paradigm, an object is a module and so is a method within an object.

To understand the importance of modularization, consider the following somewhat fanciful example. John Fence is a highly incompetent computer architect. He still has not discovered that both NAND gates and NOR gates are complete; that is, every circuit can be built with only NAND gates or with only NOR gates. John therefore decides to build an arithmetic logic unit (ALU), shifter, and 16 registers using AND, OR, and NOT gates. The resulting computer is shown in Figure 7.1. The three components are connected in a simple fashion. Now, our architect friend decides that the circuit should be fabricated on three silicon chips, so he designs the three chips shown in Figure 7.2. One chip has all the gates of the ALU, a second contains the shifter, and the third is for the registers. At this point John

**FIGURE 7.1**   The design of a computer.

**FIGURE 7.2**   The computer of Figure 7.1 fabricated on three chips.

**FIGURE 7.3** The computer of Figure 7.1 fabricated on three other chips.

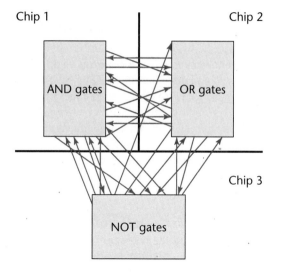

vaguely recalls that someone in a bar told him that it is best to build chips so that they have only one kind of gate, so he redesigns his chips. On chip 1 he puts all the AND gates, on chip 2 all the OR gates, and all the NOT gates go onto chip 3. The resulting "work of art" is shown schematically in Figure 7.3.

Figures 7.2 and 7.3 are functionally equivalent; that is, they do exactly the same thing. But the two designs have markedly different properties:

1. Figure 7.3 is considerably harder to *understand* than Figure 7.2. Almost anyone with a knowledge of digital logic immediately knows that the chips in Figure 7.2 form an ALU, a shifter, and a set of registers. However, even a leading hardware expert would have trouble understanding the function of the various AND, OR, and NOT gates in Figure 7.3.

2. *Corrective maintenance* of the circuits shown in Figure 7.3 is difficult. Should the computer have a design fault—and anyone capable of coming up with Figure 7.3 is undoubtedly going to make lots and lots of mistakes—it would be difficult to determine where the fault is located. On the other hand, if the design of the computer in Figure 7.2 has a fault, it can be localized by determining whether it appears to be in the way the ALU works, the way the shifter works, or the way the registers work. Similarly, if the computer of Figure 7.2 breaks down, it is relatively easy to determine which chip to replace; if the computer in Figure 7.3 breaks down, it is probably best to replace all three chips.

3. The computer of Figure 7.3 is difficult to *extend* or *enhance*. If a new type of ALU is needed or faster registers are required, it is back to the drawing board. But the design of the computer of Figure 7.2 makes it easy to replace the appropriate chip. Perhaps worst of all, the chips of Figure 7.3 cannot be *reused* in any new product. There is no way that those three specific combinations of AND, OR, and NOT gates can be utilized for any product other than the one for which they were designed. In all probability, the three chips of Figure 7.2 can be reused in other products that require an ALU, a shifter, or registers.

The point here is that software products have to be designed to look like Figure 7.2, where there is a maximal relationship within each chip and a minimal relationship between chips. A module can be likened to a chip, in that it performs an operation or series of operations and is connected to other modules. The functionality of the product as a whole is fixed; what has to be determined is how to break the product into modules. Composite/structured design [Stevens, Myers, and Constantine, 1974] provides a rationale for breaking a product into modules as a way to reduce the cost of maintenance, the major component of the total software budget, as pointed out in Chapter 1. The maintenance effort, whether corrective, perfective, or adaptive, is reduced when there is maximal interaction within each module and minimal interaction between modules. In other words, the aim of composite/structured design (C/SD) is to ensure that the module decomposition of the product resembles Figure 7.2 rather than Figure 7.3.

Myers [1978b] quantified the ideas of module **cohesion**, the degree of interaction within a module, and module **coupling**, the degree of interaction between two modules. To be more precise, Myers used the term **strength** rather than *cohesion*. However, cohesion is preferable because modules can have high strength or low strength, and something is inherently contradictory in the expression *low strength*—something that is not strong is weak. To prevent terminological inexactitude, C/SD now uses the term *cohesion*. Some authors have used the term *binding* in place of *coupling*. Unfortunately, **binding** also is used in other contexts in computer science, such as binding values to variables. But *coupling* has none of these overtones and therefore is preferable.

It is necessary at this point to distinguish between the operation of a module, the logic of a module, and the context of a module. The **operation** of a module is what it does, that is, its behavior. For example, the operation of module m is to compute the square root of its argument. The **logic** of a module is how the module performs its operation; in the case of module m, the specific way of computing the square root is Newton's method [Gerald and Wheatley, 1999]. The **context** of a module is the specific use of that module. For example, module m is used to compute the square root of a double precision integer. A key point in

C/SD is that the name assigned a module is its operation and not its logic or its context. Therefore, in C/SD, module m should be named compute_square_root;[1] its logic and its context are irrelevant from the viewpoint of its name.

# 7.2 Cohesion

Myers [1978b] defined seven categories or levels of cohesion. In the light of modern theoretical computer science, Myers's first two levels need to be interchanged because, as will be shown, informational cohesion supports reuse more strongly than functional cohesion. The resulting ranking is shown in Figure 7.4. This is not a linear scale of any sort. It is merely a relative ranking, a way of determining which types of cohesion are high (good) and which are low (bad).

To understand what constitutes a module with high cohesion, it is necessary to start at the other end and consider the lower cohesion levels.

## 7.2.1 Coincidental Cohesion

A module has **coincidental cohesion** if it performs multiple, completely unrelated operations. An example of a module with coincidental cohesion is a module named print_the_next_line, reverse_the_string_of_characters_comprising_the_second_argument, add_7_to_the_fifth_argument, convert_the_fourth_argument_to_floating_point. An obvious question is, How can such modules possibly arise in practice? The most common cause is as a consequence of rigidly enforcing rules such as "every module shall consist of between 35 and 50 executable statements." If a software organization insists that modules must be neither too big nor too small, then two undesirable things happen. First, two or more otherwise ideal smaller modules are lumped together to create a larger module with coincidental cohesion. Second, pieces hacked from well-designed modules that management considers too large are combined, again resulting in modules with coincidental cohesion.

**FIGURE 7.4**
Levels of cohesion.

| | |
|---|---|
| 7. Informational cohesion | (Good) |
| 6. Functional cohesion | |
| 5. Communicational cohesion | |
| 4. Procedural cohesion | |
| 3. Temporal cohesion | |
| 2. Logical cohesion | |
| 1. Coincidental cohesion | (Bad) |

[1] For added clarity, the underscore is used in function names like compute_square_root to highlight that the structured paradigm is used in this and the following sections. When the object-oriented paradigm is used (from Section 7.4.2 onward), the corresponding method would be named computeSquareRoot.

Why is coincidental cohesion so bad? Modules with coincidental cohesion suffer from two serious drawbacks. First, such modules degrade the maintainability of the product, both corrective maintenance and enhancement. From the viewpoint of trying to understand a product, modularization with coincidental cohesion is worse than no modularization at all [Shneiderman and Mayer, 1975]. Second, these modules are not reusable. It is extremely unlikely that the module with coincidental cohesion in the first paragraph of this section could be reused in any other product.

Lack of reusability is a serious drawback. The cost of building software is so great that it is essential to try to reuse modules wherever possible. Designing, coding, documenting, and above all, testing a module are time-consuming and hence costly processes. If an existing well-designed, thoroughly tested, and properly documented module can be used in another product, then management should insist that the existing module be reused. But there is no way that a module with coincidental cohesion can be reused, and the money spent to develop it can never be recouped. (Reuse is discussed in detail in Chapter 8.)

It is generally easy to rectify a module with coincidental cohesion—because it performs multiple operations, break the module into smaller modules that each perform one operation.

## 7.2.2 Logical Cohesion

A module has **logical cohesion** when it performs a series of related operations, one of which is selected by the calling module. All the following are examples of modules with logical cohesion.

*Example 1*    Module new_operation, which is invoked as follows:

```
function_code = 7;
new_operation (function_code, dummy_1, dummy_2, dummy_3);
// dummy_1, dummy_2, and dummy_3 are dummy variables,
// not used if function_code is equal to 7
```

In this example, new_operation is called with four arguments, but as stated in the comment lines, three of them are not needed if function_code is equal to 7. This degrades readability, with the usual implications for maintenance, both corrective and enhancement.

*Example 2*    An object that performs all input and output.

*Example 3*    A module that edits insertions, deletions, and modifications of master file records.

*Example 4*    A module with logical cohesion in an early version of OS/VS2 that performed 13 different operations; its interface contained 21 pieces of data [Myers, 1978b].

Two problems occur when a module has logical cohesion. First, the interface is difficult to understand (Example 1 is a case in point), and comprehensibility of the module as a whole may suffer as a result. Second, the code for more than one operation may be intertwined, leading to severe maintenance problems. For instance, a module that performs all input and output may be structured as shown in Figure 7.5. If a new tape unit is installed, it may be necessary to modify the sections numbered 1, 2, 3, 4, 6, 9, and 10. These changes may adversely affect other forms of input–output, such as laser printer output, because the laser printer is affected by changes to sections 1 and 3. This intertwined property is characteristic of modules with logical cohesion. A further consequence of intertwining is that it is difficult to reuse such a module in other products.

**FIGURE 7.5**
A module that performs all input and output.

| |
|---|
| 1.  Code for all input and output |
| 2.  Code for input only |
| 3.  Code for output only |
| 4.  Code for disk and tape I/O |
| 5.  Code for disk I/O |
| 6.  Code for tape I/O |
| 7.  Code for disk input |
| 8.  Code for disk output |
| 9.   Code for tape input |
| 10.  Code for tape output |
| ⋮          ⋮          ⋮ |
| 37.  Code for keyboard input |

## 7.2.3  Temporal Cohesion

A module has **temporal cohesion** when it performs a series of operations related in time. An example of a module with temporal cohesion is one named open_old_master_file, new_master_file, transaction_file, and print_file; initialize_sales_region_table; read_first_transaction_record_and_first_old_master_file_record. In the bad old days before C/SD, such a module would be called perform_initialization.

The operations of this module are related weakly to one another but more strongly to operations in other modules. Consider, for example, the sales_region_table. It is initialized in this module, but operations such as update_sales_region_table and print_sales_region_table are located in other modules. Therefore, if the structure of the sales_region_table is changed, perhaps because the organization is expanding into areas of the country where it previously had not done business, a number of modules have to be changed. Not only is there more chance of a regression fault (a fault caused by a change made to an apparently unrelated part of the product), but if the number of affected modules is large, one or two modules are likely to be overlooked. It is much better to have all the operations on the sales_region_table in one module, as described in Section 7.2.7. These operations then can be invoked, when needed, by other modules. In addition, a module with temporal cohesion is unlikely to be reusable in a different product.

## 7.2.4  Procedural Cohesion

A module has **procedural cohesion** if it performs a series of operations related by the sequence of steps to be followed by the product. An example of a module with procedural cohesion is read_part_number_from_database_and_update_repair_record_on_maintenance_file.

This clearly is better than temporal cohesion—at least the operations are related procedurally to one another. Even so, the operations are still weakly connected, and again the module is unlikely to be reusable in another product. The solution is to break a module with procedural cohesion into separate modules, each performing one operation.

## 7.2.5 Communicational Cohesion

A module has **communicational cohesion** if it performs a series of operations related by the sequence of steps to be followed by the product and if all the operations are performed on the same data. Two examples of modules with communicational cohesion are update_record_in_database_and_write_*it*_to_the_audit_trail, and calculate_new_ trajectory_and_send_*it*_to_the_printer. This is better than procedural cohesion because the operations of the module are more closely connected, but it still has the same drawback as coincidental, logical, temporal, and procedural cohesion, namely, that the module cannot be reused. Again the solution is to break such a module into separate modules, each performing one operation.

In passing, it is interesting to note that Dan Berry [personal communication, 1978] uses the term **flowchart cohesion** to refer to temporal, procedural, and communicational cohesion, because the operations performed by such modules are adjacent in the product flowchart. The operations are adjacent in the case of temporal cohesion because they are performed at the same time. They are adjacent in procedural cohesion because the algorithm requires the operations to be performed in series. They are adjacent in communicational cohesion because, in addition to being performed in series, the operations are performed on the same data, and therefore it is natural that these operations should be adjacent in the flowchart.

## 7.2.6 Functional Cohesion

A module that performs exactly one operation or achieves a single goal has **functional cohesion**. Examples of such modules are get_temperature_of_furnace; compute_ orbital_of_electron; write_to_diskette; and calculate_sales_commission.

A module with functional cohesion often can be reused because the one operation it performs frequently needs to be performed in other products. A properly designed, thoroughly tested, and well-documented module with functional cohesion is a valuable (economic and technical) asset to any software organization and should be reused as often as possible (but see Section 8.4).

Maintenance is easier to perform on a module with functional cohesion. First, functional cohesion leads to fault isolation. If it is clear that the temperature of the furnace is not being read correctly, then the fault almost certainly is in module get_temperature_of_furnace. Similarly, if the orbital of an electron is computed incorrectly, then the first place to look is in compute_orbital_of_electron.

Once the fault has been localized to a single module, the next step is to make the required changes. Because a module with functional cohesion performs only one operation, such a module generally is easier to understand than a module with lower cohesion. This ease in understanding also simplifies the maintenance. Finally, when the change is made, the chance of that change affecting other modules is slight, especially if the coupling between modules is low (Section 7.3).

Functional cohesion also is valuable when a product has to be extended. For example, suppose that a personal computer has a 40-gigabyte hard drive but the manufacturer now wishes to market a more powerful model of the computer with a 80-gigabyte hard drive instead. Reading through the list of modules, the maintenance programmer finds a module

**FIGURE 7.6**
A module with
informational
cohesion.

named write_to_hard_drive. The obvious thing to do is to replace that module with a new one called write_to_larger_hard_drive.

In passing, it should be pointed out that the three "modules" of Figure 7.2 have functional cohesion, and the arguments made in Section 7.1 for favoring the design of Figure 7.2 over that of Figure 7.3 are precisely those made in the preceding discussion for favoring functional cohesion.

### 7.2.7 Informational Cohesion

A module has **informational cohesion** if it performs a number of operations, each with its own entry point, with independent code for each operation, all performed on the same data structure. An example is given in Figure 7.6. This does not violate the tenets of structured programming; each piece of code has exactly one entry point and one exit point. A major difference between logical cohesion and informational cohesion is that the various operations of a module with logical cohesion are intertwined, whereas in a module with informational cohesion the code for each operation is completely independent.

A module with informational cohesion essentially is an implementation of an abstract data type, as explained in Section 7.5, and all the advantages of using an abstract data type are gained when a module with informational cohesion is used. Because an object essentially is an instantiation (instance) of an abstract data type (Section 7.7), an object, too, is a module with informational cohesion.[2]

### 7.2.8 Cohesion Example

For further insight into cohesion, consider the example shown in Figure 7.7. Two modules in particular merit comment. It may seem somewhat surprising that the modules initialize_sums_and_open_files and close_files_and_print_average_temperatures have been labeled as having coincidental cohesion rather than temporal cohesion. First, consider module initialize_sums_and_open_files. It performs two operations related in time, in that both have to be done before any calculations can be performed, and therefore it seems

---

[2] The discussion in this paragraph assumes that the abstract data type or object is well designed. If the methods of an object perform completely unrelated operations, then the object has coincidental cohesion.

**FIGURE 7.7** A module interconnection diagram showing the cohesion of each module.

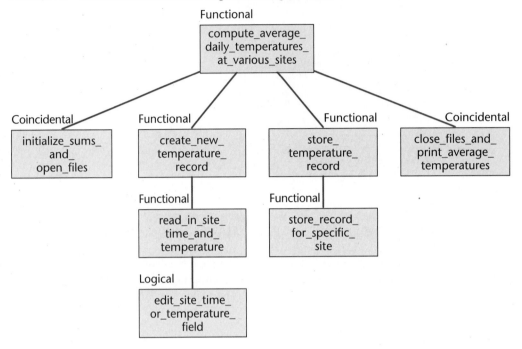

that the module has temporal cohesion. Although the two operations of initialize_sums_ and_open_files indeed are performed at the beginning of the calculation, another factor is involved. Initializing the sums is related to the problem, but opening files is a hardware issue that has nothing to do with the problem itself. The rule when two or more different levels of cohesion can be assigned to a module is to assign the lowest possible level. Consequently, because initialize_sums_and_open_files could have either temporal or coincidental cohesion, the lower of the two levels of cohesion (coincidental) is assigned to that module. That also is the reason why close_files_and_print_average_temperatures has coincidental cohesion.

# 7.3 Coupling

Recall that cohesion is the degree of interaction within a module. Coupling is the degree of interaction between two modules. As before, a number of levels can be distinguished, as shown in Figure 7.8. To highlight good coupling, the various levels are described in order from the worst to the best.

## 7.3.1 Content Coupling

Two modules are **content coupled** if one directly references the contents of the other. All the following are examples of content coupling:

***Example 1*** Module p modifies a statement of module q.

**FIGURE 7.8**
Levels of
coupling.

| | | |
|---|---|---|
| 5. | Data coupling | (Good) |
| 4. | Stamp coupling | |
| 3. | Control coupling | |
| 2. | Common coupling | |
| 1. | Content coupling | (Bad) |

This practice is not restricted to assembly language programming. The **alter** verb, now mercifully removed from COBOL, did precisely that: It modified another statement.

***Example 2***   Module p refers to local data of module q in terms of some numerical displacement within q.

***Example 3***   Module p branches to a local label of module q.

Suppose that module p and module q are content coupled. One of the many dangers is that almost any change to q, even recompiling q with a new compiler or assembler, requires a change to p. Furthermore, it is impossible to reuse module p in some new product without reusing module q as well. When two modules are content coupled, they are inextricably interlinked.

## 7.3.2 Common Coupling

Two modules are **common coupled** if both have access to the same global data. The situation is depicted in Figure 7.9. Instead of communicating with one another by passing arguments, modules cca and ccb can access and change the value of global_variable. The most common situation in which this arises is when both cca and ccb have access to the same database and can read and write the same record. For common coupling, it is necessary that both modules can read *and* write to the database; if the database access mode is read-only, then this is not common coupling. But there are other ways of implementing common coupling, including use of the C++ or Java modifier **public**.

This form of coupling is undesirable for a number of reasons:

1. It contradicts the spirit of structured programming in that the resulting code is virtually unreadable. Consider the code fragment shown in Figure 7.10. If global_variable is a global variable, then its value may be changed by module_3, module_4, or any module called by them. Determining under what conditions the loop terminates is a

**FIGURE 7.9**   An example of common coupling.

**FIGURE 7.10**   A code fragment reflecting common coupling.

```
while (global_variable == 0)
{
    if (argument_xyz > 25)
        module_3 ();
    else
        module_4 ();
}
```

nontrivial question; if a run-time failure occurs, it may be difficult to reconstruct what happened, because any of a number of modules could have changed the value of global_variable.

2. Consider the call edit_this_transaction (record_7). If there is common coupling, this call could change not just the value of record_7 but any global variable that can be accessed by that module. In short, the entire module must be read to find out precisely what it does.

3. If a maintenance change is made in one module to the declaration of a global variable, then every module that can access that global variable has to be changed. Furthermore, all changes must be consistent.

4. Another problem is that a common-coupled module is difficult to reuse because the identical list of global variables has to be supplied each time the module is reused.

5. Common coupling possesses the unfortunate property that the number of instances of common coupling between a module p and the other modules in a product can change drastically, even if module p itself never changes; this is termed *clandestine common coupling* [Schach et al., 2003a]. For example, if both module p and module q can modify global variable gv, then there is one instance of common coupling between module p and the other modules in the software product. But if 10 new modules are designed and implemented, all of which can modify global variable gv, then the number of instances of common coupling between module p and the other modules increases to 11, even though module p itself has not been changed in any way. Clandestine common coupling can have surprising consequences. For example, between 1993 and 2000, there were nearly 400 releases of Linux; 5332 versions of the 17 Linux kernel modules were unchanged between successive releases. In more than half of the 5332 versions, the number of instances of common coupling between each of those kernel modules and the rest of Linux increased or decreased, even though the kernel module itself did not change. Considerably more modules exhibited clandestine common coupling in an upward direction (2482) than downward (379) [Schach et al., 2003a]. The number of lines of code in the Linux kernel grew linearly with version number, but the number of instances of common coupling grew exponentially [Schach et al., 2002]. It seems inevitable that, at some future date, the dependencies between modules induced by clandestine common coupling will render Linux extremely hard to maintain. It will then be exceedingly hard to change one part of Linux without inducing a regression fault (an apparently unrelated fault) elsewhere in the product.

6. This problem is potentially the most dangerous. As a consequence of common coupling, a module may be exposed to more data than it needs. This defeats any attempts to control data access and ultimately may lead to computer crime. Many types of computer crime need some form of collusion. Properly designed software should not allow any one programmer access to all the data and modules needed to commit a crime. For example, a programmer writing the check printing part of a payroll product needs to have access to employee records; but, in a well-designed product, such access is exclusively in read-only mode, preventing the programmer from making unauthorized changes to his or her monthly salary. To make such changes, the programmer has to find another dishonest employee, one with access to the relevant records in update mode. But if the product has been badly designed and every module can access the payroll database

in update mode, then an unscrupulous programmer acting alone can make unauthorized changes to any record in the database.

Although we hope that these arguments will dissuade all but the most daring of readers from using common coupling, in some situations, common coupling might seem to be preferable to the alternatives. Consider, for example, a product that performs computer-aided design of petroleum storage tanks [Schach and Stevens-Guille, 1979]. A tank is specified by a large number of descriptors such as height, diameter, maximum wind speed to which the tank will be subjected, and insulation thickness. The descriptors have to be initialized but do not change in value thereafter, and most of the modules in the product need access to the values of the descriptors. Suppose that there are 55 tank descriptors. If all these descriptors are passed as arguments to every module, then the interface to each module will consist of at least 55 arguments and the potential for faults is huge. Even in a language like Ada, which requires strict type checking of arguments, two arguments of the same type still can be interchanged, a fault that would not be detected by a type checker.

One solution is to put all the tank descriptors in a database and design the product in such a way that one module initializes the values of all the descriptors, whereas all the other modules access the database exclusively in read-only mode. However, if the database solution is impractical, perhaps because the specified implementation language cannot be interfaced with the available database management system, then an alternative is to use common coupling but in a controlled way. That is, the product should be designed so that the 55 descriptors are initialized by one module, but none of the other modules changes the value of a descriptor. This programming style has to be enforced by management, unlike the database solution, where enforcement is imposed by the software. Therefore, in situations where there is no good alternative to the use of common coupling, close supervision by management can reduce some of the risks. A better solution, however, is to obviate common coupling by using information hiding, as described in Section 7.6.

## 7.3.3 Control Coupling

Two modules are **control coupled** if one passes an element of control to the other module; that is, one module explicitly controls the logic of the other. For example, control is passed when a function code is passed to a module with logical cohesion (Section 7.2.2). Another example of control coupling is when a control switch is passed as an argument.

If module p calls module q and q passes back a flag to p that says, "I am unable to complete my task," then q is passing *data*. But if the flag means, "I am unable to complete my task; accordingly, display error message ABC123," then p and q are control coupled. In other words, if q passes information back to p and p decides what action to take as a consequence of receiving that information, then q is passing data. But, if q not only passes back information but also informs module p as to what action p must take, then control coupling is present.

The major difficulty that arises as a consequence of control coupling is that the two modules are not independent; module q, the called module, has to be aware of the internal structure and logic of module p. As a result, the possibility of reuse is reduced. In addition, control coupling generally is associated with modules that have logical cohesion and includes the difficulties associated with logical cohesion.

Passing four or five different fields to a module may be slower than passing a complete record. This situation leads to a larger issue: What should be done when optimization issues (such as response time or space constraints) clash with what is generally considered to be good software engineering practice?

In my experience, this question frequently turns out to be irrelevant. The recommended approach may slow down the response time, but by only a millisecond or so, far too small to be detected by users. Therefore, in accordance with Knuth's [1974] First Law of Optimization: *Don't!*—rarely is there a need for optimization of any kind, including for performance reasons.

But what if optimization really is required? In this case, Knuth's Second Law of Optimization applies. The Second Law (labeled *for experts only*) is *Not yet!* In other words, first complete the entire product using appropriate software engineering techniques. Then, if optimization really is required, make only the necessary changes, meticulously documenting what is being changed and why. If at all possible, this optimization should be done by an experienced software engineer.

## 7.3.4 Stamp Coupling

In some programming languages, only simple variables, such as part_number, satellite_altitude, or degree_of_multiprogramming, can be passed as arguments. But many languages also support passing data structures, such as records or arrays, as arguments. In such languages, valid arguments include part_record, satellite_coordinates, or segment_table. Two modules are **stamp coupled** if a data structure is passed as an argument, but the called module operates on only some of the individual components of that data structure.

Consider, for example, the call calculate_withholding (employee_record). It is not clear, without reading the entire calculate_withholding module, which fields of the employee_record the module accesses or changes. Passing the employee's salary obviously is essential for computing the withholding, but it is difficult to see how the employee's home telephone number is needed for this purpose. Instead, only those fields that it actually needs for computing the withholding should be passed to module calculate_withholding. Not only is the resulting module, and particularly its interface, easier to understand, it is likely to be reusable in a variety of other products that also need to compute withholding. (See Just in Case You Wanted to Know Box 7.2 for another perspective on this.)

Perhaps even more important, because the call calculate_withholding (employee_record) passes more data than strictly necessary, the problems of uncontrolled data access, and conceivably computer crime, once again arise. This issue is discussed in Section 7.3.2.

Nothing is at all wrong with passing a data structure as an argument, provided all the components of the data structure are used by the called module. For example, calls like invert_matrix (original_matrix, inverted_matrix) or print_inventory_record (warehouse_record) pass a data structure as an argument, but the called modules operate on all the components of that data structure. Stamp coupling is present when a data structure is passed as an argument but only some of the components are used by the called module.

A subtle form of stamp coupling can occur in languages like C or C++ when a pointer to a record is passed as an argument. Consider the call check_altitude (pointer_to_position_record). At first sight, what is being passed is a simple variable. But the called module has access to all of the fields in the position_record pointed to by pointer_to_ position_record. Because of the potential problems, it is a good idea to examine the coupling closely whenever a pointer is passed as an argument.

### 7.3.5 Data Coupling

Two modules are **data coupled** if all arguments are homogeneous data items. That is, every argument is either a simple argument or a data structure in which all elements are used by the called module. Examples include display_time_of_arrival (flight_number), compute_product (first_number, second_number, result), and determine_job_ with_highest_priority (job_queue).

Data coupling is a desirable goal. To put it in a negative way, if a product exhibits data coupling exclusively, then the difficulties of content, common, control, and stamp coupling are not present. From a more positive viewpoint, if two modules are data coupled, then maintenance is easier, because a change to one module is less likely to cause a regression fault in the other. The following example clarifies certain aspects of coupling.

### 7.3.6 Coupling Example

Consider the example shown in Figure 7.11. The numbers on the arcs represent interfaces that are defined in greater detail in Figure 7.12. For example, when module p calls module q (interface 1), it passes one argument, the type of the aircraft. When q returns control to p, it passes back a status flag. Using the information in Figures 7.11 and 7.12, the coupling between every pair of modules can be deduced. The results are shown in Figure 7.13.

**FIGURE 7.11**
The module interconnection diagram for a coupling example.

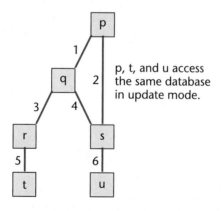

**FIGURE 7.12**
The interface description for Figure 7.11.

| Number | In | Out |
|---|---|---|
| 1 | aircraft_type | status_flag |
| 2 | list_of_aircraft_parts | — |
| 3 | function_code | — |
| 4 | list_of_aircraft_parts | — |
| 5 | part_number | part_manufacturer |
| 6 | part_number | part_name |

**FIGURE 7.13**
Coupling
between pairs
of modules of
Figure 7.11.

| | q | r | s | t | u |
|---|---|---|---|---|---|
| p | Data | — | { Data or stamp | Common | Common |
| q | | Control | { Data or stamp | — | — |
| r | | | — | Data | — |
| s | | | | — | Data |
| t | | | | | Common |

Some of the entries in Figure 7.13 are obvious. For instance, the data coupling between p and q (interface 1 in Figure 7.11), between r and t (interface 5), and between s and u (interface 6) is a direct consequence of the fact that a simple variable is passed in each direction. The coupling between p and s (interface 2) is data coupling if all the elements of the list of parts passed from p to s are used or updated, but it is stamp coupling if s operates on only certain elements of the list. The coupling between q and s (interface 4) is similar. Because the information in Figures 7.11 and 7.12 does not completely describe the function of the various modules, there is no way of determining whether the coupling is data or stamp. The coupling between q and r (interface 3) is control coupling, because a function code is passed from q to r.

Perhaps somewhat surprising are the three entries marked common coupling in Figure 7.13. The three module pairs that are farthest apart in Figure 7.11—p and t, p and u, and t and u—at first appear not to be coupled in any way. After all, no interface connects them, so the very idea of coupling between them, let alone common coupling, requires some explanation. The answer lies in the annotation on the right-hand side of Figure 7.11, namely, that p, t, and u all access the same database in update mode. The result is that a number of global variables can be changed by all three modules, and hence they are pairwise common coupled.

### 7.3.7 The Importance of Coupling

Coupling is an important metric. If module p is tightly coupled to module q, then a change to module p may require a corresponding change to module q. If this change is made, as required, during integration or postdelivery maintenance, then the resulting product functions correctly; however, progress at that stage is slower than would have been the case had the coupling been looser. On the other hand, if the required change is not made to module q at that time, then the fault manifests itself later. In the best case, the compiler or linker informs the team right away that something is amiss or a failure will occur while testing the change to module p. What usually happens, however, is that the product fails either during subsequent integration testing or after the product has been installed on the client's computer. In both cases, the failure occurs after the change to module p has been completed. There no longer is any apparent link between the change to module p and the overlooked corresponding change to module q. The fault therefore may be hard to find.

It has been shown that the stronger (more undesirable) the coupling, the greater the fault-proneness [Briand, Daly, Porter, and Wüst, 1998]. A major reason underlying this phenomenon is that dependencies within the code lead to regression faults. Furthermore, if

**FIGURE 7.14**

Key definitions of this chapter, and the sections in which they appear.

**Abstract data type:** a data type together with the operations performed on instantiations of that data type (Section 7.5)

**Abstraction:** a means of achieving stepwise refinement by suppressing unnecessary details and accentuating relevant details (Section 7.4.1)

**Class:** an abstract data type that supports inheritance (Section 7.7)

**Cohesion:** the degree of interaction within a module (Section 7.1)

**Coupling:** the degree of interaction between two modules (Section 7.1)

**Data encapsulation:** a data structure together with the operations performed on that data structure (Section 7.4)

**Encapsulation:** the gathering together into one unit of all aspects of the real-world entity modeled by that unit (Section 7.4.1)

**Information hiding:** structuring the design so that the resulting implementation details are hidden from other modules (Section 7.6)

**Object:** an instantiation of a class (Section 7.7)

a module is fault-prone, then it will have to undergo repeated maintenance, and these frequent changes are likely to compromise its maintainability. Furthermore, these frequent changes will not always be restricted to the fault-prone module itself; it is not uncommon to have to modify more than one module to fix a single fault. Thus, the fault-proneness of one module can adversely affect the maintainability of a number of other modules. In other words, it is easy to believe that strong coupling can have a deleterious effect on maintainability [Yu, Schach, Chen, and Offutt, 2004].

Given that a design in which modules have high cohesion and low coupling is a good design, the obvious question is, How can such a design be achieved? Because this chapter is devoted to theoretical concepts surrounding design, the answer to the question is presented in Chapter 13. In the meantime, those qualities that identify a good design are examined further and refined. For convenience, the key definitions in this chapter appear in Figure 7.14, together with the section in which each definition appears.

# 7.4 Data Encapsulation

Consider the problem of designing an operating system for a large mainframe computer. According to the specifications, any job submitted to the computer is classified as high priority, medium priority, or low priority. The task of the operating system is to decide which job to load into memory next, which of the jobs in memory gets the next time slice and how long that time slice should be, and which of the jobs that require disk access has highest priority. In performing this scheduling, the operating system must consider the priority of each job; the higher is the priority, the sooner that job should be assigned the resources of the computer. One way of achieving this is to maintain separate job queues for each job-priority level. The job queues have to be initialized, and facilities must exist for adding a job to a job queue when the job requires memory, CPU time, or disk access as well as for removing a job from a queue when the operating system decides to allocate the required resource to that job.

To simplify matters, consider the restricted problem of batch jobs queuing up for memory access. There are three queues for incoming batch jobs, one for each priority level. When submitted by a user, a job is added to the appropriate queue; and when the operating system decides that a job is ready to be run, it is removed from its queue and memory is allocated to it.

This portion of the product can be built in a number of different ways. One possible design, shown in Figure 7.15, depicts modules for manipulating one of the three job

**FIGURE 7.15**
One possible
design of the
job queue
portion of the
operating
system.

m_1

Definition of
job_queue

initialize_job_queue ()
{
  ⋮          ⋮
}

m_2

Definition of
job_queue

add_job_to_queue (job j)
{
  ⋮          ⋮
}

m_3

Definition of
job_queue

remove_job_from_queue (job j)
{
  ⋮          ⋮
}

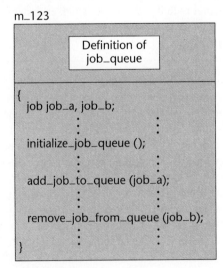

m_123

Definition of
job_queue

{
  job job_a, job_b;
    ⋮          ⋮
  initialize_job_queue ();
    ⋮          ⋮
  add_job_to_queue (job_a);
    ⋮          ⋮
  remove_job_from_queue (job_b);
    ⋮          ⋮
}

queues. A C-like pseudocode is used to highlight some of the problems that can arise in the classical paradigm. In Section 7.7, these problems are solved using the object-oriented paradigm.

Consider Figure 7.15. Function initialize_job_queue in module m_1 is responsible for the initialization of the job queue, and functions add_job_to_queue and remove_job_from_queue in modules m_2 and m_3, respectively, are responsible for the addition and deletion of jobs. Module m_123 contains invocations of all three functions in order to manipulate the job queue. To concentrate on data encapsulation, issues such as underflow (trying to remove a job from an empty queue) and overflow (trying to add a job to a full queue) have been suppressed here, as well as in the remainder of this chapter.

The modules of the design of Figure 7.15 have low cohesion, because operations on the job queue are spread all over the product. If a decision is made to change the way job_queue is implemented (for example, as a linked list of records instead of as a linear list), then modules m_1, m_2, and m_3 have to be drastically revised. Module m_123 also has to be changed; at the very least, the data structure definition has to be changed.

Now suppose that the design of Figure 7.16 is chosen instead. The module on the right-hand side of the figure has informational cohesion (Section 7.2.7), in that it performs a number of operations on the same data structure. Each operation has its own entry point and exit point and independent code. Module m_encapsulation in Figure 7.16 is an implementation of **data encapsulation**, that is, a data structure, in this case the job queue, together with the operations to be performed on that data structure.

**FIGURE 7.16**
A design of the job queue portion of the operating system using data encapsulation.

An obvious question to ask at this point is, What is the advantage of designing a product using data encapsulation? This will be answered in two ways, from the viewpoint of development and from the viewpoint of maintenance.

## 7.4.1  Data Encapsulation and Development

Data encapsulation is an example of **abstraction**. Returning to the job queue example, a data structure (the job queue) has been defined, together with three associated operations (initialize the job queue, add a job to the queue, and delete a job from the queue). The developer can conceptualize the problem at a higher level, the level of jobs and job queues, rather than at the lower level of records or arrays.

The basic theoretical concept behind abstraction, once again, is stepwise refinement. First, a design for the product is produced in terms of high-level concepts such as jobs, job queues, and the operations performed on job queues. At this stage, it is entirely irrelevant how the job queue is implemented. Once a complete high-level design has been obtained, the second step is to design the lower-level components in terms of which the data structure and operations on the data structure are implemented. In C, for example, the data structure (the job queue) is implemented in terms of records (structures) or arrays; the three operations (initialize the job queue, add a job to the queue, and remove a job from the queue) are implemented as functions. The key point is that, while this lower level is being designed, the designer totally ignores the intended use of the jobs, job queue, and operations. Therefore, during the first step, the existence of the lower level is assumed, even though at this stage no thought has been given to that level; during the second step (the design of the lower level), the existence of the higher level is ignored. At the higher level, the concern is with the behavior of the data structure, the job queue; at the lower level, the implementation of that behavior is the primary concern. Of course, a larger product has many levels of abstraction.

Different types of abstraction exist. Consider Figure 7.16. That figure has two types of abstraction. Data encapsulation (that is, a data structure together with the operations to be performed on that data structure) is an example of **data abstraction**; the C functions themselves are an example of **procedural abstraction**. *Abstraction*, to summarize, simply is a means of achieving stepwise refinement by suppressing unnecessary details and accentuating relevant details. **Encapsulation** now can be defined as the gathering into one unit of all aspects of the real-world entity modeled by that unit; this was termed *conceptual independence* in Section 1.9.

Data abstraction allows the designer to think at the level of the data structure and the operations performed on it and only later be concerned with the details of how the data structure and operations are implemented. Turning now to procedural abstraction, consider the result of defining a C function, initialize_job_queue. The effect is to extend the language by supplying the developer with another function, one that is not part of the language as originally defined. The developer can use initialize_job_queue in the same way as sqrt or abs.

The implications of procedural abstraction for design are as powerful as those of data abstraction. The designer can conceptualize the product in terms of high-level operations. These operations can be defined in terms of lower-level operations, until the lowest level is reached. At this level, the operations are expressed in terms of the predefined constructs of the programming language. At each level, the designer is concerned only with expressing

I deliberately wrote the code examples of Figures 7.17 and 7.18 as well as the subsequent code examples in this chapter in such a way as to highlight data abstraction issues at the cost of good programming practice. For example, the number 25 in the definition of **JobQueueClass** in Figures 7.17 and 7.18 certainly should be coded as a parameter, that is, as a **const** in C++ or a **public static final** variable in Java. Also, for simplicity, I omitted checks for conditions such as underflow (trying to remove an item from an empty queue) or overflow (trying to add an item to a full queue). In any real product, it is absolutely essential to include such checks.

In addition, language-specific features have been minimized. For instance, a C++ programmer usually writes

```
queueLength++;
```

to increment the value of `queueLength` by 1, rather than

```
queueLength = queueLength + 1;
```

Similarly, use of constructors and destructors has been minimized.

In summary, I wrote the code in this chapter for pedagogic purposes only. It should not be utilized for any other purpose.

---

the product in terms of operations appropriate to that level. The designer can ignore the level below, which will be handled at the next level of abstraction, that is, the next refinement step. The designer also can ignore the level above, a level irrelevant from the viewpoint of designing the current level.

## 7.4.2 Data Encapsulation and Maintenance

Approaching data encapsulation from the viewpoint of maintenance, a basic issue is to identify the aspects of a product likely to change and design the product to minimize the effects of future changes. Data structures as such are unlikely to change; if a product includes job queues, for instance, then future versions are likely to incorporate them. At the same time, the specific way that job queues are implemented may well change, and data encapsulation provides a means of coping with that change.

Figure 7.17 depicts an implementation in C++ of the job queue data structure as a **JobQueueClass**; Figure 7.18 is the corresponding Java implementation. (Just in Case You Wanted to Know Box 7.3 has comments on the programming style in Figures 7.17 and 7.18, as well as in the subsequent code examples in this chapter.) In Figure 7.17 or Figure 7.18, the queue is implemented as an array of up to 25 job numbers; the first element is queue[0] and the 25th is queue[24]. Each job number is represented as an integer. The reserved word **public** allows queueLength and queue to be visible everywhere in the operating system. The resulting common coupling is extremely poor practice and is corrected in Section 7.6.

Because they are **public**, the methods in **JobQueueClass** may be invoked from anywhere in the operating system. In particular, Figure 7.19 shows how **JobQueueClass** may be used by method queueHandler using C++, and Figure 7.20 is the corresponding Java implementation. Method queueHandler invokes methods initializeJobQueue, addJobToQueue, and removeJobFromQueue of **JobQueueClass** without having any

**FIGURE 7.17**
A C++
implementation
of **JobQueue-
Class**.
(Problems
caused by
**public**
attributes will
be solved in
Section 7.7.)

```
//
// Warning:
// This code has been written in such a way as to be accessible to readers
// who are not C++ experts, as opposed to using good C++ style. Also, vital
// features such as checks for overflow and underflow have been omitted for simplicity.
// See Just in Case You Wanted to Know Box 7.3 for details.
//
class JobQueueClass
{
    // attributes
    public:
        int queueLength;          // length of job queue
        int queue[25];            // queue can contain up to 25 jobs

    // methods
    public:
        void initializeJobQueue ()
        /*
         * an empty job queue has length 0
         */
        {
            queueLength = 0;
        }


        void addJobToQueue (int jobNumber)
        /*
         * add the job to the end of the job queue
         */
        {
            queue[queueLength] = jobNumber;
            queueLength = queueLength + 1;
        }


        int removeJobFromQueue ()
        /*
         * set jobNumber equal to the number of the job stored at the head of the queue,
         * remove the job at the head of the job queue, move up the remaining jobs,
         * and return jobNumber
         */
        {
            int jobNumber = queue[0];
            queueLength = queueLength - 1;
            for (int k = 0; k < queueLength; k++)
                queue[k] = queue[k + 1];
            return jobNumber;
        }
}// class JobQueueClass
```

**FIGURE 7.18**
A Java implementation of **class JobQueue-Class**. (Problems caused by **public** attributes will be solved in Section 7.7.)

```java
//
// Warning:
// This code has been written in such a way as to be accessible to readers
// who are not Java experts, as opposed to using good Java style.
// Also, vital features such as checks for overflow and underflow
// have been omitted for simplicity.
// See Just in Case You Wanted to Know Box 7.3 for details.
//
class JobQueueClass
{
    // attributes
    public int      queueLength;              // length of job queue
    public int      queue[ ] = new int[25];   // queue can contain up to 25 jobs

    // methods
    public void initializeJobQueue ()
    /*
     * an empty job queue has length 0
     */
    {
        queueLength = 0;
    }


    public void addJobToQueue (int jobNumber)
    /*
     * add the job to the end of the job queue
     */
    {
        queue[queueLength] = jobNumber;
        queueLength = queueLength + 1;
    }


    public int removeJobFromQueue ()
    /*
     * set jobNumber equal to the number of the job stored at the head of the queue,
     * remove the job at the head of the job queue, move up the remaining jobs,
     * and return jobNumber
     */
    {
        int jobNumber = queue[0];
        queueLength = queueLength – 1;
        for (int k = 0; k < queueLength; k++)
            queue[k] = queue[k + 1];
        return jobNumber;
    }
}// class JobQueueClass
```

**FIGURE 7.19** A C++ implementation of queueHandler.

```
class SchedulerClass
{
  . . .
  public:
    void queueHandler ()
    {
      int             jobA, jobB;
      JobQueueClass   jobQueueJ;

        // various statements
      jobQueueJ.initializeJobQueue ();
        // more statements
      jobQueueJ.addJobToQueue (jobA);
        // still more statements
      jobB = jobQueueJ.removeJobFromQueue ();
        // further statements
    }// queueHandler
  . . .
}// class SchedulerClass
```

**FIGURE 7.20** A Java implementation of queueHandler.

```
class SchedulerClass
{
  . . .
    public void queueHandler ()
    {
      int             jobA, jobB;
      JobQueueClass   jobQueueJ = new JobQueueClass ();

        // various statements
      jobQueueJ.initializeJobQueue ();
        // more statements
      jobQueueJ.addJobToQueue (jobA);
        // still more statements
      jobB = jobQueueJ.removeJobFromQueue ();
        // further statements
    }// queueHandler
  . . .
}// class SchedulerClass
```

knowledge as to how the job queue is implemented; the only information needed to use **JobQueueClass** is interface information regarding the three methods.

Now suppose that the job queue currently is implemented as a linear list of job numbers, but a decision has been made to reimplement it as a two-way linked list of job records. Each job record will have three components: the job number as before, a pointer to the job record in front of it in the linked list, and a pointer to the job record behind it. This is specified in C++ as shown in Figure 7.21 and in Java as shown in Figure 7.22. What changes must be

**FIGURE 7.21** A C++ implementation of a two-way linked **JobRecordClass**. (Problems caused by **public** attributes will be solved in Section 7.6.)

```
class JobRecordClass
{
  public:
      int              jobNo;       // number of the job (integer)
      JobRecordClass   *inFront;    // pointer to the job record in front
      JobRecordClass   *inRear;     // pointer to the job record behind
}// class JobRecordClass
```

**FIGURE 7.22** A Java implementation of a two-way linked **JobRecordClass**. (Problems caused by **public** attributes will be solved in Section 7.6.)

```
class JobRecordClass
{
    public int              jobNo;     // number of the job (integer)
    public JobRecordClass   inFront;   // reference to the job record in front
    public JobRecordClass   inRear;    // reference to the job record behind
} // class JobRecordClass
```

**FIGURE 7.23**
Outline of a
C++
implementation
of **JobQueue-
Class** using a
two-way linked
list.

```
class JobQueueClass
{
  public:
    JobRecordClass      *frontOfQueue;      // pointer to the front of the queue
    JobRecordClass      *rearOfQueue;       // pointer to the rear of the queue

    void initializeJobQueue ()
    {
      /*
       * initialize the job queue by setting frontOfQueue and rearOfQueue to NULL
       */
    }


    void addJobToQueue (int JobNumber)
    {
      /*
       * Create a new job record,
       * place jobNumber in its jobNo field,
       * set its inFront field to point to the current rearOfQueue
       * (thereby linking the new record to the rear of the queue),
       * and set its inRear field to NULL.
       * Set the inRear field of the record pointed to by the current rearOfQueue
       * to point to the new record (thereby setting up a two-way link), and
       * finally, set rearOfQueue to point to this new record.
       */
    }


    int removeJobFromQueue ()
    {
      /*
       * set jobNumber equal to the jobNo field of the record at the front of the queue,
       * update frontOfQueue to point to the next item in the queue,
       * set the inFront field of the record that is now the head of the queue to NULL,
       * and return jobNumber.
       */
    }
}// class JobQueueClass
```

made to the software product as a whole as a consequence of this modification to the way the job queue is implemented? In fact, only **JobQueueClass** itself has to be changed. Figure 7.23 shows the outline of a C++ implementation of **JobQueueClass** using the two-way linked list of Figure 7.21. Implementation details have been suppressed to highlight that the interface between **JobQueueClass** and the rest of the product (including method queueHandler) has not changed (but see Problem 7.12). That is, the three methods initializeJobQueue, addJobToQueue, and removeJobFromQueue are invoked in exactly the same way as before. Specifically, when method addJobToQueue is invoked, it still passes an integer value, and removeJobFromQueue still returns an integer value, even though the job queue itself has been implemented in an entirely different way. Consequently, the source code of method queueHandler (Figure 7.19) need not be changed at all. Accordingly, data encapsulation supports the implementation of data abstraction in a way that simplifies maintenance and reduces the chance of a regression fault.

Comparing Figures 7.17 and 7.18 and Figures 7.19 and 7.20, it is clear that, in these instances, the differences between the C++ and Java implementations essentially are syntactic. In the remainder of this chapter, we give only one implementation, together with a description of the syntactic differences in the other implementation. Specifically, the rest of the job queue code is in C++ and all the other code examples are in Java.

# 7.5   Abstract Data Types

Figure 7.17 (equivalently, Figure 7.18) is an implementation of a job queue **class**, that is, a data type together with the operations to be performed on instantiations of that data type. Such a construct is called an **abstract data type**.

Figure 7.24 shows how this abstract data type may be utilized in C++ for the three job queues of the operating system. Three job queues are instantiated: highPriorityQueue, mediumPriorityQueue, and lowPriorityQueue. (The Java version differs only in the syntax of the data declarations of the three job queues.) The statement highPriority-Queue.initializeJobQueue () means "apply method initializeJobQueue to data structure highPriorityQueue," and similarly for the other two statements.

Abstract data types are a widely applicable design tool. For example, suppose that a product is to be written in which a large number of operations have to be performed on rational numbers, that is, numbers that can be represented in the form $n/d$, where n and d are integers, $d \neq 0$. Rational numbers can be represented in a variety of ways, such as two elements of a one-dimensional array of integers or two attributes of a class. To implement rational numbers in terms of an abstract data type, a suitable representation for the data structure is chosen. In Java, it could be defined as shown in Figure 7.25, together with the various operations that are

**FIGURE 7.24**
C++ method queueHandler implemented using the abstract data type of Figure 7.17.

```
class SchedulerClass
{
   . . .
   public:
     void queueHandler ()
     {
       int              job1, job2;
       JobQueueClass    highPriorityQueue;
       JobQueueClass    mediumPriorityQueue;
       JobQueueClass    lowPriorityQueue;

         // some statements
       highPriorityQueue.initializeJobQueue ();
         // some more statements
       mediumPriorityQueue.addJobToQueue (job1);
         // still more statements
       job2 = lowPriorityQueue.removeJobFromQueue ();
         // even more statements
     }// queueHandler
   . . .
}// class SchedulerClass
```

**FIGURE 7.25**
Java abstract
data type
implementation
of a rational
number.
(Problems
caused by
**public**
attributes will
be solved in
Section 7.6.)

```java
class RationalClass
{
    public int      numerator;
    public int      denominator;

    public void sameDenominator (RationalClass r, RationalClass s)
    {
        // code to reduce r and s to the same denominator
    }

    public boolean equal (RationalClass t, RationalClass u)
    {
        RationalClass      v, w;
        v = t;
        w = u;
        sameDenominator (v, w);
        return (v.numerator == w.numerator);
    }

    // methods to add, subtract, multiply, and divide two rational numbers

}// class RationalClass
```

performed on rational numbers, such as constructing a rational number from two integers, adding two rational numbers, or multiplying two rational numbers. (The problems induced by **public** attributes such as numerator and denominator in Figure 7.25 will be fixed in Section 7.6.) The corresponding C++ implementation differs in the placement of the reserved word **public**. Also, an ampersand is needed when an argument is passed by reference.

Abstract data types support both data abstraction and procedural abstraction (Section 7.4.1). In addition, when a product is modified, it is unlikely that the abstract data types will be changed; at worst, additional operations may have to be added to an abstract data type. Therefore, from both the development and the maintenance viewpoints, abstract data types are an attractive tool for software producers.

# 7.6 Information Hiding

The two types of abstraction discussed in Section 7.4.1 (data abstraction and procedural abstraction) are in turn instances of a more general design concept put forward by Parnas, **information hiding** [Parnas, 1971, 1972a, 1972b]. Parnas's ideas are directed toward future maintenance. Before a product is designed, a list should be made of implementation decisions likely to change in the future. Modules then should be designed so that the implementation details of the resulting design are hidden from other modules. As a result, each future change is localized to one specific module. Because the details of the original implementation decision are not visible to other modules, changing the design clearly cannot affect any other module. (See Just in Case You Wanted to Know Box 7.4 for a further insight into information hiding.)

To see how these ideas can be used in practice, consider Figure 7.24, which uses the abstract data type implementation of Figure 7.17. A primary reason for using an abstract

The term *information hiding* is somewhat of a misnomer. A more accurate description would be "details hiding," because what is hidden is not information but implementation details.

data type is to ensure that the contents of a job queue can be changed only by invoking one of the three methods of Figure 7.17. Unfortunately, the nature of that implementation is such that job queues can be changed in other ways as well. Attributes queueLength and queue are both declared **public** in Figure 7.17 and therefore accessible inside queue-Handler. As a result, in Figure 7.24, it is perfectly legal C++ (or Java) to use an assignment statement such as

$$highPriorityQueue.queue[7] = -5678;$$

anywhere in queueHandler to change highPriorityQueue. In other words, the contents of a job queue can be changed without using any of the three operations of the abstract data type. In addition to the implications this might have with regard to lowering cohesion and increasing coupling, management must recognize that the product may be vulnerable to computer crime as described in Section 7.3.2.

Fortunately, there is a way out. The designers of both C++ and Java provided for information hiding within a class specification. This is shown in Figure 7.26 for C++ (the Java syntactic differences are as before). Other than changing the visibility modifier for the attributes from **public** to **private**, Figure 7.26 is identical to Figure 7.17. Now the only information visible to other modules is that **JobQueueClass** is a class and that three

**FIGURE 7.26**

A C++ abstract data type implementation with information hiding, correcting the problem of Figures 7.17, 7.18, 7.21, 7.22, and 7.25.

```
class JobQueueClass
{
    // attributes
    private:
        int     queueLength;        // length of job queue
        int     queue[25];          // queue can contain up to 25 jobs


    // methods
    public:
        void initializeJobQueue ()
        {
            // body of method unchanged from Figure 7.17
        }


        void addJobToQueue (int jobNumber)
        {
            // body of method unchanged from Figure 7.17
        }


        int removeJobFromQueue ()
        {
            // body of method unchanged from Figure 7.17
        }
}// class JobQueueClass
```

**FIGURE 7.27** Representation of an abstract data type with information hiding achieved via **private** attributes (Figure 7.26 with Figure 7.24).

**SchedulerClass**

**JobQueueClass**

```
{
    int                job1, job2;
        ⋮          ⋮
    highPriorityQueue.initializeJobQueue ();
        ⋮          ⋮
    mediumPriorityQueue.addJobToQueue (job1);
        ⋮          ⋮
    job2 = lowPriorityQueue.removeJobFromQueue ();
        ⋮          ⋮
}
```

Implementation details of

queue
queueLength
initializeJobQueue
addJobToQueue
removeJobFromQueue

Interface information regarding

initializeJobQueue
addJobToQueue
removeJobFromQueue

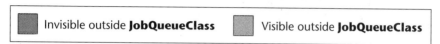

Invisible outside **JobQueueClass**    Visible outside **JobQueueClass**

operations with specified interfaces can operate on the resulting job queues. But the exact way job queues are implemented is **private**, that is, invisible to the outside. The diagram in Figure 7.27 shows how a class with **private** attributes enables a C++ or Java user to implement an abstract data type with full information hiding.

Information hiding techniques also can be used to obviate common coupling, as mentioned at the end of Section 7.3.2. Consider again the product described in that section, a computer-aided design tool for petroleum storage tanks specified by 55 descriptors. If the product is implemented with **private** operations for initializing a descriptor and **public** operations for obtaining the value of a descriptor, then there is no common coupling. This type of solution is characteristic of the object-oriented paradigm, because as described in Section 7.7, objects support information hiding. This is another strength of object technology.

## 7.7    Objects

As stated at the beginning of this chapter, objects simply are the next step in the progression shown in Figure 7.28. Nothing is special about objects; they are as ordinary as abstract data types or modules with informational cohesion. The importance of objects is that they have all the properties possessed by their predecessors in Figure 7.28, as well as additional properties of their own.

An incomplete definition of an object is that an object is an instantiation (instance) of an abstract data type. That is, a product is designed in terms of abstract data types, and the variables (objects) of the product are instantiations of the abstract data types. But defining an object as an instantiation of an abstract data type is too simplistic. Something more is

**FIGURE 7.28**
The major
concepts of
Chapter 7 and
the section in
which each is
described.

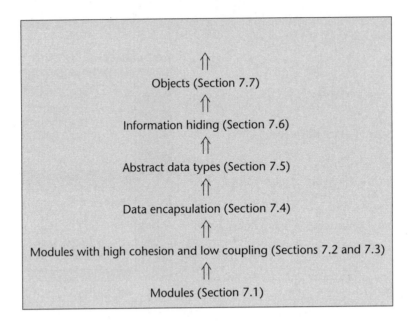

needed, namely, **inheritance**, a concept first introduced in Simula 67 [Dahl and Nygaard, 1966]. Inheritance is supported by all object-oriented programming languages, such as Smalltalk [Goldberg and Robson 1989], C++ [Stroustrup, 2003], and Java [Flanagan, 2005]. The basic idea behind inheritance is that new data types can be defined as extensions of previously defined types, rather than having to be defined from scratch [Meyer, 1986].

In an object-oriented language, a **class** can be defined as an abstract data type that supports inheritance. An **object** then is an instantiation of a class. To see how classes are used, consider the following example. Define **Human Being Class** to be a class and Joe to be an object, an instance of that class. Every instance of **Human Being Class** has certain attributes such as age and height, and values can be assigned to those attributes when describing the object Joe. Now suppose that **Parent Class** is defined to be a **subclass** (or derived class) of **Human Being Class**. This means that an instance of **Parent Class** has all the attributes of an instance of **Human Being Class** and, in addition, may have attributes of his or her own such as name of oldest child and number of children. This is depicted in Figure 7.29. In object-oriented terminology, a Parent *isA* Human Being. That is why the arrow in Figure 7.29 seems to be going in the wrong direction. In fact, the arrow depicts the *isA* relation and therefore points from the derived class to the base class. (The use of the open arrowhead to denote inheritance is a UML convention; another is that class names appear in boldface with the first letter of each word capitalized. Finally, the open rectangle with the turned over corner is a UML **note**. UML is discussed in more detail in Part 2, especially in Chapter 16.)

**Parent Class** *inherits* all the attributes of **Human Being Class**, because **Parent Class** is a derived class (or subclass) of base class **Human Being Class**. If Fred is an object (instance) of **Parent Class**, then Fred has all the attributes of an instance of **Parent Class** and also inherits all the attributes of an instance of **Human Being**

**FIGURE 7.29**
UML diagram
showing derived
types and
inheritance.

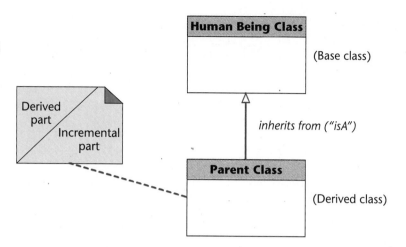

**FIGURE 7.30**
Java
implementation
of Figure 7.29.

```
class HumanBeingClass
{
    private int      age;
    private float    height;

    // public declarations of operations on HumanBeingClass

}// class HumanBeingClass


class ParentClass extends HumanBeingClass
{
    private String   nameOfOldestChild;
    private int       numberOfChildren;

    // public declarations of operations on ParentClass

}// class ParentClass
```

**Class**. A Java implementation is shown in Figure 7.30. The C++ version differs in the placement of the **private** and **public** modifiers. Also, the Java syntax **extends** is replaced in C++ by **: public** in this example.

The property of inheritance is an essential feature of all object-oriented programming languages. However, neither inheritance nor the concept of a class is supported by classical languages such as C or LISP. Therefore, the object-oriented paradigm cannot be directly implemented in these languages (but see Section 8.7.4).

In the terminology of the object-oriented paradigm, there are two other ways of looking at the relationship between **Parent Class** and **Human Being Class** in Figure 7.29. We can say that **Parent Class** is a **specialization** of **Human Being Class** or that **Human Being Class** is a **generalization** of **Parent Class**. In addition to specialization and generalization, classes have two other basic relationships [Blaha, Premerlani, and Rumbaugh, 1988]: aggregation and association. **Aggregation** refers to the components of

**FIGURE 7.31** UML aggregation example.

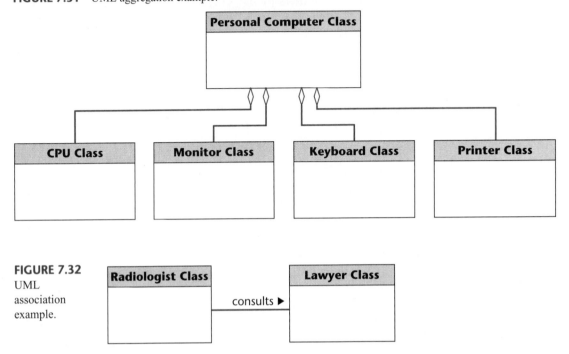

**FIGURE 7.32**
UML
association
example.

a class. For example, class **Personal Computer Class** might consist of components **CPU Class**, **Monitor Class**, **Keyboard Class**, and **Printer Class**. This is depicted in Figure 7.31; the use of a diamond to denote aggregation is another UML convention. Nothing is new about this; it occurs whenever a language supports records, such as a **struct** in C. Within the object-oriented context, however, it is used to group related items, resulting in a reusable class (Section 8.1).

**Association** refers to a relationship of some kind between two apparently unrelated classes. For example, there seems to be no connection between a radiologist and a lawyer, but a radiologist may consult a lawyer for advice regarding a contract for leasing a new MRI machine. Association is depicted using UML in Figure 7.32. The nature of the association in this instance is indicated by the word consults. In addition, the solid triangle (termed a **navigation triangle** in UML) indicates the direction of the association; after all, a lawyer with a broken ankle might consult a radiologist.

In passing, one aspect of Java and C++ notation, like that of other object-oriented languages, explicitly reflects the equivalence of operation and data. First, consider a classical language that supports records; C, for example. Suppose that record_1 is a **struct** (record) and field_2 is a field within the class. Then, the field is referred to as record_1. field_2. That is, the period . denotes membership within the record. If function_3 is a function within a C module, then function_3 ( ) denotes an invocation of that function.

In contrast, suppose that **AClass** is a **class**, with attribute attributeB and method methodC. Suppose further that ourObject is an instance of **AClass**. Then the field is referred to as ourObject.attributeB. Furthermore, ourObject.methodC ( ) denotes an invocation of the method. Hence, the period is used to denote membership within an object, whether the member is an attribute or a method.

The advantages of using objects (or, rather, classes) are precisely those of using abstract data types, including data abstraction and procedural abstraction. In addition, the inheritance aspects of classes provide a further layer of data abstraction, leading to easier and less fault-prone product development. Yet another strength follows from combining inheritance with polymorphism and dynamic binding, the subject of Section 7.8.

# 7.8  Inheritance, Polymorphism, and Dynamic Binding

Suppose that the operating system of a computer is called on to open a file. That file could be stored on a number of different media. For example, it could be a disk file, a tape file, or a diskette file. Using the classical paradigm, there would be three differently named functions, open_disk_file, open_tape_file, and open_diskette_file; this is shown in Figure 7.33(a). If my_file is declared to be a file, then at run time, it is necessary to test whether it is a disk file, a tape file, or a diskette file to determine which function to invoke. The corresponding classical code is shown in Figure 7.34(a).

In contrast, when the object-oriented paradigm is used, a class named **File Class** is defined, with three derived classes: **Disk File Class**, **Tape File Class**, and **Diskette File Class**. This is shown in Figure 7.33(b); recall that the UML open arrowhead denotes inheritance.

**FIGURE 7.33**  Operations needed to open a file. (a) Classical implementation. (b) Object-oriented file class hierarchy using UML notation.

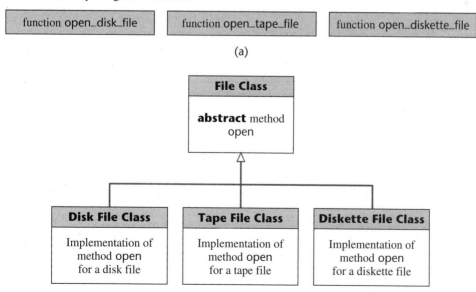

**FIGURE 7.34**
(a) Classical
code to open a
file,
corresponding
to Figure 7.33(a).
(b) Object-
oriented code
to open a file,
corresponding
to Figure 7.33(b).

```
switch (file_type)
{
    case 1:
        open_disk_file ( );          // file_type 1 corresponds to a disk file
        break;
    case 2:
        open_tape_file ( );          // file_type 2 corresponds to a tape file
        break;
    case 3:
        open_diskette_file ( );      // file_type 3 corresponds to a diskette file
        break;
}
```

(a)

```
myFile.open ( );
```

(b)

Now, suppose that method open were defined in parent class **File Class** and inherited by the three derived classes. Unfortunately, this would not work, because different operations need to be carried out to open the three different types of files.

The solution is as follows. In parent class **File Class**, a dummy method open is declared. In Java, such a method is declared to be **abstract**; in C++, the reserved word **virtual** is used instead. A specific implementation of the method appears in each of the three derived classes, and each method is given an identical name, that is, open, as shown in Figure 7.33(b). Again, suppose that myFile is declared to be a file. At run time, the message

myFile.open ( )

is sent. The object-oriented system now determines whether myFile is a disk file, a tape file, or a diskette file and invokes the appropriate version of open. That is, the system determines at run time whether object myFile is an instance of **Disk File Class**, **Tape File Class**, or **Diskette File Class** and automatically invokes the correct method. Because this has to be done at run time (dynamically) and not at compile time (statically), the act of connecting an object to the appropriate method is termed **dynamic binding**. Furthermore, because the method open can be applied to objects of different classes, it is termed **polymorphic**, which means "of many shapes." Just as carbon crystals come in many different shapes, including hard diamonds and soft graphite, so the method open comes in three different versions. In Java, these versions are denoted DiskFileClass.open, TapeFileClass.open, and DisketteFileClass.open. (In C++, the period is replaced by two colons, and the methods are denoted DiskFileClass::open, TapeFileClass::open, and DisketteFileClass::open.) However, because of dynamic binding, it is not necessary to determine which method to invoke to open a specific file. Instead, at run time, it is necessary to send only the message myFile.open ( ) and the system will determine the type (class) of myFile and invoke the correct method; this is shown in Figure 7.34(b).

**FIGURE 7.35**
A hierarchy of classes.

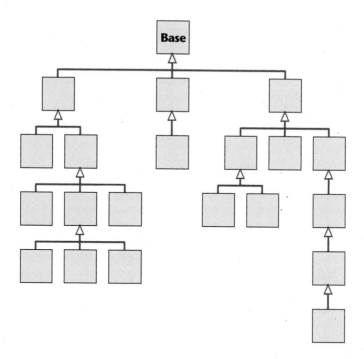

These ideas are applicable to more than just **abstract (virtual)** methods. Consider a hierarchy of classes, as shown in Figure 7.35. All classes are derived by inheritance from the **Base** class. Suppose method checkOrder (b : **Base**) takes as an argument an instance of class **Base**. Then, as a consequence of inheritance, polymorphism, and dynamic binding, it is valid to invoke checkOrder with an argument not just of class **Base** but also of any subclass of class **Base**, that is, any class derived from **Base**. All that is needed is to invoke checkOrder and everything is taken care of at run time. This technique is extremely powerful, in that the software professional need not be concerned about the precise type of an argument at the time that a message is sent.

However, polymorphism and dynamic binding also have major weaknesses.

1. It generally is not possible to determine at compilation time which version of a specific polymorphic method will be invoked at run time. Accordingly, the cause of a failure can be extremely difficult to determine.

2. Polymorphism and dynamic binding can have a negative impact on maintenance. The first task of a maintenance programmer usually is to try to understand the product (as explained in Chapter 15, the maintainer rarely is the person who developed that code). However, this can be laborious if there are multiple possibilities for a specific method. The programmer has to consider all the possible methods that could be invoked dynamically at a specific place in the code, a time-consuming task.

Thus, polymorphism and dynamic binding add both strengths and weaknesses to the object-oriented paradigm.

We conclude this chapter with a discussion of the object-oriented paradigm.

## 7.9   The Object-Oriented Paradigm

There are two ways of looking at every software product. One way is to consider just the data, including local and global variables, arguments, dynamic data structures, and files. Another way of viewing a product is to consider just the operations performed on the data, that is, the procedures and the functions. In terms of this division of software into data and operations, the classical techniques essentially fall into two groups. Operation-oriented techniques primarily consider the operations of the product. The data are of secondary importance, considered only after the operations of the product have been analyzed in depth. Conversely, data-oriented techniques stress the data of the product; the operations are examined only within the framework of the data.

A fundamental weakness of both the data- and operation-oriented approaches is that data and operation are two sides of the same coin; a data item cannot change unless an operation is performed on it, and operations without associated data are equally meaningless. Therefore, techniques that give equal weight to data and operations are needed. It should not come as a surprise that the object-oriented techniques do this. After all, an object comprises both data and operations. Recall that an object is an instance of an abstract data type (more precisely, of a class). It therefore incorporates both data and the operations performed on those data, and the data and the operations are present in objects as equal partners. Similarly, in all the object-oriented techniques, data and operations are considered of the same importance; neither takes precedence over the other.

It is inaccurate to claim that data and operations are considered simultaneously in the techniques of the object-oriented paradigm. From the material on stepwise refinement (Section 5.1), it is clear that sometimes data have to be stressed and other times operations are more critical. Overall, however, data and operations are given equal importance during the workflows of the object-oriented paradigm.

Many reasons are given in Chapter 1 and this chapter as to why the object-oriented paradigm is superior to the classical paradigm. Underlying all these reasons is that a well-designed object, that is, an object with high cohesion and low coupling, models all the aspects of one physical entity. That is, there is a clear mapping between a real-world entity and the object that models it.

The details of how this is implemented are hidden; the only communication with an object is via messages sent to that object. As a result, objects essentially are independent units with a well-defined interface. Consequently, they can be maintained easily and safely; the chance of a regression fault is reduced. Furthermore, as will be explained in Chapter 8, objects are reusable, and this reusability is enhanced by the property of inheritance. Turning now to development using objects, it is safer to construct a large-scale product by combining these fundamental building blocks of software than to use the classical paradigm. Because objects essentially are independent components of a product, development of the product, as well as management of that development, is easier and hence less likely to induce faults.

All these aspects of the superiority of the object-oriented paradigm raise a question: If the classical paradigm is so inferior to the object-oriented paradigm, why has the classical paradigm had so much success? This can be explained by realizing that the classical paradigm was adopted at a time when software engineering was not widely practiced. Instead, software was simply "written." For managers, the most important thing was for programmers to churn out lines of code. Little more than lip service was paid to the requirements and analysis (*systems analysis*) of a product, and design was almost never performed. The code-and-fix model (Section 2.9.1) was typical of the techniques of the 1970s. Therefore, use of the classical paradigm exposed the majority of software developers to methodical techniques for the first time. Small wonder, then, that the so-called structured techniques of the classical paradigm led to major improvements in the software industry worldwide. However, as software products grew in size, inadequacies of the structured techniques started to become apparent, and the object-oriented paradigm was proposed as a better alternative.

This, in turn, leads to another question: How do we know for certain that the object-oriented paradigm is superior to all other present-day techniques? No data are available that prove beyond all doubt that object-oriented technology is better than anything else currently available, and it is hard to imagine how such data could be obtained. The best we can do is to rely on the experiences of organizations that have adopted the object-oriented paradigm. Although not all reports are favorable, the majority (if not the overwhelming majority) attest that using the object-oriented paradigm is a wise decision.

For example, IBM has reported on three totally different projects that were developed using object-oriented technology [Capper, Colgate, Hunter, and James, 1994]. In almost every respect, the object-oriented paradigm greatly outperformed the classical paradigm. Specifically, there were major decreases in the number of faults detected, far fewer change requests during both development and postdelivery maintenance that were not the result of unforeseeable business changes, and significant increases in both adaptive and perfective maintainability. Also improvement in usability was found, although not as large as the previous four improvements, and no meaningful difference in performance.

A survey of 150 experienced U.S. software developers was undertaken to determine their attitudes toward the object-oriented paradigm [Johnson, 2000]. The sample consisted of 96 developers who used the object-oriented paradigm and 54 who still used the classical paradigm to develop software. Both groups felt that the object-oriented paradigm is superior, although the positive attitude of the object-oriented group was significantly stronger. Both groups essentially discounted the various weaknesses of the object-oriented paradigm.

Notwithstanding the many strengths of the object-oriented paradigm, some difficulties and problems indeed have been reported. A frequently reported problem concerns development effort and size. The first time anything new is done, it takes longer than on subsequent occasions; this initial period is sometimes referred to as the **learning curve**. But when the object-oriented paradigm is used for the first time by an organization, it often takes longer than anticipated, even allowing for the learning curve, because the size of the product is larger than when structured techniques are used. This is particularly noticeable when the product has a graphical user interface (GUI) (see Section 10.13). Thereafter, things improve greatly. First, postdelivery maintenance costs are lower, reducing the overall lifetime cost of the product. Second, the next time that a new product is developed, some of the classes from the previous project can often be reused, further reducing software costs. This has been especially significant when a GUI has been used for the first time; much of the effort that went into the GUI can be recouped in subsequent products.

Problems of inheritance are harder to solve.

1. A major reason for using inheritance is to create a new subclass that differs slightly from its parent class without affecting the parent class or any other ancestor class in the inheritance hierarchy. Conversely, however, once a product has been implemented, any

change to an existing class directly affects all its descendants in the inheritance hierarchy; this often is referred to as the **fragile base class problem**. At the very least, the affected units have to be recompiled. In some cases, the methods of the relevant objects (instantiations of the affected subclasses) have to be recoded; this can be a nontrivial task. To minimize this problem, it is important that all classes be meticulously designed during the development process. This will reduce the ripple effect induced by a change to an existing class.

2. A second problem can result from a cavalier use of inheritance. Unless explicitly prevented, a subclass inherits all the attributes of its parent class(es). Usually, subclasses have additional attributes of their own. As a consequence, objects lower in the inheritance hierarchy quickly can get large, with resulting storage problems [Bruegge, Blythe, Jackson, and Shufelt, 1992]. One way to prevent this is to change the dictum "use inheritance wherever possible" to "use inheritance wherever appropriate." In addition, if a descendent class does not need an attribute of an ancestor, then that attribute should be explicitly excluded.

3. A third group of problems stem from polymorphism and dynamic binding. These were described in Section 7.8.

4. Fourth, it is possible to write bad code in any language. However, it is easier to write bad code in an object-oriented language than in a classical language because object-oriented languages support a variety of constructs that, when misused, add unnecessary complexity to a software product. Therefore, when using the object-oriented paradigm, extra care needs to be taken to ensure that the code is always of the highest quality.

One final question is this: Someday might there be something better than the object-oriented paradigm? That is, in the future will a new technology appear in the space above the topmost arrow in Figure 7.28? Even its strongest proponents do not claim that the object-oriented paradigm is the ultimate answer to all software engineering problems. Furthermore, today's software engineers are looking beyond objects to the next major breakthrough. After all, in few fields of human endeavor are the discoveries of the past superior to anything that is being put forward today. The object-oriented paradigm is sure to be superseded by the methodologies of the future. It has been suggested that **aspect-oriented programming** (AOP) may play a role [Murphy et al., 2001]. It remains to be seen whether AOP will indeed be the next major concept in future versions of Figure 7.28 or whether some other technology will be widely adopted as the successor to the object-oriented paradigm. The important lesson is that, based on today's knowledge, the object-oriented paradigm appears to be better than the alternatives.

**Chapter Review**

The chapter begins with a description of a module (Section 7.1). The next two sections analyze what constitutes a well-designed module in terms of module cohesion and module coupling (Sections 7.2 and 7.3). Specifically, a module should have high cohesion and low coupling. A description is given of the different types of cohesion and coupling. Various types of abstraction are presented in Sections 7.4 through 7.7. In data encapsulation (Section 7.4), a module comprises a data *structure* and the actions performed on that data structure. An abstract data type (Section 7.5) is a data *type,* together with the actions performed on instances of that type. Information hiding (Section 7.6) consists of designing a module in such a way that implementation details are hidden from other modules. The progression of increasing abstraction culminates in the description of a class, an abstract data type that supports inheritance (Section 7.7). An object is an instance of a class. Inheritance, polymorphism, and dynamic binding are the subjects of Section 7.8. The chapter concludes with a discussion of the object-oriented paradigm (Section 7.9).

**For Further Reading**

Objects were first described in [Dahl and Nygaard, 1966]. Many of the ideas in this chapter originally were put forward by Parnas [1971, 1972a, 1972b]. The use of abstract data types in software development was put forward in [Liskov and Zilles, 1974]; another important early paper is [Guttag, 1977].

The primary source on cohesion and coupling is [Stevens, Myers, and Constantine, 1974]. The ideas of composite/structured design have been extended to objects [Binkley and Schach, 1997].

Introductory material on objects can be found in [Meyer, 1997]. Different types of inheritance are described in [Meyer, 1996b]. A number of short articles on the object-oriented paradigm can be found in [El-Rewini et al., 1995]. The proceedings of the annual Conference on Object-Oriented Programming Systems, Languages, and Applications (OOPSLA) include a wide selection of research papers as well as reports describing successful object-oriented projects. The successful use of the object-oriented paradigm in three IBM projects is described in [Capper, Colgate, Hunter, and James, 1994]. A survey of attitudes toward the object-oriented paradigm appears in [Johnson, 2000]. Fayad, Tsai, and Fulghum [1996] describe how to make the transition to object-oriented technology; a number of recommendations for managers are included.

The October 1992 issue of *IEEE Computer* contains a number of important articles on objects, especially [Meyer, 1992], which describes "design by contract." A variety of articles on objects can be found in the January 1993 issue of *IEEE Software*; the paper by Snyder [1993] precisely defining key terms in the field is particularly useful. Possible drawbacks of polymorphism are described in [Ponder and Bush, 1994]. The October 1995 issue of the *Communications of the ACM* contains articles on object technology, as does issue no. 2, 2005, of the *IBM Systems Journal*.

Eleven articles on aspect-oriented programming appear in the October 2001 issue of the *Communications of the ACM*; [Elrad et al., 2001] and [Murphy et al., 2001] are of particular interest. Weaknesses of aspect-oriented programming are discussed in [R. Alexander, 2003].

An investigation of the impact of inheritance on fault densities appears in [Cartwright and Shepperd, 2000].

**Key Terms**

abstract data type *202*
abstraction *196*
aggregation *207*
aspect-oriented programming (AOP) *214*
association *208*
binding *180*
class *206*
cohesion *180*
coincidental cohesion *181*
common coupling *187*
communicational cohesion *184*

content coupling *186*
context *180*
control coupling *189*
coupling *180*
data abstraction *196*
data coupling *191*
data encapsulation *195*
dynamic binding *210*
encapsulation *196*
flowchart cohesion *184*
fragile base class problem *214*
functional cohesion *184*

generalization *207*
information hiding *203*
informational cohesion *185*
inheritance *206*
isA *206*
learning curve *213*
logic *180*
logical cohesion *182*
module *178*
note *206*
navigation triangle *208*
object *206*

| | | |
|---|---|---|
| operation *180* | procedural cohesion *183* | strength *180* |
| polymorphism *210* | specialization *207* | subclass *206* |
| procedural abstraction *196* | stamp coupling *190* | temporal cohesion *183* |

**Problems**

7.1 Choose any programming language with which you are familiar. Consider the two definitions of modularity given in Section 7.1. Determine which of the two definitions includes what you intuitively understand to constitute a module in the language you have chosen.

7.2 Determine the cohesion of the following modules:

editProfitAndTaxRecord

editProfitRecordAndTaxRecord

readDeliveryRecordAndCheckSalaryPayments

computeTheOptimalCostUsingAksen'sAlgorithm

measureVaporPressureAndSoundAlarmIfNecessary

7.3 You are a software engineer involved in product development. Your manager asks you to investigate ways of ensuring that modules designed by your group will be as reusable as possible. What do you tell her?

7.4 Your manager now asks you to determine how existing modules can be reused. Your first suggestion is to break each module with coincidental cohesion into separate modules with functional cohesion. Your manager correctly points out that the separate modules have not been tested nor have they been documented. What do you say now?

7.5 What is the influence of cohesion on maintenance?

7.6 What is the influence of coupling on maintenance?

7.7 Distinguish between data encapsulation and abstract data types.

7.8 Distinguish between abstraction and information hiding.

7.9 Distinguish between polymorphism and dynamic binding.

7.10 What happens if we use polymorphism without dynamic binding?

7.11 What happens if we use dynamic binding without polymorphism?

7.12 Convert the comments in Figure 7.23 to C++ or Java, as specified by your instructor. Make sure that the resulting module executes correctly.

7.13 It has been suggested that C++ and Java support implementation of abstract data types but only at the cost of giving up information hiding. Discuss this claim.

7.14 As pointed out in Just in Case You Wanted to Know Box 7.1, objects first were put forward in 1966. Only after essentially being reinvented nearly 20 years later did objects begin to receive widespread acceptance. Can you explain this phenomenon?

7.15 Your instructor will distribute a classical software product. Analyze the modules from the viewpoints of information hiding, levels of abstraction, coupling, and cohesion.

7.16 Your instructor will distribute an object-oriented software product. Analyze the modules from the viewpoints of information hiding, levels of abstraction, coupling, and cohesion. Compare your answer with that of Problem 7.15.

7.17 What are the strengths and weaknesses of inheritance?

7.18 (Term Project) Suppose that the Osric's Office Appliances and Decor product of Appendix A was developed using the classical paradigm. Give examples of modules of functional cohesion that you would expect to find. Now suppose that the product was developed using the object-oriented paradigm. Give examples of classes that you would expect to find.

7.19 (Readings in Software Engineering) Your instructor will distribute copies of [R. Alexander, 2003]. Do you think that aspect-oriented programming will be the next major concept in future versions of Figure 7.28? Justify your answer.

**References**

[R. Alexander, 2003] R. ALEXANDER, "The Real Costs of Aspect-Oriented Programming," *IEEE Software* **20** (November/December 2003), pp. 92–93.

[Binkley and Schach, 1997] A. B. BINKLEY AND S. R. SCHACH, "Toward a Unified Approach to Object-Oriented Coupling," *Proceedings of the 35th Annual ACM Southeast Conference,* Murfreesboro, TN, April 2–4, 1997, pp. 91–97.

[Blaha, Premerlani, and Rumbaugh, 1988] M. R. BLAHA, W. J. PREMERLANI, AND J. E. RUMBAUGH, "Relational Database Design Using an Object-Oriented Methodology," *Communications of the ACM* **31** (April 1988), pp. 414–27.

[Briand, Daly, Porter, and Wüst, 1998] L. C. BRIAND, J. DALY, V. PORTER, AND J. WÜST, "A Comprehensive Empirical Validation of Design Measures for Object-Oriented Systems," *Proceedings of the Fifth International Metrics Symposium,* Bethesda, MD, November 1998, pp. 246–257.

[Bruegge, Blythe, Jackson, and Shufelt, 1992] B. BRUEGGE, J. BLYTHE, J. JACKSON, AND J. SHUFELT, "Object-Oriented Modeling with OMT," Proceedings of the Conference on Object-Oriented Programming, Languages, and Systems, OOPSLA '92, *ACM SIGPLAN Notices* **27** (October 1992), pp. 359–76.

[Capper, Colgate, Hunter, and James, 1994] N. P. CAPPER, R. J. COLGATE, J. C. HUNTER, AND M. F. JAMES, "The Impact of Object-Oriented Technology on Software Quality: Three Case Histories," *IBM Systems Journal* **33** (No. 1, 1994), pp. 131–57.

[Cartwright and Shepperd, 2000] M. CARTWRIGHT AND M. SHEPPERD, "An Empirical Investigation of an Object-Oriented Software System," *IEEE Transactions on Software Engineering* **26** (August 2000), pp. 786–95.

[Dahl and Nygaard, 1966] O.-J. DAHL AND K. NYGAARD, "SIMULA—An ALGOL-Based Simulation Language," *Communications of the ACM* **9** (September 1966), pp. 671–78.

[Elrad et al., 2001] T. ELRAD, M. AKSIT, G. KICZALES, K. LIEBERHERR, AND H. OSSHER, "Discussing Aspects of AOP," *Communications of the ACM* **44** (October 2001), pp. 33–38.

[El-Rewini et al., 1995] H. EL-REWINI, S. HAMILTON, Y.-P. SHAN, R. EARLE, S. MCGAUGHEY, A. HELAL, R. BADRACHALAM, A. CHIEN, A. GRIMSHAW, B. LEE, A. WADE, D. MORSE, A. ELMAGRAMID, E. PITOURA, R. BINDER, AND P. WEGNER, "Object Technology," *IEEE Computer* **28** (October 1995), pp. 58–72.

[Fayad, Tsai, and Fulghum, 1996] M. E. FAYAD, W.-T. TSAI, AND M. L. FULGHUM, "Transition to Object-Oriented Software Development," *Communications of the ACM* **39** (February 1996), pp. 108–21.

[Flanagan, 2005] D. FLANAGAN, *Java in a Nutshell: A Desktop Quick Reference,* 5th ed., O'Reilly and Associates, Sebastopol, CA, 2005.

[Gerald and Wheatley, 1999] C. F. GERALD AND P. O. WHEATLEY, *Applied Numerical Analysis,* 6th ed., Addison-Wesley, Reading, MA, 1999.

[Goldberg and Robson, 1989] A. GOLDBERG AND D. ROBSON, *Smalltalk-80: The Language,* Addison-Wesley, Reading, MA, 1989.

[Guttag, 1977] J. GUTTAG, "Abstract Data Types and the Development of Data Structures," *Communications of the ACM* **20** (June 1977), pp. 396–404.

[Johnson, 2000] R. A. JOHNSON, "The Ups and Downs of Object-Oriented System Development," *Communications of the ACM* **43** (October 2000), pp. 69–73.

[Knuth, 1974] D. E. KNUTH, "Structured Programming with **go to** Statements," *ACM Computing Surveys* **6** (December 1974), pp. 261–301.

[Liskov and Zilles, 1974] B. LISKOV AND S. ZILLES, "Programming with Abstract Data Types," *ACM SIGPLAN Notices* **9** (April 1974), pp. 50–59.

[Meyer, 1986] B. MEYER, "Genericity versus Inheritance," Proceedings of the Conference on Object-Oriented Programming Systems, Languages and Applications, *ACM SIGPLAN Notices* **21** (November 1986), pp. 391–405.

[Meyer, 1992] B. MEYER, "Applying 'Design by Contract'," *IEEE Computer* **25** (October 1992), pp. 40–51.

[Meyer, 1996b] B. MEYER, "The Many Faces of Inheritance: A Taxonomy of Taxonomy," *IEEE Computer* **29** (May 1996), pp. 105–8.

[Meyer, 1997] B. MEYER, *Object-Oriented Software Construction,* 2nd ed., Prentice Hall, Upper Saddle River, NJ, 1997.

[Murphy et al., 2001] G. C. MURPHY, R. J. WALKER, E. L. A. BANNIASSAD, M. P. ROBILLARD, A. LIA, AND M. A. KERSTEN, "Does Aspect-Oriented Programming Work?" *Communications of the ACM* **44** (October 2001), pp. 75–78.

[Myers, 1978b] G. J. MYERS, *Composite/Structured Design,* Van Nostrand Reinhold, New York, 1978.

[Parnas, 1971] D. L. PARNAS, "Information Distribution Aspects of Design Methodology," *Proceedings of the IFIP Congress,* Ljubljana, Yugoslavia, 1971, pp. 339–44.

[Parnas, 1972a] D. L. PARNAS, "A Technique for Software Module Specification with Examples," *Communications of the ACM* **15** (May 1972), pp. 330–36.

[Parnas, 1972b] D. L. PARNAS, "On the Criteria to Be Used in Decomposing Systems into Modules," *Communications of the ACM* **15** (December 1972), pp. 1053–58.

[Ponder and Bush, 1994] C. PONDER AND B. BUSH, "Polymorphism Considered Harmful," *ACM SIGSOFT Software Engineering Notes* **19** (April, 1994), pp. 35–38.

[Schach and Stevens-Guille, 1979] S. R. SCHACH AND P. D. STEVENS-GUILLE, "Two Aspects of Computer-Aided Design," *Transactions of the Royal Society of South Africa* **44** (Part 1, 1979), 123–26.

[Schach et al., 2002] S. R. SCHACH, B. JIN, D. R. WRIGHT, G. Z. HELLER, AND A. J. OFFUTT, "Maintainability of the Linux Kernel," *IEE Proceedings—Software* **149** (February 2002), pp. 18–23.

[Schach et al., 2003a] S. R. SCHACH, B. JIN, DAVID R. WRIGHT, G. Z. HELLER, AND J. OFFUTT, "Quality Impacts of Clandestine Common Coupling," *Software Quality Journal* **11** (July 2003), pp. 211–18.

[Shneiderman and Mayer, 1975] B. SHNEIDERMAN AND R. MAYER, "Towards a Cognitive Model of Programmer Behavior," Technical Report TR-37, Indiana University, Bloomington, 1975.

[Snyder, 1993] A. SNYDER, "The Essence of Objects: Concepts and Terms," *IEEE Software* **10** (January 1993), pp. 31–42.

[Stevens, Myers, and Constantine, 1974] W. P. STEVENS, G. J. MYERS, AND L. L. CONSTANTINE, "Structured Design," *IBM Systems Journal* **13** (No. 2, 1974), pp. 115–39.

[Stroustrup, 2003] B. STROUSTRUP, *The C++ Standard: Incorporating Technical Corrigendum No. 1,* 2nd ed., John Wiley and Sons, New York, 2003.

[Yourdon and Constantine, 1979] E. YOURDON AND L. L. CONSTANTINE, *Structured Design: Fundamentals of a Discipline of Computer Program and Systems Design,* Prentice Hall, Englewood Cliffs, NJ, 1979.

[Yu, Schach, Chen, and Offutt, 2004] L. YU, S. R. SCHACH, K. CHEN, AND J. OFFUTT, "Categorization of Common Coupling and its Application to the Maintainability of the Linux Kernel," *IEEE Transactions on Software Engineering* **30** (October 2004), pp. 694–706.

# Chapter

# Reusability and Portability

### Learning Objectives

After studying this chapter, you should be able to

- Explain why reuse is so important.
- Appreciate the obstacles to reuse.
- Describe techniques for achieving reuse during the various workflows.
- Discuss the impact of reuse on maintainability.
- Explain why portability is essential.
- Understand the obstacles to achieving portability.
- Develop portable software.

If reinventing the wheel were a criminal offense, many software professionals would today be languishing in jail. For example, there are tens of thousands (if not hundreds of thousands) of different COBOL payroll programs, all doing essentially the same thing. Surely, the world needs just one payroll program that can run on a variety of hardware and be tailored, if necessary, to cater to the specific needs of an individual organization. However, instead of utilizing previously developed payroll programs, myriad organizations all over the world have built their own payroll program from scratch. In this chapter, we investigate why software engineers delight in continually reinventing the wheel, and what can be done to achieve portable software built using reusable components. We begin by distinguishing between portability and reusability.

As explained in the Preface, the material of this chapter may be taught in parallel with Part 2.

Reuse is not restricted to software. For example, lawyers nowadays rarely draft wills from scratch. Instead, they use a word processor to store wills they have previously drafted, and then make appropriate changes to an existing will. Other legal documents, like contracts, are usually drafted in the same way from existing documents.

Classical composers frequently reused their own music. For example, in 1823 Franz Schubert wrote an entr'acte for Helmina von Chezy's play, *Rosamunde, Fürstin von Zypern* (*Rosamunde, Princess of Cyprus*) and the following year he reused that material in the slow movement of his String Quartet No. 13. Ludwig van Beethoven's Opus 66, "Variations for Cello on Mozart's *Ein Mädchen oder Weibchen*," is a good example of one great composer reusing the music of another great composer; Beethoven simply took the aria "A Girlfriend or Little Wife" from Scene 22 of Wolfgang Amadeus Mozart's opera *Der Zauberflöte* (*The Magic Flute*) and wrote a series of seven variations on that aria for the cello with piano accompaniment.

In my opinion, the greatest reuser of all time was William Shakespeare. His genius lay in reusing the plots of others—I cannot think of a single story line he made up himself. For example, his historical plays heavily reused parts of Raphael Holinshed's 1577 work, *Chronicles of England, Scotland and Ireland*. Then, Shakespeare's *Romeo and Juliet* (1594) is borrowed, on an almost line-for-line basis, from Arthur Brooke's lengthy poem *The Tragicall Historye of Romeus and Iuliet* published in 1562, two years before Shakespeare was born.

But this reuse saga didn't begin there. In fact, the earliest known version appeared around 200 CE in *Ephesiaka* (*Ephesian tale*) by the Greek novelist Xenophon of Ephesus. In 1476, Tommaso Guardati (more commonly known as Masuccio Salernitano) reused Xenophon's tale in novella 33 in his collection of 50 novellas, *Il Novellino*. In 1530, Luigi da Porto reused that story in *Historia Novellamente Ritrovata di Due Nobili Amanti* (*A Newly Found Story of Two Noble Lovers*), for the first time setting it in Verona, Italy. Brooke's poem reuses parts of *Giulietta e Romeo* (1554) by Matteo Bandello, a reuse of da Porto's version.

And this reuse saga didn't end with *Romeo and Juliet*, either. In 1957, *West Side Story* opened on Broadway. The musical, with book by Arthur Laurents, lyrics by Stephen Sondheim, and score by Leonard Bernstein, reused Shakespeare's version of the story. The Broadway musical was then reused in a Hollywood movie, which won 10 Academy Awards in 1961.

## 8.1    Reuse Concepts

A product is **portable** if it is significantly easier to modify the product as a whole to run it on another compiler–hardware–operating system configuration than to recode it from scratch. In contrast, **reuse** refers to using components of one product to facilitate the development of a different product with a different functionality. A reusable component need not necessarily be a module or a code fragment—it could be a design, a part of a manual, a set of test data, or a duration and cost estimate. (For a different view on reuse, see Just in Case You Wanted to Know Box 8.1.)

There are two types of reuse, opportunistic reuse and deliberate reuse. If the developers of a new product realize that a component of a previously developed product can be reused in the new product, then this is **opportunistic reuse**, sometimes referred to as **accidental reuse**. On the other hand, utilization of software components constructed specifically for possible future reuse is **systematic reuse** or **deliberate reuse**. A potential advantage of systematic reuse over opportunistic reuse is that components specially constructed for use in future products are more likely to be easy and safe to reuse; such components generally are robust, well documented, and thoroughly tested. In addition, they usually display a uniformity of style that makes maintenance easier. The other side of the coin is that implementing systematic reuse within a company can be expensive. It takes time to specify, design, implement, test, and document a software component. However, there can be no guarantee that such a component will be reused and thereby recoup the money invested in developing the potentially reusable component.

When computers were first constructed, nothing was reused. Every time a product was developed, items such as multiplication routines, input–output routines, or routines for computing sines and cosines were constructed from scratch. Quite soon, however, it was realized that this was a considerable waste of effort, and subroutine libraries were constructed. Programmers then simply could invoke square root or sine functions whenever they wished. These subroutine libraries have become more and more sophisticated and developed into run-time support routines. Therefore, when a programmer calls a C++ or Java method, there is no need to write code to manage the stack or pass the arguments explicitly; it is handled automatically by calling the appropriate run-time support routines. The concept of subroutine libraries has been extended to large-scale statistical libraries such as SPSS [Norušis, 2005] and numerical analysis libraries like NAG [2003]. Class libraries also play a major role in assisting users of object-oriented languages. For example, the success of Smalltalk is due at least partly to the wide variety of items in the Smalltalk library together with the presence of a browser, a CASE tool that assists the user to scan a class library. With regard to C++, a large number of different libraries are available, many in the public domain. One example is the C++ Standard Template Library (STL) [Musser and Saini, 1996].

An application programming interface (API) generally is a set of operating system calls that facilitate programming. For example, Win32 is an API for Microsoft operating systems such as Windows 2000 and Windows XP; and Cocoa is an API for Mac OS X, a Macintosh operating system. Although an API usually is implemented as a set of operating system calls, to the programmer the routines constituting the API can be viewed as a subroutine library. For example, the Java Application Programming Interface consists of a number of packages (libraries).

No matter how high the quality of a software product may be, it will not sell if it takes 2 years to get it onto the market when a competitive product can be delivered in only 1 year. The length of the development process is critical in a market economy. All other criteria as to what constitutes a "good" product are irrelevant if the product cannot compete timewise. For a corporation that has repeatedly failed to get a product to market first, software reuse offers a tempting technique. After all, if an existing component is reused, then there is no need to specify, design, implement, test, and document that component. The key point is that, on average, only about 15 percent of any software product serves a truly original purpose [Jones, 1984]. The other 85 percent of the product in theory could be standardized and reused in future products.

The figure of 85 percent is essentially a theoretical upper limit for the reuse rate; nevertheless, reuse rates on the order of 40 percent can be achieved in practice. This leads to an obvious question: If such reuse rates are attainable in practice and reuse is by no means a new idea, why do so few organizations employ reuse to shorten the development process?

## 8.2 Impediments to Reuse

There are a number of impediments to reuse:

- All too many software professionals would rather rewrite a routine from scratch than reuse a routine written by someone else, the implication being that a routine cannot be any good unless they wrote it themselves, otherwise known as the **not invented here** (NIH) **syndrome** [Griss, 1993]. NIH is a management issue, and, if management is aware of the problem, it can be solved, usually by offering financial incentives to promote reuse.

- Many developers would be willing to reuse a routine provided they could be sure that the routine in question would not introduce faults into the product. This attitude toward software quality is perfectly easy to understand. After all, every software professional has seen faulty software written by others. The solution here is to subject potentially reusable routines to exhaustive testing before making them available for reuse.

- A large organization may have hundreds of thousands of potentially useful components. How should these components be stored for effective later retrieval? For example, a reusable components database might consist of 20,000 items, 125 of which are sort routines. The database must be organized so that the designer of a new product can quickly determine which (if any) of those 125 sort routines is appropriate for the new product. Solving the storage/retrieval problem is a technical issue for which a wide variety of solutions have been proposed (e.g., [Meyer, 1987] or [Prieto-Díaz, 1991]).

- Reuse can be expensive. Tracz [1994] has stated that three costs are involved: the cost of making something reusable, the cost of reusing it, and the cost of defining and implementing a reuse process. He estimates that just making a component reusable increases its cost by at least 60 percent. Some organizations have reported cost increases of 200 percent and even up to 480 percent, whereas the cost of making a component reusable was only 11 percent in one Hewlett-Packard reuse project [Lim, 1994].

- Legal issues can arise with contract software. In terms of the type of contract usually drawn up between a client and a software development organization, the software product belongs to the client. Therefore, if the software developer reuses a component of one client's product in a new product for a different client, this essentially constitutes a violation of the first client's copyright. For internal software, that is, when the developers and client are members of the same organization, this problem does not arise.

- Another impediment arises when commercial off-the-shelf (COTS) components are reused. Rarely are developers given the source code of a COTS component, so software that reuses COTS components has limited extensibility and modifiability.

The first four impediments can be overcome, at least in principle. So, other than certain legal issues and problems with COTS components, essentially no major impediments prevent implementing reuse within a software organization (but see Just in Case You Wanted to Know Box 8.2).

The World Wide Web is a great source of "urban myths," that is, apparently true stories that somehow just do not stand up under scrutiny when they are investigated closely. One such urban myth concerns code reuse.

The story is told that the Australian Air Force set up a virtual reality training simulator for helicopter combat training. To make the scenarios as realistic as possible, programmers included detailed landscapes and (in the Northern Territory) herds of kangaroos. After all, the dust from a herd disturbed by a helicopter might reveal the position of that helicopter to the enemy.

The programmers were instructed to model both the movements of the kangaroos and their reaction to helicopters. To save time, the programmers reused code originally used to simulate the reaction of infantry to attack by a helicopter. Only two changes were made: They changed the icon from a soldier to a kangaroo, and they increased the speed of movement of the figures.

One fine day, a group of Australian pilots wanted to demonstrate their prowess with the flight simulator to some visiting American pilots. They "buzzed" (flew very low over) the virtual kangaroos. As expected, the kangaroos scattered, and then reappeared from behind a hill and launched Stinger missiles at the helicopter. The programmers had forgotten to remove that part of the code when they reused the virtual infantry implementation.

However, as reported in *The Risks Digest*, it appears that the story is not totally an urban myth—much of it actually happened [Green, 2000]. Dr. Anne-Marie Grisogono, head of the Simulation Land Operations Division at the Australian Defence Science and Technology Organisation, told the story at a meeting in Canberra, Australia, on May 6, 1999. Although the simulator was designed to be as realistic as possible (it even included over 2 million virtual trees, as indicated on aerial photographs), the kangaroos were included for fun. The programmers indeed reused Stinger missile detachments so that the kangaroos could detect the arrival of helicopters, but the behavior of the kangaroos was set to "retreat" so that the kangaroos, correctly, would flee if a helicopter approached. However, when the software team tested their simulator in their laboratory (not in front of visitors), they discovered that they had forgotten to remove both the weapons and "fire" behavior. Also, they had not specified what weapons were to be used by the simulated figures, so when the kangaroos fired on the helicopters, they fired the default weapon, which happened to be large multicolored beachballs.

Grisogono confirmed that the kangaroos were immediately disarmed and therefore it is now safe to fly over Australia. But notwithstanding this happy ending, software professionals still must take care when reusing code not to reuse too much of it.

## 8.3   Reuse Case Studies

Many published case studies show how reuse has been successfully achieved in practice; reuse case studies that have had a major impact include [Matsumoto, 1984, 1987; Selby, 1989; Prieto-Díaz, 1991; and Lim, 1994]. Here, we analyze two case studies. The first, which describes a reuse project that took place between 1976 and 1982, is important because the reuse mechanism used then for COBOL designs is the same as the reuse mechanism used today in object-oriented application frameworks (Section 8.5.2). This case study therefore serves to clarify modern reuse practices.

## 8.3.1 Raytheon Missile Systems Division

In 1976, a study was undertaken at Raytheon's Missile Systems Division to determine whether systematic reuse of designs and code was feasible [Lanergan and Grasso, 1984]. Over 5000 COBOL products in use were analyzed and classified. The researchers determined that only six basic operations are performed in a business application product. As a result, between 40 and 60 percent of business application designs and modules could be standardized and reused. The basic operations were found to be sort data, edit or manipulate data, combine data, explode data, update data, and report on data. For the next 6 years, a concerted attempt was made to reuse both design and code wherever possible.

The Raytheon approach employed reuse in two ways, what the researchers termed *functional modules* and *COBOL program logic structures*. In Raytheon's terminology a **functional module** is a COBOL code fragment designed and coded for a specific purpose, such as an edit routine, database procedure division call, tax computation routine, or date aging routine for accounts receivable. Use of the 3200 reusable modules resulted in applications that, on average, consisted of 60 percent reused code. Functional modules were carefully designed, tested, and documented. Products that used these functional modules were found to be more reliable, and less testing of the product as a whole was needed.

The modules were stored in a standard copy library and obtained with the **copy** verb. That is, the code was not physically present within the application product but included by the COBOL compiler at compilation time, a mechanism similar to **#include** in C or C++. The resulting source code therefore was shorter than if the copied code were physically present. As a consequence, maintenance was easier.

The Raytheon researchers also used what they termed a **COBOL program logic structure**. This is a framework that has to be fleshed out into a complete product. One example of a logic structure is the update logic structure. This is used to perform a sequential update, such as the mini case study in Section 5.1.1. Error handling is built in, as is sequence checking. The logic structure is 22 paragraphs (units of a COBOL program) in length. Many of the paragraphs can be filled in by using functional modules such as get-transaction, print-page-headings, and print-control-totals. Figure 8.1 is a symbolic

**FIGURE 8.1**
A symbolic representation of the Raytheon Missile Systems Division reuse mechanism.

COBOL program
logic structure

Functional module

depiction of the framework of a COBOL program logic structure with the paragraphs filled in by functional modules.

The use of such templates has many advantages. It makes the design and coding of a product quicker and easier, because the framework of the product already is present; all that is needed is to fill in the details. Fault-prone areas such as end-of-file conditions already have been tested. In fact, testing as a whole is easier. But Raytheon believed that the major advantage would occur when the users requested modifications or enhancements. Once a maintenance programmer was familiar with the relevant logic structure, it was almost as if he or she had been a member of the original development team.

By 1983, logic structures had been used over 5500 times in developing new products. About 60 percent of the code consisted of functional modules, that is, reusable code. This meant that design, coding, module testing, and documentation time also was reduced by 60 percent, leading to an estimated 50 percent increase in productivity in software product development. But, for Raytheon, the real benefit of the technique lay in the hope that the readability and understandability resulting from the consistent style would reduce the cost of maintenance by between 60 and 80 percent. Unfortunately, Raytheon closed the division before the necessary maintenance data could be obtained.

The second reuse case study is a cautionary tale, rather than a success story.

## 8.3.2 European Space Agency

On June 4, 1996, the European Space Agency launched the Ariane 5 rocket for the first time. As a consequence of a software fault, the rocket crashed about 37 seconds after liftoff. The cost of the rocket and payload was about $500 million [Jézéquel and Meyer, 1997].

The primary cause of the failure was an attempt to convert a 64-bit integer into a 16-bit unsigned integer. The number being converted was larger than $2^{16}$, so an Ada **exception** (run-time failure) occurred. Unfortunately, there was no explicit exception handler in the code to deal with this exception, so the software crashed. This caused the onboard computers to crash which, in turn, caused the Ariane 5 rocket to crash.

Ironically, the conversion that caused the failure was unnecessary. Certain computations are performed before liftoff to align the inertial reference system. These computations should stop 9 seconds before liftoff. However, if there is a subsequent hold in the countdown, resetting the inertial reference system after the countdown has recommenced can take several hours. To prevent that happening, the computations continue for 50 seconds after the start of flight mode, that is, well into the flight (notwithstanding that, once liftoff has occurred, there is no way to align the inertial reference system). This futile continuation of the alignment process caused the failure.

The European Space Agency uses a careful software development process that incorporates an effective software quality assurance component. Then, why was there no exception handler in the Ada code to handle the possibility of such an overflow? To prevent overloading the computer, conversions that could not possibly result in overflow were left unprotected. The code in question was 10 years old. It had been reused, unchanged and without any further testing, from the software controlling the Ariane 4 rocket (the precursor of the Ariane 5). Mathematical analysis had proven that the computation in question was totally safe for the Ariane 4. However, the analysis was performed on the basis of certain assumptions that were true for the Ariane 4 but not for the Ariane 5. Therefore, the analysis no longer was valid, and the code needed the protection of an exception handler to cater to the possibility of an overflow. Were it not for the performance constraint, there surely would have been exception handlers throughout the Ariane 5 Ada code. Alternatively, the use of the **assert pragma** both during testing and after the product had been installed (Section 6.5.3) could have prevented the Ariane 5 crash if the relevant module had included an assertion that the number to be converted was smaller than $2^{16}$ [Jézéquel and Meyer, 1997].

The major lesson of this reuse experience is that software developed in one context must be retested when reused in another context. That is, a reused software module does not need to be retested by itself, but it must be retested after it has been integrated into the product in which it is reused. Another lesson is that it is unwise to rely exclusively on the results of mathematical proofs, as discussed in Section 6.5.2.

We now examine the impact of the object-oriented paradigm on reuse.

# 8.4 Objects and Reuse

When the theory of composite/structured design first was put forward about 30 years ago, the claim was made that an ideal module has functional cohesion (Section 7.2.6). That is, if a module performed only one operation, it was thought to be an exemplary candidate for reuse, and maintenance of such a module was expected to be easy. The flaw in this reasoning is that a module with functional cohesion is not self-contained and independent. Instead, it has to operate on data. If such a module is reused, then the data on which it is to operate must be reused, too. If the data in the new product are not identical to those in the original, then either the data have to be changed or the module with functional cohesion has to be changed. Therefore, contrary to what we used to believe, functional cohesion is not ideal for reuse.

According to classical C/SD, the next best type of module is one with informational cohesion (Section 7.2.7). Nowadays, we appreciate that such a module essentially is an object, that is, an instance of a class. A well-designed object is the fundamental building block of software because it models all aspects of a particular real-world entity (conceptual independence, or encapsulation) but conceals the implementation of both its data and the operations that operate on the data (physical independence, or information hiding). Therefore, when the object-oriented paradigm is utilized correctly, the resulting modules (objects) have informational cohesion, and this promotes reuse.

# 8.5 Reuse during Design and Implementation

Dramatically different types of reuse are possible during design. The reused material can vary from just one or two artifacts to the architecture of the complete software product. We now examine various types of design reuse, some of which carry over into implementation.

## 8.5.1 Design Reuse

When designing a product, a member of the design team may realize that a module or class from an earlier design can be reused in the current project, with or without minor

**FIGURE 8.2** A symbolic representation of four types of design reuse. Shading denotes design reuse within (a) a library or a toolkit, (b) a framework, (c) a design pattern, and (d) a software architecture comprising a framework, a toolkit, and three design patterns.

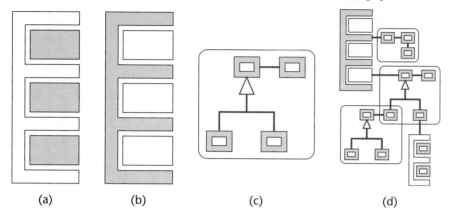

(a)  (b)  (c)  (d)

modifications. This type of reuse is particularly common in an organization that develops software in one specific application domain, such as banking or air traffic control systems. The organization can promote this type of reuse by setting up a repository of design components likely to be reused in the future and encouraging designers to reuse them, perhaps by a cash bonus for each such reuse. This type of reuse, limited though it may be, has two advantages. First, tested module designs are incorporated into the product. The overall design therefore can be produced more quickly and is likely to have a higher quality than when the entire design is produced from scratch. Second, if the design of a module can be reused, then it is likely that the implementation of that module also can be reused, if not the actual code then at least conceptually.

This approach can be extended to library reuse, depicted in Figure 8.2(a). A library is a set of related reusable routines. For example, developers of scientific software rarely write the routines to perform such common tasks as matrix inversion or finding eigenvalues. Instead, a scientific library such as LAPACK 3.0 [Anderson et al., 1999] is purchased. Then, whenever possible, the routines in the scientific library are utilized in future software. With the rise in popularity of the object-oriented paradigm, class libraries for scientific software have also been developed, such as LAPACK++ [2000].

Another example is a library for a graphical user interface. Instead of writing the GUI methods from scratch, it is far more convenient to use a GUI class library or **toolkit**, that is, a set of classes that can handle every aspect of the GUI. Many GUI toolkits of this kind are available, including the Java Abstract Windowing Toolkit [Flanagan, 2005].

A problem with library reuse is that libraries frequently are presented in the format of a set of reusable subroutines rather than reusable designs. Toolkits, too, generally promote code reuse rather than design reuse. When the object-oriented paradigm is used, however, this problem can be alleviated with the help of a browser, that is, a CASE tool for displaying the inheritance tree. The designer then can traverse the inheritance tree of the library, examine the fields of the various classes, and determine which class is applicable to the current design.

A key aspect of library and toolkit reuse is that, as depicted in Figure 8.2(a), the designer is responsible for the control logic of the product as a whole. The library or toolkit contributes to the software development process by supplying parts of the design that incorporate the specific operations of the product.

On the other hand, an application framework is the converse of a library or toolkit in that it supplies the control logic; the developers are responsible for the design of the specific operations. This is described in Section 8.5.2.

## 8.5.2 Application Frameworks

As shown in Figure 8.2(b), an **application framework** incorporates the control logic of a design. When a framework is reused, the developers have to design the application-specific operations of the product being built. The places where the application-specific operations are inserted frequently are referred to as **hot spots**.

The term **framework** nowadays usually refers to an object-oriented application framework. For example, in [Gamma, Helm, Johnson, and Vlissides, 1995], a *framework* is defined as a "set of cooperating classes that make up a reusable design for a specific class of software." However, consider the Raytheon Missiles Systems Division case study of Section 8.3.1. Figure 8.1 is identical to Figure 8.2(b). In other words, the Raytheon COBOL program logic structure of the 1970s is a classical precursor of today's object-oriented application framework.

An example of an application framework is a set of classes for the design of a compiler. The design team merely has to provide classes specific to the language and desired target machine. These classes then are inserted into the framework, as depicted by the white boxes in Figure 8.2(b). Another example of a framework is a set of classes for the software controlling an ATM. Here, the designers need to provide the classes for the specific banking services offered by the ATMs of that banking network.

Reusing a framework results in faster product development than reusing a toolkit, for two reasons. First, more of the design is reused with a framework, so there is less to design from scratch. Second, the portion of the design that is reused with a framework (the control logic) generally is harder to design than the operations, so the quality of the resulting design also is likely to be higher than when a toolkit is reused. As with library or toolkit reuse, often the implementation of the framework can be reused as well. The developers probably have to use the names and calling conventions of the framework, but that is a small price to pay. Also, the resulting product is likely to be maintained easily because the control logic has been tested in other products that reuse the application framework and the maintainer previously may have maintained another product that reused that same framework.

IBM's WebSphere (formerly known as *e-Components*, and originally as *San Francisco*) is a framework for building online information systems in Java. It utilizes Enterprise JavaBeans, that is, classes that provide services for clients distributed throughout a network.

In addition to application frameworks, many code frameworks are available. One of the first commercially successful code frameworks was MacApp, a framework for writing application software on the Macintosh. The Microsoft Foundation Class Library (MFC) is a large collection of frameworks for building GUIs in Windows-based applications. MFC applications can perform standard windowing operations, such as moving and resizing windows, processing input via dialog boxes, and handling events like mouse clicks or menu selections. Borland's Visual Component Library (VCL), an update of the ObjectWindows

One of the most influential individuals in the field of object-oriented software engineering is Christopher Alexander, a world-famous architect who freely admits to knowing little or nothing about objects or software engineering. In his books, and especially in [Alexander et al., 1977], he describes a pattern language for architecture, that is, for describing towns, buildings, rooms, gardens, and so on. His ideas were adopted and adapted by object-oriented software engineers, especially the so-called Gang of Four (Erich Gamma, Richard Helm, Ralph Johnson, and John Vlissides). Their best-selling book on design patterns [Gamma, Helm, Johnson, and Vlissides, 1995] resulted in Alexander's ideas being widely accepted by the object-oriented community.

Patterns occur in other contexts as well. For example, when approaching an airport, pilots have to know the appropriate landing pattern, that is, the sequence of directions, altitudes, and turns needed to land the plane on the correct runway. Also, a dressmaking pattern is a series of shapes that can be used repeatedly to create a particular dress. The concept of a pattern itself is by no means novel. What is new is the application of patterns to software development and especially design.

---

Library (OWL), has functionality similar to that of the MFC. However, the VCL is fully object oriented.

We now consider design patterns.

## 8.5.3 Design Patterns

Christopher Alexander (see Just in Case You Wanted to Know Box 8.3) said, "Each pattern describes a problem which occurs over and over again in our environment, and then describes the core of the solution to that problem, in such a way that you can use this solution a million times over, without ever doing it the same way twice" [Alexander et al., 1977]. Although he was writing within the context of patterns in buildings and other architectural objects, his remarks are equally applicable to design patterns.

A design pattern is a solution to a general design problem in the form of a set of interacting classes that have to be customized to create a specific design. This is depicted in Figure 8.2(c). The shaded boxes connected by lines denote the interacting classes. The white boxes inside the shaded boxes denote that these classes must be customized for a specific design.

To understand how patterns can assist with software development, consider the following example. Suppose that a software organization wishes to build a widget generator, a tool that assists developers in constructing a graphical user interface. Instead of having to develop the various **widgets** (such as windows, buttons, menus, sliders, and scroll bars) from scratch, a developer can use the set of classes created by the widget generator that define the widgets to be utilized within the application program.

The problem is that the application program (and, therefore, the widgets) may have to run under many different operating systems, including Linux, Mac OS, and Windows. The widget generator is to support all three operating systems. However, if the widget generator hard-codes routines that run under one specific system into an application program, it will be difficult to modify that application program in the future, replacing the generated routines with different routines that run under a different operating system. For example, suppose that the application program is to run under Linux. Then, every time a menu is to be generated, message create Linux menu is sent. However, if that application program now needs to run under Mac OS, every instance of create Linux menu must be replaced by create Mac OS menu. For a large application program, such a conversion from Linux to Mac OS is laborious and fault prone.

The solution is to design the widget generator in such a way that the application program is uncoupled from the specific operating system. This can be achieved using the design pattern *Abstract Factory* [Gamma, Helm, Johnson, and Vlissides, 1995]. Figure 8.3 shows the resulting design. In this figure, the names of abstract classes and their abstract (virtual)

**FIGURE 8.3**
Design of graphical user interface toolkit. The names of abstract classes and their virtual functions are italicized.

methods are in *sans serif italics*. (An abstract class is a class that cannot be instantiated although it can be used as a base class. It usually contains at least one abstract method.) At the top of Figure 8.3 is abstract class ***Abstract Widget Factory*** (as stated in Section 7.7, the UML convention is that classes appear in boldface with the first letter of each word capitalized). This abstract class contains numerous abstract methods; for simplicity, only two are shown here: *create menu* and *create window*. Moving down in the figure, **Linux Widget Factory**, **Mac OS Widget Factory**, and **Windows Widget Factory** are concrete subclasses of ***Abstract Widget Factory***. Each class contains the specific methods for creating widgets that run under a given operating system. For example, create menu within **Linux Widget Factory** causes a menu object to be created that will run under Linux.

There are also abstract classes for each widget. Two are shown here, ***Abstract Menu*** and ***Abstract Window***. Each has concrete subclasses, one for each of the three operating systems. For example, **Linux Menu** is one concrete subclass of ***Abstract Menu***. Method create menu within concrete subclass **Linux Widget Factory** causes an object of type **Linux Menu** to be created.

To create a window, a **Client** object within the application program need only send a message to method *create window* of ***Abstract Widget Factory*** and polymorphism ensures that the correct widget is created. Suppose that the application program has to run under Linux. First, an object Widget Factory of type (class) **Linux Widget Factory** is created. Then a message to abstract method *create window* of ***Abstract Widget Factory*** passing Widget Factory as a parameter is interpreted as a message to method create window within concrete subclass **Linux Widget Factory**. Method create window in turn sends a message to create a **Linux Window**; this is indicated by the leftmost vertical dashed line in Figure 8.3.

The critical aspect of this figure is that the three interfaces between the **Client** within the application program and the widget generator, classes ***Abstract Widget Factory***, ***Abstract Menu***, and ***Abstract Window***, all are abstract classes. None of these interfaces is specific to any one operating system because the methods of the abstract classes are **abstract** (**virtual** in C++). Consequently, the design of Figure 8.3 indeed has uncoupled the application program from the operating system. The design of Figure 8.3 is an instance of pattern ***Abstract Factory*** shown in Figure 8.4. To use this pattern, specific classes replace the generic names like **Concrete Factory 2** and **Product B3**. That is why Figure 8.2(c), the symbolic representation of a design pattern, contains white rectangles within the shaded rectangles; the white rectangles represent the details that have to be supplied to reuse this pattern in a design.

Patterns can interact with other patterns. This is represented symbolically in Figure 8.2(d) where the bottom-left block of the middle pattern again is a pattern. A case study of a document editor in [Gamma, Helm, Johnson, and Vlissides, 1995] contains eight interacting patterns. That is what happens in practice; it is unusual for the design of a product to contain just one pattern.

As with toolkits and frameworks, if a design pattern is reused, then an implementation of that pattern probably also can be reused. In addition, analysis patterns can assist with object-oriented analysis [Fowler, 1997]. Finally, in addition to patterns, there are antipatterns; these are described in Just in Case You Wanted to Know Box 8.4.

An antipattern is a practice that can cause a project to fail, such as "analysis paralysis" (spending far too much time and effort on the analysis workflow) or designing an object-oriented product in which just one object does almost all the work. A major motivation for writing the first antipattern book was that nearly one-third of all software projects are canceled, two-thirds of all software projects encounter cost overruns in excess of 200 percent, and over 80 percent of all software projects are deemed failures [Brown et al., 1998].

**FIGURE 8.4**
Pattern Abstract Factory. The names of abstract classes and their virtual functions are italicized.

## 8.5.4 Software Architecture

The architecture of a cathedral might be described as Romanesque, Gothic, or Baroque. Similarly, the architecture of a software product might be described as object-oriented, pipes and filters (UNIX components), or client–server (with a central server providing file storage and computing facilities for a network of client computers). Figure 8.2(d) symbolically depicts an architecture composed of a toolkit, a framework, and three design patterns.

Because it applies to the design of a product as a whole, the field of **software architecture** encompasses a variety of design issues, including the organization of the product in terms of its components; product-level control structures; issues of communication and synchronization; databases and data access; the physical distribution of the components; performance; and choice of design alternatives [Shaw and Garlan, 1996]. Accordingly, software architecture is a considerably more wide-ranging concept than design patterns.

In fact, Shaw and Garlan [1996] state, "Abstractly, software architecture involves the description of elements from which systems are built, interactions among those elements, *patterns that guide their composition,* and *constraints on those patterns*" [emphasis added]. Consequently, in addition to the many items listed in the previous paragraph, software architecture includes patterns as a subfield. This is one reason why Figure 8.2(d) shows three design patterns as components of a software architecture.

The many strengths of design reuse are even greater when a software architecture is reused. One way that reuse of architectures is achieved in practice is with **software product lines** [Lai, Weiss, and Parnas, 1999; Jazayeri, Ran, and van der Linden, 2000]. The idea is to develop a software architecture common to a number of software products and instantiate this architecture when developing a new product. For example, Hewlett-Packard manufactures a broad variety of printers, and new models constantly are being developed. Hewlett-Packard now has a firmware architecture that is instantiated for each new printer model. The results have been impressive. For example, between 1995 and 1998, the number of person-hours to develop the firmware for a new printer model decreased by a factor of 4 and the time to develop the firmware decreased by a factor of 3. Also, reuse has increased. For more recent printers, over 70 percent of the components of the firmware are reused, almost unchanged, from earlier products [Toft, Coleman, and Ohta, 2000].

## 8.5.5 Component-Based Software Engineering

The goal of **component-based software engineering** is to construct a standard collection of reusable components. Then, instead of reinventing the wheel each time, in the future all software will be constructed by choosing a standard architecture and standard reusable frameworks and inserting standard reusable code artifacts into the hot spots of the frameworks. That is, software products will be built by composing reusable components. Ideally, this will be done using an automated tool.

In this chapter, we describe the many advantages that accrue through the reuse of code artifacts, design patterns, and software architectures. Hence, achieving component-based software engineering would solve numerous problems in software development. In particular, it would lead to order-of-magnitude increases in software productivity and quality, and decreases in time to market and maintenance effort.

Unfortunately, the state of the art with regard to reuse is currently far from this ambitious target. In addition, component-based software construction has many challenges, including the definition, standardization, and retrieval of components. However, researchers in many centers are actively engaged in trying to achieve the goal of component-based software engineering [Heineman and Councill, 2001].

## 8.6  Reuse and Postdelivery Maintenance

The traditional reason for promoting reuse is that it can shorten the development process. For example, a number of major software organizations are trying to halve the time needed to develop a new product, and reuse is a primary strategy in these endeavors. However, as reflected in Figure 1.3, for every $1 spent on developing a product, $2 or more are spent on maintaining that product. Therefore, a second important reason for reuse is to reduce the time and cost of maintaining a product. In fact, reuse has a greater impact on postdelivery maintenance than on development.

Suppose now that 40 percent of a product consists of components reused from earlier products and this reuse is evenly distributed across the entire product. That is, 40 percent of the specification document consists of reused components, 40 percent of the design, 40 percent of the code artifacts, 40 percent of the manuals, and so on. Unfortunately, this does not mean that the time to develop the product as a whole will be 40 percent less than it would have been without reuse. First, some of the components have to be tailored to the new product. Suppose that one-quarter of the reused components are changed. If a component has to be changed, then the documentation for that component also has to be changed. Furthermore, the changed component has to be tested. Second, if a code artifact is reused unchanged, then unit testing of that code artifact is not required. However, integration testing of that code artifact still is needed. So, even if 30 percent of a product consists of components reused unchanged and a further 10 percent are reused changed, the time needed to develop the complete product at best is only about 27 percent less [Schach, 1992]. Suppose that, as in Figure 1.3(a), 33 percent of a software budget is devoted to development. Then, if reuse reduces development costs by 27 percent, the overall cost of that product over its 12- to 15-year lifetime is reduced by only about 9 percent as a consequence of reuse; this is reflected in Figure 8.5.

Similar but lengthier arguments can be applied to the postdelivery maintenance component of the software process [Schach, 1994]. Under the assumptions of the previous paragraph, the effect of reuse on postdelivery maintenance is an overall cost saving of about 18 percent, as shown in Figure 8.5. Clearly, the major impact of reuse is on postdelivery

**FIGURE 8.5**  Average percentage cost savings under the assumption that 40 percent of a new product consists of reused components, three-quarters of which are reused unchanged.

| Activity | Percentage of Total Cost over Product Lifetime | Percentage Savings over Product Lifetime due to Reuse |
|---|---|---|
| Development | 33% | 9.3% |
| Postdelivery maintenance | 67 | 17.9 |

maintenance rather than development. The underlying reason is that reused components generally are well designed, thoroughly tested, and comprehensively documented, thereby simplifying all three types of postdelivery maintenance.

If the actual reuse rates in a given product are lower (or higher) than assumed in this section, then the benefits of reuse are different. But the overall result is still the same: Reuse affects postdelivery maintenance more than it does development.

We turn now to portability.

# 8.7    Portability

The ever-rising cost of software makes it imperative that some means be found to contain costs. One way is to ensure that the product as a whole can be adapted easily to run on a variety of different hardware–operating system combinations. Some of the cost of writing the product may then be recouped by selling versions that run on other computers. But the most important reason for writing software that can be implemented easily on other computers is that, every 4 years or so, the client organization purchases new hardware, and all its software then must be converted to run on the new hardware. A product is considered portable if it is significantly less expensive to adapt the product to run on the new computer than to write a new product from scratch [Mooney, 1990].

More precisely, *portability* may be defined as follows: Suppose a product $P$ is compiled by compiler $C$ and then runs on the **source computer**, namely, hardware configuration $H$ under operating system $O$. A product $P'$ is needed that functionally is equivalent to $P$ but must be compiled by compiler $C'$ and run on the **target computer**, namely, hardware configuration $H'$ under operating system $O'$. If the cost of converting $P$ into $P'$ is significantly less than the cost of coding $P'$ from scratch, then $P$ is said to be *portable*.

Overall, the problem of porting software is nontrivial because of incompatibilities among different hardware configurations, operating systems, and compilers. Each of these aspects is examined in turn.

## 8.7.1 Hardware Incompatibilities

Product $P$ currently running on hardware configuration $H$ is to be installed on hardware configuration $H'$. Superficially, this is simple; copy $P$ from the hard drive of $H$ onto DAT tape and transfer it to $H'$. However, this will not work if $H'$ uses a Zip drive for backup; DAT tape cannot be read on a Zip drive.

Suppose now that the problem of physically copying the source code of product $P$ to computer $H'$ has been solved. There is no guarantee that $H'$ can interpret the bit patterns created by $H$. A number of different character codes exist, the most popular of which are Extended Binary Coded Decimal Interchange Code (EBCDIC) and American Standard Code for Information Interchange (ASCII), the American version of the 7-bit ISO code [Mackenzie, 1980]. If $H$ uses EBCDIC but $H'$ uses ASCII, then $H'$ will treat $P$ as so much garbage.

Although the original reason for these differences is historical (that is, researchers working independently for different manufacturers developed different ways of doing the same thing), there are definite economic reasons for perpetuating them. To see this, consider the following imaginary situation. MCM Computer Manufacturers has sold thousands of its

MCM-1 computer. MCM now wishes to design, manufacture, and market a new computer, the MCM-2, which is more powerful in every way than the MCM-1 but costs considerably less. Suppose further that the MCM-1 uses ASCII code and has 36-bit words consisting of four 9-bit bytes. Now, the chief computer architect of MCM decides that the MCM-2 should employ EBCDIC and have 16-bit words consisting of two 8-bit bytes. The sales force then has to tell current MCM-1 owners that the MCM-2 is going to cost them $35,000 less than any competitor's equivalent machine but will cost them up to $200,000 to convert existing software and data from MCM-1 format to MCM-2 format. No matter how good the scientific reasons for redesigning the MCM-2, marketing considerations will ensure that the new computer is compatible with the old one. A salesperson then can point out to an existing MCM-1 owner that, not only is the MCM-2 computer $35,000 less expensive than any competitor's machine, but any customer ill-advised enough to buy from a different manufacturer will be spending $35,000 too much and also will have to pay some $200,000 to convert existing software and data to the format of the non-MCM machine.

Moving from the preceding imaginary situation to the real world, the most successful line of computers to date has been the IBM System/360-370 series [Gifford and Spector, 1987]. The success of this line of computers is due largely to full compatibility between machines; a product that runs on an IBM System/360 Model 30 built in 1964 runs unchanged on an IBM eServer zSeries 990 built in 2005. However, the product that runs on the IBM System/360 Model 30 under OS/360 may require considerable modification before it can run on a totally different 2005 machine, such as a Sun Fire E25K server under Solaris. Part of the difficulty may be due to hardware incompatibilities. But part may be caused by operating system incompatibilities.

## 8.7.2 Operating System Incompatibilities

The job control languages (JCL) of any two computers usually are vastly different. Some of the difference is syntactic—the command for executing an executable load image might be @xeq on one computer, //xqt on another, and .exc on a third. When porting a product to a different operating system, syntactic differences are relatively straightforward to handle by simply translating commands from the one JCL into the other. But other differences can be more serious. For example, some operating systems support virtual memory. Suppose that a certain operating system allows products to be up to 1024 MB in size, but the actual area of main memory allocated to a particular product may be only 64 MB. What happens is that the user's product is partitioned into pages 2048 KB in size, and only 32 of these pages can be in main memory at any one time. The rest of the pages are stored on disk and swapped in and out as needed by the virtual memory operating system. As a result, products can be written with no effective constraints as to size. But, if a product that has been successfully implemented under a virtual memory operating system is to be ported to an operating system with physical constraints on product size, the entire product may have to be rewritten and then linked using overlay techniques to ensure that the size limit is not exceeded.

## 8.7.3 Numerical Software Incompatibilities

When a product is ported from one machine to another or even compiled using a different compiler, the results of performing arithmetic may differ. On a 16-bit machine, that is, a computer with a word size of 16 bits, an integer ordinarily is represented by one word

(16 bits) and a double-precision integer by two adjacent words (32 bits). Unfortunately, some language implementations do not include double-precision integers. For example, standard Pascal does not include double-precision integers. Therefore, a product that functions perfectly on a compiler–hardware–operating system configuration in which Pascal integers are represented using 32 bits may fail to run correctly when ported to a computer in which integers are represented by only 16 bits. The obvious solution—representing integers larger than $2^{16}$ by floating-point numbers (type **real**)—does not work because integers are represented exactly whereas floating-point numbers in general are only approximated using a mantissa (fraction) and exponent.

This problem can be solved in Java, because each of the eight primitive data types has been carefully specified. For example, type **int** always is implemented as a signed 32-bit two's complement integer, and type **float** always occupies 32 bits and satisfies ANSI/IEEE (Standard) 754 [1985] for floating-point numbers. The problem of ensuring that a numerical computation is performed correctly on every target hardware–operating system therefore cannot arise in Java. (For more insights into the design of Java, see Just in Case You Wanted to Know Box 8.5.) However, where a numerical computation is performed in a language other than Java, it is important, but often difficult, to ensure that numerical computations are performed correctly on the target hardware–operating system.

### 8.7.4 Compiler Incompatibilities

Portability is difficult to achieve if a product is implemented in a language for which few compilers exist. If the product has been implemented in a specialized language such as CLU [Liskov, Snyder, Atkinson, and Schaffert, 1977], it may be necessary to rewrite it in a different language if the target computer has no compiler for that language. On the other hand, if a product is implemented in a popular language such as COBOL, Fortran, Lisp, C, C++, or Java, the chances are good that a compiler or interpreter for that language can be found for a target computer.

Suppose that a product is written in a popular high-level language such as standard Fortran. In theory, there should be no problem in porting the product from one machine to another—after all, standard Fortran is standard Fortran. Regrettably, that is not the case; in practice, there is no such thing as standard Fortran. Even though there is an ISO/IEC Fortran standard, Fortran 2003 [ISO/IEC 1539–1, 2004], there is no reason for a compiler writer to adhere to it (see Just in Case You Wanted to Know Box 8.6 for more on the name Fortran 2003). For example, a decision may be taken to support additional features not usually found in Fortran so that the marketing division can tout a "new, extended Fortran compiler." Conversely, a microcomputer compiler may not be a full Fortran implementation. Also, with a deadline to produce a compiler, management may decide to bring out a less-than-complete implementation, intending to support the full standard in a later revision. Suppose that the compiler on the source computer supports a superset of Fortran 2003. Suppose further that the compiler on the target computer is an implementation of standard Fortran 2003. When a product implemented on that source computer is ported to the target, any portions of the product that use nonstandard Fortran 2003 constructs from the superset have to be recoded. Therefore, to ensure portability, programmers should use only standard Fortran language features.

Early COBOL standards were developed by the COnference on DAta SYstems Languages (CODASYL), a committee of American computer manufacturers and government and

In 1991, James Gosling of Sun Microsystems developed Java. While developing the language, he frequently stared out the window at a large oak tree outside his office. In fact, he did this so often that he decided to name his new language *Oak*. However, his choice of name was unacceptable to Sun because it could not be trademarked, and without a trademark Sun would lose control of the language.

After an intensive search for a name that could be trademarked and was easy to remember, Gosling's group came up with *Java*. During the 18th century, much of the coffee imported into England was grown in Java, the most populous island in the Dutch East Indies (now Indonesia). As a result, *Java* now is a slang word for coffee, the third most popular beverage among software engineers. Unfortunately, the names of the Big Two carbonated cola beverages are already trademarked.

To understand why Gosling designed Java, it is necessary to appreciate the source of the weaknesses he perceived in C++. And, to do that, we have to go back to C, the parent language of C++.

In 1972, the programming language C was developed by Dennis Ritchie at AT&T Bell Laboratories (now Lucent Technologies) for use in systems software. The language was designed to be extremely flexible. For example, it permits arithmetic on pointer variables, that is, on variables used to store memory addresses. From the viewpoint of the average programmer, this poses a distinct danger; the resulting programs can be extremely insecure because control can be passed to anywhere in the computer. Also, C does not embody arrays as such. Instead, a pointer to the address of the beginning of the array is used. As a result, the concept of an out-of-range array subscript is not intrinsic to C. This is a further source of possible insecurity.

These and other insecurities were no problem at Bell Labs. After all, C was designed by an experienced software engineer for use by other experienced software engineers at Bell Labs. These professionals could be relied on to use the powerful and flexible features of C in a secure way. A basic philosophy in the design of C was that the person using C knows exactly what he or she is doing. Software failures that occurred when C is used by less competent or inexperienced programmers should not be blamed on Bell Labs; there never was any intent that C should be widely employed as a general-purpose programming language, as it is today.

private users. Joint Technical Committee 1 of Subcommittee 22 of the International Organization for Standardization (ISO) and the International Electrotechnical Commission (IEC) now are responsible for COBOL standards [Schricker, 2000]. Unfortunately, COBOL standards do not promote portability. A COBOL standard has an official life of 5 years, but each successive standard is not necessarily a superset of its predecessor. Equally worrisome is that many features are left to the individual implementer, subsets may be termed *standard COBOL*, and there is no restriction on extending the language to form a superset. OO-COBOL, the language of the current COBOL standard, is object-oriented [ISO/IEC 1989, 2002], as is Fortran 2003 [ISO/IEC 1539–1, 2004].

The American National Standards Institute (ANSI) approved a standard for the programming language C [ANSI X3.159, 1989]. The standard was approved by the ISO in 1990. Most C compilers adhere quite closely to the original language specification [Kernighan and Ritchie, 1978]. This is because almost all C compiler writers use the standard front end of the portable C compiler, *pcc* [Johnson, 1979]; as a result, the language accepted by the vast majority of compilers is identical. C products, in general, are

With the rise of the object-oriented paradigm, a number of object-oriented programming languages based on C were developed, including Object C, Objective C, and C++. The idea behind these languages was to embed object-oriented constructs within C, which by then was a popular programming language. It was argued that it would be easier for programmers to learn a language based on a familiar language than to learn a totally new syntax. However, only one of the many C-based object-oriented languages became widely accepted, C++, developed by Bjarne Stroustrup, also of AT&T Bell Laboratories.

It has been suggested that the reason behind the success of C++ was the enormous financial clout of AT&T (now part of SBC Communications). However, if corporate size and financial strength were relevant features in promoting a programming language, today we would all be using PL/I, a language developed and strongly promoted by IBM. The reality is that PL/I, notwithstanding the prestige of IBM, has retreated into obscurity. The real reason for the success of C++ is that it is a true superset of C. That is, unlike any of the other C-based object-oriented programming languages, virtually any C program is also valid C++. Therefore, organizations realized that they could switch from C to C++ without changing any of their existing C software. They could advance from the classical paradigm to the object-oriented paradigm without disruption. A remark frequently encountered in the Java literature is, "Java is what C++ should have been." The implication is that, if only Stroustrup had been as smart as Gosling, C++ would have turned out to be Java. On the contrary, if C++ had not been a true superset of C, it would have gone the way of all other C-based object-oriented programming languages; that is, it essentially would have disappeared. Only after C++ had taken hold as a popular language was Java designed in reaction to perceived weaknesses in C++. Java is not a superset of C; for example, Java has no pointer variables. Therefore, it would be more accurate to say that, "Java is what C++ could not possibly have been."

Finally, it is important to realize that Java, like every other programming language, has weaknesses of its own. In addition, in some areas (such as access rules), C++ is superior to Java [Schach, 1997]. It will be interesting to see, in the coming years, whether C++ continues to be the predominant object-oriented programming language or whether it is supplanted by Java or some other language.

easily ported from one implementation to another. An aid to C portability is the *lint* processor, which can be used to determine implementation-dependent features as well as constructs that may lead to difficulties when the product is ported to a target computer. Unfortunately, *lint* checks only the syntax and the static semantics and therefore is not foolproof. However, it can be of considerable help in reducing future problems. For example, in C, it is legal to assign an integer value to a pointer and vice versa, but this is forbidden by *lint*. In some implementations, the size (number of bits) of an integer and a pointer are the same, but the sizes may be different on other implementations; this sort of potential future portability problem can be flagged by *lint* and obviated by recoding the offending portions.

The standard for C++ [ISO/IEC 14882, 1998] was unanimously approved by the various national standards committees (including ANSI) in November 1997. The standard received final ratification in 1998.

The only truly successful language standard so far has been the Ada 83 standard, embodied in the Ada Reference Manual [ANSI/MIL-STD-1815A, 1983]. (For background

Names of programming languages are spelled in uppercase when the name is an acronym. Examples include ALGOL (ALGOrithmic Language), COBOL (COmmon Business Oriented Language), and FORTRAN (FORmula TRANslator). Conversely, all other programming languages begin with an uppercase letter and the remaining letters in the name (if any) are in lowercase. Examples include Ada, C, C++, Java, and Pascal. *Ada* is not an acronym; the language was named after Ada, Countess of Lovelace (1815–1852). Daughter of the poet Lord Alfred Byron, Ada was the world's first programmer by virtue of her work on Charles Babbage's difference engine. *Pascal* is not an acronym either—this language was named after the French mathematician and philosopher, Blaise Pascal (1623–1662). And I am sure that you have read all about the name *Java* in Just in Case You Wanted to Know Box 8.5.

There is one exception: Fortran. The FORTRAN Standards Committee decided that, with effect from the 1990 version, the name of the language would thenceforth be written *Fortran*.

information on Ada, see Just in Case You Wanted to Know Box 8.6.) Until the end of 1987, the name Ada was a registered trademark of the U.S. government, Ada Joint Program Office (AJPO). As owner of the trademark, the AJPO stipulated that the name Ada legally could be used only for language implementations that complied exactly with the standard; subsets and supersets were expressly forbidden. A mechanism was set up for validating Ada compilers, and only a compiler that successfully passed the validation process could be called an Ada compiler. Thus, the trademark was used as a means of enforcing standards and hence portability.

Now that the name Ada no longer is a trademark, enforcement of the standard is being achieved via a different mechanism. There is little or no market for an Ada compiler that has not been validated. Therefore, strong economic forces encourage Ada compiler developers to have their compilers validated and hence certified as conforming to the Ada standard. This has applied to compilers for both Ada 83 [ANSI/MIL-STD-1815A, 1983] and Ada 95 [ISO/IEC 8652, 1995].

For Java to be a totally portable language, it is essential for the language to be standardized and to ensure that the standard is strictly obeyed. Sun Microsystems, like the Ada Joint Program Office, uses the legal system to achieve standardization. As mentioned in Just in Case You Wanted to Know Box 8.5, Sun chose a name for its new language that could be copyrighted so that Sun could enforce its copyright and bring legal action against alleged violators (which happened when Microsoft developed nonstandard Java classes). After all, portability is one of the most powerful features of Java. If multiple versions of Java are permitted, the portability of Java suffers; Java can be truly portable only if every Java program is handled identically by every Java compiler. To try to influence public opinion, in 1997 Sun ran a "Pure Java" advertising campaign.

Version 1.0 of Java was released early in 1997. A series of revised versions followed in response to comments and criticisms. The latest version at the time of writing is Java J2SE (Java 2 Platform, Standard Edition), version 5.0. This process of stepwise refinement of Java will continue. When the language eventually stabilizes, it is likely that a standards organization such as ANSI or ISO will publish a draft standard and elicit comments from all over the world. These comments will be used to put together the official Java standard.

## 8.8   Why Portability?

In the light of the many barriers to porting software, the reader might well wonder if it is worthwhile to port software at all. An argument in favor of portability stated in Section 8.7 is that the cost of software may be partially recouped by porting the product to a different hardware–operating system configuration. However, selling multiple variants of the software may not be possible. The application may be highly specialized, and no other client may need the software. For instance, a management information system written for one major car rental corporation may simply be inapplicable to the operations of other car rental corporations. Alternatively, the software itself may give the client a competitive advantage, and selling copies of the product would be tantamount to economic suicide. In the light of all this, is it not a waste of time and money to engineer portability into a product when it is designed?

The answer to this question is an emphatic *No*. The major reason why portability is essential is that the life of a software product generally is longer than the life of the hardware for which it was first written. Good software products can have a life of 15 years or more, whereas hardware frequently is changed every 4 years. Therefore, good software can be implemented, over its lifetime, on three or more different hardware configurations.

One way to solve this problem is to buy upwardly compatible hardware. The only expense is the cost of the hardware; the software need not to changed. Nevertheless, in some cases it may be economically more sound to port the product to different hardware entirely. For example, the first version of a product may have been implemented 7 years ago on a mainframe. Although it may be possible to buy a new mainframe on which the product can run with no changes, it may be considerably less expensive to implement multiple copies of the product on a network of personal computers, one on the desk of each user. In this instance, if the software has been written in a way that would promote portability, then porting the product to the personal computer network makes good financial sense.

But there are other kinds of software. For example, many organizations that write software for personal computers make their money by selling multiple copies of COTS software. For instance, the profit on a spreadsheet package is small and cannot possibly cover the cost of development. To make a profit, 50,000 (or even 500,000) copies may have to be sold. After this point, additional sales are pure profit. So, if the product can be ported to additional types of hardware with ease, even more money can be made.

Of course, as with all software, the product is not just the code but also the documentation, including the manuals. Porting the spreadsheet package to other hardware means changing the documentation as well. Therefore, portability also means being able to change the documentation easily to reflect the target configuration, instead of having to write new documentation from scratch. Considerably less training is needed if a familiar, existing product is ported to a new computer than if a completely new product were to be written. For this reason, too, portability is to be encouraged.

Techniques to facilitate portability now are described.

## 8.9   Techniques for Achieving Portability

One way to try to achieve portability is to forbid programmers to use constructs that might cause problems when ported to another computer. For example, an obvious principle would seem to be this: Write all software in a standard version of a high-level programming language. But how is a portable operating system to be written? After all, it is inconceivable that an operating system could be written without at least some assembler code. Similarly, a compiler has to generate object code for a specific computer. Here, too, it is impossible to avoid all implementation-dependent components.

### 8.9.1  Portable System Software

Instead of forbidding all implementation-dependent aspects, which would prevent almost all system software from being written, a better technique is to isolate any necessary implementation-dependent pieces. An example of this technique is the way the original UNIX operating system was constructed [Johnson and Ritchie, 1978]. About 9000 lines of the operating system were written in C. The remaining 1000 lines constituted the kernel. The kernel was written in assembler and had to be rewritten for each implementation. About 1000 lines of the C code consisted of device drivers; this code, too, had to be rewritten each time. However, the remaining 8000 lines of C code remained largely unchanged from implementation to implementation.

Another useful technique for increasing the portability of system software is to use levels of abstraction (Section 7.4.1). Consider, for example, graphical display routines for a workstation. A user inserts a command such as drawLine into his or her source code. The source code is compiled and then linked with graphical display routines. At run time, drawLine causes the workstation to draw a line on the screen as specified by the user. This can be implemented using two levels of abstraction. The upper level, written in a high-level language, interprets the user's command and calls the appropriate lower-level code artifact to execute that command. If the graphical display routines are ported to a new type of workstation, then no changes need be made to the user's code or the upper level of the graphical display routines. However, the lower-level code artifacts of the routines have to be rewritten, because they interface with the actual hardware, and the hardware of the new workstation is different from that of the workstation on which the package was previously implemented. This technique also has been used successfully for porting communications software that conforms to the seven levels of abstraction of the ISO-OSI model [Tanenbaum, 2002].

### 8.9.2  Portable Application Software

With regard to application software, rather than system software such as operating systems and compilers, it generally is possible to write the product in a high-level language. Section 14.1 points out that frequently no choice can be made with regard to implementation language, but that when it is possible to select a language, the choice should be made on the basis of cost–benefit analysis (Section 5.2). One factor that must enter into the cost–benefit analysis is the impact on portability.

At every stage in the development of a product, decisions can be made that result in a more portable product. For example, some compilers distinguish between uppercase and lowercase letters. For such a compiler, This_Is_A_Name and this_is_a_name are different variables. But other compilers treat the two names the same. A product that relies on differences between uppercase letters and lowercase letters can lead to hard-to-discover faults when the product is ported.

Just as frequently no choice can be made of programming language; also no choice may be allowed in the operating system. However, if at all possible, the operating system under which the product runs should be a popular one. This is an argument in favor of the UNIX operating system. UNIX has been implemented on a wide range of hardware. In addition, UNIX, or more precisely, UNIX-like operating systems, have been implemented on top of mainframe operating systems such as IBM VM/370 and VAX/VMS. For personal computers, it remains to be seen whether Linux will overtake Windows as the most widely used operating system. Just as use of a widely implemented programming language promotes portability, so too does use of a widely implemented operating system.

To facilitate the moving of software from one UNIX-based system to another, the Portable Operating System Interface for Computer Environments (POSIX) was developed [NIST 151, 1988]. POSIX standardizes the interface between an application program and a UNIX operating system. POSIX has been implemented on a number of non-UNIX operating systems as well, broadening the number of computers to which application software can be ported with little or no problem.

Language standards can play their part in achieving portability. If the coding standards of a development organization stipulate that only standard constructs may be used, then the resulting product is more likely to be portable. To this end, programmers must be provided a list of nonstandard features supported by the compiler but whose use is forbidden without prior managerial approval. Like other sensible coding standards, this one can be checked by machine.

Graphical user interfaces similarly are becoming portable via the introduction of standard GUI languages. Examples of these include Motif and X11. The standardization of GUI languages is in reaction to the growing importance of GUIs, and the resulting need for portability of human–computer interfaces.

It is also necessary to plan for potential lack of compatibility between the operating system under which the product is being constructed and any future operating systems to which the product may be ported. If at all possible, operating system calls should be localized to one or two code artifacts. In any event, every operating system call must be carefully documented. The documentation standard for operating system calls should assume that the next programmer to read the code will have no familiarity with the current operating system, often a reasonable assumption.

Documentation in the form of an installation manual should be provided to assist with future porting. That manual points out what parts of the product have to be changed when porting the product and what parts may have to be changed. In both instances, a careful explanation must be provided of what has to be done and how to do it. Finally, lists of changes that have to be made in other manuals, such as the user manual or the operator manual, also must appear in the installation manual.

### 8.9.3 Portable Data

The problem of portability of data can be vexing. Problems of hardware incompatibilities were pointed out in Section 8.7.1. But even after such problems have been solved, software incompatibilities remain. For instance, the format of an indexed-sequential file is determined by the operating system; a different operating system generally implies a different format. Many files require headers containing information such as the format of the data in that file. The format of a header almost always is unique to the specific compiler and operating system under which that file was created. The situation can be even worse when database management systems are used.

| Strengths | Impediments |
|---|---|
| **Reuse** | |
| Shorter development time (Section 8.1) | NIH syndrome (Section 8.2) |
| Lower development cost (Section 8.1) | Potential quality issues (Section 8.2) |
| Higher-quality software (Section 8.1) | Retrieval issues (Section 8.2) |
| Shorter maintenance time (Section 8.6) | Cost of making a component reusable (opportunistic reuse) (Section 8.2) |
| Lower maintenance cost (Section 8.6) | Cost of making a component for future reuse (systematic reuse) (Section 8.2) |
| | Legal issues (contract software only) (Section 8.2) |
| | Lack of source code for COTS components (Section 8.2) |
| **Portability** | |
| Software has to be ported to new hardware every 4 years or so (Section 8.8) | Potential incompatibilities: Hardware (Section 8.7.1) Operating systems (Section 8.7.2) |
| More copies of COTS software can be sold (Section 8.8) | Numerical software (Section 8.7.3) Compilers (Section 8.7.4) Data formats (Section 8.9.3) |

The safest way of porting data is to construct an unstructured (sequential) file, which can then be ported with minimal difficulty to the target machine. From this unstructured file, the desired structured file can be reconstructed. Two special conversion routines have to be written, one running on the source machine to convert the original structured file into sequential form and one running on the target machine to reconstruct the structured file from the ported sequential file. Although this solution seems simple enough, the two routines are nontrivial when conversions between complex database models have to be performed.

We conclude this chapter with a summary of the strengths of and impediments to reuse and portability (Figure 8.6); the section in which each item is discussed is stated.

**Chapter Review**

Reuse is described in Section 8.1. Various impediments to reuse are described in Section 8.2. Two reuse case studies are presented in Section 8.3. The impact of the object-oriented paradigm on reuse is analyzed in Section 8.4. Reuse during design and implementation is the subject of Section 8.5; the topics covered include frameworks, patterns, software architecture, and component-based software engineering. The impact of reuse on postdelivery maintenance is discussed in Section 8.6.

Portability is discussed in Section 8.7. Portability can be hampered by incompatibilities caused by hardware (Section 8.7.1), operating systems (Section 8.7.2), numerical software (Section 8.7.3), or compilers (Section 8.7.4). Nevertheless, it is extremely important to try to make all products as portable as possible (Section 8.8). Ways of facilitating portability include using popular high-level languages, isolating the nonportable pieces of a product (Section 8.9.1), and adhering to language standards (Section 8.9.2).

---

**For Further Reading**

A variety of reuse case studies can be found in [Lanergan and Grasso, 1984; Matsumoto, 1984, 1987; Selby, 1989; Prieto-Díaz, 1991; Lim, 1994; Jézéquel and Meyer, 1997; and Toft, Coleman, and Ohta, 2000]. Successful reuse experiences at four European companies are described in [Morisio, Tully, and Ezran, 2000]. The management of reuse is described in [Lim, 1998]. A search scheme for object retrieval and reuse is described in [Isakowitz and Kauffman, 1996]. The cost-effectiveness of reuse is described in [Barnes and Bollinger, 1991] and ways of identifying components for future reuse in [Caldiera and Basili, 1991]. Meyer [1996a] analyzes the claim that the object-oriented paradigm promotes reuse; four case studies in reuse and object technology appear in [Fichman and Kemerer, 1997]. Reuse metrics are discussed in [Poulin, 1997]. Factors that affect the success of reuse programs are presented in [Morisio, Ezran, and Tully, 2002]. Reuse strategies are discussed in [Ravichandran and Rothenberger, 2003]. A comprehensive model for evaluating software reuse alternatives is presented in [Tomer et al., 2004]. Further papers on reuse are to be found in the May 2000 issue of *IEEE Transactions on Software Engineering*.

A good source of information on frameworks is [Lewis et al., 1995]. D'Souza and Wills [1999] present a development methodology based on object-oriented frameworks and components. A series of articles on frameworks can be found in [Fayad and Johnson, 1999; Fayad and Schmidt, 1999; and Fayad, Schmidt, and Johnson, 1999]. The October 2000 issue of *Communications of the ACM* includes articles on component-based frameworks, including [Fingar, 2000] and [Kobryn, 2000], which describes how to model components and frameworks using UML. Achieving reuse via frameworks and patterns is described in [Fach, 2001].

Design patterns were put forward by Alexander within the context of architecture, as described in [Alexander et al., 1977]. A first-hand account of the origins of pattern theory appears in [Alexander, 1999]. The primary work on software design patterns is [Gamma, Helm, Johnson, and Vlissides, 1995]; a newer book is [Vlissides, 1998]. Analysis patterns are described in [Fowler, 1997], and requirements patterns in [Hagge and Lappe, 2005].

Experiments to assess the impact of design pattern documentation on maintenance are described in [Prechelt, Unger-Lamprecht, Philippsen, and Tichy, 2002]. Antipatterns are described in [Brown et al., 1998]. Patterns for designing embedded systems are discussed in [Pont and Banner, 2004]. Vokac [2004] describes the impact of patterns on fault rates in a 500-KLOC product.

The primary source of information on software architectures is [Shaw and Garlan, 1996]. Newer works on software architectures include [Bosch, 2000] and [Bass, Clements, and Kazman, 2003]. Software product lines are described in [Jazayeri, Ran, and van der Linden, 2000; Knauber, Muthig, Schmid, and Widen, 2000; Donohoe, 2000; and Clements and Northrop, 2002]. The state of the practice of software product lines is discussed in [Birk et al. 2003]. Cost–benefit analysis of software product lines is presented in [Bockle et al., 2004]. The July/August 2002 issue of *IEEE Software* contains a variety of articles on product lines.

Papers on component-based software engineering can be found in the September/October 1998 issue of *IEEE Software*, including [Weyuker, 1998], which discusses the testing of component-based software. Brereton and Budgen [2000] discuss the key issues in component-based software products. Articles on experiences with component-based software engineering include [Sparling, 2000] and [Baster, Konana, and Scott, 2001]. Strengths and weaknesses of component-based software engineering are discussed in [Vitharana, 2003]. [Heineman and Councill, 2001] is a highly recommended compendium of articles on component-based software engineering.

Strategies for achieving portability can be found in [Mooney, 1990]. Portability of C and UNIX is discussed in [Johnson and Ritchie, 1978].

**Key Terms**    accidental reuse *220*          functional module *224*          software product
                 application framework *228*      hot spot *228*                        line *233*
                 COBOL program logic              not invented here                  source computer *235*
                     structure *224*                  (NIH) syndrome *222*           systematic
                 component-based software         opportunistic reuse *220*              reuse *220*
                     engineering *233*            portable *220*                     target computer *235*
                 deliberate reuse *220*           reuse *220*                        toolkit *227*
                 framework *228*                  software architecture *233*        widget *229*

**Problems**    8.1    Explain in detail the differences between reusability and portability.

                8.2    A code artifact is reused, unchanged, in a new product. In what ways does this reuse reduce the overall cost of the product? In what ways is the cost unchanged?

                8.3    Suppose that a code artifact is reused with one change, an addition operation is changed to a subtraction. What impact does this minor change have on the savings of Problem 8.2?

                8.4    What is the influence of cohesion on reusability?

                8.5    What is the influence of coupling on reusability?

                8.6    You have just joined a large organization that manufactures a variety of pollution control products. The organization has hundreds of software products consisting of some 95,000 different Fortran modules. You have been hired to come up with a plan for reusing as many of these modules as possible in future products. What is your proposal?

                8.7    Consider an automated library circulation system. Every book has a bar code, and every borrower has a card bearing a bar code. When a borrower wishes to check out a book, the librarian scans the bar codes on the book and the borrower's card, and enters C at the computer terminal. Similarly, when a book is returned, it is again scanned and the librarian enters R. Librarians can add books (+) to the library collection or remove them (−). Borrowers can go to a terminal and determine all the books in the library by a particular author (the borrower enters A= followed by the author's name), all the books with a specific title (T= followed by the title), or all the books in a particular subject area (S= followed by the subject area). Finally, if a borrower wants a book currently checked out, the librarian can place a hold on the book so that, when it is returned, it will be held for the borrower who requested it (H= followed by the number of the book). Explain how you would ensure a high percentage of reusable code artifacts.

                8.8    You are required to build a product for determining whether a bank statement is correct. The data needed include the balance at the beginning of the month; the number, date, and amount of each check; the date and amount of each deposit; and the balance at the end of the month. Explain how you would ensure that as many code artifacts as possible of the product can be reused in future products.

                8.9    Consider an automated teller machine (ATM). The user puts a card into a slot and enters a four-digit personal identification number (PIN). If the PIN is incorrect, the card is ejected. Otherwise, the user may perform the following operations on up to four different bank accounts:

                       (i)   Deposit any amount. A receipt is printed showing the date, amount deposited, and account number.

                       (ii)  Withdraw up to $200 in units of $20 (the account may not be overdrawn). In addition to the money, the user is given a receipt showing the date, amount withdrawn, account number, and account balance after the withdrawal.

(iii) Determine the account balance. This is displayed on the screen.

(iv) Transfer funds between two accounts. Again, the account from which the funds are transferred must not be overdrawn. The user is given a receipt showing the date, amount transferred, and the two account numbers.

(v) Quit. The card is ejected.

Explain how you would ensure that as many code artifacts as possible of the product can be reused in future products.

8.10 How early in the software life cycle could the developers have caught the fault in the Ariane 5 software (Section 8.3.2)?

8.11 Section 8.5.2 states that "the Raytheon COBOL program logic structure of the 1970s is a classical precursor of today's object-oriented application framework." What are the implications of this for technology transfer?

8.12 Explain the role played by abstract classes in the design pattern of Figure 8.3.

8.13 Explain how you would ensure that the automated library circulation system (Problem 8.7) is as portable as possible.

8.14 Explain how you would ensure that the product that checks whether a bank statement is correct (Problem 8.8) is as portable as possible.

8.15 Explain how you would ensure that the software for the automated teller machine (ATM) of Problem 8.9 is as portable as possible.

8.16 Your organization is developing a real-time control system for a new type of laser that will be used in cancer therapy. You are in charge of writing two assembler modules. How will you instruct your team to ensure that the resulting code will be as portable as possible?

8.17 You are responsible for porting a 750,000-line COBOL product to your company's new computer. You copy the source code to the new machine but discover when you try to compile it that every one of the over 15,000 input–output statements has been written in a nonstandard COBOL syntax that the new compiler rejects. What do you do now?

8.18 In what ways does the object-oriented paradigm promote portability and reusability?

8.19 (Term Project) Suppose that the Osric's Office Appliances and Decor product of Appendix A is developed using the classical paradigm. What parts of the product could be reused in future products? Now suppose that the product is developed using the object-oriented paradigm. What parts of the product could be reused in future products?

8.20 (Readings in Software Engineering) Your instructor will distribute copies of [Tomer et al., 2004]. What data would you need to accumulate in order to use the model?

**References**

[Alexander, 1999] C. ALEXANDER, "The Origins of Pattern Theory," *IEEE Software* **16** (September/October 1999), pp. 71–82.

[Alexander et al., 1977] C. ALEXANDER, S. ISHIKAWA, M. SILVERSTEIN, M. JACOBSON, I. FIKSDAHL-KING, AND S. ANGEL, *A Pattern Language,* Oxford University Press, New York, 1977.

[Anderson et al., 1999] E. ANDERSON, Z. BAI, C. BISCHOF, S. BLACKFORD, J. DEMMEL, J. DONGARRA, J. DU CROZ, A. GREENBAUM, S. HAMMARLING, A. MCKENNEY, AND D. SORENSEN, *LAPACK Users' Guide,* 3rd ed., SIAM, Philadelphia, 1999.

[ANSI X3.159, 1989] *The Programming Language C*, ANSI X3.159-1989, American National Standards Institute, New York, 1989.

[ANSI/IEEE 754, 1985] *Standard for Binary Floating Point Arithmetic,* ANSI/IEEE 754, American National Standards Institute, Institute of Electrical and Electronic Engineers, New York, 1985.

[ANSI/MIL-STD-1815A, 1983] *Reference Manual for the Ada Programming Language,* ANSI/ MIL-STD-1815A, American National Standards Institute, United States Department of Defense, Washington, DC, 1983.

[Barnes and Bollinger, 1991] B. H. BARNES AND T. B. BOLLINGER, "Making Reuse Cost-Effective," *IEEE Software* **8** (January 1991), pp. 13–24.

[Bass, Clements, and Kazman, 2003] L. BASS, P. CLEMENTS, AND R. KAZMAN, *Software Architecture in Practice,* 2nd ed., Addison-Wesley, Reading, MA, 2003.

[Baster, Konana, and Scott, 2001] G. BASTER, P. KONANA, AND J. E. SCOTT, "Business Components: A Case Study of Bankers Trust Australia Limited," Communications of the ACM 44 (May 2001), pp. 92–98.

[Birk et al. 2003] A. BIRK, G. HELLER, I. JOHN, K. SCHMID, T. VON DER MASSEN, AND K. MULLER, "Product Line Engineering, the State of the Practice," *IEEE Software* **20** (November/December 2003), pp. 52–60.

[Bockle et al., 2004] G. BOCKLE, P. CLEMENTS, J. D. MCGREGOR, D. MUTHIG, AND K. SCHMID, "Calculating ROI for Software Product Lines," *IEEE Software* **21** (May/June 2004), pp. 23–31.

[Bosch, 2000] J. BOSCH, *Design and Use of Software Architectures,* Addison-Wesley, Reading, MA, 2000.

[Brereton and Budgen, 2000] P. BRERETON AND D. BUDGEN, "Component-Based Systems: A Classification of Issues," *IEEE Computer* **33** (November 2000), pp. 54–62.

[Brown et al., 1998] W. J. BROWN, R. C. MALVEAU, W. H. BROWN, H. W. MCCORMICK, III, AND T. J. MOWBRAY, *AntiPatterns: Refactoring Software, Architectures, and Projects in Crisis,* John Wiley and Sons, New York, 1998.

[Caldiera and Basili, 1991] G. CALDIERA AND V. R. BASILI, "Identifying and Qualifying Reusable Software Components," *IEEE Computer* **24** (February 1991), pp. 61–70.

[Clements and Northrop, 2002] P. CLEMENTS AND L. NORTHROP, *Software Product Lines: Practices and Patterns,* Addison-Wesley, Reading, MA, 2002.

[Donohoe, 2000] P. DONOHOE (EDITOR), *Software Product Lines: Experience and Research Directions,* Kluwer Academic Publishers, Boston, 2000.

[D'Souza and Wills, 1999] D. D'SOUZA AND A. WILLS, *Objects, Components, and Frameworks with UML: The Catalysis Approach,* Addison-Wesley, Reading, MA, 1999.

[Fach, 2001] P. W. FACH, "Design Reuse through Frameworks and Patterns," *IEEE Software* **18** (September/October 2001), pp. 71–76.

[Fayad and Johnson, 1999] M. FAYAD AND R. JOHNSON, *Domain-Specific Application Frameworks: Frameworks Experience by Industry,* John Wiley and Sons, New York, 1999.

[Fayad and Schmidt, 1999] M. FAYAD AND D. C. SCHMIDT, *Building Application Frameworks: Object-Oriented Foundations of Framework Design,* John Wiley and Sons, New York, 1999.

[Fayad, Schmidt, and Johnson, 1999] M. FAYAD, D. C. SCHMIDT, AND R. JOHNSON, *Implementing Application Frameworks: Object-Oriented Frameworks at Work,* John Wiley and Sons, New York, 1999.

[Fichman and Kemerer, 1997] R. G. FICHMAN AND C. F. KEMERER, "Object Technology and Reuse: Lessons from Early Adopters," *IEEE Computer* **30** (July 1997), pp. 47–57.

[Fingar, 2000] P. FINGAR, "Component-Based Frameworks for e-Commerce," *Communications of the ACM* **43** (October 2000), pp. 61–66.

[Flanagan, 2005] D. FLANAGAN, *Java in a Nutshell: A Desktop Quick Reference,* 5th ed., O'Reilly and Associates, Sebastopol, CA, 2005.

[Fowler, 1997] M. FOWLER, *Analysis Patterns: Reusable Object Models,* Addison-Wesley, Reading, MA, 1997.

[Gamma, Helm, Johnson, and Vlissides, 1995] E. GAMMA, R. HELM, R. JOHNSON, AND J. VLISSIDES, *Design Patterns: Elements of Reusable Object-Oriented Software,* Addison-Wesley, Reading, MA, 1995.

[Gifford and Spector, 1987] D. GIFFORD AND A. SPECTOR, "Case Study: IBM's System/360-370 Architecture," *Communications of the ACM* **30** (April 1987), pp. 292–307.

[Green, 2000] P. GREEN, "FW: Here's an Update to the Simulated Kangaroo Story," *The Risks Digest* **20** (January 23, 2000), catless.ncl.ac.uk/Risks/20.76.html.

[Griss, 1993] M. L. GRISS, "Software Reuse: From Library to Factory," *IBM Systems Journal* **32** (No. 4, 1993), pp. 548–66.

[Hagge and Lappe, 2005] L. HAGGE AND K. LAPPE, "Sharing Requirements Engineering Experience Using Patterns," *IEEE Software* **22** (January/February 2005), pp. 24–31.

[Heineman and Councill, 2001] G. T. HEINEMAN AND W. T. COUNCILL, *Component-Based Software Engineering: Putting the Pieces Together*, Addison-Wesley, Reading, MA, 2001.

[Isakowitz and Kauffman, 1996] T. ISAKOWITZ AND R. J. KAUFFMAN, "Supporting Search for Reusable Software Objects," *IEEE Transactions on Software Engineering* **22** (June 1996), pp. 407–23.

[ISO/IEC 1539–1, 2004] *Information Technology—Programming Languages—Fortran—Part 1: Base Language*, ISO/IEC 1539–1, International Organization for Standardization, International Electrotechnical Commission, Geneva, 2004.

[ISO/IEC 1989, 2002] *Information Technology—Programming Language COBOL*, ISO 1989:2002, International Organization for Standardization, International Electrotechnical Commission, Geneva, 2002.

[ISO/IEC 8652, 1995] *Programming Language Ada: Language and Standard Libraries*, ISO/IEC 8652, International Organization for Standardization, International Electrotechnical Commission, Geneva, 1995.

[ISO/IEC 14882, 1998] *Programming Language C++*, ISO/IEC 14882, International Organization for Standardization, International Electrotechnical Commission, Geneva, 1998.

[Jazayeri, Ran, and van der Linden, 2000] M. JAZAYERI, A. RAN, AND F. VAN DER LINDEN, *Software Architecture for Product Families: Principles and Practice,* Addison-Wesley, Reading, MA, 2000.

[Jézéquel and Meyer, 1997] J.-M. JÉZÉQUEL AND B. MEYER, "Put It in the Contract: The Lessons of Ariane," *IEEE Computer* **30** (January 1997), pp. 129–30.

[Johnson, 1979] S. C. JOHNSON, "A Tour through the Portable C Compiler," 7th ed., UNIX Programmer's Manual, Bell Laboratories, Murray Hill, NJ, January 1979.

[Johnson and Ritchie, 1978] S. C. JOHNSON AND D. M. RITCHIE, "Portability of C Programs and the UNIX System," *Bell System Technical Journal* **57** (No. 6, Part 2, 1978), pp. 2021–48.

[Jones, 1984] T. C. JONES, "Reusability in Programming: A Survey of the State of the Art," *IEEE Transactions on Software Engineering* **SE-10** (September 1984), pp. 488–94.

[Kernighan and Ritchie, 1978] B. W. KERNIGHAN AND D. M. RITCHIE, *The C Programming Language*, Prentice Hall, Englewood Cliffs, NJ, 1978.

[Knauber, Muthig, Schmid, and Widen, 2000] P. KNAUBER, D. MUTHIG, K. SCHMID, AND T. WIDEN, "Applying Product Line Concepts in Small and Medium-Sized Companies," *IEEE Software* **17** (September/October 2000), pp. 88–95.

[Kobryn, 2000] C. KOBRYN, "Modeling Components and Frameworks with UML," *Communications of the ACM* **43** (October 2000), pp. 31–38.

[Lai, Weiss, and Parnas, 1999] C. T. R. LAI, D. M. WEISS, AND D. L. PARNAS, *Software Product-Line Engineering: A Family-Based Software Development Process,* Addison-Wesley, Reading, MA, 1999.

[Lanergan and Grasso, 1984] R. G. LANERGAN AND C. A. GRASSO, "Software Engineering with Reusable Designs and Code," *IEEE Transactions on Software Engineering* **SE-10** (September 1984), pp. 498–501.

[LAPACK++, 2000] "LAPACK++: Linear Algebra Package in C++," at math.nist.gov/lapack++, 2000.

[Lewis et al., 1995] T. LEWIS, L. ROSENSTEIN, W. PREE, A. WEINAND, E. GAMMA, P. CALDER, G. ANDERT, J. VLISSIDES, AND K. SCHMUCKER, *Object-Oriented Application Frameworks*, Manning, Greenwich, CT, 1995.

[Lim, 1994] W. C. LIM, "Effects of Reuse on Quality, Productivity, and Economics," *IEEE Software* **11** (September 1994), pp. 23–30.

[Lim, 1998] W. C. LIM, *Managing Software Reuse*, Prentice Hall, Upper Saddle River, NJ, 1998.

[Liskov, Snyder, Atkinson, and Schaffert, 1977] B. LISKOV, A. SNYDER, R. ATKINSON, AND C. SCHAFFERT, "Abstraction Mechanisms in CLU," *Communications of the ACM* **20** (August 1977), pp. 564–76.

[Mackenzie, 1980] C. E. MACKENZIE, *Coded Character Sets: History and Development*, Addison-Wesley, Reading, MA, 1980.

[Matsumoto, 1984] Y. MATSUMOTO, "Management of Industrial Software Production," *IEEE Computer* **17** (February 1984), pp. 59–72.

[Matsumoto, 1987] Y. MATSUMOTO, "A Software Factory: An Overall Approach to Software Production," in: *Tutorial: Software Reusability*, P. Freeman (Editor), Computer Society Press, Washington, DC, 1987, pp. 155–78.

[Meyer, 1987] B. MEYER, "Reusability: The Case for Object-Oriented Design," *IEEE Software* **4** (March 1987), pp. 50–64.

[Meyer, 1996a] B. MEYER, "The Reusability Challenge," *IEEE Computer* **29** (February 1996), pp. 76–78.

[Mooney, 1990] J. D. MOONEY, "Strategies for Supporting Application Portability," *IEEE Computer* **23** (November 1990), pp. 59–70.

[Morisio, Ezran, and Tully, 2002] M. MORISIO, M. EZRAN, AND C. TULLY, "Success and Failure Factors in Software Reuse," *IEEE Transactions on Software Engineering* **28** (April 2002), pp. 340–57.

[Morisio, Tully, and Ezran, 2000] M. MORISIO, C. TULLY, AND M. EZRAN, "Diversity in Reuse Processes," *IEEE Software* **17** (July/August 2000), pp. 56–63.

[Musser and Saini, 1996] D. R. MUSSER AND A. SAINI, *STL Tutorial and Reference Guide: C++ Programming with the Standard Template Library*, Addison-Wesley, Reading, MA, 1996.

[NAG, 2003] "NAG The Numerical Algorithms Group Ltd," at www.nag.co.uk, 2003.

[NIST 151, 1988] "POSIX: Portable Operating System Interface for Computer Environments," Federal Information Processing Standard 151, National Institute of Standards and Technology, Washington, DC, 1988.

[Norušis, 2005] M. J. NORUŠIS, *SPSS 13.0 Guide to Data Analysis,* Prentice Hall, Upper Saddle Valley River, NJ, 2005.

[Pont and Banner, 2004] M. J. PONT AND M. P. BANNER, "Designing Embedded Systems Using Patterns: A Case Study," *Journal of Systems and Software* **71** (May 2004), pp. 201–213.

[Poulin, 1997] J. S. POULIN, *Measuring Software Reuse: Principles, Practice, and Economic Models*, Addison-Wesley, Reading, MA, 1997.

[Prechelt, Unger-Lamprecht, Philippsen, and Tichy, 2002] L. PRECHELT, B. UNGER-LAMPRECHT, M. PHILIPPSEN, AND W. F. TICHY, "Two Controlled Experiments in Assessing the Usefulness of Design Pattern Documentation in Program Maintenance," *IEEE Transactions on Software Engineering* **28** (June 2002), pp. 595–606.

[Prieto-Díaz, 1991] R. PRIETO-DÍAZ, "Implementing Faceted Classification for Software Reuse," *Communications of the ACM* **34** (May 1991), pp. 88–97.

[Ravichandran and Rothenberger, 2003] T. RAVICHANDRAN AND M. A. ROTHENBERGER, "Software Reuse Strategies and Component Markets," *Communications of the ACM* **46** (August 2003), pp. 109–114

[Schach, 1992] S. R. SCHACH, *Software Reuse: Past, Present, and Future*, videotape, 150 min, US-VHS format, IEEE Computer Society Press, Los Alamitos, CA, November 1992.

[Schach, 1994] S. R. SCHACH, "The Economic Impact of Software Reuse on Maintenance," *Journal of Software Maintenance—Research and Practice* **6** (July/August 1994), pp. 185–96.

[Schach, 1997] S. R. SCHACH, *Software Engineering with Java*, Richard D. Irwin, Chicago, 1997.

[Schricker, 2000] D. SCHRICKER, "Cobol for the Next Millennium," *IEEE Software* **17** (March/April 2000), pp. 48–52.

[Selby, 1989] R. W. SELBY, "Quantitative Studies of Software Reuse," in: *Software Reusability*, Vol. 2, *Applications and Experience*, T. J. Biggerstaff and A. J. Perlis (Editors), ACM Press, New York, 1989, pp. 213–33.

[Shaw and Garlan, 1996] M. SHAW AND D. GARLAN, *Software Architecture: Perspectives on an Emerging Discipline*, Prentice Hall, Upper Saddle River, NJ, 1996.

[Sparling, 2000] M. SPARLING, "Lessons Learned through Six Years of Component-Based Development," *Communications of the ACM* **43** (October 2000), pp. 47–53.

[Tanenbaum, 2002] A. S. TANENBAUM, *Computer Networks,* 4th ed., Prentice Hall, Upper Saddle River, NJ, 2002.

[Toft, Coleman, and Ohta, 2000] P. TOFT, D. COLEMAN, AND J. OHTA, "A Cooperative Model for Cross-Divisional Product Development for a Software Product Line," in: *Software Product Lines: Experience and Research Directions*, P. Donohoe (Editor), Kluwer Academic Publishers, Boston, 2000, pp. 111–32.

[Tomer et al., 2004] A. TOMER, L. GOLDIN, T. KUFLIK, E. KIMCHI, AND S. R. SCHACH, "Evaluating Software Reuse Alternatives: A Model and Its Application to an Industrial Case Study," *IEEE Transactions on Software Engineering* **30** (September 2004), 601–12.

[Tracz, 1994] W. TRACZ, "Software Reuse Myths Revisited," *Proceedings of the 16th International Conference on Software Engineering*, Sorrento, Italy, May 1994, pp. 271–72.

[Vitharana, 2003] P. VITHARANA, "Risks and Challenges of Component-Based Software Development," *Communications of the ACM* **46** (August 2003), pp. 67–72.

[Vlissides, 1998] J. VLISSIDES, *Pattern Hatching: Design Patterns Applied,* Addison-Wesley, Reading, MA, 1998.

[Vokac, 2004] M. VOKAC, "Defect Frequency and Design Patterns: An Empirical Study of Industrial Code," *IEEE Transactions on Software Engineering* **30** (December 2004), pp. 904–17.

[Weyuker, 1998] E. J. WEYUKER, "Testing Component-Based Software: A Cautionary Tale," *IEEE Software* **15** (September/October 1998), pp. 54–59.

# Chapter

# 9

# Planning and Estimating

## Learning Objectives

After studying this chapter, you should be able to

- Explain the importance of planning.
- Estimate the size and cost of building a software product.
- Appreciate the importance of updating and tracking estimates.
- Draw up a project management plan that conforms to the IEEE standard.

The challenges of constructing a software product have no easy solution. To put together a large software product takes time and resources. And, like any other large construction project, careful planning at the beginning of the project perhaps is the single most important factor that distinguishes success from failure. This initial planning, however, by no means is enough. Planning, like testing, must continue throughout the software development and maintenance process. Notwithstanding the need for continual planning, these activities reach a peak after the specifications have been drawn up but before design activities commence. At this point in the process, meaningful duration and cost estimates are computed and a detailed plan for completing the project produced.

In this chapter, we distinguish these two types of **planning** the planning that proceeds throughout the project and the intense planning that must be carried out once the specifications are complete.

As explained in the Preface, the material of this chapter may be taught in parallel with Part 2. The material of Chapter 9 is required for the software project management plan for the MSG Foundation case study (Section 11.15; Problems 11.20 and 11.21) and for the Osric's Office Appliances and Decor term project (Problem 11.16).

# 9.1   Planning and the Software Process

Ideally, we would like to plan the entire software project at the very beginning of the process, and then follow that plan until the target software finally has been delivered to the client. This is impossible, however, because we lack enough information during the initial workflows to be able to draw up a meaningful plan for the complete project. For example, during the requirements workflow, any sort of planning (other than just for the requirements workflow itself) is futile.

There is a world of difference between the information at the developers' disposal at the end of the requirements workflow and at the end of the analysis workflow, analogous to the difference between a rough sketch and a detailed blueprint. By the end of the requirements workflow, the developers at best have an informal understanding of what the client needs. In contrast, by the end of the analysis workflow, at which time the client signs a document stating precisely what is going to be built, the developers have a detailed appreciation of most (but usually still not all) aspects of the target product. This is the earliest point in the process at which accurate duration and cost estimates can be determined.

Nevertheless, in some situations, an organization may be required to produce duration and cost estimates before the specifications can be drawn up. In the worst case, a client may insist on a bid on the basis of an hour or two of preliminary discussion. Figure 9.1 shows how problematic this can be. Based on a model in [Boehm et al., 2000], it depicts the relative range of cost estimates for the various workflows of the life cycle. For example, suppose that, when a product passes its acceptance test at the end of the implementation workflow and is delivered to the client, its cost is found to be $1 million. If a cost estimate had been made midway through the requirements workflow, it is likely that it would have been somewhere in the range ($0.25 million, $4 million), as shown in Figure 9.2. Similarly, if the cost estimate had been made at the end of the requirements workflow, the range of

**FIGURE 9.1**

A model for estimating the relative range of a cost estimate for each life-cycle workflow.

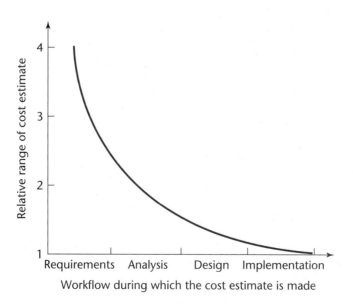

**FIGURE 9.2**

Range of cost
estimates for a
software
product that cost
$1 million to
build.

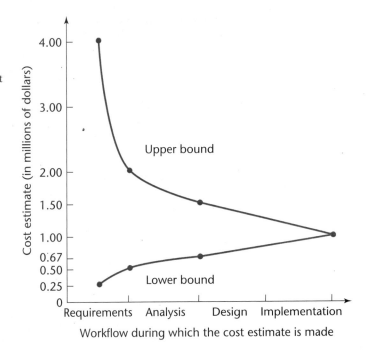

Workflow during which the cost estimate is made

likely estimates would have shrunk to ($0.5 million, $2 million). Furthermore, if the cost estimate had been made at the end of the analysis workflow, that is, at the appropriate time, the result probably would have been in the still relatively wide range of ($0.67 million, $1.5 million). All four points are marked on the upper and lower bound lines in Figure 9.2, which has a logarithmic scale on the vertical axis. This model is called the **cone of uncertainty**. It is clear from Figures 9.1 and 9.2 that cost estimation is not an exact science; reasons for this are given in Section 9.2.

The data on which the cone of uncertainty model is based are old, including five proposals submitted to the U.S. Air Force Electronic Systems Division [Devenny, 1976], and estimation techniques have improved since that time. Nevertheless, the overall shape of the curve in Figure 9.1 probably has not changed overmuch. Consequently, a premature duration or cost estimate, that is, an estimate made before the specifications have been signed off on by the client, is likely to be considerably less accurate than an estimate made when sufficient data have accumulated.

. We now examine techniques for estimating duration and cost. The assumption throughout the remainder of this chapter is that the analysis workflow has been completed; that is, meaningful estimating and planning now can be carried out.

## 9.2 Estimating Duration and Cost

The budget is an integral part of any software project management plan. Before design commences, the client needs to know how much he or she will have to pay for the product. If the development team underestimates the actual cost, the development organization can lose money on the project. On the other hand, if the development team overestimates, then the client may decide that, on the basis of cost–benefit analysis or return on investment, there is no point in having the product built. Alternatively, the client may give the job to another development organization whose estimate is more reasonable. Either way, it is clear that accurate cost estimation is critical.

In fact, two types of costs are associated with software development. The first is the **internal cost**, the **cost** to the developers; the second is the **external cost**, the **price** that the client will pay. The internal cost includes the salaries of the development teams, managers, and support personnel involved in the project; the cost of the hardware and software for developing the product; and the cost of overhead such as rent, utilities, and salaries of senior management. Although the price generally is based on the cost plus a profit margin, in some cases economic and psychological factors are important. For example, developers who desperately need the work may be prepared to charge the client at cost. A different situation arises when a contract is to be awarded on the basis of bids. The client may reject a bid that is significantly lower than all the other bids on the grounds that the quality of the resulting product probably also would be significantly lower. A development team therefore may try to come up with a bid that will be slightly, but not significantly, lower than what it believes will be the competitors' bids.

Another important part of any plan is estimating the duration of the project. The client certainly wants to know when the finished product will be delivered. If the development organization is unable to keep to its schedule, then at best the organization loses credibility, at worst penalty clauses are invoked. In all cases, the managers responsible for the software project management plan have a lot of explaining to do. Conversely, if the development organization overestimates the time needed to build the product, then there is a good chance that the client will go elsewhere.

Unfortunately, it is by no means easy to estimate cost and duration requirements accurately. Too many variables are involved to be able to get an accurate handle on either cost or duration. One big difficulty is the human factor. Over 35 years ago, Sackman and coworkers observed differences of up to 28 to 1 between pairs of programmers [Sackman, Erikson, and Grant, 1968]. It is easy to try to brush off their results by saying that experienced programmers always outperform beginners, but Sackman and his colleagues compared matched pairs of programmers. They observed, for example, two programmers with 10 years of experience on similar types of projects and measured the time it took them to perform tasks like coding and debugging. Then they observed, say, two beginners who had been in the profession for the same short length of time and had similar educational backgrounds. Comparing worst and best performances, they observed differences of 6 to 1 in product size, 8 to 1 in product execution time, 9 to 1 in development time, 18 to 1 in coding time, and 28 to 1 in debugging time. A particularly alarming observation is that the best and worst performances on one product were by two programmers, each of whom had 11 years of experience. Even when the best and worst cases were removed from Sackman et al.'s sample, observed differences were still on the order of 5 to 1. On the basis of these results, clearly, we cannot hope to estimate software cost or duration with any degree of accuracy (unless we have detailed information regarding all the skills of all the employees, which would be most unusual). It has been argued that, on a large project, differences among individuals tend to cancel out, but this perhaps is wishful thinking; the presence of one or two very good (or very bad) team members can cause marked deviations from schedules and significantly affect the budget.

Another human factor that can affect estimation is that, in a free country, there is no way of ensuring that a critical staff member will not resign during the project. Time and money then are spent attempting to fill the vacated position and integrate the replacement into the team, or in reorganizing the remaining team members to compensate for the loss. Either way, schedules slip and estimates come unstuck.

Underlying the cost estimation problem is another issue: How is the size of a product to be measured?

### 9.2.1 Metrics for the Size of a Product

The most common metric for the size of a product is the number of lines of code. Two units commonly are used: **lines of code**(LOC) and **thousand delivered source instructions** (KDSI). Many problems are associated with the use of lines of code [van der Poel and Schach, 1983].

- Creation of source code is only a small part of the total software development effort. It seems somewhat far-fetched that the time required for the requirements, analysis, design, implementation, and testing workflows (which include planning and documentation activities) can be expressed solely as a function of the number of lines of code of the final product.

- Implementing the same product in two different languages results in versions with different numbers of lines of code. Also, with languages such as Lisp or with many nonprocedural 4GLs (Section 14.2), the concept of a line of code is not defined.

- It often is unclear exactly how to count lines of code. Should only executable lines of code be counted or data definitions as well? And should comments be counted? If not, there is a danger that programmers will be reluctant to spend time on what they perceive to be "nonproductive" comments, but if comments are counted, then the opposite danger is that programmers will write reams of comments in an attempt to boost their apparent productivity. Also, what about counting job control language statements? Another problem is how changed lines or deleted lines are counted—in the course of enhancing a product to improve its performance, sometimes the number of lines of code is decreased. Reuse of code (Section 8.1) also complicates line counting: If reused code is modified, how is it counted? And, what if code is inherited from a parent class (Section 7.8)? In short, the apparently straightforward metric of lines of code is anything but straightforward to count.

- Not all the code written is delivered to the client. It is not uncommon for half the code to consist of tools needed to support the development effort.

- Suppose that a software developer uses a code generator, such as a report generator, a screen generator, or a graphical user interface (GUI) generator. After a few minutes of design activity on the part of the developer, the tool may generate many thousands of lines of code.

- The number of lines of code in the final product can be determined only when the product is completely finished. Therefore, basing cost estimation on lines of code is doubly dangerous. To start the estimation process, the number of lines of code in the finished product must be estimated. Then, this estimate is used to estimate the cost of the product. Not only is there uncertainty in every costing technique, but if the input to an uncertain cost estimator itself is uncertain (that is, the number of lines of code in a product that has not yet been built), then the reliability of the resulting cost estimate is unlikely to be very high.

Because the number of lines of code is so unreliable, other metrics must be considered. An alternative approach to estimating the size of a product is the use of metrics based on measurable quantities that can be determined early in the software process. For example, van der Poel and Schach [1983] put forward the **FFP metric** for cost estimation of medium-scale data-processing products. The three basic structural elements of a data-processing product are its files, flows, and processes; the name FFP is an acronym formed from the initial letters of those elements. A *file* is defined as a collection of logically or physically related records permanently resident in the product; transaction and temporary files are excluded. A *flow* is a data interface between the product and the environment, such as a screen or a report. A *process* is a functionally defined logical or arithmetic manipulation of data; examples include sorting, validating, or updating. Given the number of files, $Fi$, flows, $Fl$, and processes, $Pr$, in a product, its size $S$ and cost $C$ are given by

$$S = Fi + Fl + Pr \tag{9.1}$$

$$C = d \times S \tag{9.2}$$

where $d$ is a constant that varies from organization to organization. Constant $d$ is a measure of the **efficiency (productivity** ) of the software development process within that organization. The size of a product simply is the sum of the number of files, flows, and processes, a quantity that can be determined once the architectural design is complete. The cost then is proportional to the size, the constant of proportionality $d$ being determined by a least-squares fit to cost data relating to products previously developed by that organization. Unlike metrics based on the number of lines of code, the cost can be estimated before coding begins.

The validity and reliability of the FFP metric were demonstrated using a purposive sample that covered a range of medium-scale data-processing applications. Unfortunately, the metric was never extended to include databases, an essential component of many data-processing products.

A similar, but independently developed, metric for the size of a product was developed by Albrecht [1979] based on function points; Albrecht's metric is based on the number of input items, $Inp$, output items, $Out$, inquiries, $Inq$, master files, $Maf$, and interfaces, $Inf$. In its simplest form the number of **function points** , $FP$, is given by the equation

$$FP = 4 \times Inp + 5 \times Out + 4 \times Inq + 10 \times Maf + 7 \times Inf \tag{9.3}$$

Because this is a measure of the product's size, it can be used for cost estimation and productivity estimation.

Equation (9.3) is an oversimplification of a three-step calculation. First, the unadjusted function points are computed:

1. Each of the components of a product—$Inp$, $Out$, $Inq$, $Maf$, and $Inf$—must be classified as simple, average, or complex (see Figure 9.3).

2. Each component is assigned a number of function points depending on its level. For example, an average input is assigned 4 function points, as reflected in equation (9.3),

**FIGURE 9.3**

Table of function point values.

| | Level of Complexity | | |
|---|---|---|---|
| Component | Simple | Average | Complex |
| Input item | 3 | 4 | 6 |
| Output item | 4 | 5 | 7 |
| Inquiry | 3 | 4 | 6 |
| Master file | 7 | 10 | 15 |
| Interface | 5 | 7 | 10 |

**FIGURE 9.4**

Technical factors for function point computation.

1. Data communication
2. Distributed data processing
3. Performance criteria
4. Heavily utilized hardware
5. High transaction rates
6. Online data entry
7. End-user efficiency
8. Online updating
9. Complex computations
10. Reusability
11. Ease of installation
12. Ease of operation
13. Portability
14. Maintainability

but a simple input is assigned only 3, whereas a complex input is assigned 6 function points. The data needed for this step appear in Figure 9.3.

3. The function points assigned to each component are then summed, yielding the **unadjusted function points** (*UFP*).

Second, the **technical complexity factor** (*TCF*) is computed. This is a measure of the effect of 14 technical factors, such as high transaction rates, performance criteria (for example, throughput or response time), and online updating; the complete set of factors is shown in Figure 9.4. Each of these 14 factors is assigned a value from 0 ("not present or no influence") to 5 ("strong influence throughout"). The resulting 14 numbers are summed, yielding the total degree of influence (*DI*). The *TCF* is then given by

$$TCF = 0.65 + 0.01 \times DI \qquad (9.4)$$

Because *DI* can vary from 0 to 70, *TCF* varies from 0.65 to 1.35.

**FIGURE 9.5**

A comparison
of assembler
and Ada
products.

Source: [Jones, 1987].
(© 1987 IEEE.)

|  | Assembler Version | Ada Version |
|---|---|---|
| Source code size | 70 KDSI | 25 KDSI |
| Development costs | $1,043,000 | $590,000 |
| KDSI per person-month | 0.335 | 0.211 |
| Cost per source statement | $14.90 | $23.60 |
| Function points per person-month | 1.65 | 2.92 |
| Cost per function point | $3,023 | $1,170 |

Third, *FP*, the number of function points, is given by

$$FP = UFP \times TCF \qquad (9.5)$$

Experiments to measure software productivity rates have shown a better fit using function points than using KDSI. For example, Jones [1987] has stated that he observed errors in excess of 800 percent counting KDSI, but *only* [emphasis added] 200 percent in counting function points, a most revealing remark.

To show the superiority of function points over lines of code, Jones [1987] cites the example shown in Figure 9.5. The same product was coded both in assembler and in Ada and the results compared. First, consider KDSI per person-month. This metric tells us that coding in assembler is apparently 60 percent more efficient than coding in Ada, which is patently false. Third-generation languages like Ada have superseded assembler simply because it is much more efficient to code in a third-generation language. Now consider the second metric, cost per source statement. Note that one Ada statement in this product is equivalent to 2.8 assembler statements. Use of cost per source statement as a measure of efficiency again implies that again it is more efficient to code in assembler than in Ada. However, when function points per person-month is taken as the metric of programming efficiency, the superiority of Ada over assembler is reflected clearly.

On the other hand, both function points and the FFP metric of equations (9.1) and (9.2) suffer from the same weakness: Product maintenance often is inaccurately measured. When a product is maintained, major changes to the product can be made without changing the number of files, flows, and processes or the number of inputs, outputs, inquiries, master files, and interfaces. Lines of code is no better in this respect. To take an extreme case, it is possible to replace every line of a product by a completely different line without changing the total number of lines of code.

At least 40 variants of and extensions to Albrecht's function points have been proposed [Maxwell and Forselius, 2000]. Mk II function points were put forward by Symons [1991] to provide a more accurate way of computing the unadjusted function points (*UFP*). The software is decomposed into a set of component transactions, each consisting of an input, a process, and an output. The value of *UFP* then is computed from these inputs, processes, and outputs. Mk II function points are widely used all over the world [Boehm, 1997].

## 9.2.2 Techniques of Cost Estimation

Notwithstanding the difficulties with estimating size, it is essential that software developers simply do the best they can to obtain accurate estimates of both project duration and project cost, while taking into account as many as possible of the factors that can affect their estimates. These include the skill levels of the personnel, the complexity of the project, the size of the project (cost increases with size but much more than linearly), familiarity of the development team with the application area, the hardware on which the product is to be run, and availability of CASE tools. Another factor is the deadline effect. If a project has to be completed by a certain time, the effort in person-months is greater than if no constraint is placed on completion time; hence, the greater the cost. This shows that duration and cost are not independent; the shorter is the deadline, the greater the effort and, hence, the greater the cost.

From the preceding list, which is by no means comprehensive, clearly estimation is a difficult problem. A number of approaches have been used, with greater or lesser success.

### 1. Expert Judgment by Analogy

In the **expert judgment by analogy** technique, a number of experts are consulted. An expert arrives at an estimate by comparing the target product to completed products with which the expert was actively involved and noting the similarities and differences. For example, an expert may compare the target product to a similar product developed 2 years ago for which the data were entered in batch mode, whereas the target product is to have online data capture. Because the organization is familiar with the type of product to be developed, the expert reduces development time and effort by 15 percent. However, the graphical user interface is somewhat complex; this increases time and effort by 25 percent. Finally, the target product has to be developed in a language with which most of the team members are unfamiliar, thus increasing time by 15 percent and effort by 20 percent. Combining these three figures, the expert decides that the target product will take 25 percent more time and 30 percent more effort than the previous one. Because the previous product took 12 months to complete and required 100 person-months, the target product is estimated to take 15 months and consume 130 person-months.

Two other experts within the organization compare the same two products. One concludes that the target product will take 13.5 months and 140 person-months. The other comes up with the figures of 16 months and 95 person-months. How can the predictions of these three experts be reconciled? One technique is the **Delphi technique**. It allows experts to arrive at a consensus without having group meetings, which can have the undesirable side effect of one persuasive member swaying the group. In this technique, the experts work independently. Each produces an estimate and a rationale for that estimate. These estimates and rationales then are distributed to all the experts, who now produce a second estimate. This process of estimation and distribution continues until the experts can agree within an accepted tolerance. No group meetings take place during the iteration process.

Valuation of real estate frequently is done on the basis of expert judgment by analogy. An appraiser arrives at a valuation by comparing a house with similar houses that have been sold recently. Suppose that house A is to be valued, house B next door has just been sold for $205,000, and house C on the next street was sold 3 months ago for $218,000. The appraiser may reason as follows: House A has one more bathroom than house B, and the yard is 5,000 square feet larger. House C is approximately the same size as house A, but its roof is in poor condition. On the other hand, House C has a jacuzzi. After careful thought, the appraiser may arrive at a figure of $215,000 for house A.

In the case of software products, expert judgment by analogy is less accurate than real estate valuation. Recall that our first software expert claimed that using an unfamiliar language would increase time by 15 percent and effort by 20 percent. Unless the expert has some validated data from which the effect of each difference can be determined (a highly unlikely possibility), errors induced by what can be described only as guesses will result in hopelessly incorrect cost estimates. In addition, unless the experts are blessed with total recall (or have kept detailed records), their recollections of completed products may be sufficiently inaccurate as to invalidate their predictions. Finally, experts are human and, therefore, have biases that may affect their predictions. At the same time, the results of estimation by a group of experts should reflect their collective experience; if this is broad enough, the result well may be accurate.

## 2. Bottom-up Approach

One way of trying to reduce the errors resulting from evaluating a product as a whole is to break the product into smaller components. Estimates of duration and cost are made for each component separately and combined to provide an overall figure. This **bottom-up approach** has the advantage that estimating costs for several smaller components generally is quicker and more accurate than for one large one. In addition, the estimation process is likely to be more detailed than with one large, monolithic product. The weakness of this approach is that a product is more than the sum of its components.

With the object-oriented paradigm, the independence of the various classes helps the bottom-up approach. However, interactions among the various objects in the product complicate the estimation process.

## 3. Algorithmic Cost Estimation Models

In this approach, a metric, such as function points or the FFP metric, is used as input to a model for determining product cost. The estimator computes the value of the metric; duration and cost estimates then can be computed using the model. On the surface, an **algorithmic cost estimation model** is superior to expert opinion, because a human expert, as pointed out previously, is subject to biases and may overlook certain aspects of both the completed and target products. In contrast, an algorithmic cost estimation model is unbiased; every product is treated the same way. The danger with such a model is that its estimates are only as good as the underlying assumptions. For example, underlying the function point model is the assumption that every aspect of a product is embodied in the five quantities on the right-hand side of equation (9.3) and the ·14 technical factors. A further problem is that a significant amount of subjective judgment often is needed in deciding what values to assign to the parameters of the model. For example, frequently it is unclear whether a specific technical factor of the function point model should be rated a 3 or a 4.

Many algorithmic cost estimation models have been proposed. Some are based on mathematical theories as to how software is developed. Other models are statistically based; large numbers of projects are studied and empirical rules determined from the data. Hybrid models incorporate mathematical equations, statistical modeling, and expert judgment. The most important hybrid model is Boehm's COCOMO, which is described in detail in Section 9.2.3. (See Just in Case You Wanted to Know Box 9.1 for a discussion of the acronym COCOMO.)

COCOMO is an acronym formed from the first two letters of each word in COnstructive COst MOdel. Any connection with Kokomo, Indiana, is purely coincidental.

The *MO* in COCOMO stands for "model," so the phrase *COCOMO model* should not be used. That phrase falls into the same category as "ATM machine" and "PIN number," both of which were dreamed up by the Department of Redundant Information Department.

### 9.2.3 Intermediate COCOMO

**COCOMO** actually is a series of three models, ranging from a macroestimation model that treats the product as a whole to a microestimation model that treats the product in detail. In this section, a description is given of intermediate COCOMO, which has a middle level of complexity and detail. COCOMO is described in detail in [Boehm, 1981]; an overview is presented in [Boehm, 1984].

Computing development time using intermediate COCOMO is done in two stages. First, a rough estimate of the development effort is provided. Two parameters have to be estimated: the length of the product in KDSI and the product's development mode, a measure of the intrinsic level of difficulty of developing that product. There are three modes: *organic* (small and straightforward), *semidetached* (medium sized), and *embedded* (complex).

From these two parameters, the **nominal effort** can be computed. For example, if the project is judged essentially straightforward (organic), then the nominal effort (in person-months) is given by the equation

$$\text{Nominal effort} = 3.2 \times (\text{KDSI})^{1.05} \text{ person-months} \qquad \textbf{(9.6)}$$

The constants 3.2 and 1.05 are the values that best fitted the data on the organic mode products used by Boehm to develop intermediate COCOMO.

For example, if the product to be built is organic and estimated to be 12,000 delivered source statements (12 KDSI), then the nominal effort is

$$3.2 \times (12)^{1.05} = 43 \text{ person-months}$$

(but read Just in Case You Wanted to Know Box 9.2 for a comment on this value).

Next, this nominal value must be multiplied by 15 **software development effort multipliers.** These multipliers and their values are given in Figure 9.6. Each multiplier can have up to six values. For example, the product complexity multiplier is assigned the values 0.70, 0.85, 1.00, 1.15, 1.30, or 1.65, according to whether the developers rate the project complexity as very low, low, nominal (average), high, very high, or extra high. As can be seen from Figure 9.6, all 15 multipliers take on the value 1.00 when the corresponding parameter is nominal.

Boehm provides guidelines to help the developer determine whether the parameter should indeed be rated nominal or whether the rating is lower or higher. For example, consider again the module complexity multiplier. If the control operations of the module essentially consist of a sequence of the constructs of structured programming (such as **if-then-else, do-while, case**), then the complexity is rated *very low*. If these operators are nested, then the rating is *low*. Adding intermodule control and decision tables increases the rating to *nominal*. If the operators are highly nested, with compound predicates, and

One reaction to the value of the nominal effort might be, "If 43 person-months of effort are needed to produce 12,000 delivered source instructions, then on average each programmer is turning out fewer than 300 lines of code a month—I have written more than that in one night!"

A 300-line product usually is just that: 300 lines of code. In contrast, a maintainable 12,000-line product has to go through all the workflows of the life cycle. In other words, the total effort of 43 person-months is shared among many activities, including coding.

**FIGURE 9.6**    Intermediate COCOMO software development effort multipliers.

Source: [Boehm, 1984]. (© 1984 IEEE.)

| Cost Drivers | Rating | | | | | |
|---|---|---|---|---|---|---|
| | Very Low | Low | Nominal | High | Very High | Extra High |
| **Product Attributes** | | | | | | |
| Required software reliability | 0.75 | 0.88 | 1.00 | 1.15 | 1.40 | |
| Database size | | 0.94 | 1.00 | 1.08 | 1.16 | |
| Product complexity | 0.70 | 0.85 | 1.00 | 1.15 | 1.30 | 1.65 |
| **Computer Attributes** | | | | | | |
| Execution time constraint | | | 1.00 | 1.11 | 1.30 | 1.66 |
| Main storage constraint | | | 1.00 | 1.06 | 1.21 | 1.56 |
| Virtual machine volatility* | | 0.87 | 1.00 | 1.15 | 1.30 | |
| Computer turnaround time | | 0.87 | 1.00 | 1.07 | 1.15 | |
| **Personnel Attributes** | | | | | | |
| Analyst capabilities | 1.46 | 1.19 | 1.00 | 0.86 | 0.71 | |
| Applications experience | 1.29 | 1.13 | 1.00 | 0.91 | 0.82 | |
| Programmer capability | 1.42 | 1.17 | 1.00 | 0.86 | 0.70 | |
| Virtual machine experience* | 1.21 | 1.10 | 1.00 | 0.90 | | |
| Programming language experience | 1.14 | 1.07 | 1.00 | 0.95 | | |
| **Project Attributes** | | | | | | |
| Use of modern programming practices | 1.24 | 1.10 | 1.00 | 0.91 | 0.82 | |
| Use of software tools | 1.24 | 1.10 | 1.00 | 0.91 | 0.83 | |
| Required development schedule | 1.23 | 1.08 | 1.00 | 1.04 | 1.10 | |

*For a given software product, the underlying virtual machine is the complex of hardware and software (operating system, database management system) it calls on to accomplish its task.

queues and stacks, then the rating is *high*. The presence of reentrant and recursive coding and fixed-priority interrupt handling pushes the rating to *very high*. Finally, multiple resource scheduling with dynamically changing priorities and microcode-level control ensures that the rating is *extra high*. These ratings apply to control operations. A module also has to be evaluated from the viewpoint of computational operations, device-dependent operations, and data management operations. For details on the criteria for computing each of the 15 multipliers, refer to [Boehm, 1981].

To see how this works, Boehm [1984] gives the example of microprocessor-based communications processing software for a highly reliable new electronic funds transfer network, with performance, development schedule, and interface requirements. This product fits the description of embedded mode and is estimated to be 10,000 delivered source instructions (10 KDSI) in length, so the nominal development effort is given by

$$\text{Nominal effort} = 2.8 \times (\text{KDSI})^{1.20} \qquad \textbf{(9.7)}$$

(Again, the constants 2.8 and 1.20 are the values that best fitted the data on embedded products.) Because the project is estimated to be 10 KDSI in length, the nominal effort is

$$2.8 \times (10)^{1.20} = 44 \text{ person-months}$$

The estimated development effort is obtained by multiplying the nominal effort by the 15 software development effort multipliers. The ratings of these multipliers and their values are given in Figure 9.7. Using these values, the product of the multipliers is found to be 1.35, so the estimated effort for the project is

$$1.35 \times 44 = 59 \text{ person-months}$$

This number is then used in additional formulas to determine dollar costs, development schedules, phase and activity distributions, computer costs, annual maintenance costs, and other related items; for details, see [Boehm, 1981]. Intermediate COCOMO is a complete algorithmic cost estimation model, giving the user virtually every conceivable assistance in project planning.

**FIGURE 9.7**

Intermediate COCOMO effort multiplier ratings for microprocessor communications software.

Source: [Boehm, 1984]. (© 1984 IEEE.)

| Cost Drivers | Situation | Rating | Effort Multiplier |
|---|---|---|---|
| Required software reliability | Serious financial consequences of software fault | High | 1.15 |
| Data base size | 20,000 bytes | Low | 0.94 |
| Product complexity | Communications processing | Very high | 1.30 |
| Execution time constraint | Will use 70% of available time | High | 1.11 |
| Main storage constraint | 45K of 64K store (70%) | High | 1.06 |
| Virtual machine volatility | Based on commercial microprocessor hardware | Nominal | 1.00 |
| Computer turnaround time | 2 hour average turnaround time | Nominal | 1.00 |
| Analyst capabilities | Good senior analysts | High | 0.86 |
| Applications experience | 3 years | Nominal | 1.00 |
| Programmer capability | Good senior programmers | High | 0.86 |
| Virtual machine experience | 6 months | Low | 1.10 |
| Programming language experience | 12 months | Nominal | 1.00 |
| Use of modern programming practices | Most techniques in use over 1 year | High | 0.91 |
| Use of software tools | At basic minicomputer tool level | Low | 1.10 |
| Required development schedule | 9 months | Nominal | 1.00 |

Multiply = 1.35

Intermediate COCOMO has been validated with respect to a broad sample of 63 projects covering a wide variety of application areas. The results of applying intermediate COCOMO to this sample are that the actual values come within 20 percent of the predicted values about 68 percent of the time. Attempts to improve on this accuracy make little sense because in most organizations, the input data for intermediate COCOMO generally are accurate to within only about 20 percent. Nevertheless, the accuracy obtained by experienced estimators placed intermediate COCOMO at the cutting edge of cost estimation research during the 1980s; no other technique was consistently as accurate.

The major problem with intermediate COCOMO is that its most important input is the number of lines of code in the target product. If this estimate is incorrect, then every single prediction of the model may be incorrect. Because of the possibility that the predictions of intermediate COCOMO or any other estimation technique may be inaccurate, management must monitor all predictions throughout software development.

### 9.2.4  COCOMO II

COCOMO was put forward in 1981. At that time, the only life-cycle model in use was the waterfall model. Most software was run on mainframes. Technologies such as client–server and object orientation essentially were unknown. Accordingly, COCOMO did not incorporate any of these factors. However, as newer technologies began to become accepted software engineering practice, COCOMO started to become less accurate.

**COCOMO II** [Boehm et al., 2000] is a major revision of the 1981 COCOMO. COCOMO II can handle a wide variety of modern software engineering techniques, including object orientation, the various life-cycle models described in Chapter 2, rapid prototyping (Section 10.13), fourth-generation languages (Section 14.2), reuse (Section 8.1), and COTS software (Section 1.11). COCOMO II is both flexible and sophisticated. Unfortunately, to achieve this goal, COCOMO II is considerably more complex than the original COCOMO. Accordingly, the reader who wishes to utilize COCOMO II should study [Boehm et al., 2000] in detail; only an overview of the major differences between COCOMO II and intermediate COCOMO is given here.

First, intermediate COCOMO consists of one overall model based on lines of code (KDSI). On the other hand, COCOMO II consists of three different models. The **application composition model**, based on object points (similar to function points), is applied at the earliest workflows, when minimal knowledge is available regarding the product to be built. Then, as more knowledge becomes available, the **early design model** is used; this model is based on function points. Finally, when the developers have maximal information, the **postarchitecture model** is used. This model uses function points or lines of code (KDSI). The output from intermediate COCOMO is a cost and size estimate; the output from each of the three models of COCOMO II is a range of cost and size estimates. Accordingly, if the most likely estimate of the effort is $E$, then the application composition model returns the range (0.50$E$, 2.0$E$), and the postarchitecture model returns the range (0.80$E$, 1.25$E$). This reflects the increasing accuracy of the progression of models of COCOMO II.

A second difference lies in the effort model underlying COCOMO:

$$\text{Effort} = a \times (\text{size})^b \qquad \textbf{(9.8)}$$

where $a$ and $b$ are constants. In intermediate COCOMO, the exponent $b$ takes on three different values, depending on whether the mode of the product to be built is organic

($b = 1.05$), semidetached ($b = 1.12$), or embedded ($b = 1.20$). In COCOMO II, the value of $b$ varies between 1.01 and 1.26, depending on a variety of parameters of the model. These include familiarity with products of that type, process maturity level (Section 3.13), extent of risk resolution (Section 2.7), and degree of team cooperation (Section 4.1).

A third difference is the assumption regarding reuse. Intermediate COCOMO assumes that the savings due to reuse are directly proportional to the amount of reuse. COCOMO II takes into account that small changes to reused software incur disproportionately large costs (because the code has be understood in detail for even a small change and the cost of testing a modified module is relatively large).

Fourth, there now are 17 multiplicative cost drivers, instead of 15 in intermediate COCOMO. Seven of the cost drivers are new, such as required reusability in future products, annual personnel turnover, and whether the product is being developed at multiple sites.

COCOMO II has been calibrated using 83 projects from a variety of different domains. The model still is too new for there to be many results regarding its accuracy and, in particular, the extent to which it is an improvement over its predecessor, the original (1981) COCOMO.

### 9.2.5 Tracking Duration and Cost Estimates

While the product is being developed, the actual development effort constantly must be compared against predictions. For example, suppose that the estimation metric used by the software developers predicted that the **duration** of the analysis workflow would last 3 months and require 7 person-months of effort. However, 4 months have gone by and 10 person-months of effort have been expended, yet the specifications are by no means complete. Deviations of this kind can serve as an early warning that something has gone wrong and corrective action must be taken. The problem could be that the size of the product was seriously underestimated or the development team is not as competent as it was thought to be. Whatever the reason, there are going to be serious duration and cost overruns, and management must take appropriate action to minimize the effects.

Careful tracking of predictions must be done throughout the development process, irrespective of the techniques by which the predictions were made. Deviations could be due to metrics that are poor predictors, inefficient software development, a combination of both, or some other reason. The important thing is to detect deviations early and take immediate corrective action. In addition, it is essential to continually update predictions in the light of additional information as it becomes available.

Now that metrics for estimating duration and cost have been discussed, the components of the software project management plan are described.

# 9.3 Components of a Software Project Management Plan

A software project management plan has three main components: the work to be done, the resources with which to do it, and the money to pay for it all. In this section, these three ingredients of the plan are discussed. The terminology is taken from [IEEE 1058, 1998], which is discussed in greater detail in Section 9.4.

Software development requires *resources*. The major **resources** required are the people who will develop the software, the hardware on which the software is run, and the support software such as operating systems, text editors, and version control software (Section 5.7).

Use of resources such as personnel varies with time. Norden [1958] has shown that for large projects, the **Rayleigh distribution** is a good approximation of the way that resource consumption, $R_c$, varies with time, $t$, that is,

$$R_c = \frac{t}{k^2} e^{-t^2/2k^2} \qquad 0 \le t < \infty \tag{9.9}$$

Parameter $k$ is a constant, the time at which consumption is at its peak, and $\mathrm{e} = 2.71828 \ldots$, the base of Naperian (natural) logarithms. A typical Rayleigh curve is shown in Figure 9.8. Resource consumption starts small, climbs rapidly to a peak, and then decreases at a slower rate. Putnam [1978] investigated the applicability of Norden's results to software development and found that personnel and other resource consumption was modeled with some degree of accuracy by the Rayleigh distribution.

It therefore is insufficient in a software plan merely to state that three senior programmers with at least 5 years of experience are required. What is needed is something like the following:

> Three senior programmers with at least 5 years of experience in real-time programming are needed, two to start 3 months after the project commences, the third to start 6 months after that. Two will be phased out when product testing commences, the third when postdelivery maintenance begins.

The fact that resource needs depend on time applies not only to personnel but also to computer time, support software, computer hardware, office facilities, and even travel. Consequently, the software project management plan is a function of time.

The work to be done falls into two categories. First is work that continues throughout the project and does not relate to any specific workflow of software development. Such

**FIGURE 9.8**
Rayleigh curve showing how resource consumption varies with time.

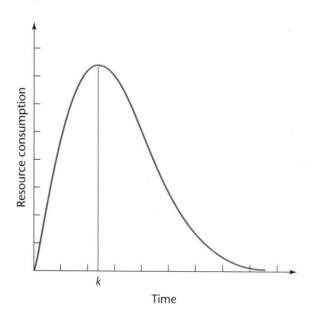

work is termed a **project function**. Examples are project management and quality control. Second is work that relates to a specific workflow in the development of the product; such work is termed an *activity* or a *task*. An **activity** is a major unit of work that has precise beginning and ending dates; consumes resources, such as computer time or person-days; and results in **work products**, such as a budget, design documents, schedules, source code, or a user's manual. An activity, in turn, comprises a set of tasks, a **task** being the smallest unit of work subject to management accountability. There are thus three kinds of work in a software project management plan: project functions carried on throughout the project, activities (major units of work), and tasks (minor units of work).

A critical aspect of the plan concerns completion of work products. The date on which a work product is deemed completed is termed a **milestone**. To determine whether a work product indeed has reached a milestone, it must first pass a series of **reviews** performed by fellow team members, management, or the client. A typical milestone is the date on which the design is completed and passes review. Once a work product has been reviewed and agreed on, it becomes a **baseline** and can be changed only through formal procedures, as described in Section 5.8.2.

In reality, there is more to a work product than merely the product itself. A **work package** defines not just the work product but also the staffing requirements, duration, resources, name of the responsible individual, and acceptance criteria for the work product. **Money** of course is a vital component of the plan. A detailed budget must be worked out and the money allocated, as a function of time, to the project functions and activities.

The issue of how to draw up a plan for software production is addressed next.

# 9.4 Software Project Management Plan Framework

There are many ways of drawing up a project management plan. One of the best is IEEE Standard 1058 [1998]. The components of the plan are shown in Figure 9.9.

- The standard was drawn up by representatives of numerous major organizations involved in software development. Input came from both industry and universities, and the members of the working group and reviewing teams had many years of experience in drawing up project management plans. The standard incorporates this experience.

- The IEEE project management plan is designed for use with all types of software products. It does not impose a specific life-cycle model or prescribe a specific methodology. The plan essentially is a framework, the contents of which are tailored by each organization for a particular domain, development team, or technique.

- The IEEE project management plan framework supports process improvement. For example, many of the sections of the framework reflect CMM key process areas (Section 3.13) such as configuration management and metrics.

- The IEEE project management plan framework is ideal for the Unified Process. For instance, one section of the plan is devoted to requirements control and another to risk management, both central aspects of the Unified Process.

On the other hand, although the claim is made in IEEE Standard 1058 [1998] that the IEEE project management plan is applicable to software projects of all sizes, some of the sections are not relevant to small-scale software. For example, Section 7.7 of the plan

**FIGURE 9.9**
The IEEE
project
management
plan framework.

1 Overview
  1.1 Project summary
    1.1.1 Purpose, scope, and objectives
    1.1.2 Assumptions and constraints
    1.1.3 Project deliverables
    1.1.4 Schedule and budget summary
  1.2 Evolution of the project management plan
2 Reference materials
3 Definitions and acronyms
4 Project organization
  4.1 External interfaces
  4.2 Internal structure
  4.3 Roles and responsibilities
5 Managerial process plans
  5.1 Start-up plan
    5.1.1 Estimation plan
    5.1.2 Staffing plan
    5.1.3 Resource acquisition plan
    5.1.4 Project staff training plan
  5.2 Work plan
    5.2.1 Work activities
    5.2.2 Schedule allocation
    5.2.3 Resource allocation
    5.2.4 Budget allocation
  5.3 Control plan
    5.3.1 Requirements control plan
    5.3.2 Schedule control plan
    5.3.3 Budget control plan
    5.3.4 Quality control plan
    5.3.5 Reporting plan
    5.3.6 Metrics collection plan
  5.4 Risk management plan
  5.5 Project close-out plan
6 Technical process plans
  6.1 Process model
  6.2 Methods, tools, and techniques
  6.3 Infrastructure plan
  6.4 Product acceptance plan
7 Supporting process plans
  7.1 Configuration management plan
  7.2 Testing plan
  7.3 Documentation plan
  7.4 Quality assurance plan
  7.5 Reviews and audits plan
  7.6 Problem resolution plan
  7.7 Subcontractor management plan
  7.8 Process improvement plan
8 Additional plans

framework is headed "Subcontractor Management Plan," but it is all but unheard of for subcontractors to be used in small-scale projects.

Accordingly, we now present the plan framework in two different ways. First, the full framework is described in Section 9.5. Second, a slightly abbreviated version of the framework is used in Appendix F for a management plan for a small-scale project, the MSG Foundation case study.

# 9.5    IEEE Software Project Management Plan

The **IEEE software project management plan** (SPMP) framework itself now is described in detail. The numbers and headings in the text correspond to the entries in Figure 9.9. The various terms used have been defined in Section 9.3.

**1 Overview.**

**1.1 Project summary.**

**1.1.1 Purpose, scope, and objectives.** A brief description is given of the purpose and scope of the software product to be delivered, as well as project objectives. Business needs are included in this subsection.

**1.1.2 Assumptions and constraints.** Any assumptions underlying the project are stated here, together with constraints, such as the delivery date, budget, resources, and artifacts to be reused.

**1.1.3 Project deliverables.** All the items to be delivered to the client are listed here, together with the delivery dates.

**1.1.4 Schedule and budget summary.** The overall schedule is presented here, together with the overall budget.

**1.2 Evolution of the project management plan.** No plan can be cast in concrete. The project management plan, like any other plan, requires continual updating in the light of experience and change within both the client organization and the software development organization. In this section, the formal procedures and mechanisms for changing the plan are described, including the mechanism for placing the project management plan itself under configuration control.

**2 Reference materials.** All documents referenced in the project management plan are listed here.

**3 Definitions and acronyms.** This information ensures that the project management plan is understood the same way by everyone.

**4 Project organization.**

**4.1 External interfaces.** No project is constructed in a vacuum. The project members have to interact with the client organization and other members of their own organization. In addition, subcontractors may be involved in a large project. Administrative and managerial boundaries between the project and these other entities must be laid down.

**4.2 Internal structure.** In this section, the structure of the development organization itself is described. For example, many software development organizations are divided into two types of groups: development groups that work on a single project and support groups that provide support functions, such as configuration management and quality assurance, on an organization-wide basis. Administrative and managerial boundaries between the project group and the support groups also must be defined clearly.

**4.3 Roles and responsibilities.** For each project function, such as quality assurance, and for each activity, such as product testing, the individual responsible must be identified.

## 5 Managerial process plans.

### 5.1 Start-up plan.

**5.1.1 Estimation plan.** The techniques used to estimate project duration and cost are listed here, as well as the way these estimates are tracked and, if necessary, modified while the project is in progress.

**5.1.2 Staffing plan.** The numbers and types of personnel required are listed, together with the durations for which they are needed.

**5.1.3 Resource acquisition plan.** The way of acquiring the necessary resources, including hardware, software, service contracts, and administrative services, is given here.

**5.1.4 Project staff training plan.** All training needed for successful completion of the project is listed in this subsection.

### 5.2 Work plan.

**5.2.1 Work activities.** In this subsection, the work activities are specified, down to the task level if appropriate.

**5.2.2 Schedule allocation.** In general, the work packages are interdependent and further dependent on external events. For example, the implementation workflow follows the design workflow and precedes product testing. In this subsection, the relevant dependencies are specified.

**5.2.3 Resource allocation.** The various resources previously listed are allocated to the appropriate project functions, activities, and tasks.

**5.2.4 Budget allocation.** In this subsection, the overall budget is broken down at the project function, activity, and task levels.

### 5.3 Control plan.

**5.3.1 Requirements control plan.** As described in Part 2 of this book, while a software product is being developed, the requirements frequently change. The mechanisms used to monitor and control the changes to the requirements are given in this section.

**5.3.2 Schedule control plan.** In this subsection, mechanisms for measuring progress are listed, together with a description of the actions to be taken if actual progress lags behind planned progress.

**5.3.3 Budget control plan.** It is important that spending should not exceed the budgeted amount. Control mechanisms for monitoring when actual cost exceeds budgeted cost, as well as the actions to be taken should this happen, are described in this subsection.

**5.3.4 Quality control plan.** The ways in which quality is measured and controlled are described in this subsection.

**5.3.5 Reporting plan.** To monitor the requirements, schedule, budget, and quality, reporting mechanisms need to be in place. These mechanisms are described in this subsection.

**5.3.6 Metrics collection plan.** As explained in Section 5.3, it is not possible to manage the development process without measuring relevant metrics. The metrics to be collected are listed in this subsection.

**5.4 Risk management plan.** Risks have to be identified, prioritized, mitigated, and tracked. All aspects of risk management are described in this section.

**5.5 Project close-out plan.** The actions to be taken once the project is completed, including reassignment of staff and archiving of artifacts, are presented here.

**6 Technical process plans.**

**6.1 Process model.** In this section, a detailed description is given of the life-cycle model to be used.

**6.2 Methods, tools, and techniques.** The development methodologies and programming languages to be used are described here.

**6.3 Infrastructure plan.** Technical aspects of hardware and software are described in detail in this section. Items that should be covered include the computing systems (hardware, operating systems, network, and software) to be used for developing the software product, as well as the target computing systems on which the software product will be run and CASE tools to be employed.

**6.4 Product acceptance plan.** To ensure that the completed software product passes its acceptance test, acceptance criteria must be drawn up, the client must agree to the criteria in writing, and the developers must then ensure that these criteria are indeed met. The way that these three stages of the acceptance process will be carried out is described in this section.

**7 Supporting process plans.**

**7.1 Configuration management plan.** In this section, a detailed description is given of the means by which all artifacts are put under configuration management.

**7.2 Testing plan.** Testing, like all other aspects of software development, needs careful planning.

**7.3 Documentation plan.** A description of documentation of all kinds, whether or not to be delivered to the client at the end of the project, is included in this section.

**7.4 Quality assurance plan.** All aspects of quality assurance, including testing, standards, and reviews, are encompassed by this section.

**7.5 Reviews and audits plan.** Details as to how reviews are conducted are presented in this section.

**7.6 Problem resolution plan.** In the course of developing a software product, problems are all but certain to arise. For example, a design review may bring to light a critical fault in the analysis workflow that requires major changes to almost all the artifacts already completed. In this section, the way such problems are handled is described.

**7.7 Subcontractor management plan.** This section is applicable when subcontractors are to supply certain work products. The approach to selecting and managing subcontractors then appears here.

**7.8 Process improvement plan.** Process improvement strategies are included in this section.

**8 Additional plans.** For certain projects, additional components may need to appear in the plan. In terms of the IEEE framework, they appear at the end of the plan. Additional components may include security plans, safety plans, data conversion plans, installation plans, and the software project postdelivery maintenance plan.

# 9.6   Planning Testing

One component of the SPMP frequently overlooked is **test planning**. Like every other activity of software development, testing must be planned. The SPMP must include resources for testing, and the detailed schedule must explicitly indicate the testing to be done during each workflow.

Without a test plan, a project can go awry in a number of ways. For example, during product testing (Section 3.7.4), the SQA group must check that every aspect of the specification document, as signed off on by the client, has been implemented in the completed product. A good way of assisting the SQA group in this task is to require that the development be traceable (Section 3.7). That is, it must be possible to connect each statement in the specification document to a part of the design, and each part of the design must be reflected explicitly in the code. One technique for achieving this is to number each statement in the specification document and ensure that these numbers are reflected in both the design and the resulting code. However, if the test plan does not specify that this is to be done, it is highly unlikely that the analysis, design, and code artifacts will be labeled appropriately. Consequently, when the product testing finally is performed, it will be extremely difficult for the SQA group to determine that the product is a complete implementation of the specifications. In fact, traceability should start with the requirements; each statement in the requirements artifacts (or each portion of the rapid prototype) must be connected to part of the analysis artifacts.

One powerful aspect of inspections is the detailed list of faults detected during an inspection. Suppose that a team is inspecting the specifications of a product. As explained in Section 6.2.3, the list of faults is used in two ways. First, the fault statistics from this inspection must be compared with the accumulated averages of fault statistics from previous specification inspections. Deviations from previous norms indicate problems within the project. Second, the fault statistics from the current specification inspection must be carried forward to the design and code inspections of the product. After all, if there are a large number of faults of a particular type, it is possible that not all of them were detected during the inspection of the specifications, and the design and code inspections provide an additional opportunity for locating any remaining faults of this type. However, unless the test plan states that details of all faults have to be carefully recorded, it is unlikely that this task will be done.

An important way of testing code modules is so-called black-box testing (Section 14.11) in which the code is executed with test cases based on the specifications. Members of the SQA group read through the specifications and draw up test cases to check whether the code obeys the specification document. The best time to draw up black-box test cases is at the end of the analysis workflow, when the details of the specification document still are fresh in the minds of the members of the SQA group that inspected it. However, unless the test plan explicitly states that the black-box test cases are to be selected at this time, in all probability only a few black-box test cases will hurriedly be thrown together later. That is, a limited number of test cases will be rapidly assembled only when pressure starts mounting from the programming team for the SQA group to approve its modules so that they can be integrated into the product as a whole. As a result, the quality of the product as a whole suffers.

Therefore, every test plan must specify what testing is to be performed, when it is to be performed, and how it is to be performed. Such a test plan is an essential part of

Section 7.2 of the SPMP. Without it, the quality of the overall product undoubtedly will suffer.

## 9.7   Planning Object-Oriented Projects

Suppose the classical paradigm is used. From a conceptual viewpoint, the resulting product generally is one large unit, even though it is composed of separate modules. In contrast, use of the object-oriented paradigm results in a product consisting of a number of relatively independent smaller components, namely, the classes. This makes planning considerably easier, in that cost and duration estimates can be computed more easily and more accurately for smaller units. Of course, the estimates must take into account that a product is more than just the sum of its parts. The separate components are not totally independent; they can invoke one another, and these effects must not be overlooked.

Are the techniques for estimating cost and duration described in this chapter applicable to the object-oriented paradigm? COCOMO II (Section 9.2.4) was designed to handle modern software technology, including object orientation, but what about earlier metrics such as function points (Section 9.2.1) and intermediate COCOMO (Section 9.2.3)? In the case of intermediate COCOMO, minor changes to some of the cost multipliers are required [Pittman, 1993]. Other than that, the estimation tools of the classical paradigm appear to work reasonably well on object-oriented projects—provided that there is no reuse. Reuse enters the object-oriented paradigm in two ways: reuse of existing components during development and the deliberate production (during the current project) of components to be reused in future products. Both forms of reuse affect the estimating process. Reuse during development clearly reduces the cost and duration. Formulas have been published showing the savings as a function of this reuse [Schach, 1994], but these results relate to the classical paradigm. At present, no information is available as to how the cost and duration change when reuse is utilized in the development of an object-oriented product.

We turn now to the goal of reusing parts of the current project. It can take about three times as long to design, implement, test, and document a reusable component as a similar nonreusable component [Pittman, 1993]. Cost and duration estimates must be modified to incorporate this additional labor, and the SPMP as a whole must be adjusted to incorporate the effect of the reuse endeavor. Therefore, the two reuse activities work in opposite directions. Reuse of existing components reduces the overall effort in developing an object-oriented product, whereas designing components for reuse in future products increases the effort. It is expected that, in the long term, the savings due to reuse of classes will outweigh the costs of the original developments, and already some evidence supports this [Lim, 1994].

## 9.8   Training Requirements

When the subject of **training** is raised in discussions with the client, a common response is, "We don't need to worry about training until the product is finished, and then we can train the users." This is a somewhat unfortunate remark, implying as it does that only users require training. In fact, training also may be needed by members of the development team, starting with training in software planning and estimating. When new software development techniques, such as new design techniques or testing procedures, are used, training must be provided to every member of the team using the new technique.

Introduction of the object-oriented paradigm has major training consequences. The introduction of hardware or software tools such as workstations or an integrated environment (see Section 14.23.2) also requires training. Programmers may need training in the operating system of the machine to be used for product development as well as in the implementation language. Documentation preparation training frequently is overlooked, as evidenced by the poor quality of so much documentation. Computer operators certainly require some sort of training to be able to run the new product; they also may require additional training if new hardware is utilized.

The required training can be obtained in a number of ways. The easiest and least disruptive is in-house training, by either fellow employees or consultants. Many companies offer a variety of training courses, and colleges often offer training courses in the evenings. World Wide Web–based courses are another alternative.

Once the training needs have been determined and the training plan drawn up, the plan must be incorporated into the SPMP.

# 9.9 Documentation Standards

The development of a software product is accompanied by a wide variety of **documentation**. Jones found that 28 pages of documentation were generated per 1000 instructions (KDSI) for an IBM internal commercial product around 50 KDSI in size, and about 66 pages per KDSI for a commercial software product of the same size. Operating system IMS/360 Version 2.3 was about 166 KDSI in size, and 157 pages of documentation per KDSI were produced. The documentation was of various types, including planning, control, financial, and technical [Jones, 1986a]. In addition to these types of documentation, the source code itself is a form of documentation; comments within the code constitute further documentation.

A considerable portion of the software development effort is absorbed by documentation. A survey of 63 development projects and 25 postdelivery maintenance projects showed that, for every 100 hours spent on activities related to code, 150 hours were spent on activities related to documentation [Boehm, 1981]. For large TRW products, the proportion of time devoted to documentation-related activities rose to 200 hours per 100 code-related hours [Boehm et al., 1984].

Standards are needed for every type of documentation. For instance, uniformity in design documentation reduces misunderstandings between team members and aids the SQA group. Although new employees have to be trained in the documentation standards, no further training is needed when existing employees move from project to project within the organization. From the viewpoint of postdelivery maintenance, uniform coding standards assist maintenance programmers in understanding source code. Standardization is even more important for user manuals, because these have to be read by a wide of variety of individuals, few of whom are computer experts. The IEEE has developed a standard for user manuals (IEEE Standard 1063 for Software User Documentation).

As part of the planning process, standards must be established for all documentation to be produced during software production. These standards are incorporated in the SPMP.

Where an existing standard is to be used, such as the ANSI/IEEE Standard for Software Test Documentation [ANSI/IEEE 829, 1991], the standard is listed in Section 2 of the SPMP (reference materials). If a standard is specially written for the development effort, then it appears in Section 6.2 (methods, tools, and techniques).

Documentation is an essential aspect of the software production effort. In a very real sense, the product *is* the documentation, because without documentation the product cannot be maintained. Planning the documentation effort in every detail, and then ensuring that the plan is adhered to, is a critical component of successful software production.

## 9.10 CASE Tools for Planning and Estimating

A number of tools are available that automate intermediate COCOMO and COCOMO II. For speed of computation when the value of a parameter is modified, several implementations of intermediate COCOMO have been written in spreadsheet languages such as Lotus 1-2-3 or Excel. For developing and updating the plan itself, a word processor is essential.

Management information tools also are useful for planning. For example, suppose that a large software organization has 150 programmers. A scheduling tool can help planners keep track of which programmers already are assigned to specific tasks and which are available for the current project.

More general types of management information also are needed. A number of commercially available management tools can be used both to assist with the planning and estimating process and monitor the development process as a whole. These include MacProject and Microsoft Project.

## 9.11 Testing the Software Project Management Plan

As pointed out at the beginning of this chapter, a fault in the software project management plan can have serious financial implications for the developers. It is critical that the development organization neither overestimate nor underestimate the cost of the project or its duration. For this reason, the entire SPMP must be checked by the SQA group before estimates are given to the client. The best way to test the plan is by a plan inspection.

The plan inspection team must review the SPMP in detail, paying particular attention to the cost and duration estimates. To reduce risks even further, irrespective of the metrics used, the duration and cost estimates should be computed independently by a member of the SQA group as soon as the members of the planning team have determined their estimates.

---

**Chapter Review**

The main theme of this chapter is the importance of planning in the software process (Section 9.1). A vital component of any software project management plan is estimating the duration and the cost (Section 9.2). Several metrics are put forward for estimating the size of a product, including function points (Section 9.2.1). Next, various metrics for cost estimation are described, especially intermediate COCOMO (Section 9.2.3) and COCOMO II (Section 9.2.4). As described in Section 9.2.5, it is essential to track all estimates. The three major components of a software project management plan—the work to be done, the resources with which to do it, and the money to pay for it—are explained in Section 9.3. One particular SPMP, the IEEE standard, is outlined in Section 9.4 and described in detail in Section 9.5. Next follow sections on planning testing (Section 9.6), planning object-oriented projects (Section 9.7), and training requirements and documentation standards and their implications for the planning process (Sections 9.8 and 9.9). CASE tools for planning and estimating are described in Section 9.10. The chapter concludes with material on testing the software project management plan (Section 9.11).

---

<table>
<tr>
<td>

**For
Further
Reading**

</td>
<td>

Weinberg's four-volume work [Weinberg, 1992; 1993; 1994; 1997] provides detailed information on many aspects of software management, as do [Bennatan, 2000] and [Reifer, 2000]. Metrics for managing software projects are discussed in [Weller, 1994].

For management of the object-oriented paradigm, [Pittman, 1993] and [Nesi, 1998] should be consulted. For further information on IEEE Standard 1058 for Software Project Management Plans, the standard itself should be read carefully [IEEE 1058, 1998]. The need for careful planning is described in [McConnell, 2001].

Sackman's classic work is described in [Sackman, Erikson, and Grant, 1968]. A more detailed source is [Sackman, 1970].

Useful information on function points can be found in [Low and Jeffrey, 1990]. A careful analysis of function points, as well as suggested improvements, appears in [Symons, 1991]. Criticisms of function points appear in [Kitchenham, 1997].

The reliability of function points is discussed in [Kemerer and Porter, 1992] and [Kemerer, 1993]. Strengths and weaknesses of function points are presented in [Furey and Kitchenham, 1997]. A comprehensive source of information on all aspects of function points is [Boehm, 1997].

The theoretical justification for intermediate COCOMO, together with full details for implementing it, appears in [Boehm, 1981]; a shorter version is found in [Boehm, 1984]. COCOMO II is described in [Boehm et al., 2000]. Ways of enhancing COCOMO predictions are presented in [Smith, Hale, and Parrish, 2001].

Briand and Wüst [2001] describe how to estimate the development effort for object-oriented products. Estimating both the size and defects of object-oriented software products is described in [Cartwright and Shepperd, 2000]. Class points, an extension of function points to classes, are introduced in [Costagliola, Ferrucci, Tortora, and Vitiello, 2005].

Errors in estimating software effort are analyzed in [Jorgensen and Molokken-Ostvold, 2004]. Software productivity data for a variety of business data processing products are presented in [Maxwell and Forselius, 2000]; the unit of productivity utilized is function points per hour. Other measures of productivity are discussed in [Kitchenham and Mendes, 2004]. Size estimation for software written in a fourth-generation language is presented in [Dolado, 2000]. A variety of articles on estimation appear in the November/December 2000 issue of *IEEE Software*.

</td>
</tr>
</table>

**Key Terms**

| | | |
|---|---|---|
| activity *268* | COCOMO *262* | early design model *265* |
| algorithmic cost | COCOMO II *265* | efficiency *257* |
| estimation model *261* | cone of uncertainty *254* | expert judgment by |
| application composition | cost *255* | analogy *260* |
| model *265* | Delphi technique *260* | external cost *255* |
| baseline *268* | documentation *275* | FFP metric *257* |
| bottom-up approach *261* | duration *266* | function point *257* |

| | | |
|---|---|---|
| IEEE software project management plan *270* | price *255* | technical complexity factor *258* |
| internal cost *255* | productivity *257* | test planning *273* |
| lines of code (LOC) *256* | project function *268* | thousand delivered source |
| milestone *268* | Rayleigh distribution *267* | instructions (KDSI) *256* |
| money *268* | resources *266* | training *274* |
| nominal effort *262* | review *268* | unadjusted function points *258* |
| planning *252* | software development | work package *268* |
| postarchitecture model *265* | effort multipliers *262* | work product *268* |
| | task *268* | |

**Problems**

9.1   Why do you think that some cynical software organizations refer to *milestones* as *millstones*? (Hint: Look up the figurative meaning of *millstone* in a dictionary.)

9.2   You are a software engineer at Bronkhorstspruit Software Developers. A year ago, your manager announced that your next product would comprise 9 files, 49 flows, and 92 processes.

   (i)   Using the FFP metric, determine its size.

   (ii)  For Bronkhorstspruit Software Developers, the constant $d$ in equation (9.2) has been determined to be $1003. What cost estimate did the FFP metric predict?

   (iii) The product recently was completed at a cost of $132,800. What does this tell you about the productivity of your development team?

9.3   A target product has 7 simple inputs, 2 average input, and 10 complex inputs. There are 56 average outputs, 8 simple inquiries, 12 average master files, and 17 complex interfaces. Determine the unadjusted function points (*UFP*).

9.4   If the total degree of influence for the product of Problem 9.3 is 49, determine the number of function points.

9.5   Why do you think that, despite its drawbacks, lines of code (LOC or KDSI) is so widely used as a metric of product size?

9.6   You are in charge of developing a 67-KDSI embedded product that is nominal except that the database size is rated very high and the use of software tools is low. Using intermediate COCOMO, what is the estimated effort in person-months?

9.7   You are in charge of developing two 33-KDSI organic-mode products. Both are nominal in every respect except that product P1 has extra-high complexity and product P2 has extra-low complexity. To develop the product, you have two teams at your disposal. Team A has very high analyst capability, applications experience, and programmer capability. Team A also has high virtual machine experience and programming language experience. Team B is rated very low on all five attributes.

   (i)   What is the total effort (in person-months) if team A develops product P1 and team B develops product P2?

   (ii)  What is the total effort (in person-months) if team B develops product P1 and team A develops product P2?

   (iii) Which of the two preceding staffing assignments makes more sense? Is your intuition backed by the predictions of intermediate COCOMO?

9.8   You are in charge of developing a 49-KDSI organic-mode product that is nominal in every respect.

   (i)   Assuming a cost of $9900 per person-month, how much is the project estimated to cost?

   (ii)  Your entire development team resigns at the start of the project. You are fortunate enough to be able to replace the nominal team with a very highly experienced and capable team, but the cost per person-month will rise to $12,900. How much money do you expect to gain (or lose) as a result of the personnel change?

9.9 You are in charge of developing the software for a product that uses a set of newly developed algorithms to compute the most cost-effective routes for a large trucking company. Using intermediate COCOMO, you determine that the cost of the product will be $470,000. However, as a check, you ask a member of your team to estimate the effort using function points. She reports that the function point metric predicts a cost of $985,000, more than twice as large as your COCOMO prediction. What do you do now?

9.10 Show that the Rayleigh distribution (equation (9.9)) attains its maximum value when $t = k$. Find the corresponding resource consumption.

9.11 A product postdelivery maintenance plan is considered an "additional component" of an IEEE software project management plan. Bearing in mind that every nontrivial product is maintained and that the cost of postdelivery maintenance, on average, is about twice or three times the cost of developing the product, how can this be justified?

9.12 Why do software development projects generate so much documentation?

9.13 (Term project) Consider the Osric's Office Appliances and Decor project described in Appendix A. Why is it not possible to estimate the cost and duration purely on the basis of the information in Appendix A?

9.14 (Readings in Software Engineering) Your instructor will distribute copies of [Costagliola, Ferrucci, Tortora, and Vitiello, 2005]. Are you convinced by the empirical validation of class points?

**References**

[Albrecht, 1979] A. J. ALBRECHT, "Measuring Application Development Productivity," *Proceedings of the IBM SHARE/GUIDE Applications Development Symposium,* Monterey, CA, October 1979, pp. 83–92.

[ANSI/IEEE 829, 1991] *Software Test Documentation*, ANSI/IEEE 829-1991, American National Standards Institute, Institute of Electrical and Electronic Engineers, New York, 1991.

[Bennatan, 2000] E. M. BENNATAN, *On Time Within Budget: Software Project Management Practices and Techniques,* 3rd ed., John Wiley and Sons, New York, 2000.

[Boehm, 1981] B. W. BOEHM, *Software Engineering Economics,* Prentice Hall, Englewood Cliffs, NJ, 1981.

[Boehm, 1984] B. W. BOEHM, "Software Engineering Economics," *IEEE Transactions on Software Engineering* **SE-10** (January 1984), pp. 4–21.

[Boehm, 1997] R. BOEHM (EDITOR), "Function Point FAQ," at ourworld.compuserve.com/homepages/softcomp/fpfaq.htm, June 25, 1997.

[Boehm et al., 1984] B. W. BOEHM, M. H. PENEDO, E. D. STUCKLE, R. D. WILLIAMS, AND A. B. PYSTER, "A Software Development Environment for Improving Productivity," *IEEE Computer* **17** (June 1984), pp. 30–44.

[Boehm et al., 2000] B. W. BOEHM, C. ABTS, A. W. BROWN, S. CHULANI, B. K. CLARK, E. HOROWITZ, R. MADACHY, D. REIFER, AND B. STEECE, *Software Cost Estimation with COCOMO II,* Prentice Hall, Upper Saddle River, NJ, 2000.

[Briand and Wüst, 2001] L. C. BRIAND AND J. WÜST, "Modeling Development Effort in Object-Oriented Systems Using Design Properties," *IEEE Transactions on Software Engineering* **27** (November 2001), pp. 963–86.

[Cartwright and Shepperd, 2000] M. CARTWRIGHT AND M. SHEPPERD, "An Empirical Investigation of an Object-Oriented Software System," *IEEE Transactions on Software Engineering* **26** (August 2000), pp. 786–95.

[Costagliola, Ferrucci, Tortora, and Vitiello, 2005] G. COSTAGLIOLA, F. FERRUCCI, G. TORTORA, AND G. VITIELLO, "Class Point: An Approach for the Size Estimation of Object-Oriented Systems," *IEEE Transactions on Software Engineering* **31** (January 2005), pp. 52–74.

[Devenny, 1976] T. DEVENNY, "An Exploratory Study of Software Cost Estimating at the Electronic Systems Division," Thesis No. GSM/SM/765-4, Air Force Institute of Technology, Dayton, OH, 1976.

[Dolado, 2000] J. J. DOLADO, "A Validation of the Component-Based Method for Software Size Estimation," *IEEE Transactions on Software Engineering* **26** (October 2000), pp. 1006–21.

[Furey and Kitchenham, 1997] S. FUREY AND B. KITCHENHAM, "Function Points," *IEEE Software* **14** (March/April 1997), pp. 28–32.

[IEEE 1058, 1998] "IEEE Standard for Software Project Management Plans," IEEE Std. 1058-1998, Institute of Electrical and Electronic Engineers, New York, 1998.

[Jones, 1986a] C. JONES, *Programming Productivity,* McGraw-Hill, New York, 1986.

[Jones, 1987] C. JONES, Letter to the Editor, *IEEE Computer* **20** (December 1987), p. 4.

[Jorgensen and Molokken-Ostvold, 2004] M. JORGENSEN AND K. MOLOKKEN-OSTVOLD, "Reasons for Software Effort Estimation Error: Impact of Respondent Role, Information Collection Approach, and Data Analysis Method," *IEEE Transactions on Software Engineering* **30** (December 2004), pp. 993–1007.

[Kemerer, 1993] C. F. KEMERER, "Reliability of Function Points Measurement: A Field Experiment," *Communications of the ACM* **36** (February 1993), pp. 85–97.

[Kemerer and Porter, 1992] C. F. KEMERER and B. S. PORTER, "Improving the Reliability of Function Point Measurement: An Empirical Study," *IEEE Transactions on Software Engineering* **18** (November 1992), pp. 1011–24.

[Kitchenham, 1997] B. KITCHENHAM, "The Problem with Function Points," *IEEE Software* **14** (March/April 1997), pp. 29, 31.

[Kitchenham and Mendes, 2004] B. KITCHENHAM AND E. MENDES, "Software Productivity Measurement Using Multiple Size Measures," *IEEE Transactions on Software Engineering* **30** (December 2004), pp. 1023–35.

[Lim, 1994] W. C. LIM, "Effects of Reuse on Quality, Productivity, and Economics," *IEEE Software* **11** (September 1994), pp. 23–30.

[Low and Jeffrey, 1990] G. C. LOW AND D. R. JEFFREY, "Function Points in the Estimation and Evaluation of the Software Process," *IEEE Transactions on Software Engineering* **16** (January 1990), pp. 64–71.

[Maxwell and Forselius, 2000] K. D. MAXWELL AND P. FORSELIUS, "Benchmarking Software Development Productivity," *IEEE Software* **17** (January/February 2000), pp. 80–88.

[McConnell, 2001] S. MCCONNELL, "The Nine Deadly Sins of Project Planning," *IEEE Software* **18** (November/December 2001), pp. 5–7.

[Nesi, 1998] P. NESI, "Managing OO Projects Better," *IEEE Software* **15** (July/August 1998), pp. 50–60.

[Norden, 1958] P. V. NORDEN, "Curve Fitting for a Model of Applied Research and Development Scheduling," *IBM Journal of Research and Development* **2** (July 1958), pp. 232–48.

[Pittman, 1993] M. PITTMAN, "Lessons Learned in Managing Object-Oriented Development," *IEEE Software* **10** (January 1993), pp. 43–53.

[Putnam, 1978] L. H. PUTNAM, "A General Empirical Solution to the Macro Software Sizing and Estimating Problem," *IEEE Transactions on Software Engineering* **SE-4** (July 1978), pp. 345–61.

[Reifer, 2000] D. J. REIFER, "Software Management: The Good, the Bad, and the Ugly," *IEEE Software* **17** (March/April 2000), pp. 73–75.

[Sackman, 1970] H. SACKMAN, *Man–Computer Problem Solving: Experimental Evaluation of Time-Sharing and Batch Processing,* Auerbach, Princeton, NJ, 1970.

[Sackman, Erikson, and Grant, 1968] H. SACKMAN, W. J. ERIKSON, AND E. E. GRANT, "Exploratory Experimental Studies Comparing Online and Offline Programming Performance," *Communications of the ACM* **11** (January 1968), pp. 3–11.

[Schach, 1994] S. R. SCHACH, "The Economic Impact of Software Reuse on Maintenance," *Journal of Software Maintenance: Research and Practice* **6** (July/August 1994), pp. 185–96.

[Smith, Hale, and Parrish, 2001] R. K. SMITH, J. E. HALE, AND A. S. PARRISH, "An Empirical Study Using Task Assignment Patterns to Improve the Accuracy of Software Effort Estimation," *IEEE Transactions on Software Engineering* **27** (March 2001), pp. 264–71.

[Symons, 1991] C. R. SYMONS, *Software Sizing and Estimating: Mk II FPA,* John Wiley and Sons, Chichester, UK, 1991.

[van der Poel and Schach, 1983] K. G. VAN DER POEL AND S. R. SCHACH, "A Software Metric for Cost Estimation and Efficiency Measurement in Data Processing System Development," *Journal of Systems and Software* **3** (September 1983), pp. 187–91.

[Weinberg, 1992] G. M. WEINBERG, *Quality Software Management: Systems Thinking,* Vol. 1, Dorset House, New York, 1992.

[Weinberg, 1993] G. M. WEINBERG, *Quality Software Management: First-Order Measurement,* Vol. 2, Dorset House, New York, 1993.

[Weinberg, 1994] G. M. WEINBERG, *Quality Software Management: Congruent Action,* Vol. 3, Dorset House, New York, 1994.

[Weinberg, 1997] G. M. WEINBERG, *Quality Software Management: Anticipating Change,* Vol. 4, Dorset House, New York, 1997.

[Weller, 1994] E. F. WELLER, "Using Metrics to Manage Software Projects," *IEEE Computer* **27** (September 1994), pp. 27–34.

# The Workflows of the Software Life Cycle

In Part 2, the workflows of the software life cycle are described in depth. For each workflow, the activities, CASE tools, metrics, and testing techniques appropriate to that workflow are presented, as well as the challenges of that workflow.

Chapter 10, "Requirements," examines the requirements workflow. The aim of this workflow is to determine the client's real needs. Various requirements analysis techniques are examined.

Once the requirements have been determined, the next step is to draw up the specifications. The classical approach is described in Chapter 11, "Classical Analysis." Three basic approaches to specifications are presented: informal, semiformal, and formal. Instances of each approach are described. Techniques described in depth and illustrated by case studies include structured systems analysis, finite state machines, Petri nets, and Z. A comparison of the various techniques is presented.

All the analysis techniques in Chapter 11 are from the classical paradigm. The object-oriented approach is described in Chapter 12, "Object-Oriented Analysis." This object-oriented technique is presented as an alternative to the classical analysis techniques of the previous chapter.

In Chapter 13, "Design," a variety of design techniques are compared, including classical techniques like data flow analysis and transaction analysis as well as object-oriented design. Particular attention is paid to object-oriented design, including case studies. Again, the emphasis is on comparison and contrast.

Implementation issues are discussed in Chapter 14, "Implementation." Areas covered include implementation, integration, good programming practice, and programming standards.

Chapter 15 is entitled "Postdelivery maintenance." Topics covered in this chapter include the importance and challenges of postdelivery maintenance. The management of postdelivery maintenance is considered in some detail.

In Chapter 16, "More on UML," additional information is provided about the Unified Modeling Language.

By the end of Part 2, you should have a clear understanding of all the workflows of the software process, the challenges associated with each workflow, and how to meet those challenges.

# Chapter 10

# Requirements

**Learning Objectives**

After studying this chapter, you should be able to

- Perform the requirements workflow.
- Draw up the initial business model.
- Draw up the requirements.
- Construct a rapid prototype.

The chances of a product being developed on time and within budget are somewhat slim unless the members of the software development team agree on what the software product is to do. The first step in achieving this unanimity is to analyze the client's current situation as precisely as possible. For example, it is inadequate to say, "The client needs a computer-aided design system because they claim their manual design system is lousy." Unless the development team knows exactly what is wrong with the current manual system, there is a high probability that aspects of the new computerized system will be equally "lousy." Similarly, if a personal computer manufacturer is contemplating development of a new operating system, the first step is to evaluate the firm's current operating system and analyze carefully exactly why it is unsatisfactory. To take an extreme example, it is vital to know whether the problem exists only in the mind of the sales manager who blames the operating system for poor sales, or whether users of the operating system are thoroughly disenchanted with its functionality and reliability. Only after a clear picture of the present situation has been gained can the team attempt to answer the critical question, What must the new product be able to do? The process of answering this question is the primary objective of the requirements workflow.

## 10.1 Determining What the Client Needs

A commonly held misconception is that, during the requirements workflow, the developers must determine what software the client *wants*. On the contrary, the real objective of the requirements workflow is to determine what software the client *needs*. One problem is that

S. I. Hayakawa (1906–1992), U.S. Senator from California, once told a group of reporters, "I know you believe you understood what you think I said, but I am not sure you realize that what you heard is not what I meant." This excuse applies equally well to the issue of requirements analysis. The software engineers hear their client's requests, but what they hear is not what the client should be saying.

That quotation has been wrongly attributed to former U.S. presidential candidate George Romney (1907–1995) who once announced at a press conference, "I didn't say that I didn't say it. I said that I didn't say I said it. I want to make that very clear." Romney's "clarification" highlights another challenge of requirements analysis—it is easy to misunderstand what the client says.

many clients do not know what they need. Furthermore, even a client who has a good idea of what is needed may have difficulty in accurately conveying these ideas to the developers, because most clients are less computer literate than the members of the development team. (For more insight into this issue, see Just in Case You Wanted to Know Box 10.1.)

Another problem is that the client may not appreciate what is going on in his or her own organization. For example, it is no use for a client to ask for a faster software product when the real reason why the current software product has such a long response time is that the database is badly designed. What needs to be done is to reorganize and improve the way that data are stored in the current software product. A new software product will be just as slow. Or, if the client operates an unprofitable chain of retail stores, the client may ask for a financial management information system that reflects such items as sales, salaries, accounts payable, and accounts receivable. Such an information system will be of little use if the real reason for the losses is shrinkage (shoplifting and theft by employees). If that is the case, then a stock control system rather than a financial management information system is required.

At first sight, determining what the client needs is straightforward—the members of the development team simply ask him or her. However, there are two reasons why this direct approach usually does not work very well.

First, as has just been stated, the client may not appreciate what is going on in his or her own organization. But the major reason why a client so often asks for the wrong software product is that software is complex. It is difficult enough for a software engineer to visualize a software product and its functionality—the problem is far worse for the client, who usually is not an expert in software engineering.

Without the assistance of a skilled software development team, the client may be a poor source of information regarding what needs to be developed. On the other hand, unless there is face-to-face communication with the client, there is no way of finding out what really is needed.

The classical attempt at solving this challenge is described in Section 10.12. The object-oriented approach is to obtain initial information from the client and future users of the target product and to use this initial information as an input to the requirements workflow of the Unified Process [Jacobson, Booch, and Rumbaugh, 1999]. This is described in Section 10.2.

## 10.2  Overview of the Requirements Workflow

The first step in the **requirements workflow** is to gain an understanding of the **application domain** (or **domain**, for short), that is, the specific environment in which the target product is to operate. The domain could be banking, space exploration, automobile manufacturing, or telemetry. Once the members of the development team understand the domain to a sufficient depth, they can build a business model, that is, use UML diagrams to describe the client's business processes. The business model is used to determine what the client's initial requirements are. Then iteration is applied.

In other words, the starting point is an initial understanding of the domain. This information is used to build the initial business model. The initial business model is utilized to draw up an initial set of the client's requirements. Then, in the light of what has been learned about the client's requirements, a deeper understanding of the domain is gained; and this knowledge is utilized in turn to refine the business model and hence the client's requirements. This iteration continues until the team is satisfied with the set of requirements. At this point, the iteration stops.

The process of discovering the client's requirements is termed **requirements elicitation** (or **requirements capture**). Once the initial set of requirements has been drawn up, the process of refining and extending them is termed **requirements analysis**.

We now examine each of these steps in detail.

## 10.3  Understanding the Domain

To elicit the client's needs, the members of the requirements team must be familiar with the application domain, that is, the general area in which the target product is to be used. For example, it is not easy to ask meaningful questions of a banker or a neurosurgeon without first acquiring some familiarity with banking or neurosurgery. Therefore, an initial task of each member of the requirements analysis team is to acquire familiarity with the application domain, unless he or she already has experience in that general area. It is particularly important to use correct terminology when communicating with the client and potential users of the target software. After all, it is hard to be taken seriously by a person working in a specific domain unless the interviewer uses the nomenclature appropriate for that domain. More important, use of an inappropriate word may lead to a misunderstanding, eventually resulting in a faulty product being delivered. The same problem can arise if the members of the requirements team do not understand the subtleties of the terminology of the domain. For example, to a layperson words like *brace, beam, girder,* and *strut* may appear to be synonyms, but to a civil engineer they are distinct terms. If a developer does not appreciate that a civil engineer is using these four terms in a precise way and if the civil engineer assumes that the developer is familiar with the distinctions among the terms, the developer may treat the four terms as equivalent; the resulting computer-aided bridge design software may contain faults that result in a bridge collapsing. Computer professionals hope that the output of every program will be scrutinized carefully by a human before decisions are made based on that program, but the growing popular faith in computers means that it is distinctly unwise to rely on the likelihood of such a check being made. So, it is by no means far-fetched that a misunderstanding in terminology could lead to the software developers being sued for negligence.

One way to address the problem with terminology is to construct a **glossary**, a list of technical words used in the domain, together with their meanings. The initial entries are inserted into the glossary while the team members are busy learning as much as they can about the application domain. Then, the glossary is updated whenever the members of the requirements team encounter new terminology. Every so often, the glossary can be printed out and distributed to team members or downloaded to a PDA (such as a Palm Pilot). Not only does such a glossary reduce confusion between client and developers, it also is useful in lessening misunderstandings between the members of the development team.

Once the requirements team has acquired familiarity with the domain, the next step is to build the business model.

# 10.4  The Business Model

A **business model** is a description of the business processes of an organization. For example, some of the business processes of a bank include accepting deposits from clients, loaning money to clients, and making investments.

The reason for building a business model first is that the business model provides an understanding of the client's business as a whole. With this knowledge, the developers can advise the client as to which portions of the client's business to computerize. Alternatively, if the task is to extend an existing software product, the developers have to understand the existing business as a whole to determine how to incorporate the extension and to learn what parts, if any, of the existing product need to be modified to add the new piece.

To build a business model, a developer needs to obtain a detailed understanding of the various business processes. These processes are now *refined,* that is, analyzed in greater detail. A number of different techniques can be used to obtain the information needed to build the business model, primarily interviewing.

## 10.4.1  Interviewing

The members of the requirements team meet with members of the client organization until they are convinced that they have elicited all relevant information from the client and future users of the target software product.

There are two basic types of question. A closed-ended question requires a specific answer. For example, the client might be asked how many salespeople the company employs or how fast a response time is required. Open-ended questions are asked to encourage the person being interviewed to speak out. For instance, asking the client, "Why is your current software product unsatisfactory?" may explain many aspects of the client's approach to business. Some of these facts might not come to light if the question were closed ended.

Similarly, there are two basic types of interview, structured and unstructured. In a **structured interview**, specific preplanned questions are asked, frequently closed ended. In an **unstructured interview**, the interviewer may start with one or two prepared closed-ended questions, but subsequent questions are posed in response to the answers he or she receives from the person being interviewed. Many of these subsequent questions are likely to be open ended in nature to provide the interviewer with wide-ranging information.

At the same time, it is not a good idea if the interview is too unstructured. Saying to the client, "Tell me about your business" is unlikely to yield much relevant knowledge. In other words, questions should be posed in such a way as to encourage the person being interviewed to give wide-ranging answers but always within the context of the specific information needed by the interviewer.

Conducting a good interview is not always easy. First, the interviewer must be fully familiar with the application domain. Second, there is no point in interviewing a member of the client organization if the interviewer has already made up his or her mind regarding the client's needs. No matter what the interviewer has previously been told or what he or she has learned by other means, the interviewer must approach every interview with the intention of listening carefully to what the person being interviewed has to say, while firmly suppressing any preconceived notions regarding the client company or the needs of the clients and the potential users of the target product to be developed.

After the interview is concluded, the interviewer must prepare a written report outlining the results of the interview. It is strongly advisable to give a copy of the report to the person who was interviewed; he or she may want to clarify certain statements or add overlooked items.

## 10.4.2 Other Techniques

Interviewing is the primary technique for obtaining information for the business model. This section describes some other techniques that may be used in conjunction with interviewing.

One way of gaining knowledge about the activities of the client organization is to send a **questionnaire** to the relevant members of the client organization. This technique is useful when the opinions of, say, hundreds of individuals need to be determined. Furthermore, a carefully thought-out written answer from an employee of the client organization may be more accurate than an immediate verbal response to a question posed by an interviewer. However, an unstructured interview conducted by a methodical interviewer who listens carefully and poses questions that elicit amplifications of initial responses usually yields far better information than a thoughtfully worded questionnaire. Because questionnaires are preplanned, there is no way that a question can be posed in response to an answer.

A different way of eliciting requirements is to examine the various **forms** used by the business. For example, a form in a printing works might reflect press number, paper roll size, humidity, ink temperature, paper tension, and so on. The various fields in this form shed light on the flow of print jobs and the relative importance of the steps in the printing process. Other documents, such as operating procedures and job descriptions, also can be powerful tools for finding out exactly what is done and how. If a software product is being used, the user manuals should also be carefully studied. A comprehensive set of different types of data regarding how the client currently does business can be extraordinarily helpful in determining the client's needs. Therefore, a good software professional carefully studies client documentation, treating it as a valuable potential source of information that can lead to an accurate assessment of the client's needs.

Another way of obtaining such information is by **direct observation** of the users, that is, by members of the requirements team observing and writing down the actions of the employees while they perform their duties. A modern version of this technique is to set up **videotape cameras** within the workplace to record (with the prior written permission of those being observed) exactly what is being done. One difficulty of this technique is that it can take a long time to analyze the tapes. In general, one or more members of the requirements team has to spend an hour playing back the tape for every hour that the cameras record. This time is in addition to what is needed to assess what was observed. More seriously, this technique has been known to backfire badly because employees may view the cameras as an unwarranted invasion of privacy. It is important that the requirements team have the full cooperation of all employees; it can be extremely difficult to obtain the necessary information if people feel threatened or harassed. The possible risks should be considered carefully before introducing cameras or, for that matter, taking any other action that has the potential to annoy or even anger employees.

**FIGURE 10.1**

The `Withdraw Money` use case of the banking software product.

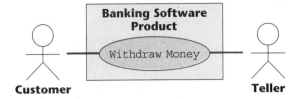

### 10.4.3 Use Cases

As stated in Section 3.2, a **model** is a set of UML diagrams that represent one or more aspects of the software product to be developed (recall that the *ML* in UML stands for "modeling language"). A primary UML diagram used in business modeling is the use case.

A **use case** models an interaction between the software product itself and the users of that software product (**actors**). For example, Figure 10.1 depicts a use case from a banking software product. There are two actors, represented by the UML stick figures, the **Customer** and the **Teller**. The label inside the oval describes the business activity represented by the use case, in this instance `Withdraw Money`.

Another way of looking at a use case is that it shows the interaction between the software product and the environment in which the software product operates. That is, an actor is a member of the world outside the software product, whereas the rectangle in the use case represents the software product itself.

It is usually easy to identify an actor.

- An actor is frequently a user of the software product. In the case of a banking software product, the users of that software product are the customers of the bank and the staff of the bank, including tellers and managers.

- In general, an actor plays a role with regard to the software product. This role may be as a user of the software product. However, an initiator of a use case or someone who plays a critical part in a use case is also playing a role and is therefore regarded as an actor, irrespective of whether that person is also a user of the software product. An example of this is given in Section 10.7.

A user of the system can play more than one role. For example, a customer of the bank can be a **Borrower** (when he or she takes out a loan) or a **Lender** (when he or she deposits money in the bank—a bank makes much of its profits by investing the money deposited by customers). Conversely, one actor can participate in multiple use cases. For example, a **Borrower** may be an actor in the `Borrow Money` use case, the `Pay Interest on Loan` use case, and the `Repay Loan Principal` use case. Also, the actor **Borrower** may stand for many thousands of bank customers.

An actor need not be a human. Recall that an actor is a user of a software product, and in many cases another software product can be a user. For example, an e-commerce information system that allows purchasers to pay with credit cards has to interact with the credit card company information system. That is, the credit card company information system is an actor from the viewpoint of the e-commerce company information system. Similarly, the e-commerce information system is an actor from the viewpoint of the credit card company information system.

**FIGURE 10.2**
Generalization
of medical staff.

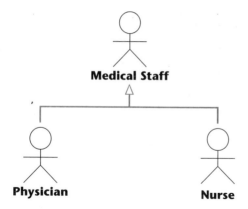

As previously stated, identification of actors is easy. Generally, the only difficulty that arises in this part of the paradigm is that an overzealous software professional sometimes identifies overlapping actors. For example, in a hospital software product, having a use case with actor **Nurse** and a different use case with actor **Medical Staff** is not a good idea, because all nurses are medical staff, but some medical staff (such as physicians) are not nurses. It would be better to have actors **Physician** and **Nurse**. Alternatively, actor **Medical Staff** can be defined with two specializations, **Physician** and **Nurse**. This is depicted in Figure 10.2. In Section 7.7, it was pointed out that inheritance is a special case of generalization. Generalization was applied to classes in Section 7.7. Figure 10.2 shows how generalization can be applied to actors, too.

## 10.5   Initial Requirements

To determine the client's requirements, initial requirements are drawn up based on the initial business model. Then, as the understanding of the domain and the business model is refined on the basis of further discussions with the client, the requirements are refined.

The requirements are dynamic. That is, there are frequent changes not just to the requirements themselves but also to the attitudes of the development team, client, and future users toward each requirement. For example, a particular requirement may first appear to the development team to be optional. After further analysis, that requirement may now seem to be critically important. However, after discussion with the client, the requirement is rejected. A good way to handle these frequent changes is to maintain a list of likely requirements, together with use cases of the requirements that have been agreed to by the members of the development team and approved by the client.

It is important to bear in mind that the object-oriented paradigm is iterative and the glossary, the business model, or the requirements therefore may have to be modified at any time. In particular, additions to the requirements list, modifications to items already on the list, and removal of items from the list can be triggered by a wide variety of events, ranging from a casual remark made by a user to a suggestion from the client at a formal meeting of the systems analysts on the requirements team. Any such change may trigger corresponding changes to the business model.

Requirements fall into two categories, functional and nonfunctional. A **functional requirement** specifies an action that the target product must be able to perform. Functional requirements are often expressed in terms of inputs and outputs: Given a specific input, the functional requirement stipulates what the output must be. Conversely, a **nonfunctional requirement** specifies properties of the target product itself, such as **platform constraints** ("The software product shall run under Linux"), **response times** ("On average, queries of Type 3B shall be answered within 2.5 seconds"), or **reliability** ("The software product shall run 99.5 percent of the time").

Functional requirements are handled while the requirements and analysis workflows are being performed, whereas some nonfunctional requirements may have to wait until the design workflow. The reason is that, to be able to handle certain nonfunctional requirements, detailed knowledge about the target software product may be needed, and this knowledge is usually not available until the requirements and analysis workflows have been completed (see Problems 10.1 and 10.2). However, wherever possible, nonfunctional requirements should also be handled during the requirements and analysis workflows.

The requirements workflow is now illustrated by a running case study.

## 10.6 Initial Understanding of the Domain: The MSG Foundation Case Study

When Martha Stockton Greengage died at the age of 87, she left her entire $2.3 billion fortune to charity. Specifically, her will set up the Martha Stockton Greengage (MSG) Foundation to assist young couples in purchasing their own homes by providing low-cost loans.

In order to reduce operating expenses, the trustees of the MSG Foundation are investigating computerization. Because none of the trustees has any experience with computers, they decide to commission a small software development organization to implement a pilot project, namely, a software product that will perform the calculations needed to determine how much money is available each week to purchase homes.

The first step, as always, is to understand the application domain, home mortgages in this instance. Not many people can afford to pay cash to buy a home. Instead, they pay a small percentage of the purchase price out of their own savings and borrow the rest of the money. This type of loan, where real estate is pledged as security for the loan, is termed a **mortgage** (see Just in Case You Wanted to Know Box 10.2).

For example, suppose that someone wishes to buy a house for $100,000. (Many houses nowadays cost much more than that, particularly in the larger cities, but the round number makes the arithmetic easier.) The person buying the house pays a **deposit** of (say) 10 percent, or $10,000, and borrows the remaining $90,000 from a financial institution such as a bank or a savings and loan company in the form of a mortgage for that amount. Thus, the **principal** (or **capital**) borrowed is $90,000.

Suppose that the terms of the mortgage are that the loan is to be repaid in monthly installments over 30 years at an interest rate of 7.5 percent per annum (or 0.625 percent

Have you ever wondered why the word *mortgage* is pronounced "more gidge" with the accent on the first syllable? The word, which was first used in Middle English in the 14th century, comes from the Old French word *mort* meaning "dead" and the Germanic word *gage* meaning "a pledge," that is, a promise to forfeit property if the debt is not paid. Strangely enough, a mortgage is a "dead pledge" in two different senses. If the loan is not repaid, the property is forfeited, or "dead" to the borrower, forever. And if the loan is repaid, then the promise to repay is dead. This two-way explanation was first given by the English judge Sir Edward Coke (1552–1634).

And the strange pronunciation? The final letter in a French word like *mort* is silent—hence the "more." And the suffix *-age* is frequently pronounced "idge" in English. Examples include the words carriage, marriage, disparage, and encourage.

---

per month). Each month, the borrower pays the finance company $629.30. Part of this amount is the interest on the outstanding balance; the rest is used to reduce the principal. This monthly payment is therefore often referred to as **P & I** (principal and **interest**). For example, in the first month the outstanding balance is $90,000. Monthly interest at 0.625 percent on $90,000 is $562.50. The remainder of the P & I payment of $629.30, namely $66.80, is used to reduce the principal. Thus, at the end of the first month, after the first payment has been made, only $89,933.20 is owed to the finance company.

The interest for the second month is 0.625 percent of $89,933.20, or $562.08. The P & I payment is $629.30, as before, and the balance of the P & I payment (now $67.22) again is used to reduce the principal, this time to $89,865.98.

After 15 years (180 months), the monthly P & I payment is still $629.30, but now the principal has been reduced to $67,881.61. The monthly interest on $67,881.61 is $424.26, so the remaining $205.04 of the P & I payment is used to reduce the principal. After 30 years (360 months), the entire loan will have been repaid.

The finance company wants to be certain that it will be repaid the $90,000 it is owed, plus interest. It ensures this in a number of different ways.

- First, the borrower signs a legal document (the mortgage deed) that states that, if the monthly payments are not made, the finance company may sell the house and use the proceeds to pay off the outstanding balance of the loan.

- Second, the finance company requires the borrower to insure the house, so that if (say) the house burns down, the insurance company will cover the loss and the check from the insurance company will then be used to repay the loan. The insurance premium is usually paid once a year by the finance company. To obtain the money for the premium from the borrower, the finance company requires the borrower to pay monthly insurance installments. It deposits the installments in an **escrow account**, essentially a savings account managed by the finance company. When the annual insurance premium is due, the money is taken from the escrow account. Real-estate taxes paid on a home are treated the same way; that is, monthly installments are deposited in the escrow account and the annual real-estate tax payment is made from that account.

- Third, the finance company wants to be sure that the borrower can afford to pay for the mortgage. Typically, a mortgage will not be granted if the total monthly

**FIGURE 10.3** The initial glossary of the MSG Foundation case study.

**Balance:** the amount of the loan still owing
**Capital:** synonym for principal
**Closing costs:** other costs involved in buying a house, such as legal costs and various taxes
**Deposit:** an initial installment toward the total cost of the house
**Escrow account:** a savings account managed by the finance company into which the weekly installments toward the annual insurance premium and annual real-estate tax payment are deposited, and from which the annual insurance premium and the annual real estate tax payment are paid
**Interest:** a cost of borrowing money, computed as a fraction of the amount owing
**Mortgage:** a loan in which real estate is pledged as security for the loan
**P & I:** abbreviation for "principal and interest"
**Points:** a cost of borrowing money, computed as a fraction of the total amount borrowed
**Principal:** the lump sum borrowed
**Principal and interest:** an installment payment consisting of the interest plus the fraction of the principal for that installment

payment (P & I plus insurance plus real-estate taxes) exceeds 28 percent of the borrower's total income.

In addition to the monthly payments, the finance company almost always wants to be paid a lump sum up front in return for lending the money to the borrower. Typically, the finance company will want 2 percent of the principal ("2 **points**"). In the case of the $90,000 loan, this amounts to $1,800.

Finally, there are other costs involved in buying a house, such as legal costs and various taxes. Thus, when the contract to buy the $100,000 house is signed (when the deal is "closed"), the **closing costs** (legal costs, taxes, and so on) plus the points can easily amount to $7000.

The initial glossary of the MSG Foundation domain is shown in Figure 10.3.

The initial business model of the MSG Foundation case study is now constructed.

## Case Study

## 10.7 Initial Business Model: The MSG Foundation Case Study

Members of the development organization interview various managers and staff members of the MSG Foundation and discover the way the Foundation operates. At the start of each week, the MSG Foundation estimates how much money will be

**FIGURE 10.4** The `Estimate Funds Available for Week` use case of the initial business model of the MSG Foundation case study.

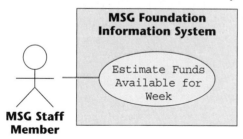

available that week to fund mortgages. Couples whose income is too low to afford a standard mortgage to buy a home can apply at any time to the MSG Foundation for a mortgage. An MSG Foundation staff member first determines whether the couple qualifies for an MSG mortgage and then determines whether the MSG Foundation still has sufficient funds on hand that week to purchase the home. If so, the mortgage is granted and the weekly mortgage repayment is computed according to the MSG Foundation's rules. This repayment amount may vary from week to week, depending on the couple's current income.

The corresponding part of the business model consists of three use cases: `Estimate Funds Available for Week`, `Apply for an MSG Mortgage`, and `Compute Weekly Repayment Amount`. These use cases are shown in Figures 10.4, 10.5, and 10.6, and the corresponding initial **use-case descriptions** appear in Figures 10.7, 10.8, and 10.9, respectively.

Consider the use case `Apply for an MSG Mortgage` (Figure 10.5). The actor on the right is **Applicants**. But is **Applicants** really an actor? Recall from Section 10.4.3 that an actor is a user of a software product. However, applicants do not use the software product. They fill in a form. Their answers are then entered into the software product by an MSG staff member. In addition, they may ask questions of the staff member or answer questions put to them by the staff member. But regardless of their interactions with MSG staff members, applicants never interact with the software product.[1]

However,

- The **Applicants** initiate the use case. That is, if a couple does not apply for a mortgage, this use case never occurs.
- Second, the information that the **MSG Staff Member** gives to the software product is provided by the **Applicants**.
- Third, in a sense, the real actor is **Applicants**; the **MSG Staff Member** is merely an agent of the **Applicants**.

For all these reasons, **Applicants** is indeed an actor.

Now consider Figure 10.6, which depicts the use case `Compute Weekly Repayment Amount`. The actor on the right is now **Borrowers**. Once an

---

[1] This will change if the MSG Foundation ever decides to accept applications over the Web. Specifically, **Applicants** will then become the only actor in Figure 10.6; **MSG Staff Member** will no longer play a role.

**FIGURE 10.5**  The `Apply for an MSG Mortgage` use case of the initial business model of the MSG Foundation case study.

**FIGURE 10.6**  The `Compute Weekly Repayment Amount` use case of the initial business model of the MSG Foundation case study.

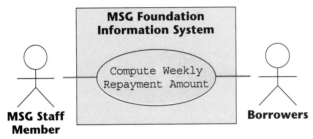

**FIGURE 10.7**  The description of the `Estimate Funds Available for Week` use case of the initial business model of the MSG Foundation case study.

| **Brief Description** |
| --- |
| The `Estimate Funds Available for Week` use case enables an MSG Foundation staff member to estimate how much money the Foundation has available that week to fund mortgages. |
| **Step-by-Step Description** |
| Not applicable at this initial stage. |

application has been granted, the couple who applied for the mortgage (the **Applicants**) become **Borrowers**. But even as borrowers they do not interact with the software product. As before, only MSG staff members can enter information into the software product. Nevertheless, again the use case is initiated by actor **Borrowers** and again the information entered by the **MSG Staff Member** is supplied by **Borrowers**. Thus, **Borrowers** is indeed an actor in the use case shown in Figure 10.6.

Another aspect of the MSG Foundation business model concerns the investments of the MSG Foundation. At this initial stage details are not yet known regarding the

**FIGURE 10.8**   The description of the `Apply for an MSG Mortgage` use case of the initial business model of the MSG Foundation case study.

---

**Brief Description**

When a couple applies for a mortgage, the `Apply for an MSG Mortgage` use case enables an MSG Foundation staff member to determine whether they qualify for an MSG mortgage and, if so, whether funds are currently available for the mortgage.

**Step-by-Step Description**

Not applicable at this initial stage.

---

**FIGURE 10.9**   The description of the `Compute Weekly Repayment Amount` use case of the initial business model of the MSG Foundation case study.

---

**Brief Description**

The `Compute Weekly Repayment Amount` use case enables an MSG Foundation staff member to compute how much borrowers have to repay each week.

**Step-by-Step Description**

Not applicable at this initial stage.

---

**FIGURE 10.10**   The `Manage an Investment` use case of the initial business model of the MSG Foundation case study.

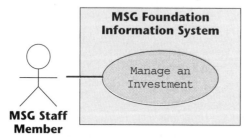

buying and selling of investments or how investment income becomes available for mortgages, but it is certainly clear that the use case `Manage an Investment` shown in Figure 10.10 is an essential part of the initial business model. The initial description appears in Figure 10.11; in a future iteration, details of how investments are handled will be inserted.

For conciseness, the four use cases of Figures 10.4, 10.5, 10.6, and 10.10 are combined into the **use-case diagram** of Figure 10.12.

Now the initial requirements have to be drawn up.

**FIGURE 10.11**   The description of the `Manage an Investment` use case of the initial business model of the MSG Foundation case study.

---

**Brief Description**

The `Manage an Investment` use case enables an MSG Foundation staff member to buy and sell investments and manage the investment portfolio.

---

**Step-by-Step Description**

Not applicable at this initial stage.

---

**FIGURE 10.12**   The use-case diagram of the initial business model of the MSG Foundation case study.

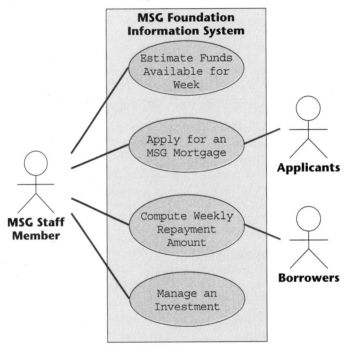

## 10.8   Initial Requirements: The MSG Foundation Case Study

The four use cases of Figure 10.12 comprise the business model of the MSG Foundation. However, it is not immediately obvious whether they are all requirements of the MSG Foundation software product that is to be developed. Recall that what the client *wants* is "a pilot project, namely, a software product that will perform the calculations needed to determine how much money is available each week to purchase homes." As always, the task of the developers is to determine, with the aid of the client, what the client *needs*. At this early stage, however, there is not enough information at the analysts' disposal to be able to decide whether just this "pilot project" will be what is needed. In situations like this, the best way to proceed is to draw up the initial requirements on the basis of what the client wants, and then iterate.

Accordingly, each of the use cases of Figure 10.12 in turn is considered. Use case `Estimate Funds Available for Week` is obviously part of the initial requirements. On the other hand, `Apply for an MSG Mortgage` does not seem to have anything to do with the pilot project, so it is excluded from the initial requirements. At first sight, the third use case, `Compute Weekly Repayment Amount`, seems equally irrelevant to the pilot project. However, the pilot project deals with the "money that is available each week to purchase homes." Part of that money surely comes from the weekly repayment of existing mortgages, so the third use case is indeed part of the initial requirements. The fourth use case, `Manage an Investment`, is also part of the initial requirements for a similar reason—income from investments also must be used to fund new mortgages.

The initial requirements then consist of three use cases and their descriptions, namely, `Estimate Funds Available for Week` (Figures 10.4 and 10.7), `Compute Weekly Repayment Amount` (Figures 10.6 and 10.9), and `Manage an Investment` (Figures 10.10 and 10.11). These three use cases appear in Figure 10.13.

The next step is to iterate the requirements workflow; that is, the steps are performed again in order to obtain a better model of the client's needs.

**FIGURE 10.13**   The use-case diagram of the initial requirements of the MSG Foundation case study.

## Continuing the Requirements Workflow: The MSG Foundation Case Study

Armed with domain knowledge and familiarity with the initial business model, members of the development team now interview the MSG Foundation managers and staff in greater depth. They discover the following information.

The MSG Foundation grants a 100 percent mortgage to buy a home under the following conditions:

- The couple has been married for at least 1 year but not more than 10 years.
- Both husband and wife are gainfully employed. Specifically, proof must be provided that both were employed full time for at least 48 weeks of the preceding year.
- The price of the home must be below the published median price for homes in that area for the past 12 months.
- The installments on a fixed-rate, 30-year, 90 percent mortgage would exceed 28 percent of their combined gross income and/or they do not have sufficient savings to pay 10 percent of the cost of the home plus $7,000. (The $7,000 is an estimate of the additional costs involved, including closing costs and points.)
- The Foundation has sufficient funds to purchase the home; this is described later in more detail.

If the application is approved, then the amount that the couple should pay the MSG Foundation every week for the next 30 years is the total of the principal and interest payment, which never changes over the life of the mortgage, and the escrow payment, which is $\frac{1}{52}$nd of the sum of the annual real-estate tax and the annual homeowner's insurance premium. If this total is greater than 28 percent of the couple's gross weekly income, then the MSG Foundation will pay the difference in the form of a grant. Thus, the mortgage is paid in full each week, but the couple will never have to pay more than 28 percent of their combined gross income.

The couple must provide a copy of their income tax return each year, so that the MSG Foundation has proof of their previous year's income. In addition, the couple may file copies of pay slips as proof of current gross income. The amount the couple has to pay for their mortgage may therefore vary from week to week.

The MSG Foundation uses the following algorithm to determine whether it has the funds to approve a mortgage application:

1. At the beginning of each week, the estimated annual income from its investments is computed and divided by 52.
2. The estimated annual MSG Foundation operating expenses are divided by 52.
3. The total of the estimated mortgage payments for that week is computed.
4. The total of the estimated grants for that week is computed.
5. The amount available at the beginning of the week is then (Item 1) − (Item 2) + (Item 3) − (Item 4).

6. During the week, if the cost of the home is no more than the amount available for mortgages, then the MSG Foundation deems that it has the funds needed to purchase the home; the amount available for mortgages that week is reduced by the cost of that home.

7. At the end of each week, any unspent funds are invested by the MSG Foundation investment advisors.

To keep the cost of the pilot project as low as possible, the developers are told that only those data items needed for the weekly funds computation should be incorporated into the software product. The rest can be added later if the MSG Foundation decides to computerize all aspects of its operation. Therefore, only three types of data are needed, namely, investment data, operating expenses data, and mortgage data.

With regard to investments, the following data are required:

Item number.

Item name.

Estimated annual return. (This figure is updated whenever new information becomes available. On average, this occurs about four times a year.)

Date estimated annual return was last updated.

With regard to operating expenses, the following data are required:

Estimated annual operating expenses. (This figure is currently determined four times a year.)

Date estimated annual operating expenses were last updated.

For each mortgage, the following data are required:

Account number.

Last name of mortgagees.

Original purchase price of home.

Date mortgage was issued.

Weekly principal and interest payment.

Current combined gross weekly income.

Date combined gross weekly income was last updated.

Annual real-estate tax.

Date annual real-estate tax was last updated.

Annual homeowner's insurance premium.

Date annual homeowner's insurance premium was last updated.

In the course of further discussions with MSG managers, the developers learn that three types of reports are needed:

The results of the funds computation for the week.

A listing of all investments (to be printed on request).

A listing of all mortgages (to be printed on request).

## 10.10 Revising the Requirements: The MSG Foundation Case Study

Recall that the initial requirements model (Section 10.8) includes three use cases, namely, `Estimate Funds Available for Week`, `Compute Weekly Repayment Amount`, and `Manage an Investment`. These use cases are shown in Figure 10.13. Now, in the light of the additional information that has been received, the initial requirements can be revised.

The formula given in Section 10.9 for determining how much money is available at the beginning of a week is as follows:

1. The estimated annual income from investments is computed and divided by 52.
2. The estimated annual MSG Foundation operating expenses are divided by 52.
3. The total of the estimated mortgage payments for that week is computed.
4. The total of the estimated grants for that week is computed.
5. The amount available is then (Item 1) − (Item 2) + (Item 3) − (Item 4).

Consider each of these items in turn.

1. *Estimated annual income from investments.* For each investment in turn, sum the estimated annual return on each investment, and divide the result by 52. To do this, an additional use case is needed, namely, `Estimate Investment Income for Week`. (Use case `Manage an Investment` is still needed for adding, deleting, and modifying investments.) This new use case is depicted in Figure 10.14 and described in Figure 10.15. In Figure 10.14, the dashed line with the open arrowhead labeled «include» denotes that use case `Estimate Investment Income for Week` is part of use case `Estimate Funds Available for Week`. The resulting first iteration of the revised use-case diagram is shown in Figure 10.16 with the new use case shaded.

2. *Estimated annual operating expenses.* Up to now, the estimated annual operating expenses have not been considered. To incorporate these expenses, two additional

**FIGURE 10.14** The `Estimate Investment Income for Week` use case of the revised requirements of the MSG Foundation case study.

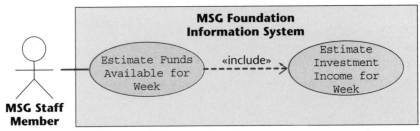

**FIGURE 10.15**   The description of the `Estimate Investment Income for Week` use case of the revised requirements of the MSG Foundation case study.

---

**Brief Description**

The `Estimate Investment Income for Week` use case enables the `Estimate Funds Available for Week` use case to estimate how much investment income is available for this week.

**Step-by-Step Description**

1. For each investment, extract the estimated annual return on that investment.
2. Sum the values extracted in Step 1 and divide the result by 52.

---

**FIGURE 10.16**   The first iteration of the use-case diagram of the revised requirements of the MSG Foundation case study. The new use case is shaded.

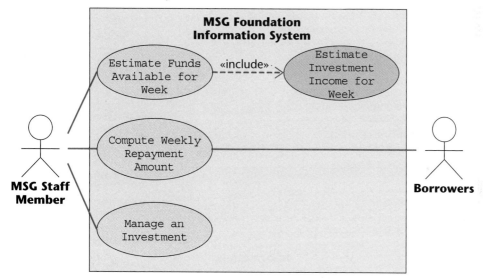

use cases are needed. Use case `Update Estimated Annual Operating Expenses` models adjustments to the value of the estimated annual operating expenses, and use case `Estimate Operating Expenses for Week` provides the estimate of the operating expenses that is required. The use cases are shown in Figures 10.17 through 10.20. In Figure 10.19, use case `Estimate Operating Expenses for Week` is similarly part of use case `Estimate Funds Available for Week`, as indicated by the dashed line with the open arrowhead labeled «include». The resulting second iteration of the revised use-case diagram is shown in Figure 10.21. The two new use cases, `Estimate Operating Expenses for Week` and `Update Estimated Annual Operating Expenses`, are shaded.

3. *Total estimated mortgage payments for the week.* (See item 4.)

**FIGURE 10.17** The Update Estimated Annual Operating Expenses use case of the revised requirements of the MSG Foundation case study.

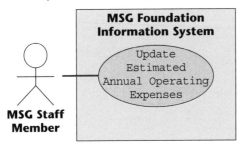

**FIGURE 10.18** The description of the Update Estimated Annual Operating Expenses use case of the revised requirements of the MSG Foundation case study.

---

**Brief Description**

The Update Estimated Annual Operating Expenses use case enables an MSG Foundation staff member to update the estimated annual operating expenses.

---

**Step-by-Step Description**

1. Update the estimated annual operating expenses.

---

**FIGURE 10.19** The Estimate Operating Expenses for Week use case of the revised requirements of the MSG Foundation case study.

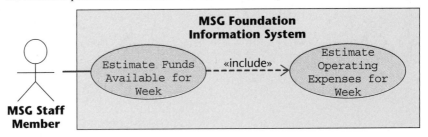

4. *Total estimated grant payments for the week.* The weekly repayment amount from use case Compute Weekly Repayment Amount is the total estimated mortgage payment less the estimated total grant payment. In other words, use case Compute Weekly Repayment Amount models the computation of both the estimated mortgage payment and the estimated grant payment for each mortgage separately. Summing these separate quantities will yield the total estimated mortgage payments for the week as well as the total estimated grant payments for the

**FIGURE 10.20**   The description of the `Estimate Operating Expenses for Week` use case of the revised requirements of the MSG Foundation case study.

---

**Brief Description**

The `Estimate Operating Expenses for Week` use case enables the `Estimate Funds Available for Week` use case to estimate the operating expenses for the week.

**Step-by-Step Description**

1. Divide the estimated annual operating expenses by 52.

---

**FIGURE 10.21**   The second iteration of the use-case diagram of the revised requirements of the MSG Foundation case study. The two new use cases, `Estimate Operating Expenses for Week` and `Update Estimated Annual Operating Expenses`, are shaded.

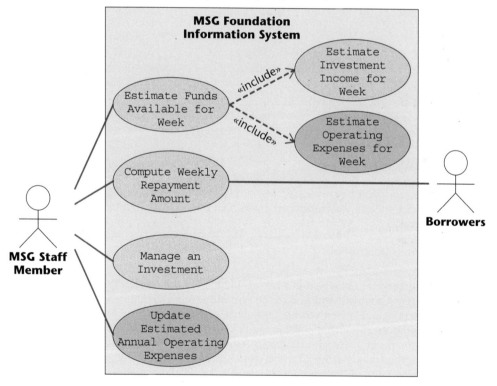

week. However, `Compute Weekly Repayment Amount` also models the borrowers changing the amount of their weekly income. Accordingly, `Compute Weekly Repayment Amount` needs to be split into two separate use cases, namely, `Estimate Payments and Grants for Week` and `Update Borrowers' Weekly Income`. The two new use cases are described in

Figures 10.22 through 10.25. Once more, one of the new use cases, namely, `Estimate Payments and Grants for Week`, is part of use case `Estimate Funds Available for Week`, as indicated by the dashed line with the open arrowhead labeled «include» in Figure 10.22. The resulting third iteration of the revised use-case diagram is shown in Figure 10.26 with the two use cases derived from use case `Compute Weekly Repayment Amount` shaded.

Consider Figure 10.26 again. Use case `Estimate Funds Available for Week` models the computation that uses the data obtained from three other use cases,

**FIGURE 10.22** The `Estimate Payments` and `Grants for Week` use case of the revised requirements of the MSG Foundation case study.

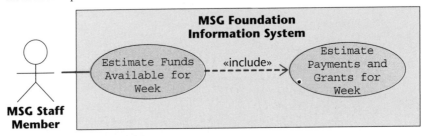

**FIGURE 10.23** The description of the `Estimate Payments and Grants for Week` use case of the revised requirements of the MSG Foundation case study.

---

**Brief Description**

The `Estimate Payments and Grants for Week` use case enables the `Estimate Funds Available for Week` use case to estimate the total estimated mortgage payments paid by borrowers to the MSG Foundation for this week and the total estimated grants paid by the MSG Foundation for this week.

**Step-by-Step Description**

1. For each mortgage:
   1.1 The amount to be paid this week is the total of the principal and interest payment and $\frac{1}{52}$nd of the sum of the annual real-estate tax and the annual homeowner's insurance premium.
   1.2 Compute 28 percent of the couple's current gross weekly income.
   1.3 If the result of Step 1.1 is greater than the result of Step 1.2, then the mortgage payment for this week is the result of Step 1.2, and the amount of the grant for this week is the difference between the result of Step 1.1 and the result of Step 1.2.
   1.4 Otherwise, the mortgage payment for this week is the result of Step 1.1 and there is no grant this week.
2. Summing the mortgage payments of Steps 1.3 and 1.4 yields the estimated mortgage payments for the week.
3. Summing the grant payments of Step 1.3 yields the estimated grant payments for the week.

**FIGURE 10.24**   The `Update Borrowers' Weekly Income` use case of the revised requirements of the MSG Foundation case study.

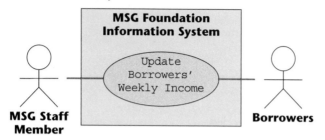

**FIGURE 10.25**   The description of the `Update Borrowers' Weekly Income` use case of the revised requirements of the MSG Foundation case study.

| **Brief Description** |
| --- |
| The `Update Borrowers' Weekly Income` use case enables an MSG Foundation staff member to update the weekly income of a couple who have borrowed money from the Foundation. |
| **Step-by-Step Description** |
| 1. Update the borrower's weekly income. |

namely, `Estimate Investment Income for Week,` `Estimate Operating Expenses for Week,` and `Estimate Payments and Grants for Week`. This is shown in Figure 10.27, which shows the second iteration of the use case `Estimate Funds Available for Week`; this figure has been extracted from the use-case diagram of Figure 10.26. Figure 10.28 is the corresponding description of the use case.

Why is it so important to indicate the **«include» relationship** in UML diagrams? For example, Figure 10.29 shows two versions of Figure 10.26, the correct version on top and an incorrect version below. The top diagram correctly models use case `Estimate Funds Available for Week` as part of use case `Estimate Payments and Grants for Week`. The bottom diagram of Figure 10.29 models use cases `Estimate Funds Available for Week` and `Estimate Payments and Grants for Week` as two independent use cases. However, as stated in Section 10.4.3, a use case models an interaction between the software product itself and users of the software product (actors). This is fine for use case `Estimate Funds Available for Week`. However, use case `Estimate Payments and Grants for Week` does not interact with an actor and, therefore, cannot be a use case in its own right. Instead, it is a portion of use case `Estimate Funds Available for Week`, as reflected in the top diagram of Figure 10.29.

**FIGURE 10.26**   The third iteration of the use-case diagram of the revised requirements of the MSG Foundation case study. The two use cases derived from use case `Compute Weekly Repayment Amount` are shaded.

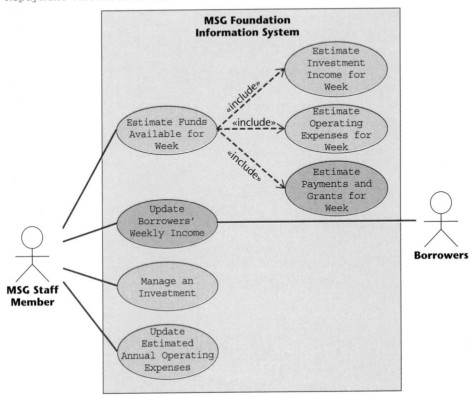

**FIGURE 10.27**   The second iteration of the `Estimate Funds Available for Week` use case of the revised requirements of the MSG Foundation case study.

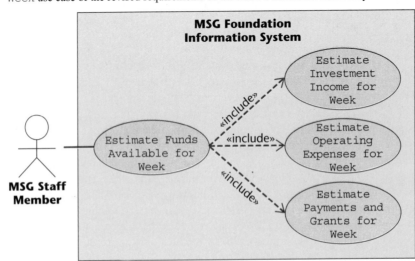

**FIGURE 10.28**  The second iteration of the description of the `Estimate Funds Available for Week` use case of the revised requirements of the MSG Foundation case study.

---

**Brief Description**

The `Estimate Funds Available for Week` use case enables an MSG Foundation staff member to estimate how much money the Foundation has available that week to fund mortgages.

---

**Step-by-Step Description**

1. Determine the estimated income from investments for the week utilizing use case `Estimate Investment Income for Week`.
2. Determine the operating expenses for the week utilizing use case `Estimate Operating Expenses for Week`.
3. Determine the total estimated mortgage payments for the week utilizing use case `Estimate Payments and Grants for Week`.
4. Determine the total estimated grants for the week utilizing use case `Estimate Payments and Grants for Week`.
5. Add the results of Steps 1 and 3 and subtract the results of Steps 2 and 4. This is the total amount available for mortgages for the current week.

---

**FIGURE 10.29**   Correct (top) and incorrect (bottom) versions of Figure 10.22.

## Case Study

### 10.11   The Test Workflow: The MSG Foundation Case Study

A common side effect of the iterative and incremental life-cycle model is that details that correctly have been postponed somehow get forgotten. That is one of the many reasons why continual testing is essential. In this instance, the details of the use case `Manage an Investment` have been overlooked. This is remedied in Figures 10.30 and 10.31.

Further review brings to light the omission of use case `Manage a Mortgage` to model the addition of a new mortgage, the modification of an existing mortgage, or the removal of an existing mortgage, analogous to use case `Manage an Investment`. Figures 10.32 and 10.33 correct this omission, and the fourth iteration of the revised use-case diagram is shown in Figure 10.34 with the new use case, `Manage a Mortgage`, shaded.

**FIGURE 10.30**   The `Manage an Investment` use case of the revised requirements of the MSG Foundation case study.

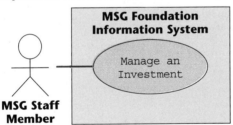

**FIGURE 10.31**   The description of the `Manage an Investment` use case of the revised requirements of the MSG Foundation case study.

---

**Brief Description**

The `Manage an Investment` use case enables an MSG Foundation staff member to add and delete investments and manage the investment portfolio.

**Step-by-Step Description**

1. Add, modify, or delete an investment.

---

**FIGURE 10.32**   The `Manage a Mortgage` use case of the revised requirements of the MSG Foundation case study.

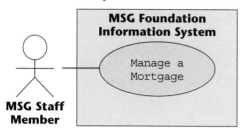

**FIGURE 10.33**   The description of the `Manage a Mortgage` use case of the revised requirements of the MSG Foundation case study.

---

**Brief Description**

The `Manage a Mortgage` use case enables an MSG Foundation staff member to add and delete mortgages and manage the mortgage portfolio.

---

**Step-by-Step Description**

1. Add, modify, or delete a mortgage.

---

Furthermore, the use case for printing the various reports has also been overlooked. Accordingly, use case `Produce a Report`, which models the printing of the three reports, is added. The details of the use case appear in Figures 10.35 and 10.36. The fifth iteration of the revised use-case diagram is shown in Figure 10.37 with the new use case, `Produce a Report`, shaded.

The revised requirements are checked yet again, and two new problems are uncovered. First, a use case has been partially duplicated. Second, two of the use cases need to be reorganized.

The first change to be made is to remove the partially duplicated use case. Consider the use case `Manage a Mortgage` (Figures 10.32 and 10.33). As stated in Figure 10.33, one of the actions of this use case is to modify a mortgage. Now consider the use case `Update Borrowers' Weekly Income` (Figures 10.24 and 10.25). The only purpose of this use case (Figure 10.25) is to update the borrowers' weekly income. But the borrowers' weekly income is an attribute of the mortgage. That is, use case `Manage a Mortgage` already includes the use case `Update Borrowers' Weekly Income`. Accordingly, use case `Update Borrowers' Weekly Income` is superfluous and should be deleted. The result is shown in Figure 10.38, the sixth iteration of the revised use-case diagram. The modified use case, `Manage a Mortgage`, is shaded.

**FIGURE 10.34**  The fourth iteration of the use-case diagram of the revised requirements of the MSG Foundation case study. The new use case, Manage a Mortgage, is shaded.

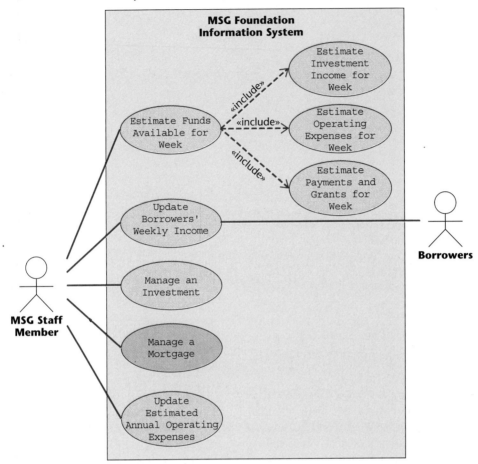

**FIGURE 10.35**  The Produce a Report use case of the revised requirements of the MSG Foundation case study.

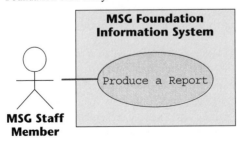

**FIGURE 10.36**    The description of the `Produce a Report` use case of the revised requirements of the MSG Foundation case study.

---

**Brief Description**

The `Produce a Report` use case enables an MSG Foundation staff member to print the results of the weekly computation of funds available for new mortgages or to print a listing of all investments or all mortgages.

---

**Step-by-Step Description**

1. The following reports must be generated:
1.1 Investments report—printed on demand:
      The information system prints a list of all investments. For each investment, the following attributes are printed:
         Item number
         Item name
         Estimated annual return
         Date estimated annual return was last updated
1.2 Mortgages report—printed on demand:
      The information system prints a list of all mortgages. For each mortgage, the following attributes are printed:
         Account number
         Name of mortgagee
         Original price of home
         Date mortgage was issued
         Principal and interest payment
         Current combined gross weekly income
         Date current combined gross weekly income was last updated
         Annual real-estate tax
         Date annual real-estate tax was last updated
         Annual homeowner's insurance premium
         Date annual homeowner's insurance premium was last updated
1.3 Results of the weekly computation—printed each week:
      The information system prints the total amount available for new mortgages during the current week

---

    This is the first iteration that has resulted in a decrement rather than an increment. That is, this is the first time in this book that the result of an iteration has been to delete an artifact (the `Update Borrowers' Weekly Income` use case). In fact, deletion occurs all too often, namely, whenever a mistake is made. Sometimes an incorrect artifact can be fixed, but frequently an artifact has to be deleted. The key point is that, when a fault is discovered, there is no need to abandon everything done

**FIGURE 10.37**   The fifth iteration of the use-case diagram of the revised requirements of the MSG Foundation case study. The new use case, `Produce a Report`, is shaded.

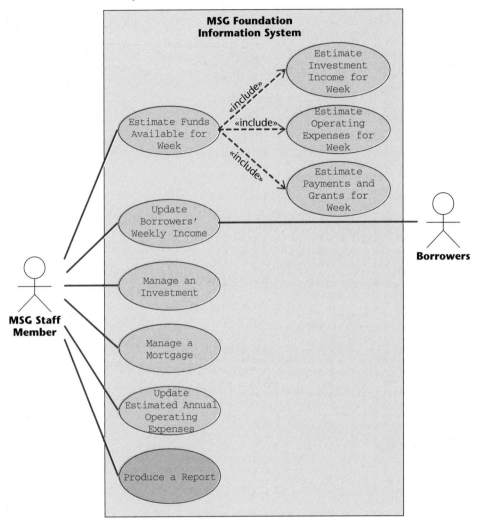

to date and start the whole requirements process from scratch. Instead, an attempt is made to fix the current iteration, as was done in this case study. If this strategy fails (because the mistake really is serious), we backtrack to the previous iteration and try to find a better way to go forward from there.

The second change that must be made to improve the requirements is to reorganize two use cases. Consider the descriptions of the use cases `Estimate Funds Available for Week` (Figure 10.28) and `Produce a Report` (Figure 10.36). Suppose that an MSG staff member wants to determine the funds available for the

**FIGURE 10.38**   The sixth iteration of the use-case diagram of the revised requirements of the MSG Foundation case study. The modified use case, `Manage a Mortgage`, is shaded.

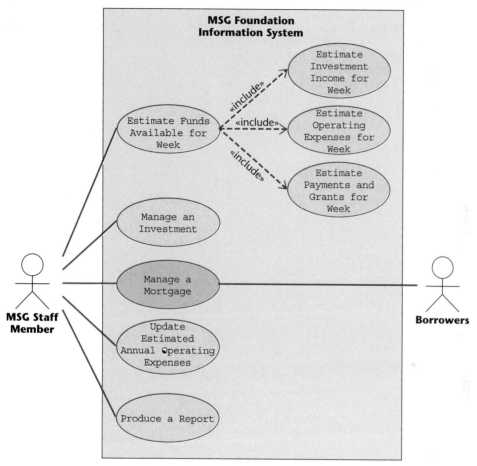

current week. Use case `Estimate Funds Available for Week` performs the calculation, and Step 1.3 of use case `Produce a Report` prints out the result of the computation. This is ridiculous. After all, there is no point in estimating the funds available unless the results are printed out.

In other words, Step 1.3 of `Produce a Report` needs to be moved from the description of that use case to the end of the description of use case `Estimate Funds Available for Week`. This does not change the use cases themselves (Figures 10.27 and 10.35) or the current use-case diagram (Figure 10.38), but the descriptions of the two use cases (Figures 10.28 and 10.36) have to be modified. The resulting modified descriptions are shown in Figures 10.39 and 10.40.

**FIGURE 10.39** The second iteration of the description of the `Produce a Report` use case of the revised requirements of the MSG Foundation case study.

---

**Brief Description**

The `Produce a Report` use case enables an MSG Foundation staff member to print a listing of all investments or all mortgages.

---

**Step-by-Step Description**

1. The following reports must be generated:
   1.1 Investments report—printed on demand:
      The information system prints a list of all investments. For each investment, the following attributes are printed:
      Item number
      Item name
      Estimated annual return
      Date estimated annual return was last updated
   1.2 Mortgages report—printed on demand:
      The information system prints a list of all mortgages. For each mortgage, the following attributes are printed:
      Account number
      Name of mortgagee
      Original price of home
      Date mortgage was issued
      Principal and interest payment
      Current combined gross weekly income
      Date current combined gross weekly income was last updated
      Annual real-estate tax
      Date annual real-estate tax was last updated
      Annual homeowner's insurance premium
      Date annual homeowner's insurance premium was last updated

---

**FIGURE 10.40** The third iteration of the description of the `Estimate Funds Available for Week` use case of the revised requirements of the MSG Foundation case study.

---

**Brief Description**

The `Estimate Funds Available for Week` use case enables an MSG Foundation staff member to estimate how much money the Foundation has available that week to fund mortgages.

---

**Step-by-Step Description**

1. Determine the estimated income from investments for the week utilizing use case `Estimate Investment Income for Week`.
2. Determine the operating expenses for the week utilizing use case `Estimate Operating Expenses for Week`.
3. Determine the total estimated mortgage payments for the week utilizing use case `Estimate Payments and Grants for Week`.
4. Determine the total estimated grants for the week utilizing use case `Estimate Payments and Grants for Week`.
5. Add the results of Steps 1 and 3 and subtract the results of Steps 2 and 4. This is the total amount available for mortgages for the current week.
6. Print the total amount available for new mortgages during the current week.

**FIGURE 10.41**   Use case `Print Tax Form` is part of three other use cases.

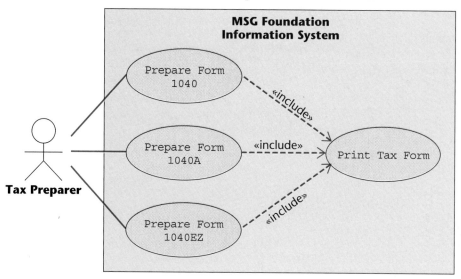

Now the use-case diagram can be improved still further. Consider the top four use cases in Figure 10.38. The three use cases on the right, namely, `Estimate Investment Income for Week`, `Estimate Operating Expenses for Week`, and `Estimate Payments and Grants for Week`, are part of the use case `Estimate Funds Available for Week`. The usual reason for an «include» relationship is where one use case is part of two or more other use cases. For example, Figure 10.41 shows that use case `Print Tax Form` is part of use cases `Prepare Form 1040`, `Prepare Form 1040A`, and `Prepare Form 1040EZ`, the three primary U.S. tax forms for individuals. In this situation, it makes sense to retain `Print Tax Form` as an independent use case. Incorporating the operations of `Print Tax Form` into the other three use cases would mean triplicating that use case.

With regard to Figure 10.38, however, all the included use cases are part of only one use case, namely, `Estimate Funds Available for Week`—there is no duplication. Accordingly, it makes sense to incorporate those three «include» use cases into `Estimate Funds Available for Week`, as shown in Figure 10.42, the seventh iteration of the use-case diagram. The resulting fourth iteration of the description of the `Estimate Funds Available for Week` use case is shown in Figure 10.43.

Now the requirements appear to be correct.

- First, they correspond to what the client has requested.
- Second, there do not seem to be any faults.
- Third, at this stage it would seem that what the client wants coincides with what the client needs.

FIGURE 10.42    The seventh iteration of the use-case diagram of the revised requirements of the MSG Foundation case study. The modified use case, `Estimate Funds Available for Week`, is shaded.

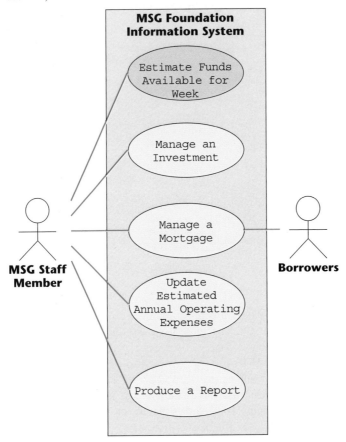

Accordingly, the requirements workflow appears to be complete, for now. Nevertheless, it is certainly possible that, during subsequent workflows, additional requirements may surface. Also, it may be necessary to split one or more of the five use cases into additional use cases. For example, in a future iteration the `Produce a Report` use case described in Figure 10.36 may be split into two separate use cases, one for the investments report, the other for the mortgages report. But for now, everything seems to be satisfactory.

This concludes the description of the requirements workflow for the MSG Foundation case study.

**FIGURE 10.43**    The fourth iteration of the description of the use case `Estimate Funds Available for Week` of the revised requirements of the MSG Foundation case study.

---

**Brief Description**

The `Estimate Funds Available for Week` use case enables an MSG Foundation staff member to estimate how much money the Foundation has available that week to fund mortgages.

---

**Step-by-Step Description**

1. For each investment, extract the estimated annual return on that investment. Summing the separate returns and dividing the result by 52 yields the estimated investment income for the week.
2. Determine the estimated MSG Foundation operating expenses for the week by extracting the estimated annual MSG Foundation operating expenses and dividing by 52.
3. For each mortgage:
   3.1 The amount to be paid this week is the total of the principal and interest payment and $\frac{1}{52}$nd of the sum of the annual real-estate tax and the annual homeowner's insurance premium.
   3.2 Compute 28 percent of the couple's current gross weekly income.
   3.3 If the result of Step 3.1 is greater than the result of Step 3.2, then the mortgage payment for this week is the result of Step 3.2, and the amount of the grant for this week is the difference between the result of Step 3.1 and the result of Step 3.2.
   3.4 Otherwise, the mortgage payment for this week is the result of Step 3.1, and there is no grant this week.
4. Summing the mortgage payments of Steps 3.3 and 3.4 yields the estimated total mortgage payments for the week.
5. Summing the grant payments of Step 3.3 yields the estimated total grant payments for the week.
6. Add the results of Steps 1 and 4 and subtract the results of Steps 2 and 5. This is the total amount available for mortgages for the current week.
7. Print the total amount available for new mortgages during the current week.

---

# 10.12    The Classical Requirements Phase

On the one hand, there is no such thing as "object-oriented requirements," nor should there be such a thing. The aim of the requirements workflow is to determine the client's needs, that is, what the functionality of the target system should be. The requirements workflow has nothing to do with how the product is to be built. From this viewpoint, it makes no sense to refer to the classical paradigm or the object-oriented paradigm within the context of the requirements workflow, any more than one can refer to a classical or object-oriented user manual. After all, the user manual describes the steps to be followed by the user when running the software product and has nothing to do with how the product was built. In the same way, the requirements workflow results in a statement of what the product is to do; the way that the product will be built does not enter into it.

On the other hand, the entire approach of Sections 10.2 through 10.11 is object oriented in nature in that it is model oriented. The use cases, together with their descriptions, form the basis of the requirements workflow. As is shown throughout Part 2 of this book, modeling is the essence of the object-oriented paradigm.

However, modeling in general (and UML modeling in particular) is not part of the classical paradigm. The classical requirements phase starts with requirements elicitation followed by requirements analysis, similarly to the object-oriented paradigm (Sections 10.3 through 10.4.2). But from that point on, the two paradigms diverge. Instead of building models, the next step in the classical requirements phase is to draw up a list of requirements. The usual step after that is to build a rapid prototype that implements the key functionality underlying those requirements, as described in Section 2.9.3. The client and future users of the target software product then experiment with the rapid prototype until the requirements team members are satisfied that the rapid prototype exhibits the key functionality of the software product the client needs.

Building a rapid prototype for the product as a whole is not part of the object-oriented paradigm, for the reasons given in Section 12.18. However, it is strongly advisable to build a rapid prototype of the user interface, as will be described.

## 10.13   Rapid Prototyping

A **rapid prototype** is hastily built software that exhibits the key functionality of the target product. For example, a product that helps to manage an apartment complex must incorporate an input screen that allows the user to enter details of a new tenant and print an occupancy report for each month. These aspects are incorporated into the rapid prototype. However, error-checking capabilities, file-updating routines, and complex tax computations probably are not included. The key point is that a rapid prototype reflects the functionality the client sees, such as input screens and reports, but omits "hidden" aspects such as file updating. (For a different way of looking at rapid prototypes, see Just in Case You Wanted to Know Box 10.3.)

The client and intended users of the product now experiment with the rapid prototype, while members of the development team watch and take notes. Based on their hands-on experience, users tell the developers how the rapid prototype satisfies their needs and, more important, identify the areas that need improvement. The developers change the rapid prototype until both sides are convinced that the needs of the client are accurately encapsulated in the rapid prototype. The rapid prototype is then used as the basis for drawing up the specifications.

An important aspect of the rapid prototyping model is embodied in the word *rapid*. The whole idea is to build the rapid prototype as quickly as possible. After all, the purpose of the rapid prototype is to provide the client an understanding of the product, and the sooner, the better. It does not matter if the rapid prototype hardly works, if it crashes every few

The idea of constructing models to show key aspects of a product goes back a long time. For example, a 1618 painting by Domenico Cresti (known as "Il Passignano" because he was born in the town of Passignano in the Chianti region of Italy) shows Michelangelo presenting a wooden model of his design for St. Peter's (in Rome) to Pope Paul IV. Such architectural models could be huge; a model of an earlier design proposal for St. Peter's by the architect Bramante is more than 20 feet long on each side.

Architectural models were used for a number of different purposes. First, as depicted in the Cresti painting (now hanging in Casa Buonarroti in Florence), models were used to try to interest a client in funding a project. This is analogous to the use of a rapid prototype to determine the client's real needs. Second, in an age before architectural drawings, the model showed the builder the structure of the building and indicated to the stonemasons how the building was to be decorated. This is similar to the way we now build a rapid prototype of the user interface, as described in Section 10.14.

It is not a good idea, however, to draw too close a parallel between such architectural models and software rapid prototypes. Rapid prototypes are used during the classical requirements phase to elicit the client's needs. Unlike architectural models, they are not used to represent either the architectural design or the detailed design; the design is produced two phases later, that is, during the classical design phase.

---

minutes, or if the screen layouts are less than perfect. The purpose of the rapid prototype is to enable the client and the developers to agree as quickly as possible on what the product is to do. Therefore, any imperfections in the rapid prototype may be ignored, provided that they do not seriously impair the functionality of the rapid prototype and thereby give a misleading impression of how the product behaves.

A second major aspect of the rapid prototyping model is that the rapid prototype must be built for change. If the first version of the rapid prototype is not what the client needs, then the prototype must be transformed rapidly into a second version that, it is hoped, better satisfies the client's requirements. To achieve rapid development throughout the rapid prototyping process, fourth-generation languages (4GL) and interpreted languages, such as Smalltalk, Prolog, and Lisp, have been used for rapid prototyping purposes. Popular rapid prototyping languages of today include HTML and Perl. Concerns have been expressed about the maintainability of certain interpreted languages, but from the viewpoint of rapid prototyping this is irrelevant. All that counts is this: Can a given language be used to produce a rapid prototype? And, can the rapid prototype be changed quickly? If the answer to both questions is Yes, then that language is probably a good candidate for rapid prototyping.

Rapid prototyping is particularly effective when developing the user interface to a product. This use is discussed in Section 10.14.

## 10.14   Human Factors

It is important that both the client and the future users of the product interact with the rapid prototype of the user interface. Encouraging users to experiment with the human–computer interface (HCI) greatly reduces the risk that the finished product will have to be altered.

In particular, this experimentation helps achieve user-friendliness, a vital objective for all software products.

The term **user-friendliness** refers to the ease with which human beings can communicate with the software product. If users have difficulty in learning how to use a product or find the screens confusing or irritating, then they will either not use the product or use it incorrectly. To try to eliminate this problem, menu-driven products were introduced. Instead of having to enter a command such as Perform computation or Print service rate report, the user merely has to select from a set of possible responses, such as

1. Perform computation
2. Print service rate report
3. Select view to be graphed

In this example, the user enters 1, 2, or 3 to invoke the corresponding command.

Nowadays, instead of simply displaying lines of text, HCIs employ graphics. Windows, icons, and pull-down menus are components of a **graphical user interface** (GUI). Because of the plethora of windowing systems, standards such as X Window have evolved. Also, **point-and-click** selection is now the norm. The user moves a mouse (that is, a hand-held pointing device) to move the screen cursor to the desired response ("point"), and pushes a mouse button ("click") to select that response.

However, even when the target product employs modern technology, the designers must never forget that the product is to be used by human beings. In other words, the HCI designers must consider **human factors** such as size of letters, capitalization, color, line length, and the number of lines on the screen.

Another example of human factors applies to the preceding menu. If the user chooses option 3. Select view to be graphed, then another menu appears with another list of choices. Unless a menu-driven system is thoughtfully designed, there is the danger that users will encounter a lengthy sequence of menus to achieve even a relatively simple operation. This delay can anger users, sometimes causing them to make inappropriate menu selections. Also, the HCI must allow the user to change a previous selection without having to return to the top-level menu and start again. This problem can exist even when a GUI is used because many graphical user interfaces are essentially a series of menus displayed in an attractive screen format.

Sometimes it is impossible for a single user interface to cater to all users. For example, if a product is to be used by both computer professionals and high-school dropouts with no previous computer experience, then it is preferable that two different sets of HCIs be designed, each carefully tailored to the skill level and psychological profile of its intended users. This technique can be extended by incorporating sets of user interfaces requiring varied levels of sophistication. If the product deduces that the user would be more comfortable with a less sophisticated user interface, perhaps because the user is making frequent mistakes or is continually invoking help facilities, then the user is automatically shown screens that are more appropriate to his or her current skill level. But, as the user becomes more familiar with the product, streamlined screens that provide less information are displayed, leading to speedier completion. This automated approach reduces user frustration and leads to increased productivity [Schach and Wood, 1986].

Many benefits can accrue when human factors are taken into account during the design of an HCI, including reduced learning times and lower error rates. Although help facilities must always be provided, they are utilized less with a carefully designed HCI. This, too, increases productivity. Uniformity of HCI appearance across a product or group of products can result in users intuitively knowing how to use a screen that they have never seen before because it is similar to other screens with which they are familiar. Designers of Macintosh software have taken this principle into account; this is one of the many reasons that software for the Macintosh is generally so user-friendly.

It has been suggested that simple common sense is all that is needed to design a user-friendly HCI. Whether or not this charge is true, it is essential that a rapid prototype of the HCI of every product be constructed. Intended users of the product can experiment with the rapid prototype of the HCI and inform the designers whether the target product indeed is user-friendly, that is, whether the designers have taken the necessary human factors into account.

In Section 10.15, reuse is discussed within the context of rapid prototyping.

## 10.15    Reusing the Rapid Prototype

After the rapid prototype has been built, it is discarded early in the software process. An alternate, but generally unwise, way of proceeding is to develop and refine the rapid prototype until it becomes the product. In theory, this approach should lead to fast software development; after all, instead of throwing away the code constituting the rapid prototype, along with the knowledge built into it, the rapid prototype is converted into the final product. However, in practice, the process is very similar to the code-and-fix approach of Figure 2.8. So, as with the code-and-fix model, the first problem with this form of the rapid prototyping model follows from the fact that, in the course of refining the rapid prototype, changes have to be made to a working product. This is an expensive way to proceed, as shown in Figure 1.6. A second problem is that a primary objective when constructing a rapid prototype is speed of building. A rapid prototype is (correctly) hurriedly put together, rather than carefully specified, designed, and implemented. In the absence of specification and design documents, the resulting code is difficult and expensive to maintain. It might seem wasteful to construct a rapid prototype and then throw it away and design the product from scratch, but it is far cheaper in both the short term and the long term to do this rather than try to convert a rapid prototype into production quality software [Brooks, 1975].

Another reason for discarding the rapid prototype is the issue of performance, particularly of real-time systems. To ensure that time constraints are met, it is necessary to design the product carefully. In contrast, a rapid prototype is constructed to display key functionality to the client; performance issues are not handled. As a result, if an attempt is made to refine a rapid prototype into a delivered product, it is unlikely that response times and other timing constraints will be met.

One way of ensuring that the rapid prototype is thrown away and the product is properly designed and implemented is to build the rapid prototype in a different language from that of the product. For example, the client may specify that the product must be written in Java. If the rapid prototype is implemented in HTML, for example, it must be discarded. First, the rapid prototype is implemented in HTML and refined until the client is satisfied that it does everything, or almost everything, the target product is to do. Next, the product is designed, relying on the knowledge and skills acquired in constructing the rapid prototype. Finally, the design is implemented in Java and the tested product handed over to the client in the usual way.

Nevertheless, there is one instance when it is permissible to refine a rapid prototype or, more specifically, portions of the rapid prototype. When portions of the rapid prototype are computer generated, those portions may be used in the final product. For example, user interfaces are often a key aspect of a rapid prototype. When CASE tools such as screen generators and report generators (Section 5.5) have been utilized to generate the user interfaces, those portions of the rapid prototype may indeed be used as part of production-quality software.

The desire not to "waste" the rapid prototype has resulted in a modified version of the rapid prototyping model being adopted by some organizations. Here, management decides *before* the rapid prototype is built that portions may be utilized in the final product, provided those portions pass the same quality assurance tests as other software components. Therefore, after the rapid prototype is complete, those sections the developers wish to continue to use must pass design and code inspections. This approach goes beyond rapid prototyping. For example, components that are of sufficiently high quality to pass design and code inspections are not usually found in a rapid prototype. Furthermore, design documents are not part of classic rapid prototyping. Nevertheless, this hybrid approach is attractive to some organizations hoping to recover some of the time and money invested in the rapid prototype. However, to ensure that the quality of the code is sufficiently high, the rapid prototype has to be built somewhat more slowly than is customary for a "rapid" prototype.

## 10.16 CASE Tools for the Requirements Workflow

The many UML diagrams in this chapter reflect the importance of having a graphical tool to assist with the requirements workflow. That is, what is needed is a drawing tool that enables the user to draw the relevant UML diagrams with ease. Such a tool has two major strengths. First, while iterating it is generally far easier to change a diagram stored in such a tool than to redraw the diagram by hand. Second, when a CASE tool of this kind is used, the details of the product are stored in the CASE tool itself. Therefore, the documentation is always available and up to date.

One weakness of such CASE tools is that they are not always user-friendly. A powerful graphical workbench or environment has so much functionality that it generally has a steep learning curve, and even experienced users sometimes have difficulty remembering how to achieve a particular outcome. A second weakness is that it is almost impossible to program a computer to draw UML diagrams that are as aesthetically pleasing as diagrams drawn by hand by humans. One alternative is to spend a considerable amount of time "tweaking" a diagram created by a tool. However, this approach is sometimes as slow as drawing the diagrams by hand. Worse, the constraints of many graphical CASE tools are such that, no matter how much time and effort is put into a diagram, it can never look as polished as a hand-drawn diagram. A third problem is that many CASE tools are expensive. It is not unusual to have to pay $5000 or more per user for a comprehensive CASE tool. On the other hand, a number of open-source CASE tools of this type can be downloaded at no cost. Overall, the two strengths of CASE tools given in the first paragraph of this section outweigh these weaknesses.

Many of the classical graphical CASE workbenches and environments, such as System Architect and Software through Pictures, have been extended to support UML diagrams. In addition, there are object-oriented CASE workbenches and environments, such as IBM Rational Rose and Together. There are also open-source CASE tools of this type, including ArgoUML.

## 10.17  Metrics for the Requirements Workflow

A key feature of the requirements workflow is how rapidly the requirements team determines the client's real needs. So, a useful metric during this workflow is a measure of requirements volatility. Keeping a record of how frequently the requirements change during the requirements workflow gives management a way of determining the rate at which the requirements team converges on the actual requirements of the product. This metric has the further advantage that it can be applied to any requirements elicitation technique, such as interviewing or forms analysis.

Another measure of how well the requirements team is doing its job is the number of requirements that change during the rest of the software development process. For each such change in requirements, it should be recorded whether that change was initiated by the client or the developers. If a large number of changes in requirements are initiated by the developers during the analysis, design, and subsequent workflows, then it is clear that the process used by the team to carry out the requirements workflow should be thoroughly reviewed. Conversely, if the client makes repeated changes to the requirements during subsequent workflows, then this metric can be used to warn the client that the moving-target problem can adversely affect the project, and future changes should be held to a minimum.

## 10.18  Challenges of the Requirements Workflow

Like every other workflow of the software development process, potential problems and pitfalls are associated with the requirements workflow. First, it is essential to have the wholehearted cooperation of the potential users of the target product from the beginning of the process. Individuals often feel threatened by computerization, fearing that the computer will take their jobs. There is some truth to that fear. Over the past 30 years or so, the impact of computerization has been to reduce the need for unskilled workers but also to generate jobs for skilled workers. Overall, the number of well-paying employment opportunities created as a direct consequence of computerization has far exceeded the number of relatively unskilled jobs made redundant, as evidenced by both decreased unemployment rates and increased average compensation. But the unparalleled economic growth of so many countries worldwide as a direct or indirect consequence of the so-called Computer Age in no way can compensate for the negative impact on those individuals who lose their jobs as a result of computerization.

It is essential that every member of the requirements team be aware at all times that the members of the client organization with whom they interact in all probability are deeply concerned about the potential impact of the target software product on their jobs. In the worst case, employees may deliberately give misleading or wrong information to try to ensure that the product does not meet the client's needs and, hence, protect those employees' jobs. But, even with no sabotage of this kind, some members of the client organization may be less than helpful simply because they have a vague feeling of being threatened by computerization.

Another challenge of the requirements workflow is the ability to **negotiate.** For example, it is often essential to scale down what the client wants. Not surprisingly, almost every client would love to have a software product that can do everything that might conceivably be needed. Such a product would take an unacceptably long time to build and cost far more than the client considers reasonable. Therefore, it often is necessary to persuade the client to accept less (sometimes far less) than he or she wants. Computing the costs and benefits (see Section 5.2) of each requirement in dispute can help in this regard.

Another example of the negotiating skill needed is the ability to arrive at a compromise among managers regarding the functionality of the target product. For example, a cunning manager may attempt to extend his or her power by including a requirement that can be implemented only by incorporating into his or her areas of responsibility certain business functions currently the responsibility of another manager. Not surprisingly, the other manager will object strongly on discovering what is going on. The requirements team must sit down with both managers and resolve the issue.

A third challenge of the requirements workflow is that, in many organizations, the individuals who possess information the requirements team needs to elicit, simply lack the time to meet for in-depth discussions. When this happens, the team must inform the client, who then must decide which is more important, the individuals' current job responsibilities or the software product to be constructed. And, if the client fails to insist that the software product comes first, the developers may have no alternative but to withdraw from a project all but doomed to failure.

Finally, flexibility and objectivity are essential for requirements elicitation. It is vital that the members of the requirements team approach each interview with no preconceived ideas. In particular, an interviewer must never make assumptions about the requirements as a result of earlier interviews and then conduct subsequent interviews within the framework of those assumptions. Instead, an interviewer must consciously suppress any information gleaned at previous interviews and conduct each interview in an impartial way. Making premature assumptions regarding the requirements is dangerous; making any assumptions during the requirements workflow regarding the software product to be built can be disastrous.

The chapter concludes with How to Perform Box 10.1, which summarizes the steps of the requirements workflow.

---

## How to Perform the Requirements Workflow    Box 10.1

- **Iterate**

  Obtain an understanding of the domain.

  Draw up the business model.

  Draw up the requirements.

- **Until** the requirements are satisfactory.

**Chapter Review**

The chapter begins with a description of the importance of determining the client's needs (Section 10.1), followed by an overview of the requirements workflow (Section 10.2). In Section 10.3, the need to understand the domain is described. How to draw up the business model is described in Section 10.4. Interviewing and other techniques of requirements extraction are discussed in Sections 10.4.1 and 10.4.2. The business model is modeled using use cases, which are introduced in 10.4.3. Drawing up the initial requirements is described in Section 10.5. The requirements workflow of the MSG Foundation case study is presented in the next six sections.

Obtaining an initial understanding of the domain is described in Section 10.6; the initial business model and the initial requirements are presented in Sections 10.7 and 10.8, respectively. The requirements are then refined in Sections 10.9 and 10.10. Finally, the test workflow for the MSG Foundation case study is described (Section 10.11). In Section 10.12, the classical requirements phase is contrasted with the requirements workflow of the Unified Process. Rapid prototyping is then discussed in greater detail in Sections 10.13 and 10.14; in the latter section, the importance of constructing a rapid prototype for the user interface is stressed. In Section 10.15, a warning is given not to reuse a rapid prototype. CASE tools for the requirements workflow (Section 10.16) and metrics for the requirements workflow (Section 10.17) are then discussed. The chapter concludes with a description of challenges of the requirements phase (Section 10.18).

**For Further Reading**

[Jackson, 1995] is an excellent introduction to requirements analysis. [Thayer and Dorfman, 1999] is a collection of papers on requirements analysis. Berry [2004] suggests that the ripple effect of the inevitable changes to the requirements is the reason why there cannot be a software engineering silver bullet (Just in Case You Wanted to Know Box 3.4). The use of cost–benefit analysis in setting priorities among requirements is described in [Karlsson and Ryan, 1997]. Nonfunctional requirements are discussed in [Cysneiros and do Prado Leite, 2004]. A variety of articles on requirements appear in the January/February 2005 issue of *IEEE Software*.

The requirements workflow of the Unified Process is described in detail in Chapters 6 and 7 of [Jacobson, Booch, and Rumbaugh, 1999]. Misuse cases (use cases that model interactions that the software should prevent) are described in [I. Alexander, 2003].

For an introduction to rapid prototyping, suggested books include [Connell and Shafer, 1989] and [Gane, 1989]. The rapid prototyping model is one version of rapid application development (RAD); a variety of articles on RAD are in the September 1995 issue of *IEEE Software*. The importance of prototyping is described in [Schrage, 2004].

A classic work on user interface design is [Shneiderman, 2003]. Methods for achieving good user interfaces are described in [Holzinger, 2005]. Articles on user interfaces can be found in the March 2002 issue of *IEEE Computer* and the March 2003 issue of *Communications of the ACM*. The proceedings of the Annual Conference on Human Factors in Computer Systems (sponsored by ACM SIGCHI) are a valuable source of information on wide-ranging aspects of human factors.

**Key Terms**

actor *290*
application domain *286*
business model *288*
closing costs *294*
direct observation *289*

domain *286*
form *289*
functional
   requirement *292*
glossary *287*

graphical user interface
  (GUI) *322*
human factors *322*
«include» relationship *307*
model *290*

negotiation *326*
nonfunctional
   requirement *292*
platform constraint *292*
point-and-click *322*
questionnaire *289*
rapid prototype *320*

reliability *292*
requirements analysis *287*
requirements capture *287*
requirements elicitation *287*
requirements workflow *286*
response time *292*
structured interview *288*

unstructured
   interview *288*
use case *290*
use-case description *295*
use-case diagram *297*
user-friendly *322*
videotape camera *289*

**Case Study
Key Terms**

capital *292*
closing costs *294*
deposit *292*

escrow account *293*
interest *293*
mortgage *292*

P & I *293*
points *294*
principal *292*

**Problems**

10.1  Give a nonfunctional requirement that can be handled without having detailed knowledge about the target software product.

10.2  Now, give a nonfunctional requirement that can be handled only after the requirements workflow has been completed.

10.3  Distinguish between a *use case* and a *use-case diagram.*

10.4  Distinguish between a *user* and an *actor.*

10.5  Draw a flowchart representing the requirements workflow.

10.6  Why does the same couple appear as two different actors (**Applicants** and **Borrowers**) in the use-case diagram of Figure 10.12?

10.7  Noting that only MSG Foundation staff members can use the software product, why do **Applicants** and **Borrowers** appear as actors in the use-case diagram of Figure 10.12?

10.8  Use a spreadsheet to show that, at the end of 30 years, monthly installments of $629.30 will pay off a loan for $90,000 with interest compounded monthly at an annual rate of 7.5 percent.

10.9  Suppose that the MSG Foundation decides that it wants its software product to include the mortgage application process. Give the description of the `Apply for an MSG Mortgage` use case. Give as many details as you can.

10.10  Sections 10.9 and 10.10 describe the restructuring of the use cases of the MSG Foundation. How would this restructuring change if, as in Problem 10.9, the `Apply for an MSG Mortgage` use case had been included in the requirements model?

10.11  You have just joined Angel & Iguassu Software as a software manager. Angel & Iguassu has been developing accounting software for small businesses for many years using the waterfall model, usually with some success. On the basis of your experience, you think that the Unified Process is a far superior way of developing software. Write a report addressed to the vice-president for software development explaining why you believe the organization should switch to the Unified Process. Remember that vice-presidents do not like reports that are more than half a page in length.

10.12  You are the vice-president for software development of Angel & Iguassu. Reply to the report of Problem 10.11.

10.13  What is the result if a rapid prototype is not constructed rapidly?

10.14  (Analysis and Design Project) Perform the requirements workflow for the automated library circulation system of Problem 8.7.

10.15 (Analysis and Design Project) Perform the requirements workflow for the product for determining whether a bank statement is correct of Problem 8.8.

10.16 (Analysis and Design Project) Perform the requirements workflow for the automated teller machine (ATM) of Problem 8.9.

10.17 (Term Project) Perform the requirements workflow for the Osric's Office Appliances and Decor project in Appendix A.

10.18 (Case Study) The trustees of the MSG Foundation have decided to expand their activities by providing scholarships for higher education to children of current borrowers with a sufficiently high grade-point average. Draw the use case `Apply for an MSG Scholarship`. Give the description of the use case, providing as much detail as you can.

10.19 (Case Study) A report of all scholarships awarded during the past year (Problem 10.18) has to be generated. Modify Figures 10.35 and 10.36 appropriately to incorporate this additional report.

10.20 (Case Study) Using the information in Sections 10.6 through 10.11, construct a rapid prototype for the MSG Foundation case study. Use the software and hardware specified by your instructor.

10.21 (Readings in Software Engineering) Your instructor will distribute copies of [Cysneiros and do Prado Leite, 2004]. In what ways did reading this article change your views on the importance of nonfunctional requirements?

## References

[I. Alexander, 2003] I. ALEXANDER, "Misuse Cases: Use Cases with Hostile Intent," *IEEE Software* **20** (January/February 2003), pp. 58–66.

[Berry, 2004] D. M. BERRY, "The Inevitable Pain of Software Development: Why There Is No Silver Bullet," in: *Radical Innovations of Software and Systems Engineering in the Future,* Lecture Notes in Computer Science, Vol. 2941, Springer-Verlag, Berlin, 2004, pp. 50–74.

[Brooks, 1975] F. P. BROOKS, JR., *The Mythical Man-Month: Essays on Software Engineering,* Addison-Wesley, Reading, MA, 1975; Twentieth Anniversary Edition, Addison-Wesley, Reading, MA, 1995.

[Browne, 1994] D. BROWNE, STUDIO: *STructured User-interface Design for Interaction Optimization,* Prentice Hall, Englewood Cliffs, NJ, 1994.

[Connell and Shafer, 1989] J. L. CONNELL AND L. SHAFER, *Structured Rapid Prototyping: An Evolutionary Approach to Software Development,* Yourdon Press, Englewood Cliffs, NJ, 1989.

[Cysneiros and do Prado Leite, 2004] L. M. CYSNEIROS AND J. C. S. DO PRADO LEITE, "Nonfunctional Requirements: From Elicitation to Conceptual Models," *IEEE Transactions on Software Engineering* **30** (May 2004), pp. 328–50.

[Dix, Finlay, Abowd, and Beale, 1993] A. DIX, J. FINLAY, G. ABOWD, AND R. BEALE, *Human-Computer Interaction,* Prentice Hall, Englewood Cliffs, NJ, 1993.

[Gane, 1989] C. GANE, *Rapid System Development: Using Structured Techniques and Relational Technology,* Prentice Hall, Englewood Cliffs, NJ, 1989.

[Holzinger, 2005] A. HOLZINGER, "Usability Engineering Methods for Software Developers," *Communications of the ACM* **48** (January 2005), pp. 71–74.

[Jackson, 1995] M. JACKSON, *Software Requirements and Specifications: A Lexicon of Practice, Principles and Prejudices,* Addison-Wesley Longman, Reading, MA, 1995.

[Jacobson, Booch, and Rumbaugh, 1999] I. JACOBSON, G. BOOCH, AND J. RUMBAUGH, The Unified Software Development Process, Addison-Wesley, Reading, MA, 1999.

[Karlsson and Ryan, 1997] J. KARLSSON AND K. RYAN, "A Cost-Value Approach for Prioritizing Requirements," *IEEE Software* **14** (September/October 1997), pp. 67–74.

[Preece, 1994] J. PREECE, *Human-Computer Interaction,* Addison-Wesley, Reading, MA, 1994.

[Schach and Wood, 1986] S. R. SCHACH AND P. T. WOOD, "An Almost Path-Free Very High-Level Interactive Data Manipulation Language for a Microcomputer-Based Database System," *Software—Practice and Experience* **16** (March 1986), pp. 243–68.

[Schrage, 2004] M. SCHRAGE, "Never Go to a Client Meeting without a Prototype," *IEEE Software* **21** (2004), pp. 42–45.

[Shneiderman, 2003] B. SHNEIDERMAN, *Designing the User Interface: Strategies for Effective Human-Computer Interaction,* 4th ed., Addison-Wesley Longman, Reading, MA, 2003.

[Thayer and Dorfman, 1999] R. H. THAYER AND M. DORFMAN, *Software Requirements Engineering,* revised 2nd ed., IEEE Computer Society Press, Los Alamitos, CA, 1999.

# Chapter

# 11

# Classical Analysis

**Learning Objectives**

After studying this chapter, you should be able to

- Perform structured systems analysis.
- Draw up formal specifications using finite state machines, Petri nets, and Z.
- Compare and contrast methods for classical analysis.

A specification document must satisfy two mutually contradictory requirements. On the one hand, this document must be clear and intelligible to the client, who probably is not a computer specialist. After all, the client is paying for the product, and unless the client believes that he or she really understands what the new product will be like, there is a good chance that the client will either decide not to authorize the development of the product or will ask some other software organization to build it.

On the other hand, the specification document must be complete and detailed, because this is virtually the sole source of information available for drawing up the design. Even if the client agrees that all needs have been determined accurately during the requirements, if the specification document contains faults such as omissions, contradictions, or ambiguities, the inevitable result will be faults in the design that are carried over into the implementation. What is needed, therefore, are techniques for representing the target product in a format sufficiently nontechnical to be intelligible to the client yet precise enough to result in a fault-free product being delivered to the client at the end of the development cycle. These analysis (specification) techniques are the subject of this chapter and Chapter 12. The emphasis in this chapter is on classical (structured) analysis techniques, whereas Chapter 12 is devoted to object-oriented analysis.

## 11.1 The Specification Document

The **specification document** is a contract between client and developer. It specifies precisely what the product must do and the **constraints** on the product. Virtually every specification document incorporates constraints that the product has to satisfy. Almost always,

**331**

a deadline is specified for delivering the product. Another common stipulation is, "The product shall be installed in such a way that it can run in parallel with the existing product," until the client is satisfied that the new product indeed satisfies every aspect of the specification document. Other constraints might include portability: The product should be constructed to run on other hardware under the same operating system or perhaps run under a variety of different operating systems. Reliability may be another constraint. If the product has to monitor patients in an intensive care unit, then it is of paramount importance that it be fully operational 24 hours a day. Rapid response time may be a requirement; a typical constraint in this category might be "95 percent of all queries of Type 4 shall be answered within 0.25 seconds." Many response-time constraints have to be expressed in probabilistic terms because the response time depends on the current load on the computer. In contrast, so-called hard real-time constraints are expressed in absolute terms. For instance, it is useless to develop software that informs a warplane pilot of an incoming missile within 0.25 seconds only 95 percent of the time—the product must meet the constraint 100 percent of the time.

A vital component of the specification document is the set of acceptance criteria. It is important from the viewpoint of both the client and the developers to spell out a series of tests that can be used to prove to the client that the product indeed satisfies its specifications and that the developer's job is done. Some of the acceptance criteria may be restatements of the constraints, whereas others address different issues. For example, the client might supply the developer with a description of the data that the product will handle. An appropriate acceptance criterion then would be that the product correctly processes data of this type and filters out nonconforming (that is, erroneous) data. Once the development team fully understands the problem, possible solution strategies can be suggested. A **solution strategy** is a general approach to building the product. For example, one possible solution strategy for a product would be to use an online database; another would be to use conventional flat files and extract the required information using overnight batch runs. When determining solution strategies, it often is a good idea to come up with strategies without worrying about the constraints in the specification document. Then, the various solution strategies can be evaluated in the light of the constraints and necessary modifications can be made. There are a number of ways of determining whether a specific solution strategy will satisfy the client's constraints. An obvious one is prototyping, which can be a good technique for resolving issues relating to user interfaces and timing constraints, as previously discussed in Chapter 10. Other techniques for determining whether constraints will be satisfied include simulation [Banks, Carson, Nelson, and Nichol, 2000] and analytic network modeling [Kleinrock and Gail, 1996].

During this process, a number of solution strategies are put forward and then discarded. It is important that a written record be kept of all discarded strategies and the reasons they were rejected. This will assist the development team if it ever is called on to justify the chosen strategy. But, more important, there is an ever-present danger during postdelivery maintenance that the process of enhancement will be accompanied by an attempt to come up with a new and unwise solution strategy. Having a record of why certain strategies were rejected during development can be extremely helpful during postdelivery maintenance.

By this point in the life cycle, the development team will have determined one or more possible solution strategies that satisfy the constraints. A two-stage decision now has to be made. First, should the client be advised to computerize? If so, which of the viable solution strategies should be adopted? The answer to the first question can best be decided on the basis of cost–benefit analysis (Section 5.2). Second, if the client decides to proceed with the project, then the client must inform the development team as to the optimization criterion to be used, such as minimizing the total cost to the client or maximizing the return on investment. The developers then advise the client as to which of the viable solution strategies best satisfies the optimization criterion.

## 11.2 Informal Specifications

In many development projects, the specification document consists of page after page of English, or some other **natural language** such as French or Xhosa. A typical paragraph of such an **informal specification** reads:

> BV.4.2.5. If the sales for the current month are below the target sales, then a report is to be printed, unless the difference between target sales and actual sales is less than half of the difference between target sales and actual sales in the previous month or if the difference between target sales and actual sales for the current month is under 5 percent.

The background leading up to that paragraph is as follows. The management of a retail chain sets a target sales figure for each shop for each month; and if a shop does not meet this target, a report is to be printed. Consider the following scenario: Suppose that the January sales target for one particular shop is $100,000, but actual sales are only $64,000, that is, 36 percent below target. In this case, a report must be printed. Now suppose further that the February target figure is $120,000 and that actual sales are only $100,000, 16.7 percent below target. Although sales are below the target figure, the percentage difference for February, 16.7 percent, is less than half of the previous month's percentage difference, 36 percent; management believes that an improvement has been made, and no report is to be printed. Next suppose that, in March, the target is again $100,000 but the shop makes $98,000, only 2 percent below target. Because the percentage difference is small, less than 5 percent, no report should be printed.

Careful rereading of the preceding specification paragraph shows some divergence from what the retail chain's management actually requested. Paragraph BV.4.2.5 speaks of the "difference between target sales and actual sales"; percentage difference is not mentioned. The difference in January was $36,000 and in February it was $20,000. The percentage difference, which is what management wanted, dropped from 36 percent in January to 16.7 percent in February, less than half of the January percentage difference. However, the actual difference dropped from $36,000 to $20,000, which is greater than half of $36,000. So if the development team had faithfully implemented the specification document, the report would have been printed, which is not what management wanted. Then the last clause speaks of a "difference . . . [of] 5 percent." What is meant, of course, is a percentage difference of 5 percent, only the word percentage does not occur anywhere in the paragraph.

Therefore, the specification document contains a number of faults. First, the wishes of the client have been ignored. Second, there is ambiguity—should the last clause read "percentage difference . . . [of] 5 percent," or "difference . . . [of] $5000," or something else entirely? In addition, the style is poor. What the paragraph says is, "If something happens, print a report. However, if something else happens, don't print it. And if a third thing happens, don't print it either." It would have been much clearer if the specifications had simply stated when the report is to be printed. All in all, paragraph BV.4.2.5 is not a very good example of how to write a specification document.

Paragraph BV.4.2.5 is fictitious but, unfortunately, typical of too many specification documents. You may think that the example is unfair and this sort of problem cannot arise if specifications are written with care by professional specification writers. To refute this charge, the mini case study of Chapter 6 resumes here.

*Mini Case Study*

 **11.2.1**   *Correctness Proof Mini Case Study Redux*

Recall from Section 6.5.2 that in 1969 Naur wrote a paper on correctness proving [Naur, 1969]. He illustrated his technique by means of a text-processing problem. Using his technique, Naur constructed an ALGOL 60 procedure to solve the problem and informally proved the correctness of his procedure. A reviewer of Naur's paper [Leavenworth, 1970] pointed out one fault in the procedure. London [1971] then detected three additional faults in Naur's procedure, presented a corrected version of the procedure, and proved its correctness formally. Goodenough and Gerhart [1975] found three further faults that London had not detected. Of the total of seven faults collectively detected by the reviewer, London, and Goodenough and Gerhart, two can be considered analysis faults. For example, Naur's specifications do not state what happens if the input includes two successive adjacent breaks (blank or newline characters). For this reason, Goodenough and Gerhart produced a new set of specifications. Their specifications were about four times longer than Naur's, which are given in Section 6.5.2.

In 1985, Meyer wrote an article on formal specification techniques [Meyer, 1985]. The main thrust of his article is that a specification document written in a natural language such as English tends to have contradictions, ambiguities, and omissions. He recommended using mathematical terminology to express specifications formally. Meyer detected some 12 faults in Goodenough and Gerhart's specifications and developed a set of mathematical specifications to correct all the problems. Meyer then paraphrased his mathematical specifications and constructed English specifications. In my opinion, Meyer's English specifications contain a fault. Meyer points out in his paper that, if the maximum number of characters per line is, say, 10, and the input is, for instance, WHO WHAT WHEN, then, in terms of both Naur's and Goodenough and Gerhart's specifications, there are two equally valid outputs: WHO WHAT on the first line and WHEN on the second or WHO on the first line and WHAT WHEN on the second. In fact, Meyer's paraphrased English specifications also contain this ambiguity.

The key point is that Goodenough and Gerhart's specifications were constructed with the greatest of care. After all, they were constructed to correct Naur's specifications. Furthermore, Goodenough and Gerhart's paper went through two versions, the first of which was published in the proceedings of a refereed conference and the second in a refereed journal [Goodenough and Gerhart, 1975]. Finally, both Goodenough and Gerhart are experts in software engineering in general and specifications in particular. Therefore, if two experts with as much time as they needed carefully produced specifications in which Meyer detected 12 faults, what chance does an ordinary computer professional working under time pressure have of producing a fault-free specification document? Worse still, the text-processing problem can be coded in 25 or 30 lines, whereas real-world products can consist of hundreds of thousands or even millions of lines of source code.

Clearly, natural language is not a good way of specifying a product. In this chapter, better alternatives are described. The order in which the analysis techniques are presented is from the informal to the more formal.

## 11.3   Structured Systems Analysis

The use of graphics to specify software was an important technique of the 1970s. Three techniques using graphics became particularly popular: those of DeMarco [1978], Gane and Sarsen [1979], and Yourdon and Constantine [1979]. All three techniques are equally good and essentially equivalent. Gane and Sarsen's approach is presented here because their notation, currently, probably is the most widely used in the industry.

As an aid to understanding the technique, consider the following mini case study.

*Mini Case Study*

### 11.3.1   *Sally's Software Shop Mini Case Study*

Sally's Software Shop buys software from various suppliers and sells it to the public. Sally stocks popular software packages and orders others as required. Sally extends credit to institutions, corporations, and some individuals. Sally's Software Shop is doing well, with a monthly turnover of 300 packages at an average retail cost of $250 each. Despite her business success, Sally has been advised to computerize. Should she?

The question, as stated, is inadequate. It should read: Which, if any, business functions—accounts payable, accounts receivable, and inventory—should be computerized? Even this is not enough—is the system to be batch or online? Is there to be an in-house computer or is outsourcing to be used? But, even if the question is refined further, it still misses the fundamental issue: What is Sally's objective in computerizing her business?

Only when Sally's objectives are known can the analysis continue. For example, if she wishes to computerize simply because she sells software, then she needs an in-house system with a variety of sound and light effects that ostentatiously shows off the possibilities of a computer. On the other hand, if she uses her business to launder "hot" money, then she needs a product that keeps four or five different sets of books and leaves no audit trail.

This example assumes that Sally wishes to computerize "to make more money." This does not help very much, but it is clear that cost–benefit analysis can determine whether to computerize each (or any) of the three sections of her business. The main danger of many standard approaches is that one is tempted to come up with the

**FIGURE 11.1**
The symbols of Gane and Sarsen's structured systems analysis.

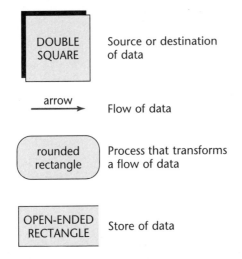

DOUBLE SQUARE — Source or destination of data

arrow → Flow of data

rounded rectangle — Process that transforms a flow of data

OPEN-ENDED RECTANGLE — Store of data

solution first, for example, a Lime III computer with a 50-gigabyte hard disk and a laser printer, and find out what the problem is later. In contrast, Gane and Sarsen [1979] use **structured systems analysis**, a nine-step technique, to analyze the client's needs. An important point is that stepwise refinement is used in many of those nine steps; this will be indicated as the technique is demonstrated.

Having determined Sally's requirements, the first step in the structured systems analysis is to determine the **logical data flow**, as opposed to the physical data flow (that is, *what* happens, as opposed to *how* it happens). This is done by drawing a **data flow diagram** (DFD). The DFD uses the four basic symbols shown in Figure 11.1. (Gane and Sarsen's notation is similar, but not identical, to that of DeMarco [1978] and Yourdon and Constantine [1979].)

*Step 1. Draw the DFD*
The DFD for any nontrivial product is likely to be large. The DFD is a pictorial representation of all aspects of the logical data flow and, as such, is guaranteed to contain considerably more than $7 \pm 2$ elements. For this reason, the DFD must be developed by stepwise refinement (Section 5.1).

A data flow diagram is constructed by identifying the **data flows** within the requirements document or rapid prototype. Each flow of data starts and ends either at a **source or destination of data** (represented by a double-square box) or at a **store of data** (represented by an open-ended rectangle). The data are transformed by one or more **processes** (represented by a rounded rectangle). At each successive refinement, either a new flow of data is added to the DFD or an existing flow of data is refined by the addition of further details.

Returning to the example, the first refinement is shown in Figure 11.2. This diagram of logical data flow can have many interpretations. Two possible implementations follow:

In Implementation 1, data store PACKAGE_DATA consists of some 900 shrink-wrapped boxes containing diskettes or CDs displayed on shelves, as well as a number

**FIGURE 11.2**

The data flow diagram for Sally's Software Shop: first refinement.

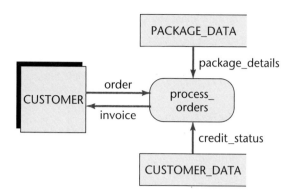

of catalogs in a desk drawer. Data store CUSTOMER_DATA is a collection of 5 × 7" cards held together by a rubber band, plus a list of customers whose payments are overdue. Process (action) process_orders is Sally looking for the appropriate package on the shelves, if necessary looking it up in a catalog, and then finding the correct 5 × 7 card and checking that the customer's name is not on the list of defaulters. This implementation is totally manual and corresponds to the way Sally currently conducts her business.

In Implementation 2, data stores PACKAGE_DATA and CUSTOMER_DATA are computer files and process_orders is Sally entering the customer's name and the name of the package at a terminal. This implementation corresponds to a fully computerized solution with all information available online.

The DFD of Figure 11.2 represents not only the preceding two implementations but also an infinity of other possibilities. The key point is that the DFD represents a flow of information—the actual package that Sally's customer wants is not important to the flow.

The DFD is now refined stepwise. The second refinement is depicted in Figure 11.3. The logical flow of data representing what happens when the customer requests a package Sally does not have on hand is added to the DFD. Specifically, details of that package are placed in the data store PENDING_ORDERS, which might be a computer file, but at this stage equally well could be a manila folder. Data store PENDING_ORDERS is scanned daily, by the computer or Sally; and if there are sufficient orders for one supplier, then a batched order is placed. Also, if an order has been waiting for 5 working days, it is ordered, regardless of how many packages are waiting to be ordered from the relevant supplier. This DFD does not show the logical flow of data when the software package arrives from the supplier nor does it show financial functions such as accounts payable and accounts receivable. These will be added in the third refinement.

Only a portion of the third refinement is shown in Figure 11.4, because the DFD is starting to become large. In this refinement, the logical flow of data relating to accounts receivable is added to the DFD.

The rest of the DFD relates to accounts payable and to the software suppliers. The final DFD will be larger still, stretching over perhaps six pages. But it will be understood easily by Sally, who will sign it off, confirming that it is an accurate

**FIGURE 11.3**   The data flow diagram for Sally's Software Shop: second refinement.

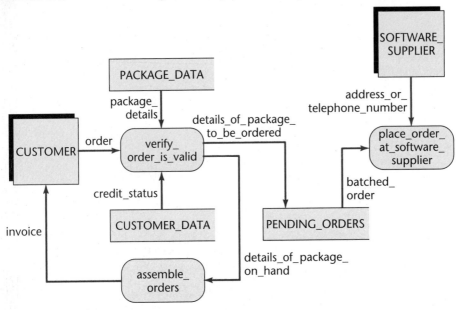

representation of the logical flow of data in her business. For a larger product, the DFD is larger. After a certain point it becomes impractical to have just one DFD, and a hierarchy of DFDs is needed. A single box at one level is expanded into a complete DFD at a lower level.

In this section, we outline the construction of the DFD for Sally's Software Shop. A more detailed example of the construction of a data flow diagram is given in Section 11.4.

### Step 2. Decide What Sections to Computerize and How (Batch or Online)

The choice of what to automate often depends on how much the client is prepared to spend. Obviously, it would be nice to automate the entire operation, but the cost of this may be prohibitive. To determine which sections to automate, cost–benefit analysis is applied to the various possible strategies for computerizing each section. For example, for each section of the DFD, a decision has to be made as to whether that group of operations should be performed in batch or online. With large volumes to process and tight controls required, batch processing is often the answer; but with small volumes and an in-house computer, online processing appears to be better. Returning to the example, one alternative is to automate accounts payable in batch and validate orders online. A second alternative is to automate everything, with the editing of the software supplier consignment notes against orders being done online or batch, and the rest of the operations done online. A key point is that the DFD corresponds to all the preceding possibilities. This is consistent with not making a commitment as to how to solve the problem during the classical analysis phase but rather waiting until the design phase.

**FIGURE 11.4**   The data flow diagram for Sally's Software Shop: part of third refinement.

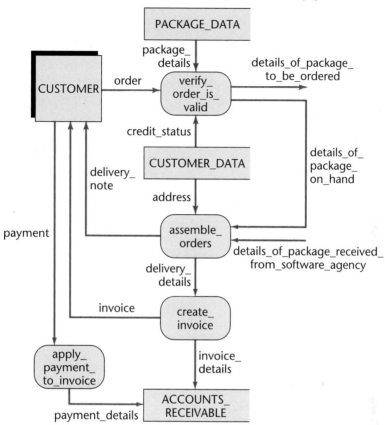

The next three stages of Gane and Sarsen's technique are the stepwise refinement of the flows of data (arrows), processes (rounded rectangles), and data stores (open rectangles).

### Step 3. Determine the Details of the Data Flows

First, decide what data items must go into the various data flows. Then, refine each flow stepwise.

In the example, the data flow **order** can be refined as follows:

order:
  order identification
  customer_details
  package_details

Next, each of the preceding components of **order** is refined further. In the case of a larger product, a data dictionary (Section 5.5) keeps track of all the data elements. Figure 11.5 shows typical information about the data elements in the computerization of Sally's Software Shop that would be stored in a data dictionary.

**FIGURE 11.5** Typical data dictionary entries for Sally's Software Shop.

| Name of Data Element | Description | Narrative |
|---|---|---|
| order | Record comprising fields<br>    order_identification<br>    customer_details<br>        customer_name<br>        customer_address<br>        . . .<br>    • package_details<br>        package_name<br>        package_price<br>        . . . | The fields contain all details of an order. |
| order_identification | 12-digit integer | Unique number generated by procedure generate_order_number. The first 10 digits contain the order number itself, the last 2 digits are check digits. |
| verify_order_is_valid | Procedure:<br>    Input parameter:<br>        order<br>    Output parameter:<br>        number_of_errors | This procedure takes order as input and checks the validity of every field; for each error found, an appropriate message is displayed on the screen (the total number of errors found is returned in parameter number_of_errors). |

**FIGURE 11.6**

A decision tree depicting Sally's Software Shop educational discount policy.

Give educational discount

Educational institution
≤ 4 packages: 10%
> 4 packages: 15%
Other: 0%

### Step 4. Define the Logic of the Processes

Now that the data elements within the product have been determined, it is time to investigate what happens within each process. Suppose that the example has a process give_educational_discount. Sally must provide the software developers with details about the discount she gives to educational institutions, for example, 10 percent on up to four packages, 15 percent on five or more. To cope with the difficulties of natural language specification documents, this should be translated from English into a decision tree. Such a tree is shown in Figure 11.6.

A decision tree makes it easy to check that all possibilities have been taken into account, especially in more complex cases. An example is shown in Figure 11.7. From this figure it is immediately obvious that the cost to an alumnus of a seat behind the end zone has not been specified.

### Step 5. Define the Data Stores

At this stage it is necessary to define the exact contents of each store and its representation (format). Therefore, if the product is to be implemented in COBOL, this

**FIGURE 11.7**
A decision tree describing seating prices for college football games.

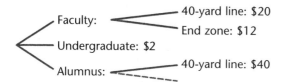

Determine football seat prices

Faculty:
— 40-yard line: $20
— End zone: $12

— Undergraduate: $2

Alumnus:
— 40-yard line: $40

**FIGURE 11.8**
The data immediate-access diagram for PACKAGE_DATA.

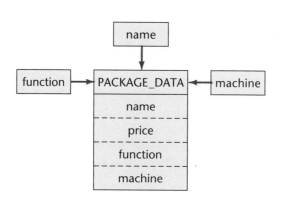

name

function → PACKAGE_DATA ← machine

name

price

function

machine

information must be provided down to the **pic** level; if Ada is to be used, the **digits** or **delta** must be specified. In addition, it is necessary to specify where immediate access is required.

The issue of immediate access depends on what queries are going to be put to the product. For example, suppose that, in the example, it is decided to validate orders online. A customer may order a package by name ("Do you have JBuilder in stock?"), by function ("What accounting packages do you have?"), or by machine ("Do you have anything new for the 786?"), but rarely by price ("What do you have for $149.50?"). Therefore, immediate access to PACKAGE DATA is required by name, function, and machine. This is depicted in the **data immediate-access diagram** (DIAD) of Figure 11.8.

### Step 6. Define the Physical Resources
Now that the developers know what is required online and the representation (format) of each element, a decision can be made regarding blocking factors. In addition, for each file, the following can be specified: file name, organization (sequential, indexed, etc.), storage medium, and records, down to the field level. If a database management system (DBMS) is to be used, then the relevant information for each table is specified here.

### Step 7. Determine the Input–Output Specifications
The input forms must be specified, at least with respect to components, if not detailed layout. Input screens must similarly be determined. The printed output also must be specified, where possible in detail, otherwise just estimated length.

### Step 8. Determine the Sizing

It is necessary to compute the numerical data that will be used in step 9 to determine the hardware requirements. This includes the volume of input (daily or hourly), the frequency of each printed report and its deadline, the size and number of records of each type that are to pass between the CPU and mass storage, and the size of each file.

### Step 9. Determine the Hardware Requirements

From the sizing information on the disk files determined in step 8, mass storage requirements can be computed. In addition, mass storage requirements for backup can be determined. From knowledge of input volumes, the needs in this area can be found. Because the number of lines and frequency of printed reports are known, output devices can be specified. If the client already has hardware, it can be determined whether this hardware is adequate or additional hardware has to be acquired. On the other hand, if the client lacks suitable hardware, a recommendation can be made as to what should be acquired and whether it should be purchased or leased. For smaller systems, advances in technology have made hardware decisions less critical; all the hardware needed for Sally's Software Store can be purchased for under $1000. However, for larger systems, the cost of hardware is nontrivial, and careful decisions need to be made.

Determining the hardware requirements is the final step of Gane and Sarsen's analysis technique. After approval by the client, the resulting specification document is handed to the design team, and the software process continues.

How to Perform Box 11.1 contains an overview of the nine steps of Gane and Sarsen's structured systems analysis.

Despite its many strengths, Gane and Sarsen's technique does not provide the answer to every question. For example, it cannot be used to determine response times. The number of input–output channels can be gauged roughly at best. Also, CPU size and timing cannot be estimated with any degree of accuracy. These are distinct drawbacks of Gane and Sarsen's technique and, to be fair, of virtually every other technique for either analysis or design. Nonetheless, at the end of the classical analysis phase, hardware decisions have to be made, whether or not accurate information is available. This situation is considerably better than what was done in the past; before methodical approaches to specifying were put forward, decisions regarding hardware were made right at the beginning of the software development process. Gane and Sarsen's technique has led to major improvements in the ways products are specified, and the fact that Gane and Sarsen and the authors of most competing techniques essentially ignore time as a variable should not detract from the advantages that these techniques have brought to the software industry.

---

## How to Perform Structured Systems Analysis    Box 11.1

- Draw the data flow diagram.
- Decide what sections to computerize and how (batch or online).
- Determine the details of the data flows.
- Define the logic of the processes.
- Define the data stores.
- Define the physical resources.
- Determine the input–output specifications.
- Perform the sizing.
- Determine the hardware requirements.

# Case Study

## 11.4   Structured Systems Analysis: The MSG Foundation Case Study

The data flow diagram of the structured systems analysis for the MSG Foundation case study (Section 10.6) is shown in Figure 11.9. As reflected in the DFD, the user can perform three different types of operations:

1. *Update investment data, mortgage data, or operating expenses data:* The USER enters an update_request. To update investment data, process perform_selected_update solicits the updated_investment_details from the USER and

**FIGURE 11.9**   The data flow diagram for MSG Foundation case study.

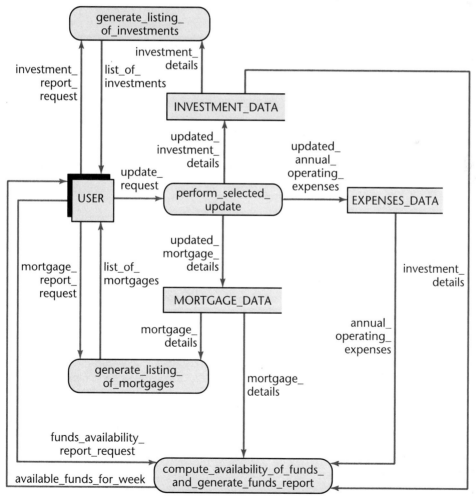

sends then to the INVESTMENT_DATA store of data. Updating mortgage data or expenses data is similar.

2. *Print a listing of investments or mortgages:* To print a list of investments, the USER enters an investment_report_request. Process generate_listing_of_investments then obtains investment data from store INVESTMENT_DATA, formats the report, and then prints the report. Printing a listing of mortgages is similar.

3. *Print a report showing available funds for mortgages for the week:* The USER enters a funds_availability_report_request. To determine how much money is available for mortgages for the current week, process compute_availability_ of_funds_and_generate_funds_report obtains:

  • investment_details from store INVESTMENT_DATA and computes the expected total annual return on investments.

  • mortgage_details from store MORTGAGE_DATA and computes the expected income for the week, expected mortgage payments for the week, and expected grants for the week.

  • annual_operating_expenses from store EXPENSES_DATA and computes the expected annual operating expenses.

  Process compute_availability_of_funds_and_generate_funds_report then uses these results to compute available_funds_for_week, formats the report, and then prints the report.

The remainder of the structured systems analysis appears in Appendix D. The organization and presentation of the material in Appendix D is such that the client can rapidly understand exactly what is going to be built.

# 11.5 Other Semiformal Techniques

Gane and Sarsen's technique clearly is more formal than writing a specification document in a natural language. At the same time, it is less formal than many of the techniques presented in the following discussion, such as Petri nets (Section 11.8) and Z (Section 11.9). Dart and her coworkers classify analysis and design techniques as informal, semiformal, or formal [Dart, Ellison, Feiler, and Habermann, 1987]. In terms of this classification, Gane and Sarsen's structured systems analysis is a **semiformal specification** technique, whereas the other two techniques mentioned in this paragraph are formal techniques.

Structured systems analysis is used widely; there is a good chance you may be employed by an organization that uses structured systems analysis or some variant of it. However, there are many other good semiformal techniques; see, for example, the proceedings of the various international workshops on software specification and design. Because of space limitations, all that will be given here is a brief description of a few well-known techniques.

**PSL/PSA** [Teichroew and Hershey, 1977] is a computer-aided technique for specifying information-processing products. The name comes from the two components of the technique: the problem statement language (PSL) used to describe the product and the problem statement analyzer (PSA) that enters the PSL description into a database and produces reports on request. PSL/PSA is still used, particularly for documenting products.

**SADT** [Ross, 1985] consists of two interrelated components, a box-and-arrow diagramming language termed **structural analysis** (SA) and a design technique (DT); hence, SADT. Stepwise refinement underlies SADT to a greater extent than with Gane and Sarsen's technique; a conscious effort has been made to adhere to Miller's Law. As Ross [1985] puts it, "Everything worth saying, about anything worth saying something about, must be expressed in six or fewer pieces." SADT has been used successfully in specifying a wide variety of products, especially complex, large-scale projects. Like many other similar semiformal techniques, its applicability to real-time systems is less clear.

On the other hand, **SREM** (the software requirements engineering method, pronounced "shrem") was designed explicitly for specifying the conditions under which certain actions are to occur [Alford, 1985]. For this reason, SREM has been particularly useful for specifying real-time systems and has been extended to distributed systems. SREM consists of a number of components. RSL is a specification language. REVS is a set of tools that perform a variety of specification-related tasks, such as translating the RSL specifications into an automated database, automatically checking for data flow consistency (ensuring that no data item is used before it has been assigned a value), and generating simulators from the specifications that can be used to ensure that the specifications are correct. In addition, SREM has a design technique, DCDS (distributed computing design system).

The power of SREM comes from the model underlying the whole technique, a finite state machine (Section 11.7). As a result of this formal model underlying SREM, it is possible to perform the consistency checking mentioned previously and to verify that performance constraints on the product as a whole can be met, given the performance of individual components. SREM has been used by the U.S. Air Force to specify two $C^3I$ software systems (command, control, communications, and intelligence) systems [Scheffer, Stone, and Rzepka, 1985]. Although SREM proved to be of great use in the classical analysis phase, it appears that the REVS tools employed later in the development cycle were considered less useful.

## 11.6   Entity-Relationship Modeling

The emphasis in structured systems analysis is on the operations, rather than the data, of the product to be built. Certainly, the data of the product are also modeled, but the data are secondary to the operations. In contrast, **entity-relationship modeling** (ERM) is a semiformal data-oriented technique for specifying a product. It has been widely used for over 30 years for specifying databases [Chen, 1976]. In that application area, the emphasis is on the data. Of course, operations are needed to access the data, and the database must be organized in such a way as to minimize access times. Nevertheless, the operations performed on the data are less significant.

A simple entity-relationship diagram is shown in Figure 11.10, which models the relationships between authors, novels, and readers. There are three entities: Author, Novel,

**FIGURE 11.10**

A simple entity-relationship diagram.

**FIGURE 11.11**

A many-to-many entity-relationship diagram.

**FIGURE 11.12**

A more complex entity-relationship diagram.

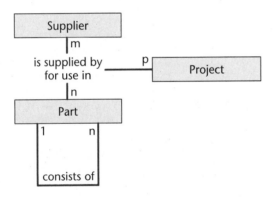

and **Reader**. The top relationship, writes, reflects that an author writes a novel. This is a one-to-many relationship, because one author can write more than one novel; this is reflected by the 1 next to **Author** and the n next to **Novel**. The entity-relationship diagram also shows two relationships between **Novel** and **Reader**. Both are one-to-many relationships. The relationship on the left models the fact that a reader may read many novels. Similarly, as shown on the right, a reader may own many novels. Two separate relationships are shown because a reader can read a novel without owning it, and a reader can buy a novel but not read it.

The next example is taken from the domain of suppliers and the parts they supply. Figure 11.11 shows a many-to-many relationship between parts and suppliers. That is, one supplier supplies many parts; conversely, a specific part can be obtained from many suppliers. This many-to-many relationship is reflected by the m next to entity **Supplier** and the n next to entity **Part**.

More complex relationships are possible as well. For example, as shown in Figure 11.12, a **Part** in turn may be viewed as consisting of a number of component **Parts**. Also, many-to-many-to-many relationships are possible. Consider the three entities **Supplier**, **Part**, and

Project shown in that figure. A particular part may be supplied by several suppliers, depending on the project. Also, the various parts supplied for a specific project may come from different suppliers. A many-to-many-to-many relationship is necessary to model such a situation accurately.

The next topic of this chapter is formal techniques. The underlying theme of the next four sections is that employing **formal specification** techniques can lead to more precise analysis artifacts than are possible with semiformal or informal techniques. However, the use of formal techniques, in general, requires lengthy training, and software engineers using formal techniques need exposure to the relevant mathematics. The following sections have been written with the mathematical content kept to a minimum. Furthermore, wherever possible, mathematical formulations are preceded by informal presentations of the same material. Nevertheless, the level of Sections 11.7 through 11.10 is higher than that of the rest of the book.

## 11.7   Finite State Machines

Consider the following example, originally formulated by the M202 team at the Open University, United Kingdom [Brady, 1977]. A safe has a combination lock that can be in one of three positions, labeled 1, 2, and 3. The dial can be turned left or right (L or R). Therefore, at any time, six dial movements are possible: 1L, 1R, 2L, 2R, 3L, and 3R. The combination to the safe is 1L, 3R, 2L; any other dial movement sets off an alarm. The situation is depicted in Figure 11.13. There is one initial state, Safe Locked. If the input is 1L, then the next state is A; but any other dial movement, 1R or 3L, say, brings it to the next state, Sound Alarm, one of the two final states. If the correct combination is chosen, then the sequence of transitions is from Safe Locked to A to B to Safe Unlocked, the other final state. Figure 11.13 shows a **state transition diagram** (STD) of a finite state machine. It is not necessary to depict a STD graphically; the same information is shown in tabular form in Figure 11.14. For each state other than the two final states, the transition to the next state is indicated, depending on the way the dial is moved.

A **finite state machine** (FSM) consists of five parts: a set of states, J; a set of inputs, K; the transition function, T, that specifies the next state given the current state and the current input; the initial state, S; and the set of final states, F. In the case of the combination lock on the safe,

The set of states J is {Safe Locked, A, B, Safe Unlocked, Sound Alarm}.
The set of inputs K is {1L, 1R, 2L, 2R, 3L, 3R}.

**FIGURE 11.13**
A finite state machine representation of a combination safe.

**FIGURE 11.14**

The transition table for the finite state machine of Figure 11.13.

| Dial Movement | Current State    Safe Locked | A | B |
|---|---|---|---|
| | **Table of Next States** | | |
| 1L | A | Sound alarm | Sound alarm |
| 1R | Sound alarm | Sound alarm | Sound alarm |
| 2L | Sound alarm | Sound alarm | Safe unlocked |
| 2R | Sound alarm | Sound alarm | Sound alarm |
| 3L | Sound alarm | Sound alarm | Sound alarm |
| 3R | Sound alarm | B | Sound alarm |

The transition function T is depicted in tabular form in Figure 11.14.

The initial state S is Safe Locked.

The set of final states F is {Safe Unlocked, Sound Alarm}.

In more formal terms, a finite state machine is a 5-tuple (J, K, T, S, F), where

J is a finite, nonempty set of **states**.

K is a finite, nonempty set of **inputs**.

T is a function from $(J \sim F) \times K$ into J, called the **transition function**.

$S \in J$ is the **initial state**.

F is the set of **final states**, $F \subseteq J$.

Use of the finite state machine approach is widespread in computing applications. For example, every menu-driven user interface is an implementation of a finite state machine. The display of a menu corresponds to a state, and entering an input at the keyboard or selecting an icon with the mouse is an **event** that causes the product to go into some other state. For example, selecting V when the main menu appears on the screen might cause a volumetric analysis to be performed on the current data set. A new menu then appears, and the user may select G, P, or R. Selecting G causes the results of the calculation to be graphed, P causes them to be printed, and R causes a return to the main menu. Each transition has the form

    **current state** [menu] and **event** [option selected] $\Rightarrow$ **next state**    **(11.1)**

To specify a product, a useful extension of FSMs is to add a sixth component to the preceding 5-tuple: a set of predicates, P, where each predicate is a function of the global state, Y, of the product [Kampen, 1987] (a **predicate** is something that is either true or false). More formally, the transition function, T, is now a function from $(J \sim F) \times K \times P$ into J. **Transition rules** now have the forms

    **current state** and **event** and **predicate** $\Rightarrow$ **next state**    **(11.2)**

Finite state machines are a powerful formalism for specifying a product that can be modeled in terms of states and transitions between states. To see how this formalism works in practice, the technique is now applied to a modified version of the so-called elevator problem; see Just in Case You Wanted to Know Box 11.1 for background information on the elevator problem.

The elevator problem truly is a classic problem of software engineering. It first appeared in print in 1968 in the first volume of Don Knuth's landmark book, *The Art of Computer Programming* [Knuth, 1968]. It is based on the single elevator in the mathematics building at the California Institute of Technology. The example was used to illustrate coroutines in the mythical programming language MIX.

By the mid-1980s, the elevator problem had been generalized to n elevators; in addition, specific properties of the solution had to be proven, for example, that an elevator eventually would arrive within a finite time. It was now *the* problem for researchers working in the area of formal specification languages, and any proposed formal specification language had to work for the elevator problem.

The problem attained broader prominence in 1986 when it was published in *ACM SIGSOFT Software Engineering Notes* in the Call for Papers for the Fourth International Workshop on Software Specification and Design [IWSSD, 1986]. The elevator problem was one of five problems to be used as examples by researchers in their submissions to the conference, held in Monterey, California, in May 1987. In the form in which it appeared in the Call for Papers, it was termed the *lift problem* and attributed to N. (Neil) Davis of STC-IDEC (a division of Standard Telecommunications and Cable, in Stevenage, United Kingdom).

Since then, the problem has attained even wider prominence and been used to demonstrate an extensive variety of techniques within software engineering in general, not just formal specification languages. It is used in this book to illustrate every technique because, as you soon will discover, the problem is by no means as simple as it looks.

## Case Study

### 11.7.1 Finite State Machines: The Elevator Problem Case Study

The problem concerns the logic required to move n elevators between m floors according to the following constraints:

1. Each **elevator** has a set of m **buttons**, one for each floor. These illuminate when pressed and cause the elevator to visit the corresponding floor. The illumination is canceled when the corresponding floor is visited by the elevator.

2. Each floor, except the first floor and the top floor, has two buttons, one to request an up-elevator and one to request a down-elevator. These buttons illuminate when pressed. The illumination is canceled when an elevator visits the floor and then moves in the desired direction.

3. When an elevator has no requests, it remains at its current floor with its doors closed.

The product now is specified using an **extended finite state machine** [Kampen, 1987]. There are two sets of buttons in the problem. In each of the n elevators, there is a set of m buttons, one for each floor. Because these n × m buttons are inside the elevators, they are referred to as **elevator buttons**. Then, on each floor

**FIGURE 11.15** The STD for an elevator button.

Source: [Kampen, 1987]. (© 1987 IEEE.)

there are two buttons, one to request an up-elevator, one to request a down-elevator. These are referred to as **floor buttons**.

The state transition diagram for an elevator button is shown in Figure 11.15. Let EB (e, f) denote the button in elevator e that is pressed to request floor f. EB (e, f) can be in two states, with the button on (**illuminated**) or off. More precisely, the states are

$$\text{EBON (e, f):} \quad \underline{\text{E}}\text{levator } \underline{\text{B}}\text{utton (e, f) } \underline{\text{ON}}$$
$$\text{EBOFF (e, f):} \quad \underline{\text{E}}\text{levator } \underline{\text{B}}\text{utton (e, f) } \underline{\text{OFF}} \tag{11.3}$$

If the button is on and the elevator has arrived at floor f, then the button is turned off. Conversely, if the button is off and it is pressed, then the button comes on. Two events are involved:

$$\text{EBP (e, f):} \quad \underline{\text{E}}\text{levator } \underline{\text{B}}\text{utton (e, f) } \underline{\text{P}}\text{ressed}$$
$$\text{EHAF (e, f):} \quad \underline{\text{E}}\text{levator e } \underline{\text{H}}\text{as } \underline{\text{A}}\text{rrived at } \underline{\text{F}}\text{loor f} \tag{11.4}$$

To define the state transition rules connecting these events and states, a predicate V (e, f) is needed.

$$\text{V (e, f):} \quad \text{Elevator e is } \underline{\text{V}}\text{isiting (stopped at) floor f} \tag{11.5}$$

Now, the formal transition rules can be stated. If elevator button (e, f) is off (current state) and elevator button (e, f) is pressed (event) and elevator e is not visiting floor f (predicate), then the button is turned on. In the format of transition rule (11.2) this becomes

$$\text{EBOFF (e, f) and EBP (e, f) and not V (e, f)} \Rightarrow \text{EBON (e, f)} \tag{11.6}$$

If the elevator is currently visiting floor f, nothing happens. In Kampen's formalism, events that do not trigger a transition indeed may occur; but if they do, then they are ignored.

Conversely, if the elevator has arrived at floor f and the elevator button is on, then it is turned off. This is expressed as

$$\text{EBON (e, f) and EHAF (e, f)} \Rightarrow \text{EBOFF (e, f)} \tag{11.7}$$

Next, the floor buttons are considered. FB (d, f) denotes the button on floor f that requests an elevator traveling in direction d. The STD for floor button FB (d, f) is shown in Figure 11.16. More precisely, the states are

$$\text{FBON (d, f):} \quad \underline{\text{F}}\text{loor } \underline{\text{B}}\text{utton (d, f) } \underline{\text{ON}}$$
$$\text{FBOFF (d, f):} \quad \underline{\text{F}}\text{loor } \underline{\text{B}}\text{utton (d, f) } \underline{\text{OFF}} \tag{11.8}$$

**FIGURE 11.16**
The STD for a
floor button.

Source: [Kampen, 1987]. (© 1987 IEEE.)

If the button is on and an elevator has arrived at floor f and is about to travel in the correct direction, d, then the button is turned off. Conversely, if the button is off and it is pressed, then the button comes on. Again, two events are involved:

$$FBP \ (d, f): \qquad \underline{F}loor \ \underline{B}utton \ (d, f) \ \underline{P}ressed$$
$$EHAF \ (1 \ . \ . \ n, f): \ \underline{E}levator \ 1 \ or \ . \ . \ . \ or \ n \ \underline{H}as \ \underline{A}rrived \ at \ \underline{F}loor \ f \qquad (11.9)$$

Note the use of 1 . . n to denote disjunction. Throughout this section an expression such as P (a, 1 . . n, b) denotes

$$P \ (a, 1, b) \ or \ P \ (a, 2, b) \ or \ . \ . \ . \ or \ P \ (a, n, b) \qquad (11.10)$$

To define the state transition rules connecting these events and states, a predicate again is needed. In this case, it is S (d, e, f), which is defined as follows:

$$S \ (d, e, f): \quad Elevator \ e \ is \ visiting \ floor \ f \ and \ the \ direction$$
$$in \ which \ it \ is \ about \ to \ move \ is \ either \ up \ (d = U), \qquad (11.11)$$
$$down \ (d = D), \ or \ no \ requests \ are \ pending \ (d = N)$$

This predicate actually is a state. In fact, the formalism allows both events and states to be treated as predicates.

Using S (d, e, f), the formal transition rules are

$$FBOFF \ (d, f) \ and \ FBP \ (d, f) \ and \ not \ S \ (d, 1 \ . \ . \ n, f) \Rightarrow$$
$$FBON \ (d, f),$$
$$FBON \ (d, f) \ and \ EHAF \ (1 \ . \ . \ n, f) \ and \ S \ (d, 1 \ . \ . \ n, f) \Rightarrow \qquad (11.12)$$
$$FBOFF \ (d, f), \ d = U \ or \ D$$

That is, if the floor button at floor f for motion in direction d is off and the button is pushed and none of the elevators currently is visiting floor f about to move in direction d, then the floor button is turned on. Conversely, if the button is on and at least one elevator has arrived at floor f and the elevator is about to move in direction d, then the floor button is turned off. The notation 1 . . n in S (d, 1 . . n, f) and EHAF (1 . . n, f) was defined in definition (11.10). The predicate V (e, f) of definition (11.5) can be defined in terms of S (d, e, f) as follows:

$$V \ (e, f) = S \ (U, e, f) \ or \ S \ (D, e, f) \ or \ S \ (N, e, f) \qquad (11.13)$$

The states of the elevator button and floor button were straightforward to define. Turning to the elevators, complications arise. The state of an elevator essentially consists of a number of component substates. Kampen [1987] identifies several, such as the elevator slowing and stopping, the door opening, the door open with a timer running, or the door closing after a **timeout**. He makes the reasonable assumption

**FIGURE 11.17** The STD for the elevator.

Source: [Kampen, 1987]. (© 1987 IEEE.)

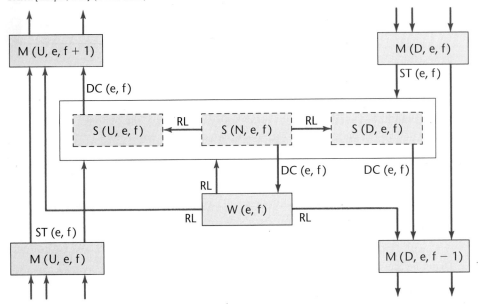

that the **elevator controller** (the mechanism that directs the motion of the elevator) initiates a state such as S (d, e, f) and that the controller then moves the elevator through the substates. Three elevator states can be defined, one of which, S (d, e, f), was defined in definition (11.11) but is included here for completeness.

$$
\begin{aligned}
&\text{M (d, e, f):} && \text{Elevator e is \underline{M}oving in direction d (floor f is next)} \\
&\text{S (d, e, f):} && \text{Elevator e is \underline{S}topped (d-bound) at floor f} && \textbf{(11.14)} \\
&\text{W (e, f):} && \text{Elevator e is \underline{W}aiting at floor f (door closed)}
\end{aligned}
$$

These states are shown in Figure 11.17. Note that the three stopped states S (U, e, f), S (N, e, f), and S (D, e, f) have been grouped into one larger state to simplify the diagram and to reduce the overall number of states.

The events that can trigger state transitions are DC (e, f), the closing of the **door** of elevator e at floor f; ST (e, f), which occurs when the sensor on the elevator is triggered as it nears floor f and the elevator controller must decide whether to stop the elevator at that floor; and RL, which occurs whenever an elevator button or a floor button is pressed and enters its ON state:

$$
\begin{aligned}
&\text{DC (e, f):} && \text{\underline{D}oor \underline{C}losed for elevator e, at floor f} \\
&\text{ST (e, f):} && \text{\underline{S}ensor \underline{T}riggered as elevator e nears floor f} && \textbf{(11.15)} \\
&\text{RL:} && \text{\underline{R}equest \underline{L}ogged (button pressed)}
\end{aligned}
$$

These events are indicated in Figure 11.17.

Finally, the state transition rules for an elevator can be presented. They can be deduced from Figure 11.17, but in some cases, additional predicates are necessary.

To be more precise, Figure 11.17 is nondeterministic; among other reasons, the predicates are necessary to make the STD deterministic. The interested reader should consult [Kampen, 1987] for the complete set of rules; for the sake of brevity, the only rules presented here are those that declare what happens when the door closes. The elevator moves up, down, or enters a wait state, depending on the current state:

$$S\ (U, e, f) \text{ and } DC\ (e, f) \Rightarrow M\ (U, e, f + 1)$$
$$S\ (D, e, f) \text{ and } DC\ (e, f) \Rightarrow M\ (D, e, f - 1) \tag{11.16}$$
$$S\ (N, e, f) \text{ and } DC\ (e, f) \Rightarrow W\ (e, f)$$

The first rule states that, if elevator e is in state S (U, e, f), that is, stopped at floor f about to go up, and the doors close, then the elevator moves up toward the next floor. The second and third rules correspond to the cases of the elevator about to go down or with no requests pending.

The format of these rules reflects the power of finite state machines for specifying complex products. Instead of having to list a complex set of preconditions that have to hold for the product to do something and then having to list all the conditions that hold after the product has done it, the specifications take the simple form

**current state** and **event** and **predicate** $\Rightarrow$ **next state**

This type of specification is easy to write, easy to validate, and easy to convert into a design and into code. In fact, it is straightforward to construct a CASE tool that will translate a finite state machine specification directly into source code. Maintenance is achieved by replay. That is, if new states or events are needed, the specifications are modified and a new version of the product generated directly from the new specifications.

The FSM approach is more precise than the graphical technique of Gane and Sarsen presented in Section 11.3.1, but it is almost as easy to understand. It has a drawback, in that for large systems, the number of (**state**, **event**, **predicate**) triples can grow rapidly. Also, like Gane and Sarsen's technique, timing considerations are not handled in Kampen's formalism.

These problems can be solved using statecharts, an extension of FSMs [Harel et al., 1990]. Statecharts are extremely powerful and are supported by a CASE workbench, Rhapsody. The approach has been successfully used for a number of large real-time systems.

Another formal technique that can handle timing issues is Petri nets.

# 11.8  Petri Nets

A major difficulty with specifying concurrent systems is coping with timing. This difficulty can manifest itself in many different ways, such as synchronization problems, race conditions, and deadlock [Silberschatz, Galvin, and Gagne, 2002]. Although timing problems can arise as a consequence of a poor design or a faulty implementation, such designs and implementations often are the consequence of poor specifications. If specifications are not properly drawn up, there is a very real risk that the corresponding design and implementation will be inadequate. One powerful technique for specifying systems with potential

**FIGURE 11.18**

A Petri net.

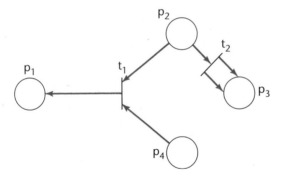

timing problems is Petri nets. A further advantage of this technique is that it can be used for the design as well.

Petri nets were invented by Carl Adam Petri [Petri, 1962]. Originally of interest only to automata theorists, Petri nets have found wide applicability in computer science, being used in such fields as performance evaluation, operating systems, and software engineering. In particular, Petri nets have proven to be useful for describing concurrent interrelated activities. But, before the use of Petri nets for specifications can be demonstrated, a brief introduction to Petri nets is given for those readers who may be unfamiliar with them.

A **Petri net** consists of four parts: a set of places, $P$; a set of transitions, $T$; an input function, $I$; and an output function, $O$. Consider the Petri net shown in Figure 11.18.

The set of places, $P$, is $\{p_1, p_2, p_3, p_4\}$.

The set of transitions, $T$, is $\{t_1, t_2\}$.

The input functions for the two transitions, represented by the arrows from places to transitions, are

$$I(t_1) = \{p_2, p_4\}$$
$$I(t_2) = \{p_2\}$$

The output functions for the two transitions, represented by the arrows from transitions to places, are

$$O(t_1) = \{p_1\}$$
$$O(t_2) = \{p_3, p_3\}$$

Note the duplication of $p_3$; there are two arrows from $t_2$ to $p_3$.

More formally [Peterson, 1981], a Petri net structure is a 4-tuple, $C = (P, T, I, O)$:

$P = \{p_1, p_2, \ldots, p_n\}$ is a finite set of **places**, $n \geq 0$.

$T = \{t_1, t_2, \ldots, t_m\}$ is a finite set of **transitions**, $m \geq 0$, with $P$ and $T$ disjoint.

$I : T \rightarrow P^\infty$ is the **input function**, a mapping from transitions to bags of places.

$O : T \rightarrow P^\infty$ is the **output function**, a mapping from transitions to bags of places.

(A **bag**, or **multiset**, is a generalization of a set that allows for multiple instances of an element.)

**FIGURE 11.19**
A marked Petri
net.

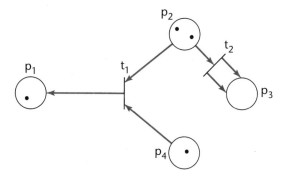

**FIGURE 11.20**
The Petri net of
Figure 11.19
after transition
$t_1$ fires.

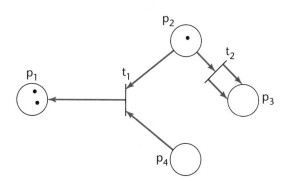

**Marking** a Petri net is the assignment of **tokens** to that Petri net. Figure 11.19 contains four tokens: one in $p_1$, two in $p_2$, none in $p_3$, and one in $p_4$. The marking can be represented by the vector (1, 2, 0, 1). Transition $t_1$ is **enabled** (ready to fire), because there are tokens in $p_2$ and in $p_4$; in general, a transition is enabled if each of its input places has as many tokens in it as there are arcs from the place to that transition. If $t_1$ were to fire, one token would be removed from $p_2$ and one from $p_4$, and one new token would be placed in $p_1$. The number of tokens is not conserved—two tokens are removed, but only one new one is placed in $p_1$. In Figure 11.19, transition $t_2$ also is enabled, because there are tokens in $p_2$. If $t_2$ were to fire, one token would be removed from $p_2$, and two new tokens would be placed in $p_3$.

Petri nets are nondeterministic; that is, if more than one transition can fire, then any one of them can be fired. Figure 11.19 has marking (1, 2, 0, 1); both $t_1$ and $t_2$ are enabled. Suppose that $t_1$ fires. The resulting marking (2, 1, 0, 0) is shown in Figure 11.20, where only $t_2$ is enabled. It fires, the enabling token is removed from $p_2$, and two new tokens are placed in $p_3$. The marking now is (2, 0, 2, 0), as shown in Figure 11.21.

More formally [Peterson, 1981], a marking, M, of a Petri net, C = (P, T, I, O), is a function from the set of places P to the set of nonnegative integers:

$$M : P \rightarrow \{0, 1, 2, \ldots\}$$

A **marked Petri net** then is a 5-tuple (P, T, I, O, M).

**FIGURE 11.21**
The Petri net of
Figure 11.20
after transition
$t_2$ fires.

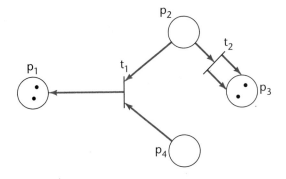

**FIGURE 11.22**
A Petri net with
an inhibitor arc.

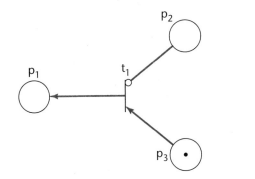

An important extension to a Petri net is an **inhibitor arc**. In Figure 11.22, the inhibitor
arc is marked by a small circle rather than an arrowhead. Transition $t_1$ is enabled because a
token is in $p_3$ but no token is in $p_2$. In general, a transition is enabled if at least one token
is on each of its (normal) input arcs and no tokens are on any of its inhibitor input arcs. This
extension is used in the Petri net specification of the elevator problem case study of Section
11.7.1 [Guha, Lang, and Bassiouni, 1987].

## *ase Study*

### 11.8.1 Petri Nets: The Elevator Problem Case Study

Recall that an n elevator system is to be installed in a building with m floors. In this
Petri net specification, each floor in the building is represented by a place, $F_f$, $1 \leq f \leq$
m, in the Petri net; an elevator is represented by a token. A token in $F_f$ denotes that an
elevator is at floor f.

*First Constraint*
Each elevator has a set of m buttons, one for each floor. These illuminate when
pressed and cause the elevator to visit the corresponding floor. The illumination is
canceled when the corresponding floor is visited by the elevator.

**FIGURE 11.23**
A Petri net representation of an elevator button.

Source: [Guha, Lang, and Bassiouni, 1987]. (© 1987 IEEE.)

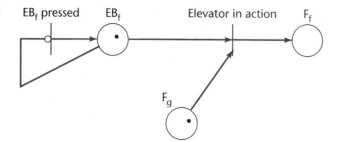

To incorporate this into the specification, additional places are needed. The elevator button for floor f is represented in the Petri net by place $EB_f$, $1 \le f \le m$. More precisely, because there are n elevators, the place should be denoted $EB_{f,e}$ with $1 \le f \le m$, $1 \le e \le n$. But, for the sake of simplicity of notation, the subscript e representing the elevator is suppressed. A token in $EB_f$ denotes that the elevator button for floor f is illuminated. Because the button must be illuminated the first time the button is pressed and subsequent button presses must be ignored, this is specified using a Petri net as shown in Figure 11.23. First, suppose that button $EB_f$ is not illuminated. Accordingly no token is in place and, because of the presence of the inhibitor arc, transition $EB_f$ **pressed** is enabled. The button now is pressed. The transition fires, and a new token is placed in $EB_f$, as shown in Figure 11.23. Now, no matter how many times the button is pressed, the combination of the inhibitor arc and the presence of the token means that transition $EB_f$ **pressed** cannot be enabled. Therefore, no more than one token can ever be in place $EB_f$.

Furthermore, suppose that the elevator is to travel from floor g to floor f. Because the elevator is at floor g, a token is in place $F_g$, as shown in Figure 11.23. Transition **Elevator in action** is enabled and fires. The tokens in $EB_f$ and $F_g$ are removed, turning off button $EB_f$, and a new token appears in $F_f$; the firing of this transition brings the elevator from floor g to floor f.

This motion from floor g to floor f cannot take place instantaneously. To handle this and similar issues, such as the physical impossibility for a button to illuminate at the very instant it is pressed, timing must be added to the Petri net model. That is, whereas in classical Petri net theory, transitions are instantaneous, in practical situations, such as the elevator problem case study, timed Petri nets [Coolahan and Roussopoulos, 1983] are needed to associate a nonzero time with a transition.

### Second Constraint

Each floor, except the first floor and top floor, has two buttons, one to request an up-elevator and one to request a down-elevator. These buttons illuminate when pressed. The illumination is canceled when an elevator visits the floor and then moves in the desired direction.

The floor buttons are represented by places $FB_f^u$ and $FB_f^d$ representing the buttons for requesting up- and down-elevators, respectively. More precisely, floor 1 has a button $FB_1^u$, floor m has a button $FB_m^d$, and the intermediate floors each have two buttons, $FB_f^u$ and $FB_f^d$, $1 < f < m$. The situation when an elevator reaches floor f from

**FIGURE 11.24**
A Petri net
representation
of floor buttons.

Source: [Guha, Lang,
and Bassiouni, 1987].
(© 1987 IEEE.)

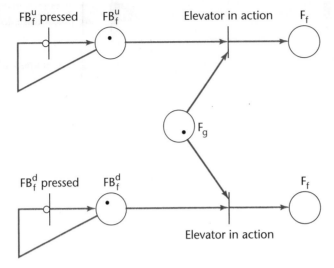

floor $g$ with one or both buttons illuminated is shown in Figure 11.24. In fact, that figure needs further refinement, because if both the buttons are illuminated, one is turned off on a nondeterministic basis. To ensure that the correct button is turned off requires a Petri net model too complicated to present here; see, for example, [Ghezzi and Mandrioli, 1987].

*Third Constraint*
When an elevator has no requests, it remains at its current floor with its doors closed.
This is achieved easily: If there are no requests, no **Elevator in action** transition is enabled.

Not only can Petri nets be used to represent the specifications, they can be used for the design as well [Guha, Lang, and Bassiouni, 1987]. However, even at this stage of the development of the product, it is clear that Petri nets possess the expressive power necessary for specifying the synchronization aspects of concurrent systems.

## 11.9 Z

A formal specification language gaining widely in popularity is **Z** [Spivey, 2001]. (For the correct pronunciation of the name Z, see Just in Case You Wanted to Know Box 11.2.) Use of Z requires knowledge of set theory, functions, and discrete mathematics, including first-order logic. Even for users with the necessary background (and this includes most computer science majors), Z initially is difficult to learn because, in addition to the usual set theoretic and logic symbols like $\exists$, $\supset$, and $\Rightarrow$, it uses many unusual special symbols, such as $\oplus$, $\lhd$, $\mapsto$, and $\rightarrowtail$.

For insight into how Z is used to specify a product, the elevator problem case study of Section 11.7.1 is considered again.

The name *Z* was given to the formal specification language by its inventor Jean-Raymond Abrial in honor of the great set theorist Ernst Friedrich Ferdinand Zermelo (1871–1953). Because it was developed at Oxford University [Abrial, 1980], the name *Z* is properly pronounced "zed," the way the British pronounce the 26th letter of the alphabet.

Lately, however, moves are afoot to acknowledge that *Z* is named after a German mathematician and to pronounce it the German way, "tzet." In response, Francophiles and Francophones point out that Abrial is a Frenchman and that the letter *Z* is pronounced "zed" in French, too.

The one totally unacceptable pronunciation is the American style, that is, "zee." The reason is that *Z* (pronounced "zee") is the name of an American fourth-generation language (see Section 14.2). However, we cannot trademark a single letter of the alphabet. Furthermore, we are free to pronounce the letter *Z* the way we wish. Nevertheless, within the programming language context, the pronunciation "zee" refers to the 4GL, not the formal specification language.

Watch this space for the next round in the Z pronunciation wars.

## *ase Study*

### 11.9.1 Z: The Elevator Problem Case Study

In its simplest form, a Z specification consists of four sections:

1. Given sets, data types, and constants.
2. State definition.
3. Initial state.
4. Operations.

Each of these sections is examined in turn.

#### 1. Given Sets
A Z specification begins with a list of **given sets**, that is, sets that need not be defined in detail. The names of any such sets appear in brackets. For the elevator problem case study, the given set will be called Button, the set of all buttons. The Z specification therefore begins.

[Button]

#### 2. State Definition
A Z specification consists of a number of schemata (plural of schema). Each **schema** consists of a group of variable declarations together with a list of predicates that constrain the possible values of the variables. The format of a schema $S$ is shown in Figure 11.25.

In the elevator problem case study, there are four subsets of Button: the floor buttons, the elevator buttons, buttons (the set of all buttons in the elevator problem case study), and pushed (the set of those buttons that have been pushed and therefore are on). Figure 11.26 depicts the schema *Button_State*, a **state definition**. The

**FIGURE 11.25**
The format of Z
schema *S*.

```
┌─────────── S ───────────┐
│ declarations            │
├─────────────────────────┤
│ predicates              │
└─────────────────────────┘
```

**FIGURE 11.26**
The Z schema
*Button_State*.

```
┌──────── Button_State ──────────────────────┐
│ floor_buttons, elevator_buttons  : P Button │
│ buttons                          : P Button │
│ pushed                           : P Button │
├─────────────────────────────────────────────┤
│ floor_buttons ∩ elevator_buttons = ∅        │
│ floor_buttons ∪ elevator_buttons = buttons  │
└─────────────────────────────────────────────┘
```

**FIGURE 11.27**
A Z
specification
of operation
*Push_Button*.

```
┌──────── Push_Button ─────────────────────────────────────────┐
│ ΔButton_State                                                 │
│ button?: Button                                               │
├───────────────────────────────────────────────────────────────┤
│ (button? ∈ buttons) ∧                                         │
│ (((button? ∉ pushed) ∧ (pushed' = pushed ∪ {button?})) ∨      │
│ ((button? ∈ pushed) ∧ (pushed' = pushed)))                    │
└───────────────────────────────────────────────────────────────┘
```

symbol **P** denotes the power set (the set of all subsets of a given set). The constraints, that is, the statements below the horizontal line, assert that the set of floor_buttons and elevator_buttons are disjoint and that together they constitute the set of buttons. (The sets floor_buttons and elevator_buttons are not needed in what follows; they are included in Figure 11.26 only to demonstrate the power of *Z*.)

*3. Initial State*
The **abstract initial state** describes the state when the system first is turned on. The abstract initial state for the elevator problem case study is

$$Button\_Init \triangleq [Button\_State' \mid pushed' = \varnothing]$$

This is a **vertical schema definition**, as opposed to a **horizontal schema definition**, such as Figure 11.26. The vertical schema asserts that, when the elevator system first is turned on, the set pushed initially is empty; that is, all the buttons are off.

*4. Operations*
If a button is pushed for the first time, then that button is turned on. The button is added to the set pushed. This is depicted in Figure 11.27, in which operation *Push_Button* is defined. The Δ in the first line of the schema denotes that this operation changes the state of *Button_State*. The operation has one input variable, button?. As in various other languages (such as CSP [Hoare, 1985]), the question mark (?) denotes an input variable, whereas an exclamation mark (!) denotes an output variable.

**FIGURE 11.28**
A Z
specification
of operation
*Floor_Arrival.*

```
┌─────── Floor_Arrival ──────────────────────────────────
│ ΔButton_State
│ button?: Button
├────────────────────────────────────────────────────────
│ (button? ∈ buttons) ∧
│ (((button? ∈ pushed) ∧ (pushed' = pushed \ {button?})) ∨
│ ((button? ∉ pushed) ∧ (pushed' = pushed)))
└────────────────────────────────────────────────────────
```

The predicate part of an **operation** consists of a group of preconditions that must hold before the operation is invoked and postconditions that must hold after the operation has completed execution. Provided the preconditions are met, the postconditions hold after completing execution. However, if the operation is invoked without the preconditions being satisfied, unspecified (and therefore unpredictable) results occur.

The first precondition of Figure 11.27 states that button? must be a member of buttons, the set of all buttons in this elevator system. If the second precondition, button? ∉ pushed, is met (that is, if the button is not on), then the set of pushed buttons is updated to include button?. In Z, the new value of a variable is denoted by a prime ('). Therefore, the postcondition says that, after operation *Push_Button* has been performed, button? must be added to the set pushed. There is no need to turn on the button explicitly; it is sufficient that button? now is an element of pushed.

The other possibility is that an already pushed button is pushed again. Because button? ∈ pushed, the third precondition holds[1] and, as required, nothing happens. This is indicated by the statement pushed' = pushed; the new state of pushed is the same as the old state.

Now, suppose an elevator arrives at a floor. If the corresponding floor button is on, then it must be turned off, and similarly for the corresponding elevator button. That is, if button? is an element of pushed, then it must be removed from the set, as shown in Figure 11.28. (The symbol \ denotes set difference.) However, if a button is not on, then set pushed is unchanged.

The solution presented in this section is an oversimplification, in that it does not distinguish between up and down floor buttons. Nevertheless, it gives an indication how Z can be used to specify the behavior of the buttons in the elevator problem case study.

## 11.9.2 Analysis of Z

Z has been used successfully in a wide variety of projects, including CASE tools [Hall, 1990], a real-time kernel [Spivey, 1990], and an oscilloscope [Delisle and Garlan, 1990].

---

[1] Without the third precondition, the specification would not state what is to happen if a button that has already been pushed is pushed again. The results would then be unspecified.

Z also has been used to specify large portions of a release of CICS, the IBM transaction-processing system [Nix and Collins, 1988].

These successes perhaps are somewhat surprising, in view of the fact that, even for the simplified version of the elevator problem case study, it is clear that Z is not straightforward to use. First is the problem caused by the notation; a new user has to learn the set of symbols and their meanings before being able to read Z specifications, let alone write them. Second, not every software engineer has the required training in mathematics to be able to use Z (although recent graduates of almost all computer science programs either know enough mathematics to use Z or could learn what they still need to know with little difficulty).

Z perhaps is the most widely used formal language of its type. Why is this, and why has Z been so successful, especially on large-scale projects? A number of different reasons have been put forward:

- It has been found that it is easy to find faults in specifications written in Z, especially during inspections of the specifications themselves and inspections of designs or code against the formal specifications [Nix and Collins, 1988; Hall, 1990].

- Writing Z specifications requires the specifier to be extremely precise; as a result of this need for exactness, there appear to be fewer ambiguities, contradictions, and omissions than with informal specifications.

- As a formal language, Z allows developers to prove specifications correct when necessary. Thus, although some organizations rarely do any correctness proving of Z, such proofs have been done, even for such practical specifications as the CICS storage manager [Woodcock, 1989].

- It has been suggested that software professionals with only high-school mathematics can be taught to write Z specifications in a relatively short period of time [Hall, 1990]. Clearly such individuals cannot prove the resulting specifications to be correct, but then formal specifications do not necessarily have to be proven to be correct.

- The use of Z has decreased the cost of software development. No doubt more time has to be spent on the specifications themselves than when informal techniques are used, but the overall time for the complete development process is decreased.

- The problem that the client cannot understand specifications written in Z has been solved in a number of ways, including rewriting the specifications in natural language. The resulting natural language specifications have been found to be clearer than informal specifications constructed from scratch. (This also was the experience with Meyer's English paraphrase of his formal specification for Naur's text-processing problem, described in Section 11.2.1.)

The bottom line is that, notwithstanding the arguments to the contrary, Z has been successfully used in the software industry for a number of large-scale projects. Although the vast majority of specifications continue to be written in languages considerably less formal than Z, there is a growing global trend toward the use of formal specifications. The use of such formal specifications traditionally has been largely a European practice. However, more and more organizations in the United States are employing formal specifications of one sort or another. The extent to which Z and similar languages will be used in the future remains to be seen.

## 11.10  Other Formal Techniques

Many other formal techniques have been proposed. These techniques are extremely varied. For example, **Anna** [Luckham and von Henke, 1985] is a formal specification language for Ada. Some formal techniques are knowledge based, such as **Gist** [Balzer, 1985]. Gist was designed so users could describe processes in a way as close as possible to the way we think about processes. This was to be achieved by formalizing the constructs used in natural languages. In practice, Gist specifications are as hard to read as most other formal specifications, so much so that a paraphraser from Gist to English has been written.

**Vienna definition method** (VDM) [Jones, 1986b] is a technique based on denotational semantics [Gordon, 1979]. The VDM can be applied, not just to the specifications, but also to the design and implementation. The VDM has been used successfully in a number of projects, most spectacularly in the Dansk Datamatik Center development of the DDC Ada Compiler System [Oest, 1986].

A different way of looking at specifications is to view them in terms of sequences of events, where an event is either a simple action or a communication that transfers data into or out of the system. For example, in the elevator problem case study, one event consists of pushing the elevator button for floor f on elevator e and its resulting illumination. Another event is elevator e leaving floor f in a downward direction and canceling the illumination of the corresponding floor button. The language **Communicating Sequential Processes** (CSP), invented by Hoare [1985], is based on the idea of describing the behavior of a system in terms of such events. In CSP, a process is described in terms of the sequences of events in which the process engages with its environment. Processes interact with each other by sending messages to one another. CSP allows processes to be combined in a wide variety of ways, such as sequentially, in parallel, or interleaved nondeterministically.

The power of CSP lies in the executable nature of CSP specifications [Delisle and Schwartz, 1987]; as a result, they can be checked for internal consistency. In addition, CSP provides a framework for going from specifications to design to implementation in a sequence of steps that preserve validity. In other words, if the specifications are correct and the transformations are performed correctly, then the design and implementation are correct as well. Going from design to implementation is particularly straightforward if the implementation language is Ada.

However, CSP also has its weaknesses. In particular, like Z, it is not an easy language to learn. An attempt was made to include a CSP specification for the elevator problem case study [Schwartz and Delisle, 1987] in this book. But the quantity of essential preliminary material and the level of detail of explanation needed to describe each CSP statement adequately were simply too great to permit inclusion in a book as general as this one. The relationship between the power of a specification language and its difficulty of use is expanded in Section 11.11.

## 11.11  Comparison of Classical Analysis Techniques

The main lesson of this chapter is that every development organization has to decide what type of specification language is appropriate for the product about to be developed. An informal technique is easy to learn but lacks the power of a semiformal or formal technique.

Conversely, each formal technique supports a variety of features that may include executability, correctness proving, or transformability to design and implementation through a series of correctness-preserving steps. Although generally the more formal the technique, the greater its power, formal techniques can be difficult to learn and use. Also, a formal specification can be difficult for the client to understand. In other words, there is a trade-off between ease of use and the power of a specification language.

In some circumstances, the choice of specification language type is easy. For example, if the vast majority of the members of the development team have no training in computer science, then it is virtually impossible to use anything other than an informal or semiformal specification technique. Conversely, where a mission-critical real-time system is being built in a research laboratory, the power of a formal specification technique almost certainly is required.

An additional complicating factor is that many of the newer formal techniques have not been tested under practical conditions. Considerable risk is involved in using such a technique. Large sums of money are needed to pay for training the relevant members of the development team, and more money will be spent while the team adjusts from using the language in the classroom to using it on the actual project. Furthermore, the language's supporting software tools might not work properly, as happened with SREM [Scheffer, Stone, and Rzepka, 1985], resulting in additional expense and time slippage. But, if everything works and the software project management plan takes into account the additional time and money needed when a new technology is used on a nontrivial project for the first time, huge gains are possible.

Which analysis technique should be used for a specific project? It depends on the project, the development team, the management team, and myriad other factors, such as the

**FIGURE 11.29**
A summary of the classical analysis methods discussed in this chapter and the section in which each is described.

| Classical Analysis Method | Category | Strengths | Weaknesses |
|---|---|---|---|
| Natural language (Section 11.2) | Informal | Easy to learn<br>Easy to use<br>Easy for the client to understand | Imprecise<br>Specifications can be ambiguous, contradictory, or incomplete |
| Entity-relationship modeling (Section 11.6)<br>PSL/PSA (Section 11.5)<br>SADT (Section 11.5)<br>SREM (Section 11.5)<br>Structured systems analysis (Section 11.3) | Semiformal | Can be understood by the client<br>More precise than informal techniques | Not as precise as formal techniques<br>Generally cannot handle timing |
| Anna (Section 11.10)<br>CSP (Section 11.10)<br>Extended finite state machines (Section 11.7)<br>Gist (Section 11.10)<br>Petri nets (Section 11.8)<br>VDM (Section 11.10)<br>Z (Section 11.9) | Formal | Extremely precise<br>Can reduce analysis faults<br>Can reduce development cost and effort<br>Can support correctness proving | Hard for the development team to learn<br>Hard to use<br>Almost impossible for most clients to understand |

client insisting that a specific method be used (or not used). As with so many other aspects of software engineering, trade-offs have to be made. Unfortunately, there is no simple rule for deciding which analysis technique to use.

Figure 11.29 is a summary of the ideas of this section.

## 11.12   Testing during Classical Analysis

During classical analysis, the functionality of the proposed product is expressed precisely in the specification document. It is vital to verify that the specification document is correct. One way to do this is by means of a walkthrough of the document (Section 6.2.1).

A more powerful mechanism for detecting faults in specification documents is an inspection (Section 6.2.3). A team of inspectors reviews the specifications against a checklist. Typical items on a specification inspection checklist are these: Have the required hardware resources been specified? Have the acceptance criteria been specified?

Inspections were suggested first by Fagan [1976] in the context of testing the design and the code. Fagan's work is described in detail in Section 6.2.3. However, inspections also have proven to be of considerable use in testing specifications. For example, Doolan [1992] used inspections to validate the specifications of a product that, when built, consisted of over 2 million lines of Fortran. From data on the cost of fixing faults in the product, he could deduce that each hour invested in inspections saved 30 hours of execution-based fault detection and correction.

When a specification has been drawn up using a formal technique, other testing techniques can be applied. For example, correctness-proving methods (Section 6.5) can be employed. Even if formal proofs are not performed, informal proof techniques such as those used in Section 6.5.1 can be an extremely useful way of highlighting specification faults. In fact, the product and its proof should be developed in parallel. In this way, faults are detected quickly.

## 11.13   CASE Tools for Classical Analysis

Two classes of CASE tools are particularly helpful during classical analysis. The first is a graphical tool. Whether a product is represented using data flow diagrams, Petri nets, entity-relationship diagrams, or any of the many other representations omitted from this book simply for reasons of space, drawing the entire product by hand is a lengthy process. In addition, making substantial changes can result in having to redraw everything from scratch. A drawing tool therefore is a great time saver. Tools of this type exist for the analysis techniques described in this chapter, as well as many other graphical representations for specifications. A second tool needed during this phase is a data dictionary. As mentioned in Section 5.5, this tool stores the name and representation (format) of every component of every data item in the product, including data flows and their components, data stores and their components, and processes (operations) and their internal variables. (Figure 11.5 shows typical information that would be stored in a data dictionary for Sally's Software Shop.) Again, a wide selection of data dictionaries run on a variety of hardware–operating system combinations.

What really is needed is not a separate graphical tool and a separate data dictionary. Instead, the two tools should be integrated, so that any change made to a data component is reflected automatically in the corresponding part of the specification document. Among the many examples of this type of tool are Analyst/Designer, Software through Pictures, and System Architect. Furthermore, many such tools also incorporate an automatic consistency checker that ensures consistency between the specification document and the corresponding design document. For example, it is possible to check that every item in the specification document is carried forward to the design document and that everything mentioned in the design has been declared in the data dictionary.

An analysis technique is unlikely to receive widespread acceptance unless a tool-rich CASE environment supports that technique. For example, SREM (Section 11.5) probably would be used far more widely today had REVS, its associated CASE tool set, performed better in the U.S. Air Force tests [Scheffer, Stone, and Rzepka, 1985]. It is not easy to specify a system correctly, even for experienced software professionals. It is only reasonable to provide specifiers with a set of state-of-the-art CASE tools to assist them in every way possible.

## 11.14 Metrics for Classical Analysis

As in all other phases, during classical analysis it is necessary to measure the five fundamental metrics: size, cost, duration, effort, and quality. One measure of the size of a specification is the number of pages in the specification document. If the same technique is used to specify a number of similar products, then differences in specification size may be significant predictors of the effort needed to build the various products.

Turning to quality, a vital aspect of specification inspections is the record of fault statistics. Noting the number of faults of each type found during an inspection is an integral part of the inspection process. Also, the rate at which faults are detected can give a measure of the efficiency of the inspection process.

Metrics for predicting the size of the target product include the number of items in the data dictionary. Several different counts should be taken, including the number of files, data items, and processes (operations). This information can give management a preliminary estimate regarding the effort required to build the product. It is important to note that this information is tentative at best. After all, during the classical design phase, a process in a DFD may be broken down into a number of different modules. Conversely, a number of processes together may constitute a single module. Nevertheless, metrics derived from the data dictionary can give management an early clue as to the eventual size of the target product.

*ase Study*

## 11.15 Software Project Management Plan: The MSG Foundation Case Study

Now that the specifications are complete, the software project management plan (SPMP) is drawn up, including estimates of cost and duration (see Chapter 9). Appendix F contains a software project management plan for development of the MSG Foundation product by a small (three-person) software organization. This plan fits the IEEE SPMP format (Section 9.5).

# 11.16    Challenges of Classical Analysis

A repeated theme of this chapter is that a specification document must be simultaneously informal enough for the client to understand and formal enough for the development team to use as the sole description of the product to be built. A major challenge of classical analysis is to resolve this contradiction. There are no easy answers. On the contrary, a permanent conflict lies between the two competing objectives, and the development team must simply do its best to steer safely between Scylla and Charybdis.

A second challenge of classical analysis is that the boundary line between analysis (what) and design (how) is all too easy to cross. The specification document should describe what the product must do; it must never say how the product is to do it. For example, suppose that the client requires a response time of no more than 0.05 seconds whenever a certain network routing computation is performed. The specification document should state exactly this—and nothing more. In particular, the specification document should *not* state which algorithm must be used to achieve this response time. That is, a specification document has to list all constraints, but it must never state how those constraints are to be achieved.

Another example of this potential pitfall arises from data flow diagrams (Section 11.3.1). A box with rounded ends denotes a process; it does not denote a module. As explained in Section 11.14, a process in a DFD may be broken down into a number of different modules and, conversely, a number of processes may be combined into a single module. The key point is that this refinement of processes into modules must take place during the classical design phase, not the classical analysis phase. The specification document has to describe the operations of the target process. It must never specify how those operations are to be implemented, not even the modules to which each is assigned. The design team's task is to study the specifications as a whole and decide on a design that will result in an optimal implementation of those specifications; this is described in Chapter 13. Until the product as a whole has been decomposed into modules, it is premature to try to assign operations to specific modules; the result is almost certain to be suboptimal.

## Chapter Review

Specifications (Section 11.1) can be expressed informally (Section 11.2), semiformally (Sections 11.3 through 11.5), or formally (Sections 11.6 through 11.10).

The major theme of this chapter is that informal techniques are easy to use but imprecise; this is demonstrated by a mini case study (Section 11.2.1). Conversely, formal techniques are powerful but require a nontrivial investment in training time (Section 11.11). One semiformal technique, Gane and Sarsen's structured systems analysis, is described in some detail (Section 11.3), followed by its application to the MSG Foundation case study (Section 11.4). Other semiformal techniques are then described (Section 11.5), including entity-relationship modeling (Section 11.6). Formal techniques presented in this chapter include finite state machines (Section 11.7), Petri nets (Section 11.8), and Z (Section 11.9). Other formal techniques are outlined in Section 11.10. Material on specification reviews appears in Section 11.12. Next follows a description of CASE tools (Section 11.13) and metrics (Section 11.14) for classical analysis. The software project management plan for the MSG Foundation case study (Section 11.15) is presented next. The chapter ends with a discussion of the challenges of classical analysis (Section 11.16).

**For Further Reading**

The classic texts on structured systems analysis are the books by DeMarco [1978], Gane and Sarsen [1979], and Yourdon and Constantine [1979]. These ideas have been updated in [Modell, 1996]. Data-oriented design, outlined in Section 13.5, is a design technique integrated with a different class of semi-formal analysis techniques; details can be found in [Jackson, 1975; Warnier, 1976; and Orr, 1981]. SADT is described in [Ross, 1985], and PSL/PSA is described in [Teichroew and Hershey, 1977]. Two sources of information on SREM are [Alford, 1985] and [Scheffer, Stone, and Rzepka, 1985].

Six formal techniques are described in [Wing, 1990]. An outstanding collection of papers on formal techniques can be found in the September 1990 issues of *IEEE Transactions on Software Engineering, IEEE Computer, IEEE Software,* and *ACM SIGSOFT Software Engineering Notes.* Of particular interest is [Hall, 1990]; the paper should be read in its entirety. [Bowen and Hinchey, 1995b] is a sequel to Hall's seminal article, and [Bowen and Hinchey, 1995a] is a list of guidelines for use of formal techniques. Additional articles on formal techniques can be found in the August 2000 issue of *IEEE Transactions on Software Engineering.* Lessons learned from applying formal specifications in industry are discussed in [Larsen, Fitzgerald, and Brookes, 1996] and [Pfleeger and Hatton, 1997]. A variety of opinions on techniques can be found in [Saiedian et al., 1996]. A maturity model for formal specifications is presented in [Fraser and Vaishnavi, 1997]. An empirical study comparing different types of formal techniques is presented in [Sobel and Clarkson, 2002]. Haxthausen and Peleska [2000] have applied formal verification to a distributed railway control system. Palshikar [2001] describes the practical use of formal specifications in real-world software development. Hall and Chapman [2002] describe the construction of a commercial secure system using formal techniques.

An early reference to the finite state machine approach is [Naur, 1964], where unfortunately it is referred to as the *Turing machine approach.* Statecharts are a powerful extension of FSMs; they are described in [Harel et al., 1990]. Object-oriented extensions of statecharts appear in [Harel and Gery, 1997].

[Peterson, 1981] is an excellent introduction to Petri nets and their applications. The use of Petri nets in prototyping is described in [Bruno and Marchetto, 1986]. Timed Petri nets are described in [Coolahan and Roussopoulos, 1983].

With regard to Z, [Diller, 1994] is a good introductory text. For the reference manual with full details about the specification language, see [Spivey, 2001]. Using the results of an experiment in reading Z specifications, Finney [1996] questions whether Z specifications are as easy to read as has been claimed by some Z proponents.

The proceedings of the International Workshops on Software Specification and Design are a preeminent source for research ideas regarding specifications.

**Key Terms**

abstract initial state *360*
Anna *363*
bag *354*
Communicating Sequential Processes (CSP) *363*
constraint *331*
data flow *336*
data flow diagram (DFD) *336*
data immediate-access diagram (DIAD) *341*
enable *355*

entity-relationship modeling (ERM) *345*
event *348*
extended finite state machine *349*
final state *348*
finite state machine (FSM) *347*
formal specification *347*
Gist *363*
given set *359*
horizontal schema definition *360*

informal specification *333*
inhibitor arc *356*
initial state *348*
input *348*
input function *354*
logical data flow *336*
marked Petri net *355*
marking *355*
multiset *354*
natural language *333*
operation *361*
output function *354*

**Case Study Key Terms**

**Problems**

11.1  Why should the following constraints not appear in a specification document?

(i) The product must reduce significantly transportation expenses that arise from distributing our beer in central Queensland.

(ii) The credit card database must be set up at a reasonable cost.

11.2  Consider the following recipe for grilled pockwester. Ingredients:

| | |
|---|---|
| 1 large onion | 2 medium-sized eggplants |
| 1 can of frozen orange juice | 1 fresh pockwester |
| Freshly squeezed juice of 1 lemon | ½ cup Pouilly Fuissé |
| 1 cup bread crumbs | 1 garlic |
| Flour | Parmesan cheese |
| Milk | 4 free-range eggs |
| 3 medium-sized shallots | |

The night before, take one lemon, squeeze it, strain the juice, and freeze it. Take one large onion and three shallots, dice them, and grill them in a skillet. When clouds of black smoke start to come off, add 2 cups of fresh orange juice. Stir vigorously. Slice the lemon into paper-thin slices and add to the mixture. In the meantime, coat the mushrooms in flour, dip them in milk, and then shake them in a paper bag with the bread crumbs. In a saucepan, heat ½ cup of Pouilly Fuissé. When it reaches 170°, add the sugar and continue to heat. When the sugar has caramelized, add the mushrooms. Blend the mixture for 10 minutes or until all lumps have been removed. Add the eggs. Now take the pockwester, and kill it by sprinkling it with frobs. Skin the pockwester, break it into bite-sized chunks, and add it to the mixture. Bring to a boil and simmer, uncovered. The eggs previously should have been vigorously stirred with a wire whisk for 5 minutes. When the pockwester is soft to the touch, place it on a serving platter, sprinkle with Parmesan cheese, and broil for not more than 4 minutes.

Determine the ambiguities, omissions, and contradictions in the preceding specification. (For the record, a pockwester is an imaginary sort of fish and *frobs* is slang for generic hors d'oeuvres.)

11.3  Correct the specification paragraph of Section 11.2 to reflect the client's wishes more accurately.

11.4  Use mathematical formulas to represent the specification paragraph of Section 11.2. Compare your answer with your answer to Problem 11.3.

11.5 Write a precise English specification for the product to determine whether a bank statement is correct (Problem 8.8).

11.6 Draw a data flow diagram for the specification you drew up for Problem 11.5. Ensure that your DFD simply reflects the flow of data and that no assumptions regarding computerization have been made.

11.7 Consider the automated library circulation system of Problem 8.7. Write down precise specifications for the library circulation system.

11.8 Draw a data flow diagram showing the operation of the library circulation system of Problem 8.7.

11.9 Complete the specification document for the library circulation system of Problem 8.7 using Gane and Sarsen's technique. Where data have not been specified (for example, the total number of books checked in and out each day), make your own assumptions, but make sure that they are indicated clearly.

11.10 A fixed-point binary number consists of an optional sign followed by one or more bits, followed by a binary point, followed by one or more bits. Examples of floating-point binary numbers include

11010.1010, −0.000001, and +1101101.0

More formally, this can be expressed as

<fixed-point binary> ::= [<sign>] <bitstring> <binary point> <bitstring>

<sign>              ::= + | −

<bitstring>         ::= <bit> [<bitstring>]

<binary point>      ::= .

<bit>               ::= 0 | 1

(The notation [. . .] denotes an optional item, and a | b denotes a or b.)

Specify a finite state machine that will take as input a string of characters and determine whether or not that string constitutes a valid fixed-point binary number.

11.11 Use the finite state machine approach to specify the library circulation system of Problem 8.7.

11.12 Show how your solution to Problem 11.11 can be used to design and implement a menu-driven product for the library circulation system (Problem 8.7).

11.13 Use a Petri net to specify the circulation of a single book through the library of Problem 8.7. Include operations $H$, $C$, and $R$ in your specification.

11.14 You are a software engineer working for a large company that specializes in computerizing library systems. Your manager asks you to specify the complete library circulation system of Problem 8.7 using Z. What is your reaction?

11.15 (Term Project) Using the technique specified by your instructor, draw up a specification document for the Osric's Office Appliances and Decor product described in Appendix A.

11.16 (Term Project) Draw up a software project management plan for the Osric's Office Appliances and Decor product described in Appendix A.

11.17 (Case Study) Draw up the requirements of the MSG Foundation product using the finite state machine approach.

11.18 (Case Study) Use the Petri net technique to specify the states through which a married couple in the MSG Foundation product passes.

11.19 (Case Study) Specify a portion of the MSG Foundation product using the Z constructs of Section 11.9.

11.20 (Case Study) The software project management plan of Section 11.15 is for a small software engineering organization consisting of three software engineers. Modify the plan so that it is appropriate for a medium-sized organization with over 1000 software engineers.

11.21  (Case Study) In what way would the software project management plan of Section 11.15 have to be modified if the MSG Foundation product had to be completed in only 8 weeks?

11.22  (Readings in Software Engineering) Your instructor will distribute copies of [Sobel and Clarkson, 2002]. In what way did this article affect your views on the strengths and weaknesses of formal techniques?

## References

[Abrial, 1980] J.-R. ABRIAL, "The Specification Language Z: Syntax and Semantics," Oxford University Computing Laboratory, Programming Research Group, Oxford, UK, April 1980.

[Alford, 1985] M. ALFORD, "SREM at the Age of Eight; The Distributed Computing Design System," *IEEE Computer* **18** (April 1985), pp. 36–46.

[Balzer, 1985] R. BALZER, "A 15 Year Perspective on Automatic Programming," *IEEE Transactions on Software Engineering* **SE-11** (November 1985), pp. 1257–68.

[Banks, Carson, Nelson, and Nichol, 2001] J. BANKS, J. S. CARSON, B. L. NELSON, AND D. M. NICHOL, *Discrete-Event System Simulation,* 3rd ed., Prentice Hall, Upper Saddle River, NJ, 1995.

[Bowen and Hinchey, 1995a] J. P. BOWEN AND M. G. HINCHEY, "Ten Commandments of Formal Methods," *IEEE Computer* **28** (April 1995), pp. 56–63.

[Bowen and Hinchey, 1995b] J. P. BOWEN AND M. G. HINCHEY, "Seven More Myths of Formal Methods," *IEEE Software* **12** (July 1995), pp. 34–41.

[Brady, 1977] J. M. BRADY, *The Theory of Computer Science,* Chapman and Hall, London, 1977.

[Bruno and Marchetto, 1986] G. BRUNO AND G. MARCHETTO, "Process-Translatable Petri Nets for the Rapid Prototyping of Process Control Systems," *IEEE Transactions on Software Engineering* **SE-12** (February 1986), pp. 346–57.

[Chen, 1976] P. CHEN, "The Entity-Relationship Model—Towards a Unified View of Data," *ACM Transactions on Database Systems* **1** (March 1976), pp. 9–36.

[Coolahan and Roussopoulos, 1983] J. E. COOLAHAN, JR., AND N. ROUSSOPOULOS, "Timing Requirements for Time-Driven Systems Using Augmented Petri Nets," *IEEE Transactions on Software Engineering* **SE-9** (September 1983), pp. 603–16.

[Dart, Ellison, Feiler, and Habermann, 1987] S. A. DART, R. J. ELLISON, P. H. FEILER, AND A. N. HABERMANN, "Software Development Environments," *IEEE Computer* **20** (November 1987), pp. 18–28.

[Delisle and Garlan, 1990] N. DELISLE AND D. GARLAN, "A Formal Description of an Oscilloscope," *IEEE Software* **7** (September 1990), pp. 29–36.

[Delisle and Schwartz, 1987] N. DELISLE AND M. SCHWARTZ, "A Programming Environment for CSP," Proceedings of the Second ACM SIGSOFT/SIGPLAN Software Engineering Symposium on Practical Software Development Environments, *ACM SIGPLAN Notices* **22** (January 1987), pp. 34–41.

[DeMarco, 1978] T. DEMARCO, *Structured Analysis and System Specification,* Yourdon Press, New York, 1978.

[Diller, 1994] A. DILLER, *Z: An Introduction to Formal Methods,* 2nd ed., John Wiley and Sons, Chichester, UK, 1994.

[Doolan, 1992] E. P. DOOLAN, "Experience with Fagan's Inspection Method," *Software—Practice and Experience* **22** (February 1992), pp. 173–82.

[Fagan, 1976] M. E. FAGAN, "Design and Code Inspections to Reduce Errors in Program Development," *IBM Systems Journal* **15** (No. 3, 1976), pp. 182–211.

[Finney, 1996] K. FINNEY, "Mathematical Notation in Formal Specification: Too Difficult for the Masses?" *IEEE Transactions on Software Engineering* **22** (1996), pp. 158–59.

[Fraser and Vaishnavi, 1997] M. D. FRASER AND V. K. VAISHNAVI, "A Formal Specifications Maturity Model," *Communications of the ACM* **40** (May 1999), pp. 95–103.

[Gane and Sarsen, 1979] C. GANE AND T. SARSEN, *Structured Systems Analysis: Tools and Techniques,* Prentice Hall, Englewood Cliffs, NJ, 1979.

[Ghezzi and Mandrioli, 1987] C. GHEZZI AND D. MANDRIOLI, "On Eclecticism in Specifications: A Case Study Centered around Petri Nets," *Proceedings of the Fourth International Workshop on Software Specification and Design,* Monterey, CA, 1987, pp. 216–24.

[Goodenough and Gerhart, 1975] J. B. GOODENOUGH AND S. L. GERHART, "Toward a Theory of Test Data Selection," *Proceedings of the Third International Conference on Reliable Software,* Los Angeles, 1975, pp. 493–510; also published in: *IEEE Transactions on Software Engineering* **SE-1** (June 1975), pp. 156–73. Revised version: J. B. Goodenough, and S. L. Gerhart, "Toward a Theory of Test Data Selection: Data Selection Criteria," in: *Current Trends in Programming Methodology,* Vol. 2, R. T. Yeh (Editor), Prentice Hall, Englewood Cliffs, NJ, 1977, pp. 44–79.

[Gordon, 1979] M. J. C. GORDON, *The Denotational Description of Programming Languages: An Introduction,* Springer-Verlag, New York, 1979.

[Guha, Lang, and Bassiouni, 1987] R. K. GUHA, S. D. LANG, AND M. BASSIOUNI, "Software Specification and Design Using Petri Nets," *Proceedings of the Fourth International Workshop on Software Specification and Design,* Monterey, CA, April 1987, pp. 225–30.

[Hall, 1990] A. HALL, "Seven Myths of Formal Methods," *IEEE Software* **7** (September 1990), pp. 11–19.

[Hall and Chapman, 2002] A. HALL AND R. CHAPMAN, "Correctness by Construction: Developing a Commercial Secure System," *IEEE Software* **19** (January/February 2002), pp. 18–25.

[Harel and Gery, 1997] D. HAREL AND E. GERY, "Executable Object Modeling with Statecharts," *IEEE Computer* **30** (July 1997), pp. 31–42.

[Harel et al., 1990] D. HAREL, H. LACHOVER, A. NAAMAD, A. PNUELI, M. POLITI, R. SHERMAN, A. SHTULL-TRAURING, AND M. TRAKHTENBROT, "STATEMATE: A Working Environment for the Development of Complex Reactive Systems," *IEEE Transactions on Software Engineering* **16** (April 1990), pp. 403–14.

[Haxthausen and Peleska, 2000] A. E. HAXTHAUSEN AND J. PELESKA, "Formal Development and Verification of a Distributed Railway Control System," *IEEE Transactions on Software Engineering* **26** (August 2000), pp. 687–701.

[Hoare, 1985] C. A. R. HOARE, *Communicating Sequential Processes,* Prentice Hall International, Englewood Cliffs, NJ, 1985.

[IWSSD, 1986] Call for Papers, Fourth International Workshop on Software Specification and Design, *ACM SIGSOFT Software Engineering Notes* **11** (April 1986), pp. 94–96.

[Jackson, 1975] M. A. JACKSON, *Principles of Program Design,* Academic Press, New York, 1975.

[Jones, 1986b] C. B. JONES, *Systematic Software Development Using VDM,* Prentice Hall, Englewood Cliffs, NJ, 1986.

[Kampen, 1987] G. R. KAMPEN, "An Eclectic Approach to Specification," *Proceedings of the Fourth International Workshop on Software Specification and Design,* Monterey, CA, April 1987, pp. 178–82.

[Kleinrock and Gail, 1996] L. KLEINROCK AND R. GAIL, *Queuing Systems: Problems and Solutions,* John Wiley and Sons, New York, 1996.

[Knuth, 1968] D. E. KNUTH, *The Art of Computer Programming,* Vol. I, *Fundamental Algorithms,* Addison-Wesley, Reading, MA, 1968.

[Larsen, Fitzgerald, and Brookes, 1996] P. G. LARSEN, J. FITZGERALD, AND T. BROOKES, "Applying Formal Specification in Industry," *IEEE Software* **13** (May 1996), pp. 48–56.

[Leavenworth, 1970] B. LEAVENWORTH, Review #19420, *Computing Reviews* **11** (July 1970), pp. 396–97.

[London, 1971] R. L. LONDON, "Software Reliability through Proving Programs Correct," *Proceedings of the IEEE International Symposium on Fault-Tolerant Computing,* Pasadena, CA, March 1971.

[Luckham and von Henke, 1985] D. C. LUCKHAM AND F. W. VON HENKE, "An Overview of Anna, a Specification Language for Ada," *IEEE Software* **2** (March 1985), pp. 9–22.

[Meyer, 1985] B. MEYER, "On Formalism in Specifications," *IEEE Software* **2** (January 1985), pp. 6–26.

[Modell, 1996] M. E. MODELL, *A Professional's Guide to Systems Analysis,* 2nd ed., McGraw-Hill, New York, 1996.

[Naur, 1964] P. NAUR, "The Design of the GIER ALGOL Compiler," in: *Annual Review in Automatic Programming,* Vol. 4, Pergamon Press, Oxford, UK, 1964, pp. 49–85.

[Naur, 1969] P. NAUR, "Programming by Action Clusters," *BIT* **9** (No. 3, 1969), pp. 250–58.

[Nix and Collins, 1988] C. J. NIX AND B. P. COLLINS, "The Use of Software Engineering, Including the Z Notation, in the Development of CICS," *Quality Assurance* **14** (September 1988), pp. 103–10.

[Oest, 1986] O. N. OEST, "VDM from Research to Practice," *Proceedings of the IFIP Congress, Information Processing '86,* 1986, pp. 527–33.

[Orr, 1981] K. ORR, *Structured Requirements Definition,* Ken Orr and Associates, Inc., Topeka, KS, 1981.

[Palshikar, 2001] G. K. PALSHIKAR, "Applying Formal Specifications to Real-World Software Development," *IEEE Software* **18** (November/December 2001), pp. 89–97.

[Peterson, 1981] J. L. PETERSON, *Petri Net Theory and the Modeling of Systems,* Prentice Hall, Englewood Cliffs, NJ, 1981.

[Petri, 1962] C. A. PETRI, "Kommunikation mit Automaten," Ph.D. Dissertation, University of Bonn, Germany, 1962. [In German.]

[Pfleeger and Hatton, 1997] S. L. PFLEEGER AND L. HATTON, "Investigating the Influence of Formal Methods," *IEEE Computer* **30** (February 1997), pp. 33–43.

[Ross, 1985] D. T. ROSS, "Applications and Extensions of SADT," *IEEE Computer* **18** (April 1985), pp. 25–34.

[Saiedian et al., 1996] H. SAIEDIAN, J. P. BOWEN, R. W. BUTLER, D. L. DILL, R. L. GLASS, D. GRIES, A. HALL, M. G. HINCHEY, C. M. HOLLOWAY, D. JACKSON, C. B. JONES, M. J. LUTZ, D. L. PARNAS, J. RUSHBY, J. WING, AND P. ZAVE, "An Invitation to Formal Methods," *IEEE Computer* **29** (April 1996), pp. 16–30.

[Scheffer, Stone, and Rzepka, 1985] P. A. SCHEFFER, A. H. STONE, III, AND W. E. RZEPKA, "A Case Study of SREM," *IEEE Computer* **18** (April 1985), pp. 47–54.

[Schwartz and Delisle, 1987] M. D. SCHWARTZ AND N. M. DELISLE, "Specifying a Lift Control System with CSP," *Proceedings of the Fourth International Workshop on Software Specification and Design,* Monterey, CA, April 1987, pp. 21–27.

[Silberschatz, Galvin, and Gagne, 2002] A. SILBERSCHATZ, P. B. GALVIN, AND G. GAGNE, *Operating System Concepts,* 6th ed., Addison-Wesley, Reading, MA, 2002.

[Sobel and Clarkson, 2002] A. E. K. SOBEL AND M. R. CLARKSON, "Formal Methods Application: An Empirical Tale of Software Development," *IEEE Transactions on Software Engineering* **28** (March 2002), pp. 308–20.

[Spivey, 1990] J. M. SPIVEY, "Specifying a Real-Time Kernel," *IEEE Software* **7** (September 1990), pp. 21–28.

[Spivey, 2001] J. M. SPIVEY, *The Z Notation: A Reference Manual*, 3rd ed., spivey.oriel.ox.ac.uk/ ~mike/zrm/, 2001.

[Teichroew and Hershey, 1977] D. TEICHROEW AND E. A. HERSHEY, III, "PSL/PSA: A Computer-Aided Technique for Structured Documentation and Analysis of Information Processing Systems," *IEEE Transactions on Software Engineering* **SE-3** (January 1977), pp. 41–48.

[Warnier, 1976] J. D. WARNIER, *Logical Construction of Programs*, Van Nostrand Reinhold, New York, 1976.

[Wing, 1990] J. WING, "A Specifier's Introduction to Formal Methods," *IEEE Computer* **23** (September 1990), pp. 8–24.

[Woodcock, 1989] J. WOODCOCK, "Calculating Properties of Z Specifications," *ACM SIGSOFT Software Engineering Notes* **14** (July 1989), pp. 43–54.

[Yourdon and Constantine, 1979] E. YOURDON AND L. L. CONSTANTINE, *Structured Design: Fundamentals of a Discipline of Computer Program and Systems Design*, Prentice Hall, Englewood Cliffs, NJ, 1979.

# Chapter

# 12

# Object-Oriented Analysis

**Learning Objectives**

After studying this chapter, you should be able to

- Perform the analysis workflow.
- Extract the boundary, control, and entity classes.
- Perform functional modeling.
- Perform class modeling.
- Perform dynamic modeling.
- Perform use-case realization.

In Chapter 11, we examined various classical analysis techniques. This chapter is the object-oriented counterpart of Chapter 11.

**Object-oriented analysis** (OOA) is a semiformal analysis technique for the object-oriented paradigm. In Chapter 11, we pointed out that a number of different techniques are used for structured systems analysis, all essentially equivalent. Similarly, well over 60 different techniques have been put forward for OOA. Again, all the techniques are largely equivalent. The "For Further Reading" section of this chapter includes references to a wide variety of techniques, as well as to published comparisons of different techniques.

However, as explained in Section 3.1, today the Unified Process [Jacobson, Booch, and Rumbaugh, 1999] is almost always the methodology of choice for object-oriented software production. For this reason, the first and last part of this chapter are devoted to the analysis workflow of the Unified Process.

Object-oriented analysis is a key component of the object-oriented paradigm. When this workflow is performed, the classes are extracted. The use cases and the classes are the basis

Most of the major advances in the object-oriented paradigm were made between 1990 and 1995. Because it usually takes some 15 years for new technology to become accepted, widespread adoption of the object-oriented paradigm should have started no sooner than 2005. However, the **millennium bug** or **Y2K problem** changed the expected timetable.

In the 1960s, when computers first started to be used for business on a widespread basis, hardware was far more expensive than it is today. As a result, the vast majority of software products of that vintage represented a date using only the last two digits for a year; the leading 19 was understood. The problem with this scheme is that the year 00 is then interpreted as 1900, not 2000.

When hardware became cheaper in the 1970s and 1980s, few managers saw any point in spending large sums of money rewriting existing software products with four-digit dates. After all, by the time the year 2000 arrived, it would be someone else's problem. As a result, **legacy systems** remained year-2000 noncompliant. However, as the deadline of January 1, 2000, neared, software organizations were forced to work against the clock to fix their software products; there was no way to postpone the arrival of Y2K.

Problems facing the maintenance programmers included a lack of documentation for many legacy software products, as well as software products written in programming languages that were now obsolete. When modifying an existing software product was impossible, the only alternative was to start again from scratch. Some companies decided to use COTS technology (Section 1.11). Others decided that new custom software products were needed. For obvious reasons, managers wanted these software products to be developed using modern technology that had already been shown to be cost effective, and that meant using the object-oriented paradigm. The Y2K problem was therefore a significant catalyst for the widespread acceptance of the object-oriented paradigm.

of the object-oriented software product to be developed. (For more insight into the object-oriented paradigm, see Just in Case You Wanted to Know Box 12.1.)

## 12.1　The Analysis Workflow

The **analysis workflow** of the Unified Process [Jacobson, Booch, and Rumbaugh, 1999] has two aims. From the viewpoint of the requirements workflow (the preceding workflow), the aim of the analysis workflow is to obtain a deeper understanding of the requirements. Conversely, from the viewpoint of the design and implementation workflows (the workflows that follow the analysis workflow), the aim of the analysis workflow is to describe those requirements in such a way that the resulting design and implementation are easy to maintain.

The Unified Process is use-case driven. During the analysis workflow, the use cases are described in terms of the classes of the software product. The Unified Process has three types of classes: entity classes, boundary classes, and control classes. An **entity class** models information that is long lived. In the case of a banking software product, **Account Class** is an entity class because information on accounts has to stay in the software product. For the MSG Foundation software product, **Investment Class** is an entity class; again, information on investments has to be long lived.

A **boundary class** models the interaction between the software product and its actors. Boundary classes are generally associated with input and output. For example, in the MSG

**FIGURE 12.1**   UML stereotypes (extensions of UML) for representing an entity class, a boundary class, and a control class.

**Entity Class**    **Boundary Class**    **Control Class**

Foundation software product, reports have to be printed listing the investments of the Foundation, as well as all the mortgages currently held. This means that boundary classes **Investments Report Class** and **Mortgages Report Class** are needed.

A **control class** models complex computations and algorithms. In the case of the MSG Foundation software product, the algorithm for estimating the funds available for the week is a control class, namely, **Estimate Funds for Week Class**.

The UML notation for these three types of classes is shown in Figure 12.1. These are **stereotypes**, that is, extensions of UML. A strength of UML is that it allows additional constructs to be defined that are not part of UML but may be needed to model a specific system accurately.

As stated at the beginning of this section, during the analysis workflow, the use cases are described in terms of the classes of the software product. The Unified Process itself does not describe how classes are to be extracted, because users of the Unified Process are expected to have a background in object-oriented analysis and design. Accordingly, this discussion of the Unified Process is temporarily suspended so that an explanation can be given of how classes are extracted; we return to the Unified Process in Section 12.15.

Entity classes, that is, classes that model long-lived information, are considered first.

## 12.2   Extracting the Entity Classes

Entity class extraction consists of three steps that are carried out iteratively and incrementally:

1. **Functional modeling.** Present scenarios of all the use cases (a **scenario** is an instance of a use case).
2. **Entity class modeling.** Determine the entity classes and their attributes. Then, determine the interrelationships and interactions between the entity classes. Present this information in the form of a class diagram.
3. **Dynamic modeling.** Determine the operations performed by or to each entity class or subclass. Present this information in the form of a statechart.

However, as with all iterative and incremental processes, the three steps are not necessarily always performed in this order; a change in one model frequently triggers corresponding revisions of the other two models.

To show how this is done, we now extract the entity classes of the elevator problem case study.

## Case Study

### 12.3 Object-Oriented Analysis: The Elevator Problem Case Study

The elevator problem case study is described in Chapter 11. For ease of reference, the problem is repeated here.

A product is to be installed to control n elevators in a building with m floors. The problem concerns the logic required to move elevators between floors according to the following constraints:

1. Each elevator has a set of m buttons, one for each floor. These illuminate when pressed and cause the elevator to visit the corresponding floor. The illumination is canceled when the corresponding floor is visited by the elevator.

2. Each floor, except the first floor and the top floor, has two buttons, one to request an up-elevator and one to request a down-elevator. These buttons illuminate when pressed. The illumination is canceled when an elevator visits the floor and then moves in the desired direction.

3. When an elevator has no requests, it remains at its current floor with its doors closed.

The first step in OOA is to model the use cases.

## Case Study

### 12.4 Functional Modeling: The Elevator Problem Case Study

A **use case** describes the interaction between the product to be constructed and the **actors**, that is, the external users of that product. The only interactions possible between a user and an elevator are the user pressing an elevator button to summon an elevator or the user pressing a floor button to request the elevator to stop at a specific floor, hence, the two use cases, `Press an Elevator Button` and `Press a Floor Button`. The two use cases are shown in the use-case diagram (Section 10.7) of Figure 12.2.

**FIGURE 12.2**
Use-case diagram for the elevator problem case study.

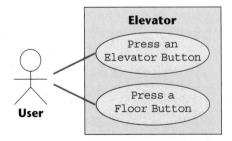

**FIGURE 12.3**   The first iteration of a normal scenario.

1. User A presses the Up floor button at floor 3 to request an elevator. User A wishes to go to floor 7.
2. The Up floor button is turned on.
3. An elevator arrives at floor 3. It contains User B, who has entered the elevator at floor 1 and pressed the elevator button for floor 9.
4. The elevator doors open.
5. The timer starts.
   User A enters the elevator.
6. User A presses the elevator button for floor 7.
7. The elevator button for floor 7 is turned on.
8. The elevator doors close after a timeout.
9. The Up floor button is turned off.
10. The elevator travels to floor 7.
11. The elevator button for floor 7 is turned off.
12. The elevator doors open to allow User A to exit from the elevator.
13. The timer starts.
    User A exits from the elevator.
14. The elevator doors close after a timeout.
15. The elevator proceeds to floor 9 with User B.

A use case provides a generic description of the overall functionality; a scenario is a specific instantiation of a use case, just as an object is an instantiation of a class. In general, there are a large number of scenarios, each representing one specific set of interactions. In this section, we consider the scenario of Figure 12.3, which incorporates instantiations of both use cases.

Figure 12.3 depicts a **normal scenario**; that is, a set of interactions between users and elevators that corresponds to the way we understand elevators should be used. Figure 12.3 was constructed after carefully observing different users interacting with elevators (or, more precisely, with elevator buttons and floor buttons). The 15 numbered events describe in detail the two interactions between User A and the buttons of the elevator system (event 1 and event 6) and the operations performed by the components of the elevator system (events 2 through 5 and 7 through 15). Two items, User A enters the elevator and User A exits from the elevator, are unnumbered. Such items essentially are comments; User A does not interact with the components of the elevator when entering or leaving an elevator.

In contrast, Figure 12.4 is an **exception scenario**. It depicts what happens when a user presses the Up button at floor 3 but actually wants to go down to floor 1. This scenario, too, was constructed by observing the actions of many users in elevators; it is unlikely that someone who has never used an elevator would realize that users sometimes press the wrong button.

The scenarios of Figures 12.3 and 12.4, plus innumerable others, are specific instances of the use cases shown in Figure 12.2. Sufficient scenarios should be studied

**FIGURE 12.4** An exception scenario.

1. User A presses the Up floor button at floor 3 to request an elevator. User A wishes to go to floor 1.
2. The Up floor button is turned on.
3. An elevator arrives at floor 3. It contains User B, who has entered the elevator at floor 1 and pressed the elevator button for floor 9.
4. The elevator doors open.
5. The timer starts.
   User A enters the elevator.
6. User A presses the elevator button for floor 1.
7. The elevator button for floor 1 is turned on.
8. The elevator doors close after a timeout.
9. The Up floor button is turned off.
10. The elevator travels to floor 9.
11. The elevator button for floor 9 is turned off.
12. The elevator doors open to allow User B to exit from the elevator.
13. The timer starts.
    User B exits from the elevator.
14. The elevator doors close after a timeout.
15. The elevator proceeds to floor 1 with User A.

to give the OOA team a comprehensive insight into the behavior of the system being modeled. This information is used in the next step, entity class modeling, to determine the entity classes.

## 12.5 Entity Class Modeling: The Elevator Problem Case Study

In this step, the entity classes and their attributes are extracted and represented in a UML class diagram. Only the attributes of an entity class are determined at this time, not the methods; the latter are assigned to the classes during the object-oriented design (OOD) workflow.

A characteristic of the whole object-oriented paradigm is that the various steps rarely are easy to carry out. Fortunately, the benefits of using objects make the effort worthwhile. So it should not come as a surprise that the first part of the analysis workflow, extracting entity classes and their attributes, usually is difficult to get right the first time.

One method of determining the entity classes is to deduce them from the use cases. That is, the developers carefully study all the scenarios, both normal and exception, and identify the components that play a role in the use cases. From just the scenarios of Figures 12.3 and 12.4, candidate entity classes are elevator buttons, floor buttons, elevators, doors, and timers. As we will see, these candidate entity classes are close to the actual classes extracted during entity class modeling. In general, however, there are many scenarios and, consequently, a large number of potential classes. An inexperienced developer may be tempted to infer too many candidate entity classes from the scenarios. This has a deleterious effect on the entity class modeling, because it is easier to add a new entity class than to remove a candidate entity class that should not have been included.

Another approach to determining the entity classes, which is effective when the developers have domain expertise, is CRC cards (Section 12.5.2). However, if the developers have little or no experience in the application domain, then it is advisable to use noun extraction, described in Section 12.5.1.

## 12.5.1 Noun Extraction

For developers with no domain expertise, a good way to proceed is to use the following two-stage **noun-extraction method** to extract candidate entity classes and then to refine the solution:

### Stage 1. Describe the Software Product in a Single Paragraph

One possible way to do this for the elevator problem case study is as follows:

> Buttons in elevators and on the floors control the movement of n elevators in a building with m floors. Buttons illuminate when pressed to request the elevator to stop at a specific floor; the illumination is canceled when the request has been satisfied. When an elevator has no requests, it remains at its current floor with its doors closed.

### Stage 2. Identify the Nouns

Identify the nouns in the informal strategy (excluding those that lie outside the problem boundary), and then use these nouns as candidate entity classes. The informal strategy is now reproduced, but this time with the identified nouns printed in a sans serif typeface.

> Buttons in elevators and on the floors control the movement of n elevators in a building with m floors. Buttons illuminate when pressed to request an elevator to stop at a specific floor; the illumination is canceled when the request has been satisfied. When an elevator has no requests, it remains at its current floor with its doors closed.

There are eight different nouns: button, elevator, floor, movement, building, illumination, request, and door. Three of these nouns—floor, building, and door—lie outside the problem boundary and therefore may be ignored. Three of the remaining nouns—movement, illumination, and request—are **abstract nouns**; that is, they identify things that have no physical existence. A useful rule of thumb is that abstract nouns rarely end up corresponding to classes. Instead, they frequently are attributes of classes. For example, illumination is an **attribute** of button. This

**FIGURE 12.5**
The first
iteration of the
class diagram
for the elevator
problem case
study.

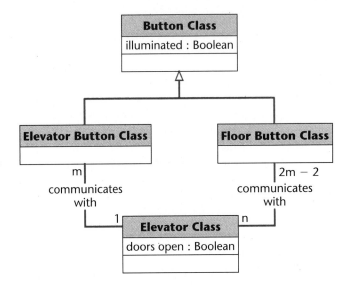

leaves two nouns and, therefore, two candidate entity classes: **Elevator Class** and **Button Class**. (The UML convention is to use boldface for class names and capitalize the initial letter of each word in a class name.)

The resulting **class diagram** is shown in Figure 12.5. **Button Class** has the Boolean attribute illuminated to model events 2, 7, 9, and 11 of the scenarios of Figures 12.3 and 12.4. The problem specifies two types of button, so two subclasses of **Button Class** are defined: **Elevator Button Class** and **Floor Button Class** (the open triangle denotes inheritance in UML). Each instance of **Elevator Button Class** and **Floor Button** communicates with the instance of **Elevator Class**. The latter class has the Boolean attribute doors open to model events 4, 8, 12, and 14 of the two scenarios.

Unfortunately, this is not a good beginning. In a real elevator, the buttons do not directly communicate with the elevators; some sort of elevator controller is needed, if only to decide which elevator to dispatch in response to a particular request. However, the problem statement makes no mention of a controller, so it was not selected as an entity class during the noun-extraction process. In other words, the technique of this section for finding candidate entity classes provides a starting point but certainly should not be relied on to do more than that.

Adding the **Elevator Controller Class** to Figure 12.5 yields Figure 12.6. This certainly makes more sense. Furthermore, there are now one-to-many relationships in Figure 12.6, as opposed to the hard to model many-to-many relationship of Figure 12.5. It therefore seems reasonable to go on to step 3 at this point, bearing in mind that it is possible to return to entity class modeling at any time, even as late as the implementation workflow. However, before proceeding with the dynamic modeling, a different technique for entity class modeling is considered.

**FIGURE 12.6**
The second
iteration of the
class diagram
for the elevator
problem case
study.

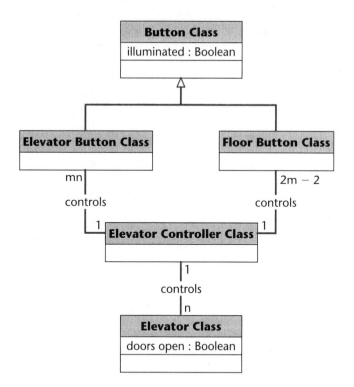

## 12.5.2 CRC Cards

For a number of years, **class–responsibility–collaboration** (CRC) **cards** have been utilized during the object-oriented analysis workflow [Wirfs-Brock, Wilkerson, and Wiener, 1990]. For each class, the software development team fills in a card showing the name of the class, its functionality (responsibility), and a list of the other classes it invokes to achieve that functionality (collaboration).

This approach subsequently has been extended. First, a CRC card often explicitly contains the attributes and methods of the class, rather than just its "responsibility" expressed in some natural language. Second, the technology has changed. Instead of using cards, some organizations put the names of the classes on Post-it Notes, which they move around on a white board; lines are drawn between the Post-it Notes to denote collaboration. Nowadays the whole process can be automated; CASE tools like System Architect include components for creating and updating CRC "cards" on the screen.

The strength of CRC cards is that, when utilized by a team, the interaction among the members can highlight missing or incorrect fields in a class, whether attributes or methods. Also, the relationships between classes are clarified when CRC cards are used. One especially powerful technique is to distribute the cards among the team members, who then act out the responsibilities of their classes. Thus, someone might say, "I am the **Date Class**, and my responsibility is to create new date objects." Another team member might then interject that he or she needs additional functionality from the **Date Class**, such as

How do we find the number of days between February 21, 1999, and August 16, 2007? Such subtractions are needed in many financial computations, such as calculating an interest payment or determining the present value of a future cash flow. The usual way this is done is to convert each date into an integer, the number of days since a specified starting date. The problem is that we cannot agree what starting date to use.

Astronomers use Julian days, the number of days since noon GMT on January 1, 4713, B.C.E. This system was invented in 1582 by Joseph Scaliger, who named it for his father, Julius Caesar Scaliger. (If you really, really have to know why January 1, 4713 B.C.E. was chosen, consult [USNO, 2000].)

A Lilian date is the number of days since October 15, 1582, the first day of the Gregorian calendar, introduced by Pope Gregory XIII. Lilian dates are named for Luigi Lilio, a leading proponent of the Gregorian calendar reform. Lilio was responsible for deriving many of the algorithms of the Gregorian calendar, including the rule for leap years.

Turning to software, COBOL intrinsic functions use January 1, 1600 as the starting date for integer dates. Almost all spreadsheets, however, use January 1, 1900, following the lead of Lotus 1-2-3.

converting a date from the conventional format to an integer, the number of days from January 1, 1900, so that finding the number of days between any two dates can be computed easily by subtracting the corresponding two integers (see Just in Case You Wanted to Know Box 12.2). Thus, acting out the responsibilities of CRC cards is an effective means of verifying that the class diagram is complete and correct.

A weakness of CRC cards is that this approach generally is not a good way of identifying entity classes unless the team members have considerable experience in the relevant application domain. On the other hand, once the developers have determined many of the classes and have a good idea of their responsibilities and collaborations, CRC cards can be an excellent way of completing the process and making sure that everything is correct. This is described in Section 12.7.

## Case Study

### 12.6 Dynamic Modeling: The Elevator Problem Case Study

The aim of dynamic modeling is to produce a **statechart**, a description of the target product similar to a finite state machine, for each class. First, consider **Elevator Controller Class**. For simplicity, only one elevator is considered. The relevant statechart for **Elevator Controller Class** is in Figure 12.7.

The notation is somewhat similar to that of the finite state machine (FSM) of Section 11.7, but there is a significant difference. An FSM as presented in Chapter 11 is an example of a formal technique. The state transition diagrams themselves are not a complete representation of the product to be built. Instead, the model consists of a set of transition rules of the form given in equation (11.2):

$$\textbf{current state} \text{ and } \textbf{event} \text{ and } \textbf{predicate} \Rightarrow \textbf{next state}$$

**FIGURE 12.7**   The first iteration of the statechart for **Elevator Controller Class**.

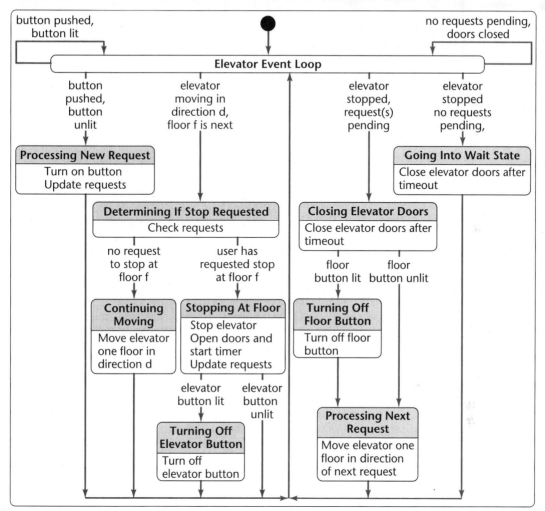

Formality is achieved by presenting the model in the form of a set of mathematical rules.

In contrast, the representation of a UML statechart is somewhat less formal. The three aspects of a state machine (state, event, and predicate) are distributed over the UML diagram. For example, the state **Going Into Wait State** in Figure 12.7 is entered if the present state is **Elevator Event Loop** and the event elevator stopped, no requests pending is true. When the state **Going Into Wait State** has been entered, operation Close elevator doors after timeout is to be carried out. Current versions of OOA are semiformal (graphical) techniques, and the intrinsic lack of formality of the statechart accordingly is no problem. However, when the object-oriented paradigm matures, it is likely that more formal versions will be developed and the corresponding dynamic models will be somewhat closer to finite state machines.

To see the equivalence of the statechart of Figure 12.7 and the STDs of Figures 11.15 through 11.17, consider various scenarios. For example, consider the first part of the scenario of Figure 12.3. Event 1 is User A presses the Up floor button at floor 3.

First consider the STD of Figure 11.16. If the floor button is off, then the button is turned on. Now consider the statechart of Figure 12.7. The solid circle denotes the start state, which takes the system into state **Elevator Event Loop**. Following the leftmost vertical line, if the button is unlit when pushed, the system enters state **Processing New Request** of Figure 12.7, and the button is turned on. The following state is **Elevator Event Loop**.

Next, the elevator nears floor 3. First consider the STD approach. In Figure 11.17, the elevator goes into state S (U, 3); that is, it stops at floor 3, about to go up. (Because the simplifying assumption has been made of only one elevator, the argument e in Figure 11.17 is suppressed here.) Now the doors close (Figure 11.17), the Up floor button is turned off (Figure 11.16), and the elevator starts to move toward floor 4.

Returning to the statechart of Figure 12.7, consider what happens when the elevator nears floor 3. Because the elevator is in motion, the next state entered is **Determining If Stop Requested**. The requests are checked and, because User A has requested the elevator to stop there, the next state is **Stopping At Floor**. The elevator stops at floor 3, the doors open, and the timer starts. The elevator button for floor 3 has not been pressed, so state **Elevator Event Loop** is next.

User A enters and presses the elevator button for floor 7. Therefore, the next state is again **Processing New Request**, followed again by **Elevator Event Loop**. The elevator has stopped and two requests are pending, so state **Closing Elevator Doors** is next and the doors close after a timeout. The floor button at floor 3 was pressed by User A, so **Turning Off Floor Button** is the following state, and the floor button is turned off. State **Processing Next Request** is next, and the elevator starts to move toward floor 4. The relevant aspects of the corresponding diagrams clearly are equivalent with respect to this scenario; you may wish to consider other possible scenarios as well.

From the preceding discussion, it should come as no surprise to learn that Figure 12.7 was constructed from the scenarios. More precisely, the specific events of the scenarios were generalized. For example, consider the first event of the scenario of Figure 12.3, User A presses the Up floor button at floor 3. This specific event is generalized to an arbitrary button (floor button or elevator button) being pushed. Then, there are two possibilities. Either the button already is lit (in which case nothing happens) or the button is unlit (in which case action must be taken to process the user's request).

To model this event, the **Elevator Event Loop** state is drawn in Figure 12.7. The case of an already lit button is modeled by the do-nothing loop with event button pushed, button lit in the top left-hand corner of Figure 12.7. The other case, an unlit button, is modeled by the arrow labeled with the event button pushed, button unlit leading to state **Processing New Request**. From event 2 of the scenario it is clear that the operation Turn on button is needed in this state. Furthermore, the purpose of the user's action of pressing an arbitrary button is to request an elevator (floor button) or request an elevator to move to a specific floor (elevator button), so operation Update requests also must be carried out in the state **Processing New Request**.

Now consider event 3 of the scenario, An elevator arrives at floor 3. This was generalized to the concept of an arbitrary elevator moving between floors. The motion of the elevator is modeled by the event elevator moving in direction d, floor f is next and the state **Determining If Stop Requested**. But there again are two possibilities, either a request to stop at floor f or no such request. In the former case, corresponding to event no request to stop at floor f, the elevator simply must be in the state of **Continuing Moving** one more floor in direction d. In the latter case (corresponding to event user has requested stop at floor f), from the scenario of Figure 12.3 it is clear that it is necessary to Stop elevator (from event 3), and then Open doors and start timer (from events 4 and 5); state **Stopping at Floor** is needed to perform these actions. Also, similar to the **Processing New Request** state, it becomes apparent that it is necessary also to Update requests in state **Stopping at Floor**. In addition, generalizing event 9 of the scenario leads to the realization that the floor button has to be turned off if it is lit. This is modeled by state **Turning Off Floor Button**, together with the two events above the box representing that state. Similarly, generalizing event 11 of the scenario similarly implies that the elevator button has to be turned off if it is lit. This is modeled by state **Turning Off Elevator Button**, together with the two events above the box representing that state.

Generalizing event 8 of the scenario of Figure 12.3 yields state **Closing Elevator Doors**; generalizing event 10 yields state **Processing Next Request**. However, the need for the state **Going into Wait State** and the event no requests pending, doors closed is deduced by generalizing an event of a different scenario, one in which the user exits from the elevator but no buttons remain lit.

The statecharts for the other classes are relatively straightforward and therefore left as an exercise (Problem 12.1).

*Case Study*

## 12.7 The Test Workflow: Object-Oriented Analysis

At this point, the functional, entity class, and dynamic models appear to be complete and the **test workflow** resumes. The next step is to review the analysis workflow to date. One component of this review, as suggested in Section 12.5.2, is to use CRC cards.

Accordingly, CRC cards are filled in for each of the entity classes, **Button Class**, **Elevator Button Class**, **Floor Button Class**, **Elevator Class**, and **Elevator Controller Class**. The CRC card for **Elevator Controller Class**, shown in Figure 12.8, is deduced from the class diagram of Figure 12.5 and the statechart of Figure 12.6. In more detail, the RESPONSIBILITY of **Elevator Controller Class** is obtained by listing all the operations in the statechart for **Elevator Controller Class** (Figure 12.7). The COLLABORATION of the **Elevator Controller Class** is determined by examining the class diagram of Figure 12.6 and noting that classes **Elevator Button Class**, **Floor Button Class**, and **Elevator Class** interact with class **Elevator Controller Class**.

**FIGURE 12.8**
The first
iteration of the
CRC card for
**Elevator
Controller
Class**.

| CLASS |
| :---: |
| **Elevator Controller Class** |
| RESPONSIBILITY |
| 1. Turn on elevator button |
| 2. Turn off elevator button |
| 3. Turn on floor button |
| 4. Turn off floor button |
| 5. Move elevator up one floor |
| 6. Move elevator down one floor |
| 7. Open elevator doors and start timer |
| 8. Close elevator doors after timeout |
| 9. Check requests |
| 10. Update requests |
| COLLABORATION |
| 1. **Elevator Button Class** |
| 2. **Floor Button Class** |
| 3. **Elevator Class** |

This CRC card highlights two major problems with the first iteration of the object-oriented analysis.

1. Consider responsibility 1. Turn on elevator button. This command is totally out of place in the object-oriented paradigm. From the viewpoint of responsibility-driven design (Section 1.9), objects (instances) of **Elevator Button Class** are responsible for turning themselves on or off. Also, from the viewpoint of information hiding (Section 7.6), the **Elevator Controller Class** should not have the knowledge of the internals of **Elevator Button Class** needed to turn on a button. The correct responsibility is this: Send a message to **Elevator Button Class** to turn itself on. Similar changes are needed for responsibilities 2 through 6 in Figure 12.8. These six corrections are reflected in Figure 12.9, the second iteration of the CRC card for the **Elevator Controller Class**.

2. A class has been overlooked. Returning to Figure 12.8, consider responsibility 7. Open elevator doors and start timer. The key concept here is the notion of **state**. The attributes of a class sometimes are termed **state variables**. The reason for this terminology is that, in most object-oriented implementations, the state of the product is determined by the values of the attributes of the various component objects. The statechart has many features in common with a finite state machine. Accordingly, it is not surprising that the concept of state plays an important role in the object-oriented paradigm. This concept can be used to help determine whether a component should be modeled as a class. If the component in question possesses a state that is changed during execution of the implementation, then it probably should be modeled as a class. Clearly, the doors of the elevator possess a state (open or closed), and **Elevator Doors Class** therefore should be a class.

**FIGURE 12.9**
The second
iteration of the
CRC card for
the class
**Elevator
Controller
Class**.

| CLASS |
|---|
| **Elevator Controller Class** |
| RESPONSIBILITY |
| 1. Send message to **Elevator Button Class** to turn on button |
| 2. Send message to **Elevator Button Class** to turn off button |
| 3. Send message to **Floor Button Class** to turn on button |
| 4. Send message to **Floor Button Class** to turn off button |
| 5. Send message to **Elevator Class** to move up one floor |
| 6. Send message to **Elevator Class** to move down one floor |
| 7. Send message to **Elevator Doors Class** to open |
| 8. Start timer |
| 9. Send message to **Elevator Doors Class** to close after timeout |
| 10. Check requests |
| 11. Update requests |
| COLLABORATION |
| 1. **Elevator Button Class** (subclass) |
| 2. **Floor Button Class** (subclass) |
| 3. **Elevator Doors Class** |
| 4. **Elevator Class** |

There is another reason why **Elevator Doors Class** should be a class. The object-oriented paradigm allows the state to be hidden within an object and hence protected from unauthorized change. If there is an **Elevator Doors Class** object, the only way that the doors of the elevator can be opened or shut is by sending a message to that **Elevator Doors Class** object. Serious accidents can be caused by opening or closing the doors of an elevator at the wrong time; see Just in Case You Wanted to Know Box 12.3. Therefore, for certain types of products, safety considerations should be added to the other strengths of objects listed in Chapters 7 and 8.

Adding **Elevator Doors Class** means that responsibilities 7 and 8 in Figure 12.8 need to be changed analogously to responsibilities 1 through 6. That is, messages should be sent to instances of the **Elevator Doors Class** to open and close themselves. But there is an additional complication. Responsibility 7 is Open elevator doors and start timer.

This must be split into two separate responsibilities. A message indeed must be sent to **Elevator Doors Class** to open. However, the timer is part of the **Elevator Controller Class**, and starting the timer therefore is the responsibility of the **Elevator Controller Class** itself. The second iteration of the CRC card for **Elevator Controller Class** (Figure 12.9) shows that this separation of responsibilities has been achieved satisfactorily.

In addition to the two major problems highlighted by the CRC card of Figure 12.8, responsibilities Check requests and Update requests of **Elevator Controller Class** require the attribute requests be added to **Elevator Controller Class**. At this stage, requests are defined simply to be of type requestType; a data structure for requests will be chosen during the design workflow.

Some years ago, I was on the 10th floor of a building, waiting impatiently for an elevator. The doors opened, I started to step forward—only no elevator was there. What saved my life was the total blackness I saw as I was about to step into the elevator shaft, and I instinctively realized that something was wrong.

Perhaps, if that elevator control system had been developed using the object-oriented paradigm, the inappropriate opening of the doors on the 10th floor might have been avoided.

The corrected class diagram is shown in Figure 12.10. Having modified the class diagram, the use-case diagram and statecharts must be reexamined to see if they, too, need further refinement. The use-case diagram clearly still is adequate. However, the operations in the statechart of Figure 12.7 must be modified to reflect the responsibilities of Figure 12.9 (the second iteration of the CRC card) and not Figure 12.8 (the first iteration). Also, the set of statecharts must be extended to include the additional class. The scenarios need to be updated to reflect these changes; Figure 12.11 shows the second iteration of the scenario of Figure 12.3. Even after all these changes have been made and checked (including the modified CRC cards), it still may be necessary during the object-oriented design workflow to return to the object-oriented analysis workflow and revise one or more of the analysis artifacts. However, at this stage it appears that the entity classes for the elevator problem case study have been correctly extracted.

**FIGURE 12.10**
The third iteration of the class diagram for the elevator problem case study.

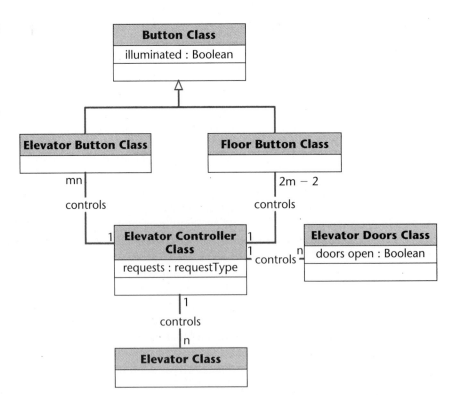

**FIGURE 12.11**   The second iteration of a normal scenario for the elevator problem case study.

1. User A presses the Up floor button at floor 3 to request an elevator. User A wishes to go to floor 7.
2. The floor button informs the elevator controller that the floor button has been pushed.
3. The elevator controller sends a message to the Up floor button to turn itself on.
4. The elevator controller sends a series of messages to the elevator to move itself up to floor 3. The elevator contains User B, who has entered the elevator at floor 1 and pressed the elevator button for floor 9.
5. The elevator controller sends a message to the elevator doors to open themselves.
6. The elevator controller starts the timer.
   User A enters the elevator.
7. User A presses elevator button for floor 7.
8. The elevator button informs the elevator controller that the elevator button has been pushed.
9. The elevator controller sends a message to the elevator button for floor 7 to turn itself on.
10. The elevator controller sends a message to the elevator doors to close themselves after a timeout.
11. The elevator controller sends a message to the Up floor button to turn itself off.
12. The elevator controller sends a series of messages to the elevator to move itself up to floor 7.
13. The elevator controller sends a message to the elevator button for floor 7 to turn itself off.
14. The elevator controller sends a message to the elevator doors to open themselves to allow User A to exit from the elevator.
15. The elevator controller starts the timer.
    User A exits from the elevator.
16. The elevator controller sends a message to the elevator doors to close themselves after a timeout.
17. The elevator controller sends a series of messages to the elevator to move itself up to floor 9 with User B.

# 12.8   Extracting the Boundary and Control Classes

Unlike entity classes, boundary classes are usually easy to extract. In general, each input screen, output screen, and printed report is modeled by its own boundary class. Recall that a class incorporates attributes (data) and operations. The boundary class modeling (say) a printed report incorporates all the various data items that can be included in the report and the various operations carried out to print the report.

Control classes are usually as easy to extract as boundary classes. In general, each nontrivial computation is modeled by a control class.

We now illustrate entity, boundary, and control class extraction by extracting the classes of the MSG Foundation case study. The starting point is the use-case diagram of Figure 10.42, reproduced here as Figure 12.12.

**FIGURE 12.12**
The seventh
iteration of the
use-case
diagram of
the MSG
Foundation case
study.

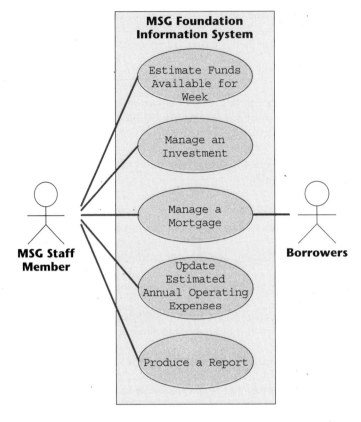

# Case Study

## 12.9 The Initial Functional Model: The MSG Foundation Case Study

As described in Section 12.2, functional modeling consists of finding the scenarios of the use cases. Recall that a scenario is an instance of a use case. Consider the use case `Manage a Mortgage` (Figures 10.32 and 10.33). One possible scenario is shown in Figure 12.13. There is a change in the annual real-estate tax to be paid on a home for which the MSG Foundation has provided a mortgage. Because the borrowers pay this tax in equal weekly payments, any change in the real-estate tax must be entered in the relevant mortgage record, so that the total weekly installment (and perhaps the grant) can be adjusted accordingly. The normal portion of the extended scenario models an MSG staff member accessing the relevant mortgage record and changing the annual real-estate tax. Sometimes, however, the staff member may not be able to locate the correct mortgage stored in the software product because he or she has

**FIGURE 12.13**   An extended scenario of managing a mortgage.

An MSG Foundation staff member wants to update the annual real-estate tax on a home for which the Foundation has provided a mortgage.
1. The staff member enters the new value of the annual real-estate tax.
2. The information system updates the date on which the annual real-estate tax was last changed.

**Possible Alternative**

A. The staff member enters the mortgage number incorrectly.

**FIGURE 12.14**   Another extended scenario of managing a mortgage.

There is a change in the weekly income of a couple who have borrowed money from the MSG Foundation. They wish to have their weekly income updated in the Foundation records by an MSG staff member so that their mortgage payments will be correctly computed.
1. The staff member enters the new value of the weekly income.
2. The information system updates the date on which the weekly income was last changed.

**Possible Alternatives**

A. The staff member enters the mortgage number incorrectly.
B. The borrowers do not bring documentation regarding their new income.

entered the mortgage number incorrectly. This possibility is modeled by the exception portion of the scenario.

A second scenario corresponding to the `Manage a Mortgage` use case (Figures 10.32 and 10.33) is shown in Figure 12.14. Here the borrowers' weekly income has changed. They would like this information to be reflected in the MSG Foundation records so that their weekly installment can be correctly computed. The normal portion of this extended scenario shows this operation proceeding as expected. The abnormal portion of this scenario shows two possibilities. First, as in the previous scenario, the staff member may enter the mortgage number incorrectly. Second, the borrowers may not bring with them adequate documentation to support their claim regarding their income, in which case the requested change is not implemented.

A third scenario (Figure 12.15) is an instance of use case `Estimate Funds Available for Week` (Figure 10.42). This scenario is directly derived from the description of the use case (Figure 10.43).

The scenarios of Figures 12.16 and 12.17 are instances of use case `Produce a Report`. Again, these scenarios are directly derived from the corresponding description of the use case (Figure 10.39). The remaining scenarios are equally straightforward and are therefore left as an exercise (Problems 12.8 and 12.9).

**FIGURE 12.15** A scenario of the `Estimate Funds Available for Week` use case.

An MSG Foundation staff member wishes to determine the funds available for mortgages this week.

1. For each investment, the information system extracts the estimated annual return on that investment. It sums the separate returns and divides the result by 52 to yield the estimated investment income for the week.
2. The information system then extracts the estimated annual MSG Foundation operating expenses and divides the result by 52.
3. For each mortgage:
   3.1 The information system computes the amount to be paid this week by adding the principal and interest payment to $\frac{1}{52}$nd of the sum of the annual real-estate tax and the annual homeowner's insurance premium.
   3.2 It then computes 28 percent of the couple's current gross weekly income.
   3.3 If the result of Step 3.1 is greater than the result of Step 3.2, then it determines the mortgage payment for the week as the result of Step 3.2, and the amount of the grant for this week as the difference between the result of Step 3.1 and the result of Step 3.2.
   3.4 Otherwise, it takes the mortgage payment for this week as the result of Step 3.1, and there is no grant for the week.
4. The information system sums the mortgage payments of Steps 3.3 and 3.4 to yield the estimated total mortgage payments for the week.
5. It sums the grant payments of Step 3.3 to yield the estimated total grant payments for the week.
6. The information system adds the results of Steps 1 and 4 and subtracts the results of Steps 2 and 5. This is the total amount available for mortgages for the current week.
7. Finally, the software product prints the total amount available for new mortgages during the current week.

**FIGURE 12.16** A scenario of the `Produce a Report` use case.

An MSG staff member wishes to print a list of all mortgages.

1. The staff member requests a report listing all mortgages.

**FIGURE 12.17** Another scenario of the `Produce a Report` use case.

An MSG staff member wishes to print a list of all investments.

1. The staff member requests a report listing all investments.

## *Case Study*

### 12.10 The Initial Class Diagram: The MSG Foundation Case Study

The second step is class modeling. The aim of this step is to extract the entity classes, determine their interrelationships, and find their attributes. The best way to start this step is usually to use the two-stage noun extraction method (Section 12.5.1).

In Stage 1 we describe the software product in a single paragraph. In the case of the MSG Foundation case study, a way to do this is

> Weekly reports are to be printed showing how much money is available for mortgages. In addition, lists of investments and mortgages must be printed on demand.

In Stage 2 we identify the nouns in this paragraph. For clarity, the nouns are printed in sans serif type.

> Weekly reports are to be printed showing how much money is available for mortgages. In addition, lists of investments and mortgages must be printed on demand.

The nouns are report, money, mortgage, list, and investment. Nouns report and list are not long lived, so they are unlikely to be entity classes (report will surely turn out to be a boundary class), and money is an abstract noun. This leaves two candidate entity classes, namely, **Mortgage Class** and **Investment Class**, as shown in Figure 12.18, the first iteration of the initial class diagram.

Now we consider interactions between these two entity classes. Looking at the descriptions of use cases Manage an Investment and Manage a Mortgage (Figures 10.31 and 10.33, respectively) it appears that the operations performed on the two entity classes are likely to be very similar, namely, insertions, deletions, and modifications. Also, the second iteration of the description of use case Produce a Report (Figure 10.39) shows all the members of both entity classes have to be printed on demand. In other words, **Mortgage Class** and **Investment Class** should probably be subclasses of some superclass. We will call that superclass **Asset Class**, because mortgages and investments are both assets of the MSG Foundation. The resulting second iteration of the initial class diagram is shown in Figure 12.19.

A useful side effect of constructing this superclass is that we can once again reduce the number of use cases. As shown in Figure 12.12, we currently have five use

**FIGURE 12.18**   The first iteration of the initial class diagram of the MSG Foundation case study.

| Mortgage Class | Investment Class |
| --- | --- |
|  |  |

**FIGURE 12.19**
The second
iteration of the
initial class
diagram of the
MSG
Foundation case
study.

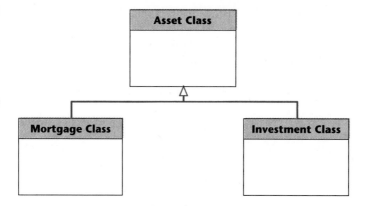

**FIGURE 12.20**
The eighth
iteration of the
use-case
diagram of the
MSG
Foundation case
study. The new
use case,
`Manage an
Asset`, is
shaded.

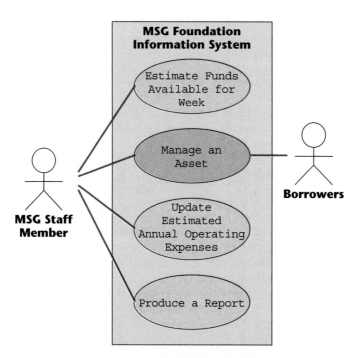

cases, including `Manage a Mortgage` and `Manage an Investment`. However, if we consider a mortgage or an investment to be a special case of an asset, we can combine the two use cases into a single use case, `Manage an Asset`. The eighth iteration of the use-case diagram is shown in Figure 12.20. The new use case is shaded. Now the attributes are added, as shown in Figure 12.21.

The phrase "iteration and *in*crementation" also includes the possibility of the need for a *de*crementation in what has been developed to date. There are two reasons for such a decrease. First, if a mistake is made, the best way to correct it may be to **backtrack** to an earlier version of the software product and find a better way of performing the step that was incorrectly carried out. When backtracking, everything

**FIGURE 12.21**   Attributes added to the second iteration of the initial class diagram of the MSG Foundation case study.

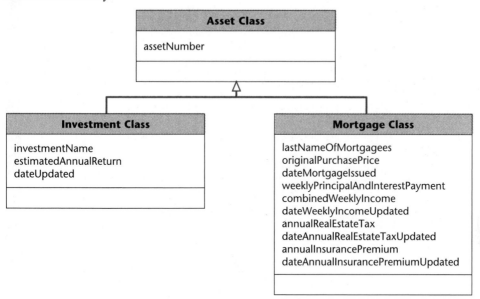

that was added in the course of the incorrect step now has to be removed. Second, as a consequence of reorganizing the models to date, one or more artifacts may have become superfluous. Developing a software product is hard. It is therefore important to remove superfluous use cases or other artifacts as soon as possible.

## *Case Study*

### 12.11 The Initial Dynamic Model: The MSG Foundation Case Study

The third step in object-oriented analysis is dynamic modeling. In this step, a statechart is drawn that reflects all the operations performed by or to that system, indicating the events that cause the transition from state to state. The major source of information regarding the relevant operations is the scenarios.

The statechart of Figure 12.22 reflects the operations of the complete MSG Foundation case study. The solid circle on the top left represents the initial state, the starting point of the statechart. The arrow from the initial state leads us to the state labeled **MSG Foundation Event Loop**; states other than the initial and final states are represented by rectangles with rounded corners. In state **MSG Foundation Event Loop**, one of five events can occur. In more detail, an MSG staff member can issue one of five commands: estimate funds for the week, manage an asset, update estimated annual operating expenses, produce a report, or quit. These possibilities are indicated by the five events estimate funds for the week selected, manage an asset

**FIGURE 12.22** The initial statechart of the MSG Foundation case study.

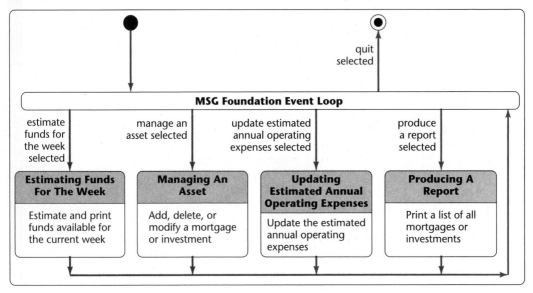

**FIGURE 12.23** Menu in the target MSG Foundation case study.

**FIGURE 12.24** Textual version of the menu of Figure 12.23.

```
                    MAIN MENU
MARTHA STOCKTON GREENGAGE FOUNDATION
      1. Estimate funds available for week
      2. Manage an asset
      3. Update estimated annual operating expenses
      4. Produce a report
      5. Quit
Type your choice and press <ENTER>:
```

selected, update estimated annual operating expenses selected, produce a report selected, and quit selected. (An **event** causes a **transition** between states.)

When the system is in state **MSG Foundation Event Loop**, any one of the five events may occur, depending on which option the MSG staff member selects from the menu, shown in Figure 12.23, that will be incorporated in the target software product. (The C++ and Java implementations of the MSG Foundation case study given in Appendices H and I, respectively, use a textual interface rather than a graphical user interface (GUI). That is, instead of clicking on a box, as shown in Figure 12.23, the user types in a choice, as shown in Figure 12.24. For example, the user types 1 to **Estimate funds available for week**, 2 to **Manage an asset**, and so on. The reason the implementations in Appendices H and I use a textual interface, such as Figure 12.24, is that a textual interface can be run on all computers; a GUI generally needs special software.)

Suppose that the MSG staff member clicks on the choice *Manage an asset* in the menu of Figure 12.23. The event manage an asset selected (second from the left below the **MSG Foundation Event Loop** box in Figure 12.22) has now occurred, so the system moves from its current state, **MSG Foundation Event Loop**, to the state **Managing An Asset**. The operations that the MSG staff member can perform in this state, namely, Add, delete, or modify a mortgage or investment, appear below the line in the box with rounded corners.

Once the operation has been performed, the system returns to the state **MSG Foundation Event Loop**, as shown by the arrows. The behavior of the rest of the statechart is equally straightforward.

In summary, the software product moves from state to state. In each state, the MSG staff member can perform the operations supported by that state, as listed below the line in the box with rounded corners that represents the state. This continues until the MSG staff member clicks on menu choice *Quit* when the software product is in the state **MSG Foundation Event Loop**. At this time the software product enters the final state (represented by the white circle containing the small black circle). When this state is entered, execution of the statechart terminates; recall that the statechart is a model of the execution of the target software product.

## Case Study
## 12.12  Revising the Entity Classes: The MSG Foundation Case Study

The initial functional model, the initial class diagram, and the initial dynamic model have now been completed. However, a check of all three models reveals that something has been overlooked.

Look at the initial statechart of Figure 12.22 and consider state **Updating Estimated Annual Operating Expenses** with operation Update the estimated annual operating expenses. This operation has to be performed on data, namely, the current value of the estimated annual operating expenses. But where is the value of the estimated annual operating expenses to be found? Looking at Figure 12.21, it would have been a serious error to have it as an attribute of **Asset Class** or either of its subclasses. On the other hand, currently there is only one class (**Asset Class**) and its two subclasses. This means that the only way a value can be stored on a long-term basis is as an attribute of an instance of that class or its subclasses.

The solution is obvious: Another entity class is needed in which the value of the estimated annual operating expenses can be stored. In fact, other values need to be stored as well; the result is shown in Figure 12.25. A new class, **MSG Application Class**, has been introduced in which the various attributes shown in the top box in the figure can be stored. In addition, the **MSG Application Class** will be assigned the task of starting the execution of the rest of the software product.

Now the class diagram of Figure 12.25 is redrawn to reflect the stereotypes. This is shown in Figure 12.26. All four classes are entity classes. The entity classes seem to be correct, at least for now. The next step is to determine the boundary classes and control classes.

**FIGURE 12.25**   The third iteration of the initial class diagram of the MSG Foundation case study.

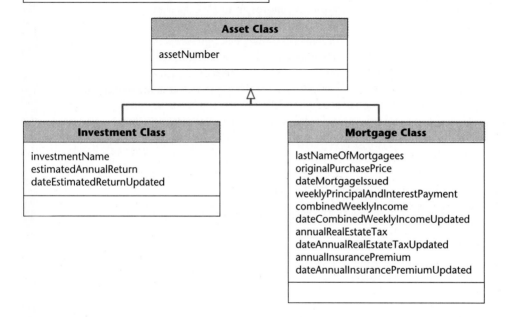

**MSG Application Class**

estimatedAnnualOperatingExpenses
dateEstimatedAnnualOperatingExpensesUpdated
availableFundsForWeek
expectedAnnualReturnOnInvestments
dateExpectedAnnualReturnOnInvestmentsUpdated
expectedGrantsForWeek
expectedMortgagePaymentsForWeek

**Asset Class**

assetNumber

**Investment Class**

investmentName
estimatedAnnualReturn
dateEstimatedReturnUpdated

**Mortgage Class**

lastNameOfMortgagees
originalPurchasePrice
dateMortgageIssued
weeklyPrincipalAndInterestPayment
combinedWeeklyIncome
dateCombinedWeeklyIncomeUpdated
annualRealEstateTax
dateAnnualRealEstateTaxUpdated
annualInsurancePremium
dateAnnualInsurancePremiumUpdated

**FIGURE 12.26**
Figure 12.25
redrawn to show
the stereotypes.

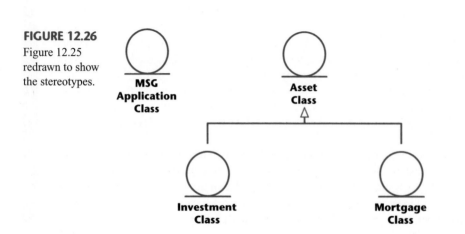

**MSG Application Class**

**Asset Class**

**Investment Class**

**Mortgage Class**

*ase Study*

### 12.13 Extracting the Boundary Classes: The MSG Foundation Case Study

Extracting entity classes is usually considerably harder than extracting boundary classes. After all, entity classes generally have interrelationships, whereas each input screen, output screen, and printed report is usually modeled by an (independent) boundary class, as pointed out in Section 12.8.

In view of the fact that the target MSG Foundation software product appears to be relatively straightforward (at least at this early stage of the Unified Process), it is reasonable to try to have just one screen that the MSG staff member can use for all four use cases: `Estimate Funds Available for Week`, `Manage an Asset`, `Update Estimated Annual Operating Expenses`, and `Produce a Report`. As more is learned about the MSG Foundation, it is certainly possible that this one screen may have to be refined into two or more screens. But the initial class extraction has just the one screen class, **User Interface Class**.

There are three reports that have to be printed, the estimated funds for the week report and the two asset reports, namely, the complete listing of all mortgages or of all investments. Each of these has to be modeled by a separate boundary class because the content of each report is different. The four corresponding initial boundary classes are then **User Interface Class**, **Estimated Funds Report Class**, **Mortgages Report Class**, and **Investments Report Class**. These four classes are displayed in Figure 12.27.

**FIGURE 12.27**
The initial boundary classes of the MSG Foundation case study.

| |
|---|
| **User Interface Class** |
| **Estimated Funds Report Class** |
| **Mortgages Report Class** |
| **Investments Report Class** |

*ase Study*

### 12.14 Extracting the Control Classes: The MSG Foundation Case Study

Control classes are generally as easy to extract as boundary classes because each nontrivial computation is almost always modeled by a control class, as stated in Section 12.8. For the MSG Foundation case study, there is just one computation, namely, estimating the funds available for the week. This yields the initial control class **Estimate Funds for Week Class** shown in Figure 12.28.

**FIGURE 12.28** The initial control class of the MSG Foundation case study.

Estimate Funds for Week Class

The next step is to check all three sets of classes: entity classes, boundary classes, and control classes. Careful examination of the classes yields no obvious discrepancies. Having completed class extraction, we now return to the Unified Process.

# Case Study

## 12.15 Use-Case Realization: The MSG Foundation Case Study

A use case is a description of an interaction between an actor and the software product. Use cases are first utilized at the beginning of the software life cycle, that is, in the requirements workflow. During the analysis and design workflows, more details are added to each use case, including a description of the classes involved in carrying out the use case. This process of extending and refining use cases is called **use-case realization**. Finally, during the implementation workflow, the use cases are implemented in code.

This terminology is somewhat confusing, because the verb *realize* can be used in at least three different senses:

- Understand ("Harvey slowly began to realize that he was in the wrong classroom").
- Receive ("Ingrid will realize a profit of $45,000 on the stock transaction").
- Accomplish ("Janet hopes to realize her dream of starting a software development organization").

In the phrase *realize a use case*, the word **realize** is used in this last sense; that is, it means to *accomplish* (or *achieve*) the use case.

An **interaction diagram** (**sequence diagram** or **collaboration diagram**) depicts the realization of a specific scenario of the use case. We first consider the use case Estimate Funds Available for Week.

### 12.15.1 Estimate Funds Available for Week **Use Case**

The use-case diagram of Figure 12.20 shows all the use cases. These include Estimate Funds Available for Week, which is shown separately in Figure 12.29. The description of that use case was given in Figure 10.43, which is reproduced here as Figure 12.30 for convenience. From the description we deduce that, as reflected in the class diagram of Figure 12.31, the classes that enter into this use case are **User Interface Class**, which models the user interface; **Estimate Funds for Week Class**, the control class that models the computation of the estimate of the funds that

**FIGURE 12.29**

The Estimate
Funds
Available
for Week use
case.

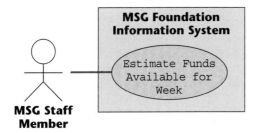

**MSG Staff
Member**

**FIGURE 12.30** The description of the Estimate Funds Available for Week use case.

---

**Brief Description**

The Estimate Funds Available for Week use case enables an MSG Foundation staff member to estimate how much money the Foundation has available that week to fund mortgages.

---

**Step-by-Step Description**

1. For each investment, extract the estimated annual return on that investment. Summing the separate returns and dividing the result by 52 yields the estimated investment income for the week.
2. Determine the estimated MSG Foundation operating expenses for the week by extracting the estimated annual MSG Foundation operating expenses and dividing by 52.
3. For each mortgage:
   3.1 The amount to be paid this week is the total of the principal and interest payment and $\frac{1}{52}$nd of the sum of the annual real-estate tax and the annual homeowner's insurance premium.
   3.2 Compute 28 percent of the couple's current gross weekly income.
   3.3 If the result of Step 3.1 is greater than the result of Step 3.2, then the mortgage payment for this week is the result of Step 3.2, and the amount of the grant for this week is the difference between the result of Step 3.1 and the result of Step 3.2.
   3.4 Otherwise, the mortgage payment for this week is the result of Step 3.1, and there is no grant this week.
4. Summing the mortgage payments of Steps 3.3 and 3.4 yields the estimated total mortgage payments for the week.
5. Summing the grant payments of Step 3.3 yields the estimated total grant payments for the week.
6. Add the results of Steps 1 and 4 and subtract the results of Steps 2 and 5. This is the total amount available for mortgages for the current week.
7. Print the total amount available for new mortgages during the current week.

---

are available to fund mortgages during that week; **Mortgage Class**, which models the estimated grants and payments for the week; **Investment Class**, which models the estimated return on investments for the week; **MSG Application Class**, which models the estimated operating expenses for the week; and **Estimated Funds Report Class**, which models the printing of the report.

**FIGURE 12.31**
Class diagram showing the classes that realize the `Estimate Funds Available for Week` use case of the MSG Foundation case study.

Figure 12.31 is a class diagram. That is, it shows the classes that participate in the realization of the use case and their relationships. A working software product, on the other hand, uses objects rather than classes. For example, a specific mortgage cannot be represented by **Mortgage Class** but rather by an object, a specific instance of **Mortgage Class**, denoted by **: Mortgage Class**. Also, the class diagram of Figure 12.31 shows the participating classes in the use case and their relationships; it does not show the sequence of events as they occur. Something more is needed to model a specific scenario such as the scenario of Figure 12.15, reproduced here as Figure 12.32.

Now consider Figure 12.33. This figure is a collaboration diagram. It therefore shows the objects that interact as well as the messages that are sent, numbered in the order in which they are sent. A collaboration diagram depicts a realization of a specific scenario of a use case. In this case, Figure 12.33 depicts the scenario of Figure 12.32. In more detail, in the scenario the staff member wants to compute the funds available for the week. This is represented by message 1: Request estimate of funds available for week from **MSG Staff Member** to **: User Interface Class**, an instance of **User Interface Class**.

Next, this request is passed on to **: Estimate Funds for Week Class**, an instance of the control class that actually performs the calculation. This is represented by message 2: Transfer request.

Four separate financial estimates are now determined by **: Estimate Funds for Week Class**. In step 1 of the scenario (Figure 12.32), the estimated annual return on investments is summed for each investment and the result divided by 52. This

**FIGURE 12.32** A scenario of the `Estimate Funds Available for Week` use case.

An MSG Foundation staff member wishes to determine the funds available for mortgages this week.

1. For each investment, the information system extracts the estimated annual return on that investment. It sums the separate returns and divides the result by 52 to yield the estimated investment income for the week.

2. The information system then extracts the estimated annual MSG Foundation operating expenses and divides the result by 52.

3. For each mortgage:

   3.1 The information system computes the amount to be paid this week by adding the principal and interest payment to $\frac{1}{52}$nd of the sum of the annual real-estate tax and the annual homeowner's insurance premium.

   3.2 It then computes 28 percent of the couple's current gross weekly income.

   3.3 If the result of Step 3.1 is greater than the result of Step 3.2, then it determines the mortgage payment for the week as the result of Step 3.2, and the amount of the grant for this week as the difference between the result of Step 3.1 and the result of Step 3.2.

   3.4 Otherwise, it takes the mortgage payment for this week as the result of Step 3.1, and there is no grant for the week.

4. The information system sums the mortgage payments of Steps 3.3 and 3.4 to yield the estimated total mortgage payments for the week.

5. It sums the grant payments of Step 3.3 to yield the estimated total grant payments for the week.

6. The information system adds the results of Steps 1 and 4 and subtracts the results of Steps 2 and 5. This is the total amount available for mortgages for the current week.

7. Finally, the software product prints the total amount available for new mortgages during the current week.

extraction of the estimated weekly return is modeled in Figure 12.33 by message 3: Request estimated return on investments for week from **: Estimate Funds for Week Class** to **: Investment Class** followed by message 4: Return estimated weekly return on investments in the reverse direction, that is, back to the object that is controlling the computation.

In step 2 of the scenario (Figure 12.32), the weekly operating expenses are estimated by taking the estimated annual operating expenses and dividing by 52. This extraction of the weekly return is modeled in Figure 12.33 by message 5: Request estimated operating expenses for week from **: Estimate Funds for Week Class** to **: MSG Application Class** followed by message 6: Return estimated operating expenses for week in the other direction.

In steps 3, 4, and 5 of the scenario (Figure 12.32), two estimates are determined, namely, the estimated grants for the week and the estimated payments for the week. This is modeled in Figure 12.33 by message 7: Request estimated grants and payments for week from **: Estimate Funds for Week Class** to **: Mortgage Class** and by message 8: Return estimated grants and payments for week in the reverse direction.

**FIGURE 12.33** A collaboration diagram of the realization of the scenario of Figure 12.32 of the `Estimate Funds Available for Week` use case of the MSG Foundation case study.

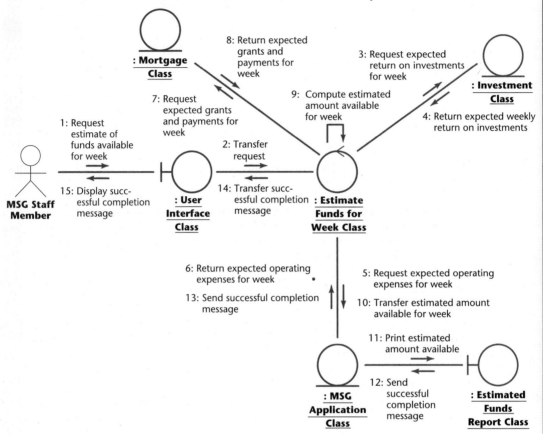

Now the arithmetic computation of step 6 of the scenario is performed. This is modeled in Figure 12.33 by message 9: Compute estimated amount available for week. This is a self-call, that is, **: Estimate Funds for Week Class** tells itself to perform the calculation. The result of the computation is stored in **: MSG Application Class** by message 10: Transfer estimated amount available for week.

Next, the result is printed in step 7 of the scenario (Figure 12.32). This is modeled in Figure 12.33 by message 11: Print estimated amount available from **: MSG Application Class** to **: Estimated Funds Report Class**.

Finally, an acknowledgment is sent to the MSG staff member that the task has been successfully completed. This is modeled in Figure 12.33 by messages 12: Send successful completion message, 13: Send successful completion message, 14: Transfer successful completion message, and 15: Display successful completion message.

**FIGURE 12.34**   The flow of events of the collaboration diagram of Figure 12.33 of the realization of the scenario of Figure 12.32 of the `Estimate Funds Available for Week` use case of the MSG Foundation case study.

> An MSG staff member requests an estimate of the funds available for mortgages for the week (1, 2). The information system estimates the return on investments for the week (3, 4), the operating expenses for the week (5, 6), and the grants and payments for the week (7, 8). Then it estimates (9), stores (10), and prints out (11–15) the funds available for the week.

No client is going to approve the specification document unless he or she understands precisely what the proposed software product will do. For this reason, a written description of the collaboration diagram is essential. This is shown in Figure 12.34, the **flow of events**. Finally, the equivalent sequence diagram of the realization of the scenario is shown in Figure 12.35. When constructing a software product, either a collaboration diagram or a sequence diagram may prove to give better insight of a realization of a use case. In some situations, both are needed to get a full understanding of a specific realization of a given use case. That is why, in this chapter, every collaboration diagram is followed by the equivalent sequence diagram. The sequence diagram of Figure 12.35 is fully equivalent to the collaboration diagram of Figure 12.33, so its flow of events is also shown in Figure 12.34.

The strength of a sequence diagram is that it shows the flow of messages unambiguously. The order of the messages is particularly clear, as are the sender and receiver of each individual message. So, when the transfer of information is the focus of attention (which is the case for much of the time when performing the analysis workflow), a sequence diagram is superior to a collaboration diagram. On the other hand, the similarity between a class diagram (such as Figure 12.31) and the collaboration diagram that realizes the relevant scenario (such as Figure 12.33) is strong. Accordingly, on those occasions when the developers are concentrating on the classes, a collaboration diagram is generally more useful than the equivalent sequence diagram.

Summarizing, Figures 12.29 through 12.35 do not depict a random collection of UML artifacts. On the contrary, these figures depict a use case and artifacts derived from that use case. In more detail:

- Figure 12.29 depicts the use case `Estimate Funds Available for Week`. That is, Figure 12.29 models all possible sets of interactions, between the actor **MSG Staff Member** (an entity that is external to the software product) and the MSG Foundation software product itself, that relate to the action of estimating funds available for the week.
- Figure 12.30 is the description of that use case; that is, it provides a written account of the details of the `Estimate Funds Available for Week` use case of Figure 12.29.
- Figure 12.31 is a class diagram showing the classes that realize the `Estimate Funds Available for Week` use case. The class diagram depicts the classes that are needed to model all possible scenarios of the use case, together with their interactions.

**FIGURE 12.35** A sequence diagram of the realization of the scenario of Figure 12.32 of the `Estimate Funds Available for Week` use case of the MSG Foundation case study. This sequence diagram is fully equivalent to the collaboration diagram of Figure 12.33, so its flow of events is also shown in Figure 12.34.

- Figure 12.32 is a scenario, that is, one specific instance of the use case of Figure 12.29.
- Figure 12.33 is a collaboration diagram of the realization of the scenario of Figure 12.32; that is, it depicts the objects and the messages sent between them in the realization of that one specific scenario.
- Figure 12.34 is the flow of events of the collaboration diagram of the realization of the scenario of Figure 12.32. That is, just as Figure 12.30 is a written description of the `Estimate Funds Available for Week` use case of Figure 12.29, Figure 12.34 is a written description of the realization of the scenario of Figure 12.32.
- Figure 12.35 is the sequence diagram that is fully equivalent to the collaboration diagram of Figure 12.33. That is, the sequence diagram depicts the objects and the messages sent between them in the realization of the scenario of Figure 12.32. Its flow of events is therefore also shown in Figure 12.34.

It has been stated many times in this book that the Unified Process is use-case driven. These bulleted items explicitly state the precise relationship between each of the artifacts of Figures 12.30 through 12.35 and the use case of Figure 12.29 that underlies each of them.

### 12.15.2 `Manage an Asset` **Use Case**

The `Manage an Asset` use case is shown in Figure 12.36 and its description in Figure 12.37. A class diagram showing the classes that realize the `Manage an Asset` use case is shown in Figure 12.38. Initially it was assumed that only one control class

**FIGURE 12.36**
The `Manage an Asset` use case.

**MSG Foundation Information System**

Manage an Asset

**MSG Staff Member**

**Borrowers**

**FIGURE 12.37**
Description of the `Manage an Asset` use case.

**Brief Description**

The `Manage an Asset` use case enables an MSG Foundation staff member to add and delete assets and manage the portfolio of assets (investments and mortgages). Managing a mortgage includes updating the weekly income of a couple who have borrowed money from the Foundation.

**Step-by-Step Description**

1. Add, modify, or delete an investment or mortgage, or update the borrower's weekly income.

**FIGURE 12.38**

A class diagram showing the classes that realize the `Manage an Asset` use case of the MSG Foundation case study.

In some scenarios, the borrowers tell the MSG staff member their current weekly income.

Borrowers

Mortgage Class

MSG Staff Member

User Interface Class

Manage an Asset Class

Investment Class

**FIGURE 12.39**

A scenario of the `Manage an Asset` use case.

> An MSG Foundation staff member wants to update the annual real-estate tax on a home for which the Foundation has provided of a mortgage.
> 1. The staff member enters the new value of the annual real-estate tax.
> 2. The information system updates the date on which the annual real-estate tax was last changed.

is needed (see Figure 12.28). However, Figure 12.38 shows that a second control class, **Manage an Asset Class**, is required; additional control classes may have to be added in subsequent iterations.

The normal part of the extended scenario of Figure 12.13 of the use case `Manage a Mortgage` (and hence of `Manage an Asset`) is reproduced as Figure 12.39. In this scenario, an MSG staff member updates the annual real-estate tax on a mortgaged home and the software product updates the date on which the tax was last changed. Figure 12.40 is the collaboration diagram of this scenario. Notice that object <u>**: Investment Class**</u> does not play an active role in this collaboration diagram because the scenario of Figure 12.39 does not involve an investment, only a mortgage. Also, the **Borrowers** do not play a role in this scenario either. The flow of

**FIGURE 12.40**   A collaboration diagram of the realization of the scenario of Figure 12.39 of the `Manage an Asset` use case of the MSG Foundation case study.

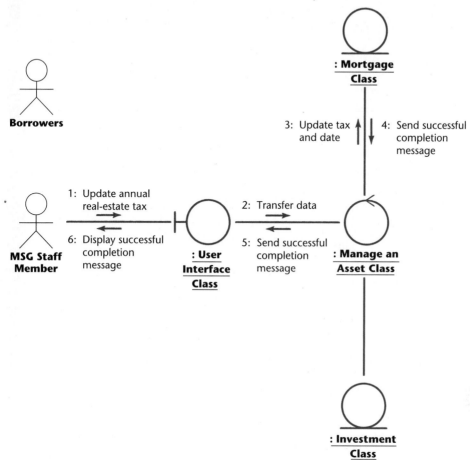

events is left as an exercise (Problem 12.10). The sequence diagram equivalent to the collaboration diagram of Figure 12.40 is shown in Figure 12.41.

Now consider a different scenario of the use case `Manage an Asset` (Figure 12.36) namely, the extended scenario of Figure 12.14, the normal part of which is reproduced here as Figure 12.42. In this scenario, at the request of the borrowers, the MSG staff member updates the weekly income of a couple who have an MSG mortgage. As explained in Section 10.7, the scenario is initiated by the **Borrowers,** and their data are entered into the software product by the **MSG Staff Member,** as stated in the note in the collaboration diagram of Figure 12.43. The flow of events is again left as an exercise (Problem 12.11). The equivalent sequence diagram is shown in Figure 12.44.

Comparing the collaboration diagrams of Figures 12.40 and 12.43 (or, equivalently, the sequence diagrams of Figures 12.41 and 12.44), we see that, other than the

**FIGURE 12.41** A sequence diagram of the realization of the scenario of Figure 12.39 of the `Manage an Asset` use case of the MSG Foundation case study.

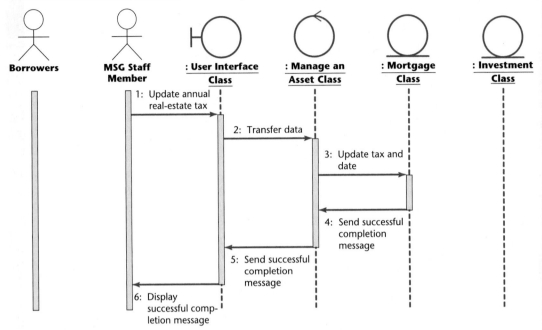

**FIGURE 12.42** A second scenario of the `Manage an Asset` use case.

> There is a change in the weekly income of a couple who have borrowed money from the MSG Foundation. They wish to have their weekly income updated in the Foundation records by an MSG staff member so that their mortgage payments will be correctly computed.
>
> 1. The staff member enters the new value of the weekly income.
> 2. The information system updates the date on which the weekly income was last changed.

actors involved, the only other difference between the two diagrams is that messages 1, 2, and 3 involve annual real-estate tax in the case of Figure 12.40 (or Figure 12.41) and weekly income in the case of Figure 12.43 (or Figure 12.44). This example highlights the difference between a use case, scenarios (instances of the use case), and collaboration or sequence diagrams of the realization of different scenarios of that use case.

Boundary class **User Interface Class** appears in all the realizations considered so far. In fact, the same screen will be used for all commands of the software product. An MSG staff member clicks on the appropriate operation in the revised menu of

**FIGURE 12.43**  A collaboration diagram of the realization of the scenario of Figure 12.42 of the `Manage an Asset` use case of the MSG Foundation case study.

Figure 12.45. (The corresponding textual interface, as implemented in Appendices H and I, is given in Figure 12.46.)

### 12.15.3 `Update Estimated Annual Operating Expenses` **Use Case**

The use case `Update Estimated Annual Operating Expenses` is shown in Figure 10.17 with a description in Figure 10.18. A class diagram showing the classes that realize the `Update Estimated Annual Operating Expenses` use case appears in Figure 12.47, and a collaboration diagram of a realization of a scenario of the use case in Figure 12.48. The equivalent sequence diagram is shown in Figure 12.49. Details of the scenario and the flow of events are left as an exercise (Problems 12.12 and 12.13).

**FIGURE 12.44** A sequence diagram of the realization of the scenario of Figure 12.42 of the `Manage an Asset` use case of the MSG Foundation case study.

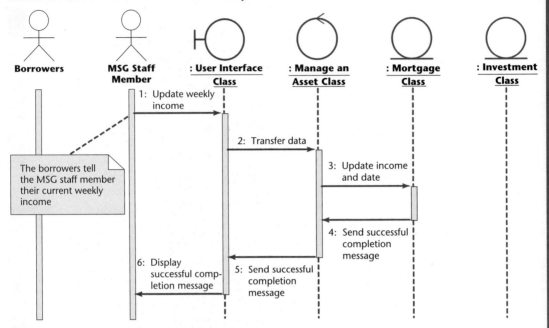

**FIGURE 12.45**
Revised menu of the target MSG Foundation case study.

Click on your choice:

*Estimate funds for the week*

*Manage a mortgage*

*Manage an investment*

*Update estimated annual operating expenses*

*Produce a mortgages report*

*Produce an investments report*

*Quit*

**FIGURE 12.46**
Textual version of the revised menu of Figure 12.45.

MAIN MENU
MARTHA STOCKTON GREENGAGE FOUNDATION
1. Estimate funds available for week
2. Manage a mortgage
3. Manage an investment
4. Update estimated annual operating expenses
5. Produce a mortgages report
6. Produce an investments report
7. Quit
Type your choice and press <ENTER>:

**FIGURE 12.47**  A class diagram showing the classes that realize the `Update Estimated Annual Operating Expenses` use case of the MSG Foundation case study.

<table>
<tr><td>MSG Staff<br>Member</td><td>User Interface<br>Class</td><td>MSG Application<br>Class</td></tr>
</table>

**FIGURE 12.48**  A collaboration diagram of the realization of a scenario of the `Update Estimated Annual Operating Expenses` use case of the MSG Foundation case study.

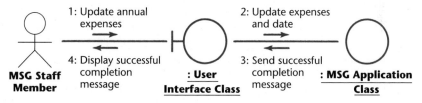

**FIGURE 12.49**  A sequence diagram of the realization of a scenario of the Update Estimated Annual Operating Expenses use case of the MSG Foundation case study.

### 12.15.4 `Produce a Report` **Use Case**

Use case `Produce a Report` is shown in Figure 12.50. The description of use case `Produce a Report` of Figure 10.39 is reproduced here as Figure 12.51. A class diagram showing the classes that realize the `Produce a Report` use case is shown in Figure 12.52.

**FIGURE 12.50**
The `Produce a Report` use case.

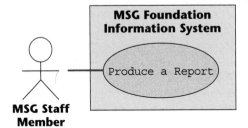

**FIGURE 12.51** Description of the `Produce a Report` use case.

| **Brief Description** |
| --- |
| The `Produce a Report` use case enables an MSG Foundation staff member to print a listing of all investments or all mortgages. |
| **Step-by-Step Description** |
| 1. The following reports must be generated:<br>  1.1 Investments report—printed on demand:<br>     The information system prints a list of all investments. For each investment, the following attributes are printed:<br>       Item number<br>       Item name<br>       Estimated annual return<br>       Date estimated annual return was last updated<br>  1.2 Mortgages report—printed on demand:<br>     The information system prints a list of all mortgages. For each mortgage, the following attributes are printed:<br>       Account number<br>       Name of mortgagees<br>       Original price of home<br>       Date mortgage was issued<br>       Principal and interest payment<br>       Current combined gross weekly income<br>       Date current combined gross weekly income was last updated<br>       Annual real-estate tax<br>       Date annual real-estate tax was last updated<br>       Annual homeowner's insurance premium<br>       Date annual homeowner's insurance premium was last updated |

**FIGURE 12.52**   A class diagram showing the classes that realize the `Produce a Report` use case of the MSG Foundation case study.

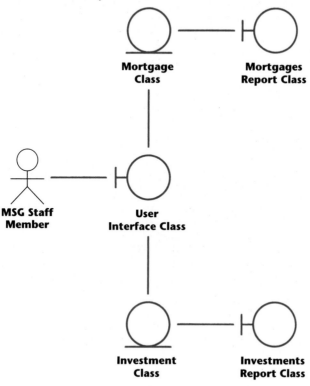

**Mortgage Class**

**Mortgages Report Class**

**MSG Staff Member**

**User Interface Class**

**Investment Class**

**Investments Report Class**

**FIGURE 12.53**   A scenario of the `Produce a Report` use case.

> An MSG staff member wishes to print a list of all mortgages.
> 1. The staff member requests a report listing all mortgages.

First consider the scenario of Figure 12.16 for listing all mortgages, reproduced here as Figure 12.53. A collaboration diagram of the realization of this scenario is shown in Figure 12.54. This realization models the listing of all mortgages. Accordingly, object **: Investment Class,** an instance of the other subclass of **Asset Class**, plays no role in this realization, and neither does **: Investments Report**

**FIGURE 12.54** A collaboration diagram of the realization of the scenario of Figure 12.53 of the `Produce a Report` use case of the MSG Foundation case study.

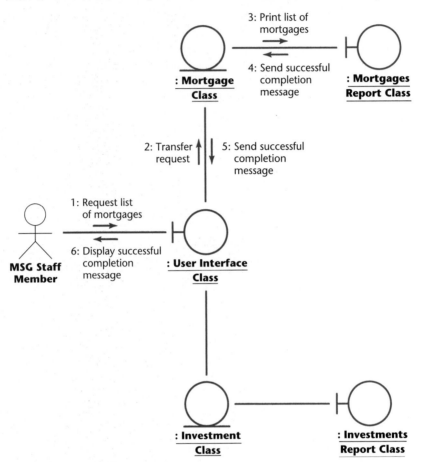

**Class**. The flow of events is left as an exercise (Problem 12.14). The equivalent sequence diagram is shown in Figure 12.55.

Now consider the scenario of Figure 12.17 for listing all investments, reproduced here as Figure 12.56. A collaboration diagram of the realization of this scenario is shown in Figure 12.57. As opposed to the previous realization, Figure 12.57 models

**FIGURE 12.55**   A sequence diagram of the realization of the scenario of Figure 12.53 of the `Produce a Report` use case of the MSG Foundation case study.

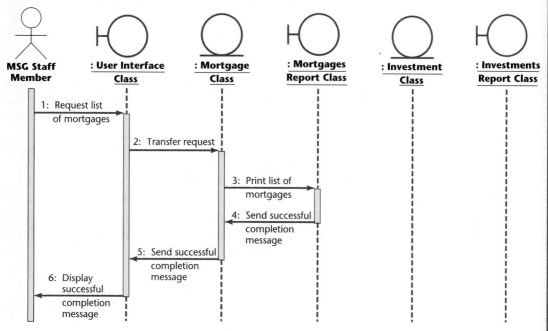

**FIGURE 12.56**   Another scenario of the `Produce a Report` use case.

> An MSG staff member wishes to print a list of all investments.
> 1. The staff member requests a report listing all investments.

the listing of the investments; mortgages are ignored here. The equivalent sequence diagram is shown in Figure 12.58.

This concludes the realization of the four use cases of Figure 12.20, the eighth iteration of the use-case diagram of the MSG Foundation case study.

FIGURE 12.57
A collaboration diagram of the realization of the scenario of Figure 12.56 of the Produce a Report use case of the MSG Foundation case study.

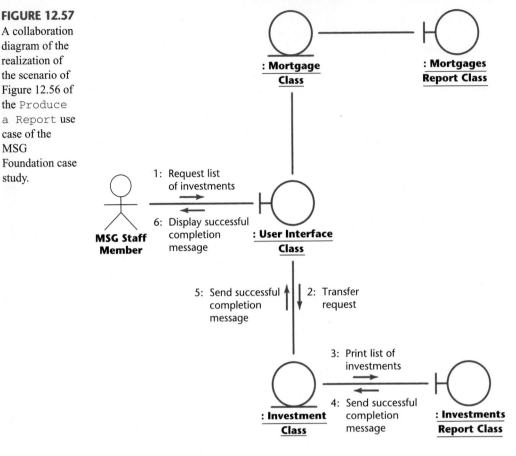

**FIGURE 12.58** A sequence diagram of the realization of the scenario of Figure 12.56 of the Produce a Report use case of the MSG Foundation case study.

## *ase Study*

### 12.16 Incrementing the Class Diagram: The MSG Foundation Case Study

The entity classes were extracted in Sections 12.9 through 12.12, yielding Figure 12.26, which shows four entity classes. The boundary classes were extracted in Section 12.13 and the two control classes in Sections 12.14 and 12.15.2. In the course of realizing the various use cases in Section 12.15, interrelationships between many of the classes became apparent; these interrelationships are reflected in the class diagrams of Figures 12.31, 12.38, 12.47, and 12.52. Figure 12.59 combines these class diagrams.

Now the class diagrams of Figures 12.26 and 12.59 are combined to yield the fourth iteration of the class diagram of the MSG Foundation case study, shown in

**FIGURE 12.59**

Class diagram combining the class diagrams of 12.31, 12.38, 12.47, and 12.52.

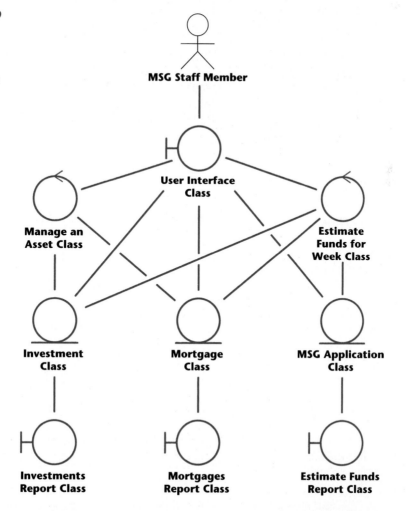

**FIGURE 12.60**

The fourth iteration of the class diagram of the MSG Foundation case study, obtained by combining the class diagrams of Figures 12.26 and 12.59.

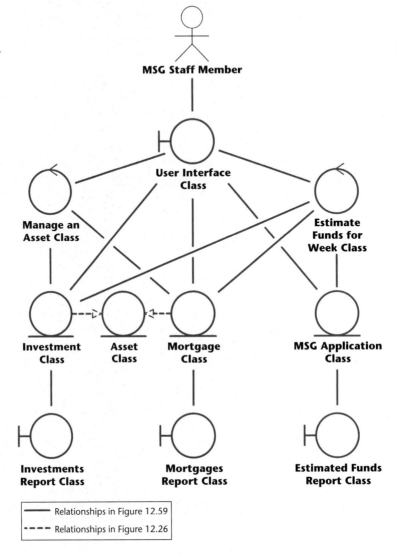

Figure 12.60. More specifically, starting with Figure 12.59, **Asset Class** of Figure 12.26 is added. Then the two inheritance (generalization) relationships in Figure 12.26 are drawn in; they are shown with dashed lines to distinguish them. The result, Figure 12.60, the fourth iteration of the class diagram, is the class diagram at the end of the analysis workflow.

The last step of the analysis workflow of the MSG Foundation case study is to draw up the software project management plan (this is done during the elaboration phase; see Section 3.10.2). Appendix F contains a software project management plan for the development of the MSG Foundation product by a small (three-person) software organization.

## Case Study

### 12.17 The Test Workflow: The MSG Foundation Case Study

The analysis workflow of the MSG Foundation case study is checked in two ways. First the entity classes are checked using CRC cards, as described in Section 12.7. Then all the artifacts of the analysis workflow are inspected (Section 6.2.3).

This concludes the analysis workflow of the MSG Foundation case study.

## 12.18 The Specification Document in the Unified Process

A primary goal of the analysis workflow is to produce the **specification document**, but at the end of Section 12.17 it was claimed that the analysis workflow is now complete. The obvious question is, Where is the specification document?

The short answer is, The Unified Process is use-case driven. In more detail, the use cases and the artifacts derived from them contain all the information that, in the traditional paradigm, appears in the specification document in text form, and more.

For example, consider the use case `Estimate Funds Available for Week`. When the requirements workflow is performed, the `Estimate Funds Available for Week` use case (Figure 10.27) and its description (Figure 10.40) are shown to the client, the trustees of the MSG Foundation. The developers must be meticulous in ensuring that the trustees fully understand these two artifacts and agree that these artifacts accurately model the software product the Foundation needs. Then, during the analysis workflow, the trustees are shown the use case `Estimate Funds Available for Week` (Figure 12.29), its description (Figure 12.30), the class diagram showing the classes that realize the use case (Figure 12.31), a scenario of the use case (Figure 12.32), the interaction diagrams of the realization of a scenario of the use case (Figures 12.33 and 12.35), and the flow of events of these interaction diagrams (Figure 12.34).

The set of artifacts just listed all appertain to only the use case `Estimate Funds Available for Week`. As shown in Figure 12.20, there are four use cases altogether. The same set of artifacts are produced for each of the scenarios of each of the use cases. The resulting collection of artifacts, some diagrammatic and some textual, convey to the client more information more accurately than the purely textual specification document of the traditional paradigm possibly could.

The traditional specification document usually plays a contractual role. That is, once it has been signed by both the developers and the client, it essentially constitutes a legal document. If the developers build a software product that satisfies the specification document, the client is obligated to pay for the software product, and conversely, if the product does not conform to its specification document, the developers are required to fix it if they want to get paid. In the case of the Unified Process, the collection of artifacts of all the scenarios of all the use cases similarly constitutes a contract. Therefore, as claimed at the end of Section 12.17, the analysis workflow of the MSG Foundation case study is indeed complete.

As stated before, the Unified Process is use-case driven. When using the Unified Process, instead of constructing a rapid prototype, the use cases, or more precisely, interaction diagrams reflecting the classes that realize the scenarios of the use cases, are shown to the client. The client can understand how the target software product will behave just as well from the interaction diagrams and their written flow of events as from a rapid prototype. After all, a scenario is a particular execution sequence of the proposed software product, as is each execution of the rapid prototype. The difference is that the rapid prototype is generally discarded, whereas the use cases are successively refined, with more information added each time.

However, there is one area where a rapid prototype is superior to a scenario, the user interface. This does not mean that a rapid prototype should be built just so that specimen screens and reports can be examined by the client and users. But specimen screens and reports need to be constructed, as described in Section 10.13, preferably with the aid of CASE tools such as screen generators and report generators (Section 5.5).

In Section 12.19, methods for determining actors and use cases are provided.

## 12.19 More on Actors and Use Cases

As stated in Section 10.4.3, a use case depicts an interaction between the software product itself and the actors (the users of that software product). Now that a number of examples of actors and use cases have been presented, it is appropriate to describe how to find actors and use cases.

To find the actors, we have to consider every **role** in which an individual can interact with the software product. For example, consider a couple who wish to obtain a mortgage from the MSG Foundation. When they apply for the mortgage, they are **Applicants**, whereas after their application has been approved and money to buy their home loaned to them, they become **Borrowers**. In other words, actors are not so much individuals as roles played by those individuals. In our example, the actors are not the couple, but rather first the couple playing the role of **Applicants** and then the couple playing the role of **Borrowers**. This means that merely listing all the individuals who will use the software product is not a satisfactory way of finding the actors. Instead, we need to find all the roles played by each user (or group of users). From the list of roles we can extract the actors.

In the terminology of the Unified Process, the term **worker** is used to denote a particular role played by an individual. This is a somewhat unfortunate term, because the word worker usually refers to an employee. In the terminology of the Unified Process, in the case of a couple with a mortgage, **Applicants** and **Borrowers** are two different workers. In this book, in the interests of clarity the word *role* is used in place of *worker*.

Within a business context, the task of finding the roles is generally straightforward. The use-case business model usually displays all the roles played by the individuals who interact with the business, thus highlighting the business actors. We then find the subset of the use-case business model that corresponds to the use-case model of the requirements. In more detail,

1. Construct the use-case business model by finding all the roles played by the individuals who interact with the business.
2. Find the subset of the use-case diagram of the business model that models the software product we wish to develop. That is, consider only those parts of the business model that correspond to the proposed software product.
3. The actors in this subset are the actors we seek.

---

**How to Perform Object-Oriented Analysis**　　　　　**Box 12.1**

- **Iterate**

  Perform functional modeling.

  Perform entity class modeling.

  Perform dynamic modeling.

- **Until** the entity classes have been satisfactorily extracted.
- Extract the boundary classes and control classes.
- Refine the use cases.
- Perform use-case realization.

---

Once the actors have been determined, finding the use cases is generally straightforward. For each role, there are one or more use cases. So, the starting point in finding the use cases of the requirements is finding the actors, as described in this section.

How to Perform Box 12.1 summarizes object-oriented analysis.

## 12.20 CASE Tools for the Object-Oriented Analysis Workflow

Bearing in mind the role played by diagrams in object-oriented analysis, it is not surprising that a number of CASE tools have been developed to support object-oriented analysis. In its basic form, such a tool is essentially a drawing tool that makes it easy to perform each of the modeling steps. More important, it is far simpler to modify a diagram constructed with a drawing tool than to attempt to change a hand-drawn figure. Thus, a CASE tool of this type supports the graphical aspects of object-oriented analysis. In addition, some tools of this type not only draw all the relevant diagrams but CRC cards as well. A strength of these tools is that a change to the underlying model is reflected automatically in all the affected diagrams; after all, the various diagrams are merely different views of the underlying model.

On the other hand, some CASE tools support not just object-oriented analysis but a considerable portion of the rest of the object-oriented life cycle as well. Nowadays virtually all of these tools support UML [Rumbaugh, Jacobson, and Booch, 1999]. Examples of such tools include IBM Rational Rose and Together. ArgoUML is a typical open-source CASE tool of this type.

## 12.21 Challenges of the Object-Oriented Analysis Workflow

Object-oriented analysis is a specific approach to analysis, so the challenges of classical analysis described in Section 11.16 apply equally to object-oriented analysis. In particular, the second challenge listed in that section is that it is easy to cross the boundary line between specifications (what) and design (how). This danger is especially acute in the case of object-oriented analysis.

Recall that, as described in Section 1.9, the transition from object-oriented analysis to object-oriented design is far smoother than the transition in the classical paradigm from the analysis phase to the design phase. In the classical paradigm, an initial task of the design phase is to decompose the product into modules. In contrast, the classes, the "modules" of the object-oriented design workflow, are extracted during the object-oriented analysis workflow, ready for refinement during the object-oriented design workflow. The presence of classes from early in the OOA workflow means that the temptation to carry the OOA too far can be extremely strong.

For example, consider the issue of allocation of methods to classes. One task of the classical analysis phase is to determine the data and operations of the target product. However, allocation of the various operations to specific modules should be delayed until the classical design phase, because as pointed out in Section 11.16, we first have to determine how the product as a whole is broken down into modules.

In the object-oriented paradigm, however, this latter task is part of the analysis workflow. That is, during the object-oriented analysis workflow, we determine the modules (classes) and their interactions; the result is depicted in the class diagram. Therefore, there is no apparent reason why we should wait until the object-oriented design workflow before allocating methods to classes.

Nevertheless, it is important to remember that object-oriented analysis is an iterative process. In the course of refining the various models, frequently large portions of the class diagram have to be reorganized. Reallocating the methods then results in unnecessary additional rework.

At each step of the OOA process it is a good idea to minimize the information that would have to be reorganized during iteration. Therefore, allocation of methods to classes should wait until the design workflow, no matter how tempting it may be to go just a little further during the object-oriented analysis workflow.

---

**Chapter Review**

Object-oriented analysis is introduced (Section 12.1). Extracting entity classes is described in Section 12.2. The technique is then applied to the elevator problem case study (Section 12.3); functional modeling, entity class modeling, and dynamic modeling are performed in Sections 12.4, 12.5, and 12.6, respectively. Next, object-oriented analysis aspects of the test workflow are covered in Section 12.7. Extraction of boundary and control classes is the subject of Section 12.8. Class extraction of the MSG Foundation case study is described in Section 12.9 (the initial functional model), Section 12.10 (the initial class diagram), Section 12.11 (the initial dynamic model), Section 12.12 (revision of the entity classes), Section 12.13 (extraction of the boundary classes), and Section 12.14 (extraction of the control classes). Application of the Unified Process to the MSG Foundation case study resumes in Section 12.15 (realization of the use cases), Section 12.16 (class diagram incrementation), and Section 12.17 (test workflow). The specification document for the Unified Process is discussed in Section 12.18. Additional information regarding actors and use cases appears in Section 12.19. CASE tools for object-oriented analysis are described in Section 12.20. The chapter concludes with a discussion of the challenges of the object-oriented analysis workflow (Section 12.21).

**For Further Reading**

Early books describing different versions of object-oriented analysis include [Coad and Yourdon, 1991a; Rumbaugh et al., 1991; Shlaer and Mellor, 1992; and Booch, 1994]. As mentioned in the chapter, these techniques (and others not listed here) are basically similar.

In addition to object-oriented analysis techniques of this type, Fusion [Coleman et al., 1994] is a second-generation OOA technique, a combination (or fusion) of a number of first-generation techniques, including OMT [Rumbaugh et al., 1991] and Objectory [Jacobson, Christerson, Jonsson, and Overgaard, 1992]. The Unified Software Development Process unifies the work of Jacobson, Booch, and Rumbaugh [1999]. Catalysis is another important object-oriented methodology [D'Souza and Mills, 1999].

ROOM is an object-oriented methodology for real-time software [Selic, Gullekson, and Ward, 1995]. Further information on real-time object-oriented technologies can be found in [Awad, Kuusela, and Ziegler, 1996].

Full details regarding UML can be found in [Booch, Rumbaugh, and Jacobson, 1999] and [Rumbaugh, Jacobson, and Booch, 1999]. The October 1999 issue of *Communications of the ACM* contains a broad variety of papers on the use of UML. UML is now under the control of the Object Management Group; the latest version of UML will be found at the OMG Web site, www.omg.org.

The noun-extraction technique used in this chapter to extract candidate classes is formalized in [Juristo, Moreno, and López, 2000]. CRC cards were first put forward in [Beck and Cunningham, 1989]. Wirfs-Brock, Wilkerson, and Wiener [1990] are a good source of information on CRC cards.

A number of comparisons of object-oriented analysis techniques have been published, including [de Champeaux and Faure, 1992; Monarchi and Puhr, 1992; and Embley, Jackson, and Woodfield, 1995]. A comparison of both object-oriented and classical analysis techniques appears in [Fichman and Kemerer, 1992].

Management of iteration in object-oriented projects is described in [Williams, 1996]. Statecharts are described in [Harel and Gery, 1997]. The reuse of specifications in the object-oriented paradigm is described in [Bellinzona, Fugini, and Pernici, 1995].

A variety of papers on formal techniques for object-oriented software appear in the July 2000 issue of *IEEE Transactions on Software Engineering*.

**Key Terms**

abstract noun *381*
actor *378*
analysis workflow *376*
attribute *381*
backtrack *396*
boundary class *376*
class diagram *382*
class–responsibility–
  collaboration (CRC)
  cards *383*
collaboration diagram *402*
control class *377*
dynamic modeling *377*
entity class *376*

entity class modeling *377*
event *398*
exception scenario *379*
flow of events *407*
functional modeling *377*
interaction diagram *402*
legacy system *376*
millennium bug *376*
normal scenario *379*
noun-extraction method *381*
object-oriented analysis *375*
realize (in the Unified
  Theory context) *402*
role *424*

scenario *377*
sequence diagram *402*
specification
  document *423*
state *388*
state variable *388*
statechart *384*
stereotype *377*
test workflow *387*
transition *398*
use case *378*
use-case realization *402*
worker *424*
Y2K problem *376*

**Problems[1]**

12.1 Complete the elevator problem case study by developing statecharts for the other classes shown in Figure 12.10.

12.2 Why cannot the finite state machine formalism of Section 11.6 be used unchanged in object-oriented analysis?

12.3 What is the latest point in the analysis workflow in which classes can be introduced without adversely affecting the project?

12.4 What is the earliest point in the Unified Process in which classes can meaningfully be introduced?

12.5 Is it possible to represent the dynamic model using a formalism other than the statechart described in this chapter? Explain your answer.

12.6 Why are the attributes of the classes but not the methods determined during object-oriented analysis?

12.7 A noun-extraction process is described in Section 12.5.1. Why do we not also extract the verbs? And what about the other six parts of speech (adjectives, adverbs, conjunctions, interjections, prepositions, and pronouns)?

12.8 Give an extended scenario of the use case **Manage an Investment** of Figures 10.30 and 10.31.

12.9 Give an extended scenario of the use case **Update Estimated Annual Operating Expenses** of Figures 10.17 and 10.18.

12.10 Give the flow of events of the interaction diagrams of Figures 12.40 and 12.41.

12.11 Give the flow of events of the interaction diagrams of Figures 12.43 and 12.44.

12.12 Check that your answer to Problem 12.9 is a possible scenario for the interaction diagrams of Figures 12.48 and 12.49. If not, modify your scenario.

12.13 Give the flow of events of the interaction diagrams of Figures 12.48 and 12.49.

12.14 Give the flow of events of the interaction diagrams of Figures 12.54 and 12.55.

12.15 (Analysis and Design Project) Perform the analysis workflow of the library software product of Problem 8.7.

12.16 (Analysis and Design Project) Perform the analysis workflow of the product for determining whether a bank statement is correct of Problem 8.8.

12.17 (Analysis and Design Project) Perform the analysis workflow of the automated teller machine of Problem 8.9. There is no need to consider the details of the constituent hardware components such as the card reader, printer, and cash dispenser. Instead, simply assume that, when the ATM sends commands to those components, they are correctly executed.

12.18 (Term Project) Perform the analysis workflow of the Osric's Office Appliances and Decor product described in Appendix A.

12.19 (Case Study) Add **Report Class** to the analysis workflow of the MSG Foundation case study (Sections 12.9 through 12.16). Is this an improvement or an unnecessary complication?

12.20 (Case Study) Determine what happens when object-oriented analysis starts with dynamic modeling. Start with the statechart of Figure 12.22 and complete the object-oriented analysis process for the MSG Foundation case study.

12.21 (Case Study) Compare and contrast the structured systems analysis of the MSG Foundation case study of Section 11.4 with the analysis workflow of Sections 12.9 through 12.16.

---

[1] Problem 11.16 (Term Project) and Problems 11.20 and 11.21 (Case Study) can be done at the end of either Chapter 11 or Chapter 12.

12.22  (Readings in Software Engineering) Your instructor will distribute copies of [Juristo, Moreno, and López, 2000]. What is your opinion of their approach to object-oriented analysis?

**References**

[Awad, Kuusela, and Ziegler, 1996] M. AWAD, J. KUUSELA, AND J. ZIEGLER, *Object-Oriented Technology for Real-Time Systems: A Practical Approach Using OMT and Fusion,* Prentice Hall, Upper Saddle River, NJ, 1996.

[Beck and Cunningham, 1989] K. BECK AND W. CUNNINGHAM, "A Laboratory for Teaching Object-Oriented Thinking," Proceedings of OOPSLA '89, *ACM SIGPLAN Notices* **24** (October 1989), pp. 1–6.

[Bellinzona, Fugini, and Pernici, 1995] R. BELLINZONA, M. G. FUGINI, AND B. PERNICI, "Reusing Specifications in OO Applications," *IEEE Software* **12** (March 1995), pp. 656–75.

[Booch, 1994] G. BOOCH, *Object-Oriented Analysis and Design with Applications,* 2nd ed., Benjamin/Cummings, Redwood City, CA, 1994.

[Booch, Rumbaugh, and Jacobson, 1999] G. BOOCH, J. RUMBAUGH, AND I. JACOBSON, *The UML Users Guide*, Addison-Wesley, Reading, MA, 1999.

[Coad and Yourdon, 1991a] P. COAD AND E. YOURDON, *Object-Oriented Analysis,* 2nd ed., Yourdon Press, Englewood Cliffs, NJ, 1991.

[Coleman et al., 1994] D. COLEMAN, P. ARNOLD, S. BODOFF, C. DOLLIN, H. GILCHRIST, F. HAYES, AND P. JEREMAES, *Object-Oriented Development: The Fusion Method*, Prentice Hall, Englewood Cliffs, NJ, 1994.

[D'Souza and Wills, 1999] D. D'SOUZA AND A. WILLS, *Objects, Components, and Frameworks with UML: The Catalysis Approach*, Addison-Wesley, Reading, MA, 1999.

[de Champeaux and Faure, 1992] D. DE CHAMPEAUX AND P. FAURE, "A Comparative Study of Object-Oriented Analysis Methods," *Journal of Object-Oriented Programming* **5** (March/April 1992), pp. 21–33.

[Embley, Jackson, and Woodfield, 1995] D. W. EMBLEY, R. B. JACKSON, AND S. N. WOODFIELD, "OO Systems Analysis: Is It or Isn't It?" *IEEE Software* **12** (July 1995), pp. 18–33.

[Fichman and Kemerer, 1992] R. G. FICHMAN AND C. F. KEMERER, "Object-Oriented and Conventional Analysis and Design Methodologies: Comparison and Critique," *IEEE Computer* **25** (October 1992), pp. 22–39.

[Harel and Gery, 1997] D. HAREL AND E. GERY, "Executable Object Modeling with Statecharts," *IEEE Computer* **30** (July 1997), pp. 31–42.

[Jacobson, Booch, and Rumbaugh, 1999] I. JACOBSON, G. BOOCH, AND J. RUMBAUGH, *The Unified Software Development Process*, Addison-Wesley, Reading, MA, 1999.

[Jacobson, Christerson, Jonsson, and Overgaard, 1992] I. JACOBSON, M. CHRISTERSON, P. JONSSON, AND G. OVERGAARD, *Object-Oriented Software Engineering: A Use Case Driven Approach*, ACM Press, New York, 1992.

[Juristo, Moreno, and López, 2000] N. JURISTO, A. M. MORENO, AND M. LÓPEZ, "How to Use Linguistic Instruments for Object-Oriented Analysis," *IEEE Software* **17** (May/June 2000), pp. 80–89.

[Monarchi and Puhr, 1992] D. E. MONARCHI AND G. I. PUHR, "A Research Typology for Object-Oriented Analysis and Design," *Communications of the ACM* **35** (September 1992), pp. 35–47.

[Rumbaugh et al., 1991] J. RUMBAUGH, M. BLAHA, W. PREMERLANI, F. EDDY, AND W. LORENSEN, *Object-Oriented Modeling and Design*, Prentice Hall, Englewood Cliffs, NJ, 1991.

[Rumbaugh, Jacobson, and Booch, 1999] J. RUMBAUGH, I. JACOBSON, AND G. BOOCH, *The Unified Modeling Language Reference Manual,* Addison-Wesley, Reading, MA, 1999.

[Selic, Gullekson, and Ward, 1995] B. SELIC, G. GULLEKSON, AND P. T. WARD, *Real-Time Object-Oriented Modeling*, John Wiley and Sons, New York, 1995.

[Shlaer and Mellor, 1992] S. SHLAER AND S. MELLOR, *Object Lifecycles: Modeling the World in States,* Yourdon Press, Englewood Cliffs, NJ, 1992.

[USNO, 2000] "The 21st Century and the Third Millennium—When Will They Begin?" U.S. Naval Observatory, Astronomical Applications Department, at aa.usno.navy.mil/AA/faq/docs/millennium.html, February 22, 2000.

[Williams, 1996] J. D. WILLIAMS, "Managing Iteration in OO Projects," *IEEE Computer* **29** (September 1996), pp. 39–43.

[Wirfs-Brock, Wilkerson, and Wiener, 1990] R. WIRFS-BROCK, B. WILKERSON, AND L. WIENER, *Designing Object-Oriented Software*, Prentice Hall, Englewood Cliffs, NJ, 1990.

# Chapter

# 13

# Design

**Learning Objectives**

After studying this chapter, you should be able to

- Perform the design workflow.
- Perform object-oriented design.
- Perform data flow analysis and transaction analysis.

Over the past 40 or so years, hundreds of design techniques have been put forward. Some are variations on existing techniques; others are radically different from anything previously proposed. A few design techniques have been used by tens of thousands of software engineers; many have been used by only their authors. Some design strategies, particularly those developed by academics, have a firm theoretical basis. Others, including many drawn up by academics, are more pragmatic in nature; they were put forward because their authors found that they worked well in practice. Most design techniques are manual, but automation increasingly is becoming an important aspect of design, if only to assist in the management of documentation.

Notwithstanding this plethora of design techniques, a certain underlying pattern emerges. A major theme of this book is that two essential aspects of a product are its operations and the data on which the operations act. Therefore, the two basic ways of designing a product are operation-oriented design and data-oriented design. In **operation-oriented design**, the emphasis is on the operations. An example is data flow analysis (Section 13.3), where the objective is to design modules with high cohesion (Section 7.2). In **data-oriented design**, the data are considered first. For example, in Jackson's technique (Section 13.5), the structure of the data is determined first and then the procedures are designed to conform to the structure of the data.

A weakness of operation-oriented design techniques is that they concentrate on the operations; the data are of only secondary importance. Data-oriented design techniques similarly emphasize the data, to the detriment of the operations. The solution is to use object-oriented techniques, which give equal weight to operations and data. In this chapter, operation- and data-oriented design are described first, and then object-oriented design. Just as an object incorporates both operation and data, so object-oriented design combines features of operation-oriented and data-oriented design. Therefore, a basic understanding of operation- and data-oriented design is needed to get a full understanding of object-oriented design.

Before specific design techniques are examined, some general remarks must be made regarding design.

## 13.1   Design and Abstraction

The classical design phase consists of three activities: architectural design, detailed design, and design testing. The input to the design process is the specification document, a description of *what* the product is to do. The output is the design document, a description of *how* the product is to achieve this.

During **architectural design** (also known as **general design**, **logical design**, or **high-level design**), a modular decomposition of the product is developed. That is, the specifications are carefully analyzed, and a module structure that has the desired functionality is produced. The output from this activity is a list of the modules and a description of how they are to be interconnected. From the viewpoint of abstraction, during architectural design, the existence of certain modules is assumed; the design then is developed in terms of those modules.

When the object-oriented paradigm is used, however, as explained in Section 1.9, the architectural design activity is performed during the object-oriented analysis workflow (Chapter 12). This is because the first step in the analysis workflow is to determine the classes. Because a class is a type of module, the modular decomposition has been performed during the analysis workflow.

The next activity in the classical design phase and a major activity of the object-oriented design workflow is **detailed design**, also known as **modular design, physical design**, or **low-level design**, during which each module (or class) is designed in detail. For example, specific algorithms are selected and data structures are chosen. Again, from the viewpoint of abstraction, during this activity the fact that the modules (or classes) are to be interconnected to form a complete product is ignored.

It was stated previously that the classical design phase has three activities and that the third activity is testing. The word *activity* was used, rather than *stage* or *step,* to emphasize that testing is an integral part of design, just as it is an integral part of the entire software development and maintenance process. Testing is not something performed only after the architectural design and detailed design have been completed. Similarly, in the case of object-oriented design, the test workflow is performed concurrently with the design workflow.

A variety of design techniques now are described, first operation-oriented techniques, then data-oriented techniques, and finally object-oriented techniques.

## 13.2   Operation-Oriented Design

Sections 7.2 and 7.3 made a theoretical case for decomposing a product into modules with high cohesion and low coupling. We now describe two practical classical techniques for achieving this design objective, data flow analysis (Section 13.3) and transaction analysis

(Section 13.4). In theory, data flow analysis can be applied whenever the specifications can be represented by a data flow diagram, and because (at least in theory) every product can be represented by a DFD, data flow analysis is universally applicable. In practice, however, in a number of situations, there are more appropriate design techniques, specifically for designing products where the flow of data is secondary to other considerations. Examples where other design techniques are indicated include rule-based systems (expert systems), databases, and transaction-processing products. (Transaction analysis, described in Section 13.4, is a good way of decomposing transaction-processing products into modules.)

## 13.3   Data Flow Analysis

**Data flow analysis** (DFA) is a classical design technique for achieving modules with high cohesion. It can be used in conjunction with most analysis techniques. Here, DFA is presented in conjunction with structured systems analysis (Section 11.3). The input to the technique is a data flow diagram. A key point is that, once the DFD has been completed, the software designer has precise and complete information regarding the input to and output from the product.

Consider the flow of data in the product represented by the DFD of Figure 13.1. The product somehow transforms input into output. At some point in the DFD, the input ceases to be input and becomes some sort of internal data. Then, at some further point, these internal data take on the quality of output. This is shown in more detail in Figure 13.2. The point at which the input loses the quality of being input and simply becomes internal data operated on by the product is termed the **point of highest abstraction of input**. The **point of highest abstraction of output** is similarly the first point in the flow of data at which the output can be identified as such, rather than as some sort of internal data.

Using the points of highest abstraction of input and output, the product is decomposed into three modules: input_module, transform_module, and output_module. Now each module is taken in turn, its points of highest abstraction found, and the module

**FIGURE 13.1**   A data flow diagram showing flow of data and operations of product.

**FIGURE 13.2**   Points of highest abstraction of input and output.

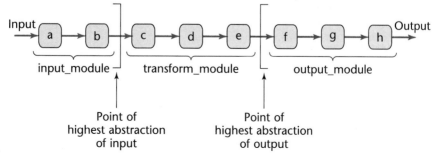

decomposed again. This procedure is continued stepwise until each module performs a single operation; that is, the design consists of modules with high cohesion. Thus, stepwise refinement, the foundation of so many other software engineering techniques, also underlies data flow analysis.

In fairness, it should be pointed out that minor modifications might have to be made to the decomposition to achieve the lowest possible coupling. Data flow analysis is a way of achieving high cohesion. The aim of composite/structured design is high cohesion but also low coupling. To achieve the latter, sometimes it is necessary to make minor modifications to the design. For example, because DFA does not take coupling into account, control coupling may arise inadvertently in a design constructed using DFA. In such a case, all that is needed is to modify the two modules involved so that data, and not control, are passed between them.

*Mini*  *ase Study*

### 13.3.1   *Word Counting*

Consider the problem of designing a product that takes as input a file name and returns the number of words in that file, similarly to the UNIX wc utility.

Figure 13.3 depicts the data flow diagram. There are five modules. Module read_file_name reads the name of the file, which then is validated by validate_file_name. The validated name is passed to count_number_of_words, which does precisely that. The word count is passed on to format_word_count, and the formatted word count finally is passed to display_word_count for output.

Examining the data flow, the initial input is file_name. When this becomes validated_file_name, it still is a file name and therefore has not lost its quality of being input data. But consider module count_number_of_words. Its input is validated_file_name, and its output is word_count. The output from this module is totally different in quality from the input to the product as a whole. It is clear that the point of highest abstraction of input is as indicated on Figure 13.3. Similarly, even though the output from count_number_of_words undergoes some sort of formatting, it is essentially *output* from the time it emerges from module count_number_of_words. The point of highest abstraction of output therefore is as shown in Figure 13.3.

**FIGURE 13.3**   The first refinement of the data flow diagram.

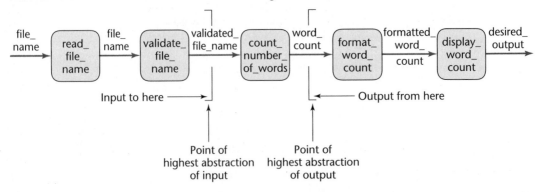

The result of decomposing the product using these two points of highest abstraction is shown in the structure chart of Figure 13.4. This figure also reveals that the data flow diagram of Figure 13.3 is somewhat too simplistic. The DFD does not show the logical flow corresponding to what happens if the file specified by the user does not exist. Module read_and_validate_file_name must return a status_flag to perform_word_count. If the name is invalid, then it is ignored by perform_word_count and an error message of some sort is printed. But, if the name is valid, it is passed on to count_number_of_words. In general, wherever there is a conditional data flow, a corresponding control flow is needed.

In Figure 13.4, two modules have communicational cohesion (Section 7.2.5), read_and_validate_file_name and format_and_display_word_count. These must be decomposed further. The final result is shown in Figure 13.5. All eight modules have functional cohesion, with either data coupling or no coupling between them.

**FIGURE 13.4**
The first refinement of the structure chart.

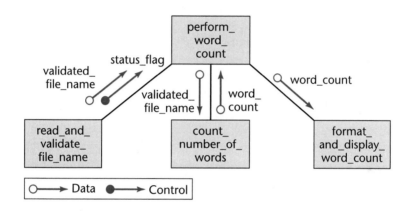

**FIGURE 13.5** The second refinement of the structure chart.

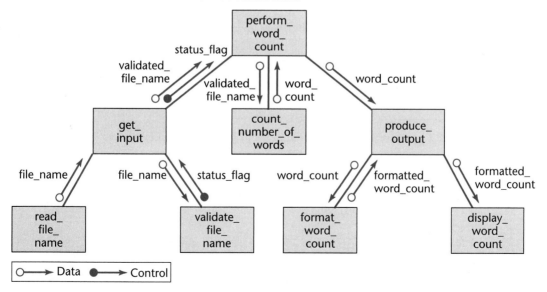

Now that the architectural design has been completed, the next step is the detailed design. Here, data structures are chosen and algorithms selected. The detailed design of each module then is handed to a programmer for implementation. Just as with virtually every other phase of software production, time constraints usually require that the implementation be done by a team, rather than having a single programmer responsible for coding all the modules. For this reason, the detailed design of each module must be presented so it can be understood without reference to any other module. The detailed design of four of the eight modules appears in Figure 13.6; the other four modules are presented in a different format.

**FIGURE 13.6**
The detailed design of four modules of the example.

| | |
|---|---|
| Module name | **read_file_name** |
| Module type | Function |
| Return type | **string** |
| Input arguments | None |
| Output arguments | None |
| Error messages | None |
| Files accessed | None |
| Files changed | None |
| Modules called | None |
| Narrative | The product is invoked by the user by means of the command string |
| | <div align="center">**word_count <file_name>**</div> |
| | Using an operating system call, this module accesses the contents of the command string input by the user, extracts **<file_name>**, and returns it as the value of the module. |

| | |
|---|---|
| Module name | **validate_file_name** |
| Module type | Function |
| Return type | **Boolean** |
| Input arguments | **file_name : string** |
| Output arguments | None |
| Error messages | None |
| Files accessed | None |
| Files changed | None |
| Modules called | None |
| Narrative | This module makes an operating system call to determine whether file **file_name** exists. The module returns **true** if the file exists and **false** otherwise. |

**FIGURE 13.6**
(*continued*)

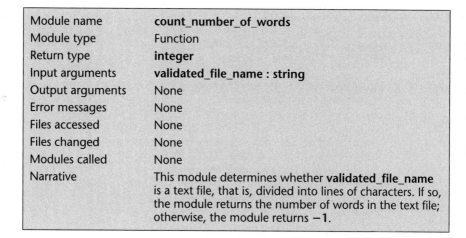

| Module name | **count_number_of_words** |
|---|---|
| Module type | Function |
| Return type | **integer** |
| Input arguments | **validated_file_name : string** |
| Output arguments | None |
| Error messages | None |
| Files accessed | None |
| Files changed | None |
| Modules called | None |
| Narrative | This module determines whether **validated_file_name** is a text file, that is, divided into lines of characters. If so, the module returns the number of words in the text file; otherwise, the module returns **−1**. |

| Module name | **produce_output** |
|---|---|
| Module type | Function |
| Return type | **void** |
| Input arguments | **word_count : integer** |
| Output arguments | None |
| Error messages | None |
| Files accessed | None |
| Files changed | None |
| Modules called | **format_word_count**<br>        arguments:  **word_count : integer**<br>                        **formatted_word_count : string**<br>**display_word_count**<br>        arguments:  **formatted_word_count : string** |
| Narrative | This module takes the integer **word_count** passed to it by the calling module and calls **format_word_count** to have that integer formatted according to the specifications. Then it calls **display_word_count** to have the line printed. |

The design of Figure 13.6 is independent of the programming language. However, if management decides on an implementation language before the detailed design is started, the use of a **program description language** (PDL) for representing the detailed design is an attractive alternative (**pseudocode** is an earlier name for PDL). PDL essentially consists of comments connected by the control statements of the chosen implementation language. Figure 13.7 shows a detailed design for the remaining four modules of the product written in a PDL with the flavor of C++ or Java. A PDL

**FIGURE 13.7**
PDL
(pseudocode)
representation
of the detailed
design of four
methods of the
example.

```
void perform_word_count()
{
  String                validate_file_name;
  int                   word_count;

  if (get_input (validate_file_name) is false)
     print "error 1: file does not exist";
  else
  {
     set word_count equal to count_number_of_words (validate_file_name);
     if (word_count is equal to -1)
        print "error 2: file is not a text file";
     else
        produce_output (word_count);
  }
}


Boolean get_input (String validate_file_name)
{
  String                file_name;

  file_name = read_file_name ();
  if (validate_file_name (file_name) is true)
  {
     set validate_file_name equal to file_name;
     return true;
  }
  else
     return false;
}


void display_word_count (String formatted_word_count)
{
  print formatted_word_count, left justified;
}


String format_word_count (int word_count);
{
  return "File contains" word_count "words";
}
```

has the advantage that it generally is clear and concise, and the implementation step usually consists merely of translating the comments into the relevant programming language. The weakness is that sometimes there is a tendency for the designers to go into too much detail and produce a complete code implementation of a module rather than a PDL detailed design.

After it has been fully documented and successfully tested, the detailed design is handed over to the implementation team for coding. The product then proceeds through the remaining phases of the classical software life cycle.

**How to Perform Data Flow Analysis**                    **Box 13.1**

- **Iterate**

  Find the point of highest abstraction of input of each input stream.

  Find the point of highest abstraction of output of each output stream.

  Decompose the data flow diagram using these points of highest abstraction.

- **Until** the resulting modules have high cohesion.
- If a resulting coupling is too high, adjust the design.

**FIGURE 13.8**
The data flow diagram with multiple input and output streams.

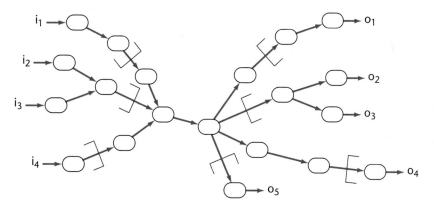

### 13.3.2 Data Flow Analysis Extensions

The reader may well feel that this example is somewhat artificial, in that the data flow diagram (Figure 13.3) has only one input stream and one output stream. To see what happens in more complex situations, consider Figure 13.8. Now there are four input streams and five output streams, a situation that corresponds more closely to reality.

When there are multiple input and output streams, the way to proceed is to find the point of highest abstraction of input for each input stream and the point of highest abstraction of output for each output stream. Use these points to decompose the given data flow diagram into modules with fewer input–output streams than the original. Continue this way until each resulting module has high cohesion. Finally, determine the coupling between each pair of modules and make any necessary adjustments.

Data flow analysis is summarized in How to Perform Box 13.1.

## 13.4   Transaction Analysis

A **transaction** is an operation from the viewpoint of the user of the product, such as "process a request" or "print a list of today's orders." Data flow analysis is inappropriate for the transaction-processing type of product, in which a number of related operations, similar in outline but differing in detail, must be performed. A typical example is the software controlling an automated teller machine. The customer inserts a magnetized card into a

---

## How to Perform Transaction Analysis       Box 13.2

- Design the architecture in terms of two components:
    - The analyzer.
    - The dispatcher.
- **For** each set of related operations
    - Design one basic module and instantiate it as many times as necessary.

---

slot, keys in a password, and then performs operations such as deposit to a checking, savings, or credit card account; withdraw from an account; or determine the balance in an account. This type of product is depicted in Figure 13.9. A good way to design such a product is to break it into two pieces, the analyzer and the dispatcher. The analyzer determines the transaction type and passes this information to the dispatcher, which performs the transaction.

A poor design of this type is shown in Figure 13.10, which has two modules with logical cohesion, edit_any_transaction and update_any_file. On the other hand, it seems a waste of effort to have five very similar edit modules and five very similar update modules. The solution is software reuse (Section 8.1): A basic edit module should be designed, coded, documented, tested, and then instantiated five times. Each version is slightly different, but the differences are small enough to make this approach worthwhile. Similarly, a basic update module can be instantiated five times and slightly modified to cater to the five different update types. The resulting design has high cohesion and low coupling.

**Transaction analysis** is summarized in How to Perform Box 13.2.

**FIGURE 13.9**   A typical transaction-processing system.

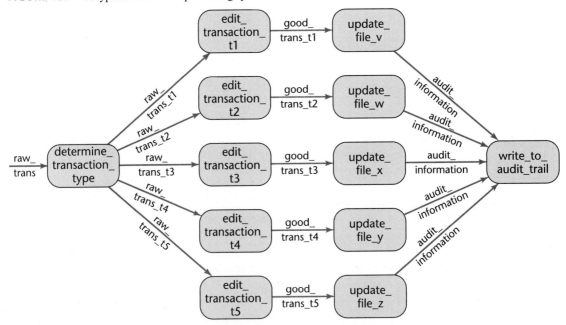

**FIGURE 13.10**
A poor design
of a transaction-
processing
system.

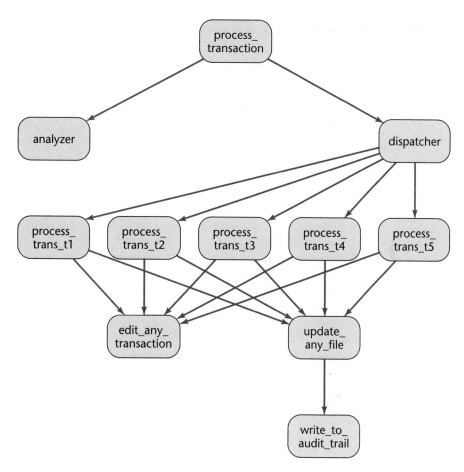

# 13.5   Data-Oriented Design

The basic principle behind data-oriented design is to design the product according to the structure of the data on which it is to operate. That is, first the structure of the data is determined. Then each procedure is given the same structure as the data on which it operates. There are a number of data-oriented techniques of this type; the most well known are those of Michael Jackson [1975], Warnier [1976], and Orr [1981]. The three techniques share many similarities.

Data-oriented design was never as popular as operation-oriented design and, with the rise of the object-oriented paradigm, largely has fallen out of fashion. For reasons of space, data-oriented design is not discussed further in this book; the interested reader should consult the references cited in the previous paragraph.

## 13.6 Object-Oriented Design

As previously stated, the Unified Process assumes previous knowledge of **object-oriented design** (OOD). Accordingly, we now describe OOD and then discuss the design workflow of the Unified Process in Section 13.9.

The aim of OOD is to design the product in terms of objects, that is, instantiations of the classes and subclasses extracted during object-oriented analysis. Classical languages, such as C, and older (pre-2000) versions of COBOL and Fortran do not support objects as such. This might seem to imply that OOD is accessible only to users of object-oriented languages like Smalltalk [Goldberg and Robson, 1989], C++ [Stroustrup, 2003], Ada 95 [ISO/IEC 8652, 1995], and Java [Flanagan, 2005].

That is not the case. Although OOD as such is not supported by classical languages, a large subset of OOD can be used. As explained in Section 7.7, a class is an abstract data type with inheritance and an object is an instance of a class. When using an implementation language that does not support inheritance, the solution is to utilize those aspects of OOD that can be achieved in the programming language used in the project, that is, to use **abstract data type design**. Abstract data types can be implemented in virtually any language that supports **type** statements. Even in a classical language that does not support type statements as such, and hence cannot support abstract data types, it still may be possible to implement data encapsulation. Figure 7.28 depicts a hierarchy of design concepts starting with modules and ending with objects. In those cases where full OOD is not possible, the developers should endeavor to ensure that their design uses the highest possible concept in the hierarchy of Figure 7.28 that their implementation language supports.

The two key steps of OOD are to complete the class diagram and perform the detailed design. With regard to the first step, completing the **class diagram**, the formats of the attributes need to be determined, and the methods need to be assigned to the relevant classes. The formats of the attributes can generally be deduced directly from the analysis artifacts. For example, in the United States the specifications may state that a date such as December 3, 1947, is represented as 12/03/1947 (mm/dd/yyyy format) or in Europe as 03/12/1947 (dd/mm/yyyy format). But, irrespective of which date convention is used, a total of 10 characters is needed.

The information for determining the formats is obtained during the analysis workflow, so the formats could certainly be added to the class diagram at that time. However, the object-oriented paradigm is iterative. Each iteration results in a change to what has already been completed. For practical reasons, then, information should be added to UML models as late as possible. Consider, for example, Figures 12.18, 12.19, 12.25, and 12.60, which show the first four iterations of the class diagram of the MSG Foundation case study. None of those four iterations show the attributes of the classes. If the attributes had been determined earlier, they would probably have had to be modified, as well as possibly moved from class to class, until the analysis team was satisfied with the class diagram. Instead, all that had to be modified was the classes themselves. In general, it makes little sense to add an item to a class diagram (or any other UML diagram) before it is absolutely essential to do so, because adding the item will make the next iteration unnecessarily burdensome. In particular, it makes little sense to specify formats before they are strictly needed.

The other major component of the first step of OOD is to assign methods (implementations of operations) to classes. Determination of all the operations of the product is performed by examining the interaction diagrams of every scenario. This is straightforward. The hard part is to determine how to decide which methods should be associated with each class.

A method can be assigned to either a class or to a client that sends a message to an object of that class. (A client of an object is a program unit that sends a message to that object.) One principle that can be employed to assist in deciding how to assign an operation is information hiding (Section 7.6). That is, the state variables of a class should be declared **private** (accessible only within an object of that class) or **protected** (accessible only within an object of that class or a subclass of that class). Accordingly, operations performed on state variables must be local to that class.

A second principle is that, if a particular operation is invoked by a number of different clients of an object, it makes sense to have a single copy of that operation implemented as a method of the object, rather than have a copy in each client of that object.

A third principle that can be employed to assist in deciding where to locate a method is to use responsibility-driven design. As explained in Section 1.9, **responsibility-driven design** is a key aspect of the object-oriented paradigm. If a client sends a message to an object, then that object is responsible for every aspect of carrying out the request of the client. The client does not know how the request will be carried out and is not permitted to know. Once the request has been carried out, control returns to the client. At that point, all the client knows is that the request has been carried out; it still has no idea how this was achieved.

To see how these principles are utilized, we now illustrate OOD by means of two examples. As before, the elevator problem case study is presented, with just one elevator for simplicity. Then, we return to the MSG Foundation case study. By using the same examples, you are able to compare different approaches without having to worry about the ramifications of the problem itself.

## 13.7  Object-Oriented Design: The Elevator Problem Case Study

### Step 1. Complete the Class Diagram

A design workflow class diagram (Figure 13.11) is obtained by adding the operations (methods) to the class diagram of Figure 12.10. (In the case of a Java implementation, two additional classes are needed. **Elevator Application Class** corresponds to the C++ main function, and **Elevator Utilities Class** contains the Java routines that correspond to the C++ functions declared external to the C++ classes.)

Consider the second iteration of the CRC card for the elevator controller (Figure 12.9). The responsibilities fall into two groups. Three responsibilities—**8. Start timer, 10. Check requests**, and **11. Update requests**—are assigned the elevator controller on the basis of responsibility-driven design; those tasks are carried out by the elevator controller itself.

**FIGURE 13.11** The detailed class diagram for the elevator problem case study.

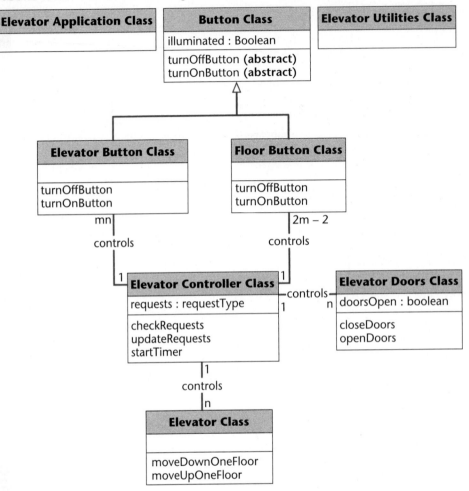

On the other hand, the remaining eight responsibilities (events 1 through 7 and event 9) have the form "Send a message to another class to tell it to do something." This implies the principle that should be used in assigning the relevant method to classes again should be responsibility-driven design. In addition, because of safety concerns, the principle of information hiding is equally applicable in all eight cases.

For these two reasons, methods closeDoors and openDoors are assigned to **Elevator Doors Class**. That is, a client of **Elevator Doors Class** (in this case, an object of **Elevator Controller Class**) sends a message to an object of **Elevator Doors Class** to close or open the doors of the elevator, and that request is then carried out by the relevant method. Every aspect of those two methods is encapsulated within **Elevator Doors Class**. In addition, information hiding results in a truly independent **Elevator Doors Class**, instances of which can undergo detailed design and implementation independently and be reused later in other products.

The same two design principles are applied to methods moveDownOneFloor and moveUpOneFloor, and they are assigned to **Elevator Class**. There is no need for an explicit instruction to cause an elevator to stop. If neither of its two methods is invoked, an elevator cannot move; there is no way to change the state of an elevator other than by invoking one of its two methods.

Finally, methods turnOffButton and turnOnButton are assigned to both **Elevator Button Class** and **Floor Button Class**. The reasoning here is the same as for the methods assigned to **Elevator Doors Class** and **Elevator Class**.

**FIGURE 13.12**
The detailed design of method elevatorEvent-Loop.

```
void elevatorEventLoop (void)
{
   while (TRUE)
   {
      if (a button has been pressed)
         if (button is not on)
         {
            updateRequests;
            button::turnOnButton;
         }
      else if (elevator is moving up)
      {
         if (there is no request to stop at floor f)
            elevator::moveUpOneFloor;
         else
         {
            stop elevator by not sending a message to move;
            elevatorDoors::openDoors;
            startTimer;
            if (elevatorButton is on)
               elevatorButton::turnOffButton;
            updateRequests;
         }
      }
      else if (elevator is moving down)
         [similar to up case]
      else if (elevator is stopped and request is pending)
      {
         elevatorDoors::closeDoors;
         determine direction of next request;
         if (appropriate floorButton is on)
            floorButton::turnOffButton;
         elevator::moveUp/DownOneFloor;
      }
      else if (elevator is at rest and not (request is pending))
         elevatorDoors::closeDoors;
      else
         there are no requests, elevator is stopped with elevatorDoors closed, so do nothing;
   }
}
```

First, the principle of responsibility-driven design requires that the buttons have full control over whether they are on or off. Second, the principle of information hiding requires the internal state of a button to be hidden. The methods that turn an elevator button on or off therefore must be local to **Elevator Button Class**, and similarly for **Floor Button Class**. To make use of polymorphism and dynamic binding, methods turnOffButton and turnOnButton are declared **abstract (virtual)** in the base class **Button Class** for the reasons stated in Section 7.8. At run time, the correct version of method turnOffButton or turnOnButton will then be invoked.

### Step 2. Perform the Detailed Design

A detailed design now is developed for all the classes. Any suitable technique may be used, such as the stepwise refinement described in Chapter 5. The detailed design of method elevatorEventLoop is shown in Figure 13.12. Here PDL (pseudocode) was used, but a tabular representation (such as that of Figure 13.6) can be equally effective.

Figure 13.12 is constructed from the statechart of Figure 12.7. For example, the event button pushed, button unlit is implemented by the two nested **if** statements at the beginning of Figure 13.12. The two operations of the state **Process Requests** then follow. The **else-if** condition corresponds to the next event leading from state **Elevator Event Loop**, elevator moving in direction d, floor f is next. The remainder of the detailed design is equally straightforward.

Now we consider the object-oriented design of the MSG Foundation case study.

## 13.8    Object-Oriented Design: The MSG Foundation Case Study

As described in Section 13.6, object-oriented design consists of two steps.

### Step 1. Complete the Class Diagram

The final class diagram for the MSG Foundation case study is shown in Figure 13.13. The user-defined **Date Class** is drawn dashed to denote that it is needed for only a C++ implementation; Java has built-in classes for handling dates, including **java.text.Dateformat** and **java.util.Calendar**.

Next, the formats for the attributes of the classes are deduced from discussions with the client and users; examination of forms (Section 10.4.2) is also extremely useful in this regard. A portion of the result is shown in Figure 13.14.

The methods of the product are found in the various interaction diagrams. The task of the designer is to decide to which class each method should be assigned. For example, the convention in an object-oriented software product is that associated with each attribute of a class are **mutator** method setAttribute, used to assign a specific value to that attribute, and **accessor** method getAttribute, which returns the current value of that attribute.

**FIGURE 13.13**   The overall class diagram for the MSG Foundation case study.

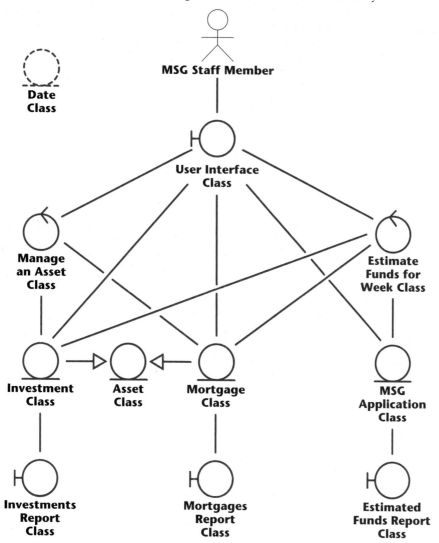

For example, consider method setAssetNumber, used to assign a number to an asset (investment or mortgage). In the classical paradigm, we would need separate functions set_investment_number and set_mortgage_number. However, the object-oriented paradigm supports inheritance. Therefore, method setAssetNumber should be assigned to **Asset Class**. Then, as reflected in Figure 13.15, the method can then be applied not only to instances of **Asset Class** but also, as a consequence of inheritance, to instances of every subclass of **Asset Class**, that is, to instances of **Investment Class** and **Mortgage Class**. Similarly, method getAssetNumber should also be allocated to the superclass **Asset Class**.

**FIGURE 13.14** Part of the overall class diagram for the MSG Foundation case study with the attribute formats added.

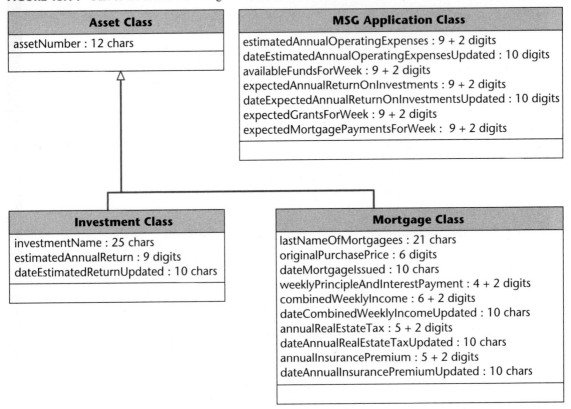

| **Asset Class** |
| --- |
| assetNumber : 12 chars |
| |

| **MSG Application Class** |
| --- |
| estimatedAnnualOperatingExpenses : 9 + 2 digits |
| dateEstimatedAnnualOperatingExpensesUpdated : 10 digits |
| availableFundsForWeek : 9 + 2 digits |
| expectedAnnualReturnOnInvestments : 9 + 2 digits |
| dateExpectedAnnualReturnOnInvestmentsUpdated : 10 digits |
| expectedGrantsForWeek : 9 + 2 digits |
| expectedMortgagePaymentsForWeek : 9 + 2 digits |
| |

| **Investment Class** |
| --- |
| investmentName : 25 chars |
| estimatedAnnualReturn : 9 digits |
| dateEstimatedReturnUpdated : 10 chars |
| |

| **Mortgage Class** |
| --- |
| lastNameOfMortgagees : 21 chars |
| originalPurchasePrice : 6 digits |
| dateMortgageIssued : 10 chars |
| weeklyPrincipleAndInterestPayment : 4 + 2 digits |
| combinedWeeklyIncome : 6 + 2 digits |
| dateCombinedWeeklyIncomeUpdated : 10 chars |
| annualRealEstateTax : 5 + 2 digits |
| dateAnnualRealEstateTaxUpdated : 10 chars |
| annualInsurancePremium : 5 + 2 digits |
| dateAnnualInsurancePremiumUpdated : 10 chars |
| |

**FIGURE 13.15** Part of the class diagram for the MSG Foundation case study with methods setAsset Number and getAssetNumber assigned to **Asset Class**.

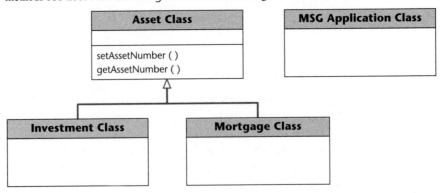

| **Asset Class** |
| --- |
| |
| setAssetNumber ( ) |
| getAssetNumber ( ) |

| **MSG Application Class** |
| --- |
| |
| |

| **Investment Class** |
| --- |
| |

| **Mortgage Class** |
| --- |
| |

**FIGURE 13.16**
The detailed design of method compute-Estimated-Funds of class Estimate-FundsForWeek of the MSG Foundation case study.

**public static void** computeEstimatedFunds( )

*This method computes the estimated funds available for the week.*

{

    **float** expectedWeeklyInvestmentReturn;        *(expected weekly investment return)*

    **float** expectedTotalWeeklyNetPayments = (**float**) 0.0;

                                                    *(expected total mortgage payments less total weekly grants)*

    **float** estimatedFunds = (**float**) 0.0;        *(total estimated funds for week)*

*Create an instance of an investment record.*

    Investment inv = **new** Investment ( );

*Create an instance of a mortgage record.*

    Mortgage mort = **new** Mortgage ( );

*Invoke method totalWeeklyReturnOnInvestment.*

    expectedWeeklyInvestmentReturn = inv.totalWeeklyReturnOnInvestment ( );

*Invoke method expectedTotalWeeklyNetPayments*    *(see Figure 13.17)*

    expectedTotalWeeklyNetPayments = mort.totalWeeklyNetPayments ( );

*Now compute the estimated funds for the week.*

    estimatedFunds = (expectedWeeklyInvestmentReturn

         – (MSGApplication.getAnnualOperatingExpenses ( ) / (**float**) 52.0)

         + expectedTotalWeeklyNetPayments);

*Store this value in the appropriate location.*

    MSGApplication.setEstimatedFundsForWeek (estimatedFunds);

} // computeEstimatedFunds

 

Assigning the other methods to the appropriate classes is equally straightforward. The resulting design is shown in Appendix G.

## Step 2. Perform the Detailed Design

Next, the detailed design is built by taking each method and determining what it does. Figures 13.16 shows the detailed design (in a PDL for Java) of method computeEstimatedFunds of class **EstimateFundsForWeek** of the MSG Foundation case study. This method invokes method totalWeeklyNetPayments of class **Mortgage** shown in Figure 13.17.

**FIGURE 13.17**
The detailed design of method totalWeekly-NetPayments of class **Mortgage** of the MSG Foundation case study.

**public float** totalWeeklyNetPayments ( )

*This method computes the net total weekly payments made by the mortgagees, that is, the expected total weekly mortgage amount less the expected total weekly grants.*

{

    File mortgageFile = **new** File ("mortgage.dat");    *( file of mortgage records)*

    **float** expectedTotalWeeklyMortgages = (**float**) 0.0;    *(expected total weekly mortgage payments)*

    **float** expectedTotalWeeklyGrants = (**float**) 0.0;    *(expected total weekly grants)*

    **float** capitalRepayment;    *(capital repayment)*

    **float** interestPayment;    *(interest payment)*

    **float** escrowPayment;    *(escrow payment)*

    **float** tempMortgage;    *(temporary value)*

    **float** maximumPermittedMortgagePayment;    *(maximum amount the couple may pay)*

*Open the file of mortgages, name it* inFile, *and read each element in turn.*

    {

      read (inFile);

*Compute the capital repayment, interest payment, and escrow payment for this mortgage.*

      capitalRepayment = price / NUMBER_OF_MORTGAGE_PAYMENTS;

      interestPayment = mortgageBalance * INTEREST_RATE / WEEKS_IN_YEAR ;

      escrowPayment = (annualPropertyTax + annualInsurancePremium) / WEEKS_IN_YEAR;

*First assume that the couple can pay the mortgage in full, without a grant.*

      tempMortgage = capitalRepayment + interestPayment + escrowPayment;

*Add this amount to the running total of mortgage payments.*

      expectedTotalWeeklyMortgages += tempMortgage;

*Now determine how much the couple can actually pay.*

      maximumPermittedMortgagePayment = currentWeeklyIncome *

            MAXIMUM_PERC_OF_INCOME;

*If a grant needed, add the grant amount to the running total of grants.*

      **if** (tempMortgage > maximumPermittedMortgagePayment)

      expectedTotalWeeklyGrants += tempMortgage − maximumPermittedMortgagePayment;

    }

*Close the file of mortgages. Return the total expected net payments for the week.*

    **return** (expectedTotalWeeklyMortgages − expectedTotalWeeklyGrants);

} // totalWeeklyNetPayments

| How to Perform Object-Oriented Design | Box 13.3 |
|---|---|

- Complete the class diagram.
- Perform the detailed design.

The steps of object-oriented design are summarized in How to Perform Box 13.3.

# 13.9 The Design Workflow

The input to the **design workflow** is the analysis workflow artifacts (Chapter 12). During the design workflow, these artifacts are iterated and incremented until they are in a format that can be utilized by the programmers.

One aspect of this iteration and incrementation is the identification of methods and their allocation to the appropriate classes. Another aspect is performing the detailed design. These two steps constitute the object-oriented design component of the design workflow.

In addition to performing the object-oriented design, many decisions have to be made as part of the design workflow. One such decision is the selection of the programming language in which the software product will be implemented. This process is described in detail in Chapter 14. Another decision is how much of existing software products to reuse in the new software product to be developed. Reuse is described in Chapter 8. Portability is another important design decision; this topic, too, is described in Chapter 8. Also, large software products are often implemented on a network of computers; yet another design decision is the allocation of each software component to the hardware component on which it is to run.

The major motivation behind the development of the Unified Process was to present a methodology that could be used to develop large-scale software products, typically, 500,000 lines of code or more. On the other hand, the implementations of the MSG Foundation case study in Appendices H and I are less than 5000 lines of C++ and Java, respectively. In other words, the Unified Process is intended primarily for software products at least 100 times larger than the MSG Foundation case study presented in this book. Accordingly, many aspects of the Unified Process are inapplicable to this case study. For instance, an important part of the analysis workflow is to partition the software product into analysis packages. Each **package** consists of a set of related classes, usually of relevance to a small subset of the actors, that can be implemented as a single unit. For example, accounts payable, accounts receivable, and general ledger are typical analysis packages. The concept underlying analysis packages is that it is much easier to develop smaller software products than larger software products. Accordingly, a large software product is easier to develop if it can be decomposed into relatively independent packages.

This idea of decomposing a large workflow into relatively independent smaller workflows is carried forward to the design workflow. Here, the objective is to break up the upcoming implementation workflow into manageable pieces, termed **subsystems**. Again, it does not make sense to break up the MSG Foundation case study into subsystems; the case study is just too small.

There are two reasons why larger workflows are broken into subsystems:

1. As previously explained, it is easier to implement a number of smaller subsystems than one large system.
2. If the subsystems to be implemented are indeed relatively independent, then they can be implemented by programming teams working in parallel. This results in the software product as a whole being delivered sooner.

Recall from Section 8.5.4 that the *architecture* of a software product includes the various components and how they fit together. The allocation of components to subsystems is a major part of the architectural task. Deciding on the architecture of a software product is by no means easy and, in all but the smallest software products, is performed by a specialist, the software **architect**.

In addition to being a technical expert, an architect needs to know how to make **trade-offs**. A software product has to satisfy the functional requirements, that is, the use cases. It also needs to satisfy the nonfunctional requirements, including portability (Chapter 8), reliability (Section 6.4.2), robustness (Section 6.4.3), maintainability, and security. But it needs to do all these things within budget and time constraints. It is almost never possible to develop a software product that satisfies all its requirements, both functional and nonfunctional, and finish the project within the cost and time constraints; compromises almost always have to be made. The client has to relax some of the requirements, increase the budget, or move the delivery deadline, or do more than one of these. The architect must assist the client's decision making by clearly mapping out the trade-offs.

In some cases the trade-offs are obvious. For example, the architect may point out that a set of security requirements that conform to a new high-security standard are going to take a further 3 months and $350,000 to incorporate in the software product. If the product is an international banking network, the issue is moot—there is no way that the client could possibly agree to compromise on security in any way. However, in other instances, the client needs to make critical determinations regarding trade-offs and has to rely on the technical expertise of the architect to assist in coming to the right business decision. For example, the architect might point out that deferring a particular requirement until the software product has been delivered and is being maintained may save $150,000 now but will cost $300,000 to incorporate later (see Figure 1.6). The decision as to whether or not to defer a requirement can be made by only the client, but he or she needs the technical expertise of the architect to assist in coming to the correct decision.

The architecture of a software product is a vital factor as to whether the delivered product is a success or a failure. And, the critical decisions regarding the architecture have to be made while performing the design workflow. If the requirements workflow is badly performed, it is still possible to have a successful project, provided additional time and money are spent on the analysis workflow. Similarly, if the analysis workflow is inadequate, it is possible to recover by making an extra effort as part of the design workflow. But, if the architecture is suboptimal, there is no way to recover; the architecture must immediately be redesigned. It is therefore essential that the development team include an architect with the necessary technical expertise and people skills.

## 13.10  The Test Workflow: Design

The goal of testing the design is to verify that the specifications have been accurately and completely incorporated into the design as well as to ensure the correctness of the design itself. For example, the design must have no logic faults and all interfaces must be correctly defined. It is important that any faults in the design be detected before coding commences; otherwise, the cost of fixing the faults will be considerably higher, as reflected in Figure 1.6. Design faults can be detected by means of design inspections as well as design walk-throughs. Design inspections are discussed in the remainder of this section, but the remarks apply equally to design walkthroughs.

When the product is transaction oriented (Section 13.4), the design inspection should reflect this [Beizer, 1990]. Inspections that include all possible transaction types should be scheduled. The reviewer should relate each transaction in the design to the specifications, showing how the transaction arises from the specification document. For example, if the application is an automated teller machine, a transaction corresponds to each operation the customer can perform, such as deposit to or withdraw from a credit card account. In other instances, the correspondence between specifications and transactions is not necessarily one to one. In a traffic-light control system, for example, if an automobile driving over a sensor pad results in the system deciding to change a particular light from red to green in 15 seconds, then further impulses from that sensor pad may be ignored. Conversely, to speed traffic flow, a single impulse may cause a whole series of lights to be changed from red to green.

Restricting reviews to **transaction-driven inspections** does not detect cases where the designers have overlooked instances of transactions required by the specifications. To take an extreme example, the specifications for the traffic-light controller may stipulate that between 11:00 P.M. and 6:00 A.M. all lights are to flash yellow in one direction and red in the other direction. If the designers overlooked this stipulation, then clock-generated transactions at 11:00 P.M. and 6:00 A.M. would not be included in the design; and if these transactions were overlooked, they could not be tested in a design inspection based on transactions. Therefore, it is not adequate to schedule design inspections that are just transaction driven; specification-driven inspections also are essential to ensure that no statement in the specification document has been either overlooked or misinterpreted.

## 13.11  The Test Workflow: The MSG Foundation Case Study

Now that the design is apparently complete, all aspects of the design of the MSG Foundation case study must be checked by means of a design inspection (Section 6.2.3). In particular, each design artifact must be examined. Even if no faults are found, it is possible that the design will change again, perhaps radically, when the MSG Foundation case study is implemented.

## 13.12   Formal Techniques for Detailed Design

One technique for detailed design has already been presented. In Section 5.1, a description of stepwise refinement was given. It then was applied to detailed design using flowcharts. In addition to stepwise refinement, formal techniques can be used to advantage in detailed design. Chapter 6 suggests that implementing a complete product and then proving it correct could be counterproductive. However, developing the proof and the detailed design in parallel and carefully testing the code as well is quite a different matter. Formal techniques applied to detailed design can greatly assist in three ways:

1. The state of the art in proving correctness is such that, although it generally cannot be applied to a product as a whole, it can be applied to module-sized pieces of a product.
2. Developing a proof together with the detailed design should lead to a design with fewer faults than if correctness proofs were not used.
3. If the same programmer is responsible for both the detailed design and the implementation, then that programmer will feel confident that the detailed design is correct. This positive attitude toward the design should lead to fewer faults in the code.

## 13.13   Real-Time Design Techniques

As explained in Section 6.4.4, **real-time software** is characterized by hard time constraints, that is, time constraints of such a nature that, if a constraint is not met, information is lost. In particular, each input must be processed before the next input arrives. An example of such a system is a computer-controlled nuclear reactor. Inputs such as the temperature of the core and the level of the water in the reactor chamber continually are being sent to the computer that reads the value of each input and performs the necessary processing before the next input arrives. Another example is a computer-controlled intensive care unit. There are two types of patient data: routine information such as heart rate, temperature, and blood pressure of each patient, and emergency information, when the system deduces that the condition of a patient has become critical. When such emergencies occur, the software must process both the routine inputs and the emergency-related inputs from one or more patients.

A characteristic of many real-time systems is that they are implemented on distributed hardware. For example, software controlling a fighter aircraft may be implemented on five computers: one to handle navigation, another the weapons system, a third for electronic countermeasures, a fourth to control the flight hardware such as wing flaps and engines, and the fifth to propose tactics in combat. Because hardware is not totally reliable, there may be additional backup computers that automatically replace a malfunctioning unit. Not only does the design of such a system have major communications implications, but timing issues, over and above those of the type just described, arise as a consequence of the distributed nature of the system. For example, under combat conditions, the tactical computer might suggest that the pilot should climb, whereas the weapons computer recommends that the pilot go into a dive so that a particular weapon may be launched under optimal conditions. However, the human pilot decides to move the stick to the right, thereby sending a signal to the flight hardware computer to make the necessary adjustments so that the plane banks in the indicated direction. All this information must be managed carefully in such a way that the actual motion of the plane takes precedence in every way over suggested maneuvers. Furthermore, the actual motion must be relayed to the tactical and weapons computers so that new suggestions can be formulated in the light of actual, rather than suggested, conditions.

A further difficulty with real-time systems is the problem of synchronization. Suppose that a real-time system is to be implemented on distributed hardware. Situations such as deadlock (or deadly embrace) can arise when two operations each have exclusive use of a data item and each requests exclusive use of the other's data item in addition. Of course, deadlock does not occur only in real-time systems, implemented on distributed hardware. But it is particularly troublesome in real-time systems where there is no control over the order or timing of the inputs, and the situation can be complicated by the distributed nature of the hardware. In addition to deadlock, other synchronization problems are possible, including race conditions; for details, the reader may refer to [Silberschatz, Galvin, and Gagne, 2002] or other operating systems textbooks.

From these examples it is clear that the major difficulty with regard to the design of real-time systems is ensuring that the timing constraints are met by the design. That is, the design technique should provide a mechanism for checking that, when implemented, the design is able to read and process incoming data at the required rate. Furthermore, it should be possible to show that synchronization issues in the design also have been addressed correctly.

Since the beginning of the computer age, advances in hardware technology have outstripped, in almost every respect, advances in software technology. Therefore, although the hardware exists to handle every aspect of the real-time systems described previously, software design technology has lagged behind considerably. In some areas of real-time software engineering, major progress has been made. For instance, many of the analysis techniques of Chapters 11 and 12 can be used to specify real-time systems. Unfortunately, software design has not yet reached the same level of sophistication. Great strides indeed are being made, but the state of the art is not yet comparable to what has been achieved with regard to analysis techniques. Because almost any design technique for real-time systems is preferable to no technique at all, a number of real-time design techniques are used in practice. But, there still is a long way to go before it will be possible to design real-time systems such as those described previously and be certain that, before the system has been implemented, every real-time constraint will be met and synchronization problems cannot arise.

Older real-time design techniques are extensions of non-real-time techniques to the real-time domain. For example, structured development for real-time systems (SDRTS) [Ward and Mellor, 1985] essentially is an extension of structured systems analysis (Section 11.3), data flow analysis (Section 13.3), and transaction analysis (Section 13.4) to real-time software. The development technique includes a component for real-time design. Newer techniques are described in [Liu, 2000] and [Gomaa, 2000].

As stated previously, it is unfortunate that the state of the art of real-time design is not as advanced as one would wish. Nevertheless, efforts are under way to improve the situation.

# 13.14 CASE Tools for Design

As stated in Section 13.10, a critical aspect of design is testing that the design artifacts accurately incorporate all aspects of the analysis. What therefore is needed is a CASE tool that can be used both for the analysis artifacts and the design artifacts, a so-called front-end or upperCASE tool (as opposed to a back-end or lowerCASE tool, which assists with the implementation artifacts).

A number of upperCASE tools are on the market. Some of the more popular ones include Analyst/Designer, Software through Pictures, and System Architect. UpperCASE tools generally are built around a data dictionary. The CASE tool can check that every field of every record in the dictionary is mentioned somewhere in the design or that every item in the design is reflected in the data flow diagram. In addition, many upperCASE tools incorporate a consistency checker that uses the data dictionary to determine that every item in the design has been declared in the specifications and conversely that every item in the specifications appears in the design.

Furthermore, many upperCASE tools incorporate screen and report generators. That is, the client can specify what items are to appear in a report or on an input screen and where and how each item is to appear. Because full details regarding every item are in the data dictionary, the CASE tool easily can generate the code for printing the report or displaying the input screen according to the client's wishes. Some upperCASE products also incorporate management tools for estimating and planning.

With regard to object-oriented design, Together, IBM Rational Rose, and Software through Pictures provide support for this workflow within the context of the complete object-oriented life cycle. Open-source CASE tools of this type include ArgoUML.

## 13.15 Metrics for Design

A variety of metrics can be used to describe aspects of the design. For example, the number of code artifacts (modules or classes) is a crude measure of the size of the target product. Cohesion and coupling are measures of the quality of the design, as are fault statistics. As with all other types of inspection, it is vital to keep a record of the number and type of design faults detected during a design inspection. This information is used during code inspections of the product and in design inspections of subsequent products.

The **cyclomatic complexity** $M$ of a detailed design is the number of binary decisions (predicates) plus 1 [McCabe, 1976] or, equivalently, the number of branches in the code artifact. It has been suggested that cyclomatic complexity is a metric of design quality; the lower the value of $M$, the better. A strength of this metric is that it is easy to compute. However, it has an inherent problem. Cyclomatic complexity is a measure purely of the control complexity; the data complexity is ignored. That is, $M$ does not measure the complexity of a code artifact that is data driven, such as by the values in a table. For example, suppose a designer is unaware of the C++ library function toascii and designs a code artifact from scratch that reads a character input by the user and returns the corresponding ASCII code (an integer between 0 and 127). One way of designing this is by means of a 128-way branch implemented by means of a **switch** statement. A second way is to have an array containing the 128 characters in ASCII code order and utilize a loop to compare the character input by the user with each element of the array of characters; the loop is exited when a match is obtained. The current value of the loop variable then is the corresponding ASCII code. The two designs are equivalent in functionality but have cyclomatic complexities of 128 and 1, respectively.

When the classical paradigm is used, a related class of metrics for the design phase is based on representing the architectural design as a directed graph with the modules represented by nodes and the flows between modules (procedure and function calls) represented by arcs. The **fan-in** of a module can be defined as the number of flows into the module plus the number of global data structures accessed by the module. The **fan-out** similarly is the number of flows out of the module plus the number of global data structures updated by the module. A measure of complexity of the module then is given by *length* $\times$ (*fan-in* $\times$ *fan-out*)$^2$ [Henry and Kafura, 1981], where **length** is a measure of the size of the module (Section 9.2.1). Because the definitions of *fan-in* and *fan-out* incorporate global data, this metric has a data-dependent component. Nevertheless, experiments have shown that this metric is no better a measure of complexity than simpler metrics, such as cyclomatic complexity [Kitchenham, Pickard, and Linkman, 1990; Shepperd, 1990].

The issue of design metrics is complicated even more when the object-oriented paradigm is used. For example, the cyclomatic complexity of a class usually is low, because many classes typically include a large number of small, straightforward methods. Furthermore, as previously pointed out, cyclomatic complexity ignores data complexity. Because data and operations are equal partners within the object-oriented paradigm, cyclomatic complexity overlooks a major component that could contribute to the complexity of an object. Therefore, metrics for classes that incorporate cyclomatic complexity generally are of little use.

A number of object-oriented design metrics have been put forward, for example, in [Chidamber and Kemerer, 1994]. These and other metrics have been questioned on both theoretical and experimental grounds [Binkley and Schach, 1996; 1997; 1998].

## 13.16   Challenges of the Design Workflow

As pointed out in Sections 11.16 and 12.21, it is important not to do too much in the analysis workflow; that is, the analysis team must not prematurely start parts of the design workflow. In the design workflow, the design team can go wrong in two ways: by doing too much and by doing too little.

Consider the PDL (pseudocode) detailed design of Figure 13.7. The temptation is strong for a designer who enjoys programming to write the detailed design in C++ or Java, rather than PDL. That is, instead of sketching the detailed design in pseudocode, the designer may all but code the class. This takes longer to write than just outlining the class and longer to fix if a fault is detected in the design (see Figure 1.6). Like the analysis team, the members of the design team must firmly resist the urge to do more than what is required of them.

At the same time, the design team must be careful not to do too little. Consider the tabular detailed design of Figure 13.6. If the design team is in a hurry, it may decide to shrink the detailed design to just the narrative box. The team even may decide that the programmers should do the detailed design by themselves. Either of these decisions would be a mistake. A primary reason for the detailed design is to ensure that all interfaces are correct. The narrative box by itself is inadequate for this purpose; no detailed design at all clearly is even less helpful. Therefore, one challenge of the design workflow is for the designers to do just the correct amount of work.

In addition, there is a much more significant challenge. In "No Silver Bullet" (see Just in Case You Wanted to Know Box 3.4), Brooks [1986] decries the lack of what he terms *great designers*, that is, designers who are significantly more outstanding than the other members of the design team. In Brooks's opinion, the success of a software project depends critically on whether the design team is led by a great designer. Good design can be taught; great design is produced only by great designers, and they are "very rare."

The challenge, then, is to grow great designers. They should be identified as early as possible (the best designers are not necessarily the most experienced), assigned a mentor, provided a formal education as well as apprenticeships to great designers, and allowed to interact with other designers. A specific career path should be available for these designers, and the rewards they receive should be commensurate with the contribution that only a great designer can make to a software development project.

| | |
|---|---|
| **Chapter Review** | The design workflow is introduced in Section 13.1. There are three basic approaches to design: operation-oriented design (Section 13.2), data-oriented design (Section 13.5), and object-oriented design (Section 13.6). Two instances of operation-oriented design are described, data flow analysis (Section 13.3) and transaction analysis (Section 13.4). Object-oriented design is applied to the elevator problem case study in Section 13.7 and to the MSG Foundation case study in Section 13.8. The design workflow is presented in Section 13.9. The design aspects of the test workflow are described in Section 13.10 and applied to the MSG Foundation case study in Section 13.11. Formal techniques for detailed design are discussed in Section 13.12. Real-time system design is described in Section 13.13. CASE tools and metrics for the design workflow are presented in Sections 13.14 and 13.15, respectively. The chapter concludes with a discussion of the challenges of the design workflow (Section 13.16). |
| **For Further Reading** | Data flow analysis and transaction analysis are described in books such as [Gane and Sarsen, 1979] and [Yourdon and Constantine, 1979]. Jackson's technique is described in [Jackson, 1975]. For readers interested in Warnier's work, the original source is [Warnier, 1976]. Orr's approach can be found in [Orr, 1981]. |

Turning now to object-oriented design, information can be obtained from [Wirfs-Brock, Wilkerson, and Wiener, 1990; Coad and Yourdon, 1991b; Shlaer and Mellor, 1992; and Jacobson, Booch, and Rumbaugh, 1999]. Comparisons of a variety of techniques for object-oriented design appear in [Monarchi and Puhr, 1992] and [Walker, 1992]. Briand, Bunse, and Daly [2001] discuss the maintainability of object-oriented designs. A comparison of both object-oriented and classical design techniques appears in [Fichman and Kemerer, 1992]. The redesign of an air traffic control system is described in [Jackson and Chapin, 2000]. Design techniques for high-performance, reliable systems are given in [Stolper, 1999].

Formal design techniques are described in [Hoare, 1987].

With regard to reviews during the design process, the original paper on design inspections is [Fagan, 1976]; detailed information can be obtained from that paper. Later advances in review techniques are described in [Fagan, 1986]. The use of walkthroughs to test user interface design is described in [Bias, 1991]. Architecture reviews are discussed in [Maranzano et al., 2005].

With regard to real-time design, specific techniques are to be found in [Liu, 2000] and [Gomaa, 2000]. A comparison of four real-time design techniques is found in [Kelly and Sherif, 1992]. A documentation-driven approach to the design of complex real-time systems is described in [Luqi, Zhang, Berzins, and Qiao, 2004]. The design of concurrent systems is described in [Magee and Kramer, 1999]. The March/April 2005 issue of *IEEE Software* contains a number of papers on design.

Metrics for design are described in [Henry and Kafura, 1981] and [Zage and Zage, 1993]. Metrics for object-oriented design are discussed in [Chidamber and Kemerer, 1994] and in [Binkley and Schach, 1996]. A model for object-oriented quality is presented in [Bansiya and Davis, 2002].

The proceedings of the International Workshops on Software Specification and Design are a comprehensive source for information on design techniques.

## Key Terms

abstract data type design *442*
accessor *446*
architect *452*
architectural design *432*
class diagram *442*
cyclomatic complexity *456*
data flow analysis (DFA) *433*
data-oriented design *431*
design workflow *451*
detailed design *432*
fan-in *457*
fan-out *457*
general design *432*
high-level design *432*

length *457*
logical design *432*
low-level design *432*
modular design *432*
mutator *446*
object-oriented design
   (OOD) *442*
operation-oriented design *431*
package *451*
physical design *432*
point of highest abstraction of
   input *433*
point of highest abstraction of
   output *433*

program description language
   (PDL) *437*
pseudocode *437*
real-time software *454*
responsibility-driven
   design *433*
subsystem *451*
trade-off *452*
transaction *439*
transaction analysis *440*
transaction-driven
   inspections *453*

## Problems

13.1   Starting with your DFD for Problem 11.6, use data flow analysis to design a product for determining whether a bank statement is correct.

13.2   Use transaction analysis to design the software to control an ATM (Problem 8.9). At this stage omit error-handling capabilities.

13.3   Now take your design for Problem 13.2 and add modules to perform error handling. Carefully examine the resulting design and determine the cohesion and coupling of the modules. Be on the lookout for situations such as that depicted in Figure 13.10.

13.4   Two different techniques for depicting a detailed design are presented in Section 13.3.1 (Figures 13.6 and 13.7). Compare and contrast the two techniques.

13.5   Starting with your data flow diagram for the automated library circulation system (Problem 11.8), design the circulation system using data flow analysis.

13.6   Repeat Problem 13.5 using transaction analysis. Which of the two techniques did you find to be more appropriate?

13.7   (Analysis and Design Project) Starting with your object-oriented analysis for the automated library circulation system (Problem 12.15), design the library system using object-oriented design.

13.8   (Analysis and Design Project) Starting with your object-oriented analysis for the product for determining whether a bank statement is correct (Problem 12.16), design the software using object-oriented design.

13.9   (Analysis and Design Project) Starting with your object-oriented analysis for the ATM software (Problem 12.17), design the ATM software using object-oriented design.

13.10  (Term Project) Starting with your specifications of Problem 11.15 or 12.18, design the Osric's Office Appliances and Decor product (Appendix A). Use the design technique specified by your instructor.

13.11 (Case Study) Redesign the MSG Foundation product using data flow analysis.

13.12 (Case Study) Redesign the MSG Foundation product using transaction analysis.

13.13 (Case Study) The detailed design of Figures 13.16 and 13.17 is represented in PDL form. Represent the design using a tabular format. Which representation is superior? Give reasons for your answer.

13.14 (Readings in Software Engineering) Your instructor will distribute copies of [Luqi, Zhang, Berzins, and Qiao, 2004]. Would you use this approach for developing real-time systems? Give reasons for your answer.

**References**

[Bansiya and Davis, 2002] J. BANSIYA AND C. G. DAVIS, "A Hierarchical Model for Object-Oriented Design Quality Assessment," *IEEE Transactions on Software Engineering* **28** (January 2002), pp. 4–17.

[Beizer, 1990] B. BEIZER, *Software Testing Techniques,* 2nd ed., Van Nostrand Reinhold, New York, 1990.

[Bias, 1991] R. BIAS, "Walkthroughs: Efficient Collaborative Testing," *IEEE Software* **8** (September 1991), pp. 94–95.

[Binkley and Schach, 1996] A. B. BINKLEY AND S. R. SCHACH, "A Comparison of Sixteen Quality Metrics for Object-Oriented Design," *Information Processing Letters* **57** (No. 6, June 1996), pp. 271–75.

[Binkley and Schach, 1997] A. B. BINKLEY AND S. R. SCHACH, "Toward a Unified Approach to Object-Oriented Coupling," *Proceedings of the 35th Annual ACM Southeast Conference*, Murfreesboro, TN, April 2–4, 1997, pp. 91–97.

[Binkley and Schach, 1998] A. B. BINKLEY AND S. R. SCHACH, "Validation of the Coupling Dependency Metric as a Predictor of Run-Time Failures and Maintenance Measures," *Proceedings of the 20th International Conference on Software Engineering*, Kyoto, Japan, April 1988, pp. 542–55.

[Briand, Bunse, and Daly, 2001] L. C. BRIAND, C. BUNSE, AND J. W. DALY, "A Controlled Experiment for Evaluating Quality Guidelines on the Maintainability of Object-Oriented Designs," *IEEE Transactions on Software Engineering* **27** (June 2001), pp. 513–30.

[Brooks, 1986] F. P. BROOKS, JR., "No Silver Bullet," in: *Information Processing '86*, H.-J. Kugler (Editor), Elsevier North-Holland, New York, 1986; reprinted in: *IEEE Computer* **20** (April 1987), pp. 10–19.

[Chidamber and Kemerer, 1994] S. R. CHIDAMBER AND C. F. KEMERER, "A Metrics Suite for Object Oriented Design," *IEEE Transactions on Software Engineering* **20** (June 1994), pp. 476–93.

[Coad and Yourdon, 1991b] P. COAD AND E. YOURDON, *Object-Oriented Design*, Yourdon Press, Englewood Cliffs, NJ, 1991.

[Fagan, 1976] M. E. FAGAN, "Design and Code Inspections to Reduce Errors in Program Development," *IBM Systems Journal* **15** (No. 3, 1976), pp. 182–211.

[Fagan, 1986] M. E. FAGAN, "Advances in Software Inspections," *IEEE Transactions on Software Engineering* **SE-12** (July 1986), pp. 744–51.

[Fichman and Kemerer, 1992] R. G. FICHMAN AND C. F. KEMERER, "Object-Oriented and Conventional Analysis and Design Methodologies: Comparison and Critique," *IEEE Computer* **25** (October 1992), pp. 22–39.

[Flanagan, 2005] D. FLANAGAN, *Java in a Nutshell: A Desktop Quick Reference*, 5th ed., O'Reilly and Associates, Sebastopol, CA, 2005.

[Gane and Sarsen, 1979] C. GANE AND T. SARSEN, *Structured Systems Analysis: Tools and Techniques*, Prentice Hall, Englewood Cliffs, NJ, 1979.

[Goldberg and Robson, 1989] A. GOLDBERG AND D. ROBSON, *Smalltalk-80: The Language,* Addison-Wesley, Reading, MA, 1989.

[Gomaa, 2000] H. GOMAA, *Designing Concurrent, Distributed, and Real-Time Applications with UML*, Addison-Wesley, Reading, MA, 2000.

[Henry and Kafura, 1981] S. M. HENRY AND D. KAFURA, "Software Structure Metrics Based on Information Flow," *IEEE Transactions on Software Engineering* **SE-7** (September 1981), pp. 510–18.

[Herbsleb and Grinter, 1999] J. D. HERBSLEB AND R. E. GRINTER, "Architectures, Coordination, and Distance: Conway's Law and Beyond," *IEEE Software* **16** (September/October 1999), pp. 63–70.

[Hoare, 1987] C. A. R. HOARE, "An Overview of Some Formal Methods for Program Design," *IEEE Computer* **20** (September 1987), pp. 85–91.

[ISO/IEC 8652, 1995] *Programming Language Ada: Language and Standard Libraries*, ISO/IEC 8652, International Organization for Standardization, International Electrotechnical Commission, Geneva, Switzerland, 1995.

[Jackson, 1975] M. A. JACKSON, *Principles of Program Design*, Academic Press, New York, 1975.

[Jackson and Chapin, 2000] D. JACKSON AND J. CHAPIN, "Redesigning Air Traffic Control: An Exercise in Software Design," *IEEE Software* **17** (May/June 2000), pp. 63–70.

[Jacobson, Booch, and Rumbaugh, 1999] I. JACOBSON, G. BOOCH, AND J. RUMBAUGH, *The Unified Software Development Process*, Addison-Wesley, Reading, MA, 1999.

[Kelly and Sherif, 1992] J. C. KELLY AND J. S. SHERIF, "A Comparison of Four Design Methods for Real-Time Software Development," *Information and Software Technology* **34** (February 1992), pp. 74–82.

[Kitchenham, Pickard, and Linkman, 1990] B. A. KITCHENHAM, L. M. PICKARD, AND S. J. LINKMAN, "An Evaluation of Some Design Metrics," *Software Engineering Journal* **5** (January 1990), pp. 50–58.

[Liu, 2000] J. W. S. LIU, *Real Time Systems*, Prentice Hall, Upper Saddle River, NJ, 2000.

[Luqi, Zhang, Berzins, and Qiao, 2004] LUQI, L. ZHANG, V. BERZINS, AND Y. QIAO, "Documentation Driven Development for Complex Real-Time Systems," *IEEE Transactions on Software Engineering* **30** (December 2004), pp. 936–52.

[Magee and Kramer, 1999] J. MAGEE AND J. KRAMER, *Concurrency: State Models & Java Programs*, John Wiley and Sons, New York, 1999.

[Maranzano et al., 2005] J. F. MARANZANO, S. A. ROZSYPAL, G. H. ZIMMERMAN, G. W. WARNKEN, P. E. WIRTH, AND D. M. WEISS, "Architecture Reviews: Practice and Experience," *IEEE Software* **22** (March/April 2005), pp. 34–43.

[McCabe, 1976] T. J. MCCABE, "A Complexity Measure," *IEEE Transactions on Software Engineering* **SE-2** (December 1976), pp. 308–20.

[Monarchi and Puhr, 1992] D. E. MONARCHI AND G. I. PUHR, "A Research Typology for Object-Oriented Analysis and Design," *Communications of the ACM* **35** (September 1992), pp. 35–47.

[Orr, 1981] K. ORR, *Structured Requirements Definition*, Ken Orr and Associates, Topeka, KS, 1981.

[Shepperd, 1990] M. SHEPPERD, "Design Metrics: An Empirical Analysis," *Software Engineering Journal* **5** (January 1990), pp. 3–10.

[Shlaer and Mellor, 1992] S. SHLAER AND S. MELLOR, *Object Lifecycles: Modeling the World in States,* Yourdon Press, Englewood Cliffs, NJ, 1992.

[Silberschatz, Galvin, and Gagne, 2002] A. SILBERSCHATZ, P. B. GALVIN, AND G. GAGNE, *Operating System Concepts,* 6th ed., Addison-Wesley, Reading, MA, 2002.

[Stolper, 1999] S. A. STOLPER, "Streamlined Design Approach Lands Mars Pathfinder," *IEEE Software* **16** (September/October 1999), pp. 52–62.

[Stroustrup, 2003] B. STROUSTRUP, *The C++ Standard: Incorporating Technical Corrigendum No. 1*, 2nd ed., John Wiley and Sons, New York, 2003.

[Walker, 1992] I. J. WALKER, "Requirements of an Object-Oriented Design Method," *Software Engineering Journal* **7** (March 1992), pp. 102–13.

[Ward and Mellor, 1985] P. T. WARD AND S. MELLOR, *Structured Development for Real-Time Systems*, Vols. 1, 2, and 3, Yourdon Press, New York, 1985.

[Warnier, 1976] J. D. WARNIER, *Logical Construction of Programs*, Van Nostrand Reinhold, New York, 1976.

[Wirfs-Brock, Wilkerson, and Wiener, 1990] R. WIRFS-BROCK, B. WILKERSON, AND L. WIENER, *Designing Object-Oriented Software*, Prentice Hall, Englewood Cliffs, NJ, 1990.

[Yourdon and Constantine, 1979] E. YOURDON AND L. L. CONSTANTINE, *Structured Design: Fundamentals of a Discipline of Computer Program and Systems Design*, Prentice Hall, Englewood Cliffs, NJ, 1979.

[Zage and Zage, 1993] W. M. ZAGE AND D. M. ZAGE, "Evaluating Design Metrics on Large-Scale Software," *IEEE Software* **10** (July 1993), pp. 75–81.

# Chapter  14

# Implementation

**Learning Objectives**

After studying this chapter, you should be able to

- Perform the implementation workflow.
- Perform black-box, glass-box, and non-execution-based unit testing.
- Perform integration testing, product testing, and acceptance testing.
- Appreciate the need for good programming practices and programming standards.

Implementation is the process of translating the detailed design into code. When this is done by a single individual, the process is relatively well understood. But, most real-life products today are too large to be implemented by one programmer within the given time constraints. Instead, the product is implemented by a team, working at the same time on different components of the product; this is termed **programming-in-the-many**. Issues associated with programming-in-the-many are examined in this chapter.

## 14.1  Choice of Programming Language

In most cases, the issue of which programming language to choose for the implementation simply does not arise. Suppose the client wants a product to be written in, say, Smalltalk. Perhaps, in the opinion of the development team, Smalltalk is entirely unsuitable for the product. Such an opinion is irrelevant to the client. Management of the development organization has only two choices: Implement the product in Smalltalk or turn down the job.

Similarly, if the product has to be implemented on a specific computer and the only language available on that computer is assembler, then again there is no choice. If no other language is available, either because no compiler has yet been written for any high-level language on that computer or management is not prepared to pay for a new C++ compiler for the stipulated computer, then again clearly the issue of choice of programming language is not relevant.

A more interesting situation is this: A contract specifies that the product is to be implemented in "the most-suitable" programming language. What language should be chosen? To answer this question, consider the following scenario. QQQ Corporation has been writing COBOL products for over 30 years. The entire 200-member software staff of QQQ, from the most junior programmer to the vice-president for software, has COBOL expertise. Why on earth should the most suitable programming language be anything but COBOL? The introduction of a new language, Java, for example, would mean having to hire new programmers, or, at the very least, existing staff would have to be intensively retrained. Having invested all that money and effort in Java training, management might well decide that future products also should be written in Java. Nevertheless, all the existing COBOL products would have to be maintained. There then would be two classes of programmers, COBOL maintenance programmers and Java programmers writing the new applications. Quite undeservedly, maintenance almost always is considered inferior to developing new applications, so there would be distinct unhappiness among the ranks of the COBOL programmers. This unhappiness would be compounded by the fact that Java programmers usually are paid more than COBOL programmers because Java programmers are in short supply. Although QQQ has excellent development tools for COBOL, a Java compiler would have to be purchased, as well as appropriate Java CASE tools. Additional hardware may have to be purchased or leased to run this new software. Perhaps most serious of all, QQQ has accumulated hundreds of person-years of COBOL expertise, the kind of expertise that can be gained only through hands-on experience, such as what to do when a certain cryptic error message appears on the screen or how to handle the quirks of the compiler. In brief, it would seem that "the most suitable" programming language could be only COBOL—any other choice would be financial suicide, either from the viewpoint of the cost involved or as a consequence of plummeting staff morale leading to poor-quality code.

And yet, the most suitable programming language for QQQ Corporation's latest project may indeed be some language other than COBOL. Notwithstanding its position as the world's most widely used programming language (see Just in Case You Wanted to Know Box 14.1), COBOL is suited for only one class of software products, data-processing applications. If QQQ Corporation has software needs outside this class, then COBOL rapidly loses its attractiveness. For example, if QQQ wishes to construct a knowledge-based product using artificial intelligence (AI) techniques, then an AI language such as Lisp could be used; COBOL is totally unsuitable for AI applications. If large-scale communications software is to be built, perhaps because QQQ requires satellite links to hundreds of branch offices all over the world, then a language such as Java would prove far more suitable than COBOL. If QQQ is to go into the business of writing systems software, such as operating systems, compilers, and linkers, then COBOL very definitely is unsuitable. And, if QQQ Corporation decides to go into defense contracting, management will soon discover that COBOL simply cannot be used for real-time embedded software.

The issue of which programming language to use often can be decided by using cost–benefit analysis (Section 5.2). That is, management must compute the dollar cost of an implementation in COBOL as well as the dollar benefits, present and future, of using COBOL. This computation must be repeated for every language under consideration. The language with the largest expected gain (that is, the difference between estimated benefits and estimated costs) is then the appropriate implementation language. Another way of

Far more code has been written in COBOL than all other programming languages put together. COBOL is the most widely used language primarily because COBOL is a product of the U.S. Department of Defense (DoD). Developed under the direction of the late Rear-Admiral Grace Murray Hopper, COBOL was approved by the DoD in 1960. Thereafter, the DoD would not buy hardware for running data-processing applications unless that hardware had a COBOL compiler [Sammet, 1978]. The DoD was, and still is, the world's largest purchaser of computer hardware; and in the 1960s, a considerable proportion of DoD software was written for data processing. As a result, COBOL compilers were written as a matter of urgency for virtually every computer. This widespread availability of COBOL, at a time when the only alternative language usually was assembler, resulted in COBOL becoming the world's most popular programming language.

Languages such as C, C++, Java, and the 4GLs undoubtedly are growing in popularity for new applications. Nevertheless, postdelivery maintenance still is the major software activity, and this maintenance is being performed on existing COBOL software. In short, the DoD put its stamp onto the world's software via its first major programming language, COBOL.

Another reason for the popularity of COBOL is that COBOL frequently is the best language for implementing a data-processing product. In particular, COBOL generally is the language of choice when money is involved. Financial books have to balance, so rounding errors cannot be allowed to creep in. Therefore, all computations have to be performed using integer arithmetic. COBOL supports integer arithmetic on very large numbers (that is, billions of dollars). In addition, COBOL can handle very small numbers, such as fractions of a cent. Banking regulations require interest computations to be calculated to at least four decimal places of a cent, and COBOL can do this arithmetic with ease as well. Finally, COBOL probably has the best formatting, sorting, and report generation facilities of any third-generation language (or high-level language, see Section 14.2). All these reasons have made COBOL an excellent choice for implementing a data-processing product.

As mentioned in Section 8.7.4, the current COBOL language standard is for an object-oriented language. This standard surely will further boost the popularity of COBOL.

---

deciding which programming language to select is to use risk analysis. For each language under consideration, a list is made of the potential risks and ways of resolving them. The language for which the overall risk is the smallest then is selected.

Currently, software organizations are under pressure to develop new software in an object-oriented language—any object-oriented language. The question that arises is this: Which is the appropriate object-oriented language? Twenty years ago, there really was only one choice, Smalltalk. Today, however, the most widely used object-oriented programming language is C++ [Borland, 2002], with Java in second place. There are a number of reasons for the popularity of C++. One is the widespread availability of C++ compilers. In fact, some C++ compilers simply translate the source code from C++ into C, and then invoke the C compiler. Therefore, any computer with a C compiler essentially can handle C++.

But the real explanation for the popularity of C++ is its apparent similarity to C. This is unfortunate, in that a number of managers view C++ as a superset of C and, therefore, conclude that any programmer who knows C can quickly pick up the additional pieces. Indeed, from just a syntactical viewpoint, C++ essentially is a superset of C. After all, virtually any C program can be compiled using a C++ compiler. Conceptually, however, C++ is totally different from C. C is a product of the classical paradigm, whereas C++ is for the object-oriented paradigm. Using C++ makes sense only if object-oriented techniques have been used and if the product is organized around objects and classes, not functions.

Therefore, before an organization adopts C++, it is essential that the relevant software professionals be trained in the object-oriented paradigm. It is particularly important that the information of Chapter 7 be taught. Unless it is clear to all involved, and particularly to management, that the object-oriented paradigm is a different way of developing software and what the precise differences are, the classical paradigm just will continue to be used but with the code written in C++ rather than C. When organizations are disappointed with the results of switching from C to C++, a major contributory factor is a lack of education in the object-oriented paradigm.

Suppose that an organization decides to adopt Java. In that case it is not possible to move gradually from the classical paradigm to the object-oriented paradigm. Java is a pure object-oriented programming language; it does not support the functions and procedures of the classical paradigm. Unlike a hybrid object-oriented language such as C++, Java programmers have to use the object-oriented paradigm (and only the object-oriented paradigm) from the very beginning. Because of the necessity of an abrupt transition from the one paradigm to the other, education and training is even more important when adopting Java (or other pure object-oriented language, such as Smalltalk) than if the organization were to switch to a hybrid object-oriented language like C++ or OO-COBOL.

## 14.2    Fourth-Generation Languages

The first computers had neither interpreters nor compilers. They were programmed in binary, either hardwired with plug boards or by setting switches. Such a binary machine code was a **first-generation language**. The **second-generation languages** were assemblers, developed in the late 1940s and early 1950s. Instead of having to program in binary, instructions could be expressed in symbolic notation such as

mov        $17, next

In general, each assembler instruction is translated into one machine code instruction. So, although assembler was easier to write than machine code and easier for postdelivery maintenance programmers to comprehend, the assembler source code was the same length as the machine code.

The idea behind a **third-generation language** (or high-level language), such as C, C++, Pascal, or Java, is that one statement of a high-level language is compiled to as many as 5 or 10 machine code instructions (this is another example of abstraction; see Section 7.4.1). High-level language code is hence considerably shorter than the equivalent assembler code. It is also simpler to understand and, therefore, easier to maintain than assembler code. The fact that the high-level language code may not be quite as efficient as the equivalent assembler code generally is a small price to pay for ease in postdelivery maintenance.

This concept was taken further in the late 1970s. A major objective in the design of a **fourth-generation language** (4GL) is that each 4GL statement should be equivalent to 30, or even 50, machine code instructions. Products written in a 4GL such as Focus or Natural are shorter and hence quicker to develop and easier to maintain.

Some years ago I hailed a cab outside Grand Central Station in New York City and said to the driver, "Please take me to Lincoln Center." This was a *nonprocedural* request, because I expressed the desired result but left it to the driver to decide how to achieve that result. It turned out that the driver was an immigrant from Central Europe who had been in America less than 2 months and knew virtually nothing about the geography of New York City or the English language. As a result, I quickly replaced my nonprocedural request by a **procedural** request of the form, "Straight, straight. Take a right at the next light. I said right. Right, here, yes, right! Now straight. Slow down, please. I said slow down. For heaven's sake, slow down!" and so on, until we finally reached Lincoln Center.

---

It is difficult to program in machine code. It is somewhat easier to program in assembler, and easier still to use a high-level language. A second major design objective of a 4GL is ease in programming. In particular, many 4GLs are **nonprocedural** (see Just in Case You Wanted to Know Box 14.2 for an insight into this term). For example, consider the command

**for every** surveyor
**if** rating **is** excellent
**add** 6500 **to** salary

It is up to the compiler of the 4GL to translate this nonprocedural instruction into a sequence of machine code instructions that can be executed procedurally.

Success stories abound from organizations that have switched to a 4GL. A few that previously used COBOL reported a 10-fold increase in productivity through use of a 4GL. Many organizations found that their productivity indeed increased through use of a 4GL but not spectacularly so. Other organizations tried a 4GL and were bitterly disappointed with the results.

One reason for this inconsistency is that it is unlikely that one 4GL will be appropriate for all products. On the contrary, it is important to select the correct 4GL for the specific product. For example, Playtex used IBM's Application Development Facility (ADF) and reported an 80 to 1 productivity increase over COBOL. Notwithstanding this impressive result, Playtex subsequently returned to COBOL for products deemed by management to be less well suited to ADF [Martin, 1985].

A second reason for these inconsistent results is that many 4GLs are supported by powerful CASE workbenches and environments (Section 5.5). CASE workbenches and environments can be both a strength and a weakness. As explained in Section 5.10, it is inadvisable to introduce large-scale CASE within an organization with a low maturity level. The reason is that the purpose of a CASE workbench or environment is to support the software process. An organization at level 1 has no software process in place. If at this point CASE is introduced as part of the transition to a 4GL, this imposes a process onto an organization not ready for any sort of process. The usual consequences at best are unsatisfactory and can be disastrous. In fact, a number of reported 4GL failures can be ascribed to the effects of the associated CASE environment rather than to the 4GL itself.

The attitudes of 43 organizations to 4GLs are reported in [Guimaraes, 1985]. This research found that use of a 4GL reduced user frustration because the data-processing department could respond more quickly when a user needed information extracted from the organization's database. However, there also were a number of problems. Some 4GLs proved to be slow and inefficient, with long response times. One product consumed 60 percent of the CPU cycles on an IBM 4331 mainframe, while supporting, at most, 12 concurrent users. Overall, the 28 organizations that had been using a 4GL for over 3 years felt that the benefits outweighed the costs.

No one 4GL dominates the software market. Instead, there are hundreds of 4GLs; some of them, including DB2, Oracle, and PowerBuilder, have sizable user groups. This widespread proliferation of 4GLs is further evidence that care has to be taken in selecting the correct 4GL. Of course, few organizations can afford to support more than one 4GL. Once a 4GL has been chosen and used, the organization must either use that 4GL for subsequent products or fall back on the language used before the 4GL was introduced.

Notwithstanding the potential productivity gain, there could be danger in using a 4GL the wrong way. Many organizations currently have a large backlog of products to be developed and a long list of postdelivery maintenance tasks to be performed. A design objective of many 4GLs is **end-user programming**, that is, programming by the person who will use the product. For example, before the advent of 4GLs, the investment manager of an insurance company would ask the data-processing manager for a product that would display certain information regarding the bond portfolio. The investment manager then would wait a year or so for the data-processing group to find the time to develop the product. A 4GL was desired that would be so simple to use that the investment manager, previously untrained in programming, could write the desired product unaided. End-user programming was intended to help reduce the development backlog, leaving the professionals to maintain existing products.

In practice, end-user programming can be dangerous. First, consider the situation when all product development is performed by computer professionals. Computer professionals are trained to mistrust computer output. After all, probably less than 1 percent of all output during product development is correct. On the other hand, the user is told to trust all computer output, because no product should be delivered to the user until it is fault free. Now consider the situation when end-user programming is encouraged. When a user who is inexperienced in programming writes code with a user-friendly, nonprocedural 4GL, the natural tendency is for that user to believe the output. After all, for years the user has been instructed to trust computer output. As a result, many business decisions have been based on data generated by hopelessly incorrect end-user code. In some cases, the user-friendliness of certain 4GLs has led to financial catastrophes.

Another potential danger lies in the tendency, in some organizations, to allow users to write 4GL products that update the organization's database. A programming mistake made by a user eventually may result in the corruption of the entire database. The lesson is clear: Programming by inexperienced or inadequately trained users can be exceedingly dangerous, if not fatal, to the financial health of a corporation.

The ultimate choice of a 4GL is made by management. In making such a decision, management should be guided by the many success stories resulting from the use of a 4GL. At the same time, management should carefully analyze the failures caused by using an inappropriate 4GL, by premature introduction of a CASE environment, and by poor management of the development process. For example, a common cause of failure is neglecting to train the development team thoroughly in all aspects of the 4GL, including relational database theory [Date, 2003] where appropriate. Management should study both

In the late 1970s, a small software organization in Johannesburg, South Africa, consisted of two programming teams. Team A was made up of èmigrès from Mozambique. They were of Portuguese extraction, and their native language was Portuguese. Their code was well written. Variable names were meaningful but unfortunately only to a speaker of Portuguese. Team B comprised Israeli immigrants whose native language was Hebrew. Their code was equally well written, and the names they chose for their variables were equally meaningful—but only to a speaker of Hebrew.

One day, team A resigned en masse, together with its team leader. Team B was totally unable to maintain any of the excellent code that team A had written, because they spoke no Portuguese. The variable names, meaningful as they were to Portuguese speakers, were incomprehensible to the Israelis, whose linguistic abilities were restricted to Hebrew and English. The owner of the software organization was unable to hire enough Portuguese-speaking programmers to replace team A, and the company soon went into bankruptcy, under the weight of numerous lawsuits from disgruntled customers whose code was now essentially unmaintainable.

The situation could have been avoided easily. The head of the company should have insisted from the start that all variable names be in English, the language understood by every South African computer professional. Variable names then would have been meaningful to any maintenance programmer.

the successes and failures in the specific application area and learn from past mistakes. Choosing the correct 4GL can mean the difference between a major success and dismal failure.

Having decided on the implementation language, the next issue is how software engineering principles can lead to better-quality code.

## 14.3    Good Programming Practice

Many recommendations on good coding style are language specific. For example, suggestions regarding use of COBOL 88-level entries or parentheses in Lisp are of little interest to programmers implementing a product in Java. In contrast, recommendations regarding language-independent good programming practice are now given.

### 14.3.1  Use of Consistent and Meaningful Variable Names

As stated in Chapter 1, on average at least two-thirds of a software budget is devoted to postdelivery maintenance. This implies that the programmer developing a code artifact is merely the first of many who will work on that code artifact. It is counterproductive for a programmer to give names to variables that are meaningful to only that programmer; within the context of software engineering, the term meaningful variable names means "meaningful from the viewpoint of future maintenance programmers." This point is amplified in Just in Case You Wanted to Know Box 14.3.

In addition to the use of meaningful variable names, it is equally essential that consistent variable names be chosen. For example, the following four variables are declared in a code artifact: averageFreq, frequencyMaximum, minFr, and frqncyTotl. A maintenance programmer who is trying to understand the code has to know if freq, frequency, fr, and frqncy all refer to the same thing. If yes, then the identical word should be used, preferably frequency, although freq or frqncy is marginally acceptable; fr is not. But if one or more variable names refer to a different quantity, then a totally different name, such as rate, should be used. Conversely, do not use two different names to denote the identical concept; for example, both average and mean should not be used in the same program.

A second aspect of consistency is the ordering of the components of variable names. For example, if one variable is named frequencyMaximum, then the name minimumFrequency would be confusing; it should be frequencyMinimum. To make the code clear and unambiguous for future maintenance programmers, the four variables listed previously should be named frequencyAverage, frequencyMaximum, frequencyMinimum, and frequencyTotal, respectively. Alternatively, the frequency component can appear at the end of all four variable names, yielding the variable names averageFrequency, maximumFrequency, minimumFrequency, and totalFrequency. It clearly does not matter which of the two sets is chosen; what is important is that all the names be from one set or the other.

A number of different naming conventions have been put forward that are intended to make it easier to understand the code. The idea is that the name of a variable should incorporate type information. For example, ptrChTmp might denote a temporary variable (Tmp) of type pointer (ptr) to an character (Ch). The best known of such schemes are the Hungarian Naming Conventions [Klunder, 1988]. (If you want to know why they are called Hungarian, see Just in Case You Wanted to Know Box 14.4.) One drawback of many of such schemes is that the effectiveness of code inspections (Section 14.14) can be reduced when participants are unable to pronounce the names of variables. It is extremely frustrating to have to spell out variable names, letter by letter.

## 14.3.2 The Issue of Self-Documenting Code

When asked why their code contains no comments whatsoever, programmers often proudly reply, "I write **self-documenting code**." The implication is that their variable names are chosen so carefully and their code crafted so exquisitely that there is no need for comments. Self-documenting code does exist, but it is exceedingly rare. Instead, the usual scenario is that the programmer appreciates every nuance of the code at the time the code artifact is written. It is conceivable that the programmer uses the same style for every code artifact and that in 5 years' time the code still is crystal clear in every respect to the original programmer. Unfortunately, this is irrelevant. The important point is whether the code artifact can be understood easily and unambiguously by all the other programmers who have to read it, starting with the software quality assurance group and including a number of different postdelivery maintenance programmers. The problem becomes more acute in the light of the unfortunate practice of assigning postdelivery maintenance tasks to inexperienced programmers and not supervising them closely. The undocumented code of the artifact may be only partially comprehensible to an experienced programmer. How much worse, then, is the situation when the maintenance programmer is inexperienced.

To see the sort of problems that can arise, consider the variable xCoordinateOf-PositionOfRobotArm. Such a variable name undoubtedly is self-documenting in every sense of the word, but few programmers are prepared to use a 31-character variable name, especially if that name is used frequently. Instead, a shorter name is used, xCoord, for example. The reasoning behind this is that if the entire code artifact deals with the movement of the arm of a robot, xCoord can refer only to the *x* coordinate of the position of the arm of the robot. Although that argument holds water within the context of the development process, it is not necessarily true for postdelivery maintenance. The maintenance programmer may not have sufficient knowledge of the product as a whole to realize that, within this code artifact, xCoord refers to the arm of the robot or may not have the necessary documentation to understand the workings of the code artifact. The way to avoid this sort of problem is to insist that every variable name be explained at the beginning of the code artifact, in the **prologue comments**. If this rule is followed, the maintenance programmer quickly will understand that variable xCoord is used for the *x* coordinate of the position of the robot arm.

Prologue comments are mandatory in every code artifact. The minimum information that must be provided at the top of every code artifact is listed in Figure 14.1.

Even if a code artifact is clearly written, it is unreasonable to expect someone to have to read every line to understand what the code artifact does and how it does it. Prologue comments make it easy for others to understand the key points. Only a member of the SQA group or a maintenance programmer modifying a specific code artifact should be expected to have to read every line of that code artifact.

**FIGURE 14.1**
Minimal prologue comments for a code artifact.

The name of the code artifact
A brief description of what the code artifact does
The programmer's name
The date the code artifact was coded
The date the code artifact was approved
The name of the person who approved the code artifact
The arguments of the code artifact
A list of the name of each variable of the code artifact, preferably in alphabetical order, and a brief description of its use
The names of any files accessed by this code artifact
The names of any files changed by this code artifact
Input–output, if any
Error-handling capabilities
The name of the file containing test data (to be used later for regression testing)
A list of each modification made to the code artifact, the date the modification was made, and who approved the modification
Any known faults

In addition to prologue comments, inline comments should be inserted into the code to assist maintenance programmers in understanding that code. It has been suggested that inline comments should be used only when the code is written in a nonobvious way or uses some subtle aspect of the language. On the contrary, confusing code should be rewritten in a clearer way. Inline comments are a means of helping maintenance programmers and should not be used to promote or excuse poor programming practice.

### 14.3.3  Use of Parameters

There are very few genuine constants, that is, variables whose values *never* change. For instance, satellite photographs have caused changes to be made in submarine navigation systems incorporating the latitude and longitude of Pearl Harbor, Hawaii, to reflect more accurate geographic data regarding the exact location of Pearl Harbor. To take another example, sales tax is not a genuine constant; legislators tend to change the sales tax rate from time to time. Suppose that the sales tax rate currently is 6.0 percent. If the value 6.0 has been hard coded in a number of code artifacts of a product, then changing the product is a major exercise, with the likely outcome of one or two instances of the "constant" 6.0 being overlooked and, perhaps, changing an unrelated 6.0 by mistake. A better solution is a C++ declaration such as

**const float** salesTaxRate = 6.0;

or, in Java,

**public static final float** salesTaxRate = (**float**) 6.0;

Then, wherever the value of the sales tax rate is needed, the constant salesTaxRate should be used and not the number 6.0. If the sales tax rate changes, then only the line containing the value of salesTaxRate need be altered using an editor. Better still, the value of the sales tax rate should be read in from a parameter file at the beginning of the run. All such apparent constants should be treated as parameters. If a value should change for any reason, this change can be implemented quickly and effectively.

### 14.3.4  Code Layout for Increased Readability

It is relatively simple to make a code artifact easy to read. For example, no more than one statement should appear on a line, even though many programming languages permit more than one. Indentation is perhaps the most important technique for increasing readability. Just imagine how difficult it would be to read the code examples in Chapter 7 if indentation had not been used to assist in understanding the code. In C++ or Java, indentation can be used to connect corresponding { . . . } pairs. Indentation also shows which statements belong in a given block. In fact, correct indentation is too important to be left to humans. Instead, as described in Section 5.6, CASE tools should be used to ensure that indentation is done correctly.

Another useful aid is blank lines. Methods should be separated by blank lines; in addition, it often is helpful to break up large blocks of code with blank lines. The extra "white space" makes the code easier to read and, hence, comprehend.

### 14.3.5  Nested if Statements

Consider the following example. A map consists of two squares, as shown in Figure 14.2. It is required to write code to determine whether a point on the Earth's surface lies in

**FIGURE 14.2**
Coordinates for
a map.

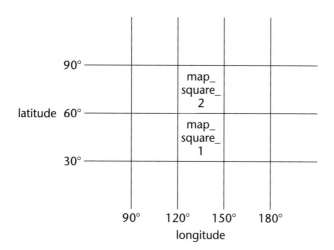

latitude

longitude

**FIGURE 14.3**
Badly formatted
nested **if**
statements.

**if** (latitude > 30 && longitude > 120) {**if** (latitude <= 60 && longitude <= 150)
mapSquareNo = 1; **else if** (latitude <= 90 && longitude <= 150) mapSquareNo = 2
**else** *print* "Not on the map";} **else** *print* "Not on the map";

**FIGURE 14.4**
Well-formatted
but badly
constructed
nested **if**
statements.

```
if (latitude > 30 && longitude > 120)
{
   if (latitude <= 60 && longitude <= 150)
      mapSquareNo = 1;
   else
      if (latitude <= 90 && longitude <= 150)
         mapSquareNo = 2;
      else
         print "Not on the map";
}
else
   print "Not on the map";
```

**FIGURE 14.5**
Acceptably
nested **if**
statements.

```
if (longitude > 120 && longitude <= 150 && latitude > 30 && latitude <= 60)
   mapSquareNo = 1;
else
   if (longitude > 120 && longitude <= 150 && latitude > 60 && latitude <= 90)
      mapSquareNo = 2;
   else
      print "Not on the map";
```

map_square_1, map_square_2, or not on the map at all. The solution of Figure 14.3 is
so badly formatted that it is incomprehensible. A properly formatted version appears in
Figure 14.4. Notwithstanding this, the combination of **if-if** and **if-else-if** constructs is so
complex that it is difficult to check whether the code fragment is correct. This is fixed in
Figure 14.5.

When faced with complex code containing the **if-if** construct, one way to simplify it is to use the fact that the **if-if** combination

**if** <*condition* 1>
**if** <*condition* 2>

is equivalent to the single condition

**if** <*condition* 1> **and** <*condition* 2>

provided that <*condition* 2> is defined even if <*condition* 1> does not hold. For example, <*condition* 1> might check that a pointer is not null and, if so, then <*condition* 2> can use that pointer. (This problem does not arise in Java or C++. The && operator is defined such that if <*condition* 1> is false, then <*condition* 2> is not evaluated.)

Another problem with the **if-if** construct is that nesting **if** statements too deeply leads to code that can be difficult to read. As a rule of thumb, **if** statements nested to a depth greater than three is poor programming practice and should be avoided.

## 14.4 Coding Standards

**Coding standards** can be both a blessing and a curse. Section 7.2.1 pointed out that modules with coincidental cohesion generally arise as a consequence of rules such as, "Every module will consist of between 35 and 50 executable statements." Instead of stating a rule in such a dogmatic fashion, a better formulation is, "Programmers should consult their managers before constructing a module with fewer than 35 or more than 50 executable statements." The point is that no coding standard can be applicable under all possible circumstances.

Coding standards imposed from above tend to be ignored. As mentioned previously, a useful rule of thumb is that **if** statements should not be nested to a depth greater than three. If programmers are shown examples of unreadable code resulting from nesting **if** statements too deeply, then it is likely that they will conform to such a regulation. But they are unlikely to adhere to a list of coding rules imposed on them with no discussion or explanation. Furthermore, such standards are likely to lead to friction between programmers and their managers.

In addition, unless a coding standard can be checked by machine, it is going to either waste a lot of the SQA group's time or simply be ignored by the programmers and SQA group alike. On the other hand, consider the following rules:

- Nesting of **if** statements should not exceed a depth of three, except with prior approval from the team leader.
- Modules should consist of between 35 and 50 statements, except with prior approval from the team leader.
- The use of **goto** statements should be avoided. However, with prior approval from the team leader, a forward **goto** may be used for error handling.

Such rules may be checked by machine, provided some mechanism is set up for capturing the data relating to permission to deviate from the standard.

The aim of coding standards is to make maintenance easier. However, if the effect of a standard is to make the life of software developers difficult, then such a standard should be modified, even in the middle of a project. Overly restrictive coding standards are counter-productive, in that the quality of software production inevitably must suffer if programmers have to develop software within such a framework. On the other hand, standards such as those just listed regarding nesting of **if** statements, module size, and **goto** statements, coupled with a mechanism for deviating from those standards, can lead to improved software quality, which, after all, is a major goal of software engineering.

## 14.5   Code Reuse

Reuse was presented in detail in Chapter 8. In fact, the material on reuse could have appeared virtually anywhere in this book, because artifacts from all workflows of the software process are reused, including portions of specifications, contracts, plans, designs, and code artifacts. That is why the material on reuse was put into the first part of the book, rather than tying it to one or another specific workflow. In particular, it was important that the material on reuse not be presented in this chapter to underline the fact that, even though reuse of code is by far the most common form of reuse, more than just code can be reused.

## 14.6   Integration

Consider the product depicted in Figure 14.6. One approach to **integration** of the product is to code and test each code artifact separately, link together all 13 code artifacts, and test the product as a whole. There are two difficulties with this approach. First, consider artifact a. It cannot be tested on its own, because it calls artifacts b, c, and d. Therefore, to unit test artifact a, artifacts b, c, and d must be coded as **stubs**. In its simplest form, a stub is an empty artifact. A more effective stub prints a message such as artifact displayRadarPattern called. Best of all, a stub should return values corresponding to preplanned test cases.

**FIGURE 14.6**
A typical
interconnection
diagram.

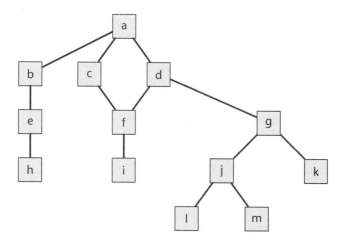

Now consider artifact h. To test it on its own requires a **driver**, a code artifact that calls it one or more times, if possible checking the values returned by the artifact under test. Similarly, testing artifact d requires a driver and two stubs. Therefore, one problem that arises with separate implementation and integration is that effort has to be put into constructing stubs and drivers, all of which are thrown away after unit testing is completed.

The second, and much more important, difficulty that arises when implementation is completed before integration starts is lack of fault isolation. If the product as a whole is tested against a specific test case and the product fails, then the fault could lie in any of the 13 code artifacts or 13 interfaces. In a large product with, say, 103 code artifacts and 108 interfaces, the fault might lie in no fewer than 211 places.

The solution to both difficulties is to combine unit and integration testing.

## 14.6.1 Top-down Integration

In **top-down integration**, if code artifact mAbove sends a message to artifact mBelow, then mAbove is implemented and integrated before mBelow. Suppose that the product shown in Figure 14.6 is implemented and integrated top down. One possible top-down ordering is a, b, c, d, e, f, g, h, i, j, k, l, and m. First, artifact a is coded and tested with b, c, and d implemented as stubs. Next stub b is expanded into artifact b, linked to artifact a, and tested with artifact e implemented as a stub. Implementation and integration proceed in this way until all the artifacts have been integrated into the product. Another possible top-down ordering is a, b, e, h, c, d, f, i, g, j, k, l, and m. With this ordering, portions of the integration can proceed in parallel in the following way. After a has been coded and tested, one programmer can use artifact a to implement and integrate b, e, and h, while another programmer can use a to work in parallel on c, d, f, and i. Once d and f are completed, a third programmer can start work on g, j, k, l, and m.

Suppose that artifact a by itself executes correctly on a specific test case. However, when the same test data are submitted after b has been coded and integrated into the product, now consisting of artifacts a and b linked together, the test fails. The fault can be in one of two places, in artifact b or the interface between artifacts a and b. In general, whenever a code artifact mNew is added to what has been tested so far and a previously successful test case fails, the fault almost certainly lies either in mNew or in the interface(s) between mNew and the rest of the product. Thus, top-down integration supports fault isolation.

Another strength of top-down integration is that major design flaws show up early. The artifacts of a product can be divided into two groups, logic artifacts and operational artifacts. **Logic artifacts** essentially incorporate the decision-making flow of control aspects of the product. The logic artifacts generally are those situated close to the root in the interconnection diagram. For example, in Figure 14.6, it is reasonable to expect artifacts a, b, c, d, and perhaps g and j to be logic artifacts. The **operational artifacts**, on the other hand, perform the actual operations of the product. For example, an operational artifact may be named getLineFromTerminal or measureTemperatureOfReactorCore. The operational artifacts generally are found in the lower levels, close to the leaves, of the interconnection diagram. In Figure 14.6, artifacts e, f, h, i, k, l, and m are operational artifacts.

It always is important to code and test the logic artifacts before coding and testing the operational artifacts. This ensures that any major design faults show up early. Suppose the whole product is completed before a major fault is detected. Large parts of the product have to be rewritten, especially the logic artifacts that embody the flow of control. Many of the operational artifacts probably are reusable in the rebuilt product; for example, an artifact like getLineFromTerminal or measureTemperatureOfReactorCore is needed no matter how the product is restructured. However, the way the operational artifacts are connected to the other artifacts in the product may have to be changed, resulting in unnecessary work. Therefore, the earlier a design fault is detected, the quicker and less costly it is to correct the product and get back on the development schedule. The order in which artifacts are implemented and integrated using the top-down strategy essentially ensures that logic artifacts indeed are implemented and integrated before operational artifacts, because logic artifacts almost always are the ancestors of operational artifacts in the interconnection diagram. This is a major strength of top-down integration.

Nevertheless, top-down integration has a weakness: Potentially reusable code artifacts may not be adequately tested, as will be explained. Reuse of an artifact that is thought, incorrectly, to have been thoroughly tested is likely to be less cost-effective than writing that artifact from scratch, because the assumption that an artifact is correct can lead to wrong conclusions when the product fails. Instead of suspecting the insufficiently tested, reused artifact, the tester may think that the fault lies elsewhere, resulting in a waste of effort.

Logic artifacts are likely to be somewhat problem specific and hence unusable in another context. However, operational artifacts, particularly if they have informational cohesion (Section 7.2.7), probably are reusable in future products and, therefore, require thorough testing. Unfortunately, the operational artifacts generally are the lower-level code artifacts in the interconnection diagram and hence are not tested as frequently as the upper-level artifacts. For example, if there are 184 artifacts, the root artifact is tested 184 times, whereas the last artifact to be integrated into the product is tested only once. Top-down integration makes reuse a risky undertaking as a consequence of inadequate testing of operational artifacts.

The situation is exacerbated if the product is well designed; in fact, the better the design, the less thoroughly the artifacts are likely to be tested. To see this, consider an artifact computeSquareRoot. This artifact takes two arguments, a floating-point number x whose square root is to be determined and an errorFlag that is set to true if x is negative. Suppose further that computeSquareRoot is invoked by artifact a3 and that a3 contains the statement

$$\textbf{if } (x > = 0)$$
$$y = \text{computeSquareRoot (x, errorFlag)};$$

In other words, computeSquareRoot is never invoked unless the value of x is nonnegative; therefore, the artifact can never be tested with negative values of x to see if it behaves correctly. The type of design where the calling artifact includes a safety check of this kind is referred to as **defensive programming**. As a result of defensive programming, subordinate operational artifacts are unlikely to be thoroughly tested if integrated top down. An alternative to defensive programming is the use of responsibility-driven design (Section 1.9). Here, the necessary safety checks are built into the invoked artifact, rather than the invoker. Another approach is the use of assertions in the invoked artifact (Section 6.5.3).

### 14.6.2 Bottom-up Integration

In **bottom-up integration**, if artifact mAbove sends a message to artifact mBelow, then mBelow is implemented and integrated before mAbove. In Figure 14.6, one possible bottom-up ordering is l, m, h, i, j, k, e, f, g, b, c, d, and a. To have the product coded by a team, a better bottom-up ordering is as follows: h, e, and b are given to one programmer and i, f, and c to another. The third programmer starts with l, m, j, k, and g, and then implements d and integrates his or her work with the work of the second programmer. Finally, when b, c, and d have been successfully integrated, a can be implemented and integrated.

The operational artifacts thus are tested thoroughly when a bottom-up strategy is used. In addition, the testing is done with the aid of drivers, rather than by fault-shielding, defensively programmed artifacts. Although bottom-up integration solves the major difficulty of top-down integration and shares with top-down integration the advantage of fault isolation, it unfortunately has a difficulty of its own. Specifically, major design faults are detected late in the implementation workflow. The logic artifacts are integrated last; hence, if there is a major design fault, it will be picked up at the end of the implementation workflow with the resulting huge cost of redesigning and recoding large portions of the product.

Therefore, both top-down and bottom-up integration have their strengths and weaknesses. The solution for product development is to combine the two strategies in such a way as to use their strengths and minimize their weaknesses. This leads to the idea of sandwich integration.

### 14.6.3 Sandwich Integration

Consider the interconnection diagram shown in Figure 14.7. Six of the code artifacts—a, b, c, d, g, and j—are logic artifacts and therefore should be integrated top down. Seven are

**FIGURE 14.7**
The product of Figure 14.6 developed using sandwich integration.

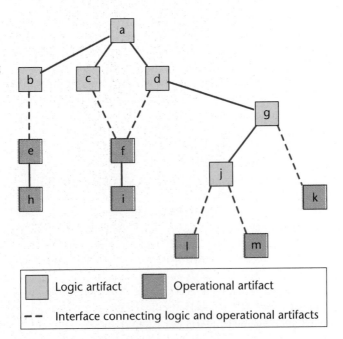

operational artifacts—e, f, h, i, k, l, and m—and should be integrated bottom up. Because neither top-down nor bottom-up integration is suitable for all the artifacts, the solution is to partition them. The six logic artifacts are integrated top down, and any major design faults can be caught early. The seven operational artifacts are integrated bottom up. They thus receive a thorough testing, unshielded by defensively programmed artifacts that invoke them, and therefore can be reused with confidence in other products. When all artifacts have been appropriately integrated, the interfaces between the two groups of artifacts are tested, one by one. There is fault isolation at all times during this process, called **sandwich integration** (see Just in Case You Wanted to Know Box 14.5).

Figure 14.8 summarizes the strengths and weaknesses of sandwich integration, as well as the other integration techniques previously discussed in this chapter.

Sandwich integration is summarized in How to Perform Box 14.1.

## 14.6.4 Integration of Object-Oriented Products

Objects can be integrated either bottom up or top down. If top-down integration is chosen, stubs are used for each method in the same way as with classical modules.

If bottom-up integration is used, the objects that do not send messages to other objects are implemented and integrated first. Then, the objects that send messages to those objects

**FIGURE 14.8**

A summary of the integration approaches presented in this chapter and the section in which each is described.

| Approach | Strengths | Weaknesses |
|---|---|---|
| Implementation then integration (Section 14.6) | — | No fault isolation<br>Major design faults show up late<br>Potentially reusable code artifacts are not adequately tested |
| Top-down integration (Section 14.6.1) | Fault isolation<br>Major design faults show up early | Potentially reusable code artifacts are not adequately tested |
| Bottom-up integration (Section 14.6.2) | Fault isolation<br>Potentially reusable code artifacts are adequately tested | Major design faults show up late |
| Sandwich integration (Section 14.6.3) | Fault isolation<br>Major design faults show up early<br>Potentially reusable code artifacts are adequately tested | — |

## How to Perform Sandwich Integration                    Box 14.1

- **In parallel,**
  Implement and integrate the logic artifacts top down.
  Implement and integrate the operational artifacts bottom up.
- Test the interfaces between the logic artifacts and the operational artifacts.

are implemented and integrated, and so on, until all the objects in the product have been implemented and integrated. (This process must be modified if there is recursion.)

Because both top-down and bottom-up integration are supported, sandwich integration also can be used. If the product is implemented in a hybrid object-oriented language like C++, the classes generally are operational artifacts and therefore integrated bottom up. Many of the artifacts that are not classes are logic artifacts. These are implemented and integrated in a top-down manner. The other artifacts are operational, so they are implemented and integrated bottom up. Finally, all the nonobject artifacts are integrated with the objects.

Even when the product is implemented using a pure object-oriented language like Java, class methods (sometimes referred to as **static methods**) such as main and utility methods usually are similar in structure to logic modules of the classical paradigm. Therefore, class methods also are also implemented top down and then integrated with the other objects. In other words, when implementing and integrating an object-oriented product, variants of sandwich integration are used.

### 14.6.5 Management of Integration

A problem for management is discovering, at integration time, that the code artifacts simply do not fit together. For example, suppose that programmer 1 coded object o1, and programmer 2 coded object o2. In the version of the design documentation used by programmer 1, object o1 sends a message to object o2 passing four arguments, but the version of the design documentation used by programmer 2 states clearly that only three arguments are passed to o2. A problem like this can arise when a change is made to only one copy of the design document, without informing all the members of the development group. Both programmers know that they are in the right; neither is prepared to compromise, because the programmer who gives in must recode large portions of the product.

To solve these and similar problems of incompatibility, the entire integration process should be run by the SQA group. Furthermore, as with testing during other workflows, the SQA group has the most to lose if the integration testing is performed improperly. The SQA group therefore is the most likely to ensure that the testing is performed thoroughly. Hence, the manager of the SQA group should have responsibility for all aspects of integration testing. He or she must decide which artifacts are implemented and integrated top down and which bottom up and assign integration-testing tasks to the appropriate individuals. The SQA group, which will have drawn up the integration test plan in the software project management plan, is responsible for implementing that plan.

At the end of the integration process, all the code artifacts will have been tested and combined into a single product.

## 14.7  The Implementation Workflow

The aim of the **implementation workflow** is to implement the target software product in the selected implementation language. More precisely, as explained in Section 13.9, a large software product is partitioned into smaller subsystems, which are then implemented in parallel by coding teams. The subsystems, in turn, consist of **components** or **code artifacts**.

As soon as a code artifact has been coded, the programmer tests it; this is termed **unit testing**. Once the programmer is satisfied that the code artifact is correct, it is passed onto the quality assurance group for further testing. This testing by the quality assurance group is part of the test workflow, described in Sections 14.20 through 14.22.

*Case Study*

### 14.8  The Implementation Workflow: The MSG Foundation Case Study

Complete implementations of the MSG Foundation product in both C++ and Java can be downloaded from www.mhhe.com/schach. The programmers included a variety of comments to aid the postdelivery maintenance programmers.

Testing during the implementation workflow is examined next.

## 14.9  The Test Workflow: Implementation

A number of different types of testing have to be performed during the implementation workflow, including unit testing, integration testing, product testing, and acceptance testing. These types of testing are discussed in the following sections.

As pointed out in Section 6.6, code artifacts (modules, classes) undergo two types of testing: informal unit testing performed by the programmer while developing the code artifact and methodical unit testing carried out by the SQA group after the programmer is satisfied that the artifact appears to function correctly. This methodical testing is described in Sections 14.10 through 14.14. In turn, there are two basic types of methodical testing, **non-execution-based testing**, in which the artifact is reviewed by a team, and **execution-based testing** in which the artifact is run against test cases. Techniques for selecting test cases now are described.

It is reasonable to ask why so many different names are given for the same testing concept. As so often happens in software engineering, the same concept was discovered, independently, by a number of different researchers, each of whom invented his or her own term. By the time the software engineering community realized that these were different names for the identical concept it was too late—the diverse names had crept into the software engineering vocabulary.

In this book, I use the terms *black-box testing* and *glass-box testing*. These terms are particularly descriptive. When we test to specifications, we treat the code as a totally opaque black box. Conversely, when we test to code, we need to be able to see inside the box, hence the term *glass-box testing*. I avoid the term *white-box testing* because it is somewhat confusing. After all, a box painted white is just as opaque as one painted black.

## 14.10    Test Case Selection

The worst way to test a code artifact is to use haphazard test data. The tester sits in front of the keyboard, and whenever the artifact requests input, the tester responds with arbitrary data. As will be shown, there is never time to test more than the tiniest fraction of all possible test cases, which easily can number many more than $10^{100}$. The few test cases that can be run, perhaps, on the order of 1000, are too valuable to waste on haphazard data. Worse, there is a tendency when the machine solicits input to respond more than once with the same data, wasting even more test cases. It is clear that **test case selection** must be performed systematically.

### 14.10.1  Testing to Specifications versus Testing to Code

Test data for unit testing can be constructed systematically in two basic ways. The first is to **test to specifications**. This technique also is called **black-box**, **behavioral**, **data-driven**, **functional**, and **input/output-driven testing**. In this approach, the code itself is ignored; the only information used in drawing up test cases is the specification document. The other extreme is to **test to code** and to ignore the specification document when selecting test cases. Other names for this technique are **glass-box**, **white-box**, **structural**, **logic-driven**, and **path-oriented testing** (for an explanation of why there are so many different terms, see Just in Case You Wanted to Know Box 14.6).

We now consider the feasibility of each of these two techniques, starting with testing to specifications.

### 14.10.2  Feasibility of Testing to Specifications

Consider the following example. Suppose that the specifications for a certain data-processing product state that five types of commission and seven types of discount must be incorporated. Testing every possible combination of just commission and discount requires 35 test cases. It is no use saying that commission and discount are computed in two entirely separate code artifacts and hence may be tested independently—in black-box testing, the product is treated as a black box, and its internal structure therefore is completely irrelevant.

This example contains only two factors, commission and discount, taking on five and seven different values, respectively. Any realistic product has hundreds, if not thousands, of different factors. Even if there are only 20 factors, each taking on only four different values, a total of $4^{20}$ or $1.1 \times 10^{12}$ different test cases must be examined.

To see the implications of over a trillion test cases, consider how long it would take to test them all. If a team of programmers could be found that could generate, run, and examine test cases at an average rate of one every 30 seconds, then it would take more than a million years to test the product exhaustively.

Therefore, exhaustive testing to specifications is impossible in practice because of the combinatorial explosion. There simply are too many test cases to consider. Testing to code now is examined.

## 14.10.3 Feasibility of Testing to Code

The most common form of testing to code requires that each path through the code artifact be executed at least once.

- To see the infeasibility of this, consider the code fragment of Figure 14.9. The corresponding flowchart is shown in Figure 14.10. Even though the flowchart appears to be almost trivial, it has over $10^{12}$ different paths. There are five possible paths through the central group of six shaded boxes, and the total number of possible paths through the flowchart therefore is

$$5^1 + 5^2 + 5^3 + \cdots + 5^{18} = \frac{5 \times (5^{18} - 1)}{(5 - 1)} = 4.77 \times 10^{12}$$

If there can be this many paths through a simple flowchart containing a single loop, it is not difficult to imagine the total number of different paths in a code artifact of reasonable size and complexity, let alone a large artifact with many loops. In short, the huge number of possible paths renders exhaustive testing to code as infeasible as exhaustive testing to specifications.

**FIGURE 14.9**
A code fragment.

```
read (kmax)                        // kmax is an integer between 1 and 18
for (k = 0; k < kmax; k++) do
{
    read (myChar)                  // myChar is the character A, B, or C
    switch (myChar)
    {
      case 'A':
        blockA;
        if (cond1) blockC;
        break;
      case 'B':
        blockB;
        if (cond2) blockC;
        break;
      case 'C':
        blockC;
        break;
    }
    blockD;
}
```

**FIGURE 14.10**

A flowchart
with over $10^{12}$
possible paths.

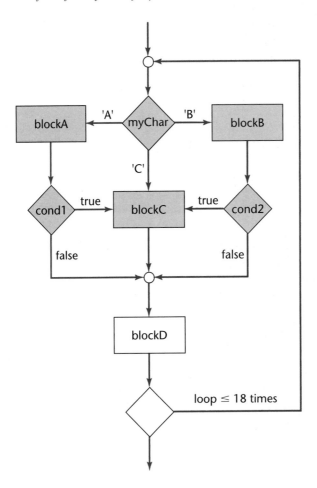

- Furthermore, testing to code requires the tester to exercise every path. It is possible to exercise every path without detecting every fault in the product; that is, testing to code is not reliable. To see this, consider the code fragment shown in Figure 14.11 [Myers, 1976]. The fragment was written to test the equality of three integers, x, y, and z, using the totally fallacious assumption that if the average of three numbers is equal to the first number, then the three numbers are equal. Two test cases are shown in Figure 14.11. In the first test case the value of the average of the three numbers is 6/3 or 2, which is not equal to 1. The product therefore correctly informs the tester that x, y, and z are unequal. The integers x, y, and z all equal 2 in the second test case, so the product computes their average as 2, which is equal to the value of x, and the product correctly concludes that the three numbers are equal. Thus, both paths through the product have been exercised without the fault being detected. Of course, the fault would come to light if test data such as x = 2, y = 1, z = 3 are used.
- A third difficulty with path testing is that a path can be tested only if it is present. Consider the code fragment shown in Figure 14.12(a). Clearly, two paths are to be

**FIGURE 14.11**
An incorrect
code fragment
for determining
if three integers
are equal,
together with
two test cases.

```
if ((x + y + z)/3 == x)
    print "x, y, z are equal in value";
else
    print "x, y, z are unequal";


Test case 1:    x = 1, y = 2, z = 3
Test case 2:    x = y = z = 2
```

**FIGURE 14.12**
Two code
fragments for
computing a
quotient.

```
if (d == 0)
    zeroDivisionRoutine ();
else
    x = n/d;
              (a)
```

```
x = n/d;
        (b)
```

tested, corresponding to the cases $d = 0$ and $d \neq 0$. Next, consider the single statement of Figure 14.12(b). Now there is only one path, and this path can be tested without the fault being detected. In fact, a programmer who omits checking whether $d = 0$ in his or her code is likely to be unaware of the potential danger, and the case $d = 0$ will not be included in the programmer's test data. This problem is an additional argument for having an independent software quality assurance group whose job includes detecting faults of this type.

These examples show conclusively that the criterion "exercise all paths in the product" is not **reliable**, as products exist for which some data exercising a given path detect a fault and different data exercising the same path do not. However, path-oriented testing is **valid**, because it does not inherently preclude selecting test data that might reveal the fault.

Because of the combinatorial explosion, neither exhaustive testing to specifications nor exhaustive testing to code is feasible. A compromise is needed, using techniques that highlight as many faults as possible, while accepting that there is no way to guarantee that all faults have been detected. A reasonable way to proceed is to use black-box test cases first (testing to specifications) and then develop additional test cases using glass-box techniques (testing to code).

# 14.11    Black-Box Unit-Testing Techniques

Exhaustive black-box testing generally requires billions and billions of test cases. The art of testing is to devise a small, manageable set of test cases to maximize the chances of detecting a fault while minimizing the chances of wasting a test case by having the same fault detected by more than one test case. Every test case must be chosen to detect a previously undetected fault. One such black-box technique is equivalence testing combined with boundary value analysis.

## 14.11.1 Equivalence Testing and Boundary Value Analysis

Suppose the specifications for a database product state that the product must be able to handle any number of records from 1 through 16,383 ($2^{14} - 1$). If the product can handle 34 records and 14,870 records, then the chances are good that it will work fine for, say, 8252 records. In fact, the chances of detecting a fault, if present, are likely to be equally good if any test case from 1 through 16,383 records is selected. Conversely, if the product works correctly for any one test case in the range from 1 through 16,383, then it probably will work for any other test case in the range. The range from 1 through 16,383 constitutes an **equivalence class**, that is, a set of test cases such that any one member of the class is as good a test case as any other. To be more precise, the specified range of numbers of records that the product must be able to handle defines three equivalence classes:

Equivalence class 1. Less than 1 record.

Equivalence class 2. From 1 through 16,383 records.

Equivalence class 3. More than 16,383 records.

Testing the database product using the technique of equivalence classes then requires that one test case from each equivalence class be selected. The test case from equivalence class 2 should be handled correctly, whereas error messages should be printed for the test cases from class 1 and class 3.

A successful test case detects a previously undetected fault. To maximize the chances of finding such a fault, a high-payoff technique is **boundary value analysis**.

Experience has shown that, when a test case on or just to one side of the boundary of an equivalence class is selected, the probability of detecting a fault increases. Therefore, when testing the database product, seven test cases should be selected:

Test case 1.   0 records: Member of equivalence class 1 and adjacent to boundary value.

Test case 2.   1 record: Boundary value.

Test case 3.   2 records: Adjacent to boundary value.

Test case 4.   723 records: Member of equivalence class 2.

Test case 5.   16,382 records: Adjacent to boundary value.

Test case 6.   16,383 records: Boundary value.

Test case 7.   16,384 records: Member of equivalence class 3 and adjacent to boundary value.

This example applies to the input specifications. An equally powerful technique is to examine the output specifications. For example, in 2006, the minimum Social Security deduction or, more precisely, the minimum Old-Age, Survivors, and Disability Insurance (OASDI) deduction from any one paycheck permitted by the U.S. tax code was $0 and the maximum was $5840.40, the latter corresponding to gross earnings of $94,200. Therefore,

# How to Perform Equivalence Testing

## Box 14.2

- **For** both the input and output specifications

    **For** each range ($L$, $U$)

    Select five test cases: less than $L$, equal to $L$, greater than $L$ but less than $U$, equal to $U$, and greater than $U$.

    **For** each set $S$

    Select two test cases: a member of $S$ and a nonmember of $S$.

    **For** each precise value $P$

    Select two cases: $P$ and anything else.

when testing a payroll product, the test cases for the Social Security deduction from paychecks should include input data that are expected to result in deductions of exactly $0 and $5840.40. In addition, test data should be set up that might result in deductions of less than $0 or more than $5840.40.

In general, for each range ($R_1$, $R_2$) listed in either the input or the output specifications, five test cases should be selected, corresponding to values less than $R_1$, equal to $R_1$, greater than $R_1$ but less than $R_2$, equal to $R_2$, and greater than $R_2$. Where it is specified that an item has to be a member of a certain set (for example, the input must be a letter), two equivalence classes must be tested, a member of the specified set and a nonmember of the set. Where the specifications lay down a precise value (for example, the response must be followed by a # sign), then again there are two equivalence classes, the specified value and anything else.

The use of equivalence classes, together with boundary value analysis, to test both the input specifications and the output specifications is a valuable technique for generating a relatively small set of test data with the potential of uncovering a number of faults that might well remain hidden if less powerful techniques for test data selection were used.

The process of equivalence testing is summarized in How to Perform Box 14.2.

## 14.11.2 Functional Testing

An alternative form of black-box testing is to base the test data on the functionality of a code artifact. In functional testing [Howden, 1987], each item of functionality or function implemented in the code artifact is identified. Typical functions in a classical module for a computerized warehouse product might be get_next_database_record or determine_whether_quantity_on_hand_is_below_the_reorder point. In a weapons control system, a module might include the function compute_trajectory. In a module of an operating system, one function might be determine_whether_file_is_empty.

After determining all the functions of a code artifact, test data are devised to test each function separately. Now, the functional testing is taken a step further. If the code artifact consists of a hierarchy of lower-level functions, connected by the control structures of structured programming, then functional testing proceeds recursively. For example, if a

higher-level function is of the form

$$\textit{<higher-level function>} ::= \textbf{if} \textit{ <conditional expression>}$$
$$\textit{<lower-level function 1>;}$$
$$\textbf{else}$$
$$\textit{<lower-level function 2>;}$$

then, because *<conditional expression>*, *<lower-level function 1>*, and *<lower-level function 2>* have been subjected to functional testing, *<higher-level function>* can be tested using branch coverage, a glass-box technique described in Section 14.13.1. Note that this form of structural testing is a hybrid technique—the lower-level functions are tested using a black-box technique, but the higher-level functions are tested using a glass-box technique.

In practice, however, higher-level functions are not constructed in such a structured fashion from lower-level functions. Instead, the lower-level functions usually are intertwined in some way. To determine faults in this situation, **functional analysis** is required, a somewhat complex procedure; for details, see [Howden, 1987]. A further complicating factor is that functionality frequently does not coincide with code artifact boundaries. Therefore, the distinction between unit testing and integration testing becomes blurred; one code artifact cannot be tested without, at the same time, testing the other code artifacts whose functionality it uses. This problem also arises in the object-oriented paradigm when a method of one object sends a message to (invokes) a method of a different object.

The random interrelationships between code artifacts from the viewpoint of functional testing may have unacceptable consequences for management. For example, milestones and deadlines can become somewhat ill defined, making it difficult to determine the status of the product with respect to the software project management plan.

## Case Study
## 14.12 Black-Box Test Cases: The MSG Foundation Case Study

Figures 14.13 and 14.14 contain black-box test cases for the MSG Foundation case study. First consider test cases derived from equivalence classes and boundary value analysis. The first test case in Figure 14.13 tests whether the product detects an error if the itemName of an investment does not begin with an alphabetic character. The next set of five test cases checks that an itemName consists of between 1 and 25 characters. Similar test cases check other statements in the specifications, as reflected in Figure 14.13.

Turning now to functional testing, 10 functions are listed in the specification document, as shown in Figure 14.14. An additional 11 test cases correspond to misuses of these functions.

It is important to be aware that these test cases could have been developed as soon as the analysis workflow was complete; the only reason that they appear here is that

**FIGURE 14.13**
Black-box test
cases for the
MSG
Foundation case
study derived
from
equivalence
classes and
boundary value
analysis.

**Investment data**:

Equivalence classes for itemName.

| | |
|---|---|
| 1. First character not alphabetic | Error |
| 2. < 1 character | Error |
| 3. 1 character | Acceptable |
| 4. Between 1 and 25 characters | Acceptable |
| 5. 25 characters | Acceptable |
| 6. > 25 characters | Error (name too long) |

Equivalence classes for itemNumber.

| | |
|---|---|
| 1. Character instead of digit | Error (not a number) |
| 2. < 12 digits | Acceptable |
| 3. 12 digits | Acceptable |
| 4. > 12 digits | Error (too many digits) |

Equivalence classes for estimatedAnnualReturn and expectedAnnualOperatingExpenses.

| | |
|---|---|
| 1. < $0.00 | Error |
| 2. $0.00 | Acceptable |
| 3. $0.01 | Acceptable |
| 4. Between $0.01 and $999,999,999.97 | Acceptable |
| 5. $999,999,999.98 | Acceptable |
| 6. $999,999,999.99 | Acceptable |
| 7. $1,000,000,000.00 | Error |
| 8. > $1,000,000,000.00 | Error |
| 9. Character instead of digit | Error (not a number) |

**Mortgage information:**

Equivalence classes for accountNumber are same as for itemNumber above.

Equivalence classes for last name of mortgagees

| | |
|---|---|
| 1. First character not alphabetic | Error |
| 2. < 1 character | Error |
| 3. 1 character | Acceptable |
| 4. Between 1 and 21 characters | Acceptable |
| 5. 21 characters | Acceptable |
| 6. > 21 characters | Acceptable (truncated to 21 characters) |

Equivalence classes for original price of home, current family income, and mortgage balance.

| | |
|---|---|
| 1. < $0.00 | Error |
| 2. $0.00 | Acceptable |
| 3. $0.01 | Acceptable |
| 4. Between $0.01 and $999,999.98 | Acceptable |
| 5. $999,999.98 | Acceptable |
| 6. $999,999.99 | Acceptable |
| 7. $1,000,000.00 | Error |
| 8. > $1,000,000.00 | Error |
| 9. Character instead of digit | Error (not a number) |

**FIGURE 14.13**
(*continued*)

Equivalence classes for annual property tax and annual home-owner's premium.

| | |
|---|---|
| 1.  < $0.00 | Error |
| 2.  $0.00 | Acceptable |
| 3.  $0.01 | Acceptable |
| 4.  Between $0.01 and $99,999.98 | Acceptable |
| 5.  $99,999.98 | Acceptable |
| 6.  $99,999.99 | Acceptable |
| 7.  $100,000.00 | Error |
| 8.  > $100,000.00 | Error |
| 9.  Character instead of digit | Error (not a number) |

**FIGURE 14.14**

Functional analysis test cases for the MSG Foundation case study.

The functions outlined in the specifications document are used to create test cases:

1.  Add a mortgage.
2.  Add an investment.
3.  Modify a mortgage.
4.  Modify an investment.
5.  Delete a mortgage.
6.  Delete an investment.
7.  Update operating expenses.
8.  Compute funds to purchase houses.
9.  Print list of mortgages.
10.  Print list of investments.

In addition to these direct tests, it is necessary to perform the following additional tests:

11.  Attempt to add a mortgage that is already on file.
12.  Attempt to add an investment that is already on file.
13.  Attempt to delete a mortgage that is not on file.
14.  Attempt to delete an investment that is not on file.
15.  Attempt to modify a mortgage that is not on file.
16.  Attempt to modify an investment that is not on file.
17.  Attempt to delete twice a mortgage that is already on file.
18.  Attempt to delete twice an investment that is already on file.
19.  Attempt to update each field of a mortgage twice and check that the second version is stored.
20.  Attempt to update each field of an investment twice and check that the second version is stored.
21.  Attempt to update operating expenses twice and check that second version is stored.

test case selection is a topic of this chapter, rather than an earlier chapter. A major component of every test plan should be a stipulation that black-box test cases be drawn up as soon as the analysis artifacts have been approved, for use by the SQA group during the implementation workflow.

# 14.13   Glass-Box Unit-Testing Techniques

In glass-box techniques, test cases are selected on the basis of examination of the code rather than the specifications. There are a number of different forms of glass-box testing, including statement, branch, and path coverage.

## 14.13.1   Structural Testing: Statement, Branch, and Path Coverage

The simplest form of glass-box unit testing is **statement coverage**, that is, running a series of test cases during which every statement is executed at least once. To keep track of which statements are still to be executed, a CASE tool keeps a record of how many times each statement has been executed over the series of tests; PureCoverage is an example of such a tool.

A weakness of this approach is that there is no guarantee that all outcomes of branches are properly tested. To see this, consider the code fragment of Figure 14.15. The programmer made a mistake; the compound conditional s > 1 && t == 0 should read s > 1 || t == 0. The test data shown in the figure allow the statement x = 9 to be executed without the fault being highlighted.

An improvement over statement coverage is **branch coverage**, that is, running a series of tests to ensure that all branches are tested at least once. Again, a tool usually is needed to help the tester keep track of which branches have or have not been tested; Generic Coverage Tool (*gct*) is an example of a branch coverage tool for C programs. Techniques such as statement or branch coverage are termed **structural tests**.

The most powerful form of structural testing is **path coverage**, that is, testing all paths. As shown previously, in a product with loops, the number of paths can be very large indeed. As a result, researchers have been investigating ways of reducing the number of paths to be examined while uncovering more faults than would be possible using branch coverage. One criterion for selecting paths is to restrict test cases to **linear code sequences** [Woodward, Hedley, and Hennell, 1980]. To do this, first identify the set of points $L$ from which control flow may jump. The set $L$ includes entry and exit points and branch statements such as an **if** or **goto** statement. The linear code sequences are those paths that begin at an element of $L$ and end at an element of $L$. The technique has been successful in that it has uncovered many faults without having to test every path.

Another way of reducing the number of paths to test is **all-definition-use-path coverage** [Rapps and Weyuker, 1985]. In this technique, each occurrence of a variable pqr, say, in the source code is labeled either as a *definition* of the variable, such as pqr = 1 or read (pqr), or a *use* of the variable, such as y = pqr + 3 or **if** (pqr < 9) errorB (). All paths between the definition of a variable and the use of that definition are identified, nowadays by means of an automatic tool. Finally, a test case is set up for each such path. All-definition-use-path coverage is an excellent test technique in that large numbers of faults frequently are detected by relatively few test cases. However, all-definition-use-path coverage has the weakness that the upper bound on the number of paths is $2^d$, where $d$ is the number of decision statements (branches) in the product. Examples can be constructed exhibiting the upper bound. However, it has been shown that, for real products as opposed to artificial examples, this upper bound is not reached, and the actual number of paths is proportional to $d$ [Weyuker, 1988a]. In other words, the number of test cases needed for

**FIGURE 14.15**
Code fragment
with test data.

```
if (s > 1 && t == 0)
    x = 9;
```

Test case:    s = 2, t = 0.

**FIGURE 14.16**
Two examples
of infeasible
paths.

```
if (k < 2)
{
    if (k > 3)              [should be k > −3]
          ↑
        x = x * k;
}
                    (a)
```

```
for (j = 0; j < 0; j++)  [should be j < 10]
      ↑
    total = total + value[j];
                (b)
```

all-definition-use-path coverage generally is much smaller than the theoretical upper bound. Therefore, all-definition-use-path coverage is a practical test case selection technique.

When using structural testing, the tester simply might not come up with a test case that exercises a specific statement, branch, or path. What may have happened is that an infeasible path ("dead code") is in the code artifact, that is, a path that cannot possibly be executed for any input data. Figure 14.16 shows two examples of infeasible paths. In Figure 14.16(a) the programmer omitted a minus sign. If k is less than 2, then k cannot possibly be greater than 3, so the statement x = x * k cannot be reached. Similarly, in Figure 14.16(b), j is never less than 0, so the statement total = total + value[j] can never be reached; the programmer had intended the test to be j < 10, but made a typing mistake. A tester using statement coverage would soon realize that neither statement could be reached, and the faults would be found.

## 14.13.2 Complexity Metrics

The quality assurance viewpoint provides another approach to glass-box unit testing. Suppose a manager is told that code artifact m1 is more complex than code artifact m2. Irrespective of the precise way in which the term *complex* is defined, the manager intuitively believes that m1 is likely to have more faults than m2. Following this idea, computer scientists have developed a number of metrics of software **complexity** as an aid in determining which code artifacts are most likely to have faults. If the complexity of a code artifact is found to be unreasonably high, a manager may direct that the artifact be redesigned and reimplemented on the grounds that it probably is less costly and faster to start from scratch than to attempt to debug a fault-prone code artifact.

A simple metric for predicting numbers of faults is lines of code. The underlying assumption is that there is a constant probability, $p$, that a line of code contains a fault. If a tester believes that, on average, a line of code has a 2 percent chance of containing a fault, and the artifact under test is 100 lines long, then this implies that the artifact is expected to contain two faults; and an artifact that is twice as long is likely to have four faults. Basili and Hutchens [1983] as well as Takahashi and Kamayachi [1985] showed that the number of faults indeed is related to the size of the product as a whole.

Attempts have been made to find more sophisticated predictors of faults based on measures of product complexity. A typical contender is McCabe's [1976] measure of **cyclomatic complexity**, the number of binary decisions (predicates) plus 1. As described in Section 13.14, the cyclomatic complexity essentially is the number of branches in the code artifact. Accordingly, cyclomatic complexity can be used as a metric for the number of test cases needed for branch coverage of a code artifact. This is the basis for so-called **structured testing** [Watson and McCabe, 1996].

McCabe's metric can be computed almost as easily as lines of code. In some cases, it has been shown to be a good metric for predicting faults; the higher the value of $M$, the greater is the chance that a code artifact contains a fault. For example, Walsh [1979] analyzed 276 modules in the Aegis system, a shipboard combat system. Measuring the cyclomatic complexity, $M$, he found that 23 percent of the modules with $M$ greater than or equal to 10 had 53 percent of the faults detected. In addition, the modules with $M$ greater than or equal to 10 had 21 percent more faults per line of code than the modules with smaller $M$ values. However, the validity of McCabe's metric has been questioned seriously on both theoretical grounds and the basis of the many different experiments cited in [Shepperd, 1988], and [Shepperd and Ince, 1994].

Musa, Iannino, and Okumoto [1987] analyzed the data available on fault densities. They concluded that most complexity metrics, including McCabe's, show a high correlation with the number of lines of code or, more precisely, the number of deliverable, executable source instructions. In other words, when researchers measure what they believe to be the complexity of a code artifact or a product, the result they obtain largely may be a reflection of the number of lines of code, a measure that correlates strongly with the number of faults. In addition, complexity metrics provide little improvement over lines of code for predicting fault rates. Other problems with complexity are discussed in [Shepperd and Ince, 1994].

## 14.14 Code Walkthroughs and Inspections

Section 6.2 made a strong case for the use of walkthroughs and inspections in general. The same arguments hold for code walkthroughs and inspections. In brief, the fault-detecting power of these two non-execution-based techniques leads to rapid, thorough, and early fault detection. The additional time required for code walkthroughs or inspections is more than repaid by increased productivity due to the presence of fewer faults when integration is performed. Furthermore, code inspections have led to a reduction of up to 95 percent in corrective maintenance costs [Crossman, 1982].

Another reason why code inspections should be performed is that the alternative, execution-based testing (test cases), can be extremely expensive in two ways. First, it is time consuming. Second, inspections lead to detection and correction of faults earlier in the life cycle than with execution-based testing. As reflected in Figure 1.6, the earlier a fault is detected and corrected, the less it costs. An extreme case of the high cost of running test cases is that 80 percent of the budget for the software of the NASA Apollo Program was consumed by testing [Dunn, 1984].

Further arguments in favor of walkthroughs and inspections are given in Section 14.15.

## 14.15 Comparison of Unit-Testing Techniques

A number of studies have compared strategies for unit testing. Myers [1978a] compared black-box testing, a combination of black-box and glass-box testing, and three-person code walkthroughs. The experiment was performed using 59 highly experienced programmers testing the same product. All three techniques were equally effective in finding faults, but code walkthroughs proved to be less cost effective than the other two techniques. Hwang [1981] compared black-box testing, glass-box testing, and code reading by one person. All three techniques were found to be equally effective, with each technique having its own strengths and weaknesses.

A major experiment was conducted by Basili and Selby [1987]. The techniques compared were the same as in Hwang's experiment: black-box testing, glass-box testing, and one-person code reading. The subjects were 32 professional programmers and 42 advanced students. Each tested three products, using each testing technique once. Fractional factorial design [Basili and Weiss, 1984] was used to compensate for the different ways the products were tested by different participants; no participant tested the same product in more than one way. Different results were obtained from the two groups of participants. The professional programmers detected more faults with code reading than with the other two techniques, and the fault detection rate was faster. Two groups of advanced students participated. In one group, no significant difference was found among the three techniques; in the other, code reading and black-box testing were equally good and both outperformed glass-box testing. However, the rate at which students detected faults was the same for all techniques. Overall, code reading led to the detection of more interface faults than the other two techniques, whereas black-box testing was most successful at finding control faults. The main conclusion that can be drawn from this experiment is that code inspection is at least as successful at detecting faults as glass-box and black-box testing.

A development technique that makes good use of this conclusion is the Cleanroom software development technique.

## 14.16   Cleanroom

The **Cleanroom** technique [Linger, 1994] is a combination of a number of different software development techniques, including an incremental life-cycle model, formal techniques for analysis and design, and non-execution-based unit-testing techniques, such as code reading [Mills, Dyer, and Linger, 1987] and code walkthroughs and inspections (Section 14.14). A critical aspect of Cleanroom is that a code artifact is not compiled until it has passed inspection. That is, a code artifact should be compiled only after non-execution-based testing has been successfully completed.

The technique has had a number of great successes. For example, a prototype automated documentation system was developed for the U.S. Naval Underwater Systems Center using Cleanroom [Trammel, Binder, and Snyder, 1992]. Altogether 18 faults were detected while the design underwent "functional verification," a review process in which correctness-proving techniques are employed (Section 6.5). Informal proofs such as the one presented in Section 6.5.1 were used as much as possible; full mathematical proofs were developed only when participants were unsure of the correctness of the portion of the design being inspected. Another 19 faults were detected during walkthroughs of the 1820 lines of FoxBASE code; when the code was then compiled, there were no compilation errors. Furthermore, there were no failures at execution time. This is an additional indication of the power of non-execution-based testing techniques.

This certainly is an impressive result. But, as has been pointed out, results that apply to small-scale software products cannot necessarily be scaled up to large-scale software. In the case of Cleanroom, however, results for larger products also are impressive. The relevant metric is the **testing fault rate**, that is, the total number of faults detected per KLOC (thousand lines of code), a relatively common metric in the software industry. Yet, there is a critical difference in the way this metric is computed when Cleanroom is used as opposed to traditional development techniques.

As pointed out in Section 6.6, when traditional development techniques are used, a code artifact is tested informally by its programmer while it is being developed and thereafter it is tested methodically by the SQA group. Faults detected by the programmer while developing the code are not recorded. However, from the time the artifact leaves the private workspace of the programmer and is handed over to the SQA group for execution-based and non-execution-based testing, a tally is kept of the number of faults detected. In contrast, when Cleanroom is used, "testing faults" are counted from the time of compilation. Fault counting then continues through execution-based testing. In other words, when traditional development techniques are used, faults detected informally by the programmer do not count toward the testing fault rate. When Cleanroom is used, faults detected during the inspections and other non-execution-based testing procedures that precede compilation are recorded, but they do not count toward the testing fault rate.

A report on 17 Cleanroom products appears in [Linger, 1994]. For example, Cleanroom was used to develop the 350,000-line Ericsson Telecom OS32 operating system. The product was developed in 18 months by a team of 70. The testing fault rate was only 1.0 fault per KLOC. Another product was the prototype automated documentation system described previously; the testing fault rate was 0.0 faults per KLOC for the 1820-line program. The 17 products together total nearly 1 million lines of code. The weighted average testing fault rate was 2.3 faults per KLOC, which Linger describes as a remarkable quality achievement. That praise certainly is no exaggeration.

## 14.17  Potential Problems When Testing Objects

One of the many reasons put forward for using the object-oriented paradigm is that it reduces the need for testing. Reuse via inheritance is a major strength of the paradigm; once a class has been tested, the argument goes, there is no need to retest it. Furthermore, new methods defined within a subclass of such a tested class have to be tested, but inherited methods need no further testing.

In fact, both claims are only partially true. In addition, the testing of objects poses certain problems that are specific to object orientation. These issues are discussed here.

To begin, it is necessary to clarify an issue regarding the testing of classes and of objects. As explained in Section 7.7, a class is an abstract data type that supports inheritance, and an object is an instance of a class. That is, a class has no concrete realization, whereas an object is a physical piece of code executing within a specific environment. Therefore, it is impossible to perform execution-based testing on a class; only non-execution-based testing, such as an inspection, can be done.

Information hiding and the fact that many methods consist of relatively few lines of code can have a significant impact on testing. First, consider a product developed using the classical paradigm. Nowadays, such a product generally consists of modules of roughly 50 executable instructions. The interface between a module and the rest of the product is the argument list. Arguments are of two kinds, input arguments supplied to the module when it is invoked and output arguments returned by the module when it returns control to the calling module. Testing a module consists of supplying values to the input arguments and invoking the module and then comparing the values of the output arguments to the predicted results of the test.

In contrast, a "typical" object contains perhaps 30 methods, many of which are relatively small, frequently just two or three executable statements [Wilde, Matthews, and Huitt, 1993]. These methods do not return a value to the caller but rather change the state of the object. That is, these methods modify attributes (state variables) of the object. The difficulty here is that, to test that the change of state has been performed correctly, it is necessary to send additional messages to the object. For example, consider the bank account object described in Section 1.9. The effect of method deposit is to increase the value of state variable accountBalance. However, as a consequence of information hiding, the only way to test whether a particular deposit method has been executed correctly is to invoke method determineBalance both before and after invoking method deposit and see how the bank balance changes.

The situation is worse if the object does not include methods that can be invoked to determine the values of all the state variables. One alternative is to include additional methods for this purpose, and then use conditional compilation to ensure that they are unavailable except for testing purposes (in C++, this can be implemented using #ifdef). The test plan (Section 9.6) should stipulate that the value of every state variable be accessible during testing. To satisfy this requirement, additional methods that return the values of the state variables may have to be added to the relevant classes during the design workflow. As a result, it is possible to test the effect of invoking a specific method of an object by querying the value of the applicable state variable.

Surprisingly enough, an inherited method still may have to be tested. That is, even if a method has been adequately tested, it may require thorough testing when inherited, unchanged, by a subclass. To see this latter point, consider the class hierarchy shown in Figure 14.17. Two methods are defined in the base class **RootedTreeClass**, namely, displayNodeContents and printRoutine, where method displayNodeContents uses method printRoutine.

Next consider subclass **BinaryTreeClass**. This subclass inherits method printRoutine from its base class **RootedTreeClass**. In addition, a new method, displayNodeContents, is defined that overrides the method defined in **RootedTreeClass**. This new method still uses printRoutine. In Java notation, BinaryTreeClass.displayNodeContents uses RootedTreeClass.printRoutine.

Now consider the subclass **BalancedBinaryTreeClass**. This subclass inherits method displayNodeContents from its superclass **BinaryTreeClass**. However, a new method printRoutine is defined that overrides the one defined in **RootedTreeClass**. When displayNodeContents uses printRoutine within the context of **Balanced-BinaryTreeClass**, the scope rules of C++ and Java specify that the local version of printRoutine is to be used. In Java notation, when method BinaryTreeClass.displayNodeContents is invoked within the lexical scope of **BalancedBinaryTreeClass**, it uses method BalancedBinaryTreeClass.printRoutine.

**FIGURE 14.17**
A Java
implementation
of a tree
hierarchy.

```
class RootedTreeClass
{
   ...
   void displayNodeContents (Node a);
   void printRoutine (Node b);
//
// method displayNodeContents uses method printRoutine
//
   ...
}

class BinaryTreeClass extends RootedTreeClass
{
   ...
   void displayNodeContents (Node a);
//
// method displayNodeContents defined in this class uses
// method printRoutine inherited from ClassRootedTree
//
   ...
}

class BalancedBinaryTreeClass extends BinaryTreeClass
{
   ...
   void printRoutine (Node b);
//
// method displayNodeContents (inherited from BinaryTreeClass) uses this
// local version of printRoutine within class BalancedBinaryTreeClass
//
   ...
}
```

Therefore, the actual code (method printRoutine) executed when displayNode-Contents is invoked within instantiations of **BinaryTreeClass** is different from what is executed when displayNodeContents is invoked within instantiations of **Balanced-BinaryTreeClass**. This holds notwithstanding that the method displayNodeContents itself is inherited, unchanged, by **BalancedBinaryTreeClass** from **BinaryTreeClass**. Therefore, even if method displayNodeContents has been thoroughly tested within a **BinaryTreeClass** object, it has to be retested from scratch when reused within a **BalancedBinaryTreeClass** environment. To make matters even more complex, there are theoretical reasons why it needs to be retested with different test cases [Perry and Kaiser, 1990].

It must be pointed out immediately that these complications are no reason to abandon the object-oriented paradigm. First, they arise only through the interaction of methods (displayNodeContents and printRoutine in the example). Second, it is possible to determine when this retesting is needed [Harrold, McGregor, and Fitzpatrick, 1992].

Suppose an instantiation of a class has been thoroughly tested. Any new or redefined methods of a subclass then need to be tested, together with methods flagged for retesting because of their interaction with other methods. In short, then, the claim that use of the object-oriented paradigm reduces the need for testing largely is true.

Some management implications of unit testing now are considered.

## 14.18   Management Aspects of Unit Testing

An important decision that must be made during the development of every code artifact is how much time, and therefore money, to spend on testing that artifact. As with so many other economic issues in software engineering, cost–benefit analysis (Section 5.2) can play a useful role. For example, the decision as to whether the cost of correctness proving exceeds the benefit of the assurance that a specific product satisfies its specifications can be decided on the basis of cost–benefit analysis. Cost–benefit analysis also can be used to compare the cost of running additional test cases against the cost of failure of the delivered product caused by inadequate testing.

There is another approach for determining whether testing of a specific code artifact should continue or it is likely that virtually all the faults have been removed. The techniques of reliability analysis can be used to provide statistical estimates of how many faults remain. A variety of different techniques have been proposed for determining statistical estimates of the number of remaining faults. The basic idea underlying these techniques is the following. Suppose a code artifact is tested for 1 week. On Monday, 23 faults are found and 7 more on Tuesday. On Wednesday, five more faults are found, two on Thursday, and none on Friday. Because the rate of fault detection decreases steadily from 23 faults per day to none, it seems likely that most faults have been found, and testing of that code artifact could be halted. Determining the probability that there are no more faults in the code requires a level of mathematical statistics beyond that required for readers of this book. Details therefore are not given here; the reader interested in reliability analysis should consult Grady [1992].

## 14.19   When to Rewrite Rather than Debug a Code Artifact

When a member of the SQA group detects a failure (erroneous output), as stated previously, the code artifact must be returned to the original programmer for **debugging**, that is, detection of the fault and correction of the code. On some occasions, it is preferable for the code artifact to be thrown away and redesigned and recoded from scratch, either by the original programmer or by another, possibly more senior, member of the development team.

To see why this may be necessary, consider Figure 14.18. The graph shows the counter-intuitive concept that the probability of the existence of more faults in a code artifact is proportional to the number of faults already found in that code artifact [Myers, 1979]. To see why this should be so, consider two code artifacts, a1 and a2. Suppose that both code artifacts are approximately the same length and both have been tested for the same number of hours. Suppose further that only 2 faults were detected in a1, but 48 faults were detected in a2. It is likely that more faults remain to be rooted out of a2 than out of a1. Furthermore, additional testing and debugging of a2 is likely to be a lengthy process, and the suspicion that a2 is still not perfect will remain. In both the short run and the long run, it is preferable to discard a2, redesign it, and then recode it.

**FIGURE 14.18**
Graph showing that the probability that faults are still to be found is proportional to the number of faults already detected.

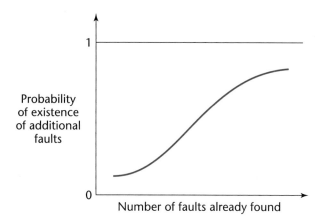

Probability of existence of additional faults

1

0

Number of faults already found

The distribution of faults in modules certainly is not uniform. Myers [1979] cites the example of faults found by users in OS/370. It was found that 47 percent of the faults were associated with only 4 percent of the modules. An earlier study by Endres [1975] regarding internal tests of DOS/VS (Release 28) at IBM Laboratories, Böblingen, Germany, showed similar nonuniformity. Of the total of 512 faults detected in 202 modules, only 1 fault was detected in each of 112 of the modules. On the other hand, some modules were found to have 14, 15, 19, and 28 faults, respectively. Endres points out that the latter three modules were three of the largest modules in the product, each comprising over 3000 lines of DOS macro assembler language. However, the module with 14 faults was a relatively small module previously known to be extremely unstable. This type of module is a prime candidate for being discarded and recoded.

The way for management to cope with this sort of situation is to predetermine the maximum number of faults permitted during development of a given code artifact; when that maximum is reached, the code artifact must be thrown away and then redesigned and recoded, preferably by an experienced software professional. This maximum varies from application domain to application domain and from code artifact to code artifact. After all, the maximum permitted number of faults detected in a code artifact that reads a record from a database and checks the validity of the part number should be far smaller than the number of faults in a complex code artifact from a tank weapons control system that must coordinate data from a variety of sensors and direct the aim of the main gun toward the intended target. One way to decide on the maximum fault figure for a specific code artifact is to examine fault data on similar code artifacts that have required corrective maintenance. But, whatever estimation technique is used, management must ensure that the code artifact is scrapped if that figure is exceeded (but see Just in Case You Wanted to Know Box 14.7.)

## 14.20    Integration Testing

Each new code artifact must be tested when it is added to what has already been integrated; this is termed **integration testing**. The key point here is first to test the new code artifact as described in Sections 14.10 through 14.14 (unit testing) and then to check that the rest

The discussion regarding the maximum permitted number of faults detected during development of a code artifact means precisely that: the maximum number permitted *during development*. The maximum permitted number of faults detected after the product has been delivered to the client should be *zero* for all code artifacts of all products. That is, it should be the aim of every software engineer to deliver fault-free code to the client.

of the partial product continues to behave as it did before the new code artifact was integrated into it.

When the product has a graphical user interface, special issues can arise with regard to integration testing. In general, testing a product usually can be simplified by storing the input data for a test case in a file. The product then is executed, and the relevant data submitted to it. With the aid of a CASE tool, the whole process can be automated; that is, a set of test cases is set up, together with the expected outcome of each case. The CASE tool runs each test case, compares the actual results with the expected results, and reports to the user on each case. The test cases then are stored, for use in regression testing whenever the product is modified. SilkTest is an example of a tool of this kind.

However, when a product incorporates a graphical user interface, this approach does not work. Specifically, test data for pulling down a menu or clicking on a mouse button cannot be stored in a file in the same way as conventional test data. At the same time, it is time consuming and boring to test a GUI manually. The solution to this problem is to use a special CASE tool that keeps a record of mouse clicks, key presses, and so on. The GUI is tested once manually so that the CASE tool can set up the test file. Thereafter, this file is used in subsequent tests. A number of CASE tools support testing GUIs, including QARun and XRunner.

When the integration process is complete, the product as a whole is tested; this is termed **product testing**. When the developers are confident about the correctness of every aspect of the product, it is handed over to the client for **acceptance testing**. These two forms of testing are now described in more detail.

## 14.21    Product Testing

The fact that the last code artifact has been integrated successfully into the product does not mean that the task of the developers is complete. The SQA group still must perform a number of testing tasks to ascertain that the product will be successful. There are two main types of software, commercial off-the-shelf (COTS) software (Section 1.11) and custom software. The aim of COTS product testing is to ensure that the product as a whole is free of faults. When the product testing is complete, the product undergoes alpha and beta testing, as described in Section 3.7. That is, preliminary versions are shipped to selected prospective buyers of the product to get feedback, particularly regarding residual faults overlooked by the SQA team.

Custom software, on the other hand, undergoes somewhat different product testing. The SQA group performs a number of testing tasks to be certain that the product will not fail its acceptance test, the final hurdle that the custom software development team must overcome. The failure of a product to pass its acceptance test almost always is a poor reflection on the management capabilities of the development organization. The client may conclude that the developers are incompetent, which all but guarantees that the client will do everything to avoid employing those developers again. Worse, the client may believe that the developers are dishonest and deliberately handed over substandard software to finish the contract and be paid as quickly as possible. If the client genuinely believes this and tells other potential clients, then the developers face a major public relations problem. It is up to the SQA group to make sure the product passes the acceptance test with flying colors.

To ensure a successful acceptance test, the SQA group must test the product using tests that the SQA group believes closely approximate the forthcoming acceptance tests:

- Black-box test cases for the product as a whole must be run. Up to now, test cases have been set up on an artifact-by-artifact or class-by-class basis, ensuring that each code artifact or class individually satisfies its specifications.

- The robustness of the product as a whole must be tested. Again, the robustness of individual code artifacts and classes was tested during integration; now productwide robustness is the issue for which test cases must be set up and run. In addition, the product must be subjected to **stress testing**, that is, making sure that it behaves correctly when operating under a peak load, such as all terminals trying to log on at the same time or customers operating all the automated teller machines simultaneously. The product also must be subjected to **volume testing**, for example, making sure that it can handle large input files.

- The SQA group must check that the product satisfies all its constraints. For example, if the specifications state that the response time for 95 percent of queries when the product is working under full load must be under 3 seconds, then it is the responsibility of the SQA group to verify that this indeed is the case. There is no question that the client will check constraints during acceptance testing; and if the product fails to meet a major constraint, then the development organization will lose a considerable amount of credibility. Similarly, storage constraints and security constraints must be checked.

- The SQA group must review all documentation to be handed over to the client together with the code. The SQA group must check that the documentation conforms to the standards laid down in the SPMP. In addition, the documentation must be checked against the product. For instance, the SQA group has to determine that the user manual indeed reflects the correct way of using the product and that the product functions as specified in the user manual.

Once the SQA group assures management that the product can handle anything the acceptance testers can throw at it, the product (that is, the code plus all the documentation) is handed to the client organization for acceptance testing.

## 14.22    Acceptance Testing

The purpose of acceptance testing is for the client to determine whether the product indeed satisfies its specifications as claimed by the developer. Acceptance testing is done by either the client organization, the SQA group in the presence of client representatives, or an independent SQA group hired by the client for this purpose. Acceptance testing naturally includes correctness testing, but in addition, it is necessary to test performance and robustness. The four major components of acceptance testing—testing correctness, robustness, performance, and documentation—are exactly what is done by the developer during product testing; this is not surprising, because product testing is a comprehensive rehearsal for the acceptance test.

A key aspect of acceptance testing is that it must be performed on actual data rather than on test data. No matter how well test cases are set up, by their very nature they are artificial. More important, test data should be a true reflection of the corresponding actual data, but in practice, this is not always the case. For example, the member of the specification team responsible for characterizing the actual data may perform this task incorrectly. Alternatively, even if the data are specified correctly, the SQA group member who uses that data specification may misunderstand or misinterpret it. The resulting test cases are not a true reflection of the actual data, leading to an inadequately tested product. For these reasons, acceptance testing must be performed on actual data. Furthermore, because the development team endeavors to ensure that the product testing duplicates every aspect of the acceptance testing, as much of the product testing as possible should also be performed on actual data.

When a new product is to replace an existing one, the specification document almost always includes a clause to the effect that the new product must be installed to run in parallel with the existing product. The reason is that there is a very real possibility that the new product may be faulty in some way. The existing product works correctly but is inadequate in some respects. If the existing product is replaced by a new product that works incorrectly, then the client is in trouble. Therefore, both products must run in parallel until the client is satisfied that the new product can take over the functions of the existing product. Successful parallel running concludes acceptance testing, and the existing product can be retired.

When the product has passed its acceptance test, the task of the developers is complete. Any changes now made to that product constitute postdelivery maintenance.

## 14.23 The Test Workflow: The MSG Foundation Case Study

The C++ and Java implementations of the MSG Foundation product (available for download at www.mhhe.com/schach) were tested against the black-box test cases of Figures 14.13 and 14.14, as well as the glass-box test cases of Problems 14.30 through 14.34.

## 14.24 CASE Tools for Implementation

CASE tools to support implementation of code artifacts were described in some detail in Chapter 5. For integration, version-control tools, build tools, and configuration management tools are needed (Chapter 5). The reason is that code artifacts under test change continually as a consequence of faults being detected and corrected, and these CASE tools are essential to ensure that the appropriate version of each artifact is compiled and linked. Commercially available configuration-control workbenches include PVCS and SourceSafe. A popular open-source configuration-control tool is CVS.

In each chapter so far, CASE tools and workbenches specific to that workflow have been described. Now that all workflows of the development process have been described, it is appropriate to consider CASE tools for the process as a whole.

## 14.24.1 CASE Tools for the Complete Software Process

There is a natural progression within CASE. As described in Section 5.5, the simplest CASE device is a single **tool**, such as an online interface checker or a build tool. Next, tools can be combined, leading to a **workbench** that supports one or two activities within the software process, such as configuration control or coding. However, such a workbench might not provide management information even for the limited portion of the software process to which it is applicable, let alone for the project as a whole. Finally, an **environment** provides computer-aided support for most, if not all, of the process.

Ideally, every software development organization should utilize an environment. But the cost of an environment can be large—not just the package itself but the hardware on which to run it. For a smaller organization, a workbench, or perhaps just a set of tools, may suffice. But, if at all possible, an **integrated environment** should be utilized to support the development and maintenance effort.

## 14.24.2 Integrated Development Environments

The most common meaning of the word *integrated* within the CASE context is in terms of **user interface integration**. That is, all the tools in the environment share a common user interface. The idea behind this is that, if all the tools have the same visual appearance, the user of one tool should have little difficulty in learning and using another tool in the environment. This has been successfully achieved on the Macintosh, where most applications have a similar "look and feel." Although this is the usual meaning, there are other types of integration as well.

The term **tool integration** means that all the tools communicate via the same data format. For example, in the UNIX Programmer's Workbench, the UNIX pipe formalism assumes that all data are in the form of an ASCII stream. It thus is easy to combine two tools by directing the output stream from one tool to the input stream of the other tool. Eclipse is an open-source environment for tool integration.

**Process integration** refers to an environment that supports one specific software process. A subset of this class of environment is the **technique-based environment** (but see Just in Case You Wanted to Know Box 14.8). An environment of this type supports only a specific technique for developing software, rather than a complete process. Environments exist for a variety of the techniques discussed in this book, such as Gane and Sarsen's structured systems analysis (Section 11.3), Jackson system development (Section 13.5), and Petri nets (Section 11.8). The majority of these environments provide graphical support for analysis and design and incorporate a data dictionary. Some consistency checking usually is provided. Support for managing the development process frequently is incorporated into the environment. Many environments of this type are commercially available, including Analyst/Designer and Rhapsody. Analyst/Designer is specific to Yourdon's methodology [Yourdon, 1989], and Rhapsody supports statecharts [Harel et al., 1990]. With regard to object-oriented methodologies, IBM Rational Rose supports the Unified Process [Jacobson, Booch, and Rumbaugh, 1999]. In addition, some older environments have been extended to support the object-oriented paradigm; Software through Pictures is an example of this type. Almost all object-oriented environments now support UML.

The emphasis in most technique-based environments is on the support and formalization of the manual operations for software development laid down by the technique. That is, these environments force users to utilize the technique step by step in the way intended by its author, while assisting the user by providing graphical tools, a data dictionary, and consistency checking. This computerized framework is a strength of technique-based environments in that users are forced to use a specific technique and use it correctly. But it can be a weakness as well. Unless the software process of the organization incorporates this specific technique, use of a technique-based environment can be counterproductive.

## 14.24.3 Environments for Business Applications

An important class of environments is used for building business-oriented products. The emphasis is on ease of use, achieved in a number of ways. In particular, the environment incorporates a number of standard screens, and these can be modified endlessly via a user-friendly GUI generator. One popular feature of such environments is a code generator. The lowest level of abstraction of a product then is the detailed design. The detailed design is the input to a code generator that automatically generates code in a language such as C, C++, or Java. This automatically generated code is compiled; no "programming" of any kind is performed on it.

Languages for specifying the detailed design could well be the programming languages of the future. The level of abstraction of programming languages rose from the physical machine level of first- and second-generation languages to the abstract machine level of third- and fourth-generation languages. Today, the level of abstraction of environments of this type is the detailed design level, a portable level. Section 14.2 stated that one objective in using a fourth-generation language is shorter code, and hence quicker development and easier postdelivery maintenance. The use of code generators takes these goals even further, in that the programmer has to provide fewer details to a code generator than to an interpreter or compiler for a 4GL. Therefore, it is expected that use of business-oriented environments that support code generators will increase productivity.

A number of environments of this type are currently available, including Oracle Developer Suite. Bearing in mind the size of the market for business-oriented CASE environments, it is likely that many more environments of this type will be developed in future years.

### 14.24.4 Public Tool Infrastructures

The European Strategic Programme for Research in Information Technology (ESPRIT) developed an infrastructure for supporting CASE tools. Despite its name, the **portable common tool environment** (PCTE) [Long and Morris, 1993] is *not* an environment. Instead, it is an infrastructure that provides the services needed by CASE tools, in much the same way that UNIX provides the operating system services needed by user products. (The word *common* in PCTE is in the sense of "public" or "not copyrighted.")

PCTE has gained widespread acceptance. For example, PCTE and the C and Ada interfaces to PCTE were adopted as ISO/IEC Standard 13719 in 1995. Implementations of PCTE include those of Emeraude and IBM.

The hope is that, in the future, many more CASE tools will conform to the PCTE standard and that PCTE itself will be implemented on a wider variety of computers. A tool that conforms to PCTE would run on any computer that supports PCTE. Accordingly, this should result in the widespread availability of a broad range of CASE tools. This, in turn, should lead to better software processes and better-quality software.

### 14.24.5 Potential Problems with Environments

No one environment is ideal for all products and all organizations, any more than one programming language can be considered "the best." Every environment has its strengths and its weaknesses, and choosing an inappropriate environment can be worse than using no environment at all. For example, as explained in Section 14.24.2, a technique-based environment essentially automates a manual process. If an organization chooses to use an environment that enforces a technique inappropriate for it as a whole or for a current software product under development, then use of that CASE environment is counterproductive.

A worse situation occurs when an organization chooses to ignore the advice of Section 5.10, that the use of a CASE environment should be firmly avoided until the organization has attained CMM level 3. Of course, every organization should use CASE tools, and there generally is little harm in using a workbench. However, an environment imposes an automated software process on an organization that uses it. If a good process is being used, that is, the organization is at level 3 or higher, then use of the environment assists in all aspects of software production by automating that process. But, if the organization is at the crisis-driven level 1 or even at level 2, then no process as such is in place. Automation of this nonexistent process, that is, the introduction of a CASE environment (as opposed to a CASE tool or CASE workbench), can lead only to chaos.

## 14.25 CASE Tools for the Test Workflow

Numerous CASE tools are available to support the different types of testing that are performed during the implementation workflow. First consider unit testing. The XUnit testing frameworks, including JUnit for Java and CppUnit for C++, are a set of open-source automated tools for unit testing; that is, they are utilized to test each class in turn. A set of test cases is prepared, and the tool checks that each of the messages sent to the class results in the expected answer being returned. Commercial tools of this type are produced by many vendors, including Parasoft.

We now turn to integration testing. Examples of commercial tools that support automated integration testing (as well as unit testing) include SilkTest and IBM Rational Functional Tester. It is common for tools of this kind to pool the unit testing test cases and utilize the resulting set of test cases for integration testing and regression testing.

During the test workflow, it is essential for management to know the status of all defects. In particular, it is vital to know which defects have been detected but have not yet been corrected. The best-known defect-tracking tool is Bugzilla, an open-source product.

Returning to Figure 1.6 yet again, it is vital to detect coding faults as soon as possible. One way to achieve this is to use a CASE tool to analyze the code, looking for common syntactic and semantic faults, or constructs that could lead to problems later. Examples of such tools include *lint* (for C—see Section 8.7.4), IBM Rational Purify, Sun's Jackpot Source Code Metrics, and three Microsoft tools: PREfix, PREfast, and SLAM.

The Hyades project (otherwise known as the Eclipse test and performance tools project) is an open-source integrated test, trace, and monitoring environment that currently can be used with Java and C++. It has facilities for a variety of different testing tools. As more and more tool vendors adapt their tools to work under Eclipse, users will be able to select from a wider choice of testing tools, all of which will work in conjunction with one another.

# 14.26  Metrics for the Implementation Workflow

A number of different complexity metrics for the implementation workflow are discussed in Section 14.13.2, including lines of code and McCabe's cyclomatic complexity.

From a testing viewpoint, the relevant metrics include the total number of test cases and the number of test cases that resulted in a failure. The usual fault statistics must be maintained for code inspections. The total number of faults is important, because if the number of faults detected in a code artifact exceeds a predetermined maximum, then that code artifact must be redesigned and recoded, as discussed in Section 14.19. In addition, detailed statistics need to be kept regarding the types of faults detected. Typical fault types include misunderstanding the design, lack of initialization, and inconsistent use of variables. The fault data can be incorporated into the checklists to be used during code inspections of future products.

A number of metrics specific to the object-oriented paradigm have been put forward, for example, the height of the inheritance tree [Chidamber and Kemerer, 1994]. Many of these metrics have been questioned on both theoretical and experimental grounds [Binkley and Schach, 1996; 1997]. Furthermore, Alshayeb and Li [2003] have shown that, whereas object-oriented metrics can relatively accurately predict the number of lines of code added, changed, and deleted in agile processes, they are of little use in predicting the same measures in a framework-based process (see Section 8.5.2). It remains to be shown that there is a need for specifically object-oriented metrics, as opposed to classical metrics that can be applied equally to object-oriented software.

# 14.27   Challenges of the Implementation Workflow

Paradoxically, a major challenge of the implementation workflow has to be met in the workflows that precede it. As explained in Chapter 8, code reuse is an effective way of reducing software development cost and delivery time. However, it is hard to achieve code reuse if it is attempted as late as the implementation workflow.

For example, suppose the decision is made to implement a product in language L. Now, after half the code artifacts have been implemented and tested, management decides to utilize package P for the graphical user interfaces of the software product. No matter how powerful the routines of P may be, if they are written in a language that is hard to interface with L, then they cannot be reused in the software product.

Even if language interoperability is not an issue, there is little point in trying to reuse an existing code artifact unless the item to be reused fits the design exactly. More work may be needed to modify the existing code artifact than to create a new code artifact from scratch.

Code reuse therefore has to be built into a software product from the very beginning. Reuse has to be a user requirement as well as a constraint of the specification document. The software project management plan (Section 9.4) must incorporate reuse. Also, the design document must state which code artifacts are to be implemented and which are to be reused.

So, as stated at the beginning of this section, even though code reuse is an important challenge of implementation, code reuse has to be incorporated into the requirements, analysis, and design workflows.

From a purely technical viewpoint, the implementation workflow is relatively straightforward. If the requirements, analysis, and design workflows were carried out satisfactorily, the task of implementation should pose few problems to competent programmers. However, management of integration is of critical importance; the challenges of the implementation workflow are to be found in this area.

Typical make-or-break issues include use of the appropriate CASE tools (Section 14.24), test planning once the specifications have been signed off on by the client (Section 9.6), ensuring that changes to the design are communicated to all relevant personnel (Section 14.6.5), and deciding when to stop testing and deliver the product to the client (Section 6.1.2).

---

**Chapter Review**

This chapter presents various issues relating to the implementation of a product by a team. These include choice of programming language (Section 14.1). The issue of fourth-generation languages is discussed in some detail in Section 14.2. Good programming practice is described in Section 14.3, and the need for practical coding standards is presented in Section 14.4. Then, comments are made regarding code reuse (Section 14.5). Implementation and integration activities must be carried out in parallel (Section 14.6). Top-down, bottom-up, and sandwich integration are described and compared (Sections 14.6.1 through 14.6.3). Integration of object-oriented products is discussed in Section 14.6.4, and management of integration in Section 14.6.5. The implementation workflow is presented in Section 14.7 and applied to the MSG Foundation case study in Section 14.8. Next, implementation aspects of the test workflow are presented (Section 14.9). Test cases must be selected systematically (Section 14.10). Various black-box, glass-box, and non-execution-based unit-testing techniques are described (Sections 14.11, 14.13, and 14.14, respectively) and then compared (Section 14.15). Black-box testing of the MSG Foundation case study is presented in Section 14.12. The Cleanroom technique is described in Section 14.16.

Testing objects is discussed in Section 14.17, followed by a discussion of the managerial implications of unit testing (Section 14.18). Another problem is when to rewrite rather than debug a code artifact (Section 14.19). Integration testing is described in Section 14.20, product testing in Section 14.21, and acceptance testing in Section 14.22. The test workflow for the MSG Foundation case study is outlined in Section 14.23. CASE tools for the implementation workflow are described in Section 14.24. In more detail, CASE tools for the complete process are discussed in Section 14.24.1 and integrated development environments in Section 14.24.2. Environments for business applications are presented in Section 14.24.3. Section 14.24.4 is devoted to public tool infrastructures. Next, potential problems with environments are discussed (Section 14.24.5). Now CASE tools for the test workflow are described (Section 14.25). Metrics for the implementation workflow are discussed in Section 14.26. The chapter concludes with an analysis of the challenges of the implementation workflow (Section 14.27).

**For Further Reading**

A wide-ranging source of information on 4GLs is [Martin, 1985]. The attitudes of 43 organizations to 4GLs are reported in [Guimaraes, 1985]. Klepper and Bock [1995] describe how McDonnell Douglas obtained higher productivity with 4GLs than with 3GLs.

Excellent books on good programming practice include [Kernighan and Plauger, 1974] and [McConnell, 1993].

Some of the dangers of end-user programming are presented in [Harrison, 2004]. A wide variety of papers on end-user programming appear in the November 2004 issue of the *Communications of the ACM*.

Probably the most important early work on execution-based testing is [Myers, 1979]. A comprehensive source of information on testing in general is [Beizer, 1990]. Functional testing is described in [Howden, 1987]; structural techniques are compared in [Clarke, Podgurski, Richardson, and Zeil, 1989]. Black-box testing is described in detail in [Beizer, 1995]. The design of black-box test cases is presented in [Yamaura, 1998]. The relationship between the various coverage measures of structural testing and software quality is discussed in [Horgan, London, and Lyu, 1994]. A formal approach to glass-box testing is described in [Stocks and Carrington, 1996]. Elbaum, Malishevsky, and Rothermel [2002] discuss setting test case priorities.

Cleanroom is described in [Linger, 1994]. The use of Cleanroom during postdelivery maintenance is presented in [Sherer, Kouchakdjian, and Arnold, 1996]. A criticism of Cleanroom is given in [Beizer, 1997].

A good introduction to software reliability is [Musa and Everett, 1990]. In addition, the proceedings of the annual International Symposium on Software Reliability Engineering contain a wide variety of articles on software reliability.

The proceedings of the International Symposia on Software Testing and Analysis cover a particularly broad range of testing issues; selected papers for the 2000 International Symposium appear in the February 2002 issue of *IEEE Transactions on Software Engineering*.

A survey of different approaches to the testing of objects can be found in [Turner, 1994]. Two important papers on the subject are [Perry and Kaiser, 1990] and [Harrold, McGregor, and Fitzpatrick, 1992]. [Beizer, 1995], mentioned previously, also covers black-box testing of object-oriented software. With regard to the object-oriented paradigm, Jorgensen and Erickson [1994] describe the integration testing of object-oriented software.

With regard to metrics for implementation, McCabe's cyclomatic complexity was first presented in [McCabe, 1976]. Extensions of the metric to design appear in [McCabe and Butler, 1989]. Articles questioning the validity of cyclomatic complexity include [Shepperd, 1988; Weyuker, 1988b; and Shepperd and Ince, 1994]. Metrics for managing code inspections are described in [Barnard and Price, 1994]. The validity of object-oriented metrics is discussed in [Alshayeb and Li, 2003].

Selection of test data for integration testing appears in [Harrold and Soffa, 1991]. The generation of test cases for testing GUIs is described in [Memon, Pollack, and Soffa, 2001].

Every 2 or 3 years, ACM SIGSOFT and SIGPLAN sponsor a Symposium on Practical Software Development Environments. The proceedings provide information on a broad spectrum of toolkits and environments. Also useful are the proceedings of the annual International Workshops on Computer-Aided Software Engineering.

With regard to PCTE, [Long and Morris, 1993] contains a number of information sources on that topic.

## Key Terms

acceptance testing *500*
all-definition-use-path coverage *491*
behavioral testing *482*
black-box testing *482*
bottom-up integration *478*
boundary value analysis *486*
branch coverage *491*
Cleanroom *494*
code artifact *481*
coding standards *474*
complexity *492*
component *481*
consistent variable names *469*
cyclomatic complexity *492*
data-driven testing *482*
debugging *498*
defensive programming *477*
driver *476*
end-user programming *468*
environment *503*
equivalence class *486*
execution-based testing *481*
first-generation language *466*
fourth-generation language (4GL) *466*
functional analysis *488*
functional testing *482*

glass-box testing *482*
good programming practice *469*
Hungarian Naming Conventions *470*
implementation workflow *481*
input/output-driven testing *482*
integrated environment *503*
integration *475*
integration testing *499*
linear code sequences *491*
logic artifact *476*
logic-driven testing *482*
meaningful variable names *469*
method-based environment *504*
non-execution-based testing *481*
nonprocedural *467*
operational artifact *476*
path coverage *491*
path-oriented testing *482*
portable common tool environment (PCTE) *505*
procedural *467*
process integration *503*
product testing *500*
programming-in-the-many *463*
prologue comments *471*

reliable *485*
sandwich integration *479*
second-generation language *466*
self-documenting code *470*
statement coverage *491*
static method *479*
stress testing *501*
structural test *491*
structural testing *482*
structured testing *492*
stub *475*
technique-based environment *503*
test case selection *482*
testing fault rate *495*
testing to code *482*
testing to specifications *482*
third-generation language *466*
tool *503*
tool integration *503*
top-down integration *476*
unit testing *481*
user interface integration *503*
valid *485*
volume testing *501*
white-box testing *482*
workbench *503*

## Problems

14.1  Your instructor has asked you to implement the Osric's Office Appliances and Decor product (Appendix A). Which language would you choose for implementing the product, and why? Of the various languages available to you, list their benefits and their costs. Do not attempt to attach dollar values to your answers.

14.2  Repeat Problem 14.1 for the elevator problem (Section 11.7.1).

14.3  Repeat Problem 14.1 for the automated library circulation system (Problem 8.7).

14.4  Repeat Problem 14.1 for the product that determines whether a bank statement is correct (Problem 8.8).

14.5  Repeat Problem 14.1 for the automated teller machine (Problem 8.9).

14.6  Add prologue comments to a code artifact that you have recently written.

14.7   How do coding standards for a one-person software production company differ from those in organizations with 300 software professionals?

14.8   How do coding standards for a software company that develops and maintains software for intensive-care units differ from those in an organization that develops and maintains accounting products?

14.9   Set up black-box test cases for Naur's text-processing problem (Section 6.5.2). For each test case, state what is being tested and the expected outcome of that test case.

14.10  Using your solution to Problem 6.15 (or code distributed by your instructor), set up statement coverage test cases. For each test case, state what is being tested and the expected outcome of that test case.

14.11  Repeat Problem 14.10 for branch coverage.

14.12  Repeat Problem 14.10 for all-definition-use-path coverage.

14.13  Repeat Problem 14.10 for path coverage.

14.14  Repeat Problem 14.10 for linear code sequences.

14.15  Draw a flowchart of your solution to Problem 6.15 (or code distributed by your instructor). Determine its cyclomatic complexity. If you are unable to determine the number of branches, consider the flowchart as a directed graph. Determine the number of edges $e$, nodes $n$, and connected components $c$. (Each method constitutes a connected component.) The cyclomatic complexity $V$ is then given by the formula [McCabe, 1976]

$$V = e - n + 2c$$

14.16  You are the owner and sole employee of One-Person Software Company. You bought the programming workbench described in Section 5.6. List its five capabilities in order of importance to you, giving reasons.

14.17  You are now the vice-president for software technology of Very Big Software Company; there are 17,500 employees in your organization. How do you rank the capabilities of the programming workbench described in Section 5.6? Explain any differences between your answer to this problem and that of Problem 14.16.

14.18  As SQA manager for a software development organization, you are responsible for determining the maximum number of faults that may be found in a given code artifact during testing. If this maximum is exceeded, then the code artifact must be redesigned and recoded. What criteria would you use to determine the maximum for a given code artifact?

14.19  Explain the difference between logic artifacts and operational artifacts.

14.20  Defensive programming is good software engineering practice. At the same time, it can prevent operational artifacts from being tested thoroughly enough for reuse purposes. How can this apparent contradiction be resolved?

14.21  What are the similarities between product testing and acceptance testing? What are the major differences?

14.22  What is the role of the SQA group during implementation?

14.23  You are the owner and sole employee of One-Person Software Company. You decide that to be competitive you must buy CASE tools. You therefore apply for a bank loan for $15,000. Your bank manager asks you for a statement no more than one page in length (preferably shorter) explaining in lay terms why you need CASE tools. Write the statement.

14.24  The newly appointed vice-president for software development of Ye Olde Fashioned Software Corporation has hired you to help her change the way the company develops software. There are 650 employees, all writing COBOL code without the assistance of any CASE tools. Write a memo to the vice-president stating what sort of CASE equipment the company should purchase. Justify your choice.

14.25 You and a friend decide to start Personal Computer Software Programs 'R Us, developing software for personal computers on personal computers. Then a distant cousin dies, leaving you $1 million on condition that you spend the money on a business-oriented environment and the hardware needed to run it and that you keep the environment for at least 5 years. What do you do, and why?

14.26 You are a computer science professor at an excellent small liberal arts college. Programming assignments for computer science courses are done on a network of 35 personal computers. Your dean asks you whether to use the limited software budget to buy CASE tools, bearing in mind that, unless some sort of site license can be obtained, 35 copies of every CASE tool have to be purchased. What do you advise?

14.27 You have just been elected mayor of a major city. You discover that no CASE tools are being used to develop software for the city. What do you do?

14.28 (Term Project) Draw up black-box test cases for the product you specified in Problem 11.15 or 12.18. For each test case, state what is being tested and the expected outcome of that test case.

14.29 (Term Project) Implement and integrate the Osric's Office Appliances and Decor product (Appendix A). Use the programming language specified by your instructor. Your instructor will tell you whether to build a Web-based user interface, a graphical user interface, or a text-based user interface. Remember to utilize the black-box test cases you developed in Problem 14.28 for testing your code.

14.30 (Case Study) Download a copy of the implementation of the MSG Foundation product described in Section 14.8. Draw up statement coverage test cases for the product. For each test case, state what is being tested and the expected outcome of that test case.

14.31 (Case Study) Repeat Problem 14.30 for branch coverage.

14.32 (Case Study) Repeat Problem 14.30 for all-definition-use-path coverage.

14.33 (Case Study) Repeat Problem 14.30 for path coverage.

14.34 (Case Study) Repeat Problem 14.30 for linear code sequences.

14.35 (Case Study) Starting with the detailed design of Section 13.10, code the MSG Foundation case study in an object-oriented language other than C++ or Java.

14.36 (Case Study) Recode the MSG Foundation case study (Section 14.8) in pure C, with no C++ features. Although C does not support inheritance, object-based concepts such as encapsulation and information hiding can be achieved relatively easily. How would you implement polymorphism and dynamic binding?

14.37 (Case Study) To what extent is the documentation of the code of the implementation of Section 14.8 inadequate? Make any necessary additions.

14.38 (Readings in Software Engineering) Your instructor will distribute copies of [Alshayeb and Li, 2003]. Does this paper give you confidence in the validity of object-oriented metrics?

**References**   [Alshayeb and Li, 2003] M. ALSHAYEB, AND W. LI, "An Empirical Validation of Object-Oriented Metrics in Two Different Iterative Software Processes," *IEEE Transactions on Software Engineering* **29** (November 2003), pp. 1043–49.

[Barnard and Price, 1994] J. BARNARD AND A. PRICE, "Managing Code Inspection Information," *IEEE Software* **11** (March 1994), pp. 59–69.

[Basili and Hutchens, 1983] V. R. BASILI AND D. H. HUTCHENS, "An Empirical Study of a Syntactic Complexity Family," *IEEE Transactions on Software Engineering* **SE-9** (November 1983), pp. 664–72.

[Basili and Selby, 1987] V. R. BASILI AND R. W. SELBY, "Comparing the Effectiveness of Software Testing Strategies," *IEEE Transactions on Software Engineering* **SE-13** (December 1987), pp. 1278–96.

[Basili and Weiss, 1984] V. R. BASILI AND D. M. WEISS, "A Methodology for Collecting Valid Software Engineering Data," *IEEE Transactions on Software Engineering* **SE-10** (November 1984), pp. 728–38.

[Beizer, 1990] B. BEIZER, *Software Testing Techniques,* 2nd ed., Van Nostrand Reinhold, New York, 1990.

[Beizer, 1995] B. BEIZER, *Black-Box Testing: Techniques for Functional Testing of Software and Systems,* John Wiley and Sons, New York, 1995.

[Beizer, 1997] B. BEIZER, "Cleanroom Process Model: A Critical Examination," *IEEE Software* **14** (March/April 1997), pp. 14–16.

[Binkley and Schach, 1996] A. B. BINKLEY AND S. R. SCHACH, "A Comparison of Sixteen Quality Metrics for Object-Oriented Design," *Information Processing Letters* **57** (No. 6, June 1996), pp. 271–75.

[Binkley and Schach, 1997] A. B. BINKLEY AND S. R. SCHACH, "Toward a Unified Approach to Object-Oriented Coupling," *Proceedings of the 35th Annual ACM Southeast Conference,* Murfreesboro, TN, April 2–4, 1997, pp. 91–97.

[Borland, 2002] BORLAND, "Press Release: Borland Unveils C++ Application Development Strategy for 2002," www.borland.com/news/press_releases/2002/01_28_02_cpp.strategy.html, January 28, 2002.

[Chidamber and Kemerer, 1994] S. R. CHIDAMBER AND C. F. KEMERER, "A Metrics Suite for Object Oriented Design," *IEEE Transactions on Software Engineering* **20** (June 1994), pp. 476–93.

[Clarke, Podgurski, Richardson, and Zeil, 1989] L. A. CLARKE, A. PODGURSKI, D. J. RICHARDSON, AND S. J. ZEIL, "A Formal Evaluation of Data Flow Path Selection Criteria," *IEEE Transactions on Software Engineering* **15** (November 1989), pp. 1318–32.

[Crossman, 1982] T. D. CROSSMAN, "Inspection Teams, Are They Worth It?" *Proceedings of the Second National Symposium on EDP Quality Assurance*, Chicago, November 1982.

[Date, 2003] C. J. DATE, *An Introduction to Database Systems,* 8th ed., Addison-Wesley, Reading, MA, 2003.

[Dunn, 1984] R. H. DUNN, *Software Defect Removal*, McGraw-Hill, New York, 1984.

[Elbaum, Malishevsky, and Rothermel, 2002] S. ELBAUM, A. G. MALISHEVSKY, AND G. ROTHERMEL, "Test Case Prioritization: A Family of Empirical Studies," *IEEE Transactions on Software Engineering* **28** (February 2002), pp. 159–82.

[Endres, 1975] A. ENDRES, "An Analysis of Errors and Their Causes in System Programs," *IEEE Transactions on Software Engineering* **SE-1** (June 1975), pp. 140–49.

[Grady, 1992] R. B. GRADY, *Practical Software Metrics for Project Management and Process Improvement*, Prentice Hall, Englewood Cliffs, NJ, 1992.

[Guimaraes, 1985] T. GUIMARAES, "A Study of Application Program Development Techniques," *Communications of the ACM* **28** (May 1985), pp. 494–99.

[Harel et al., 1990] D. HAREL, H. LACHOVER, A. NAAMAD, A. PNUELI, M. POLITI, R. SHERMAN, A. SHTULL-TRAURING, AND M. TRAKHTENBROT, "STATEMATE: A Working Environment for the Development of Complex Reactive Systems," *IEEE Transactions on Software Engineering* **16** (April 1990), pp. 403–14.

[Harrison, 2004] W. HARRISON, "The Dangers of End-User Programming," *IEEE Software* **21** (July/August 2004), pp. 5–7.

[Harrold and Soffa, 1991] M. J. HARROLD AND M. L. SOFFA, "Selecting and Using Data for Integration Testing," *IEEE Software* **8** (1991), pp. 58–65.

[Harrold, McGregor, and Fitzpatrick, 1992] M. J. HARROLD, J. D. MCGREGOR, AND K. J. FITZPATRICK, "Incremental Testing of Object-Oriented Class Structures," *Proceedings of the 14th International Conference on Software Engineering*, Melbourne, Australia, May 1992, pp. 68–80.

[Horgan, London, and Lyu, 1994] J. R. HORGAN, S. LONDON, AND M. R. LYU, "Achieving Software Quality with Testing Coverage Measures," *IEEE Computer* **27** (1994), pp. 60–69.

[Howden, 1987] W. E. HOWDEN, *Functional Program Testing and Analysis*, McGraw-Hill, New York, 1987.

[Hwang, 1981] S.-S. V. HWANG, "An Empirical Study in Functional Testing, Structural Testing, and Code Reading Inspection," Scholarly Paper 362, Department of Computer Science, University of Maryland, College Park, 1981.

[Jacobson, Booch, and Rumbaugh, 1999] I. JACOBSON, G. BOOCH, AND J. RUMBAUGH, *The Unified Software Development Process*, Addison-Wesley, Reading, MA, 1999.

[Jorgensen and Erickson, 1994] P. C. JORGENSEN AND C. ERICKSON, "Object-Oriented Integration Testing," *Communications of the ACM* **37** (September 1994), pp. 30–38.

[Kernighan and Plauger, 1974] B. W. KERNIGHAN AND P. J. PLAUGER, *The Elements of Programming Style,* McGraw-Hill, New York, 1974.

[Klepper and Bock, 1995] R. KLEPPER AND D. BOCK, "Third and Fourth Generation Productivity Differences," *Communications of the ACM* **38** (September, 1995), pp. 69–79.

[Klunder, 1988] D. KLUNDER, "Hungarian Naming Conventions," Technical Report, Microsoft Corporation, Redmond, WA, January 1988.

[Linger, 1994] R. C. LINGER, "Cleanroom Process Model," *IEEE Software* **11** (March 1994), pp. 50–58.

[Long and Morris, 1993] F. LONG AND E. MORRIS, "An Overview of PCTE: A Basis for a Portable Common Tool Environment," Technical Report CMU/SEI–93–TR–1, Software Engineering Institute, Carnegie Mellon University, Pittsburgh, January 1993.

[Martin, 1985] J. MARTIN, *Fourth-Generation Languages,* Vols. 1, 2, and 3, Prentice Hall, Englewood Cliffs, NJ, 1985.

[McCabe, 1976] T. J. MCCABE, "A Complexity Measure," *IEEE Transactions on Software Engineering* **SE-2** (December 1976), pp. 308–20.

[McCabe and Butler, 1989] T. J. MCCABE AND C. W. BUTLER, "Design Complexity Measurement and Testing," *Communications of the ACM* **32** (December 1989), pp. 1415–25.

[McConnell, 1993] S. MCCONNELL, *Code Complete: A Practical Handbook of Software Construction,* Microsoft Press, Redmond, WA, 1993.

[Memon, Pollack, and Soffa, 2001] A. M. MEMON, M. E. POLLACK, AND M. L. SOFFA, "Hierarchical GUI Test Case Generation Using Automated Planning," *IEEE Transactions on Software Engineering* **27** (February 2001), pp. 144–55.

[Mills, Dyer, and Linger, 1987] H. D. MILLS, M. DYER, AND R. C. LINGER, "Cleanroom Software Engineering," *IEEE Software* **4** (September 1987), pp. 19–25.

[Musa and Everett, 1990] J. D. MUSA AND W. W. EVERETT, "Software-Reliability Engineering: Technology for the 1990s," *IEEE Software* **7** (November 1990), pp. 36–43.

[Musa, Iannino, and Okumoto, 1987] J. D. MUSA, A. IANNINO, AND K. OKUMOTO, *Software Reliability: Measurement, Prediction, Application*, McGraw-Hill, New York, 1987.

[Myers, 1976] G. J. MYERS, *Software Reliability: Principles and Practices,* Wiley-Interscience, New York, 1976.

[Myers, 1978a] G. J. MYERS, "A Controlled Experiment in Program Testing and Code Walkthroughs/ Inspections," *Communications of the ACM* **21** (September 1978), pp. 760–68.

[Myers, 1979] G. J. MYERS, *The Art of Software Testing*, John Wiley and Sons, New York, 1979.

[Perry and Kaiser, 1990] D. E. PERRY AND G. E. KAISER, "Adequate Testing and Object-Oriented Programming," *Journal of Object-Oriented Programming* **2** (January/February 1990), pp. 13–19.

[Rapps and Weyuker, 1985] S. RAPPS AND E. J. WEYUKER, "Selecting Software Test Data Using Data Flow Information," *IEEE Transactions on Software Engineering* **SE-11** (April 1985), pp. 367–75.

[Sammet, 1978] J. E. SAMMET, "The Early History of COBOL," *Proceedings of the History of Programming Languages Conference,* Los Angeles, 1978, pp. 199–276.

[Shepperd, 1988] M. SHEPPERD, "A Critique of Cyclomatic Complexity as a Software Metric," *Software Engineering Journal* **3** (March 1988), pp. 30–36.

[Shepperd and Ince, 1994] M. SHEPPERD AND D. C. INCE, "A Critique of Three Metrics," *Journal of Systems and Software* **26** (September 1994), pp. 197–210.

[Sherer, Kouchakdjian, and Arnold, 1996] S. W. SHERER, A. KOUCHAKDJIAN, AND P. G. ARNOLD, "Experience Using Cleanroom Software Engineering," *IEEE Software* **13** (May 1996), pp. 69–76.

[Stocks and Carrington, 1996] P. STOCKS AND D. CARRINGTON, "A Framework for Specification-Based Testing," *IEEE Transactions on Software Engineering* **22** (November 1996), pp. 777–93.

[Takahashi and Kamayachi, 1985] M. TAKAHASHI AND Y. KAMAYACHI, "An Empirical Study of a Model for Program Error Prediction," *Proceedings of the Eighth International Conference on Software Engineering*, London, 1985, pp. 330–36.

[Trammel, Binder, and Snyder, 1992] C. J. TRAMMEL, L. H. BINDER, AND C. E. SNYDER, "The Automated Production Control Documentation System: A Case Study in Cleanroom Software Engineering," *ACM Transactions on Software Engineering and Methodology* **1** (January 1992), pp. 81–94.

[Turner, 1994] C. D. TURNER, "State-Based Testing: A New Method for the Testing of Object-Oriented Programs," Ph.D. thesis, Computer Science Division, University of Durham, Durham, UK, November, 1994.

[Walsh, 1979] T. J. WALSH, "A Software Reliability Study Using a Complexity Measure," *Proceedings of the AFIPS National Computer Conference*, New York, 1979, pp. 761–68.

[Watson and McCabe, 1996] A. H. WATSON AND T. J. MCCABE, "Structured Testing: A Testing Methodology Using the Cyclomatic Complexity Metric," NIST Special Publication 500–235, Computer Systems Laboratory, National Institute of Standards and Technology, Gaithersburg, MD, 1996.

[Weyuker, 1988a] E. J. WEYUKER, "An Empirical Study of the Complexity of Data Flow Testing," *Proceedings of the Second Workshop on Software Testing, Verification, and Analysis*, Banff, Canada, July 1988, pp. 188–95.

[Weyuker, 1988b] E. WEYUKER, "Evaluating Software Complexity Measures," *IEEE Transactions on Software Engineering* **14** (September 1988), pp. 1357–65.

[Wilde, Matthews, and Huitt, 1993] N. WILDE, P. MATTHEWS, AND R. HUITT, "Maintaining Object-Oriented Software," *IEEE Software* **10** (January 1993), pp. 75–80.

[Woodward, Hedley, and Hennell, 1980] M. R. WOODWARD, D. HEDLEY, AND M. A. HENNELL, "Experience with Path Analysis and Testing of Programs," *IEEE Transactions on Software Engineering* **SE-6** (May 1980), pp. 278–86.

[Yamaura, 1998] T. YAMAURA, "How to Design Practical Test Cases," *IEEE Software* **15** (November/December 1998), pp. 30–36.

[Yourdon, 1989] E. YOURDON, *Modern Structured Analysis*, Yourdon Press, Englewood Cliffs, NJ, 1989.

# Chapter

# 15

# Postdelivery Maintenance

## Learning Objectives

After studying this chapter, you should be able to

- Perform postdelivery maintenance.
- Appreciate the importance of postdelivery maintenance.
- Describe the challenges of postdelivery maintenance.
- Describe the maintenance implications of the object-oriented paradigm.
- Describe the skills needed for maintenance.

A major theme of this book is the vital importance of postdelivery maintenance. Therefore, it is somewhat surprising that this is a relatively short chapter. The reason is that maintainability has to be built into a product from the very beginning and must not be compromised at any time during the development process. Accordingly, in a very real sense, all the previous chapters have been devoted to the subject of postdelivery maintenance. What is described in this chapter is how to ensure that maintainability is not compromised during postdelivery maintenance itself.

## 15.1 Development and Maintenance

Once the product has passed its acceptance test, it is handed over to the client. The product is installed and used for the purpose for which it was constructed. Any useful product, however, is almost certain to undergo **postdelivery maintenance**, either to fix faults (corrective maintenance) or extend the functionality of the product (enhancement).

Because a product consists of more than just the source code, any changes to the documentation, manuals, or any other component of the product after it has been delivered to the client are examples of postdelivery maintenance. Some computer scientists prefer to use the term **evolution** rather than maintenance to indicate that a product evolves over time. In fact, some view the entire software life cycle, from beginning to end, as an evolutionary process.

This is how maintenance is viewed by the Unified Process. In fact, the word *maintenance* hardly occurs anywhere in Jacobson, Booch, and Rumbaugh [1999]. Instead, maintenance is implicitly treated merely as another increment of the software product. However, there is a basic difference between development and maintenance, a difference that will be illustrated by means of the following example.

Suppose that a woman has her portrait painted when she is 18. The oil painting depicts just her head and shoulders. Twenty years later she marries and now wants the portrait to be modified so that it depicts both her new husband and herself. There are four difficulties that would arise if the portrait were to be changed in this way.

- The canvas is not large enough for her husband's head to be added.
- The original portrait was hung where sunlight fell on it much of the day, so the colors have faded somewhat. In addition, the brand of oil paint that was used for the original painting is no longer manufactured. For both these reasons, it will be hard to achieve consistency of color.
- The original artist has retired, so it will be hard to achieve consistency of style.
- The woman's face has aged 20 years since the original portrait was painted, so considerable work will have to be done to ensure that the modified painting is an accurate likeness.

For all these reasons, it would be laughable even to think about modifying the original portrait. Instead, a new artist will paint a new portrait of the couple from scratch (but see Just in Case You Wanted to Know Box 15.1).

Now consider the maintenance of a software product that originally cost $2 million to develop. There are four difficulties that have to be solved:

- Unfortunately, the disk on which the database is stored is all but full—the current disk is not large enough for more data to be added.
- The company that manufactured the original disk is no longer in business, so a larger disk will have to be bought from a different manufacturer. However, there are hardware incompatibilities between the new disk and the existing software product (Section 8.7.1), and it will cost about $100,000 to make all the changes needed to use the new disk.
- The original developers left the company some years ago, so the changes to the software product will have to be made by a team of maintainers who have never seen the software product before.
- The original software product was developed using the classical paradigm. Nowadays, the object–oriented paradigm (and specifically the Unified Process) is commonly used.

There is a clear correspondence between each portrait bullet point and the corresponding software product bullet point. The inescapable conclusion regarding the oil painting is to paint a new portrait from scratch. Does that mean that, instead of performing a $100,000 maintenance task, we should develop a totally new software product at a cost of $2 million?

The National Gallery in London contains a masterpiece that was ruined when an additional head was added to a portrait. In 1515, the artist Lorenzo Lotto (ca. 1480–after 1556) painted a picture of Giovanni Agostino della Torre, a physician who lived in Bergamo, then in the State of Venice, Italy. Download the picture [Lotto, 1515] and examine it. It certainly appears as if the artist added della Torre's son, Niccolò, after the original portrait had been completed, thereby irreparably marring the painting.

The answer is that analogies should never be taken too far. Just as it is obvious that a new portrait should be painted, it is equally obvious that the existing software product should undergo maintenance at 5 percent of the cost of a new software product.

Nevertheless, there is an important lesson to be learned from this otherwise poor analogy. Whether we are dealing with portraits or software products, it is easier to create a new version than to modify an existing version. In the case of the portrait, not only was it all but impossible to modify the existing portrait, but the cost of doing so would surely have been more than the cost of painting a new portrait from scratch. In the case of the software product, not only were the changes feasible, but the cost of doing them would be a fraction of the cost of developing a new software product from scratch. In other words, even though it is harder to make changes to existing artifacts than to construct new artifacts from scratch, economic considerations make maintenance far preferable to redevelopment.

## 15.2   Why Postdelivery Maintenance Is Necessary

There are three main reasons for making changes to a product:

1. A fault needs correcting, whether an analysis fault, design fault, coding fault, documentation fault, or any other type of fault. This is termed **corrective maintenance**.
2. In **perfective maintenance**, a change is made to the code to improve the effectiveness of the product. For instance, the client may wish additional functionality or request that the product be modified so that it runs faster. Improving the maintainability of a product is another example of perfective maintenance.
3. In **adaptive maintenance**, a change is made to the product to react to a change in the environment in which the product operates. For example, a product almost certainly has to be modified if it is ported to a new compiler, operating system, or hardware. With each change to the tax code, a product that prepares tax returns has to be modified accordingly. When the U.S. Postal Service introduced nine-digit ZIP codes in 1981, products that had allowed for only five-digit ZIP codes had to be changed. Adaptive maintenance is not requested by a client; instead, it is externally imposed on the client.

## 15.3   What Is Required of Postdelivery Maintenance Programmers?

During the software life cycle, more time is spent on postdelivery maintenance than on any other activity. In fact, on average, at least 67 percent of the total cost of a product can be attributed to postdelivery maintenance, as shown in Figure 1.3. But many organizations, even today, assign the task of postdelivery maintenance to beginners and less competent programmers, leaving the "glamorous" job of product development to better or more experienced programmers.

In fact, postdelivery maintenance is the most difficult of all aspects of software production. A major reason is that postdelivery maintenance incorporates aspects of all the other workflows of the software process. Consider what happens when a defect report is handed to a maintenance programmer (recall from Section 1.11 that a **defect** is a generic term for a fault, failure, or error). A defect report is filed if, in the opinion of the user, the product is not working as specified in the user manual. A number of causes are possible. First, nothing at all could be wrong; perhaps the user has misunderstood the user manual or is using the product incorrectly. Alternatively, if there is a fault in the product, it simply might be that the user manual has been badly worded and nothing is wrong with the code itself. Usually, however, there is a fault in the code. But, before making any changes, the maintenance programmer has to determine exactly where the fault lies, using the defect report filed by the user, the source code, and often nothing else. Therefore, the maintenance programmer needs to have far above average debugging skills, because the fault could lie anywhere within the product. And the original cause of the defect might lie in the by now nonexistent analysis or design artifacts.

Suppose that the maintenance programmer has located a fault and must fix it without inadvertently introducing another fault elsewhere in the product, that is, a **regression fault**. If regression faults are to be minimized, detailed documentation for the product as a whole and each individual code artifact must be available. However, software professionals are notorious for their dislike of paperwork of all kinds, especially documentation; and it is quite common for the documentation to be incomplete, erroneous, or totally missing. In these cases, the maintenance programmer has to deduce from the source code itself, the only valid form of documentation available, all the information needed to avoid introducing a regression fault.

Having determined the probable fault and tried to correct it, the maintenance programmer now must test that the modification works correctly and no regression faults have been introduced. To check the modification itself, the maintenance programmer must construct special test cases; checking for regression faults is done using the set of test data stored precisely for performing **regression testing** (Section 3.8). Then the test cases constructed for checking the modification must be added to the set of stored test cases to be used for future regression testing of the modified product. In addition, if changes to the analysis or design had to be made to correct the fault, then these changes also must be checked. Expertise in testing therefore is an additional prerequisite for postdelivery maintenance. Finally, it is essential that the maintenance programmer document every change. The preceding discussion relates to corrective maintenance. For that task, the maintenance programmer primarily must be a superb diagnostician to determine if there is a fault and, if so, an expert technician to fix it.

The other major maintenance tasks are adaptive and perfective maintenance. To perform these, the maintenance programmer must perform the requirements, analysis, design, and implementation workflows, taking the existing product as the starting point. For some types of changes, additional code artifacts have to be designed and implemented. In other cases, changes to the design and implementation of existing code artifacts are needed. Therefore, whereas specifications frequently are produced by analysis experts, designs by design experts, and code by programming experts, a maintenance programmer has to be an expert in all three areas. Perfective and adaptive maintenance are adversely affected by a lack of adequate documentation, just like corrective maintenance. Furthermore, the ability to design suitable test cases and write good documentation is needed for perfective and

In *Practical Software Maintenance*, Tom Pigoski [1996] describes how he set up a U.S. Navy postdelivery maintenance organization in Pensacola, Florida. His idea was that, if prospective employees were told in advance that they were to work as maintainers, they would have a positive attitude toward postdelivery maintenance. In addition, he tried to keep morale high by ensuring that all employees received plenty of training and had the opportunity to travel all over the world in the course of their work. The beautiful nearby beaches certainly helped, as did the brand-new building they occupied.

Nevertheless, within 6 months of starting work at the postdelivery maintenance organization, every employee asked when he or she could do some development work. It seems that it is extremely hard to change the attitudes of individuals toward postdelivery maintenance.

---

adaptive maintenance, just as in corrective maintenance. Therefore, none of the forms of maintenance is a task for a less experienced programmer unless a top-rank computer professional supervises the process.

From the preceding discussion, it is clear that maintenance programmers have to possess almost every technical skill that a software professional could have. But what does he or she get in return?

- Postdelivery maintenance is a thankless task in every way. Maintainers deal with dissatisfied users; if the user were happy with the product, it would not need maintenance.
- The user's problems have frequently been caused by the individuals who developed the product, not the maintainer.
- The code itself may be badly written, adding to the frustrations of the maintainer.
- Postdelivery maintenance is looked down on by many software developers, who consider development to be a glamorous job and maintenance to be drudge work fit only for junior programmers or incompetents.

Postdelivery maintenance can be likened to after-sales service. The product has been delivered to the client. But the client is dissatisfied, because the product does not work correctly, it does not do everything that the client currently wants, or the circumstances for which the product was built have changed in some way. Unless the software organization provides good maintenance service, the client will take all future product development business elsewhere. When the client and software group are part of the same organization, and hence inextricably tied from the viewpoint of future work, a dissatisfied client may use every means, fair or foul, to discredit the software group. This, in turn, leads to an erosion of confidence, from both outside and inside the software group, and resignations and dismissals. It is important for every software organization to keep its clients happy by providing excellent postdelivery maintenance service. So, for product after product, postdelivery maintenance is the most challenging aspect of software production—and frequently the most thankless.

How can this situation be changed? Managers must restrict postdelivery maintenance tasks to programmers with all the skills needed to perform maintenance. They must make it known that only top computer professionals merit maintenance assignments in their organization and pay them accordingly. If management believes that postdelivery maintenance is a challenge and good maintenance is critical for the success of the organization, attitudes toward postdelivery maintenance will slowly improve (but see Just in Case You Wanted to Know Box 15.2).

Some of the problems that maintenance programmers face are now highlighted in a mini case study.

*Mini Case Study*

### 15.4   *Postdelivery Maintenance Mini Case Study*

In countries with centralized economies, the government controls the distribution and marketing of agricultural products. In one such country, temperate fruits, such as peaches, apples, and pears, were the responsibility of the Temperate Fruit Committee (TFC). One day, the chairman of the TFC asked a government computer consultant to computerize the operations of the TFC. The chairman informed the consultant that there are exactly seven temperate fruits: apples, apricots, cherries, nectarines, peaches, pears, and plums. The database was to be designed for those seven fruits, no more and no less. After all, that was the way that the world was, and the consultant was not to waste time and money allowing for any sort of expandability.

The product was duly delivered to the TFC. About a year later, the chairman summoned the maintenance programmer responsible for the product. "What do you know about kiwi fruit?" asked the chairman. "Nothing," replied the mystified programmer. "Well," said the chairman, "it seems that kiwi fruit is a temperate fruit that has just started to be grown in our country, and the TFC is responsible for it. Please change the product accordingly."

The maintenance programmer discovered that the consultant fortunately had not carried out the chairman's original instructions to the letter. The good practice of allowing for some sort of future expansion was too ingrained, and the consultant had provided a number of unused fields in the relevant database records. By slightly rearranging certain items, the maintenance programmer was able to incorporate kiwi fruit, the eighth temperate fruit, into the product.

Another year went by, and the product functioned well. Then the maintenance programmer again was called to the chairman's office. The chairman was in a good mood. He jovially informed the programmer that the government had reorganized the distribution and marketing of agricultural products. His committee was now responsible for all fruit produced in that country, not just temperate fruit, and so the product now had to be modified to incorporate the 26 additional kinds of fruit on the list he handed to the maintenance programmer. The programmer protested, pointing out that this change would take almost as long as rewriting the product from scratch. "Nonsense," replied the chairman. "You had no trouble adding kiwi fruit. Just do the same thing another 26 times!"

A number of important lessons are to be learned from this:

- The problem with the product, no provision for expansion, was caused by the developer, not the maintainer. The developer made the mistake of obeying the chairman's instruction regarding future expandability of the product, but the maintenance programmer suffered the consequences. In fact, unless she reads this book, the consultant who developed the original product may never realize that her product was anything but a success. One of the more annoying aspects of postdelivery maintenance is that the maintainer is responsible for fixing other people's mistakes. The person who caused the problem either has other duties or has left the organization, but the maintenance programmer is left holding the baby.

- The client frequently does not understand that postdelivery maintenance can be difficult or, in some instances, all but impossible. The problem is exacerbated when the maintenance programmer has successfully carried out previous perfective and adaptive maintenance tasks but suddenly protests that a new assignment cannot be done, even though superficially it seems no different from what has been done before with little difficulty.

- All software development must be carried out with an eye on future postdelivery maintenance. If the consultant had designed the product for an arbitrary number of different kinds of fruit, there would have been no difficulty in incorporating first the kiwi fruit and then the 26 other kinds of fruit.

As stated many times, postdelivery maintenance is a vital aspect of software production, and the one that consumes the most resources. During product development, it is essential that the development team never forget the maintenance programmer, who will be responsible for the product once it has been installed.

## 15.5 Management of Postdelivery Maintenance

Issues regarding management of postdelivery maintenance are now considered.

### 15.5.1 Defect Reports

The first thing needed when maintaining a product is a mechanism for changing the product. With regard to corrective maintenance, that is, removing residual faults, if the product appears to be functioning incorrectly, then a **defect report** should be filed by the user. This must include enough information to enable the maintenance programmer to re-create the problem, which usually is some sort of software failure. In addition, the maintenance programmer must indicate the severity of the defect; typical severity categories include critical, major, normal, minor, and trivial.

Ideally, every defect reported by a user should be fixed immediately. In practice, programming organizations usually are understaffed, with a backlog of work, both development and maintenance. If the defect is critical, such as if a payroll product crashes the day before payday or overpays or underpays employees, immediate corrective action must be taken. Otherwise, each defect report must at least receive an immediate preliminary investigation.

The maintenance programmer should first consult the defect report file. This contains all reported defects that have not yet been fixed, together with suggestions for working around them, that is, ways for the user to bypass the portion of the product that apparently is responsible for the failure, until such time as the defect can be fixed. If the defect has been reported previously, any information in the defect report file should be given to the user. But, if what the user reports appears to be a new defect, then the maintenance programmer should study the problem and attempt to find the cause and a way to fix it. In addition, an attempt should be made to find a way to work around the problem, because it may take 6 or 9 months before someone can be assigned to make the necessary changes to the software. In the light of the serious shortage of programmers and in particular programmers good enough to perform maintenance, suggesting a way to live with the defect until it can be solved often is the only way to deal with defect reports that are not true emergencies.

The maintenance programmer's conclusions should be added to the defect report file, together with any supporting documentation, such as listings, designs, and manuals used to arrive at those conclusions. The manager in charge of postdelivery maintenance should consult the file regularly, setting priorities for the various fixes. The file also should contain the client's requests for perfective and adaptive maintenance. The next modification made to the product then will be the one with the highest priority.

When copies of a product have been distributed to a variety of sites, copies of defect reports must be circulated to all users of the product, together with an estimate of when each defect can be fixed. Then, if the same failure occurs at another site, the user can consult the relevant defect report to determine if it is possible to work around the defect and when it will be fixed. It would be preferable to fix every defect immediately and distribute a new version of the product to all sites, of course. Given the current worldwide shortage of good programmers and the realities of postdelivery software maintenance, distributing defect reports probably is the best that can be done.

There is another reason why defects usually are not fixed immediately. It almost always is cheaper to make a number of changes, test them all, change the documentation, and install the new version than it is to perform each change separately, test it, document it, install the new version, and then repeat the entire cycle for the next change. This is particularly true if every new version has to be installed on a significant number of computers (such as a large number of clients in a client–server network) or when the software is running at different sites. As a result, organizations prefer to accumulate noncritical maintenance tasks and then implement the changes as a group.

## 15.5.2 Authorizing Changes to the Product

Once a decision has been made to perform corrective maintenance, a maintenance programmer is assigned the task of determining the fault that caused the failure and repairing it. After the code has been changed, the repair must be tested, as must the product as a whole (regression testing). Then, the documentation must be updated to reflect the changes. In particular, a detailed description of what was changed, why it was changed, by whom, and when must be added to the prologue comments of any changed code artifact (Figure 14.1). If necessary, analysis or design artifacts also are changed. A similar set of steps is followed when performing perfective or adaptive maintenance; the only real difference is that perfective and adaptive maintenance are initiated by a change in requirements rather than by a defect report.

At this point all that would seem to be needed would be to distribute the new version to the users. But, what if the maintenance programmer has not tested the repair adequately? Before the product is distributed, it must be subjected to software quality assurance performed by an independent group; that is, the members of the maintenance SQA group must not report to the same manager as the maintenance programmer. It is important that the SQA group remain managerially independent (Section 6.1.2).

Reasons were given previously as to why postdelivery maintenance is difficult. For those same reasons, maintenance also is fault prone. Testing during postdelivery maintenance is difficult and time consuming, and the SQA group should not underestimate the implications of software maintenance with regard to testing. Once the new version has been approved by the SQA group, it can be distributed.

Another area in which management must ensure that procedures are followed carefully is when the technique of baselines and private copies (Section 5.8.2) is used. Suppose a programmer wishes to change **Tax Provision Class.** The programmer makes copies of **Tax Provision Class** and all the other code artifacts needed to perform the required maintenance task; often this includes all the other classes in the product. The programmer makes the necessary changes to **Tax Provision Class** and tests them. Now, the previous version of **Tax Provision Class** is frozen, and the modified version of **Tax Provision Class** incorporating the changes is installed in the baseline. But, when the modified product is delivered to the user, it immediately crashes. What went wrong is that the maintenance programmer tested the modified version of **Tax Provision Class** using his or her private workspace copies, that is, the copies of the other code artifacts that were in the baseline at the time that maintenance of **Tax Provision Class** was started. In the meantime, certain other code artifacts were updated by other maintenance programmers working on the same product. The lesson is clear: Before installing a code artifact, it must be tested using the current baseline versions of all the other code artifacts and not the programmer's private versions. This is a further reason for stipulating an independent SQA group— members of the SQA group simply have no access to programmers' private workspaces. A third reason is that it has been estimated that the initial correction of a fault is itself incorrect some 70 percent of the time [Parnas, 1999].

## 15.5.3  Ensuring Maintainability

Postdelivery maintenance is not a one-time effort. A well-written product goes through a series of versions over its lifetime. As a result, it is necessary to plan for postdelivery maintenance during the entire software process. During the design workflow, for example, information-hiding techniques (Section 7.6) should be employed; during implementation, variable names should be selected that will be meaningful to future maintenance programmers (Section 14.3). Documentation should be complete, correct, and reflect the current version of every component code artifact of the product.

During postdelivery maintenance, it is important not to compromise the maintainability that has been built into the product from the very beginning. In other words, just as software development personnel always should be conscious of the inevitable postdelivery maintenance, so software maintenance personnel always should be conscious of the equally inevitable further future postdelivery maintenance. The principles established for maintainability during development apply equally to postdelivery maintenance.

## 15.5.4  Problem of Repeated Maintenance

One of the more frustrating difficulties of software development is the **moving-target problem** (Section 2.4). As fast as the developer constructs the product, the client can change the requirements. Not only is this frustrating to the development team, frequent changes can result in a poorly constructed product. In addition, such changes add to the cost of the product.

The problem is exacerbated during postdelivery maintenance. The more a completed product is changed, the more it deviates from its original design, and the more difficult further changes become. Under repeated maintenance, the documentation is likely to become even less reliable than usual, and the regression testing files may not be up to date. If still more maintenance is done, the product as a whole may first have to be completely rewritten.

The problem of the moving target clearly is a management problem. In theory, if management is sufficiently firm with the client and explains the problem at the beginning of the project, then the requirements can be frozen from the time the specifications are signed off on until the product is delivered. Again, after each request for perfective maintenance, the requirements can be frozen for, say, 3 months or 1 year. In practice, it does not work that way. For example, if the client happens to be the president of the corporation and the development organization is the software division of that corporation, then the president can order changes every Monday and Thursday and they will be implemented. The old proverb, "He who pays the piper calls the tune," unfortunately is all too relevant in this situation. Perhaps, the best that the vice-president for software can do is to try to explain to the president the effect on the product of repeated maintenance, and then simply have the complete product rewritten whenever further maintenance would be hazardous to the integrity of the product.

Trying to discourage additional maintenance by ensuring that the requested changes are implemented slowly may mean that the relevant personnel are replaced by others prepared to do the job faster. In short, if the person who requests repeated changes has sufficient clout, there is no solution to the problem of the moving target.

## 15.6   Maintenance of Object-Oriented Software

One reason put forward for using the object-oriented paradigm is that it promotes maintainability. After all, an object is an independent unit of a program. More specifically, a well-designed object exhibits conceptual independence, otherwise known as **encapsulation** (Section 7.4). Every aspect of the product that relates to the portion of the real world modeled by that object is localized to the object itself. In addition, objects exhibit physical independence; information hiding is employed to ensure that implementation details are not visible outside that object (Section 7.6). The only form of communication permitted is sending a message to the object to invoke a specific method.

As a consequence, the argument goes, it is easy to maintain an object for two reasons. First, conceptual independence means it is easy to determine which part of a product must be changed to achieve a specific maintenance goal, be it enhancement or corrective maintenance. Second, information hiding ensures that a change made to an object has no impact outside that object, and hence the number of regression faults is reduced greatly.

In practice, however, the situation is not quite this idyllic. In fact, three obstacles are specific to the maintenance of object-oriented software. One of the problems can be solved through use of appropriate CASE tools, but the others are less tractable:

1. Consider the C++ class hierarchy shown in Figure 15.1. Method displayNode is defined in **UndirectedTreeClass**, inherited by **DirectedTreeClass**, and then redefined in **RootedTreeClass**. This redefined version is inherited by **BinaryTreeClass** and

**FIGURE 15.1**
C++ implementation of a class hierarchy.

```
class UndirectedTreeClass
{
    ...
    void displayNode (Node a);
    ...
}// class UndirectedTreeClass

class DirectedTreeClass : public UndirectedTreeClass
{

    ...
}// class DirectedTreeClass

class RootedTreeClass : public DirectedTreeClass
{

    ...
    void displayNode (Node a);
    ...
}// class RootedTreeClass

class BinaryTreeClass : public RootedTreeClass
{

    ...
}// class BinaryTreeClass

class BalancedBinaryTreeClass : public BinaryTreeClass
{
    Node        hhh;
    displayNode (hhh);
}// class BalancedBinaryTreeClass
```

**BalancedBinaryTreeClass** and utilized in **BalancedBinaryTreeClass**. Therefore, a maintenance programmer has to study the complete inheritance hierarchy to understand **BalancedBinaryTreeClass**. Worse, the hierarchy may not be displayed in the linear fashion of Figure 15.1 but generally is spread over the entire product. So, to understand what displayNode does in **BalancedBinaryTreeClass**, the maintenance programmer may have to peruse a major proportion of the product. This is a far cry from the "independent" object described at the beginning of this section. The solution to this problem is straightforward: use the appropriate CASE tool. Just as a C++ compiler can resolve precisely the version of displayNode within instances of the class **BalancedBinaryTreeClass**, so a programming workbench can provide a "flattened" version of a class, that is, a definition of the class with all features inherited directly or indirectly appearing explicitly, with any renaming or redefinition incorporated. The flattened form of **BalancedBinaryTreeClass** of Figure 15.1 includes the definition of displayNode from **RootedTreeClass**.

2. Another obstacle to the maintenance of a product implemented using an object-oriented language is less easy to solve. It arises as a consequence of polymorphism and dynamic binding, concepts explained in Section 7.8. An example was given in that section, a base class named **File Class**, together with three subclasses: **Disk File Class**, **Tape File**

**FIGURE 15.2**
Definition of
base class **File
Class** with
derived classes
**Disk File
Class**, **Tape
File Class**, and
**Diskette File
Class**.

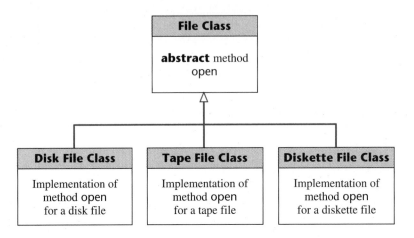

**Class**, and **Diskette File Class**. This is shown in Figure 7.33(b), reproduced here for convenience as Figure 15.2. In base class **File Class**, a dummy (**abstract** or **virtual**) method open is declared. Then, a specific implementation of the method appears in each of the three subclasses; each method is given the identical name, open, as shown in Figure 15.2. Suppose that myFile is declared to be an object, an instance of **File Class**, and the code to be maintained contains the message myFile.open (). As a consequence of polymorphism and dynamic binding, at run time, myFile could be a member of any of the three derived classes of **File Class**, that is, a disk file, a tape file, or a diskette file. Once the run-time system has determined in which derived class it is, the appropriate version of open is invoked. This can have adverse consequences for maintenance. If a maintenance programmer encounters the call myFile.open () in the code, then, to understand that part of the product, he or she has to consider what would happen if myFile were an instance of each of the three subclasses. A CASE tool cannot help here, because, in general, there is no way to resolve dynamic binding issues using static methods. The only way to determine which of a number of dynamic bindings actually occurs in a particular set of circumstances is to trace through the code, either by running it on a computer or tracing through it manually. Polymorphism and dynamic binding indeed are extremely powerful aspects of object-oriented technology that promote the development of an object-oriented product. However, they can have a deleterious impact on maintenance, by forcing the maintenance programmer to investigate a wide variety of possible bindings that might occur at run time and hence determine which of a number of different methods could be invoked at that point in the code.

3. The final problem arises as a consequence of **inheritance**. Suppose a particular base class does most, but not all, of what is required for the design of a new product. A derived class now is defined, that is, a class identical to the base class in many ways, but new features may be added and existing features renamed, reimplemented, suppressed, or changed in other ways. Furthermore, these changes may be made without having an effect on the base class or any other derived classes. However, suppose now that the base class itself is changed. If this happens, all derived classes are changed in the same way. In other words, the strength of inheritance is that new leaves can be added

to the inheritance tree (or graph, if the implementation language supports multiple inheritance, as C++ does) without altering any other class in the tree. But, if an interior node of the tree is changed in any way, then this change is propagated to all its descendants (the **fragile base class problem**).

Thus, inheritance is another feature of object-oriented technology that can have a major positive influence on development but a negative impact on maintenance.

## 15.7  Postdelivery Maintenance Skills versus Development Skills

Earlier in this chapter, much was said about the skills needed for postdelivery maintenance.

- For corrective maintenance, the ability to determine the cause of a failure of a large product was deemed essential. But this skill is not needed exclusively for postdelivery maintenance. It is used throughout integration and product testing.
- Another vital skill is the ability to function effectively without adequate documentation. Again, the documentation rarely is complete while integration and product testing are under way.
- Also stressed was that skills with regard to analysis, design, implementation, and testing are essential for adaptive and perfective maintenance. These activities also are carried out during the development process, and each requires specialized skills if it is to be performed correctly.

In other words, the skills a postdelivery maintenance programmer needs are in no way different from those needed by software professionals specializing in other aspects of software production. The key point is that a maintenance programmer must not be merely skilled in a broad variety of areas but *highly* skilled in *all* those areas. Although the average software developer can specialize in one area of software development, such as design or testing, the software maintainer must be a specialist in virtually every area of software production. After all, postdelivery maintenance is the same as development, only more so.

## 15.8  Reverse Engineering

As has been pointed out, sometimes the only documentation available for postdelivery maintenance is the source code itself. (This happens all too frequently when maintaining **legacy systems**, that is, software in current use but developed some 15 or 20 years ago, if not earlier.) Under these circumstances, maintaining the code can be extremely difficult. One way of handling this problem is to start with the source code and attempt to re-create the design documents or even the specifications. This process is called **reverse engineering**.

CASE tools can assist with this process. One of the simplest is a pretty printer (Section 5.6), which may help display the code more clearly. Other tools construct diagrams, such as flowcharts or UML diagrams, directly from the source code; these visual aids can help in the process of design recovery.

Once the maintenance team has reconstructed the design, there are two possibilities. One alternative is to attempt to reconstruct the specifications, modify the reconstructed specifications to reflect the necessary changes, and reimplement the product the usual way. (Within the context of reverse engineering, the usual development process that proceeds from analysis through design to implementation is called **forward engineering**. The process of reverse engineering followed by forward engineering sometimes is called **reengineering**.) In practice, reconstruction of the specifications is an extremely hard task. More frequently, the reconstructed design is modified and the modified design then is forward engineered.

A related activity often performed during maintenance is restructuring. Reverse engineering takes the product from a lower level of abstraction to a higher level of abstraction, for example, from code to design. Forward engineering takes the product from a higher level of abstraction to a lower level. **Restructuring**, however, takes place at the same level. It is the process of improving the product without changing its functionality. Pretty printing is one form of restructuring, and so is converting code from unstructured to structured form. In general, restructuring is performed to make the source code (or design or even the database) easier to maintain. When an agile process (Section 2.9.5) is used, the design modification known as **refactoring** is another example of restructuring.

A worse situation occurs if the source code is lost and the executable version of the product is all that is available. At first sight, it might seem that the only possible way to re-create the source code is to use a disassembler to create assembler code and then to build a tool (that might be termed a *reverse compiler*) to try to re-create the original high-level language code. A number of virtually insurmountable problems accompany this approach:

- The names of the variables will have been lost as a consequence of the original compilation.
- Many compilers optimize the code in some way, making it extremely difficult to attempt to re-create the source code.
- A construct such as a loop in the assembler could correspond to a number of different possible constructs in the source code.

In practice, therefore, the existing product is treated as a black box and reverse engineering is used to deduce the specifications from the behavior of the current product. The reconstructed specifications are modified as required, and a new version of the product is forward engineered from those specifications.

## 15.9 Testing during Postdelivery Maintenance

While the product is being developed, many members of the development team have a broad overview of the product as a whole, but as a result of the rapid personnel turnover in the computer industry, it is unlikely that members of the postdelivery maintenance team have been involved in the original development. Therefore, the maintainer tends to see the product as a set of loosely related components and generally is not aware that a change to one code artifact may seriously affect one or more other artifacts and hence the product as a whole. Even if the maintainer wished to understand every aspect of the product, the pressures to fix or to extend the product generally are such that no time is allowed for the detailed study needed to achieve this. Furthermore, in many cases, little or no documentation is available to assist in gaining that understanding. One way of trying to minimize this diffi-culty is to use regression testing, that is, testing the changed product against previous test cases to ensure that it still works correctly.

For this reason, it is vital to store all test cases, together with their expected outcomes, in machine-readable form. As a result of changes made to the product, certain stored test cases may have to be modified. For example, if salary withholding percentages change as a consequence of tax legislation, then the correct output from a payroll product for each test case involving withholding changes, too. Similarly, if satellite observations lead to correc-tions in the latitude and longitude of an island, then the correct output from a product that calculates the position of an aircraft using the coordinates of the island must correspond-ingly change. Depending on the maintenance performed, some valid test cases become invalid. But the computations that need to be made to correct the stored test cases are essentially the same as would have to be made to set up new test data for checking that the maintenance has been correctly performed. No additional work therefore is involved in maintaining the file of test cases and their expected outcomes.

It can be argued that regression testing is a waste of time because regression testing requires the complete product to be retested against a host of test cases, most of which apparently have nothing to do with the code artifacts modified in the course of product maintenance. The word *apparently* in the previous sentence is critical. The dangers of unwitting side effects of maintenance (that is, the introduction of regression faults) are too great for that argument to hold water; regression testing is an essential aspect of mainte-nance in all situations.

## 15.10  CASE Tools for Postdelivery Maintenance

It is unreasonable to expect maintenance programmers to keep track manually of the vari-ous revision numbers and assign the next revision number each time a code artifact is up-dated. Unless the operating system incorporates version control, a version-control tool such as the UNIX tools *sccs* (source code control system) [Rochkind, 1975] and *rcs* (revision control system) [Tichy, 1985], or open-source product CVS (concurrent versions system) [Loukides and Oram, 1997], is needed. It is equally unreasonable to expect manual control of the freezing technique described in Chapter 5 or any other manual way of ensuring that revisions are updated appropriately. A configuration-control tool is needed. Typical exam-ples of commercial tools are CCC (change and configuration control) and IBM Rational ClearCase. Even if the software organization does not wish to purchase a complete configuration-control tool, at the very least a build tool must be used in conjunction with a version-control tool. Another category of CASE tool virtually essential during postdelivery maintenance is a defect-tracking tool that keeps a record of reported defects not yet fixed.

Section 15.8 described some categories of CASE tools that can assist in reverse engi-neering and reengineering. Examples of such tools that assist by creating visual displays of the structure of the product include IBM Rational Rose and Together. Doxygen is an open-source tool of this kind.

Defect tracking is an important aspect of postdelivery maintenance. It is vital to be able to determine the current status of every reported defect. IBM Rational ClearQuest is a commercial **defect-tracking tool**, and Bugzilla is a popular open-source tool. Such tools can be used to record the severity of a defect (Section 15.5.1) and its status (essentially, whether or not the defect has been fixed). In addition, some defect-tracking tools can link a defect report to the configuration management tool so that, when a new version is built, the maintenance programmer can select specific defect report fixes to be included in the build.

Postdelivery maintenance is difficult and frustrating. The very least that management can do is to provide the maintenance team the tools needed for efficient and effective product maintenance.

## 15.11 Metrics for Postdelivery Maintenance

The activities of postdelivery maintenance essentially are analysis, design, implementation, testing, and documentation. Therefore, the metrics that measure these activities are equally applicable to maintenance. For example, the complexity metrics of Section 14.13.2 are relevant to postdelivery maintenance, in that a code artifact with high complexity is a likely candidate for inducing a regression fault. Particular care must be taken in modifying such a code artifact.

In addition, metrics specific to postdelivery maintenance include measures relating to software defect reports, such as the total number of defects reported and classification of those defects by severity and type. In addition, information regarding the current status of the defect reports is needed. For example, there is a considerable difference between having 13 critical defects reported and fixed during 2006 and having only 2 critical defects reported during that year but neither of them fixed.

## 15.12 Postdelivery Maintenance: The MSG Foundation Case Study

A number of faults have been seeded in the source code of the MSG Foundation case study. In addition, perfective maintenance must be performed. These maintenance tasks are left as exercises (Problems 15.11 through 15.16).

## 15.13 Challenges of Postdelivery Maintenance

This chapter describes numerous challenges of postdelivery maintenance. The toughest one to change is that maintenance is generally harder than development, yet maintenance programmers are often looked down on by developers and all too frequently are paid less than developers.

## Chapter Review

The chapter begins with a comparison of development and maintenance (Section 5.1). Postdelivery maintenance is an important and challenging software activity (Sections 15.2 and 15.3). This is illustrated by means of the mini case study of Section 15.4. Issues relating to the management of post-delivery maintenance are described (Section 15.5), including the problem of repeated maintenance (Section 15.5.4). Postdelivery maintenance of object-oriented software is discussed in Section 15.6. The skills that a maintenance programmer needs are the same as those of a developer; the difference is that a developer can specialize in one aspect of the software process, whereas the maintainer must be an expert in all aspects of software production (Section 15.7). A description of reverse engineering is given in Section 15.8. Next follows a description of testing during postdelivery maintenance (Section 15.9) and CASE tools for postdelivery maintenance (Section 15.10). Metrics for postdelivery maintenance are described in Section 15.11. Postdelivery maintenance of the MSG Foundation case study, discussed in Section 15.12, is left as an exercise. The chapter concludes with a discussion of the challenges of postdelivery maintenance (Section 15.13).

## For Further Reading

A classic source of information on postdelivery maintenance is [Lientz and Swanson, 1978], although some of the results are now being questioned (see Just in Case You Wanted to Know Box 1.3). Regression test case selection is discussed in [Harrold, Rosenblum, Rothermel, and Weyuker, 2001] and setting priorities of regression test cases in [Rothermel, Untch, Chu, and Harrold, 2001]. Regression testing in an industrial environment is discussed in [Onoma, Tsai, Poonawala, and Suganuma, 1998]. A method for estimating staffing needs during postdelivery maintenance is described in [Antoniol, Cimitile, Di Lucca, and Di Penta, 2004].

Planning reengineering is covered in [Sneed, 1995], one of the many articles on reengineering in the January 1995 issue of *IEEE Software*. The costs and benefits of reengineering are discussed in [Adolph, 1996]. Charette, Adams, and White [1997] describe risk management within the framework of postdelivery maintenance, and von Mayrhauser and Vana [1997] discuss various mechanisms of program comprehension for postdelivery maintenance of large-scale products.

A profile of successful reengineering projects is given in [Teng, Jeong, and Grover, 1998]. Maintenance of legacy software products is described in [Bisbal, Lawless, Wu, and Grimson, 1999]. Fioravanti and Nesi [2001] present metrics for estimating adaptive maintenance effort. Problems of comprehension of legacy systems are discussed in [Rajlich, Wilde, Buckellew, and Page, 2001]. The importance of traceability within the context of reengineering is the subject of [Ebner and Kaindl, 2002]. The use of metrics within the context of maintainability is discussed in [Bandi, Vaishnavi, and Turk, 2003]. Problems that can arise in the maintenance of open-source software are presented in [Samoladas, Stamelos, Angelis, and Oikonomou, 2005].

The impact on postdelivery maintenance of the use of objects is described in [Henry and Humphrey, 1990] and [Mancl and Havanas, 1990]. Postdelivery maintenance of specific object-oriented products is described in [Lejter, Meyers, and Reiss, 1992] and [Wilde, Matthews, and Huitt, 1993]. Briand, Bunse, and Daly [2001] discuss the maintainability of object-oriented designs. Experiments to assess the impact of design pattern documentation on postdelivery maintenance are described in [Prechelt, Unger-Lamprecht, Philippsen, and Tichy, 2002]. The maintainability of object-oriented software is discussed in [Lim, Jeong, and Schach, 2005] and [Freeman and Schach, 2005].

Papers on software maintenance appear in the May 1994 issue of *Communications of the ACM*. The July/August 1998 issue of *IEEE Software* contains a number of articles on legacy systems, especially [Rugaber and White, 1998]. The proceedings of the annual Conference on Software Maintenance are a broadly based source of information on all aspects of maintenance.

**Key Terms**

adaptive maintenance *517*
corrective maintenance *517*
defect *518*
defect report *521*
defect-tracking tool *530*
encapsulation *524*
evolution *516*

forward engineering *528*
fragile base class problem *527*
inheritance *526*
legacy system *527*
moving-target problem *523*
perfective maintenance *517*
postdelivery maintenance *515*

reengineering *528*
refactoring *528*
regression fault *518*
regression testing *518*
restructuring *528*
reverse engineering *527*

**Problems**

15.1 Why do you think that the mistake is frequently made of considering postdelivery software maintenance to be inferior to software development?

15.2 Consider a product that determines whether a computer is virus free. Describe why such a product is likely to have multiple variations of many of its code artifacts. What are the implications for postdelivery maintenance? How can the resulting problems be solved?

15.3 Repeat Problem 15.2 for the automated library circulation system of Problem 8.7.

15.4 Repeat Problem 15.2 for the product of Problem 8.8 that checks whether a bank statement is correct.

15.5 Repeat Problem 15.2 for the automated teller machine of Problem 8.9.

15.6 You are the manager in charge of postdelivery maintenance in a large software organization. What qualities do you look for when hiring new employees?

15.7 What are the implications of postdelivery maintenance for a one-person software production organization?

15.8 You have been asked to build a computerized defect report file. What sort of data would you store in the file? What sort of queries could be answered by your tool? What sort of queries could not be answered by your tool?

15.9 You receive a memo from the vice-president for software maintenance of Ye Olde Fashioned Software Corporation (Problem 14.24), pointing out that, for the foreseeable future, Olde Fashioned will have to maintain tens of millions of lines of COBOL code and asking your advice with regard to CASE tools for such postdelivery maintenance. What do you reply?

15.10 (Term Project) Suppose that the product for Osric's Office Appliances and Decor of Appendix A has been implemented exactly as described. Now Osric wants the product to be modified so that the priority of a customer in the queue can be manually changed. In what ways will the existing product have to be modified? Would it be better to discard everything and start again from scratch? Compare your answer to the answer you gave to Problem 1.17.

15.11 (Case Study) Improve the aesthetic appearance of the reports in the implementation of Section 14.8 by adjusting the horizontal alignment of the various components.

15.12 (Case Study) Suppose that the requirements of the MSG Foundation are changed so that a couple will never have to pay more than 26 percent of their gross income each week to the MSG Foundation (rather than 28 percent as currently stipulated). In how many places does the implementation of Section 14.8 have to be changed?

15.13 (Case Study) The MSG Foundation has decided that it will now operate on a monthly basis, rather than a weekly basis. Modify the implementation of Section 14.8 accordingly.

15.14 (Case Study) Replace the menu-driven input routines in the implementation of Section 14.8 with a graphical user interface (GUI).

15.15 (Case Study) Modify the implementation of Section 14.8 to make it Web-based.

15.16 (Readings in Software Engineering) Your instructor will distribute copies of [Freeman and Schach, 2005]. Do you feel that the paper resolves the question of whether object orientation promotes maintainability? Justify your answer.

**References**   [Adolph, 1996] W. S. ADOLPH, "Cash Cow in the Tar Pit: Reengineering a Legacy System," *IEEE Software* **13** (May 1996), pp. 41–47.

[Antoniol, Cimitile, Di Lucca, and Di Penta, 2004] G. ANTONIOL, A. CIMITILE, G. A. DI LUCCA, AND M. DI PENTA, "Assessing Staffing Needs for a Software Maintenance Project through Queuing Simulation," *IEEE Transactions on Software Engineering* **30** (January 2004), pp. 43–58.

[Bandi, Vaishnavi, and Turk, 2003] R. K. BANDI, V. K. VAISHNAVI, AND D. E. TURK, "Predicting Maintenance Performance Using Object-Oriented Design Complexity Metrics," *IEEE Transactions on Software Engineering* **29** (January 2003), pp. 77–87.

[Bisbal, Lawless, Wu, and Grimson, 1999] J. BISBAL, D. LAWLESS, B. WU, AND J. GRIMSON, "Legacy Software Products: Issues and Directions," *IEEE Software* **16** (September/October 1999), pp. 103–111.

[Briand, Bunse, and Daly, 2001] L. C. BRIAND, C. BUNSE, AND J. W. DALY, "A Controlled Experiment for Evaluating Quality Guidelines on the Maintainability of Object-Oriented Designs," *IEEE Transactions on Software Engineering* **27** (June 2001), pp. 513–30.

[Charette, Adams, and White, 1997] R. N. CHARETTE, K. M. ADAMS, AND M. B. WHITE, "Managing Risk in Software Maintenance," *IEEE Software* **14** (May/June 1997), pp. 43–50.

[Ebner and Kaindl, 2002] G. EBNER AND H. KAINDL, "Tracing All Around in Reengineering," *IEEE Software* **19** (May/June 2002), pp. 70–77.

[Fioravanti and Nesi, 2001] F. FIORAVANTI AND P. NESI, "Estimation and Prediction Metrics for Adaptive Maintenance Effort of Object-Oriented Systems," *IEEE Transactions on Software Engineering* **27** (December 2001), pp. 1062–84.

[Freeman and Schach, 2005] G. L. FREEMAN, JR., AND S. R. SCHACH, "The Task-Dependent Nature of the Maintenance of Object-Oriented Programs," *Journal of Systems and Software* **76** (May 2005), pp. 195–206.

[Harrold, Rosenblum, Rothermel and Weyuker, 2001] M. J. HARROLD, D. ROSENBLUM, G. ROTHERMEL, AND E. WEYUKER, "Empirical Studies of a Prediction Model for Regression Test Selection," *IEEE Transactions on Software Engineering* **27** (March 2001), pp. 248–63.

[Henry and Humphrey, 1990] S. M. HENRY AND M. HUMPHREY, "A Controlled Experiment to Evaluate Maintainability of Object-Oriented Software," *Proceedings of the IEEE Conference on Software Maintenance*, San Diego, CA, November 1990, pp. 258–65.

[Jacobson, Booch, and Rumbaugh, 1999] I. JACOBSON, G. BOOCH, AND J. RUMBAUGH, *The Unified Software Development Process*, Addison-Wesley, Reading, MA, 1999.

[Lejter, Meyers, and Reiss, 1992] M. LEJTER, S. MEYERS, AND S. P. REISS, "Support for Maintaining Object-Oriented Programs," *IEEE Transactions on Software Engineering* **18** (December 1992), pp. 1045–52.

[Lientz, Swanson, and Tompkins, 1978] B. P. LIENTZ, E. B. SWANSON, AND G. E. TOMPKINS, "Characteristics of Application Software Maintenance," *Communications of the ACM* **21** (June 1978), pp. 466–71.

[Lim, Jeong, and Schach, 2005] J. S. LIM, S. R. JEONG, AND S. R. SCHACH, "An Empirical Investigation of the Impact of the Object-Oriented Paradigm on the Maintainability of Real-World Mission-Critical Software," *Journal of Systems and Software* **77** (August 2005), pp. 131–38.

[Lotto, 1515] L. LOTTO, *Giovanni Agostino della Torre and his Son, Niccolò*, oil on canvas, 1515, www.nationalgallery.org.uk/cgi-bin/WebObjects.dll/CollectionPublisher.woa/wa/largeImage?workNumber=NG699.

[Loukides and Oram, 1997] M. K. LOUKIDES AND A. ORAM, *Programming with GNU Software*, O'Reilly and Associates, Sebastopol, CA, 1997.

[Mancl and Havanas, 1990] D. MANCL AND W. HAVANAS, "A Study of the Impact of C++ on Software Maintenance," *Proceedings of the IEEE Conference on Software Maintenance*, San Diego, CA, November 1990, pp. 63–69.

[Onoma, Tsai, Poonawala, and Suganuma, 1998] A. K. ONOMA, W.-T. TSAI, M. H. POONAWALA, AND H. SUGANUMA, "Regression Testing in an Industrial Environment," *Communications of the ACM* **42** (May 1998), pp. 81–86.

[Parnas, 1999] D. L. PARNAS, "Ten Myths about Y2K Inspections," *Communications of the ACM* **42** (May 1999), p. 128.

[Pigoski, 1996] T. M. PIGOSKI, *Practical Software Maintenance: Best Practices for Managing Your Software Investment*, John Wiley and Sons, New York, 1996.

[Prechelt, Unger-Lamprecht, Philippsen, and Tichy, 2002] L. PRECHELT, B. UNGER-LAMPRECHT, M. PHILIPPSEN, AND W. F. TICHY, "Two Controlled Experiments in Assessing the Usefulness of Design Pattern Documentation in Program Maintenance," *IEEE Transactions on Software Engineering* **28** (June 2002), pp. 595–606.

[Rajlich, Wilde, Buckellew, and Page, 2001] V. RAJLICH, N. WILDE, M. BUCKELLEW, AND H. PAGE, "Software Cultures and Evolution," *IEEE Computer* **34** (September 2001), pp. 24–28.

[Rochkind, 1975] M. J. ROCHKIND, "The Source Code Control System," *IEEE Transactions on Software Engineering* **SE-1** (October 1975), pp. 255–65.

[Rothermel, Untch, Chu, and Harrold, 2001] G. ROTHERMEL, R. H. UNTCH, C. CHU, AND M. J. HARROLD, "Prioritizing Test Cases for Regression Test Cases," *IEEE Transactions on Software Engineering* **27** (October 2001), pp. 929–48.

[Rugaber and White, 1998] S. RUGABER AND J. WHITE, "Restoring a Legacy: Lessons Learned," *IEEE Software* **15** (July/August 1998), pp. 28–33.

[Samoladas, Stamelos, Angelis, and Oikonomou, 2005] I. SAMOLADAS, I. STAMELOS, L. ANGELIS, AND A. OIKONOMOU, "Open Source Software Development Should Strive for Even Greater Code Maintainability," *Communications of the ACM* **47** (October 2004), pp. 83–87.

[Sneed, 1995] H. M. SNEED, "Planning the Reengineering of Legacy Systems," *IEEE Software* **12** (January 1995), pp. 24–34.

[Teng, Jeong, and Grover, 1998] J. T. C. TENG, S. R. JEONG, AND V. GROVER, "Profiling Successful Reengineering Projects," *Communications of the ACM* **41** (June 1999), pp. 96–102.

[Tichy, 1985] W. F. TICHY, "RCS—A System for Version Control," *Software—Practice and Experience* **15** (July 1985), pp. 637–54.

[von Mayrhauser and Vana, 1997] A. VON MAYRHAUSER AND A. M. VANA, "Identification of Dynamic Comprehension Processes during Large Scale Maintenance," *IEEE Transactions on Software Engineering* **22** (June 1996), pp. 424–37.

[Wilde, Matthews, and Huitt, 1993] N. WILDE, P. MATTHEWS, AND R. HUITT, "Maintaining Object-Oriented Software," *IEEE Software* **10** (January 1993), pp. 75–80.

# Chapter 16

# More on UML

### Learning Objectives

After studying this chapter, you should be able to

- Model software using UML use cases, class diagrams, notes, use-case diagrams, interaction diagrams, statecharts, activity diagrams, packages, component diagrams, and deployment diagrams.
- Appreciate that UML is a language, *not* a methodology.

During the course of this book, various elements of UML [Booch, Rumbaugh, and Jacobson, 1999] have been introduced. Specifically, the notation for class diagrams, inheritance, aggregation, and association was described in Chapter 7. In Chapter 10, use cases, use-case diagrams, and notes were introduced; in Chapter 12, statecharts, collaboration diagrams, and sequence diagrams were added.

This subset of UML is adequate for understanding this book and for doing all the exercises, as well as the term project of Appendix A. However, real-world software products are, unfortunately, much larger and considerably more complex than the MSG Foundation case study or the term project of Appendix A. Accordingly, in this chapter more material on UML is presented, as preparation for entering the real world.

Before reading this chapter, it is necessary to be aware that UML, like all state-of-the-art computer languages, is constantly changing. When this book was written, the latest version of UML was Version 2.0. By this time, however, some aspects of UML may have changed. As explained in Just in Case You Wanted to Know Box 3.2, UML is now under the control of the Object Management Group. Before proceeding, it would probably be a good idea to check for updates to UML at the OMG website, www.omg.org.

## 16.1 UML Is *Not* a Methodology

Before looking at UML in more detail, it is essential to clarify what UML is and, more importantly, what UML is not. UML is an acronym for Unified Modeling Language. That is, UML is a *language*. Consider a language like English. English can be used to write novels, encyclopedias, poems, prayers, news reports, and even textbooks on software engineering. That is, a language is simply a tool for expressing ideas. A specific language does not constrain the types of ideas that can be described by that language or the way that they can be described.

As a language, UML can be used to describe software developed using the traditional paradigm or any of the many versions of the object-oriented paradigm, including the Unified Process. In other words, UML is a notation, not a methodology. It is a notation that can be used in conjunction with any methodology.

In fact, UML is not merely *a* notation; it is *the* notation. It is hard to imagine a modern book on software engineering that does not use UML to describe software. UML has become a world standard, so much so that someone unfamiliar with UML would have difficulty functioning today as a software professional.

The title of this chapter is "More on UML." Bearing in mind the central role played by UML, it would seem essential for all of UML to be presented here. However, the manual for Version 2.0 of UML is over 1200 pages long, so complete coverage would probably not be a good idea. But is it possible to be a competent software professional without knowing every single aspect of UML?

The key point is that UML is a language. The English language has over 100,000 words, but almost all speakers of English seem to manage perfectly well with just a subset of the complete English vocabulary. In the same way, in this chapter all the types of UML diagrams are described, together with many (but by no means all) of the various options for each of those diagrams. The small subset of UML presented in Chapters 7, 10, and 12 is adequate for the purposes of this book. In the same way, the larger subset of UML presented in this chapter is adequate for the development and maintenance of most software products.

# 16.2 Class Diagrams

The simplest possible **class diagram** is shown in Figure 16.1. It depicts the **Bank Account Class**. More details of **Bank Account Class** are shown in the class diagram of Figure 16.2. A key aspect of UML is that both Figures 16.1 and 16.2 are valid class diagrams. In other words, in UML as many or as few details may be added as are judged appropriate for the current iteration and incrementation.

**FIGURE 16.2** The class diagram of Figure 16.1 with an attribute and two operations added.

**FIGURE 16.1** The simplest possible class diagram.

| Bank Account Class |
|---|
| |
| |

| Bank Account Class |
|---|
| accountBalance |
| deposit ( ) withdraw ( ) |

This freedom of notation extends to objects. The notation **bank account** may be informally used for one specific object of this class. The full UML notation is

<u>bank account : Bank Account Class</u>

That is, **bank account** is an object, an instance of a class **Bank Account Class**. In more detail, the underlining denotes an object, the colon denotes "an instance of," and the boldface and initial uppercase letters in **Bank Account Class** denote this is a class. However, UML allows us to use a shorter notation, **bank account**, when there is no ambiguity.

Now suppose we wish to model the concept of an arbitrary bank account. That is, we do not wish to refer to one specific object of **Bank Account Class**. The UML notation for this is

<u>: Bank Account Class</u>

As just pointed out, the colon means "an instance of," so **: Bank Account Class** means "an instance of class **Bank Account Class**," which is precisely what we wanted to model. This notation is widely used in Chapter 12. Conversely, in Figure 12.48, a collaboration diagram for the realization of a scenario of the use case `Update Estimated Annual Operating Expenses` of the MSG Foundation software product, the actor is labeled **MSG Staff Member** and not **: MSG Staff Member** (the labeling of other items in that diagram) precisely because **MSG Staff Member** denotes that MSG Staff Member is an actor, whereas **: MSG Staff Member** would denote "an instance of the [nonexistent] **MSG Staff Member Class**."

Section 7.6 introduced the concept of information hiding. In UML, the prefix + indicates that an attribute or operation is **public**, and similarly the prefix – denotes that the attribute or operation is **private**. This notation is used in Figure 16.3. The attribute of **Bank Account Class** is declared to be **private** (so that we can achieve information hiding), whereas both the operations are **public** so that they can be invoked from anywhere in the software product. A third standard type of visibility, **protected**, uses the prefix #. If an attribute is **public**, it is visible everywhere; if it is **private**, it is visible only in the class in which it is defined, and if it is **protected**, it is visible either within the class in which it is defined or within subclasses of that class.

Up to now in this chapter, class diagrams containing only one class have been presented. Section 16.2.1 considers class diagrams with more than one class.

## 16.2.1 Aggregation

Consider Figure 16.4, which models the statement: "A car consists of a chassis, an engine, wheels, and seats." Recall that the open diamonds denote aggregation. **Aggregation** is the UML term for the **part–whole relationship**; the parts of a car are the chassis, engine,

**FIGURE 16.3**
The class diagram of Figure 16.2 with visibility prefixes added.

| Bank Account |
| --- |
| – accountBalance |
| + deposit ( )<br>+ withdraw ( ) |

**FIGURE 16.4**   An aggregation example.

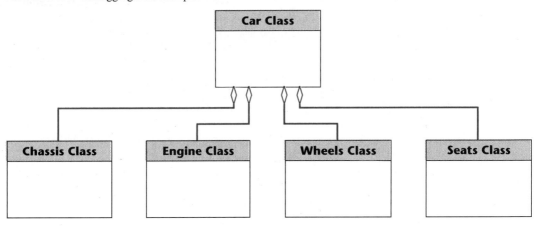

**FIGURE 16.5**   Aggregation example with multiplicities.

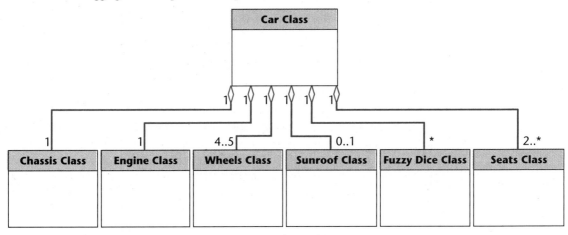

wheels, and seats. The diamond is placed at the "whole" (car) end, not the "part" (chassis, engine, wheels, or seats) end of the line connecting a part to the whole.

## 16.2.2 Multiplicity

Now suppose that we want to use UML to model the statement: "A car consists of one chassis, one engine, four or five wheels, an optional sunroof, zero or more fuzzy dice hanging from the rearview mirror, and two or more seats." This is shown in Figure 16.5. The numbers next to the ends of the lines denote **multiplicity**, the number of times that the one class is associated with the other class.

First consider the line connecting **Chassis Class** to **Car Class**. The 1 at the "part" end of the line denotes that one chassis is involved in this relationship, and the 1 at the "whole" end denotes that one car is involved; that is, each car has one chassis. Similar observations hold for the line connecting **Engine Class** to **Car Class**.

Stephen Kleene laid the foundations of recursive function theory, a branch of mathematical logic that has had a major influence on computer science. The Kleene star (the asterisk that denotes "zero or more" in diagrams like Figure 16.5) is named after him.

The Kleene star is well known among mathematicians and computer scientists. What is considerably less well known is that Kleene pronounced his last name as if it were written "Clay knee" (with the accent on the first syllable), and *not* "Clean knee."

Now consider the line connecting **Wheels Class** to **Car Class**. The 4..5 at the "part" end together with the 1 at the "whole" end denotes that each car has from four to five wheels (the fifth wheel is the spare). Because instances of classes come in whole numbers only, this means that the UML diagram models the statement that a car has four or five wheels, as required.

In general, the two dots .. denote a range. Thus, 0..1 means zero or one, which is the UML way of denoting "optional." That is why there is the 0..1 next to the line connecting **Sun Roof Class** to **Car Class**.

Now look at the line connecting **Fuzzy Dice Class** to **Car Class**. At the "part" end, the label is *. An asterisk by itself denotes "zero or more." Thus, the * in Figure 16.5 means that a car has zero or more fuzzy dice hanging from the rearview mirror. (If you want to know more about that asterisk, see Just in Case You Wanted to Know Box 16.1.)

Now look at the line connecting **Seats Class** to **Car Class**. At the "part" end, the label is 2..*. An asterisk by itself denotes "zero or more"; an asterisk in a range denotes "or more." Thus, the 2..* in Figure 16.5 means that a car has two or more seats.

Therefore, in UML if the exact multiplicity is known, that number is used. An example is the 1 that appears in eight places in Figure 16.5. If the range is known, the range notation is used, as with the 0..1 or 4..5 in Figure 16.5. And if the number is unspecified, the asterisk is used. If the upper limit in a range is unspecified, the range notation is combined with the asterisk notation, as with the 2..* in Figure 16.5. In passing, the multiplicity notation of UML is based on the entity–relationship diagrams of traditional database theory (see Section 11.6).

## 16.2.3  Composition

Another example of aggregation is shown in Figure 16.6, which models the relationship between a chessboard and its squares; every chessboard consists of 64 squares. In fact, this relationship goes further; it is an example of **composition**, a stronger form of aggregation. As previously stated, association models the part–whole relationship. When there is composition, then, in addition, every part may belong to only one whole, and if the whole is deleted, so are the parts. In the example, if there are a number of different chessboards, each square belongs to only one board, and if a chessboard is thrown away, all 64 squares

**FIGURE 16.6**
Another aggregation example (but see Figure 16.7).

**FIGURE 16.7**
Composition
example.

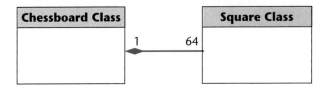

**FIGURE 16.8**
Generalization
(inheritance)
example with
an explicit
discriminator.

**FIGURE 16.9**
An association.

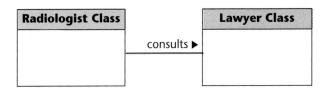

on that board go as well. Composition, an extension of aggregation, is depicted with a solid diamond, as in Figure 16.7.

### 16.2.4 Generalization

Inheritance is a required feature of object orientation. It is a special case of **generalization**. The UML notation for generalization is an open triangle. Sometimes we choose to label that open triangle with a **discriminator**. Consider Figure 16.8, which models two types of investments, bonds and stocks. The notation *investmentType* next to the open triangle means that every instance of **Investment Class** or its two subclasses has an attribute investmentType, and this attribute can be used to distinguish between instances of bonds and instances of stocks.

### 16.2.5 Association

In Section 7.7, an example of **association** involving two classes was presented in which the direction of the association had to be clarified by means of a navigation arrow in the form of a solid triangle. Figure 7.32 is reproduced here as Figure 16.9.

**FIGURE 16.10**   An association class.

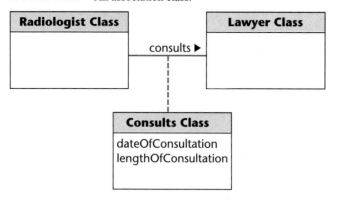

**FIGURE 16.11**
Generalization
of an actor.

In some cases, the association between the two classes may itself need to be modeled as a class. For example, suppose the radiologist in Figure 16.9 consults the lawyer on a number of different occasions, on each occasion for a different length of time. To enable the lawyer to bill the radiologist correctly, a class diagram such as that depicted in Figure 16.10 is needed. Now consults has become a class, **Consults Class**, called an **association class** (because it is both an association and a class).

# 16.3   Notes

When we want to include a comment in a UML diagram, we put it in a **note** (a rectangle with the top right-hand corner bent over). A dashed line is then drawn from the note to the item to which the note refers. Figure 12.38 shows a note.

# 16.4   Use-Case Diagrams

As described in Section 10.4.3, a **use case** is a model of the interaction between external users of a software product (**actors**) and the software product itself. More precisely, an actor is a user playing a specific role. A **use-case diagram** is a set of use cases.

In Section 10.4.3, generalization within the context of actors was described, as depicted in Figure 10.2. Figure 16.11 is another example; it shows that a **Manager** is a special case of an **Employee**. As with classes, the open triangle points toward the more general case.

# 16.5   Stereotypes

The three primary tax forms for U.S. personal income tax are Forms 1040, 1040A, and 1040EZ. Figure 16.12 shows that use cases Prepare Form 1040, Prepare Form

**FIGURE 16.12**
The use cases
`Prepare
Form 1040,`
`Prepare
Form 1040A,`
and `Prepare
Form 1040EZ`
incorporate the
use case `Print
Tax Form.`

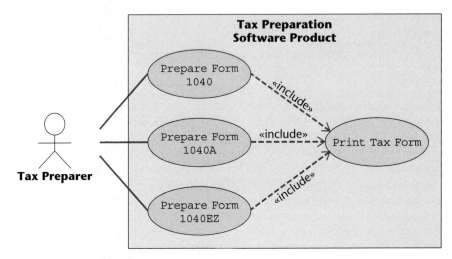

**FIGURE 16.13** Use case `Order a Burger` showing the variation when the customer turns down the fries.

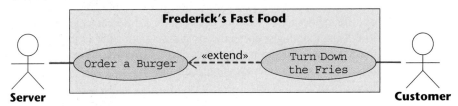

`1040A`, and `Prepare Form 1040EZ` all incorporate the use case `Print Tax Form`, as indicated by the include relationship, represented by a stereotype.

A **stereotype** in UML is a way of extending UML. That is, if we need to define a construct that is not in UML, we can do it. Three stereotypes were presented in Chapter 12: boundary, control, and entity classes. In general, the names of stereotypes appear between **guillemets**, for example, «this is my own construct». Thus, instead of using the special symbol for a boundary class, the standard rectangular symbol for a class could have been used with the notation «boundary class» inside the rectangle and similarly for control and entity classes.

The **include relationship** shown in Figure 16.12 is treated in UML as a stereotype, hence the notation «include» in that figure to denote common functionality, in this instance the use case `Print Tax Form` (Figure 10.41). Another relationship is the **extend relationship**, where one use case is a variation of the standard use case. For example, we may wish to have a separate use case to model the situation of a customer ordering a burger but turning down the fries. The notation «extend» is similarly used for this purpose, as shown in Figure 16.13. However, for this relationship, the open-headed arrow goes in the other direction.

# 16.6   Interaction Diagrams

**Interaction diagrams** show the way that the objects in the software product interact with one another. In Chapter 12, both types of interaction diagram supported by UML were presented: sequence diagrams and collaboration diagrams.

First, consider **sequence diagrams**. Suppose that someone interactively orders an item over the Internet, but when the overall total, including sales tax and delivery charges, is displayed, the buyer decides that the price is too high and cancels the order. Figure 16.14 depicts the dynamic creation and subsequent dynamic destruction of the order.

1. Consider the lifelines in Figure 16.14. When an object is active, this is denoted by a thin rectangle (**activation box**) in place of the dashed line. For example, the **: Price Class**

**FIGURE 16.14**

A sequence diagram showing dynamic creation and destruction of an object, return, and explicit activation.

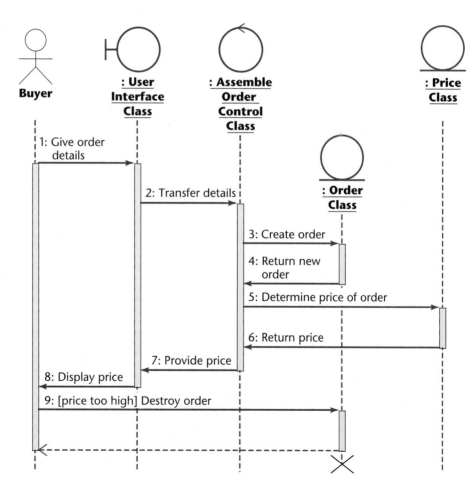

object is active from message 5: Determine price of order until message 6: Return price, and similarly for the other objects.

2. The **: Order Class** object is created only when the **: Assemble Order Control Class** sends message 3: Create order to the **: Order Class** object. This is denoted by the lifeline starting at only the point of dynamic creation,

3. Figure 16.14 also shows the destruction of the **: Order Class** object after the **: Order Class** object receives the message 9: Destroy object. The destruction is denoted by the heavy **X**.

4. This destruction takes place after a return has taken place, denoted by the dashed horizontal line below event 9, terminated by an open arrow. In the rest of the sequence diagram, each message is eventually followed by a message sent back to the object that sent the original message. In fact, this reciprocity is optional; it is perfectly valid to send a message without eventually receiving any sort of reply. Even if there is a reply, it is not necessary that a specific new message be sent back. Instead, a dashed line ending in an open arrow is drawn (a **return**) to indicate a return from the original message, as opposed to a new message.

5. There is a guard on message 9: [price too high] Destroy order. That is, message 9 is sent only if the buyer decides not to purchase the item because the price is too high. A **guard** (condition) is something that is true or false; only if it is true is the message sent. In Section 16.7, guards are described within the context of statecharts, but here they are used in a sequence diagram.

(In Figure 16.14, the message 9 [price too high] Destroy order should be sent from the **Buyer** to the **: User Interface Class** object, and the latter should then send a message to the **: Assemble Order Control Class** object. Next, the **: Assemble Order Control Class** object should send a message to the **: Order Class** object, instructing it to destroy the order. To highlight dynamic destruction of an object, these details have been suppressed in Figure 16.14.)

Many other options are supported by UML interaction diagrams. For example, suppose we model an elevator going up. We do not know in advance which elevator button will be pressed, so we have no idea how many floors up the elevator will go. We model this iteration by labeling the relevant message *move up one floor, as shown in Figure 16.15. The asterisk is, once again, the Kleene star (see Just in Case You Wanted to Know Box 16.1). So this message means, "move up zero or more floors."

An object can send a message to itself. This is termed a **self-call**. For example, suppose that the elevator has arrived at a floor. The elevator controller sends a message to the elevator doors to open. Once the return has been received, the elevator controller sends a message to itself to start its timer; this self-call is also shown in Figure 16.15. At the end of the time period, the elevator controller sends a message to the doors to close. When the second return has been received (that is, when the doors have been safely closed), the elevator is instructed to move again.

Turning now to **collaboration diagrams**, it was stated in Section 12.15.1 that collaboration diagrams are equivalent to sequence diagrams. So, all the features of sequence diagrams presented in this section are equally applicable to collaboration diagrams, such as Figure 12.33.

**FIGURE 16.15**
A sequence diagram showing iteration and self-call.

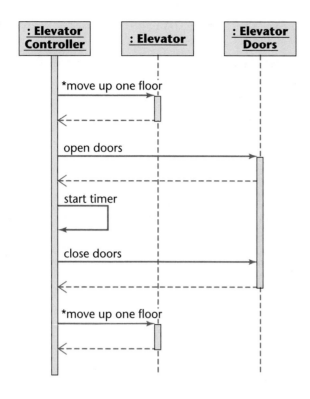

## 16.7 Statecharts

Consider the **statechart** of Figure 16.16. This is similar to the statechart of Figure 12.22, but modeled using guards instead of events. It shows the start state (the solid circle) with an unlabeled **transition** leading to state **MSG Foundation Event Loop**. Five transitions lead from that state, each with a guard, that is, a condition that is true or false. When one of the guards becomes true, the corresponding transition takes place.

An **event** also causes transitions between states. A common event is the receipt of a message. Consider Figure 16.17, which depicts a part of a statechart for an elevator. The elevator is in state **Elevator Moving**. It stays in motion, performing operation Move up one floor, while guard [no message received yet] remains true, until it receives the message Elevator has arrived at floor. The receipt of this message (event) causes the guard to be false and also enables a transition to state **Stopped At Floor**. In this state, the activity Open the elevator doors is performed.

So far, transition labels have been in the form of [guard] or event. In fact, the most general form of a transition label is

$$\text{event [guard] / action}$$

That is, if event has taken place and [guard] is true, then the transition occurs and, while it is occurring, action is performed. An example of such a transition label is shown

**FIGURE 16.16** A statechart for the MSG Foundation case study.

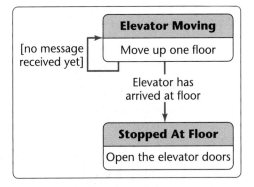

**FIGURE 16.17**
A portion of a statechart for an elevator.

in Figure 16.18, which is equivalent to Figure 16.17. The transition label is Elevator has arrived at floor [a message has been received] / Open the elevator doors. The *guard* [a message has been received] is true when the *event* Elevator has arrived at floor has occurred and a message to this effect has been sent. The **action** to be taken, indicated by the instruction following the slash /, is Open the elevator doors.

Comparing Figures 16.17 and 16.18, we see that there are two places where an action can be performed in a statechart. First, as reflected in state **Stopped At Floor** in Figure 16.17, an action can be performed when a state is entered. Such an action is called an **activity** in UML. Second, as shown in Figure 16.18, an action can take place as part of a transition. (Technically, there is a slight difference between an activity and an action.

**FIGURE 16.18**   A statechart equivalent to Figure 16.17.

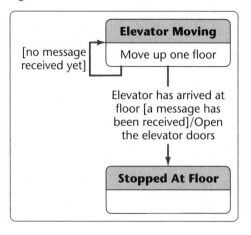

**FIGURE 16.19**   Statechart (a) without and (b) with superstate.

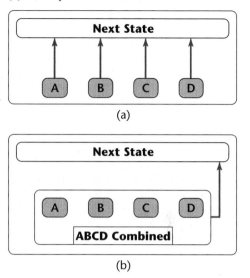

An action is assumed to take place essentially instantaneously, but an activity may take place less quickly, perhaps over several seconds.)

UML supports a wide variety of different types of actions and events in statecharts. For instance, an event can be specified in terms of words like when or after. Therefore, an event might stipulate when (cost > 1000) or after (2.5 seconds).

A statechart with a large number of states tends to have a large number of transitions. The many arrows representing these transitions soon make the statechart look like a large bowl of spaghetti. One technique for dealing with this is to use a **superstate**. Consider the statechart of Figure 16.19(a). The four states **A**, **B**, **C**, and **D** all have transitions to **Next State**. Figure 16.19(b) shows how these four states can be combined into one superstate, **ABCD Combined**, which needs only one transition, as opposed to the four in Figure 16.19(a). This reduces the number of arrows from four to only one. At the same time, states **A**, **B**, **C**, and **D** still exist in their own right, so any existing actions associated with those states are not affected nor are any existing transitions into those states. Another example of a superstate is shown in Figure 16.20, where the four lower states of Figure 16.16 are unified into one superstate, **MSG Foundation Combined**, leading to a cleaner and clearer diagram.

# 16.8   Activity Diagrams

**Activity diagrams** show how various events are coordinated. They are therefore used when activities are carried out in parallel.

Suppose a couple seated at a restaurant orders their meal. One orders a chicken dish; the other orders fish. The waiter writes down their order and hands the order to the chef so that she knows what dishes to prepare. It does not matter which dish is completed first because the meal is served only when both dishes have been prepared. This is shown in Figure 16.21. The

**FIGURE 16.20** Figure 16.16 with four states combined into a superstate, **MSG Foundation Combined**.

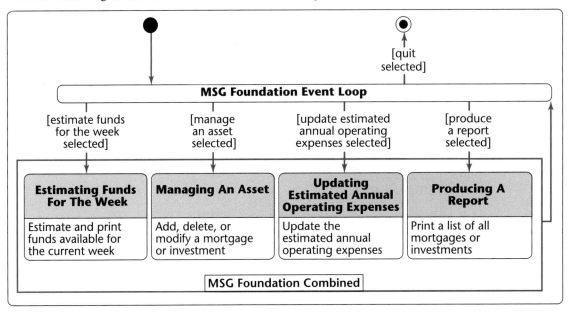

**FIGURE 16.21**
An activity
diagram for a
restaurant order
for two diners.

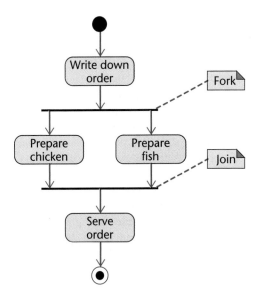

upper heavy horizontal line is called a *fork*, and the lower one is called a *join*. In general, a **fork** has one incoming transition and many outgoing transitions, each of which starts an activity to be executed in parallel with the other activities. Conversely, a **join** has many incoming transitions, each of which lead from an activity executed in parallel with the other activities, and one outgoing transition that is started when all the parallel activities have been completed.

**FIGURE 16.22**
An activity
diagram for a
computer
assembly
company.

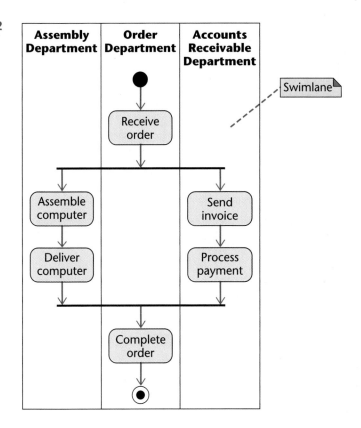

Activity diagrams are useful for modeling businesses where a number of activities are carried out in parallel. For example, consider a company that assembles computers as specified by the customer. As shown in the activity diagram of Figure 16.22, when an order is received, it is passed on to the **Assembly Department**. It is also passed to the **Accounts Receivable Department**. The order is complete when the computer has been assembled and delivered and the customer's payment has been processed. Each of the three departments involved, the **Assembly Department**, the **Order Department**, and the **Accounts Receivable Department**, is in its own swimlane. In general, the combination of forks, joins, and swimlanes shows clearly which branches of an organization are involved in each specific activity, which tasks are carried out in parallel, and which tasks have to be completed in parallel before the next task can be started.

# 16.9   Packages

As explained in Section 13.9, the way to handle a large software product is to decompose it into relatively independent **packages**. The UML notation for a package is a rectangle with a name tag, as shown in Figure 16.23. This figure shows that My Package is a package, but the rectangle is empty. This is a valid UML diagram—the diagram simply models the fact that My Package is a package. Figure 16.24 is more interesting—it shows the contents of

**FIGURE 16.23** The UML notation for a package.

**FIGURE 16.24** The package of Figure 16.23 with more details shown.

**FIGURE 16.25** Component diagram.

My Package, including a class, an entity class, and another package. We can continue to supply more details until the package is at the appropriate level of detail for the current iteration and incrementation.

## 16.10 Component Diagrams

A **component diagram** shows dependencies among software components, including source code, compiled code, and executable load images. For example, the component diagram of Figure 16.25 shows source code (represented by a note) and the executable load image created from the source code.

## 16.11 Deployment Diagrams

A **deployment diagram** shows on which hardware component each software component is installed (or deployed). It also shows the communication links among the hardware components. A simple deployment diagram is shown in Figure 16.26.

**FIGURE 16.26** A deployment diagram.

# 16.12    Review of UML Diagrams

A wide variety of different UML diagrams have been presented in this chapter. In the interests of clarity, here is a list of some of the diagram types that might be confused:

- A *use case* models the interaction between actors (external users of a software product) and the software product itself.
- A *use-case diagram* is a single diagram that incorporates a number of use cases.
- A *class diagram* is a model of the classes showing the static relationships among them, including association and generalization.
- A *statechart* shows states (specific values of attributes of objects), events that cause transitions between states (subject to guards), and actions and activities performed by objects. A statechart is therefore a dynamic model—it reflects the behavior of objects, that is, the way they react to specific events.
- An *interaction diagram* (*sequence diagram* or *collaboration diagram*) shows the way that objects interact with one another as messages are passed between them. This is another dynamic model; that is, it also shows how objects behave.
- An *activity diagram* shows how events that occur at the same time are coordinated. This is yet another dynamic model.

# 16.13    UML and Iteration

Consider a statechart. The transitions can be labeled with a guard, an event, an action, or all three. Now consider a sequence diagram. The lifelines may or may not include activation boxes, there may or may not be returns, and there may or may not be guards on the messages.

A wide range of options are available for every UML diagram. That is, a valid UML diagram consists of a small required part plus any number of options. UML diagrams have so many options for two reasons. First, not every feature of UML is applicable to every software product, so there has to be freedom with regard to choice of options. Second, we cannot perform the iteration and incrementation of the Unified Process unless we are permitted to add features stepwise to diagrams, rather than create the complete final diagram at the beginning. That is, UML allows us to start with a basic diagram. We can then add optional features as we wish, bearing in mind that, at all times, the resulting UML diagram is still valid. This is one of the many reasons why UML is so well suited to the Unified Process.

**Chapter Review**

It is explained in Section 16.1 that UML is a language, not a methodology. Class diagrams are described in Section 16.2. Specific aspects of class diagrams are discussed, including aggregation (Section 16.2.1), multiplicity (Section 16.2.2), composition (Section 16.2.3), generalization (Section 16.2.4), and association (Section 16.2.5). Next, a variety of UML diagrams are presented, including notes (Section 16.3), use-case diagrams (Section 16.4), stereotypes (Section 16.5), interaction diagrams (both sequence diagrams and collaboration diagrams; Section 16.6), statecharts (Section 16.7), activity diagrams (Section 16.8), packages (Section 16.9), component diagrams (Section 16.10), and deployment diagrams (Section 16.11). The chapter concludes with a review of UML diagrams (Section 16.12) and a discussion of why UML is so suitable for the Unified Process (Section 16.13).

**For Further Reading**

There is no substitute for reading the current version of the UML manual, to be found at the OMG website, www.omg.org. Two good introductory texts on UML are [Fowler and Scott, 2000], and [Stevens and Pooley, 2000].

**Key Terms**

| | | |
|---|---|---|
| action *546* | discriminator *540* | part–whole |
| activation box *543* | event *545* | relationship *537* |
| activity *546* | extend relationship *542* | return *544* |
| activity diagram *547* | fork *548* | self-call *544* |
| actor *541* | generalization *540* | sequence diagram *543* |
| aggregation *537* | guard *544* | statechart *545* |
| association *540* | guillemets *542* | stereotype *542* |
| association class *541* | include relationship *542* | superstate *547* |
| class diagram *536* | interaction diagram *543* | swimlane *549* |
| collaboration diagram *544* | join *548* | transition *545* |
| component diagram *550* | multiplicity *538* | use case *541* |
| composition *539* | note *541* | use-case |
| deployment diagram *550* | package *549* | diagram *541* |

**Problems**

16.1  Use UML to model airports. (Hint: Do not show any more details than are strictly needed to answer the question.)

16.2  Use UML to model chocolate cakes. A chocolate cake is made with eggs, flour, sugar, baking powder, milk, and cocoa. A chocolate cake is mixed, baked, frosted, and then eaten. To prevent unauthorized individuals from baking a chocolate cake, the ingredients are private, as are all but the last operation.

16.3  Use UML to model dining rooms. Every dining room has to have a table, four or more chairs, and a sideboard. Optionally, it may also have a fireplace.

16.4  Model the dining rooms of Problem 16.3 using a combination of aggregation and composition.

16.5  Modify your UML model of Problem 16.3 to reflect that a dining room is a specific type of room.

16.6  Add a note to your diagram of Problem 16.2 pointing out that the cake you modeled is a chocolate cake.

16.7  Use UML to model John Cage's somewhat controversial 1952 piano composition entitled *4'33"*. The piece consists of three silent movements, of length 30 seconds, 2 minutes 23 seconds, and 1 minute 40 seconds, respectively. (The title of the piece comes from its total length.) The pianist walks onto the stage holding a stopwatch and the score (in conventional music notation but with blank measures). The pianist sits down on the piano stool, puts the score and the stopwatch on the piano, opens the score, starts the stopwatch, and then signals the start of the first movement by lowering the lid of the piano. At the end of the first movement (that is, after 30 seconds of silence during which the pianist carefully follows the blank score, turning the page when necessary), the lid of the piano is raised to signal the end of the first movement. These actions are repeated for the second movement (2 minutes 23 seconds) and the third movement (1 minute 40 seconds). The pianist then closes the score, picks up the score and the stopwatch, gets up, and leaves the stage.

**References**   [Booch, Rumbaugh, and Jacobson, 1999] G. BOOCH, J. RUMBAUGH, AND I. JACOBSON, *The UML Users Guide,* Addison-Wesley, Reading, MA, 1999.

[Fowler and Scott, 2000] M. FOWLER WITH K. SCOTT, *UML Distilled,* 2nd ed., Addison-Wesley, Upper Saddle River, NJ, 2000.

[Stevens and Pooley, 2000] P. STEVENS WITH R. POOLEY, *Using UML: Software Engineering with Objects and Components,* updated edition, Addison-Wesley, Upper Saddle River, NJ, 2000.

# Bibliography

The chapter number in parentheses denotes the chapter in which the item has been referenced.

[Abrial, 1980] J.-R. ABRIAL, "The Specification Language Z: Syntax and Semantics," Oxford University Computing Laboratory, Programming Research Group, Oxford, UK, April 1980. (Chapter 11)

[Ackerman, Buchwald, and Lewski, 1989] A. F. ACKERMAN, L. S. BUCHWALD, AND F. H. LEWSKI, "Software Inspections: An Effective Verification Process," *IEEE Software* **6** (May 1989), pp. 31–36. (Chapter 6)

[Adolph, 1996] W. S. ADOLPH, "Cash Cow in the Tar Pit: Reengineering a Legacy System," *IEEE Software* **13** (May 1996), pp. 41–47. (Chapter 15)

[Albrecht, 1979] A. J. ALBRECHT, "Measuring Application Development Productivity," *Proceedings of the IBM SHARE/GUIDE Applications Development Symposium*, Monterey, CA, October 1979, pp. 83–92. (Chapter 9)

[Alexander, 1999] C. ALEXANDER, "The Origins of Pattern Theory," *IEEE Software* **16** (September/October 1999), pp. 71–82. (Chapter 8)

[I. Alexander, 2003] I. ALEXANDER, "Misuse Cases: Use Cases with Hostile Intent," *IEEE Software* **20** (January/February 2003), pp. 58–66. (Chapter 10)

[R. Alexander, 2003] R. ALEXANDER, "The Real Costs of Aspect-Oriented Programming," *IEEE Software* **20** (November/December 2003), pp. 92–93. (Chapter 7)

[Alexander et al., 1977] C. ALEXANDER, S. ISHIKAWA, M. SILVERSTEIN, M. JACOBSON, I. FIKSDAHL-KING, AND S. ANGEL, *A Pattern Language*, Oxford University Press, New York, 1977. (Chapter 8)

[Alford, 1985] M. ALFORD, "SREM at the Age of Eight; The Distributed Computing Design System," *IEEE Computer* **18** (April 1985), pp. 36–46. (Chapter 11)

[Alshayeb and Li, 2003] M. ALSHAYEB, AND W. LI "An Empirical Validation of Object-Oriented Metrics in Two Different Iterative Software Processes," *IEEE Transactions on Software Engineering* **29** (November 2003), pp. 1043–49. (Chapters 5 and 14)

[Anderson et al., 1999] E. ANDERSON, Z. BAI, C. BISCHOF, S. BLACKFORD, J. DEMMEL, J. DONGARRA, J. DU CROZ, A. GREENBAUM, S. HAMMARLING, A. MCKENNEY, AND D. SORENSEN, *LAPACK Users' Guide*, 3rd ed., SIAM, Philadelphia, 1999. (Chapter 8)

[ANSI X3.159, 1989] *The Programming Language C*, ANSI X3.159-1989, American National Standards Institute, New York, 1989. (Chapter 8)

[ANSI/IEEE 754, 1985] *Standard for Binary Floating Point Arithmetic*, ANSI/IEEE 754, American National Standards Institute, Institute of Electrical and Electronic Engineers, New York, 1985. (Chapter 8)

[ANSI/IEEE 829, 1991] *Software Test Documentation*, ANSI/IEEE 829-1991, American National Standards Institute, Institute of Electrical and Electronic Engineers, New York, 1991. (Chapter 9)

[ANSI/MIL-STD-1815A, 1983] *Reference Manual for the Ada Programming Language*, ANSI/MIL-STD-1815A, American National Standards Institute, United States Department of Defense, Washington, DC, 1983. (Chapter 8)

[Antoniol, Cimitile, Di Lucca, and Di Penta, 2004] G. ANTONIOL, A. CIMITILE, G. A. DI LUCCA, AND M. DI PENTA, "Assessing Staffing Needs for a Software Maintenance Project through Queuing Simulation," *IEEE Transactions on Software Engineering* **30** (January 2004), pp. 43–58. (Chapter 15)

[Awad, Kuusela, and Ziegler, 1996] M. AWAD, J. KUUSELA, AND J. ZIEGLER, *Object-Oriented Technology for Real-Time Systems: A Practical Approach Using OMT and Fusion,* Prentice Hall, Upper Saddle River, NJ, 1996. (Chapter 12)

[Baber, 1987] R. L. BABER, *The Spine of Software: Designing Provably Correct Software: Theory and Practice*, John Wiley and Sons, New York, 1987. (Chapter 6)

[Babich, 1986] W. A. BABICH, *Software Configuration Management: Coordination for Team Productivity*, Addison-Wesley, Reading, MA, 1986. (Chapter 5)

[Baetjer, 1996] H. BAETJER, *Software as Capital: An Economic Perspective on Software Engineering,* IEEE Computer Society Press, Los Alamitos, CA, 1996. (Chapter 1)

[Baker, 1972] F. T. BAKER, "Chief Programmer Team Management of Production Programming," *IBM Systems Journal* **11** (No. 1, 1972), pp. 56–73. (Chapter 4)

[Balzer, 1985] R. BALZER, "A 15 Year Perspective on Automatic Programming," *IEEE Transactions on Software Engineering* **SE-11** (November 1985), pp. 1257–68. (Chapter 11)

[Bamberger, 1997] J. BAMBERGER, "Essence of the Capability Maturity Model," *IEEE Computer* **30** (June 1997), pp. 112–14. (Chapter 3)

[Bamford and Deibler, 1993a] R. C. BAMFORD AND W. J. DEIBLER, II, "Comparing, Contrasting ISO 9001 and the SEI Capability Maturity Model," *IEEE Computer* **26** (October 1993), pp. 68–70. (Chapter 3)

[Bamford and Deibler, 1993b] R. C. BAMFORD AND W. J. DEIBLER, II, "A Detailed Comparison of the SEI Software Maturity Levels and Technology Stages to the Requirements for ISO 9001 Registration," Software Systems Quality Consulting, San Jose, CA, 1993. (Chapter 3)

[Bandi, Vaishnavi, and Turk, 2003] R. K. BANDI, V. K. VAISHNAVI, AND D. E. TURK, "Predicting Maintenance Performance Using Object-Oriented Design Complexity Metrics," *IEEE Transactions on Software Engineering* **29** (January 2003), pp. 77–87. (Chapter 15)

[Banks, Carson, Nelson, and Nichol, 2001] J. BANKS, J. S. CARSON, B. L. NELSON, AND D. M. NICHOL, *Discrete-Event System Simulation,* 3rd ed., Prentice Hall, Upper Saddle River, NJ, 1995. (Chapter 11)

[Bansiya and Davis, 2002] J. BANSIYA AND C. G. DAVIS, "A Hierarchical Model for Object-Oriented Design Quality Assessment," *IEEE Transactions on Software Engineering* **28** (January 2002), pp. 4–17. (Chapter 13)

[Barnard and Price, 1994] J. BARNARD AND A. PRICE, "Managing Code Inspection Information," *IEEE Software* **11** (March 1994), pp. 59–69. (Chapter 14)

[Barnes and Bollinger, 1991] B. H. BARNES AND T. B. BOLLINGER, "Making Reuse Cost-Effective," *IEEE Software* **8** (January 1991), pp. 13–24. (Chapter 8)

[Basili and Hutchens, 1983] V. R. BASILI AND D. H. HUTCHENS, "An Empirical Study of a Syntactic Complexity Family," *IEEE Transactions on Software Engineering* **SE-9** (November 1983), pp. 664–72. (Chapter 14)

[Basili and Selby, 1987] V. R. BASILI AND R. W. SELBY, "Comparing the Effectiveness of Software Testing Strategies," *IEEE Transactions on Software Engineering* **SE-13** (December 1987), pp. 1278–96. (Chapter 14)

[Basili and Weiss, 1984] V. R. BASILI AND D. M. WEISS, "A Methodology for Collecting Valid Software Engineering Data," *IEEE Transactions on Software Engineering* **SE-10** (November 1984), pp. 728–38. (Chapter 14)

[Bass, Clements, and Kazman, 2003] L. BASS, P. CLEMENTS, AND R. KAZMAN, *Software Architecture in Practice,* 2nd ed., Addison-Wesley, Reading, MA, 2003. (Chapter 8)

[Baster, Konana, and Scott, 2001] G. BASTER, P. KONANA, AND J. E. SCOTT, "Business Components: A Case Study of Bankers Trust Australia Limited," Communications of the ACM 44 (May 2001), pp. 92–98. (Chapter 8)

[Beck, 2000] K. BECK, *Extreme Programming Explained: Embrace Change,* Addison-Wesley Longman, Reading, MA, 2000. (Chapters 2 and 4)

[Beck and Cunningham, 1989] K. BECK AND W. CUNNINGHAM, "A Laboratory for Teaching Object-Oriented Thinking," Proceedings of OOPSLA '89, *ACM SIGPLAN Notices* **24** (October 1989), pp. 1–6. (Chapter 12)

[Beck et al., 2001] K. BECK, M. BEEDLE, A. COCKBURN, W. CUNNINGHAM, M. FOWLER, J. GRENNING, J. HIGHSMITH, A. HUNT, R. JEFFRIES, J. KERN, B. MARICK, R. C. MARTIN, S. MELLOR, K. SCHWABER, J. SUTHERLAND, D. THOMAS, AND A. VAN BENNEKUM, *Manifesto for Agile Software Development,* agilemanifesto.org, 2001. (Chapters 2 and 4)

[Beizer, 1990] B. BEIZER, *Software Testing Techniques,* 2nd ed., Van Nostrand Reinhold, New York, 1990. (Chapters 3, 6, 13, and 14)

[Beizer, 1995] B. BEIZER, *Black-Box Testing: Techniques for Functional Testing of Software and Systems,* John Wiley and Sons, New York, 1995. (Chapter 14)

[Beizer, 1997] B. BEIZER, "Cleanroom Process Model: A Critical Examination," *IEEE Software* **14** (March/April 1997), pp. 14–16. (Chapter 14)

[Bellinzona, Fugini, and Pernici, 1995] R. BELLINZONA, M. G. FUGINI, AND B. PERNICI, "Reusing Specifications in OO Applications," *IEEE Software* **12** (March 1995), pp. 656–75. (Chapter 12)

[Bennatan, 2000] E. M. BENNATAN, *On Time Within Budget: Software Project Management Practices and Techniques*, 3rd ed., John Wiley and Sons, New York, 2000. (Chapter 9)

[Berry, 2004] D. M. BERRY, "The Inevitable Pain of Software Development: Why There Is No Silver Bullet," in: *Radical Innovations of Software and Systems Engineering in the Future*, Lecture Notes in Computer Science, Vol. 2941, Springer-Verlag, Berlin, 2004, pp. 50–74. (Chapter 10)

[Berry and Wing, 1985] D. M. BERRY AND J. M. WING, "Specifying and Prototyping: Some Thoughts on Why They Are Successful," in: *Formal Methods and Software Development, Proceedings of the International Joint Conference on Theory and Practice of Software Development*, Vol. 2, Springer-Verlag, Berlin, 1985, pp. 117–28. (Chapter 6)

[Bianchi, Caivano, Marengo, and Visaggio, 2003] A. BIANCHI, D. CAIVANO, V. MARENGO, AND G. VISAGGIO, "Iterative Reengineering of Legacy Systems," *IEEE Transactions on Software Engineering* **29** (March 2003), pp. 225–41. (Chapter 2)

[Bias, 1991] R. BIAS, "Walkthroughs: Efficient Collaborative Testing," *IEEE Software* **8** (September 1991), pp. 94–95. (Chapter 13)

[Binkley and Schach, 1996] A. B. BINKLEY AND S. R. SCHACH, "A Comparison of Sixteen Quality Metrics for Object-Oriented Design," *Information Processing Letters* **57** (No. 6, June 1996), pp. 271–75. (Chapters 13 and 14)

[Binkley and Schach, 1997] A. B. BINKLEY AND S. R. SCHACH, "Toward a Unified Approach to Object-Oriented Coupling," *Proceedings of the 35th Annual ACM Southeast Conference*, Murfreesboro, TN, April 2–4, 1997, pp. 91–97. (Chapters 7, 13, and 14)

[Binkley and Schach, 1998] A. B. BINKLEY AND S. R. SCHACH, "Validation of the Coupling Dependency Metric as a Predictor of Run-Time Failures and Maintenance Measures," *Proceedings of the 20th International Conference on Software Engineering*, Kyoto, Japan, April 1988, pp. 542–55. (Chapter 13)

[Birk et al. 2003] A. BIRK, G. HELLER, I. JOHN, K. SCHMID, T. VON DER MASSEN, AND K. MULLER, "Product Line Engineering, the State of the Practice," *IEEE Software* **20** (November/December 2003), pp. 52–60. (Chapter 8)

[Bisbal, Lawless, Wu, and Grimson, 1999] J. BISBAL, D. LAWLESS, B. WU, AND J. GRIMSON, "Legacy Software Products: Issues and Directions," *IEEE Software*

**16** (September/October 1999), pp. 103–111. (Chapter 15)

[Blaha, Premerlani, and Rumbaugh, 1988] M. R. BLAHA, W. J. PREMERLANI, AND J. E. RUMBAUGH, "Relational Database Design Using an Object-Oriented Methodology," *Communications of the ACM* **31** (April 1988), pp. 414–27. (Chapter 7)

[Blanco, Gutiérrez, and Satriani, 2001] M. BLANCO, P. GUTIÉRREZ, AND G. SATRIANI, "SPI Patterns: Learning from Experience," *IEEE Software* **18** (May/June 2001), pp. 28–35. (Chapter 3)

[Bockle et al., 2004] G. BOCKLE, P. CLEMENTS, J. D. MCGREGOR, D. MUTHIG, AND K. SCHMID, "Calculating ROI for Software Product Lines," *IEEE Software* **21** (May/June 2004), pp. 23–31. (Chapters 5 and 8)

[Boehm, 1976] B. W. BOEHM, "Software Engineering," *IEEE Transactions on Computers* **C-25** (December 1976), pp. 1226–41. (Chapters 1 and 3)

[Boehm, 1979] B. W. BOEHM, "Software Engineering, R & D Trends and Defense Needs," in: *Research Directions in Software Technology*, P. Wegner (Editor), The MIT Press, Cambridge, MA, 1979. (Chapter 1)

[Boehm, 1980] B. W. BOEHM, "Developing Small-Scale Application Software Products: Some Experimental Results," *Proceedings of the Eighth IFIP World Computer Congress,* October 1980, pp. 321–26. (Chapter 1)

[Boehm, 1981] B. W. BOEHM, *Software Engineering Economics.* Prentice Hall, Englewood Cliffs, NJ. 1981. (Chapters 1 and 9)

[Boehm, 1984] B. W. BOEHM, "Software Engineering Economics," *IEEE Transactions on Software Engineering* **SE-10** (January 1984), pp. 4–21. (Chapter 9)

[Boehm, 1988] B. W. BOEHM, "A Spiral Model of Software Development and Enhancement," *IEEE Computer* **21** (May 1988), pp. 61–72. (Chapter 2)

[Boehm, 1997] R. BOEHM (EDITOR), "Function Point FAQ," at ourworld.compuserve.com/homepages/softcomp/fpfaq.htm, June 25, 1997. (Chapter 9)

[Boehm, 2002] B. W. BOEHM, "Get Ready for Agile Methods, with Care," *IEEE Computer* **35** (January 2002), pp. 64–69. (Chapters 2 and 4)

[Boehm and Basili, 2001] B. BOEHM AND V. R. BASILI, "Software Defect Reduction Top Ten List," *IEEE Computer* **34** (January 2001), pp. 135–37. (Chapter 6)

[Boehm and Huang, 2003] B. BOEHM AND L. G. HUANG, "Value-Based Software Engineering: A Case Study," *IEEE Computer* **36** (March 2003), pp. 33–41. (Chapter 1)

[Boehm and Turner, 2003] B. BOEHM AND R. TURNER, *Balancing Agility and Discipline: A Guide for the Perplexed*, Addison-Wesley Professional, Boston, MA, 2003. (Chapter 2)

[Boehm et al., 1984] B. W. BOEHM, M. H. PENEDO, E. D. STUCKLE, R. D. WILLIAMS, AND A. B. PYSTER, "A Software Development Environment for Improving Productivity," *IEEE Computer* **17** (June 1984), pp. 30–44. (Chapters 2 and 9)

[Boehm et al., 2000] B. W. BOEHM, C. ABTS, A. W. BROWN, S. CHULANI, B. K. CLARK, E. HOROWITZ, R. MADACHY, D. REIFER, AND B. STEECE, *Software Cost Estimation with COCOMO II*, Prentice Hall, Upper Saddle River, NJ, 2000. (Chapter 9)

[Booch, 1994] G. BOOCH, *Object-Oriented Analysis and Design with Applications,* 2nd ed., Benjamin/Cummings, Redwood City, CA, 1994. (Chapters 3 and 12)

[Booch, 2000] G. BOOCH, "The Future of Software Engineering," keynote address, International Conference on Software Engineering, Limerick, Ireland, May 2000. (Chapter 2)

[Booch, Rumbaugh, and Jacobson, 1999] G. BOOCH, J. RUMBAUGH, AND I. JACOBSON, *The UML Users Guide*, Addison-Wesley, Reading, MA, 1999. (Chapters 3, 12, and 16)

[Borjesson and Mathiassen, 2004] A. BORJESSON AND L. MATHIASSEN, "Successful Process Implementation," *IEEE Software* **21** (July/August 2004), pp. 36–44. (Chapter 3)

[Borland, 2002] BORLAND, "Press Release: Borland Unveils C++ Application Development Strategy for 2002," www.borland.com/news/press_releases/2002/01_28_02_cpp.strategy.html, January 28, 2002. (Chapter 14)

[Bosch, 2000] J. BOSCH, *Design and Use of Software Architectures,* Addison-Wesley, Reading, MA, 2000. (Chapter 8)

[Bowen and Hinchey, 1995a] J. P. BOWEN AND M. G. HINCHEY, "Ten Commandments of Formal Methods," *IEEE Computer* **28** (April 1995), pp. 56–63. (Chapter 11)

[Bowen and Hinchey, 1995b] J. P. BOWEN AND M. G. HINCHEY, "Seven More Myths of Formal Methods," *IEEE Software* **12** (July 1995), pp. 34–41. (Chapter 11)

[Brady, 1977] J. M. BRADY, *The Theory of Computer Science*, Chapman and Hall, London, 1977. (Chapter 11)

[Brereton and Budgen, 2000] P. BRERETON AND D. BUDGEN, "Component-Based Systems: A Classification of Issues," *IEEE Computer* **33** (November 2000), pp. 54–62. (Chapter 8)

[Brereton et al., 1999] P. BRERETON, D. BUDGEN, K. BENNETT, M. MUNRO, P. LAYZELL, L. MACAULAY, D. GRIFFITHS, AND C. STANNETT, "The Future of Software," *Communications of the ACM* **42** (December 1999), pp. 78–84. (Chapter 1)

[Briand and Wüst, 2001] L. C. BRIAND AND J. WÜST, "Modeling Development Effort in Object-Oriented Systems Using Design Properties," *IEEE Transactions on Software Engineering* **27** (November 2001), pp. 963–86. (Chapters 5 and 9)

[Briand, Bunse, and Daly, 2001] L. C. BRIAND, C. BUNSE, AND J. W. DALY, "A Controlled Experiment for Evaluating Quality Guidelines on the Maintainability of Object-Oriented Designs," *IEEE Transactions on Software Engineering* **27** (June 2001), pp. 513–30. (Chapters 13 and 15)

[Briand, Daly, Porter, and Wüst, 1998] L. C. BRIAND, J. DALY, V. PORTER, AND J. WÜST, "A Comprehensive Empirical Validation of Design Measures for Object-Oriented Systems," *Proceedings of the Fifth International Metrics Symposium*, Bethesda, MD, November 1998, pp. 246–257. (Chapter 7)

[Brooks, 1975] F. P. BROOKS, JR., *The Mythical Man-Month: Essays on Software Engineering,* Addison-Wesley, Reading, MA, 1975; Twentieth Anniversary Edition, Addison-Wesley, Reading, MA, 1995. (Chapters 1, 3, 4, and 10)

[Brooks, 1986] F. P. BROOKS, JR., "No Silver Bullet," in: *Information Processing '86*, H.-J. Kugler (Editor), Elsevier North-Holland, New York, 1986; reprinted in *IEEE Computer* **20** (April 1987), pp. 10–19. (Chapters 3 and 13)

[Brooks et al., 1987] F. P. BROOKS, V. BASILI, B. BOEHM, E. BOND, N. EASTMAN, D. L. EVANS, A. K. JONES, M. SHAW, AND C. A. ZRAKET, "Report of the Defense Science Board Task Force on Military Software," Department of Defense, Office of the Under Secretary of Defense for Acquisition, Washington, DC, September 1987. (Chapter 3)

[Brown et al., 1998] W. J. BROWN, R. C. MALVEAU, W. H. BROWN, H. W. MCCORMICK, III, AND T. J. MOWBRAY, *AntiPatterns: Refactoring Software, Architectures, and Projects in Crisis,* John Wiley and Sons, New York, 1998. (Chapter 8)

[Brownsword, Oberndorf, and Sledge, 2000] L. BROWNSWORD, T. OBERNDORF, AND C. A. SLEDGE, "Developing New Process for COTS-Based Systems," *IEEE Software* **17** (July/August 2000), pp. 40–47. (Chapter 1)

[Bruegge, Blythe, Jackson, and Shufelt, 1992] B. BRUEGGE, J. BLYTHE, J. JACKSON, AND J. SHUFELT, "Object-Oriented Modeling with OMT," Proceedings of the Conference on Object-Oriented Programming, Languages, and Systems, OOPSLA '92, *ACM SIG-PLAN Notices* **27** (October 1992), pp. 359–76. (Chapter 7)

[Bruno and Marchetto, 1986] G. BRUNO AND G. MARCHETTO, "Process-Translatable Petri Nets for the Rapid Prototyping of Process Control Systems," *IEEE Transactions on Software Engineering* **SE-12** (February 1986), pp. 346–57. (Chapter 11)

[Budd, 2002] T. A. BUDD, *An Introduction to Object-Oriented Programming,* 3rd ed., Addison-Wesley, Reading, MA, 2002. (Chapter 1)

[Bush, 1990] M. BUSH, "Improving Software Quality: The Use of Formal Inspections at the Jet Propulsion Laboratory," *Proceedings of the 12th International Conference on Software Engineering*, Nice, France, March 1990, pp. 196–99. (Chapter 6)

[Business Week Online, 1999] *Business Week Online*, www.businessweek.com/1999/99_08/b3617025 .htm, February 2, 1999. (Chapter 4)

[Caldiera and Basili, 1991] G. CALDIERA AND V. R. BASILI, "Identifying and Qualifying Reusable Software Components," *IEEE Computer* **24** (February 1991), pp. 61–70. (Chapter 8)

[Capper, Colgate, Hunter, and James, 1994] N. P. CAPPER, R. J. COLGATE, J. C. HUNTER, AND M. F. JAMES, "The Impact of Object-Oriented Technology on Software Quality: Three Case Histories," *IBM Systems Journal* **33** (No. 1, 1994), pp. 131–57. (Chapters 1 and 7)

[Cartwright and Shepperd, 2000] M. CARTWRIGHT AND M. SHEPPERD, "An Empirical Investigation of an Object-Oriented Software System," *IEEE Transactions on Software Engineering* **26** (August 2000), pp. 786–95. (Chapters 7 and 9)

[Ceschi, Sillitti, Succi, and De Panfilis, 2005] M. CESCHI, A. SILLITTI, G. SUCCI, AND S. DE PANFILIS, "Project Management in Plan-Based and Agile Companies,"

*IEEE Software* **22** (May/June 2005), pp. 21-27. (Chapter 2)

[Charette, Adams, and White, 1997] R. N. CHARETTE, K. M. ADAMS, AND M. B. WHITE, "Managing Risk in Software Maintenance," *IEEE Software* **14** (May/June 1997), pp. 43–50. (Chapter 15)

[Chen, 1976] P. CHEN, "The Entity-Relationship Model— Towards a Unified View of Data," *ACM Transactions on Database Systems* **1** (March 1976), pp. 9–36. (Chapter 11)

[Chidamber and Kemerer, 1994] S. R. CHIDAMBER AND C. F. KEMERER, "A Metrics Suite for Object Oriented Design," *IEEE Transactions on Software Engineering* **20** (June 1994), pp. 476–93. (Chapters 13 and 14)

[Ciolkowski, Laitenberger, and Biffl, 2003] M. CIOLKOWSKI, O. LAITENBERGER, S. BIFFL, "Software Reviews, the State of the Practice," *IEEE Software* **20** (November/ December 2003), pp. 46–51. (Chapter 6)

[Clarke, Podgurski, Richardson, and Zeil, 1989] L. A. CLARKE, A. PODGURSKI, D. J. RICHARDSON, AND S. J. ZEIL, "A Formal Evaluation of Data Flow Path Selection Criteria," *IEEE Transactions on Software Engineering* **15** (November 1989), pp. 1318–32. (Chapter 14)

[Clements and Northrop, 2002] P. CLEMENTS AND L. NORTHROP, *Software Product Lines: Practices and Patterns*, Addison-Wesley, Reading, MA, 2002. (Chapter 8)

[CNN.com, 2003] "Russia: Software Bug Made Soyuz Stray," edition.cnn.com/2003/TECH/space/05/06/ soyuz.landing.ap/. (Chapter 3)

[Coad and Yourdon, 1991a] P. COAD AND E. YOURDON, *Object-Oriented Analysis,* 2nd ed., Yourdon Press, Englewood Cliffs, NJ, 1991. (Chapter 12)

[Coad and Yourdon, 1991b] P. COAD AND E. YOURDON, *Object-Oriented Design*, Yourdon Press, Englewood Cliffs, NJ, 1991. (Chapter 13)

[Cockburn, 2001] A. COCKBURN, *Agile Software Development*, Addison-Wesley Professional, Reading, MA, 2001. (Chapter 2)

[Coleman et al., 1994] D. COLEMAN, P. ARNOLD, S. BODOFF, C. DOLLIN, H. GILCHRIST, F. HAYES, AND P. JEREMAES, *Object-Oriented Development: The Fusion Method*, Prentice Hall, Englewood Cliffs, NJ, 1994. (Chapter 12)

[Connell and Shafer, 1989] J. L. CONNELL AND L. SHAFER, *Structured Rapid Prototyping: An Evolutionary Approach to Software Development,*

Yourdon Press, Englewood Cliffs, NJ, 1989. (Chapters 1, 2, and 10)

[Conradi and Fuggetta, 2002] R. CONRADI AND A. FUGGETTA, "Improving Software Process Improvement," *IEEE Software* **19** (July/August 2002), pp. 92–99. (Chapter 3)

[Coolahan and Roussopoulos, 1983] J. E. COOLAHAN, JR., AND N. ROUSSOPOULOS, "Timing Requirements for Time-Driven Systems Using Augmented Petri Nets," *IEEE Transactions on Software Engineering* **SE-9** (September 1983), pp. 603–16. (Chapter 11)

[Costagliola, Ferrucci, Tortora, and Vitiello, 2005] G. COSTAGLIOLA, F. FERRUCCI, G. TORTORA, AND G. VITIELLO, "Class Point: An Approach for the Size Estimation of Object-Oriented Systems," *IEEE Transactions on Software Engineering* **31** (January 2005), pp. 52–74. (Chapter 9)

[Crossman, 1982] T. D. CROSSMAN, "Inspection Teams, Are They Worth It?" *Proceedings of the Second National Symposium on EDP Quality Assurance*, Chicago, November 1982. (Chapter 14)

[Curtis, Hefley, and Miller, 2002] B. CURTIS, W. E. HEFLEY, AND S. A. MILLER, *The People Capability Maturity Model: Guidelines for Improving the Workforce*, Addison-Wesley, Reading, MA, 2002. (Chapter 4)

[Cusumano and Selby, 1995] M. A. CUSUMANO AND R. W. SELBY, *Microsoft Secrets: How the World's Most Powerful Software Company Creates Technology, Shapes Markets, and Manages People*, The Free Press/Simon and Schuster, New York, 1995. (Chapters 2 and 4)

[Cusumano and Selby, 1997] M. A. CUSUMANO AND R. W. SELBY, "How Microsoft Builds Software," *Communications of the ACM* **40** (June 1997), pp. 53–61. (Chapters 2 and 4)

[Cutter Consortium, 2002] Cutter Consortium, "78% of IT Organizations Have Litigated," *The Cutter Edge*, www.cutter.com/research/2002/edge020409 .html, April 09, 2002. (Chapter 1)

[Cysneiros and do Prado Leite, 2004] L. M. CYSNEIROS AND J. C. S. DO PRADO LEITE, "Nonfunctional Requirements: From Elicitation to Conceptual Models," *IEEE Transactions on Software Engineering* **30** (May 2004), pp. 328–50. (Chapter 10)

[Dahl and Nygaard, 1966] O.-J. DAHL AND K. NYGAARD, "SIMULA—An ALGOL-Based Simulation Language," *Communications of the ACM* **9** (September 1966), pp. 671–78. (Chapter 7)

[Daly, 1977] E. B. DALY, "Management of Software Development," *IEEE Transactions on Software Engineering* **SE-3** (May 1977), pp. 229–42. (Chapter 1)

[Dart, Ellison, Feiler, and Habermann, 1987] S. A. DART, R. J. ELLISON, P. H. FEILER, AND A. N. HABERMANN, "Software Development Environments," *IEEE Computer* **20** (November 1987), pp. 18–28. (Chapter 11)

[Date, 2003] C. J. DATE, *An Introduction to Database Systems,* 8th ed., Addison-Wesley, Reading, MA, 2003. (Chapter 14)

[Dawood, 1994] M. DAWOOD, "It's Time for ISO 9000," *CrossTalk* (March 1994) pp. 26–28. (Chapter 3)

[de Champeaux and Faure, 1992] D. DE CHAMPEAUX AND P. FAURE, "A Comparative Study of Object-Oriented Analysis Methods," *Journal of Object-Oriented Programming* **5** (March/April 1992), pp. 21–33. (Chapter 12)

[Delisle and Garlan, 1990] N. DELISLE AND D. GARLAN, "A Formal Description of an Oscilloscope," *IEEE Software* **7** (September 1990), pp. 29–36. (Chapter 11)

[Delisle and Schwartz, 1987] N. DELISLE AND M. SCHWARTZ, "A Programming Environment for CSP," Proceedings of the Second ACM SIGSOFT/SIGPLAN Software Engineering Symposium on Practical Software Development Environments, *ACM SIGPLAN Notices* **22** (January 1987), pp. 34–41. (Chapter 11)

[DeMarco, 1978] T. DEMARCO, *Structured Analysis and System Specification*, Yourdon Press, New York, 1978. (Chapter 11)

[DeMarco and Boehm, 2002] T. DEMARCO AND B. BOEHM, "The Agile Methods Fray," *IEEE Computer* **35** (June 2002), pp. 90–92. (Chapters 2 and 4)

[DeMarco and Lister, 1987] T. DEMARCO AND T. LISTER, *Peopleware: Productive Projects and Teams*, Dorset House, New York, 1987. (Chapter 1 and 4)

[DeMillo, Lipton, and Perlis, 1979] R. A. DEMILLO, R. J. LIPTON, AND A. J. PERLIS, "Social Processes and Proofs of Theorems and Programs," *Communications of the ACM* **22** (May 1979), pp. 271–80. (Chapter 6)

[DeMillo, Lipton, and Sayward, 1978] R. A. DEMILLO, R. J. LIPTON, AND F. G. SAYWARD, "Hints on Test Data Selection: Help for the Practicing Programmer," *IEEE Computer* **11** (April 1978), pp. 34–43. (Chapter 6)

[Deming, 1986] W. E. DEMING, *Out of the Crisis*, MIT Center for Advanced Engineering Study, Cambridge, MA, 1986. (Chapter 3)

[DeRemer and Kron, 1976] F. DeRemer and H. H. Kron, "Programming-in-the-Large versus Programming-in-the-Small," *IEEE Transactions on Software Engineering* **SE-2** (June 1976), pp. 80–86. (Chapter 5)

[Devenny, 1976] T. Devenny, "An Exploratory Study of Software Cost Estimating at the Electronic Systems Division," Thesis No. GSM/SM/765–4, Air Force Institute of Technology, Dayton, OH, 1976. (Chapter 9)

[Devlin, 2001] K. Devlin, "The Real Reason Why Software Engineers Need Math," *Communications of the ACM* **44** (October 2001), pp. 21–22. (Chapter 1)

[Diaz and Sligo, 1997] M. Diaz and J. Sligo, "How Software Process Improvement Helped Motorola," *IEEE Software* **14** (September/October 1997), pp. 75–81. (Chapter 3)

[Dijkstra, 1968] E. W. Dijkstra, "A Constructive Approach to the Problem of Program Correctness," *BIT* **8** (No. 3, 1968), pp. 174–86. (Chapter 6)

[Dijkstra, 1972] E. W. Dijkstra, "The Humble Programmer," *Communications of the ACM* **15** (October 1972), pp. 859–66. (Chapter 6)

[Dijkstra, 1976] E. W. Dijkstra, *A Discipline of Programming,* Prentice Hall, Englewood Cliffs, NJ, 1976. (Chapter 5)

[Diller, 1994] A. Diller, *Z: An Introduction to Formal Methods*, 2nd ed., John Wiley and Sons, Chichester, UK, 1994. (Chapter 11)

[Dion, 1993] R. Dion, "Process Improvement and the Corporate Balance Sheet," *IEEE Software* **10** (July 1993), pp. 28–35. (Chapter 3)

[Dolado, 2000] J. J. Dolado, "A Validation of the Component-Based Method for Software Size Estimation," *IEEE Transactions on Software Engineering* **26** (October 2000), pp. 1006–21. (Chapter 9)

[Donohoe, 2000] P. Donohoe (Editor), *Software Product Lines: Experience and Research Directions*, Kluwer Academic Publishers, Boston, 2000. (Chapter 8)

[Doolan, 1992] E. P. Doolan, "Experience with Fagan's Inspection Method," *Software—Practice and Experience* **22** (February 1992), pp. 173–82. (Chapter 11)

[Dooley and Schach, 1985] J. W. M. Dooley and S. R. Schach, "FLOW: A Software Development Environment Using Diagrams," *Journal of Systems and Software* **5** (August 1985), pp. 203–19. (Chapter 5)

[Drobka, Noftz, and Raghu, 2004] J. Drobka, D. Noftz, and R. Raghu, "Piloting XP on Four Mission-Critical Projects," *IEEE Software* **21** (November/December 2004), pp. 70–75. (Chapters 2 and 4)

[D'Souza and Wills, 1999] D. D'Souza and A. Wills, *Objects, Components, and Frameworks with UML: The Catalysis Approach*, Addison-Wesley, Reading, MA, 1999. (Chapters 8 and 12)

[Dunn, 1984] R. H. Dunn, *Software Defect Removal*, McGraw-Hill, New York, 1984. (Chapter 14)

[Dunsmore, Roper, and Wood, 2003] A. Dunsmore, M. Roper, and M. Wood, "The Development and Evaluation of Three Diverse Techniques for Object-Oriented Code Inspection," *IEEE Transactions on Software Engineering* **29** (August 2003), pp. 677–86. (Chapter 6)

[Dybå, 2005] T. Dybå, "An Empirical Investigation of the Key Factors for Success in Software Process Improvement," *IEEE Transactions in Software Engineering* **31** (May 2005), pp. 410–24. (Chapter 3)

[Ebert, Matsubara, Pezzé, and Bertelsen, 1997] C. Ebert, T. Matsubara, M. Pezzé, and O. W. Bertelsen, "The Road to Maturity: Navigating between Craft and Science," *IEEE Software* **14** (November/December 1997), pp. 77–88. (Chapters 1 and 3)

[Ebner and Kaindl, 2002] G. Ebner and H. Kaindl, "Tracing All Around in Reengineering," *IEEE Software* **19** (May/June 2002), pp. 70–77. (Chapter 15)

[Eickelmann, 2003] N. Eickelmann, "An Insider's View of CMM Level 5," *IEEE Software* **20** (July/August 2003), pp. 79–81. (Chapter 3)

[Eickelmann and Anant, 2003] N. Eickelmann and A. Anant, "Statistical Process Control: What You Don't Know Can Hurt You!" *IEEE Software* **20** (March/April 2003), pp. 49–51. (Chapter 3)

[Elbaum, Malishevsky, and Rothermel, 2002] A. Elbaum, A. G. Malishevsky, and G. Rothermel, "Test Case Prioritization: A Family of Empirical Studies," *IEEE Transactions on Software Engineering* **28** (2002), pp. 159–82. (Chapters 6 and 14)

[El Emam, Benlarbi, Goel, and Rai, 2001] K. El Emam, S. Benlarbi, N. Goel, and S. N. Rai, "The Confounding Effect of Class Size on the Validity of Object-Oriented Metrics," *IEEE Transactions on Software Engineering* **27** (July 2001), pp. 630–50. (Chapter 5)

[Elrad et al., 2001] T. Elrad, M. Aksit, G. Kiczales, K. Lieberherr, and H. Ossher, "Discussing Aspects of AOP," *Communications of the ACM* **44** (October 2001), pp. 33–38. (Chapter 7)

[El-Rewini et al., 1995] H. EL-REWINI, S. HAMILTON, Y.-P. SHAN, R. EARLE, S. MCGAUGHEY, A. HELAL, R. BADRACHALAM, A. CHIEN, A. GRIMSHAW, B. LEE, A. WADE, D. MORSE, A. ELMAGRAMID, E. PITOURA, R. BINDER, AND P. WEGNER, "Object Technology," *IEEE Computer* **28** (October 1995), pp. 58–72. (Chapter 7)

[Elshoff, 1976] J. L. ELSHOFF, "An Analysis of Some Commercial PL/I Programs," *IEEE Transactions on Software Engineering* **SE-2** (June 1976), pp. 113–20. (Chapter 1)

[Embley, Jackson, and Woodfield, 1995] D. W. EMBLEY, R. B. JACKSON, AND S. N. WOODFIELD, "OO Systems Analysis: Is It or Isn't It?" *IEEE Software* **12** (July 1995), pp. 18–33. (Chapter 12)

[Endres, 1975] A. ENDRES, "An Analysis of Errors and Their Causes in System Programs," *IEEE Transactions on Software Engineering* **SE-1** (June 1975), pp. 140–49. (Chapter 14)

[Erdogmus, Morisio, and Torchiano, 2005] H. ERDOGMUS, M. MORISIO, AND M. TORCHIANO, "On the Effectiveness of the Test-First Approach to Programming," *IEEE Transactions on Software Engineering* **31** (March 2005), pp. 226–237. (Chapter 2)

[Fach, 2001] P. W. FACH, "Design Reuse through Frameworks and Patterns," *IEEE Software* **18** (September/October 2001), pp. 71–76. (Chapter 8)

[Fagan, 1974] M. E. FAGAN, "Design and Code Inspections and Process Control in the Development of Programs," Technical Report IBM-SSD TR 21.572, IBM Corporation, December 1974. (Chapter 1)

[Fagan, 1976] M. E. FAGAN, "Design and Code Inspections to Reduce Errors in Program Development," *IBM Systems Journal* **15** (No. 3, 1976), pp. 182–211. (Chapters 6, 11, and 13)

[Fagan, 1986] M. E. FAGAN, "Advances in Software Inspections," *IEEE Transactions on Software Engineering* **SE-12** (July 1986), pp. 744–51. (Chapters 6 and 13)

[Fayad and Johnson, 1999] M. FAYAD AND R. JOHNSON, *Domain-Specific Application Frameworks: Frameworks Experience by Industry,* John Wiley and Sons, New York, 1999. (Chapter 8)

[Fayad and Schmidt, 1999] M. FAYAD AND D. C. SCHMIDT, *Building Application Frameworks: Object-Oriented Foundations of Framework Design,* John Wiley and Sons, New York, 1999. (Chapter 8)

[Fayad, Schmidt, and Johnson, 1999] M. FAYAD, D. C. SCHMIDT, AND R. JOHNSON, *Implementing Application Frameworks: Object-Oriented Frameworks at Work,* John Wiley and Sons, New York, 1999. (Chapter 8)

[Fayad, Tsai, and Fulghum, 1996] M. E. FAYAD, W.-T. TSAI, AND M. L. FULGHUM, "Transition to Object-Oriented Software Development," *Communications of the ACM* **39** (February 1996), pp. 108–21. (Chapter 7)

[Feldman, 1979] S. I. FELDMAN, "Make—A Program for Maintaining Computer Programs," *Software—Practice and Experience* **9** (April 1979), pp. 225–65. (Chapter 5)

[Fenton and Pfleeger, 1997] N. E. FENTON AND S. L. PFLEEGER, *Software Metrics: A Rigorous and Practical Approach*, 2nd ed., IEEE Computer Society, Los Alamitos, CA, 1997. (Chapter 5)

[Ferguson and Sheard, 1998] J. FERGUSON AND S. SHEARD, "Leveraging Your CMM Efforts for IEEE/EIA 12207," *IEEE Software* **15** (September/October 1998), pp. 23–28. (Chapter 3)

[Ferguson et al., 1997] P. FERGUSON, W. S. HUMPHREY, S. KHAJENOORI, S. MACKE, AND A. MATVYA, "Results of Applying the Personal Software Process," *IEEE Computer* **30** (May 1997), pp. 24–31. (Chapter 3)

[Fichman and Kemerer, 1992] R. G. FICHMAN AND C. F. KEMERER, "Object-Oriented and Conventional Analysis and Design Methodologies: Comparison and Critique," *IEEE Computer* **25** (October 1992), pp. 22–39. (Chapters 12 and 13)

[Fichman and Kemerer, 1997] R. G. FICHMAN AND C. F. KEMERER, "Object Technology and Reuse: Lessons from Early Adopters," *IEEE Computer* **30** (July 1997), pp. 47–57. (Chapters 1 and 8)

[Fingar, 2000] P. FINGAR, "Component-Based Frameworks for e-Commerce," *Communications of the ACM* **43** (October 2000), pp. 61–66. (Chapter 8)

[Finkelstein, 2000] A. FINKELSTEIN (Editor), *The Future of Software Engineering*, IEEE Computer Society Press, Los Alamitos, CA, 2000. (Chapter 1)

[Finney, 1996] K. FINNEY, "Mathematical Notation in Formal Specification: Too Difficult for the Masses?" *IEEE Transactions on Software Engineering* **22** (1996), pp. 158–59. (Chapter 11)

[Fioravanti and Nesi, 2001] F. FIORAVANTI AND P. NESI, "Estimation and Prediction Metrics for Adaptive Maintenance Effort of Object-Oriented Systems," *IEEE Transactions on Software Engineering* **27** (December 2001), pp. 1062–84. (Chapter 15)

[Flanagan, 2005] D. FLANAGAN, *Java in a Nutshell: A Desktop Quick Reference*, 5th ed., O'Reilly and

Associates, Sebastopol, CA, 2005. (Chapters 7, 8, and 13)

[Florac, Carleton, and Barnard, 2000] W. A. FLORAC, A. D. CARLETON, AND J. BARNARD, "Statistical Process Control: Analyzing a Space Shuttle Onboard Software Process," *IEEE Software* **17** (July/August 2000), pp. 97–106. (Chapter 3)

[*Florida Today*, 1999] "Milstar Satellite Lost during Air Force Titan 4b Launch from Cape," *Florida Today*, www.floridatoday.com/space/explore/uselv/titan/b32/, June 5, 1999. (Chapter 3)

[Fowler, 1986] P. J. FOWLER, "In-Process Inspections of Workproducts at AT&T," *AT&T Technical Journal* **65** (March/April 1986), pp. 102–12. (Chapter 6)

[Fowler, 1997] M. FOWLER, *Analysis Patterns: Reusable Object Models*, Addison-Wesley, Reading, MA, 1997. (Chapter 8)

[Fowler and Scott, 2000] M. FOWLER WITH K. SCOTT, *UML Distilled*, 2nd ed., Addison-Wesley, Upper Saddle River, NJ, 2000. (Chapter 16)

[Fowler et al., 1999] M. FOWLER WITH K. BECK, J. BRANT, W. OPDYKE, AND D. ROBERTS, *Refactoring: Improving the Design of Existing Code*, Addison-Wesley, Reading, MA, 1999. (Chapter 2)

[Fraser and Vaishnavi, 1997] M. D. FRASER AND V. K. VAISHNAVI, "A Formal Specifications Maturity Model," *Communications of the ACM* **40** (May 1999), pp. 95–103. (Chapter 11)

[Freeman and Schach, 2005] G. L. FREEMAN, JR., AND S. R. SCHACH, "The Task-Dependent Nature of the Maintenance of Object-Oriented Programs," *Journal of Systems and Software* **76** (May 2005), pp. 195–206. (Chapter 15)

[Fuggetta, 1993] A. FUGGETTA, "A Classification of CASE Technology," *IEEE Computer* **26** (December 1993), pp. 25–38. (Chapter 5)

[Furey and Kitchenham, 1997] S. FUREY AND B. KITCHENHAM, "Function Points," *IEEE Software* **14** (March/April 1997), pp. 28–32. (Chapter 9)

[Gamma, Helm, Johnson, and Vlissides, 1995] E. GAMMA, R. HELM, R. JOHNSON, AND J. VLISSIDES, *Design Patterns: Elements of Reusable Object-Oriented Software*, Addison-Wesley, Reading, MA, 1995. (Chapter 8)

[Gane and Sarsen, 1979] C. GANE AND T. SARSEN, *Structured Systems Analysis: Tools and Techniques*, Prentice Hall, Englewood Cliffs, NJ, 1979. (Chapters 11 and 13)

[Gane, 1989] C. GANE, *Rapid System Development: Using Structured Techniques and Relational Technology*, Prentice Hall, Englewood Cliffs, NJ, 1989. (Chapter 10)

[Garman, 1981] J. R. GARMAN, "The 'Bug' Heard 'Round the World," *ACM SIGSOFT Software Engineering Notes* **6** (October 1981), pp. 3–10. (Chapter 3)

[Gelperin and Hetzel, 1988] D. GELPERIN AND B. HETZEL, "The Growth of Software Testing," *Communications of the ACM* **31** (June 1988), pp. 687–95. (Chapter 6)

[Gerald and Wheatley, 1999] C. F. GERALD AND P. O. WHEATLEY, *Applied Numerical Analysis*, 6th ed., Addison-Wesley, Reading, MA, 1999. (Chapter 7)

[Ghezzi and Mandrioli, 1987] C. GHEZZI AND D. MANDRIOLI, "On Eclecticism in Specifications: A Case Study Centered around Petri Nets," *Proceedings of the Fourth International Workshop on Software Specification and Design*, Monterey, CA, 1987, pp. 216–24. (Chapter 11)

[Gifford and Spector, 1987] D. GIFFORD AND A. SPECTOR, "Case Study: IBM's System/360-370 Architecture," *Communications of the ACM* **30** (April 1987), pp. 292–307. (Chapter 8)

[GJSentinel.com, 2003] "Sallie Mae's Errors Double Some Bills," www.gjsentinel.com/news/content/coxnet/headlines/0522_salliemae.html, May 22, 2003. (Chapter 1)

[Glass, 1998] R. L. GLASS, "Is There Really a Software Crisis?" *IEEE Software* **15** (January/February 1998), pp. 104–5. (Chapter 1)

[Goldberg and Robson, 1989] A. GOLDBERG AND D. ROBSON, *Smalltalk-80: The Language,* Addison-Wesley, Reading, MA, 1989. (Chapters 7 and 13)

[Gomaa, 2000] H. GOMAA, *Designing Concurrent, Distributed, and Real-Time Applications with UML*, Addison-Wesley, Reading, MA, 2000. (Chapter 13)

[Goodenough, 1979] J. B. GOODENOUGH, "A Survey of Program Testing Issues," in: *Research Directions in Software Technology*, P. Wegner (Editor), The MIT Press, Cambridge, MA, 1979, pp. 316–40. (Chapter 6)

[Goodenough and Gerhart, 1975] J. B. GOODENOUGH AND S. L. GERHART, "Toward a Theory of Test Data Selection," *Proceedings of the Third International Conference on Reliable Software*, Los Angeles, 1975, pp. 493–510; also published in *IEEE Transactions on Software Engineering* **SE-1** (June 1975), pp. 156–73.

Revised version: J. B. Goodenough and S. L. Gerhart, "Toward a Theory of Test Data Selection: Data Selection Criteria," in: *Current Trends in Programming Methodology,* Vol. 2, R. T. Yeh (Editor), Prentice Hall, Englewood Cliffs, NJ, 1977, pp. 44–79. (Chapters 6 and 11)

[Gordon, 1979] M. J. C. GORDON, *The Denotational Description of Programming Languages: An Introduction*, Springer-Verlag, New York, 1979. (Chapter 11)

[Gorla and Lam, 2004] N. GORLA AND Y. W. LAM, "Who Should Work with Whom?" *Communications of the ACM* **47** (June 2004), pp. 79–82. (Chapter 4)

[Goth, 2000] G. GOTH, "New Air Traffic Control Software Takes an Incremental Approach," *IEEE Software* **17** (July/August 2000), pp. 108–111. (Chapter 2)

[Grady, 1992] R. B. GRADY, *Practical Software Metrics for Project Management and Process Improvement*, Prentice Hall, Englewood Cliffs, NJ, 1992. (Chapter 14)

[Grady, 1994] R. B. GRADY, "Successfully Applying Software Metrics," *IEEE Computer* **27** (September 1994), pp. 18–25. (Chapter 1)

[Gramlich, 1997] E. M. GRAMLICH, *A Guide to Benefit–Cost Analysis*, 2nd ed., Waveland Books, Prospect Heights, IL, 1997. (Chapter 5)

[Green, 2000] P. GREEN, "FW: Here's an Update to the Simulated Kangaroo Story," *The Risks Digest* **20** (January 23, 2000), catless.ncl.ac.uk/Risks/20.76.html. (Chapter 8)

[Griss, 1993] M. L. GRISS, "Software Reuse: From Library to Factory," *IBM Systems Journal* **32** (No. 4, 1993), pp. 548–66. (Chapter 8)

[Guerrero and Eterovic, 2004] F. GUERRERO AND Y. ETEROVIC, "Adopting the SW-CMM in a Small IT Organization," *IEEE Software* **21** (July/August 2004), pp. 29–35. (Chapter 3)

[Guha, Lang, and Bassiouni, 1987] R. K. GUHA, S. D. LANG, AND M. BASSIOUNI, "Software Specification and Design Using Petri Nets," *Proceedings of the Fourth International Workshop on Software Specification and Design*, Monterey, CA, April 1987, pp. 225–30. (Chapter 11)

[Guimaraes, 1985] T. GUIMARAES, "A Study of Application Program Development Techniques," *Communications of the ACM* **28** (May 1985), pp. 494–99. (Chapter 14)

[Guinan, Cooprider, and Sawyer, 1997] P. J. GUINAN, J. G. COOPRIDER, AND S. SAWYER, "The Effective Use of Automated Application Development Tools," *IBM Systems Journal* **36** (No. 1, 1997), pp. 124–39. (Chapter 5)

[Guttag, 1977] J. GUTTAG, "Abstract Data Types and the Development of Data Structures," *Communications of the ACM* **20** (June 1977), pp. 396–404. (Chapter 7)

[Hagge and Lappe, 2005] L. HAGGE AND K. LAPPE, "Sharing Requirements Engineering Experience Using Patterns," *IEEE Software* **22** (January/February 2005), pp. 24–31. (Chapter 8)

[Haley, 1996] T. J. HALEY, "Raytheon's Experience in Software Process Improvement," *IEEE Software* **13** (November 1996), pp. 33–41. (Chapter 3)

[Hall, 1990] A. HALL, "Seven Myths of Formal Methods," *IEEE Software* **7** (September 1990), pp. 11–19. (Chapter 11)

[Hall and Chapman, 2002] A. HALL AND R. CHAPMAN, "Correctness by Construction: Developing a Commercial Secure System," *IEEE Software* **19** (January/February 2002), pp. 18–25. (Chapter 11)

[Harel and Gery, 1997] D. HAREL AND E. GERY, "Executable Object Modeling with Statecharts," *IEEE Computer* **30** (July 1997), pp. 31–42. (Chapters 11 and 12)

[Harel et al., 1990] D. HAREL, H. LACHOVER, A. NAAMAD, A. PNUELI, M. POLITI, R. SHERMAN, A. SHTULL-TRAURING, AND M. TRAKHTENBROT, "STATEMATE: A Working Environment for the Development of Complex Reactive Systems," *IEEE Transactions on Software Engineering* **16** (April 1990), pp. 403–14. (Chapters 11 and 14)

[Harrison, 2004] W. HARRISON, "The Dangers of End-User Programming," *IEEE Software* **21** (July/August 2004), pp. 5–7. (Chapter 14)

[Harrold and Soffa, 1991] M. J. HARROLD AND M. L. SOFFA, "Selecting and Using Data for Integration Testing," *IEEE Software* **8** (1991), pp. 58–65. (Chapter 14)

[Harrold, McGregor, and Fitzpatrick, 1992] M. J. HARROLD, J. D. MCGREGOR, AND K. J. FITZPATRICK, "Incremental Testing of Object-Oriented Class Structures," *Proceedings of the 14th International Conference on Software Engineering*, Melbourne, Australia, May 1992, pp. 68–80. (Chapter 14)

[Harrold, Rosenblum, Rothermel and Weyuker, 2001] M. J. HARROLD, D. ROSENBLUM, G. ROTHERMEL, AND E. WEYUKER, "Empirical Studies of a Prediction Model for Regression Test Selection," *IEEE Transactions on*

*Software Engineering* **27** (March 2001), pp. 248–63. (Chapter 15)

[Hatton, 1998] L. HATTON, "Does OO Sync with How We Think?" *IEEE Software* **15** (May/June 1998), pp. 46–54. (Chapter 1)

[Haxthausen and Peleska, 2000] A. E. HAXTHAUSEN AND J. PELESKA, "Formal Development and Verification of a Distributed Railway Control System," *IEEE Transactions on Software Engineering* **26** (August 2000), pp. 687–701. (Chapter 11)

[Hayes, 2004] F. HAYES, "Chaos Is Back," *Computerworld*, www.computerworld.com/management-topics/ management/project/story/0,10801,97283,00 .html, November 8, 2004. (Chapters 1 and 2)

[Heineman and Councill, 2001] G. T. HEINEMAN AND W. T. COUNCILL, *Component-Based Software Engineering: Putting the Pieces Together*, Addison-Wesley, Reading, MA, 2001. (Chapter 8)

[Henry and Humphrey, 1990] S. M. HENRY AND M. HUMPHREY, "A Controlled Experiment to Evaluate Maintainability of Object-Oriented Software," *Proceedings of the IEEE Conference on Software Maintenance,* San Diego, CA, November 1990, pp. 258–65. (Chapter 15)

[Henry and Kafura, 1981] S. M. HENRY AND D. KAFURA, "Software Structure Metrics Based on Information Flow," *IEEE Transactions on Software Engineering* **SE-7** (September 1981), pp. 510–18. (Chapter 13)

[Herbsleb et al., 1997] J. HERBSLEB, D. ZUBROW, D. GOLDENSON, W. HAYES, AND M. PAULK, "Software Quality and the Capability Maturity Model," *Communications of the ACM* **40** (June 1997), pp. 30–40. (Chapter 3)

[Hetzel, 1988] W. HETZEL, *The Complete Guide to Software Testing,* 2nd ed., QED Information Systems, Wellesley, MA, 1988. (Chapter 6)

[Highsmith and Coburn, 2001] J. HIGHSMITH AND A. COCKBURN, "Agile Software Development: The Business of Innovation," *IEEE Computer* **34** (September 2001), pp. 120–22. (Chapter 2)

[Hoare, 1969] C. A. R. HOARE, "An Axiomatic Basis for Computer Programming," *Communications of the ACM* **12** (October 1969), pp. 576–83. (Chapter 6)

[Hoare, 1981] C. A. R. HOARE, "The Emperor's Old Clothes," *Communications of the ACM* **24** (February 1981), pp. 75–83. (Chapter 6)

[Hoare, 1985] C. A. R. HOARE, *Communicating Sequential Processes*, Prentice Hall International, Englewood Cliffs, NJ, 1985. (Chapter 11)

[Hoare, 1987] C. A. R. HOARE, "An Overview of Some Formal Methods for Program Design," *IEEE Computer* **20** (September 1987), pp. 85–91. (Chapter 13)

[Holzinger, 2005] A. HOLZINGER, "Usability Engineering Methods for Software Developers," *Communications of the ACM* **48** (January 2005), pp. 71–74. (Chapter 10)

[Horgan, London, and Lyu, 1994] J. R. HORGAN, S. LONDON, AND M. R. LYU, "Achieving Software Quality with Testing Coverage Measures," *IEEE Computer* **27** ( 1994), pp. 60–69. (Chapter 14)

[Howden, 1987] W. E. HOWDEN, *Functional Program Testing and Analysis*, McGraw-Hill, New York, 1987. (Chapter 14)

[Humphrey, 1989] W. S. HUMPHREY, *Managing the Software Process*, Addison-Wesley, Reading, MA, 1989. (Chapter 3)

[Humphrey, 1996] W. S. HUMPHREY, "Using a Defined and Measured Personal Software Process," *IEEE Software* **13** (May 1996), pp. 77–88. (Chapter 3)

[Humphrey, 1999] W. S. HUMPHREY, "Pathways to Process Maturity: The Personal Software Process and Team Software Process," *SEI Interactive* **2** (No. 4, December 1999), interactive.sei.cmu.edu/Features/ 1999/June/Background/Background.jun99.htm. (Chapter 3)

[Humphrey, Snider, and Willis, 1991] W. S. HUMPHREY, T. R. SNIDER, AND R. R. WILLIS, "Software Process Improvement at Hughes Aircraft," *IEEE Software* **8** (July 1991), pp. 11–23. (Chapter 3)

[Hwang, 1981] S.-S. V. HWANG, "An Empirical Study in Functional Testing, Structural Testing, and Code Reading Inspection," Scholarly Paper 362, Department of Computer Science, University of Maryland, College Park, 1981. (Chapter 14)

[IEEE 1028, 1997] *Standard for Software Reviews*, IEEE 1028, Institute of Electrical and Electronic Engineers, New York, 1997. (Chapter 6)

[IEEE 1058, 1998] "IEEE Standard for Software Project Management Plans," IEEE Std. 1058-1998, Institute of Electrical and Electronic Engineers, New York, 1998. (Chapter 9)

[IEEE 610.12, 1990] "A Glossary of Software Engineering Terminology," IEEE 610.12-1990, Institute of Electrical and Electronic Engineers, New York, 1990. (Chapters 1 and 6)

[IEEE Standards, 2003] "Products and Projects Status Report," standards.ieee.org/db/status/status.txt, June 3, 2003. (Chapter 1)

[IEEE/ACM, 1999] "Software Engineering Code of Ethics and Professional Practice, Version 5.2, as Recommended by the IEEE-CS/ACM Joint Task Force on Software Engineering Ethics and Professional Practice," www.computer.org/tab/seprof/code.htm, 1999. (Chapter 1)

[IEEE/EIA 12207.0-1996, 1998] "IEEE/EIA 12207.0-1996 Industry Implementation of International Standard ISO/IEC 12207:1995," Institute of Electrical and Electronic Engineers, Electronic Industries Alliance, New York, 1998. (Chapters 1 and 3)

[Isakowitz and Kauffman, 1996] T. ISAKOWITZ AND R. J. KAUFFMAN, "Supporting Search for Reusable Software Objects," *IEEE Transactions on Software Engineering* **22** (June 1996), pp. 407–23. (Chapter 8)

[ISO 9000-3, 1991] "ISO 9000-3, Guidelines for the Application of ISO 9001 to the Development, Supply, and Maintenance of Software," International Organization for Standardization, Geneva, 1991. (Chapter 3)

[ISO 9001, 1987] "ISO 9001, Quality Systems—Model for Quality Assurance in Design/Development, Production, Installation, and Servicing," International Organization for Standardization, Geneva, 1987. (Chapter 3)

[ISO/IEC 12207, 1995] "ISO/IEC 12207:1995, Information Technology—Software Life-Cycle Processes," International Organization for Standardization, International Electrotechnical Commission, Geneva, 1995. (Chapters 1, 2, and 3)

[ISO/IEC 14882, 1998] *Programming Language C++*, ISO/IEC 14882, International Organization for Standardization, International Electrotechnical Commission, Geneva, 1998. (Chapter 8)

[ISO/IEC 1539–1, 2004] *Information Technology— Programming Languages—Fortran—Part 1: Base Language*, ISO/IEC 1539–1, International Organization for Standardization, International Electrotechnical Commission, Geneva, 2004. (Chapter 8)

[ISO/IEC 1989, 2002] *Information Technology— Programming Language COBOL*, ISO 1989:2002, International Organization for Standardization, International Electrotechnical Commission, Geneva, 2002. (Chapter 8)

[ISO/IEC 8652, 1995] *Programming Language Ada: Language and Standard Libraries*, ISO/IEC 8652, International Organization for Standardization, International Electrotechnical Commission, Geneva, 1995. (Chapters 8 and 13)

[IWSSD, 1986] Call for Papers, Fourth International Workshop on Software Specification and Design, *ACM SIGSOFT Software Engineering Notes* **11** (April 1986), pp. 94–96. (Chapter 11)

[Jackson, 1975] M. A. JACKSON, *Principles of Program Design*, Academic Press, New York, 1975. (Chapters 11 and 13)

[Jackson, 1995] M. JACKSON, *Software Requirements and Specifications: A Lexicon of Practice, Principles and Prejudices,* Addison-Wesley Longman, Reading, MA, 1995. (Chapter 10)

[Jackson and Chapin, 2000] D. JACKSON AND J. CHAPIN, "Redesigning Air Traffic Control: An Exercise in Software Design," *IEEE Software* **17** (May/June 2000), pp. 63–70. (Chapter 13)

[Jacobson, Booch, and Rumbaugh, 1999] I. JACOBSON, G. BOOCH, AND J. RUMBAUGH, *The Unified Software Development Process*, Addison-Wesley, Reading, MA, 1999. (Chapters 2, 3, 10, 12, 13, 14, and 15)

[Jacobson, Christerson, Jonsson, and Overgaard, 1992] I. JACOBSON, M. CHRISTERSON, P. JONSSON, AND G. OVERGAARD, *Object-Oriented Software Engineering: A Use Case Driven Approach*, ACM Press, New York, 1992. (Chapter 12)

[Jalote, Palit, Kurien, and Peethamber, 2004] P. JALOTE, A. PALIT, P. KURIEN AND V. T. PEETHAMBER, "Timeboxing: A Process Model for Iterative Software Development," *Journal of Systems and Software* **70** (February 2004), pp. 117–27. (Chapter 2)

[Jazayeri, Ran, and van der Linden, 2000] M. JAZAYERI, A. RAN, AND F. VAN DER LINDEN, *Software Architecture for Product Families: Principles and Practice,* Addison-Wesley, Reading, MA, 2000. (Chapter 8)

[Jézéquel and Meyer, 1997] J.-M. JÉZÉQUEL AND B. MEYER, "Put It in the Contract: The Lessons of Ariane," *IEEE Computer* **30** (January 1997), pp. 129–30. (Chapter 8)

[Johnson, 1979] S. C. JOHNSON, "A Tour through the Portable C Compiler," 7th ed., UNIX Programmer's Manual, Bell Laboratories, Murray Hill, NJ, January 1979. (Chapter 8)

[Johnson, 2000] R. A. JOHNSON, "The Ups and Downs of Object-Oriented System Development," *Communications of the ACM* **43** (October 2000), pp. 69–73. (Chapters 1 and 7)

[Johnson and Brodman, 2000] D. JOHNSON AND J. G. BRODMAN, "Applying CMM Project Planning

Practices to Diverse Environments," *IEEE Software* **17** (July/August 2000), pp. 40–47. (Chapter 3)

[Johnson and Disney, 1998] P. M. JOHNSON AND A. M. DISNEY, "The Personal Software Process: A Cautionary Tale," *IEEE Software* **15** (November/December 1998), pp. 85–88. (Chapter 3)

[Johnson and Ritchie, 1978] S. C. JOHNSON AND D. M. RITCHIE, "Portability of C Programs and the UNIX System," *Bell System Technical Journal* **57** (No. 6, Part 2, 1978), pp. 2021–48. (Chapter 8)

[Jones, 1978] T. C. JONES, "Measuring Programming Quality and Productivity," *IBM Systems Journal* **17** (No. 1, 1978), pp. 39–63. (Chapter 6)

[Jones, 1984] T. C. JONES, "Reusability in Programming: A Survey of the State of the Art," *IEEE Transactions on Software Engineering* **SE-10** (September 1984), pp. 488–94. (Chapter 8)

[Jones, 1986a] C. JONES, *Programming Productivity,* McGraw-Hill, New York, 1986. (Chapter 9)

[Jones, 1986b] C. B. JONES, *Systematic Software Development Using VDM*, Prentice Hall, Englewood Cliffs, NJ, 1986. (Chapter 11)

[Jones, 1987] C. JONES, Letter to the Editor, *IEEE Computer* **20** (December 1987), p. 4. (Chapter 9)

[Jones, 1994] C. JONES, "Software Metrics: Good, Bad, and Missing," *IEEE Computer* **27** (September 1994), pp. 98–100. (Chapter 5)

[Jorgensen and Erickson, 1994] P. C. JORGENSEN AND C. ERICKSON, "Object-Oriented Integration Testing," *Communications of the ACM* **37** (September 1994), pp. 30–38. (Chapter 14)

[Jorgensen and Molokken-Ostvold, 2004] M. Jorgensen and K. Molokken-Ostvold, "Reasons for Software Effort Estimation Error: Impact of Respondent Role, Information Collection Approach, and Data Analysis Method," *IEEE Transactions on Software Engineering* **30** (December 2004), pp. 993–1007. (Chapter 9)

[Josephson, 1992] M. JOSEPHSON, *Edison, A Biography*, John Wiley and Sons, New York, 1992. (Chapter 1)

[Juran, 1988] J. M. JURAN, *Juran on Planning for Quality*, Macmillan, New York, 1988. (Chapter 3)

[Juristo, Moreno, and López, 2000] N. JURISTO, A. M. MORENO, AND M. LÓPEZ, "How to Use Linguistic Instruments for Object-Oriented Analysis," *IEEE Software* **17** (May/June 2000), pp. 80–89. (Chapter 12)

[Kampen, 1987] G. R. KAMPEN, "An Eclectic Approach to Specification," *Proceedings of the Fourth International Workshop on Software Specification and Design*, Monterey, CA, April 1987, pp. 178–82. (Chapter 11)

[Kan et al., 1994] S. H. KAN, S. D. DULL, D. N. AMUNDSON, R. J. LINDNER, AND R. J. HEDGER, "AS/400 Software Quality Management," *IBM Systems Journal* **33** (No. 1, 1994), pp. 62–88. (Chapter 1)

[Karlsson and Ryan, 1997] J. KARLSSON AND K. RYAN, "A Cost-Value Approach for Prioritizing Requirements," *IEEE Software* **14** (September/October 1997), pp. 67–74. (Chapter 10)

[Karlström and Runeson, 2005] D. KARLSTRÖM AND P. RUNESON, "Combining Agile Methods with Stage-Gate Project Management," *IEEE Software* **22** (May/June 2005), pp. 43–49. (Chapter 2)

[Keeni, 2000] G. KEENI, "The Evolution of Quality Processes at Tata Consultancy Services," *IEEE Software* **17** (July/August 2000), pp. 79–88. (Chapter 3)

[Keil and Tiwana, 2005] M. KEIL AND A. TIWANA, "Beyond Cost: The Drivers of COTS Application Value," IEEE Software **22** (May/June 2005), pp. 64–69. (Chapter 1)

[Kelly and Sherif, 1992] J. C. KELLY AND J. S. SHERIF, "A Comparison of Four Design Methods for Real-Time Software Development," *Information and Software Technology* **34** (February 1992), pp. 74–82. (Chapter 13)

[Kelly, Sherif, and Hops, 1992] J. C. KELLY, J. S. SHERIF, AND J. HOPS, "An Analysis of Defect Densities Found during Software Inspections," *Journal of Systems and Software* **17** (January 1992), pp. 111–17. (Chapters 1 and 6)

[Kemerer, 1993] C. F. KEMERER, "Reliability of Function Points Measurement: A Field Experiment," *Communications of the ACM* **36** (February 1993), pp. 85–97. (Chapter 9)

[Kemerer and Porter, 1992] C. F. KEMERER AND B. S. PORTER, "Improving the Reliability of Function Point Measurement: An Empirical Study," *IEEE Transactions on Software Engineering* **18** (November 1992), pp. 1011–24. (Chapter 9)

[Kernighan and Plauger, 1974] B. W. KERNIGHAN AND P. J. PLAUGER, *The Elements of Programming Style,* McGraw-Hill, New York, 1974. (Chapter 14)

[Kernighan and Ritchie, 1978] B. W. KERNIGHAN AND D. M. RITCHIE, *The C Programming Language*, Prentice Hall, Englewood Cliffs, NJ, 1978. (Chapter 8)

[Khan, Al-A'ali, and Girgis, 1995] E. H. KHAN, M. AL-A'ALI, AND M. R. GIRGIS, "Object-Oriented Programming for Structured Procedural Programming," *IEEE Computer* **28** (October 1995), pp. 48–57. (Chapter 1)

[Kilpi, 2001] T. KILPI, "Implementing a Software Metrics Program at Nokia," *IEEE Software* **18** (November/December 2001), pp. 72–76. (Chapter 5)

[Kitchenham, 1997] B. KITCHENHAM, "The Problem with Function Points," *IEEE Software* **14** (March/April 1997), pp. 29, 31. (Chapter 9)

[Kitchenham and Mendes, 2004] B. KITCHENHAM AND E. MENDES, "Software Productivity Measurement Using Multiple Size Measures," *IEEE Transactions on Software Engineering* **30** (December 2004), pp. 1023–35. (Chapter 9)

[Kitchenham, Pickard, and Linkman, 1990] B. A. KITCHENHAM, L. M. PICKARD, AND S. J. LINKMAN, "An Evaluation of Some Design Metrics," *Software Engineering Journal* **5** (January 1990), pp. 50–58. (Chapter 13)

[Kitchenham, Pickard, and Pfleeger, 1995] B. KITCHENHAM, L. PICKARD, AND S. L. PFLEEGER. "Case Studies for Method and Tool Evaluation," *IEEE Software* **12** (July 1995), pp. 52–62. (Chapter 5)

[Kleinrock and Gail, 1996] L. KLEINROCK AND R. GAIL, *Queuing Systems: Problems and Solutions*, John Wiley and Sons, New York, 1996. (Chapter 11)

[Klepper and Bock, 1995] R. KLEPPER AND D. BOCK, "Third and Fourth Generation Productivity Differences," *Communications of the ACM* **38** (September, 1995), pp. 69–79. (Chapter 14)

[Klunder, 1988] D. KLUNDER, "Hungarian Naming Conventions," Technical Report, Microsoft Corporation, Redmond, WA, January 1988. (Chapter 14)

[Knauber, Muthig, Schmid, and Widen, 2000] P. KNAUBER, D. MUTHIG, K. SCHMID, AND T. WIDEN, "Applying Product Line Concepts in Small and Medium-Sized Companies," *IEEE Software* **17** (September/October 2000), pp. 88–95. (Chapter 8)

[Knuth, 1968] D. E. KNUTH, *The Art of Computer Programming,* Vol. I, *Fundamental Algorithms*, Addison-Wesley, Reading, MA, 1968. (Chapter 11)

[Knuth, 1974] D. E. KNUTH, "Structured Programming with **go to** Statements," *ACM Computing Surveys* **6** (December 1974), pp. 261–301. (Chapter 7)

[Kobryn, 2000] C. KOBRYN, "Modeling Components and Frameworks with UML," *Communications of the ACM* **43** (October 2000), pp. 31–38. (Chapter 8)

[Kroeker et al., 1999] K. K. KROEKER, L. WALL, D. A. TAYLOR, C. HORN, P. BASSETT, J. K. OUSTERHOUT, M. L. GRISS, R. M. SOLEY, J. WALDO, AND C. SIMONYI, "Software [R]evolution: A Roundtable," *IEEE Computer* **32** (May 1999), pp. 48–57. (Chapter 1)

[Kung, Hsia, and Gao, 1998] D. C. KUNG, P. HSIA, AND J. GAO, *Testing Object-Oriented Software*, IEEE Computer Society Press, Los Alamitos, CA, 1998. (Chapter 6)

[Kurki-Suonio, 1993] R. KURKI-SUONIO, "Stepwise Design of Real-Time Systems," *IEEE Transactions on Software Engineering* **19** (January 1993), pp. 56–69. (Chapter 5)

[Lai, Weiss, and Parnas, 1999] C. T. R. LAI, D. M. WEISS, AND D. L. PARNAS, *Software Product-Line Engineering: A Family-Based Software Development Process,* Addison-Wesley, Reading, MA, 1999. (Chapter 8)

[Landwehr, 1983] C. E. LANDWEHR, "The Best Available Technologies for Computer Security," *IEEE Computer* **16** (July 1983), pp. 86–100. (Chapter 6)

[Lanergan and Grasso, 1984] R. G. LANERGAN AND C. A. GRASSO, "Software Engineering with Reusable Designs and Code," *IEEE Transactions on Software Engineering* **SE-10** (September 1984), pp. 498–501. (Chapter 8)

[LAPACK++, 2000] "LAPACK++: Linear Algebra Package in C++," at math.nist.gov/lapack++, 2000. (Chapter 8)

[Larman and Basili, 2003] C. LARMAN AND V. R. BASILI, "Iterative and Incremental Development: A Brief History," *IEEE Computer* **36** (June 2003), pp. 47–56. (Chapter 2)

[Larsen, Fitzgerald, and Brookes, 1996] P. G. LARSEN, J. FITZGERALD, AND T. BROOKES, "Applying Formal Specification in Industry," *IEEE Software* **13** (May 1996), pp. 48–56. (Chapter 11)

[Leavenworth, 1970] B. LEAVENWORTH, Review #19420, *Computing Reviews* **11** (July 1970), pp. 396–97. (Chapters 6 and 11)

[Lejter, Meyers, and Reiss, 1992] M. LEJTER, S. MEYERS, AND S. P. REISS, "Support for Maintaining Object-Oriented Programs," *IEEE Transactions on Software Engineering* **18** (December 1992), pp. 1045–52. (Chapter 15)

[Leveson and Turner, 1993] N. G. LEVESON AND C. S. TURNER, "An Investigation of the Therac-25 Accidents," *IEEE Computer* **26** (July 1993), pp. 18–41. (Chapter 1)

[Lewis et al., 1995] T. LEWIS, L. ROSENSTEIN, W. PREE, A. WEINAND, E. GAMMA, P. CALDER, G. ANDERT, J. VLISSIDES, AND K. SCHMUCKER, *Object-Oriented Application Frameworks*, Manning, Greenwich, CT, 1995. (Chapter 8)

[Lieberman and Fry, 2001] H. LIEBERMAN AND C. FRY, "Will Software Ever Work?" *Communications of the ACM* **44** (March 2001), pp. 122–24. (Chapter 6)

[Lientz, Swanson, and Tompkins, 1978] B. P. LIENTZ, E. B. SWANSON, AND G. E. TOMPKINS, "Characteristics of Application Software Maintenance," *Communications of the ACM* **21** (June 1978), pp. 466–71. (Chapters 1 and 15)

[Lim, 1994] W. C. LIM, "Effects of Reuse on Quality, Productivity, and Economics," *IEEE Software* **11** (September 1994), pp. 23–30. (Chapters 8 and 9)

[Lim, 1998] W. C. LIM, *Managing Software Reuse*, Prentice Hall, Upper Saddle River, NJ, 1998. (Chapter 8)

[Lim, Jeong, and Schach, 2005] J. S. LIM, S. R. JEONG, AND S. R. SCHACH, "An Empirical Investigation of the Impact of the Object-Oriented Paradigm on the Maintainability of Real-World Mission-Critical Software," *Journal of Systems and Software* **77** (August 2005), pp. 131–38. (Chapter 15)

[Linger, 1994] R. C. LINGER, "Cleanroom Process Model," *IEEE Software* **11** (March 1994), pp. 50–58. (Chapter 14)

[Liskov and Zilles, 1974] B. LISKOV AND S. ZILLES, "Programming with Abstract Data Types," *ACM SIGPLAN Notices* **9** (April 1974), pp. 50–59. (Chapter 7)

[Liskov, Snyder, Atkinson, and Schaffert, 1977] B. LISKOV, A. SNYDER, R. ATKINSON, AND C. SCHAFFERT, "Abstraction Mechanisms in CLU," *Communications of the ACM* **20** (August 1977), pp. 564–76. (Chapter 8)

[Liu, 2000] J. W. S. LIU, *Real Time Systems*, Prentice Hall, Upper Saddle River, NJ, 2000. (Chapter 13)

[London, 1971] R. L. LONDON, "Software Reliability through Proving Programs Correct," *Proceedings of the IEEE International Symposium on Fault-Tolerant Computing,* March 1971. (Chapters 6 and 11)

[Long and Morris, 1993] F. LONG AND E. MORRIS, "An Overview of PCTE: A Basis for a Portable Common Tool Environment," Technical Report CMU/SEI–93–TR–1, Software Engineering Institute, Carnegie Mellon University, Pittsburgh, January 1993. (Chapter 14)

[Longstaff, Chittister, Pethia, and Haimes, 2000] T. A. LONGSTAFF, C. CHITTISTER, R. PETHIA, AND Y. Y. HAIMES, "Are We Forgetting the Risks of Information Technology?" *IEEE Computer* **33** (December 2000), pp. 43–51. (Chapters 1 and 2)

[Lotto, 1515] L. LOTTO, *Giovanni Agostino della Torre and his Son, Niccolò*, oil on canvas, 1515 www.nationalgallery.org.uk/cgi-bin/WebObjects .dll/CollectionPublisher.woa/wa/largeImage? workNumber=NG699. (Chapter 15)

[Loukides and Oram, 1997] M. K. LOUKIDES AND A. ORAM, *Programming with GNU Software*, O'Reilly and Associates, Sebastopol, CA, 1997. (Chapters 5 and 15)

[Low and Jeffrey, 1990] G. C. LOW AND D. R. JEFFREY, "Function Points in the Estimation and Evaluation of the Software Process," *IEEE Transactions on Software Engineering* **16** (January 1990), pp. 64–71. (Chapter 9)

[Luckham and von Henke, 1985] D. C. LUCKHAM AND F. W. VON HENKE, "An Overview of Anna, a Specification Language for Ada," *IEEE Software* **2** (March 1985), pp. 9–22. (Chapter 11)

[Luqi, Zhang, Berzins, and Qiao, 2004] LUQI, L. ZHANG, V. BERZINS, AND Y. QIAO, "Documentation Driven Development for Complex Real-Time Systems," *IEEE Transactions on Software Engineering* **30** (December 2004), pp. 936–52. (Chapter 13)

[Mackenzie, 1980] C. E. MACKENZIE, *Coded Character Sets: History and Development*, Addison-Wesley, Reading, MA, 1980. (Chapter 8)

[Mackey, 1999] K. MACKEY, "Stages of Team Development," *IEEE Software* **16** (July/August 1999), pp. 90–91. (Chapter 4)

[Madanmohan and De', 2004] T. R. MADANMOHAN AND R. DE', "Open Source Reuse in Commercial Firms," *IEEE Software* **21** (November/December 2004), pp. 62–69. (Chapter 1)

[Magee and Kramer, 1999] J. MAGEE AND J. KRAMER, *Concurrency: State Models & Java Programs*, John Wiley and Sons, New York, 1999. (Chapter 13)

[Mancl and Havanas, 1990] D. MANCL AND W. HAVANAS, "A Study of the Impact of C++ on Software Maintenance," *Proceedings of the IEEE Conference on Software Maintenance,* San Diego, CA, November 1990, pp. 63–69. (Chapter 15)

[Manna and Pnueli, 1992] Z. MANNA AND A. PNUELI, *The Temporal Logic of Reactive and Concurrent Systems,* Springer-Verlag, New York, 1992. (Chapter 6)

[Manna and Waldinger, 1978] Z. MANNA AND R. WALDINGER, "The Logic of Computer Programming," *IEEE Transactions on Software Engineering* **SE-4** (1978), pp. 199–229. (Chapter 6)

[Mantei, 1981] M. MANTEI, "The Effect of Programming Team Structures on Programming Tasks," *Communications of the ACM* **24** (March 1981), pp. 106–13. (Chapter 4)

[Manzoni and Price, 2003] L. V. MANZONI AND R. T. PRICE, "Identifying Extensions Required by RUP (Rational Unified Process) to Comply with CMM (Capability Maturity Model) Levels 2 and 3," *IEEE Transactions on Software Engineering* **29** (February 2003), pp. 181–92. (Chapter 3)

[Maranzano et al., 2005] J. F. MARANZANO, S. A. ROZSYPAL, G. H. ZIMMERMAN, G. W. WARNKEN, P. E. WIRTH, AND D. M. WEISS, "Architecture Reviews: Practice and Experience," *IEEE Software* **22** (March/April 2005), pp. 34–43. (Chapter 13)

[Maring, 1996] B. MARING, "Object-Oriented Development of Large Applications," *IEEE Software* **13** (May 1996), pp. 33–40. (Chapter 1)

[Martin, 1985] J. MARTIN, *Fourth-Generation Languages,* Vols. 1, 2, and 3, Prentice Hall, Englewood Cliffs, NJ, 1985. (Chapter 14)

[Matsumoto, 1984] Y. MATSUMOTO, "Management of Industrial Software Production," *IEEE Computer* **17** (February 1984), pp. 59–72. (Chapter 8)

[Matsumoto, 1987] Y. MATSUMOTO, "A Software Factory: An Overall Approach to Software Production," in: *Tutorial: Software Reusability*, P. Freeman (Editor), Computer Society Press, Washington, DC, 1987, pp. 155–78. (Chapter 8)

[Maxwell and Forselius, 2000] K. D. MAXWELL AND P. FORSELIUS, "Benchmarking Software Development Productivity," *IEEE Software* **17** (January/February 2000), pp. 80–88. (Chapter 9)

[McCabe, 1976] T. J. MCCABE, "A Complexity Measure," *IEEE Transactions on Software Engineering* **SE-2** (December 1976), pp. 308–20. (Chapters 13 and 14)

[McCabe and Butler, 1989] T. J. MCCABE AND C. W. BUTLER, "Design Complexity Measurement and Testing," *Communications of the ACM* **32** (December 1989), pp. 1415–25. (Chapter 14)

[McConnell, 1993] S. MCCONNELL, *Code Complete: A Practical Handbook of Software Construction,* Microsoft Press, Redmond, WA, 1993. (Chapter 14)

[McConnell, 1996] S. MCCONNELL, "Daily Build and Smoke Test," *IEEE Software* **13** (July/August 1996), pp. 144, 143. (Chapters 2 and 4)

[McConnell, 2001] S. MCCONNELL, "The Nine Deadly Sins of Project Planning," *IEEE Software* **18** (November/December 2001), pp. 5–7. (Chapter 9)

[McGarry and Decker, 2002] F. MCGARRY AND B. DECKER, "Attaining Level 5 in CMM Process Maturity," *IEEE Software* **19** (2002), pp. 87–96. (Chapter 3)

[Mellor, 1994] P. MELLOR, "CAD: Computer-Aided Disaster," Technical Report, Centre for Software Reliability, City University, London, July 1994. (Chapter 1)

[Memon, Pollack, and Soffa, 2001] A. M. MEMON, M. E. POLLACK, AND M. L. SOFFA, "Hierarchical GUI Test Case Generation Using Automated Planning," *IEEE Transactions on Software Engineering* **27** (February 2001), pp. 144–55. (Chapter 14)

[Mens, 2002] T. MENS, "A State-of-the-Art Survey on Software Merging," *IEEE Transactions on Software Engineering* **28** (May 2002), pp. 449–62. (Chapter 5)

[Mens and Tourwe, 2004] T. MENS AND T. TOURWE, "A Survey of Software Refactoring," *IEEE Transactions on Software Engineering* **30** (February 2004), pp. 126–39. (Chapter 2)

[Meyer, 1985] B. MEYER, "On Formalism in Specifications," *IEEE Software* **2** (January 1985), pp. 6–26. (Chapter 11)

[Meyer, 1986] B. MEYER, "Genericity versus Inheritance," Proceedings of the Conference on Object-Oriented Programming Systems, Languages and Applications, *ACM SIGPLAN Notices* **21** (November 1986), pp. 391–405. (Chapter 7)

[Meyer, 1987] B. MEYER, "Reusability: The Case for Object-Oriented Design," *IEEE Software* **4** (March 1987), pp. 50–64. (Chapter 8)

[Meyer, 1992] B. MEYER, "Applying 'Design by Contract'," *IEEE Computer* **25** (October 1992), pp. 40–51. (Chapters 1 and 7)

[Meyer, 1996a] B. MEYER, "The Reusability Challenge," *IEEE Computer* **29** (February 1996), pp. 76–78. (Chapter 8)

[Meyer, 1996b] B. MEYER, "The Many Faces of Inheritance: A Taxonomy of Taxonomy," *IEEE Computer* **29** (May 1996), pp. 105–8. (Chapter 7)

[Meyer, 1997] B. MEYER, *Object-Oriented Software Construction*, 2nd ed., Prentice Hall, Upper Saddle River, NJ, 1997. (Chapters 1 and 7)

[Miller, 1956] G. A. MILLER, "The Magical Number Seven, Plus or Minus Two: Some Limits on Our Capacity for Processing Information," *The Psychological Review* **63** (March 1956), pp. 81–97; reprinted in: www.well.com/user/smalin/miller.html. (Chapters 2, 3, and 5)

[Miller and Yin, 2004] J. MILLER AND Z. YIN, "A Cognitive-Based Mechanism for Constructing Software Inspection Teams," *IEEE Transactions on Software Engineering* **30** (November 30), pp. 811–25. (Chapter 6)

[Mills, Dyer, and Linger, 1987] H. D. MILLS, M. DYER, AND R. C. LINGER, "Cleanroom Software Engineering," *IEEE Software* **4** (September 1987), pp. 19–25. (Chapter 14)

[Modell, 1996] M. E. MODELL, *A Professional's Guide to Systems Analysis*, 2nd ed., McGraw-Hill, New York, 1996. (Chapter 11)

[Monarchi and Puhr, 1992] D. E. MONARCHI AND G. I. PUHR, "A Research Typology for Object-Oriented Analysis and Design," *Communications of the ACM* **35** (September 1992), pp. 35–47. (Chapters 12 and 13)

[Mooney, 1990] J. D. MOONEY, "Strategies for Supporting Application Portability," *IEEE Computer* **23** (November 1990), pp. 59–70. (Chapter 8)

[Moran, 1981] T. P. MORAN (Editor), Special Issue: The Psychology of Human-Computer Interaction, *ACM Computing Surveys* **13** (March 1981). (Chapter 5)

[Morisio, Ezran, and Tully, 2002] M. MORISIO, M. EZRAN, AND C. TULLY, "Success and Failure Factors in Software Reuse," *IEEE Transactions on Software Engineering* **28** (April 2002), pp. 340–57. (Chapter 8)

[Morisio, Tully, and Ezran, 2000] M. MORISIO, C. TULLY, AND M. EZRAN, "Diversity in Reuse Processes," *IEEE Software* **17** (July/August 2000), pp. 56–63. (Chapter 8)

[Murphy et al., 2001] G. C. MURPHY, R. J. WALKER, E. L. A. BANNIASSAD, M. P. ROBILLARD, A. LIA, AND M. A. KERSTEN, "Does Aspect-Oriented Programming Work?" *Communications of the ACM* **44** (October 2001), pp. 75–78. (Chapter 7)

[Murru, Deias, and Mugheddu, 2003] O. MURRU, R. DEIAS, AND G. MUGHEDDU, "Assessing XP at a European Internet Company," *IEEE Software* **20** (May/June, 2003), pp. 37–43. (Chapters 2 and 4)

[Murugappan and Keeni, 2003] M. MURUGAPPAN AND G. KEENI, "Blending CMM and Six Sigma to Meet Business Goals," *IEEE Software* **20** (March/April 2003), pp. 42–48. (Chapter 3)

[Musa and Everett, 1990] J. D. MUSA AND W. W. EVERETT, "Software-Reliability Engineering: Technology for the 1990s," *IEEE Software* **7** (November 1990), pp. 36–43. (Chapter 14)

[Musa, Iannino, and Okumoto, 1987] J. D. MUSA, A. IANNINO, AND K. OKUMOTO, *Software Reliability: Measurement, Prediction, Application*, McGraw-Hill, New York, 1987. (Chapter 14)

[Musser and Saini, 1996] D. R. MUSSER AND A. SAINI, *STL Tutorial and Reference Guide: C++ Programming with the Standard Template Library*, Addison-Wesley, Reading, MA, 1996. (Chapter 8)

[Myers, 1976] G. J. MYERS, *Software Reliability: Principles and Practices,* Wiley-Interscience, New York, 1976. (Chapter 14)

[Myers, 1978a] G. J. MYERS, "A Controlled Experiment in Program Testing and Code Walkthroughs/Inspections," *Communications of the ACM* **21** (September 1978), pp. 760–68. (Chapter 14)

[Myers, 1978b] G. J. MYERS, *Composite/Structured Design*, Van Nostrand Reinhold, New York, 1978. (Chapter 7)

[Myers, 1979] G. J. MYERS, *The Art of Software Testing*, John Wiley and Sons, New York, 1979. (Chapters 6 and 14)

[Myers, 1992] W. MYERS, "Good Software Practices Pay off—or Do They?" *IEEE Software* **9** (March 1992), pp. 96–97. (Chapter 5)

[NAG, 2003] "NAG The Numerical Algorithms Group Ltd," at www.nag.co.uk, 2003. (Chapter 8)

[Naur, 1964] P. NAUR, "The Design of the GIER ALGOL Compiler," in: *Annual Review in Automatic Programming,* Vol. 4, Pergamon Press, Oxford, UK, 1964, pp. 49–85. (Chapter 11)

[Naur, 1969] P. NAUR, "Programming by Action Clusters," *BIT* **9** (No. 3, 1969), pp. 250–58. (Chapters 6 and 11)

[Naur, Randell, and Buxton, 1976] P. NAUR, B. RANDELL, AND J. N. BUXTON (Editors), *Software Engineering: Concepts and Techniques: Proceedings of the NATO Conferences*, Petrocelli-Charter, New York, 1976. (Chapter 1)

[Nerur, Mahapatra, and Mangalaraj, 2005] S. NERUR, R. MAHAPATRA, G. MANGALARAJ, "Challenges of Migrating to Agile Methodologies," *Communications of the ACM* **48** (May 2005), pp. 72–78. (Chapter 2)

[Nesi, 1998] P. NESI, "Managing OO Projects Better," *IEEE Software* **15** (July/August 1998), pp. 50–60. (Chapter 9)

[Neumann, 1980] P. G. NEUMANN, Letter from the Editor, *ACM SIGSOFT Software Engineering Notes* **5** (July 1980), p. 2. (Chapter 1)

[Neumann, 1995] P. G. NEUMANN, *Computer-Related Risks*, Addison-Wesley, Reading, MA, 1995. (Chapter 1)

[NIST 151, 1988] "POSIX: Portable Operating System Interface for Computer Environments," Federal Information Processing Standard 151, National Institute of Standards and Technology, Washington, DC, 1988. (Chapter 8)

[Nix and Collins, 1988] C. J. NIX AND B. P. COLLINS, "The Use of Software Engineering, Including the Z Notation, in the Development of CICS," *Quality Assurance* **14** (September 1988), pp. 103–10. (Chapter 11)

[Norden, 1958] P. V. NORDEN, "Curve Fitting for a Model of Applied Research and Development Scheduling," *IBM Journal of Research and Development* **2** (July 1958), pp. 232–48. (Chapter 9)

[Norušis, 2005] M. J. NORUŠIS, *SPSS 13.0 Guide to Data Analysis,* Prentice Hall, Upper Saddle Valley River, NJ, 2005. (Chapter 8)

[Oest, 1986] O. N. OEST, "VDM from Research to Practice," *Proceedings of the IFIP Congress, Information Processing '86,* 1986, pp. 527–33. (Chapter 11)

[Onoma, Tsai, Poonawala, and Suganuma, 1998] A. K. ONOMA, W.-T. TSAI, M. H. POONAWALA, AND H. SUGANUMA, "Regression Testing in an Industrial Environment," *Communications of the ACM* **42** (May 1998), pp. 81–86. (Chapter 15)

[Orr, 1981] K. ORR, *Structured Requirements Definition*, Ken Orr and Associates, Inc., Topeka, KS, 1981. (Chapters 11 and 13)

[Palshikar, 2001] G. K. PALSHIKAR, "Applying Formal Specifications to Real-World Software Development," *IEEE Software* **18** (November/December 2001), pp. 89–97. (Chapter 11)

[Parnas, 1971] D. L. PARNAS, "Information Distribution Aspects of Design Methodology," *Proceedings of the IFIP Congress*, Ljubljana, Yugoslavia, 1971, pp. 339–44. (Chapter 7)

[Parnas, 1972a] D. L. PARNAS, "A Technique for Software Module Specification with Examples," *Communications of the ACM* **15** (May 1972), pp. 330–36. (Chapter 7)

[Parnas, 1972b] D. L. PARNAS, "On the Criteria to Be Used in Decomposing Systems into Modules," *Communications of the ACM* **15** (December 1972), pp. 1053–58. (Chapter 7)

[Parnas, 1994] D. L. PARNAS, "Software Aging," *Proceedings of the 16th International Conference on Software Engineering*, Sorrento, Italy, May 1994, pp. 279–87. (Chapter 1)

[Parnas, 1999] D. L. PARNAS, "Ten Myths about Y2K Inspections," *Communications of the ACM* **42** (May 1999), p. 128. (Chapter 15)

[Parnas and Lawford, 2003] D. L. PARNAS AND M. LAWFORD, "The Role of Inspection in Software Quality Assurance," *IEEE Transactions on Software Engineering* **29** (August 2003), pp. 674–76. (Chapter 6)

[Paulk, 1995] M. C. PAULK, "How ISO 9001 Compares with the CMM," *IEEE Software* **12** (January 1995), pp. 74–83. (Chapter 3)

[Paulk, Weber, Curtis, and Chrissis, 1995] M. C. PAULK, C. V. WEBER, B. CURTIS, AND M. B. CHRISSIS, *The Capability Maturity Model: Guidelines for Improving the Software Process*, Addison-Wesley, Reading, MA, 1995. (Chapter 3)

[Paulson, Succi, and Eberlein, 2004] J. W. PAULSON, G. SUCCI, AND A. EBERLEIN, "An Empirical Study of Open-Source and Closed-Source Software Products," *IEEE Transactions on Software Engineering* **30** (April 2004), pp. 246–56. (Chapter 1)

[Perry and Kaiser, 1990] D. E. PERRY AND G. E. KAISER, "Adequate Testing and Object-Oriented Programming," *Journal of Object-Oriented Programming* **2** (January/February 1990), pp. 13–19. (Chapter 14)

[Perry et al., 2002] D. E. PERRY, A. PORTER, M. W. WADE, L G. VOTTA, AND J. PERPICH, "Reducing Inspection Interval in Large-Scale Software Development," *IEEE Transactions on Software Engineering* **28** (July 2002), pp. 695–705. (Chapter 6)

[Peterson, 1981] J. L. PETERSON, *Petri Net Theory and the Modeling of Systems*, Prentice Hall, Englewood Cliffs, NJ, 1981. (Chapter 11)

[Petri, 1962] C. A. PETRI, "Kommunikation mit Automaten," Ph.D. Dissertation, University of Bonn, Germany, 1962. [In German.] (Chapter 11)

[Pfleeger and Hatton, 1997] S. L. PFLEEGER AND L. HATTON, "Investigating the Influence of Formal Methods," *IEEE Computer* **30** (February 1997), pp. 33–43. (Chapter 11)

[Pfleeger, Jeffrey, Curtis, and Kitchenham, 1997] S. L. PFLEEGER, R. JEFFREY, B. CURTIS, AND B. KITCHENHAM, "Status Report on Software Measurement,"

*IEEE Software* **14** (March/April 1997), pp. 33–44. (Chapter 5)

[Pigoski, 1996] T. M. PIGOSKI, *Practical Software Maintenance: Best Practices for Managing Your Software Investment,* John Wiley and Sons, New York, 1996. (Chapter 15)

[Pitterman, 2000] B. PITTERMAN, "Telecordia Technologies: The Journey to High Maturity," *IEEE Software* **17** (July/August 2000), pp. 89–96. (Chapter 3)

[Pittman, 1993] M. PITTMAN, "Lessons Learned in Managing Object-Oriented Development," *IEEE Software* **10** (January 1993), pp. 43–53. (Chapter 9)

[Ponder and Bush, 1994] C. PONDER AND B. BUSH, "Polymorphism Considered Harmful," *ACM SIGSOFT Software Engineering Notes* **19** (April, 1994), pp. 35–38. (Chapter 7)

[Pont and Banner, 2004] M. J. PONT AND M. P. BANNER, "Designing Embedded Systems Using Patterns: A Case Study," *Journal of Systems and Software* **71** (May 2004), pp. 201–213. (Chapter 8)

[Poulin, 1997] J. S. POULIN, *Measuring Software Reuse: Principles, Practice, and Economic Models,* Addison-Wesley, Reading, MA, 1997. (Chapter 8)

[Prechelt and Unger, 2000] L. PRECHELT AND B. UNGER, "An Experiment Measuring the Effects of Personal Software Process (PSP) Training," *IEEE Transactions on Software Engineering* **27** (May 2000), pp. 465–72. (Chapter 3)

[Prechelt, Unger-Lamprecht, Philippsen, and Tichy, 2002] L. PRECHELT, B. UNGER-LAMPRECHT, M. PHILIPPSEN, AND W. F. TICHY, "Two Controlled Experiments in Assessing the Usefulness of Design Pattern Documentation in Program Maintenance," *IEEE Transactions on Software Engineering* **28** (June 2002), pp. 595–606. (Chapters 8 and 15)

[Prieto-Díaz, 1991] R. PRIETO-DÍAZ, "Implementing Faceted Classification for Software Reuse," *Communications of the ACM* **34** (May 1991), pp. 88–97. (Chapter 8)

[Putnam, 1978] L. H. PUTNAM, "A General Empirical Solution to the Macro Software Sizing and Estimating Problem," *IEEE Transactions on Software Engineering* **SE-4** (July 1978), pp. 345–61. (Chapter 9)

[Radin, 1996] G. RADIN, "Object Technology in Perspective," *IBM Systems Journal* **35** (No. 2, 1996), pp. 124–26. (Chapter 1)

[Rajlich and Bennett, 2000] V. RAJLICH AND K. H. BENNETT, "A Staged Model for the Software Life Cycle," *IEEE Computer* **33** (July 2000), pp. 66–71. (Chapter 2)

[Rajlich, Wilde, Buckellew, and Page, 2001] V. RAJLICH, N. WILDE, M. BUCKELLEW, AND H. PAGE, "Software Cultures and Evolution," *IEEE Computer* **34** (September 2001), pp. 24–28. (Chapter 15)

[Rapps and Weyuker, 1985] S. RAPPS AND E. J. WEYUKER, "Selecting Software Test Data Using Data Flow Information," *IEEE Transactions on Software Engineering* **SE-11** (April 1985), pp. 367–75. (Chapter 14)

[Rasmussen, 2003] J. RASMUSSON, "Introducing XP into Greenfield Projects: Lessons Learned," *IEEE Software* **20** (May/June, 2003), pp. 21–29. (Chapter 2)

[Ravichandran and Rothenberger, 2003] T. RAVICHANDRAN AND M. A. ROTHENBERGER, "Software Reuse Strategies and Component Markets," *Communications of the ACM* **46** (August 2003), pp. 109–114

[Raymond, 2000] E. S. RAYMOND, *The Cathedral and the Bazaar: Musings on Linux and Open Source by an Accidental Revolutionary,* O'Reilly & Associates, Sebastopol, CA, 2000; also available at www.catb .org/~esr/writings/cathedral-bazaar/cathedral-bazaar/. (Chapters 1 and 2)

[Reifer, 2000] D. J. REIFER, "Software Management: The Good, the Bad, and the Ugly," *IEEE Software* **17** (March/April 2000), pp. 73–75. (Chapter 9)

[Reifer, Maurer, and Erdogmus, 2003] D. REIFER, F. MAURER, AND H. ERDOGMUS, "Scaling Agile Methods," *IEEE Software* **20** (July/August 2004), pp. 12–14. (Chapter 2)

[Rochkind, 1975] M. J. ROCHKIND, "The Source Code Control System," *IEEE Transactions on Software Engineering* **SE-1** (October 1975), pp. 255–65. (Chapters 5 and 15)

[Ropponen and Lyttinen, 2000] J. ROPPONEN AND K. LYTTINEN, "Components of Software Development Risk: How to Address Them? A Project Manager Survey," *IEEE Transactions on Software Engineering* **26** (February 2000), pp. 96–111. (Chapter 2)

[Ross, 1985] D. T. ROSS, "Applications and Extensions of SADT," *IEEE Computer* **18** (April 1985), pp. 25–34. (Chapter 11)

[Rothermel, Untch, Chu, and Harrold, 2001] G. ROTHERMEL, R. H. UNTCH, C. CHU, AND M. J. HARROLD, "Prioritizing Test Cases for Regression Test Cases," *IEEE Transactions on Software Engineering* **27** (October 2001), pp. 929–48. (Chapter 15)

[Royce, 1970] W. W. ROYCE, "Managing the Development of Large Software Systems: Concepts and Techniques," *1970 WESCON Technical Papers, Western Electronic Show and Convention*, Los Angeles, August 1970, pp. A/1-1–A/1-9; reprinted in: *Proceedings of the 11th International Conference on Software Engineering*, Pittsburgh, May 1989, IEEE, pp. 328–38. (Chapter 2)

[Royce, 1998] W. ROYCE, *Software Project Management: A Unified Framework*, Addison-Wesley, Reading, MA, 1998. (Chapters 2 and 4)

[Rugaber and White, 1998] S. RUGABER AND J. WHITE, "Restoring a Legacy: Lessons Learned," *IEEE Software* **15** (July/August 1998), pp. 28–33. (Chapter 15)

[Rumbaugh et al., 1991] J. RUMBAUGH, M. BLAHA, W. PREMERLANI, F. EDDY, AND W. LORENSEN, *Object-Oriented Modeling and Design*, Prentice Hall, Englewood Cliffs, NJ, 1991. (Chapters 3 and 12)

[Rumbaugh, Jacobson, and Booch, 1999] J. RUMBAUGH, I. JACOBSON, AND G. BOOCH, *The Unified Modeling Language Reference Manual,* Addison-Wesley, Reading, MA, 1999. (Chapter 12)

[Sackman, 1970] H. SACKMAN, *Man–Computer Problem Solving: Experimental Evaluation of Time-Sharing and Batch Processing,* Auerbach, Princeton, NJ, 1970. (Chapter 9)

[Sackman, Erikson, and Grant, 1968] H. SACKMAN, W. J. ERIKSON, AND E. E. GRANT, "Exploratory Experimental Studies Comparing Online and Offline Programming Performance," *Communications of the ACM* **11** (January 1968), pp. 3–11. (Chapter 9)

[Saiedian and Kuzara, 1995] H. SAIEDIAN AND R. KUZARA, "SEI Capability Maturity Model's Impact on Contractors," *IEEE Computer* **28** (January 1995), pp. 16–26. (Chapter 3)

[Saiedian et al., 1996] H. SAIEDIAN, J. P. BOWEN, R. W. BUTLER, D. L. DILL, R. L. GLASS, D. GRIES, A. HALL, M. G. HINCHEY, C. M. HOLLOWAY, D. JACKSON, C. B. JONES, M. J. LUTZ, D. L. PARNAS, J. RUSHBY, J. WING, AND P. ZAVE, "An Invitation to Formal Methods," *IEEE Computer* **29** (April 1996), pp. 16–30. (Chapter 11)

[Sammet, 1978] J. E. SAMMET, "The Early History of COBOL," *Proceedings of the History of Programming Languages Conference,* Los Angeles, 1978, pp. 199–276. (Chapter 14)

[Samoladas, Stamelos, Angelis, and Oikonomou, 2005] I. SAMOLADAS, I. STAMELOS, L. ANGELIS, AND

A. OIKONOMOU, "Open Source Software Development Should Strive for Even Greater Code Maintainability," *Communications of the ACM* **47** (October 2004), pp. 83–87. (Chapter 15)

[Schach, 1992] S. R. SCHACH, *Software Reuse: Past, Present, and Future*, videotape, 150 min, US-VHS format, IEEE Computer Society Press, Los Alamitos, CA, November 1992. (Chapter 8)

[Schach, 1994] S. R. SCHACH, "The Economic Impact of Software Reuse on Maintenance," *Journal of Software Maintenance—Research and Practice* **6** (July/August 1994), pp. 185–96. (Chapters 8 and 9)

[Schach, 1997] S. R. SCHACH, *Software Engineering with Java*, Richard D. Irwin, Chicago, 1997. (Chapter 8)

[Schach and Stevens-Guille, 1979] S. R. SCHACH AND P. D. STEVENS-GUILLE, "Two Aspects of Computer-Aided Design," *Transactions of the Royal Society of South Africa* **44** (Part 1, 1979), 123–26. (Chapter 7)

[Schach and Wood, 1986] S. R. SCHACH AND P. T. WOOD, "An Almost Path-Free Very High-Level Interactive Data Manipulation Language for a Microcomputer-Based Database System," *Software—Practice and Experience* **16** (March 1986), pp. 243–68. (Chapter 10)

[Schach et al., 2002] S, R. SCHACH, B. JIN, D. R. WRIGHT, G. Z. HELLER, AND A. J. OFFUTT, "Maintainability of the Linux Kernel," *IEE Proceedings—Software* **149** (February 2002), pp. 18–23. (Chapters 1 and 7)

[Schach et al., 2003a] S. R. SCHACH, B. JIN, DAVID R. WRIGHT, G. Z. HELLER, AND J. OFFUTT, "Quality Impacts of Clandestine Common Coupling," *Software Quality Journal* **11** (July 2003), pp. 211–18. (Chapter 7)

[Schach et al., 2003b] S. R. SCHACH, B. JIN, G. Z. HELLER, L. YU, AND J. OFFUTT, "Determining the Distribution of Maintenance Categories: Survey versus Measurement," *Empirical Software Engineering* **8** (December 2003), pp. 351–66. (Chapter 1)

[Scheffer, Stone, and Rzepka, 1985] P. A. SCHEFFER, A. H. STONE, III, AND W. E. RZEPKA, "A Case Study of SREM," *IEEE Computer* **18** (April 1985), pp. 47–54. (Chapter 11)

[Schrage, 2004] M. SCHRAGE, "Never Go to a Client Meeting without a Prototype," *IEEE Software* **21** (2004), pp. 42–45. (Chapter 10)

[Schricker, 2000] D. SCHRICKER, "Cobol for the Next Millennium," *IEEE Software* **17** (March/April 2000), pp. 48–52. (Chapter 8)

[Schwaber, 2001] K. SCHWABER, *Agile Software Development with Scrum*, Prentice Hall, Upper Saddle River, NJ, 2001. (Chapter 2)

[Schwartz and Delisle, 1987] M. D. SCHWARTZ AND N. M. DELISLE, "Specifying a Lift Control System with CSP," *Proceedings of the Fourth International Workshop on Software Specification and Design*, Monterey, CA, April 1987, pp. 21–27. (Chapter 11)

[Scott and Vessey, 2002] J. E. SCOTT AND I. VESSEY, "Managing Risks in Enterprise Systems Implementations," *Communications of the ACM* **45** (April 2002), pp. 74–81. (Chapters 1 and 2)

[Sedigh-Ali and Paul, 2001] S. SEDIGH-ALI AND R. A. PAUL, "Software Engineering Metrics for COTS-Based Systems," *IEEE Computer* **34** (May 2001), pp. 44–50. (Chapter 5)

[SEI, 2002] "CMMI Frequently Asked Questions (FAQ)," Software Engineering Institute, Carnegie Mellon University, Pittsburgh, June 2002. (Chapter 3)

[Selby, 1989] R. W. SELBY, "Quantitative Studies of Software Reuse," in: *Software Reusability,* Vol. 2, *Applications and Experience*, T. J. Biggerstaff and A. J. Perlis (Editors), ACM Press, New York, 1989, pp. 213–33. (Chapter 8)

[Selic, Gullekson, and Ward, 1995] B. SELIC, G. GULLEKSON, AND P. T. WARD, *Real-Time Object-Oriented Modeling*, John Wiley and Sons, New York, 1995. (Chapter 12)

[Shapiro, 1994] F. R. SHAPIRO, "The First Bug," *Byte* **19** (April 1994), p. 308. (Chapter 1)

[Sharma and Rai, 2000] S. SHARMA AND A. RAI, "CASE Deployment in IS Organizations," *Communications of the ACM* **43** (January 2000), pp. 80–88. (Chapter 5)

[Shaw and Garlan, 1996] M. SHAW AND D. GARLAN, *Software Architecture: Perspectives on an Emerging Discipline*, Prentice Hall, Upper Saddle River, NJ, 1996. (Chapter 8)

[Shepperd, 1988] M. SHEPPERD, "A Critique of Cyclomatic Complexity as a Software Metric," *Software Engineering Journal* **3** (March 1988), pp. 30–36. (Chapter 14)

[Shepperd, 1990] M. SHEPPERD, "Design Metrics: An Empirical Analysis," *Software Engineering Journal* **5** (January 1990), pp. 3–10. (Chapter 13)

[Shepperd, 1996] M. SHEPPERD, *Foundations of Software Measurement*, Prentice Hall, Upper Saddle River, NJ, 1996. (Chapter 5)

[Shepperd and Ince, 1994] M. SHEPPERD AND D. C. INCE, "A Critique of Three Metrics," *Journal of Systems and Software* **26** (September 1994), pp. 197–210. (Chapter 14)

[Sherer, Kouchakdjian, and Arnold, 1996] S. W. SHERER, A. KOUCHAKDJIAN, AND P. G. ARNOLD, "Experience Using Cleanroom Software Engineering," *IEEE Software* **13** (May 1996), pp. 69–76. (Chapter 14)

[Shlaer and Mellor, 1992] S. SHLAER AND S. MELLOR, *Object Lifecycles: Modeling the World in States*, Yourdon Press, Englewood Cliffs, NJ, 1992. (Chapters 12 and 13)

[Shneiderman, 1980] B. SHNEIDERMAN, *Software Psychology: Human Factors in Computer and Information Systems*, Winthrop Publishers, Cambridge, MA, 1980. (Chapter 1)

[Shneiderman, 2003] B. SHNEIDERMAN, *Designing the User Interface: Strategies for Effective Human-Computer Interaction*, 4th ed., Addison-Wesley Longman, Reading, MA, 2003. (Chapter 10)

[Shneiderman and Mayer, 1975] B. SHNEIDERMAN AND R. MAYER, "Towards a Cognitive Model of Programmer Behavior," Technical Report TR-37, Indiana University, Bloomington, 1975. (Chapter 7)

[Silberschatz, Galvin, and Gagne, 2002] A. SILBERSCHATZ, P. B. GALVIN, AND G. GAGNE, *Operating System Concepts*, 6th ed., Addison-Wesley, Reading, MA, 2002. (Chapters 11 and 13)

[Smith, Hale, and Parrish, 2001] R. K. SMITH, J. E. HALE, AND A. S. PARRISH, "An Empirical Study Using Task Assignment Patterns to Improve the Accuracy of Software Effort Estimation," *IEEE Transactions on Software Engineering* **27** (March 2001), pp. 264–71. (Chapter 9)

[Sneed, 1995] H. M. SNEED, "Planning the Reengineering of Legacy Systems," *IEEE Software* **12** (January 1995), pp. 24–34. (Chapter 15)

[Snyder, 1993] A. SNYDER, "The Essence of Objects: Concepts and Terms," *IEEE Software* **10** (January 1993), pp. 31–42. (Chapter 7)

[Sobel and Clarkson, 2002] A. E. K. SOBEL AND M. R. CLARKSON, "Formal Methods Application: An Empirical Tale of Software Development," *IEEE Transactions on Software Engineering* **28** (March 2002), pp. 308–20. (Chapter 11)

[Sobell, 1995] M. G. SOBELL, *A Practical Guide to the UNIX System*, 3rd ed., Benjamin/Cummings, Menlo Park, CA, 1995. (Chapter 5)

[Softwaremag.com, 2004] "Standish: Project Success Rates Improved Over 10 Years," www.softwaremag .com/L.cfm?Doc=newsletter/2004-01-15/ Standish, January 15, 2004. (Chapter 2)

[Sparling, 2000] M. SPARLING, "Lessons Learned through Six Years of Component-Based Development," *Communications of the ACM* **43** (October 2000), pp. 47–53. (Chapter 8)

[Spiegel Online, 2004] "Rheinbrücke mit Treppe— 54 Zentimeter Höhenunterschied," www.spiegel .de/ panorama/0,1518,281837,00.html. (Chapter 1)

[Spivey, 1990] J. M. SPIVEY, "Specifying a Real-Time Kernel," *IEEE Software* **7** (September 1990), pp. 21–28. (Chapter 11)

[Spivey, 1992] J. M. SPIVEY, *The Z Notation: A Reference Manual*, Prentice Hall, New York, 1992. (Chapter 2)

[Spivey, 2001] J. M. SPIVEY, *The Z Notation: A Reference Manual*, 3rd ed., spivey.oriel.ox.ac.uk/~mike/zrm/, 2001. (Chapter 11)

[St. Petersburg Times Online, 2003] "Thousands of Federal Checks Uncashable," www.sptimes.com/ 2003/02/07/Worldandnation/Thousands_of_ federal_.shtml, February 07, 2003. (Chapter 1)

[Standish, 2003] STANDISH GROUP INTERNATIONAL, "Introduction," www.standishgroup.com/ chaos/introduction.pdf, 2003. (Chapter 2)

[Stephens and Rosenberg, 2003] M. STEPHENS AND D. ROSENBERG, *Extreme Programming Refactored: The Case against XP*, Apress, Berkeley, CA, 2003. (Chapter 2)

[Stephenson, 1976] W. E. STEPHENSON, "An Analysis of the Resources Used in Safeguard System Software Development," Bell Laboratories, Draft Paper, August 1976. (Chapter 1)

[Stevens and Pooley, 2000] P. STEVENS WITH R. POOLEY, *Using UML Software Engineering with Objects and Components,* updated edition, Addison-Wesley, Upper Saddle River, NJ, 2000. (Chapter 16)

[Stevens, Myers, and Constantine, 1974] W. P. STEVENS, G. J. MYERS, AND L. L. CONSTANTINE, "Structured Design," *IBM Systems Journal* **13** (No. 2, 1974), pp. 115–39. (Chapter 7)

[Stocks and Carrington, 1996] P. STOCKS AND D. CARRINGTON, "A Framework for Specification-Based Testing," *IEEE Transactions on Software Engineering* **22** (November 1996), pp. 777–93. (Chapter 14)

[Stolper, 1999] S. A. STOLPER, "Streamlined Design Approach Lands Mars Pathfinder," *IEEE Software* **16** (September/October 1999), pp. 52–62. (Chapter 13)

[Stroustrup, 2003] B. STROUSTRUP, *The C++ Standard: Incorporating Technical Corrigendum No. 1*, 2nd ed., John Wiley and Sons, New York, 2003. (Chapters 7 and 13)

[Sykes and McGregor, 2000] D. A. SYKES AND J. D. MCGREGOR, *Practical Guide to Testing Object-Oriented Software*, Addison-Wesley, Reading, MA, 2000. (Chapter 6)

[Symons, 1991] C. R. SYMONS, *Software Sizing and Estimating: Mk II FPA*, John Wiley and Sons, Chichester, UK, 1991. (Chapter 9)

[Takahashi and Kamayachi, 1985] M. TAKAHASHI AND Y. KAMAYACHI, "An Empirical Study of a Model for Program Error Prediction," *Proceedings of the Eighth International Conference on Software Engineering*, London, 1985, pp. 330–36. (Chapter 14)

[Tanenbaum, 2002] A. S. TANENBAUM, *Computer Networks*, 4th ed., Prentice Hall, Upper Saddle River, NJ, 2002. (Chapter 8)

[Teichroew and Hershey, 1977] D. TEICHROEW AND E. A. HERSHEY, III, "PSL/PSA: A Computer-Aided Technique for Structured Documentation and Analysis of Information Processing Systems," *IEEE Transactions on Software Engineering* **SE-3** (January 1977), pp. 41–48. (Chapter 11)

[Teng, Jeong, and Grover, 1998] J. T. C. TENG, S. R. JEONG, AND V. GROVER, "Profiling Successful Reengineering Projects," *Communications of the ACM* **41** (June 1999), pp. 96–102. (Chapter 15)

[Thayer and Dorfman, 1999] R. H. THAYER AND M. DORFMAN, *Software Requirements Engineering*, revised 2nd ed., IEEE Computer Society Press, Los Alamitos, CA, 1999. (Chapter 10)

[Tichy, 1985] W. F. TICHY, "RCS—A System for Version Control," *Software—Practice and Experience* **15** (July 1985), pp. 637–54. (Chapters 5 and 15)

[Toft, Coleman, and Ohta, 2000] P. TOFT, D. COLEMAN, AND J. OHTA, "A Cooperative Model for Cross-Divisional Product Development for a Software Product Line," in: *Software Product Lines: Experience and Research Directions*, P. Donohoe (Editor), Kluwer Academic Publishers, Boston, 2000, pp. 111–32. (Chapter 8)

[Tomer and Schach, 2000] A. TOMER AND S. R. SCHACH, "The Evolution Tree: A Maintenance-Oriented

Software Development Model," in: *Proceedings of the Fourth European Conference on Software Maintenance and Reengineering (CSMR 2000)*, Zürich, Switzerland, February/March 2000, pp. 209–14. (Chapter 2)

[Tomer and Schach, 2002] A. TOMER AND S. R. SCHACH, "A Three-Dimensional Model for System Design Evolution," *Systems Engineering* **5** (No. 4, 2002), pp. 264–273. (Chapter 5)

[Tomer et al., 2004] A. TOMER, L. GOLDIN, T. KUFLIK, E. KIMCHI, AND S. R. SCHACH, "Evaluating Software Reuse Alternatives: A Model and Its Application to an Industrial Case Study," *IEEE Transactions on Software Engineering* **30** (September 2004), 601–12. (Chapter 8)

[Tracz, 1979] W. J. TRACZ, "Computer Programming and the Human Thought Process," *Software—Practice and Experience* **9** (February 1979), pp. 127–37. (Chapter 5)

[Tracz, 1994] W. TRACZ, "Software Reuse Myths Revisited," *Proceedings of the 16th International Conference on Software Engineering*, Sorrento, Italy, May 1994, pp. 271–72. (Chapter 8)

[Trammel, Binder, and Snyder, 1992] C. J. TRAMMEL, L. H. BINDER, AND C. E. SNYDER, "The Automated Production Control Documentation System: A Case Study in Cleanroom Software Engineering," *ACM Transactions on Software Engineering and Methodology* **1** (January 1992), pp. 81–94. (Chapter 14)

[Turner, 1994] C. D. TURNER, "State-Based Testing: A New Method for the Testing of Object-Oriented Programs," Ph.D. thesis, Computer Science Division, University of Durham, Durham, UK, November, 1994. (Chapter 14)

[Tyran and George, 2002] C. K. TYRAN AND J. F. GEORGE, "Improving Software Inspections with Group Process Support," *Communications of the ACM* **45** (September 2002), pp. 87–92. (Chapter 6)

[Ulkuniemi and Seppanen, 2004] P. ULKUNIEMI, AND V. SEPPANEN, "COTS Component Acquisition in an Emerging Market," *IEEE Software* **21** (November/December 2004), pp. 76–82. (Chapter 1)

[USNO, 2000] "The 21st Century and the Third Millennium—When Will They Begin?" U.S. Naval Observatory, Astronomical Applications Department, at aa.usno.navy.mil/AA/faq/docs/millennium.html, February 22, 2000. (Chapter 12)

[van der Hoek, Carzaniga, Heimbigner, and Wolf, 2002] A. VAN DER HOEK, A. CARZANIGA, D. HEIMBIGNER, AND A. L. WOLF, "A Testbed for Configuration Management Policy Programming," *IEEE Transactions on Software Engineering* **28** (January 2002), pp. 79–99. (Chapter 5)

[van der Poel and Schach, 1983] K. G. VAN DER POEL AND S. R. SCHACH, "A Software Metric for Cost Estimation and Efficiency Measurement in Data Processing System Development," *Journal of Systems and Software* **3** (September 1983), pp. 187–91. (Chapter 9)

[van Solingen, 2004] R. VAN SOLINGEN, "Measuring the ROI of Software Process Improvement," *IEEE Software* **21** (May/June 2004), pp. 32–38. (Chapters 3 and 5)

[van Wijngaarden et al., 1975] A. VAN WIJNGAARDEN, B. J. MAILLOUX, J. E. L. PECK, C. H. A. KOSTER, M. SINTZOFF, C. H. LINDSEY, L. G. L. T. MEERTENS, AND R. G. FISKER, "Revised Report on the Algorithmic Language ALGOL 68," *Acta Informatica* **5** (1975), pp. 1–236. (Chapter 3)

[Vitharana, 2003] P. VITHARANA, "Risks and Challenges of Component-Based Software Development," *Communications of the ACM* **46** (August 2003), pp. 67–72. (Chapter 8)

[Vitharana and Ramamurthy, 2003] P. VITHARANA AND K. RAMAMURTHY, "Computer-Mediated Group Support, Anonymity and the Software Inspection Process: An Empirical Investigation," *IEEE Transactions on Software Engineering* **29** (March 2003), pp. 167–80. (Chapter 6)

[Vlissides, 1998] J. VLISSIDES, *Pattern Hatching: Design Patterns Applied*, Addison-Wesley, Reading, MA, 1998. (Chapter 8)

[Voas, 1999] J. VOAS, "Software Quality's Eight Greatest Myths," *IEEE Software* **16** (September/October 1999), pp. 118–20. (Chapter 6)

[Vokac, 2004] M. VOKAC, "Defect Frequency and Design Patterns: An Empirical Study of Industrial Code," *IEEE Transactions on Software Engineering* **30** (December 2004), pp. 904–17. (Chapter 8)

[von Mayrhauser and Vana, 1997] A. VON MAYRHAUSER AND A. M. VANA, "Identification of Dynamic Comprehension Processes during Large Scale Maintenance," *IEEE Transactions on Software Engineering* **22** (June 1996), pp. 424–37. (Chapter 15)

[Walker, 1992] I. J. WALKER, "Requirements of an Object-Oriented Design Method," *Software Engineering Journal* **7** (March 1992), pp. 102–13. (Chapter 13)

[Walrad and Strom, 2002] C. WALRAD AND D. STROM, "The Importance of Branching Models in SCM," *IEEE Computer* **35** (September 2002), pp. 31–38. (Chapter 5)

[Walsh, 1979] T. J. WALSH, "A Software Reliability Study Using a Complexity Measure," *Proceedings of the AFIPS National Computer Conference*, New York, 1979, pp. 761–68. (Chapter 14)

[Ward and Mellor, 1985] P. T. WARD AND S. MELLOR, *Structured Development for Real-Time Systems*, Vols. 1, 2, and 3, Yourdon Press, New York, 1985. (Chapter 13)

[Warnier, 1976] J. D. WARNIER, *Logical Construction of Programs*, Van Nostrand Reinhold, New York, 1976. (Chapters 11 and 13)

[Wasserman, 1996] A. I. WASSERMAN, "Toward a Discipline of Software Engineering," *IEEE Software* **13** (November/December 1996), pp. 23–31. (Chapters 1 and 3)

[Watson and McCabe, 1996] A. H. WATSON AND T. J. MCCABE, "Structured Testing: A Testing Methodology Using the Cyclomatic Complexity Metric," NIST Special Publication 500–235, Computer Systems Laboratory, National Institute of Standards and Technology, Gaithersburg, MD, 1996. (Chapter 14)

[Webster, 1995] B. F. WEBSTER, *Pitfalls of Object-Oriented Development*, M&T Books, New York, 1995. (Chapter 1)

[Weinberg, 1971] G. M. WEINBERG, *The Psychology of Computer Programming*, Van Nostrand Reinhold, New York, 1971. (Chapters 1 and 4)

[Weinberg, 1992] G. M. WEINBERG, *Quality Software Management: Systems Thinking*, Vol. 1, Dorset House, New York, 1992. (Chapter 9)

[Weinberg, 1993] G. M. WEINBERG, *Quality Software Management: First-Order Measurement*, Vol. 2, Dorset House, New York, 1993. (Chapter 9)

[Weinberg, 1994] G. M. WEINBERG, *Quality Software Management: Congruent Action*, Vol. 3, Dorset House, New York, 1994. (Chapter 9)

[Weinberg, 1997] G. M. WEINBERG, *Quality Software Management: Anticipating Change*, Vol. 4, Dorset House, New York, 1997. (Chapter 9)

[Weller, 1994] E. F. WELLER, "Using Metrics to Manage Software Projects," *IEEE Computer* **27** (September 1994), pp. 27–34. (Chapter 9)

[Weller, 2000] E. F. WELLER, "Practical Applications of Statistical Process Control," *IEEE Software* **18** (May/June 2000), pp. 48–55. (Chapter 3)

[Weyuker, 1988a] E. J. WEYUKER, "An Empirical Study of the Complexity of Data Flow Testing," *Proceedings of the Second Workshop on Software Testing, Verification, and Analysis*, Banff, Canada, July 1988, pp. 188–95. (Chapter 14)

[Weyuker, 1988b] E. WEYUKER, "Evaluating Software Complexity Measures," *IEEE Transactions on Software Engineering* **14** (September 1988), pp. 1357–65. (Chapter 14)

[Weyuker, 1998] E. J. WEYUKER, "Testing Component-Based Software: A Cautionary Tale," *IEEE Software* **15** (September/October 1998), pp. 54–59. (Chapter 8)

[Whitgift, 1991] D. WHITGIFT, *Methods and Tools for Software Configuration Management*, John Wiley and Sons, New York, 1991. (Chapter 5)

[Whittaker, 2000] J. A. WHITTAKER, "What Is Software Testing? And Why Is It So Hard?" *IEEE Software* **17** (January/February 2000), pp. 70–79. (Chapter 6)

[Whittaker and Voas, 2000] J. A. WHITTAKER AND J. VOAS, "Toward a More Reliable Theory of Software Reliability," *IEEE Computer* **33** (December 2000), pp. 36–42. (Chapter 6)

[Wilde, Matthews, and Huitt, 1993] N. WILDE, P. MATTHEWS, AND R. HUITT, "Maintaining Object-Oriented Software," *IEEE Software* **10** (January 1993), pp. 75–80. (Chapters 14 and 15)

[Williams, 1996] J. D. WILLIAMS, "Managing Iteration in OO Projects," *IEEE Computer* **29** (September 1996), pp. 39–43. (Chapter 12)

[Williams, Kessler, Cunningham, and Jeffries, 2000] L. WILLIAMS, R. R. KESSLER, W. CUNNINGHAM, AND R. JEFFRIES, "Strengthening the Case for Pair Programming," *IEEE Software* **17** (July/August 2000), pp. 19–25. (Chapters 2 and 4)

[Wing, 1990] J. WING, "A Specifier's Introduction to Formal Methods," *IEEE Computer* **23** (September 1990), pp. 8–24. (Chapter 11)

[Wirfs-Brock, Wilkerson, and Wiener, 1990] R. WIRFS-BROCK, B. WILKERSON, AND L. WIENER, *Designing Object-Oriented Software*, Prentice Hall, Englewood Cliffs, NJ, 1990. (Chapters 1, 12, and 13)

[Wirth, 1971] N. WIRTH, "Program Development by Stepwise Refinement," *Communications of the ACM* **14** (April 1971), pp. 221–27. (Chapters 5 and 6)

[Wirth, 1975] N. WIRTH, *Algorithms + Data Structures = Programs,* Prentice Hall, Englewood Cliffs, NJ, 1975. (Chapter 5)

[Wohlwend and Rosenbaum, 1993] H. WOHLWEND AND S. ROSENBAUM, "Software Improvements in an International Company," *Proceedings of the 15th International Conference on Software Engineering*, Baltimore, MD, May 1993, pp. 212–20. (Chapter 3)

[Woodcock, 1989] J. WOODCOCK, "Calculating Properties of Z Specifications," *ACM SIGSOFT Software Engineering Notes* **14** (July 1989), pp. 43–54. (Chapter 11)

[Woodward, Hedley, and Hennell, 1980] M. R. WOODWARD, D. HEDLEY, AND M. A. HENNELL, "Experience with Path Analysis and Testing of Programs," *IEEE Transactions on Software Engineering* **SE-6** (May 1980), pp. 278–86. (Chapter 14)

[Yamaura, 1998] T. YAMAURA, "How to Design Practical Test Cases," *IEEE Software* **15** (November/December 1998), pp. 30–36. (Chapter 14)

[Yourdon, 1989] E. YOURDON, *Modern Structured Analysis*, Yourdon Press, Englewood Cliffs, NJ, 1989. (Chapter 14)

[Yourdon, 1992] E. YOURDON, *The Decline and Fall of the American Programmer*, Yourdon Press, Upper Saddle River, NJ, 1992. (Chapter 1)

[Yourdon and Constantine, 1979] E. YOURDON AND L. L. CONSTANTINE, *Structured Design: Fundamentals of a Discipline of Computer Program and Systems Design*, Prentice Hall, Englewood Cliffs, NJ, 1979. (Chapters 7, 11, and 13)

[Yu, Schach, Chen, and Offutt, 2004] L. YU, S. R. SCHACH, K. CHEN, AND J. OFFUTT, "Categorization of Common Coupling and its Application to the Maintainability of the Linux Kernel," *IEEE Transactions on Software Engineering* **30** (October 2004), pp. 694–706. (Chapters 2 and 7)

[Zage and Zage, 1993] W. M. ZAGE AND D. M. ZAGE, "Evaluating Design Metrics on Large-Scale Software," *IEEE Software* **10** (July 1993), pp. 75–81. (Chapter 13)

[Zelkowitz, Shaw, and Gannon, 1979] M. V. ZELKOWITZ, A. C. SHAW, AND J. D. GANNON, *Principles of Software Engineering and Design,* Prentice Hall, Englewood Cliffs, NJ, 1979. (Chapter 1)

[Zvegintzov, 1998] N. ZVEGINTZOV, "Frequently Begged Questions and How to Answer Them," *IEEE Software* **15** (January/February 1998), pp. 93–96. (Chapter 1)

# Appendix

# Term Project: Osric's Office Appliances and Decor

Osric Ormondsey owns Osric's Office Appliances and Decor (OOA&D). Osric has a highly successful career decorating the offices of top business executives. He employs a number of subcontractors and technicians so that he can provide a complete turnkey service, including telecommunications (telephone, fax, high-speed data link, and so on). His success is largely due to the speed with which he responds to a customer's request; he has been known to completely redecorate a large executive suite in only two days.

Osric's customers frequently comment effusively about the skills of his two telecommunications technicians, in the light of their many bad experiences with technicians of the local telephone company. Osric realizes that he can expand his business by adding a telecommunications division. He decides to hire the best technicians he can find, offer them an exorbitant salary plus bonuses, and advertise their services to the executives whose offices he has decorated. The executives realize that it is far more effective for their companies to pay Osric's high rates for a highly skilled technician who arrives within an hour or two and fixes the problem quickly than to wait two or three days for an incompetent technician to come and make the problem worse.

Osric's idea has succeeded beyond his wildest dreams. His technicians are in constant high demand, so much so that the waiting time for an OOA&D technician is sometimes more than two days, despite the fact that Osric has technicians on call 24 hours a day. This is unacceptable to both Osric and his customers, so Osric tries to rectify the situation. He has been unable to hire enough technicians with the necessary high level of skills, so he has decided to ration their services. Specifically, he decides to prioritize his customers so that, when someone calls to request service, Osric can decide where to put them on the waiting list for a technician.

Each customer company has a five-digit customer number and is assigned a priority.

*Priority 4:* A company that has hired Osric to decorate an executive office.

*Priority 3:* A company that has had three or more previous telecommunications service calls.

*Priority 2:* A company that has had one or two previous telecommunications service calls.

*Priority 1:* A company calling for service for the first time.

When someone calls for service, the assistant asks the caller for his or her company's customer number. If the customer does not know the customer number, the assistant asks for the company name. If the name is not found, the software assumes that this is a new customer. A new customer is assigned a number only if it is put on the waiting list (see the following).

When there is a request for service, the company is added to the waiting list. The companies on the waiting list are sorted by priority, and by date and time of call within priority.

Osric's technicians work 8-hour shifts. He currently has seven technicians on the day shift and two on each of the two night shifts, but this could change. Osric has observed that the durations of the service calls are normally distributed with a mean of 5.5 hours and a standard deviation of 9.8 hours. However, the shortest time for a job was 1.9 hours, and the longest time was 23.1 hours.[1] At 8 A.M. a technician is assigned to each of the top seven companies on the waiting list, and similarly at 12 noon, provided that there are no incomplete jobs, as described in the next paragraph.

If a job is completed within its assigned 4-hour block, the customer is charged for the 4-hour block and the technician returns to OOA&D. If a job has not been completed by 12 noon, the same technician is assigned a further 4-hour block to complete it, reducing the number of technicians available for new jobs.

Osric provides service 24 hours a day. At night, however, the assistant on duty does not accept new service requests; his or her sole task is to supervise the night technicians. At 4 P.M. the assistant on duty checks if there are jobs that have not been completed. If so, he or she calls each company to ask if they want a night technician to continue the job (at double rates), or whether they want the same technician to continue in the morning. Because there are fewer night technicians than day technicians, it may not be possible to honor all requests for night service. Accordingly, the assistant calls the companies with outstanding jobs in waiting list order, that is, by priority, and by date and time of call within priority.

---

[1] Many programming languages support pseudorandom number generators. In Java, function nextGaussian generates numbers from a distribution that is normally distributed with mean 0 and standard deviation 1. In C++, function rand generates numbers uniformly distributed between 0 and 1; the Box-Muller transformation can then be used to generate normally distributed pseudorandom numbers (see G. E. P. Box and M. E. Muller, "A Note on the Generation of Random Normal Deviates," *Annals of Mathematical Statistics* **29** (1958), pp. 610–11). Alternatively, many free Gaussian pseudorandom number generators for C++ can be downloaded from the Web, including gsl_ran_Gaussian in the GNU Scientific Library (GSL).

If $x$ is a number generated from a distribution that is normally distributed with mean 0 and standard deviation 1, then $\mu + x \times \sigma$ will be from a distribution that is normally distributed with mean $\mu$ and standard deviation $\sigma$. Outliers (numbers that are too high or too low) can then be rejected.

Again, work is assigned and charged at night on the basis of 4-hour blocks. A night job can continue the following day, if necessary, at day rates. In this case, too, the same day technician as before will be assigned to the job.

After a company has been on the waiting list for 2 full day blocks, its priority is *temporarily* increased by 1 before technicians are assigned to their next job. As a result, Priority-4 customers usually get service within 4 hours, but new (Priority 1) customers may have to wait until the fourth day for service.

When a customer calls for service, the software product estimates how soon service will be available based on the time taken so far on each of the current jobs, the length of the current waiting list, and the average time to complete a job. It also gives a worst-case estimate, based on the time it will take if the company has to reach Priority 4 before receiving service. The assistant gives this information to the customer, and asks if the company is prepared to wait, if necessary. Each morning the assistant calls all the customers on the waiting list to inform them how soon they can expect service. Again, this information is computed by the product, using the information available at that time.

If a new company requests a service call, this must first be approved by a manager. Ordinarily, such approval will not be given if the number of customers on the waiting list exceeds twice the number of day technicians. Occasionally, however, Osric will want to add a specific new company to his customer list. Accordingly, decisions regarding new customers have to be made by a manager who will give an immediate response when called by the assistant.

When the technician has completed the service call, he or she hands the job card to the assistant, who enters the customer number and the number of day and night blocks that the job required. The software product first uses this information to update the company's priority, if applicable. Then the data are used to generate a bill to be mailed to the customer; the cost per block is $480 during the day, and $960 at night. Osric's billing address is Suite 16, Kronborg Castle, Helsingør, Sjælland, Denmark (see Just in Case You Wanted to Know Box A.1).

You are required to determine the effectiveness of Osric's scheme by simulating it. First, generate a job mix, that is, a set of jobs. For each job in the mix, specify the necessary attributes, including the time the call is made, the company priority, and the duration; other attributes will also be needed. As each job is called in, it is added to the queue. At the start of each block, jobs are removed from the queue and assigned to available technicians. When a job is finished, the technician is released, either to begin a job at the start of the second block of the shift or to go home.

In order to assess the effectiveness of the scheme, certain statistics need to be kept, including the average waiting time before a job is started; the average queue length; the percentage of time the queue is empty, both day and night; the number of blocks when a technician is idle (and hence no income accrues to OOA&D); and the number of jobs that cannot be continued at night because no technician is available.

Now, using the same job mix, determine the same statistics without Osric's scheme, that is, on a pure first-come–first-served basis, including new customers. Determine the average waiting time for customers with each priority. Repeat with different sets of jobs and different numbers of technicians. Decide whether Osric's scheme is cost effective for Osric, and whether it reduces the customers' waiting time.

# Appendix B

# Software Engineering Resources

There are two good ways to get more information on software engineering topics: by reading journals and conference proceedings, and via the Internet and World Wide Web.

Journals dedicated exclusively to software engineering are available, such as *IEEE Transactions on Software Engineering*, as well as journals of a more general nature, such as *Communications of the ACM,* in which significant articles on software engineering are published. For reasons of space, only a selection of journals of both classes follows. The journals have been chosen on a subjective basis, those I currently find to be the most useful.

*ACM Computing Reviews*
*ACM Computing Surveys*
*ACM SIGSOFT Software Engineering Notes*
*ACM Transactions on Computer Systems*
*ACM Transactions on Programming Languages and Systems*
*ACM Transactions on Software Engineering and Methodology*
*Communications of the ACM*
*Computer Journal*
*Empirical Software Engineering*
*IBM Systems Journal*
*IEEE Computer*
*IEEE Software*
*IEEE Transactions on Software Engineering*

*Journal of Systems and Software*
*Software Engineering Journal*
*Software—Practice and Experience*
*Software Quality Journal*

In addition, proceedings of many conferences contain important articles on software engineering topics. Again, a subjective selection follows. Most of the conferences are referred to by their acronym or name of sponsoring organization; these appear in parentheses.

*ACM SIGPLAN Annual Conference (SIGPLAN)*
*ACM SIGSOFT Symposium on the Foundations of Software Engineering (FSE)*
*Conference on Human Factors in Computing Systems (CHI)*
*Conference on Object-Oriented Programming Systems, Languages, and Applications (OOPSLA)*
*International Computer Software and Applications Conference (COMPSAC)*
*International Conference on Software Engineering (ICSE)*
*International Conference on Software Maintenance (ICSM)*
*International Conference on Software Reuse (ICSR)*
*International Conference on the Software Process (ICSP)*
*International Software Architecture Workshop (ISAW)*
*International Symposium on Software Testing and Analysis (ISSTA)*
*International Workshop on Software Configuration Management (SCM)*
*International Workshop on Software Specification and Design (IWSSD)*

The Internet is another valuable source of information on software engineering. With regard to Usenet news groups, the following two have been consistently useful to me:

comp.object
comp.software-eng

Other newsgroups that sometimes have items that I find relevant include the following:

comp.lang.c++.moderated
comp.lang.java.programmer
comp.risks
comp.software.config-mgmt

# C

# Requirements Workflow: The MSG Foundation Case Study

The requirements workflow for the MSG Foundation case study appears in Chapter 10.

# D

# Structured Systems Analysis: The MSG Foundation Case Study

**Step 1. Draw the Data Flow Diagram** See Figure 11.9.

**Step 2. Decide What Sections to Computerize and How** Computerize the complete pilot project online. However, if the weekly computation regarding availability of funds to purchase homes turns out to be time consuming, it may be better to perform it the night before it is required.

**Step 3. Put in the Details of the Data Flows**

| | |
|---|---|
| investment_details | |
| investment_number | (12 characters) |
| investment_name | (25 characters) |
| expected_return | (9 + 2 digits) |
| date_expected_return_updated | (8 characters) |
| | |
| mortgage_details | |
| mortgage_number | (12 characters) |
| mortgage_name | (21 characters) |
| price | (6 + 2 digits) |
| date_mortgage_issued | (8 characters) |
| weekly_income | (6 + 2 digits) |
| date_weekly_income_was_updated | (8 characters) |
| annual_property_tax | (5 + 2 digits) |

| | |
|---|---|
| annual_insurance_premium | (5 + 2 digits) |
| mortgage_balance | (6 + 2 digits) |
| available_funds_for_week | (9 + 2 digits) |
| annual_operating_expenses | (9 + 2 digits) |
| update_request | (1 character) |

## Step 4. Define the Logic of the Processes

compute_availability_of_funds_and_generate_funds_report

Determine the expected income for the week by adding the expected_return of each investment in INVESTMENT_DATA.

Determine the expected mortgage payments for the week by adding the expected mortgage payment of each mortgage in MORTGAGE_DATA.

Determine the expected grants for the week by adding the expected grant for each mortgage in MORTGAGE_DATA.

Compute available_funds_for_week =
   expected income for the week
   − annual_operating_expenses / 52
   + expected mortgage payments for the week
   − expected grants for the week

generate_listing_of_investments

For each investment in INVESTMENT_DATA
   Print investment_details

generate_listing_of_mortgages

For each mortgage in MORTGAGE_DATA
   Print mortgage_details

perform_selected_update

Use the value of update_request to determine whether MORTGAGE_DATA, INVESTMENT_DATA, or EXPENSES_DATA are to be updated.
Perform the update.

## Step 5. Define the Data Stores

EXPENSES_DATA
annual_operating_expenses [defined in Step 3]

INVESTMENT_DATA
investment_details [defined in Step 3]

MORTGAGE_DATA
mortgage_details [defined in Step 3]

All files are sequential, and hence there is no DIAD.

## Step 6.  Define the Physical Resources

EXPENSES DATA
>    Sequential file
>    Stored on disk

INVESTMENT DATA
>    Sequential file
>    Stored on disk

MORTGAGE DATA
>    Sequential file
>    Stored on disk

## Step 7.  Determine the Input–Output Specifications   Input screens are designed for the following processes:

>    update_investment,  update_mortgage,  update_annual_operating_expenses,
>    compute_availability_of_funds_and_generate_funds_report

The following reports are displayed:

>    list_of_investments, list_of_mortgages, available_funds_for_week

The screens and reports of the rapid prototype will be used as a basis for the preceding. The exact format of all screens and reports is subject to approval by the MSG Foundation.

## Step 8.  Perform Sizing   Approximately 4 megabytes of storage are needed for the software. Each investment record requires approximately 50 bytes of storage. Each mortgage record requires approximately 90 bytes of storage. The storage requirements can be computed on the basis of the number of investments and mortgages owned by the MSG Foundation.

## Step 9.  Determine the Hardware Requirements

>    Desktop computer with hard disk, running Linux.
>    Zip drive for backups.
>    Laser printer for printing reports.

# Appendix E

## Analysis Workflow: The MSG Foundation Case Study

The analysis workflow is presented in Chapter 12.

# Appendix F

# Software Project Management Plan: The MSG Foundation Case Study

The plan presented here is for development of the MSG product by a small software organization consisting of three individuals: Almaviva, the owner of the company, and two software engineers, Bartolo and Cherubini.

*1 Overview.*

*1.1 Project Summary.*

*1.1.1 Purpose, Scope, and Objectives.* The objective of this project is to develop a software product that will assist the Martha Stockton Greengage (MSG) Foundation in making decisions regarding home mortgages for married couples. The product will allow the client to add, modify, and delete information regarding the Foundation's investments, operating expenses, and individual mortgage information. The product will perform the required calculations in these areas and produce reports listing investments, mortgages, and weekly operating expenses.

*1.1.2 Assumptions and Constraints.* Constraints include the following:

The deadline must be met.

The budget constraint must be met.

The product must be reliable.

The architecture must be open so that additional functionality may be added later.

The product must be user-friendly.

***1.1.3  Project Deliverables.***   The complete product, including user manual, will be delivered 10 weeks after the project commences.

***1.1.4  Schedule and Budget Summary.***   The duration, personnel requirements, and budget of each workflow are as follows:

> Requirements workflow (1 week, two team members, $3740)
>
> Analysis workflow (2 weeks, two team members, $7480)
>
> Design workflow (2 weeks, two team members, $7480)
>
> Implementation workflow (3 weeks, three team members, $16,830)
>
> Testing workflow (2 weeks, three team members, $11,220)

The total development time is 10 weeks, and the total internal cost is $46,750.

***1.2  Evolution of the Project Management Plan.***   All changes in the project management plan must be agreed to by Almaviva before they are implemented. All changes should be documented in order to keep the project management plan correct and up to date.

***2  Reference Materials.***   All artifacts will conform to the company's programming, documentation, and testing standards.

***3  Definitions and Acronyms.***   MSG—Martha Stockton Greengage; the MSG Foundation is our client.

***4  Project Organization.***

***4.1  External Interfaces.***   All the work on this project will be performed by Almaviva, Bartolo, and Cherubini. Almaviva will meet weekly with the client to report progress and discuss possible changes and modifications.

***4.2  Internal Structure.***   The development team consists of Almaviva (owner), Bartolo, and Cherubini.

***4.3  Roles and Responsibilities.***   Bartolo and Cherubini will perform the design workflow. Almaviva will implement the class definitions and report artifacts, Bartolo will construct the artifacts to handle investments and operating expenses, and Cherubini will develop the artifacts that handle mortgages. Each member is responsible for the quality of the artifacts he or she produces. Almaviva will oversee integration and the overall quality of the software product and will liaise with the client.

***5  Managerial Process Plans.***

***5.1  Start-up Plan.***

***5.1.1  Estimation Plan.***   As previously stated, the total development time is estimated to be 10 weeks and the total internal cost to be $46,750. These figures were obtained by expert judgment by analogy, that is, by comparison with similar projects.

***5.1.2  Staffing Plan.***   Almaviva is needed for the entire 10 weeks, for the first 5 weeks in only a managerial capacity and the second 5 weeks as both manager and programmer. Bartolo and Cherubini are needed for the entire 10 weeks, for the first 5 weeks as systems analysts and designers and for the second 5 weeks as programmers and testers.

**5.1.3 Resource Acquisition Plan.** All necessary hardware, software, and CASE tools for the project are already available. The product will be delivered to the MSG Foundation installed on a desktop computer that will be leased from our usual supplier.

**5.1.4 Project Staff Training Plan.** No additional staff training is needed for this project.

**5.2 Work Plan.**

**5.2.1–2 Work Activities and Schedule Allocation.**

Week 1.  (Completed) Met with client, and determined requirements artifacts. Inspected requirements artifacts.

Weeks 2, 3.  (Completed) Produced analysis artifacts, and inspected analysis artifacts. Showed artifacts to client, who approved them. Produced software project management plan, and inspected software project management plan.

Weeks 4, 5.  Produce design artifacts, and inspect design artifacts.

Weeks 6–10.  Implementation and inspection of each class, unit testing and documentation, integration of each class, integration testing, product testing, and documentation inspection.

**5.2.3 Resource Allocation.** The three team members will work separately on their assigned artifacts. Almaviva's assigned role will be to monitor the daily progress of the other two, oversee implementation, be responsible for overall quality, and interact with the client. Team members will meet at the end of each day and discuss problems and progress. Formal meetings with the client will be held at the end of each week to report progress and determine if any changes need to be made. Almaviva will ensure that schedule and budget requirements are met. Risk management will also be Almaviva's responsibility.

Minimizing faults and maximizing user-friendliness will be Almaviva's top priorities. Almaviva has overall responsibility for all documentation and has to ensure that it is up to date.

**5.2.4 Budget Allocation.** The budget for each workflow is as follows:

| | |
|---|---|
| Requirements workflow | $ 3,740 |
| Analysis workflow | 7,480 |
| Design workflow | 7,480 |
| Implementation workflow | 16,830 |
| Testing workflow | 11,220 |
| Total | $46,750 |

**5.3 Control Plan.** Any major changes that affect the milestones or the budget have to be approved by Almaviva and documented. No outside quality assurance personnel are involved. The benefits of having someone other than the individual who carried out the development task do the testing will be accomplished by each person testing another person's work products.

Almaviva will be responsible for ensuring that the project is completed on time and within budget. This will be accomplished through daily meetings with the team members. At each meeting, Bartolo and Cherubini will present the day's progress and problems.

Almaviva will determine whether they are progressing as expected and whether they are following the specification document and the project management plan. Any major problems faced by the team members will immediately be reported to Almaviva.

*5.4  Risk Management Plan.*   The risk factors and the tracking mechanisms are as follows.

There is no existing product with which the new product can be compared. Accordingly, it will not be possible to run the product in parallel with an existing one. Therefore, the product should be subjected to extensive testing.

The client is assumed to be inexperienced with computers. Therefore, special attention should be paid to the analysis workflow and communication with the client. The product has to be made as user-friendly as possible.

Because of the ever-present possibility of a major design fault, extensive testing will be performed during the design workflow. Also, each of the team members will initially test his or her own code and then test the code of another member. Almaviva will be responsible for integration testing and in charge of product testing.

The information must meet the specified storage requirements and response times. This should not be a major problem because of the small size of the product, but it will be monitored by Almaviva throughout development.

There is a slim chance of hardware failure, in which case another machine will be leased. If there is a fault in the compiler, it will be replaced. These are covered in the warranties received from the hardware and compiler suppliers.

*5.5  Project Close-out Plan.*   Not applicable here.

*6  Technical Process Plans.*

*6.1  Process Model.*   The Unified Process will be used.

*6.2  Methods, Tools, and Techniques.*   The workflows will be performed in accordance with the Unified Process. The product will be implemented in Java.

*6.3  Infrastructure Plan.*   The product will be developed using ArgoUML running under Linux on a personal computer.

*6.4  Product Acceptance Plan.*   Acceptance of the product by our client will be achieved by following the steps of the Unified Process.

*7  Supporting Process Plan*

*7.1  Configuration Management Plan.*   CVS will be used throughout for all artifacts.

*7.2  Testing Plan.*   The testing workflow of the Unified Process will be performed.

*7.3  Documentation Plan.*   Documentation will be produced as specified in the Unified Process.

*7.4–5  Quality Assurance Plan and Reviews and Audits Plan.*   Bartolo and Cherubini will test each other's code, and Almaviva will conduct integration testing. Extensive product testing will then be performed by all three.

*7.6  Problem Resolution Plan.*   As stated in 5.3, any major problems faced by the team members will immediately be reported to Almaviva.

*7.7  Subcontractor Management Plan.*    Not applicable here.

*7.8  Process Improvement Plan.*    All activities will be conducted in accord with the company plan to advance from CMM level 2 to level 3 within 2 years.

*8.  Additional Plans.*    Additional components:

**Security.**    A password will be needed to use the product.

**Training.**    Training will be performed by Almaviva at time of delivery. Because the product is straightforward to use, 1 day should be sufficient for training. Almaviva will answer questions at no cost for the first year of use.

**Maintenance.**    Corrective maintenance will be performed by the team at no cost for a period of 12 months. A separate contract will be drawn up regarding enhancement.

# Design Workflow: The MSG Foundation Case Study

This appendix contains the final version of the class diagram for the MSG Foundation case study (Figure G.1). The overall class diagram is followed by UML diagrams for the 10 component classes, in alphabetical order. These UML diagrams show the attributes and the methods. As explained in Section 16.2, the UML visibility prefixes are − for **private**, + for **public**, and # for **protected.** The attributes and methods are shown in a PDL for Java. Accordingly, there is no **Date Class** (see Section 13.8).

**FIGURE G.1**

The final class diagram for the MSG Foundation case study.

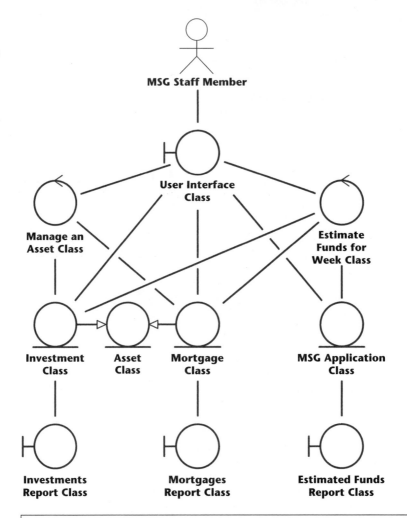

| «entity class» **Asset Class** | | |
|---|---|---|
| # assetNumber : string | | |
| + getAssetNumber ( ) : string<br>+ setAssetNumber (a : string) : void<br>+ **abstract** read (fileName : RandomAccessFile) : void<br>+ **abstract** obtainNewData ( ) : void<br>+ **abstract** performDeletion ( ) : void<br>+ **abstract** write (fileName : RandomAccessFile) : void<br>+ **abstract** save ( ) : void<br>+ **abstract** print ( ) : void<br>+ **abstract** find (s : string) : Boolean<br>+ delete ( ) : void<br>+ add ( ) : void | | |

| «control class» |
| :---: |
| **Estimate Funds for Week Class** |
| |
| + <<static>> compute ( ) : void |

| «boundary class» |
| :---: |
| **Estimate Funds Report Class** |
| |
| + <<static>> printReport ( ) : void |

| «entity class» |
| :---: |
| **Investment Class** |

| |
| :--- |
| – investmentName : string |
| – expectedAnnualReturn : float |
| – expectedAnnualReturnUpdated : string |

| |
| :--- |
| + getInvestmentName ( ) : string |
| + setInvestmentName (n : string) : void |
| + getExpectedAnnualReturn ( ) : float |
| + setExpectedAnnualReturn (r : float) : void |
| + getExpectedAnnualReturnUpdated ( ) : string |
| + setExpectedAnnualReturnUpdated (d : string) : void |
| + totalWeeklyReturnOnInvestment ( ) : float |
| + find (findInvestmentID : string) : Boolean |
| + read (fileName : RandomAccessFile) : void |
| + write (fileName : RandomAccessFile) : void |
| + save ( ) : void |
| + print ( ) : void |
| + printAll ( ) : void |
| + obtainNewData ( ) : void |
| + performDeletion ( ) : void |
| + readInvestmentData ( ) : void |
| + updateInvestmentName ( ) : void |
| + updateExpectedReturn ( ) : void |

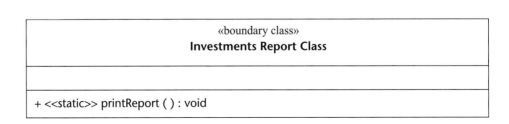

| «boundary class» |
| :---: |
| **Investments Report Class** |
| |
| + <<static>> printReport ( ) : void |

| «control class» |
| --- |
| **Manage an Asset Class** |
| |
| + <<static>> manageInvestment ( ) : void<br>+ <<static>> manageMortgage ( ) : void |

| «entity class» |
| --- |
| **Mortgage Class** |
| – mortgageeName : string<br>– price : float<br>– dateMortgageIssued : string<br>– currentWeeklyIncome : float<br>– weeklyIncomeUpdated : string<br>– annualPropertyTax : float<br>– annualInsurancePremium : float<br>– mortgageBalance : float<br>+ <<static final>> INTEREST_RATE : float<br>+ <<static final>> MAX_PER_OF_INCOME : float<br>+ <<static final>> NUMBER_OF_MORTGAGE_PAYMENTS : int<br>+ <<static final>> WEEKS_IN_YEAR : float<br>+ getMortgageeName ( ) : string<br>+ setMortgageeName (n : string) : void<br>+ getPrice ( ) : float<br>+ setPrice (p : float) : void<br>+ getDateMortgageIssued ( ) : string<br>+ setDateMortgageIssued (w : string) : void<br>+ getCurrentWeeklyIncome ( ) : float<br>+ setCurrentWeeklyIncome (i : float) : void<br>+ getWeeklyIncomeUpdated ( ) : string<br>+ setWeeklyIncomeUpdated (w : string) : void<br>+ getAnnualPropertyTax ( ) : float<br>+ setAnnualPropertyTax (t : float) : void<br>+ getAnnualInsurancePremium ( ) : float<br>+ setAnnualInsurancePremium (p : float) : void<br>+ getMortgageBalance ( ) : float<br>+ setMortgageBalance (m : float) : void<br>+ totalWeeklyNetPayments ( ) : float<br>+ find (findMortgageID : string) : Boolean<br>+ read (fileName : RandomAccessFile) : void<br>+ write (fileName : RandomAcessFile) : void<br>+ obtainNewData ( ) : void<br>+ performDeletion ( ) : void<br>+ print ( ) : void<br>+ <<static>> printAll ( ) : void |

+ save ( ) : void
+ readMortgageData ( ) : void
+ updateBalance ( ) : void
+ updateDate ( ) : void
+ updateInsurancePremium ( ) : void
+ updateMortgageeName ( ) : void
+ updatePrice ( ) : void
+ updatePropertyTax ( ) : void
+ updateWeeklyIncome ( ) : void

---

«boundary class»
**Mortgages Report Class**

---

+ <<static>> printReport ( ) : void

---

«entity class»
**MSG Application Class**

---

– <<static>> estimatedAnnualOperatingExpenses : float
– <<static>> estimatedFundsForWeek : float

---

– <<static>> getAnnualOperatingExpenses ( ) : float
– <<static>> setAnnualOperatingExpenses (e : float) : void
+ <<static>> getEstimatedFundsForWeek ( ) : float
+ <<static>> setEstimatedFundsForWeek (e : float) : void
+ <<static>> initializeApplication ( ) : void
+ <<static>> updateAnnualOperatingExpenses ( ) : void
+ <<static>> main ( )

---

«boundary class»
**User Interface Class**

---

+ <<static>> clearScreen ( ) : void
+ <<static>> pressEnter ( ) : void
+ <<static>> displayMainMenu ( ) : void
+ <<static>> displayInvestmentMenu ( ) : void
+ <<static>> displayMortgageMenu ( ) : void
+ <<static>> displayReportMenu ( ) : void
+ <<static>> getChar ( ) : char
+ <<static>> getString ( ) : string
+ <<static>> getInt ( ) : int

Appendix

# H

## Implementation Workflow: The MSG Foundation Case Study (C++ Version)

The complete C++ source code for the MSG Foundation product is available on the World Wide Web at www.mhhe.com/schach.

# Appendix

# I

# Implementation Workflow: The MSG Foundation Case Study (Java Version)

The complete Java source code for the MSG Foundation product is available on the World Wide Web at www.mhhe.com/schach.

# Appendix J

## Test Workflow: The MSG Foundation Case Study

The test workflow of the MSG Foundation case study is presented in four sections:

Section 10.11 (requirements)
Section 12.17 (analysis)
Section 13.11 (design)
Section 14.23 (implementation)

# Author Index

This index includes only authors cited in the actual text.

# Subject Index

## A

abstract data type, 185, 202–3, 495

abstract data type design, 442

abstract initial state, 360

**abstract** method, 525

abstract noun, 381

abstraction, 196–202, 432

acceptance criteria, 332

acceptance testing, 9, 83, 153, 500, 501–2

accessor, 446

accidental reuse, 220

action, 598
definition, 598

activation box, 595

activity, 132, 268, 598

activity diagram, 599–601, 603

actor, 290–91, 295–97, 379, 424–25, 593, 603
definition, 290
elevator problem case study, 379
MSG Foundation case study, 295–97

Ada, 189, 239–40, 259, 341, 363, 505

Ada 83 (language), 239, 240

Ada 95 (language), 240, 442

Ada Joint Program Office (AJPO), 240

Ada reference manual, 239

Ada standard, 239–40

adaptive maintenance, 9, 137, 517, 518–19, 522, 527
definition, 517

ADF, 467

aggregation, 207, 589

Agile Alliance, 58

agile processes, 57–60, 115

Alexander, Christopher, 229

ALGOL, 240

algorithm, 300–301

all-definition-use-path coverage, 491–92

alpha release, 83

alpha testing, 84, 500

**alter** verb, 186

ambiguity, 78, 333

analysis. *See* analysis workflow; classical analysis phase; object-oriented analysis

analysis artifacts, 81–82
review, 82

analysis fault, 13–15, 517

analysis phase. *See* classical analysis phase

analysis testing, 82

analysis workflow, 23, 42–45, 77–79, 376–425, 589
challenges, 425–26
elevator problem case study, 378–90
MSG Foundation case study, 392–422, 589

Analyst/Designer, 366, 456, 503

analytic network modeling, 332

Anna, 363

Ant, 142

antipattern, 232

Apache project, 142

Apache Web server, 24

application composition model, 265

application domain, 73, 76, 286, 287

application framework, 228–29

application programming interface (API), 221

architect, 452

architectural design, 9, 22, 79, 432–36

architecture, 47, 87. *See also* software architecture

ArgoUML, 324, 425, 456

Ariane 5 rocket, 225–26

artifact, 19, 39, 130

ASCII, 235

aspect-oriented programming (AOP), 214

assembler, 242, 259, 466, 499, 528

**assert** statement, 169, 226

assertion, 163, 165, 169

association, 208, 592

association class, 593

asterisk, 591

AT&T Bell Laboratories, 238

ATM, 262

attribute, 19–23, 206, 381, 496

## B

Babbage, Charles, 240

back-end CASE tool, 131, 456

backtrack, 314, 396

backup programmer, 108–9, 110

bag, 354

baseline, 39, 140–41, 268, 523

Basili, 42

Beethoven, Ludwig van, 220

behavioral testing, 482

beta release, 83, 89

beta testing, 84, 500

binding, 180

black-box testing, 273, 482. *See also* black-box unit testing
origin of term, 482

black-box unit testing, 485–90, 493–95

Booch's method, 74

Borland, 24

bottom-up integration, 477–78
strengths, 478
weaknesses, 478

boundary class, 391, 401
definition, 376
MSG Foundation case study, 401

boundary value analysis, 486–87

bounds checking, 169

branch coverage, 491–92

Brooks's Law, 105

browser, 221

budget, 79, 254, 268

bug, 26, 106
first use in computer context, 26

Bugzilla, 506, 530

build tool, 141–42, 529

business case, 87–89